Anonymus

The Songs of Scotland

Chronologically Arranged with Introduction and Biographical Notes

Anonymus

The Songs of Scotland
Chronologically Arranged with Introduction and Biographical Notes

ISBN/EAN: 9783741184307

Manufactured in Europe, USA, Canada, Australia, Japa

Cover: Foto ©Angelika Wolter / pixelio.de

Manufactured and distributed by brebook publishing software (www.brebook.com)

Anonymus

The Songs of Scotland

THE SONGS OF SCOTLAND

CHRONOLOGICALLY ARRANGED

WITH INTRODUCTION AND BIOGRAPHICAL

NOTES

LONDON
BELL AND DALDY, YORK ST. COVENT GARDEN
GLASGOW: OGLE AND COMPANY

NOTE.

THE Editor has to acknowledge his indebtedness to ROBERT CHAMBERS, Esq., LL.D., for his kindness in allowing several extracts to be taken from his valuable "History of the Rebellion of 1745-6;" to Dr. BUCHAN for permission to print his continuation of Tannahill's song, "In the Spring time o' the year;" and to Mr. DAVID ROBERTSON, publisher, Glasgow, and Messrs. WOOD & Co., of Edinburgh, for allowing the insertion of several pieces of which they hold the copyright. To nearly every preceding work on the subject this Collection has been more or less indebted, but the Editor has tried always to acknowledge this in the body of the work.

It may be as well to state that, the plan of the work here submitted to the public is to print only genuine Scotish productions; to omit every piece which could not be read or sung in the family circle, and to arrange the pieces, as far as possible, in chronological order. The Jacobite Songs referring to a distinct subject are arranged together in a separate section, according to the event known or presumed to be celebrated in the song. Long notes and critical remarks are, as a rule, avoided as useless; and an introductory essay is prefixed, gathering together the fragments of early pieces, and giving an account of the principal printed Collections.

INDEX OF FIRST LINES.

	PAGE.
A canty sang, O, a canty sang	433
A cogie o' yill	265
A cock laird fu' cadgie	59
A friend o' mine came here yestreen	170
A laddie and a lassie fair	136
A lass that was laden with care	162
A lassie cam' to our gate yestreen	452
A rose bud by my early walk	212
A soldier for gallant achievements renown'd	106
A Southland Jenny, that was right bonnie	168
A steed, a steed, of matchless speede	483
A weary lot is mine, fair maid	387
A wee bird cam' to our ha' door	569
A wet sheet and a flowing sea	446
About the cloxin' o' the day	481
Accuse me not inconstant fair	886
Adieu to rock and to waterfall	407
Admiring nature's simple charms	469
As fond kiss, and then we sever	211
As morn last ouk as I gaed out	342
Again rejoicing nature sees	244
Ah Mary, sweetest maid farewell!	358
Ah! the poor shepherd's mournful fate	115
Alake for the lassie, she's no right ava'	399
Alas my son you little know	150
Allen-a-dale has no faggot for burning	387
All joy was bereft me the day that you left me	391
All lovely on the sultry beach	176
Although his back be at the wa'	578
Although I be but a country lass	45
Amang the birks sae blythe and gay	369
An' a' that ere my Jenny had	50
An' oh! for ane an' twenty Tam	280
An' thou wert my ain thing	75
And are ye sure the news is true	168
And can thy bosom bear the thought	878
And fare ye weel my auld wife	28
And I'll owre the muir to Maggy	91

INDEX OF FIRST LINES.

	PAGE
And oh! my Eppie	254
Argyll is my name, and you may think it strange	127
As I cam' by Loch Erroch-side	287
As I cam' down the Canongate	550
As I cam' in by Teviot side	35
As I came by Lochmaben gate	516
As I came through Glendochart vale	275
As I sail'd past green Jura's Isle	446
As I was walking ae May morning	159
As I went forth to view the plain	98
As Jenny sat down wi' her wheel by the fire	289
As Patie cam' up frae the glen	154
As walking forth to view the plain	42
At Polwarth on the green	76
At setting day and rising-morn	97
At Willie's wedding on the green	561
Auld gudeman, ye're a drucken carle	363
Auld Rob Morris that wons in yon glen	48
Auld Rob the Laird o' muckle land	261
Awake my love! with genial ray	156
Awa' Whigs awa'	507
Awa' wi' your witchcraft o' beauty's alarms	229
Bannocks o' bear meal, bannocks o' barley	576
Behave yoursel' before folk	474
Behind yon hills where Lugar flows	199
Beneath a beach's grateful shade	104
Beneath a green shade, a lovely young swain	175
Bird of the wilderness	425
Blink o'er the burn sweet Betty	26
Blythe, blythe, and merry was she	120
Blythe, blythe, and merry was she—Second version	249
Blythe, blythe, around the nappie	404
Blythe are we set wi' ither	349
Blythe was the time when he fee'd wi' my father O	528
Blythe young Bess to Jean did say	141
Bonny Charlie's now awa'	574
Bonnie lassie will ye go	235
Bonnie Mary Halliday	443
Bonnie wee thing, cannie wee thing	216
Braw, braw lads o' Gala water	28
Busk ye, busk ye, my bonny bonny bride	110
By Carnoustie's auld wa's at the close o' the day	504
By Logan's streams that rin sae deep	290
By Pinkie house oft let me walk	142
By smooth winding Tay, a swain was reclining	40
By yon castle wa' at the close o' the day	504
Ca' the yowes to the knowes	189
Caledonia! thou land of the mountain and rock	426
Can I behave, can I behave	475
Carle an' the king come	492

INDEX OF FIRST LINES.

	PAGE
Cauld blaws the wind, frae north to south	343
Cauld kail in Aberdeen	129
Chaunt no more thy roundelay	452
Chill the wintry winds were blowing	323
Clavers an' his Highlandmen	495
Come all ye jolly shepherds	410
Come along my brave clans	533
Come boat me o'er, come row me o'er	589
Come, gie's a sang, Montgomery cried	177
Come hame to your lingels ye neer-do-weel loon	880
Come o'er the stream, Charlie, dear Charlie, brave Charlie	539
Come under my plaidie, the night's gaun to fa'	809
Come ye by Athol, lad wi' the philabeg	535
Comin' through the Craigs o' Kyle	191
Contented wi' little an' canty wi' mair	219
Cope sent a challenge frae Dunbar	545
Dark lowers the night o'er the wild stormy main	841
Dear Doctor, be clever, an' fling off your beaver	418
Dear land of my birth, of my friends, of my love	882
Dear Roger if your Jenny geck	95
Did ever swain a nymph adore	107
Do you weep for the woes of poor wandering Nelly	845
Does haughty Gaul invasion threat	239
Donald Caird's come again	894
Donald's gane up the hill hard and hungry	514
Doon i' the glen by the lowan o' the trees	461
Dorothy sits in the cauld ingle neuk	824
Dumbarton's drums beat bonnie O	55
Duncan Gray cam' here to woo	252
Down in yon meadow a couple did tarry	137
Earl March look'd on his dying child	462
Fair lady mourn the memory	588
Fair modest flower of matchless worth	856
Far frae the giddy court of mirth	821
Far lone amang the Highland hills	316
Far o'er yon hills of the heather so green	576
Farewell thou fair day, thou green earth and ye skies	249
Farewell to a' our Scottish fame	503
Farewell to Glen-Shalloch	562
Farewell to Lochaber, and farewell to my Jean	77
Farewell to pleasant Ditson Hall	529
Fare-thee-weel, my native cot	568
Farewell ye dungeons dark and strong	255
First when Maggy was my care	248
Flow gently, sweet Afton, amang thy green braes	201
Fly we to some distant isle	826
For lack of gold she has left me O	134
For mony lang year I hae heard frae my granny	274
Fortune frowning most severe	820
From Roslin Castle's echoing walls	125

INDEX OF FIRST LINES.

	PAGE
Frae the friends and the land I love	567
From thee, Eliza, I must go	206
From the rude bustling camp, to the calm rural plain	324
From the village of Lesly, with a heart fu' o' glee	341
Fy let us a' to the bridal	81
Gae bring my gude auld harp ance mair	477
Gane is the day, an' mirk's the nicht	216
General Cope is now come down	546
Geordie sits in Charlie's chair	588
Get up gudewife, don on your claise	26
Gie me a lass wi' a lump o' land	74
Gin a body meet a body	403
Gin I had a wee house, an' a canty wee fire	161
Gin ye meet a bonnie lassie	78
Gloomy winter's now awa'	317
Go fetch to me a pint o' wine	213
Go to Berwick, Johnnie	344
Go to him then if thou canst go	365
Gude day now bonnie robin	24
Ha's ye seen in the calm dewy morning	435
Had I a cave on some wild distant shore	254
Hame, hame, hame, hame fain wad I be	581
Happy's the love which meets return	88
Hard fate that I should banish'd be	527
Hark yonder eagle lonely wails	268
Harken and I will tell you how	9
Have ye ony pots or pans	22
Hay I now the day dawis	8
Hear me ye nymphs, and every swain	102
Heard ye e'er o' Donald Gunn	448
He is gone on the mountain	886
Here around the ingle bleezin	258
Here awa' there awa' here awa', Willie	58
Here awa' there awa' wandering Willie	160
Here's to the year that's awa'	461
Here's to the King, Sir	498
He's a terrible man, John Tod, John Tod	278
He's owre the hills' that I lo'e weel	543
Hersell be Highland shentleman	132
Here's a health to them that's awa'	577
Hey how Johnnie lad	169
Hey Donald, how Donald	262
Hey for bobbing John	305
Hey the bonnie, how the bonnie	261
Hey the dusty miller	252
His bonnie lassie blink over the burn	132
Hoo are ye, kimmer	27
How brightly beams the bonnie moon	478
How blythe ilk morn was I to see	116
How dear to think on former days	429

INDEX OF FIRST LINES.

	PAGE
How lang shall our land thus suffer distresses	530
How pleasant the banks of the clear winding Devon	246
How sweetly smells the simmer green	71
How sweet the modest light to view	408
Husband, husband cease your strife	241
I am a puir silly auld man	43
I chanc'd to meet an airy blade	188
I do confess thou'rt smooth and fair	11
I dream'd I lay where flowers were springing	196
I gae'd a waefu' gate yestreen	241
I ha'e a wife o' my ain	211
I ha'e laid a herring in saut	287
I ha'e nae kith, I ha'e nae kin	502
I ha'e seen great anes, and sat in great ha's	427
I heard the evening linnet's voice, the woodland tufts amang	209
I lately lived in quiet case	412
I lo'ed ne'er a laddie but ane	310
I loved thee once, I love thee no more	12
I mark'd a gem o' pearly dew	384
I married wi' a scolding wife	224
I may sit in my wee croo-house	506
I wadna' gie my ain wife	468
I was ance a weel tochered lass	119
I will awa' wi' my love	84
I winna gang back to my mammy again	274
I winna lo'e the laddie that ca's the cart and pleugh	480
I wish I were where Helen lies	19
———— Second version	20
If doughty deeds my ladye please	190
If my dear wife should chance to gang	171
I'll aye ca' in by yon town	210
I'll gar oor guidman trow	54
I'll hie me to the shieling hill	826
I'll sing o' yon glen o' red heather	423
I'm now a gude farmer, I've acres o' land	295
I'm owre yonng to marry yet	222
I'm wearing awa', John	281
I met four chaps yon birks amang	860
In a saft simmer gloaming	488
In April when primroses paint the sweet plain	80
In Scotland there liv'd a humble beggar	156
In summer I maw'd my meadow	26
In the garb of old Gaul with the fire of old Rome	128
In the land of Fife there liv'd a wicked wife	188
In winter when the rain rain'd cauld	16
Is there for honest povertie	237
It fell about the Martinmas time	158
It fell on a morning when we were thrang	353
It was in and about the Martinmas time	87
It was at a wedding near Tranent	367
It was upon a Lammas night	200

INDEX OF FIRST LINES.

	PAGE
It's Geordie's now come hereabout	510
It's Hanover, Hanover, fast as you can over	513
It's no that thou'rt bonnie, it's no that thou'rt braw	472
I've heard a lilting at our yowe milking	184
I've seen the smiling	128
I've spent my time in rioting	99
I've wandered east, I've wandered west	486
It wasna for our rightfu' King	497
Jenny's heart was frank and free	292
Jocky fou, Jenny fain	65
Jock he came here to woo	160
Jocky said to Jenny, Jenny wilt thou do't?	49
John Anderson my Jo, John	239
John Grumlie swore by the light of the moon	441
Keen blaws the wind o'er the braes o' Gleniffer	314
Land of my fathers, though no mangrove here	405
Langsyne beside the woodland burn	318
Lassies, look na sourly meek	371
Lassie wi' the lint-white locks	242
Last May a braw wooer cam' doon the lang glen	231
Late in an evening forth I went	47
Let us go, lassie, go	314
Let us haste to Kelvin grove, bonnie lassie O	438
Like bees that suck the morning dew	76
Little wat ye wha's comin'	518
Lo, what it is to lufe	5
Long have I pined for thee	582
Look where my Hamilla smiles	105
Loose the yett, and let me in	424
Louder than the tramp o' fame	312
Loudon's bonnie woods and braes	318
Love never more shall give me pain	103
Love's goddess in a myrtle grove	89
March, march, Ettrick and Teviotdale	350
March, march, why the deil do ye na march	25
Mark yonder pomp of costly fashion	248
Mary, why thus waste thy youth time in sorrow	335
Maxwelltown banks are bonnie	45
May morning had shed her first streamers on high	580
Meg muckin at Geordie's byre	206
Merry may the maid be	67
My daddy had a riding mare	512
My daddie is a cankert carle	145
My daddie left me gear enough	18
My dear little lassie why what's a' the matter	298
My dear and only love, I pray	21
My father was a farmer, upon the Carrick border	198
My gudeman says aye to me	471
My Harry was a gallant gay	256

	PAGE
My hawk is tired of perch and hood	898
My heart is a breaking, dear Tittie	225
My heart's in the Highlands, my heart is not here	257
My laddie is gane far away o'er the plain	262
My heart is sair, I daurna tell	219
My heart is sair, I daurna tell	582
My love come let us wander	430
My love's in Germany	805
My love she's but a lassie yet	232
My love she's but a lassie yet	419
My love was born in Aberdeen	556
My love was once a bonnie lad	126
My Mary is a bonnie lassie	328
My mither's aye glowrin ower me	71
My mither ment my auld breeks	476
My name is Donald MacDonald	416
My Patie is a lover gay	96
My Peggie is a young thing	96
My sheep I neglected, I lost my sheep hook	135
My sweetest May, let love incline thee	99
My wife's a wanton wee thing	164
Nae Gentle dames thoe'er sae fair	208
Nancy's to the Greenwood gane	15
Neath the wave thy lover sleeps	430
Never wedding, ever wooing	462
Nith, trembling to the reapers sang	444
No Churchman am I for to rail and to write	217
Now Charles asserts his father's right	548
Now fy let us a' to the treaty	508
Now in her green mantle blythe nature arrays	231
Now, Jenny lass, my bonnie bird	800
Now rosy May comes in wi' flowers	226
Now smiling summer's balmy breeze	370
Now the sun's gaen out o' sight	83
Now there's peace on the shore, now there's calm on the sea	457
Now wat ye wha I met yestreen	70
Now winter wi' his cloudy brow	331
O Allister McAllister	400
O, an ye were dead gudeman	285
O, are ye sleepin, Maggie	816
O, Bell thy looks hae killed my heart	81
O, Bessie Bell and Mary Gray	80
O cam ye here the fight to shun	524
O can ye sew cushions	264
O come awa, come awa	64
O gin my love were yon red rose	59
O how could I venture to love one like thee	122
O hush thee my babie, thy sire was a knight	895
O, I had a wee bit mailin	499
O Kenmure's on, and awa, Willie	523

	PAGE
O ken ye Meg o' Marley glen	422
O lassie I loe dearest	372
O Logie, of Buchan, O Logie the laird	131
O lovers' eyes are sharp to see	396
O lustie May with Flora queue	6
O mother tell the laird o't	421
O my lassie, our joy to complete again	411
O once I lov'd a bonnie lass	195
O sair I rue the witless wish	325
O Sandy why leave thou thy Nelly to mourn	89
O saw ye my wee thing, saw ye my ain thing	303
O saw ye my father, saw ye my mither	166
O say is there ane wha does not rejoice	278
O say not love will never	467
O say not my love, with that mortified air	396
O the ewe buchting's bonnie baith e'ening and morn ...	58, 456
O the sun frae the eastward was peeping	376
O this is no my ain house	500
O waly, waly, up the bank	41
O weel may I mind on the folk at Lindores	381
O weel may the boatie row	284
O were I able to rehearse	180
O wha are sae happy as me and my Janet	432
O wha's for Scotland and Charlie	536
O wha's that at my chamber door	91
O what will a' the lads do	425
O what's the rhyme to Porringer	500
O when she cam ben she bobbit fu' low	259
O where, tell me where, is your highland laddie gone ...	348
O why should old age so much wound us, O	184
O wilt thou go wi' me, sweet Tibbie Dunbar	253
Och hey Johnnie lad	333
October winds wi' biting breath	317
Of a' the airts the wind can blaw	209
Of all the days that's in the year	515
Oh aye my wife she dang me	251
Oh dinna ask me gin I loe thee	431
Oh dinna think, bonnie lassie, I'm gaun to leave thee ...	304
Oh how can I be blythe and glad	222
Oh I am come to the low countrie	568
Oh lay thy loof in mine lass	223
Oh leeze me on my spinning wheel	228
Oh love will venture in, where it daurna weel be seen ...	234
Oh Logan sweetly didst thou glide	213
Oh Mally's meek, Mally's sweet	246
Oh Mary at thy window be	197
Oh meikle thinks my love o' my beauty	229
Oh mirk, mirk, is this midnight hour	251
Oh my love's like a red, red rose	218
Oh neighbours what had I ado for to marry	364
Oh open the door, some pity to show	224

	PAGE
Oh pity an auld Highlan' piper	435
Oh poortith cauld, and restless love	221
Oh Rowan tree, oh Rowan tree	283
Oh saw ye bonnie Lesley	248
Oh send Lewie Gordon hame	577
Oh sisters there are midnight dreams	479
Oh take me to yon sunny isle that stands in Fortha's sea	434
Oh tell me, oh tell me bonnie young lassie	806
Oh Tibbie, I hae seen the day	217
Oh the auld house, the auld house	281
Oh this is no my ain lassie	230
Oh was be to the orders that march'd my love awa	400
Oh weel befa' the busy toon	426
Oh! were I on Parnassus hill	220
Oh! whistle, and I'll come to you my lad	226
Oh why left I my hame; why did I cross the deep	482
Oh Willie brew'd a peck o' mant	234
O'er the mist shrouded clifts of the gray mountain straying	872
On Cessnock banks there lives a lass	198
On Ettrick banks as simmer's night	63
On Gallia's shore we sat and wept	561
On the banks of the burn, while I pensively wander	398
On the blyth Beltane as I went	150
On the wild braes of Calder, I found a fair lily	470
One day I heard Mary say	105
One night as young Colin lay musing in bed	176
Once on a morning of sweet recreation	595
Our bonnie Scots lads in their green tartan plaids	327
Our gallant Prince is now come hame	547
Our goodman cam hame at e'en	151
Our gudewife's awa'	440
Our native land, our native vale	455
Our's is the land of gallant hearts	478
Ower the hills and far away	531
Pardon now the bold outlaw	402
Pibroch of Donuil Dhu	389
Powers Celestial! whose protection	203
Preserve us a'; what shall we do	267
Quoth Rab to Kate, my sonsy dear	801
Return thee hameward, heart again	5
Rising o'er the heaving billow	845
Robin is my only jo	166
Robin shure in hairst	257
Rob's Jock tam to woo our Jenny	7
Row weel my boatie, row weel	369
Royal Charlie's now awa	573
Roy's wife o' Aldivalloch	302
Sae flaxen were her ringlets	215
Saw ye Johnny comin', quoth she	62

INDEX OF FIRST LINES.

	PAGE
Saw ye nae my Peggie	61
Scotia's thistle guards the grave	482
Scotland and England must now be	158
Scots, wha hae wi' Wallace bled	235
See the glow-worm lits her fairy lamp	487
See the moon o'er cloudless Jura	492
See aff and awa' like the lang summer days	485
She's fair and fause that causes my smart	256
She is a winsome wee thing	211
She was a sunbeam in the storm	468
Should old acquaintance be forgot	15
Should auld acquaintance be forgot	73
Should auld acquaintance be forgot	217
Simmer's a pleasant time	250
Since all thy vows, false maid	89
Since uncle's death, I've lads anew	451
Sing a' ye bards wi' loud acclaims	475
Sing on, sing on, my bonnie bird	415
Sir John Cope rode to the north right far	544
Sit ye down here my cronies and gie us your crack	305
Soldier rest! thy warfare o'er	388
Some say that kissing's a sin	50
Surrounded wi' bent and wi' heather	392
Symon Brodie had a cow	140
Sweet is the eve on Craigieburn	250
Sweet sir, let your courtesie	99
Sweet is the dew-deck'd rose in June	374
Tarry woo, tarry woo	118
Taste life's glad moments	363
That life's a faught; there is nae doubt	454
The auld man's near dead	97
The auld Stuarts back again	517
The bride cam' oot o' the byre	44
The bride she is winsome and bonnie	352
The bloom hath fled thy cheek, Mary	488
The blude red rose at yule may blow	223
The bonnie bracket lassie	235
The Campbells are comin', O ho, O ho	260
The Catrine woods were yellow seen	206
The collier has a daughter	73
The cronach stills the dowie heart	356
The cuckoo's a bonny bird, when he comes hame	513
The day returns, my bosom burns	250
The deil cam fiddling through the town	249
The e'e o' the dawn, Eliza	406
The gloomy night is gath'ring fast	208
The gowan glitters on the sward	361
The grass had nae freedom o' growin'	379
The heath this night must be my bed	394
The highlandmen came down the hill	555
The laird o' Cockpen, he's proud and he's great	280

	PAGE
The lass of Patie's mill	94
The lassies a' laugh an' the carlin flate	838
The last time I cam' owre the muir	86
The Lawland lads think they are fine	82
The love that I had chosen	124
The lovely lass o' Inverness	564
The meal was dear short syne	50
The midges dance aboon the burn	882
The moon had climbed the highest hill	144
The moon's on the lake, and the mist's on the brae	890
The moon was fair, saft was the air	102
The murmur of the merry brook	489
The news frae Moidart cam' yestreen	587
The night is mirk, and the wind blaws schill	485
The pawkie auld carle came o'er the lea	1
The piper came to our town	542
The ploughman he's a bonnie lad	52
The small birds rejoice in the green leaves returning	512
The smiling morn, the breathing spring	124
The smiling plain profusely gay	126
The spring time returns, and clothes the gay plain	121
The storm is raging o'er the Kyle	570
The sun has gone down o'er the lofty Ben Lomond	812
The sun rise see rosy the green hills adorning	805
The standard on the braes o' Mar	519
The tears I shed must ever fall	884
The Thames flows proudly to the sea	247
The widow can bake, an' the widow can brew	79
The wind comes frae the land I lo'e	538
The winter sat lang on the spring o' the year	292
The wren scho lyes in care's bed	26
The year is wearin' to the wane	416
The yellow haired laddie sat down on yon brae	59
The youth that should hae been our King	579
Their groves of sweet myrtle let foreign lands reckon	210
There are twa bonnie maidens	571
There cam a braw lad to my daddie's door	166
There dwelt a man into the west	448
There grows a bonnie brier bush in our kail yard	552
There lived a lass in Inverness	564
There lives a landart laird in Fife	867
There lives a lassie on the brae	185
There lives a young lassie	439
There was a lad was born in Kyle	195
There was a lass, they ca'd her Meg	215
There was a wife wound in a glen	64
There was an auld wife had a wee pickle tow	171
There was aince a maid and she loo'd na men	57
There were twa dogs sat in a dookit	279
There's Auld Rob Morris that wons in yon glen	253
There's braw braw lads on Yarrow braes	219

INDEX OF FIRST LINES.

	PAGE
There's Cauld Kail in Aberdeen	180
There's Cauld Kail in Aberdeen	347
There's fowth o' braw Jockies and Jennies	146
There's kames o' hinnie 'tween my love's lips	442
There's nae laddie comin' for thee, my dear Jean	420
There's nae covenant now lassie	453
There's nought but care on every han'	201
There's some say that we wan	520
There's waefu' news in yon town	272
There's was a wee bit wifukie was comin' frae the fair	268
They lighted a taper at the dead of night	463
They say that Jockey'll speed weel o't	172
Thickest night o'erhange my dwelling	221
This is no mine ain house	78
Tho' summer smiles on bank and brae	837
Thou art gane awa', thou art gane awa'	262
Thou bonnie wood o' Craigielea	817
Thou cauld gloomy Feber'war	837
Thou dark winding Carron once pleasing to see	812
Thou hast left me ever Jamie, thou hast left me ever	227
Thou ling'ring star with less'ning ray	205
Though dowie's the winter sae gloomy and drear	468
Though Geordie reigns wi' Jamie's stead	578
Through Crookston Castle's lanely wa's	815
Thy cheek is o' the rose's hue	271
Tibby has a store of charms	90
Tibbie Fowler o' the glen	140
Ts hinns ye heard man o' Barrochan Jean	329
'Tis no very lang sinsyne	167
Tune your fiddles, tune them sweetly	183
To curb usurpation by th' assistance of France	340
To daunton me, to daunton me	497
To daunton me, an' me sae young	541
To your arms, to your arms, my bonnie Highland lads	551
To the Lords of Convention, 'twas Claverhouse spoke	493
Touch once more a sober measure	458
Turn again, thou fair Eliza	205
'Twas even, the dewy fields were green	207
'Twas na her bonnie blue e'e was my ruin	247
'Twas on a Monday morning	549
'Twas on a summer afternoon	283
'Twas summer, and saftly the breezes were blowing	149
'Twas summer tide! the Cushat sang	408
'Twas when the wan leaf frae the birk tree was fa'in	897
Up amang yon cliffy rocks	840
Up, and rin awa, Hawley	554
Up in the morning's no for me	230
Upon a summer's afternoon	402
Was ever old warrior of sufferings so weary	419
Weary is' yon Duncan Gray	260

INDEX OF FIRST LINES.   xix

	PAGE
We'll hap and row, we'll hap and row	288
We'll meet beside the dusky glen, on yon burnside	331
Wha the deil hae we gotten for a king	508
Wha wadna be in love	32
Wha wadna fight for Charlie	536
Wha will ride wi gallant Murray	534
Wha'll buy my caller herrin'	377
Whar hae ye been a' day	508
Whare hae ye been sae braw lads	499
What beauties does Flora disclose	101
What can a young lassie, what shall a young lassie	227
What gude the present day can gie	274
What ails you now my dauntie Pate	289
What's this wi' voice o' music sweet	278
Where live ye my bonnie lass	268
When a' ither bairnies are hush'd to their hame	456
When cities of old days	465
When first I cam' to be a man of twenty years or so	181
When first my dear laddie gaed to the greenhill	95
When France had her assistance lent	553
When gloamin o'er the welkin steals	381
When gowans sprinkled a' the lea	353
When I began the world first	179
When I had a saxpence under my thumb	49
When innocent pastime our pleasures did crown	87
When I think on the sweet smiles o' my lassie	364
When I think on the world's pelf	61
When I upon thy bosom lean	187
When I was a miller in Fife	449
When I left thee bonnie Scotland	600
When John and me were married	333
When Katie was scarce out nineteen	357
When lonely thon wandered along by the wildwood	884
When Maggie and me were acquaint	58
When my flocks upon the heathy hill are lying a' at rest	477
When o'er the hill the eastern star	213
When our ancient forefathers agreed with the laird	188
When Phoebus bright the azure skyes	35
When poortith cauld, and sour disdain	330
When Rosie was faithful how happy was I	333
When shall the lover rest	322
When summer comes the swains on Tweed	117
When the sheep are in the fauld, and the kye a' at hame	276
When trees did bud and fields were green	106
When we gaed to the braes o' Mar	526
When we think on the days of auld	501
When white was my o'erlay as foam o' the linn	356
When wild war's deadly blast was blawn	285
Whare Cart rins rowin to the sea	308
Where is your daddie gane, my little May	563
Where Quair rins sweet amang the flowers	298

	PAGE.
While fups in saft Italian verse	108
While frequent on Tweed and on Tay	143
While the gray pinioned lark early mounts to the skies	328
Why hangs that cloud upon thy brow	114
Why, my Charlie, dost thou leave me	575
Why weep ye by the tide, ladye	385
Wi' a hundred pipers an' a' an' a'	552
Will ye gae to the ewe buchts, Marion	53
Will ye gang o'er the lea rig	148
Will ye gang wi' me, lassie	414
Will ye gang wi' me, Lizzie Lindsay	259
Will ye go to the Indies, my Mary	202
Will ye come to the board I've prepared for you	522
Willie was a wanton wag	98
Willie Wastle dwelt on Tweed	240
Willy's rare, and Willy's fair	118
With broken words and downcast eyes	92
With tuneful pipe and hearty glee	157
With waefu' heart and sorrowing e'e	334
Ye banks and braes, and streams around	204
Ye banks and braes o' bonnie Doon	208
Ye echoes that ring 'round the woods of Bowgreen	320
Ye gales that gently wave the sea	84
Ye gallants bright, I rede ye right	253
Ye gods was Strephon's picture blest	113
Ye rivers so limpid and clear	174
Ye shepherds and nymphs that adorn the gay plain	118
Ye sunny braes that skirt the Clyde	327
Ye watchful guardian of the fair	93
Ye whigs are a rebellious crew	509
Ye wooer lads wha greet and grane	310
Ye'll a' ha'e heard tell o' Rab Roryson's bonnet	322
You may sing o' your Wallace, and brag o' your Bruce	401
Young Charlie is a gallant lad	541
Young Peggie blooms our bonniest lass	214
Youre welcome, whigs, from Bothwell Brigs	492
You've surely heard o' famous Neil	355

INTRODUCTION.

A song is generally the earliest form in which the literary taste of a nation is to be found, and the collected songs of a country placed before a critical reader is probably the most severe test of its excellence in literature. To write a mere song, or words to accompany a given air is a comparatively easy matter, but to write one which will touch the heart or the passions, and stand the test of time, after all the best test of poetic merit, is a gift comparatively rare. To be popular with the masses, its language must be simple and unaffected: nothing, in Scotish Song especially, is more nonsensical than the introduction of Phillis, Adonis, Miranda, or Strephon, or any of these classical beauties and exquisites. To be remembered, it must be short; and its sentiments whether amorous, bacchanalian, warlike, or domestic, must not be extravagant, but rather given with subdued power, while to please the critical reader its rhyme must be smooth and its rhythm faultless.

That these conditions are fulfilled by the majority of our best Scotch songs may be seen by glancing at the collection here submitted to the public. To select a few, what could be finer or more pleasing to critics and readers than "O waly waly up the bank," "Auld Robin Gray," "I've heard a lilting," "Brume o' the Cowdenknowes," "Tam Glen," "My Nannie's awa," "Land o' the Leal," "Lucy's Flittin'," and many others?

There is one thing which cannot fail to strike the reader of these songs, and it is the fact that the great majority of our best songs are from the pens of writers born in the poorer ranks of society, and whose education was generally comparatively imperfect. Ramsay, Burns, Allan Cunningham, Mayne, Tannahill, Hogg, Gall, Laidlaw, may serve to illustrate this in the later period of the annals of our song. For the earlier period the song writers are generally unknown, but from various circumstances we must infer that the same fact is visible here also, especially when we remember that in the works of Sir David Lindsay, Gawain Douglas, or Dunbar, we do not find any piece which could be included in a collection of Scotish song; and assuredly these writers give us no name distinguished in their time for excellence in this department of their craft. Why this should be, we leave some future investigator into the Curiosities of Literature to determine.

We purpose devoting this introduction to an examination of the remains of our early songs, so as to give the reader such an idea of our earliest pieces as may be derived from an enumeration of the titles, which is almost wholly all that has come down to us. Where a fragment has been fortunate enough to escape the fate of its fellows, we shall faithfully and gladly give it. We will also take a glance at the most important printed collections, from Ramsay's Tea Table Miscellany onward.

The songs of Scotland, so far as they are left to us, begin at the period when the ancient minstrels, on whose social position so much valuable time, paper, and temper has been wasted, had fallen into the deepest disgrace, and were classed in Acts of Parliament along with beggars, rogues, and vagabonds. The decline of their influence, and in all likelihood the comparative worthlessness of their later compositions, caused the people generally to cherish more fondly the songs and ballads that had arisen amongst themselves, no one could tell how, and which better assisted their varying mood than the long rhymes of the strolling bard, and enabled them to keep men of the questionable character, which the representatives of the old minstrels had won for themselves, away from their dwellings and merry meetings.

The pastoral life which, in the fifteenth and sixteenth centuries, was followed by the majority of the people of the lowlands, would also favour the growth of song; and in each little community one man's success doubtless excited the emulation of his neighbour, and each would strive to be reckoned best at rhyming,[1] particularly if some rustic beauty were the prize to be won. However it may be, there is now hardly a village, river, or glen without a song in its honour; all the favourite names of the lassies, Mary, Kate, Jean, Meg, or Annie, are duly enshrined ; every battlefield has been celebrated or wailed, while the popular enemies of the country, whether internal or external, are bedecked in satire which, justly or not, has sent them down to all posterity with an evil prominence that can never be removed.

A collection like this can only deal with the songs of the Lowlands. Could the Highland minstrelsy be collected and edited, it would be seen that the north is not behind the south in little pieces that touch the heart and fire the soul. Many of the Gaelic Airs especially, convey the impressions of love, sorrow, grief, and triumph in a manner at once beautiful, musical, and impressive.[2]

Prior to the publication of the Tea Table Miscellany in 1725, Scotish Song was preserved only in the precarious keeping of

---

[1] We know how well pleased the Ettrick Shepherd was at the title given him by the country lassies of "Jamie the Poeter."

[2] The bagpipe is commonly put down by Englishmen as a nuisance, but they never heard the pipers at a grave side, where, as each dull thud of earth falls on the coffin lid, a low plaintive wail is given forth at once touching and heart-rending.

the people, who, with each succeeding generation, altered the
songs bequeathed by them to suit their own tastes. The words
of course were first altered, then the ideas, till often the mere
name of the original song given to us as the original name of
an air, is all that remains to afford us an idea of the early words.
Sufficient evidence of this will be given further on, when we
detail the titles of the old tunes to which words in keeping with
the titles cannot now be produced.

The earliest scrap of song which has been preserved occurs
in Wynton's Orygynale Cronykil (which is supposed to have
been written early in the fifteenth century), and seems to form
part of a lament for the death of Alexander III., A.D. 1285:—

> "Quhen Alysander oure kynge wes dede
> That Scotland led in luwe and le,
> Away wes sons off ale and brede
> Off wyne and wax, off gamyn and gle;
> Oure gold was changyd into lede,
> Cryst, borne into vergynyte,
> Succour Scotland and remede,
> That stad in his perplexite."

With the death of Alexander began the intrigues of the English
king for the sovereignty of Scotland, and the next scrap we
have refers to the first expedition of Edward I. into the northern
kingdom. The town of Berwick-on-Tweed was in the possession
of the Scotch and was strongly garrisoned by them. This of
course had to be taken and was besieged. The inhabitants
were so much elated at a temporary success (the burning of
two English ships, assisting in the attack from the sea side),
that the following was sung by them in derision at the attempts
of the English:—

> Wend Kyng Edewarde, with his lange shankes,
> To have gete Berwicke, al our unthankes?
> Gas pikes hym,
> And after Gas dikes hym.[1]

"This pleasantry, however," says Ritson, "was in the present
instance somewhat ill-timed; for as soon as the King heard of
it, he assaulted the town with such fury that he carried it with
the loss of 25,700 Scots."

The battle of Bannockburn, fought July, 1314, was naturally
the subject of a great rejoicing in Scotland, and we have a
short fragment of a song which appears to have been popular
at the time:—

---

[1] Harleian MSS. quoted by Ritson. Mr. Chambers, Songs of Scotland, vol. I.
p. 5, suggests that the word Gas is an error for Gar, a suggestion very likely to be
correct.

> Maydens of Englande are may ye morne
> For your lemmans ye have lost at Banokysborne,
>   With hane a lowe
> What weayth the Kynge of Englande
> To have got Scotlonde
>   Wyth rumbylowe ? [1]

That a song was a very popular method of celebrating a victory is made known to us by a reference in Barbour's Bruce, where the poet forbears to enter into particulars, as

> Quhas liks they may her
> Young women, quhen thai will play,
> Syng it amang thaim ilk day. [2]

The feeling against the English was not removed by the marriage of a Scotish King with an English Princess, for in 1328 at the time of the marriage of David II. with the Princess Jane, this pasquil was in great favour with the Scotch :—

> Long beerdis hartles,
> Paynted hoodes wytlos,
> Gay cottes graceles,
> Maketh Englande thryfteles.

We now come to the reign of James I., unquestionably the ablest of all the Stewart race of kings. As is well known to every reader of Scotish History, James, while on his way to France, to which court he was sent for his education, was captured by an English Cruiser and detained for nineteen years a prisoner in England. During his captivity he received the best education that could be given, and which, if not far beyond what he would have had in France, was at least greatly superior to that of any of his predecessors on the throne. He returned to Scotland with ideas as to government and refinement far beyond his age. He was also, so far as we know, the best Scotch poet of his age; and although the "Kingis Quair" is the only work we can ascribe to him with any degree of certainty, still it is but reasonable to believe that other pieces came from his pen, and from his love of music that these pieces comprised many songs. Fordun, a contemporary historian, has highly extolled his talents as a musician, and Mr. Tytler, one of his editors and biographers, says "From the genius of King James, his profound skill in the principles of music, and great performance on the harp, we may esteem him the inventor and reformer of the Scottish Vocal Music."[3]

---

[1] Preserved in the Chronicle of St. Alban's. The words Heualogh and Rombelogh were probably, as remarked by Ritson, an ordinary burdan for ballads in the time.
[2] Barbour's Bruce. Jamieson's ed. Glasgow, 1869.
[3] Works of King James I.; Glasgow, 12mo, no date, page 173.

Major in his De Gestis Scotorum, mentions two songs by King James entitled—
Yas Sen.[1]
At Beltayn.[2]

In one of the poems attributed to the king, entitled Peblis to the Play, two songs are mentioned as being struck up by the merry-makers—

Their fure[3] ane man to the holt[4]
Their sall be mirth at our melting yet.[5]

A curious poem entitled Cockelbie's Sow (which will be found printed in Laing's Select Remains of the Ancient Popular Poetry of Scotland; Edinburgh, 1822, 4to), seems to have been written about the year 1450. A man called Cockelbie had a sow "which he sold for the reasonable sum of threepence; and a detail of the various effects connected with the disbursement of this sum, constitutes the substance of the poem."[6] One of the pennies was lost, and was found by a woman who determined to expend it to the best advantage, by buying a pig with it and inviting her acquaintances to partake. The pig, however, escaped before being killed. The fortunes of the other two pennies are treated in their turn in the poem, but it is with the first only we have at present to deal. The list of the parties invited by the woman to discuss the pig is very curious, and contains also the following list of songs, which were given at the meeting:—

Joly Lemmane.
Trus and Trenass.
The Bass.
Perdolly.
Trolly Lolly.[7]
Cok thou crawis quhill day.
Twysbank.[8]
Terway.
Lincolne.
Lindsay.
Joly Lemmane dawis it not day.

---

[1] Supposed to be the song printed in Pinkerton's Ancient Scottish Poems, vol. ii., page 214, and Sibbald's Chronicle, vol. iv., page 55, beginning "Sen that [the] eyne that workis my welfair." If this, however, be the case, the piece in question can hardly be called a song, consisting as it does of thirteen stanzas of nine lines each.

[2] In all likelihood, as has been remarked by Ritson, Chambers, and others, this refers to the poem of "Peblis to the Play," which begins, "At Beltane when ilk body bound is."   [3] Went.   [4] Wood.

[5] All trace of the words of these songs is now unfortunately lost.

[6] Irving's History of Scotish Poetry, edited by Carlyle, Edinburgh, 1861; 8vo, page 179.

[7] Mr. Chambers thinks this is the same as "Trolles Jolles lemmaudo," mentioned in the Complaynt of Scotland, and to be the same as that printed under his same title by Ritson in his ancient songs.

[8] Supposed to be the same piece as the ballad preserved in the Bannatyne MS., and printed in Laing's Ancient Popular Poetry.

Be you wodsyd.
Lait, late in evinnyngis.
Joly Martene with a mok.
Lulalow lute Cok.
My deir derling.[1]

In 1513, Gawin Douglas, Bishop of Dunkeld, completed his celebrated translation of Virgil's Æneid, the first translation of a classic which appeared in Britain. Poetical prologues to each book were added by the translator, and these prologues are now considered, and that justly, as the most interesting part of the work. To these prologues we are indebted for the names of four old songs:—

"The ship sails ower the saut faem,
Will bring thir merchants and my lemman hame."
—— "I will be blythe and licht,
My heart is lent upon sae guid a wicht."
"I come hidder to wow,"[2]
"The joly day now dawis."[3]

In one of his poems, Dunbar mentions a tune, entitled—
Into Juna,
but no vestige of it remains.

King James V., whose reign covers what has been termed the Augustan age of early Scotish Poetry, is credited with two songs—
The Gaberlunzie Man.[4]
The Jolly Beggars.[5]

---

[1] This is given as the name of a dance, but probably appropriate words were attached to the air.

[2] In all likelihood this refers to an early version of the favourite song, "I ha'e laid three herring in saut."

[3] This appears to have been always a favourite in Scotland. It is mentioned by Dunbar. Montgomery has a song of a similar character; see page 3 of this collection. In the Muses Threnodie, 1774, the words are quoted as the title of a celebrated old song; and in the poem on the "Life and Death of Habbie Simpson" (Watson's collection, part I., 1706), it is asked—
"Now wha shall play, the day it dawis."
Ritson expresses a doubt as to whether the "song or tune" be actually, or at least originally, Scotish, as he found in the Fairfax MSS. (circa 1500) a song of two stanzas, written in praise of Queen Elizabeth, beginning—
This day day dawis,
This gauntil day dawis,
And I must gone home;
but we see no reason for the doubt, as it is quite as likely that the English poet was acquainted with the Scotish song. He also admits that the music which accompanies the English song is poor, "so that it would seem as if either the English harmonist had entirely spoiled the Scotish tune, or the Scotish piper had improved the English one."

[4] See page 1 of this collection.

[5] This song we were reluctantly obliged to omit on account of its indecency; and besides, we had great doubts as to its ascribed authorship being correct. It seems to us to have been written long after the time of James V., though it is likely intended to illustrate one of his wandering exploits.

INTRODUCTION.

In 1549 was published at St. Andrews the now celebrated Complaynt of Scotland, a work to which inquirers into early Scotish song and music are more indebted than to any other early production. The author of this production is quite unknown; Leyden, who edited the work in 1801, claiming it for Sir David Lindsay, while others ascribe it to James Inglis, Abbot of Culross, and to David Wedderburn of Dundee. It is probable that the question will never now be satisfactorily settled. Besides being remarkable for the knowledge it gives us of domestic life in Scotland, it is deeply valuable to the antiquary as being an excellent specimen of early Scotch prose, and to the book-worm as the earliest prose work printed in Scotland. The plan of the work is very curious. "It is divided," says Leyden, "into three parts, of which the first may be properly denominated the complaint of the author; the second, the monologue of the author; and the third, the dream of the author, or the complaynt of Scotland. In the first, the author, deeply afflicted by the miseries of his country, begins to speculate concerning their cause. In the second, which has little connection with the first or third, a variety of rural scenes and occupations are depicted, which are ingeniously diversified with a sea-fight, and a dissertation on Natural Philosophy. This diversion is terminated by the author going into a profound sleep, during the unsuccessful experiment of shutting his eyes and looking through his eyelids; and in the third part he relates his dream or vision. The subject of the third part is the same with that of the first—the miseries of Scotland; but the description is more particular, and the machinery more allegorical."[1] Nothing could be more tedious to an ordinary reader than a perusal of the piece, but it conveys a valuable legacy to the student of Scotish song, containing, as it does, the titles of thirty-seven songs, popular in their time. The author, tired of study, goes to the fields for relaxation, and there meets with some shepherds, who, for his amusement, sing to him a great number of their favourite songs; and in the work we have a list of their titles, as under:—

    Pastance with gude cumpanye,[2]
    The breir byndis me soir.
    Stil vnder the leyuis grene.[3]

---

[1] The Complaynt of Scotland; edited by John Leyden: 8vo, 1801; Intro., p. 74.

[2] Said to be a song composed by Henry VIII., Ritson having a manuscript of that time where a song is printed, entitled "The King's Ballet," beginning—

    Pasetyme with good cumpanye,
    I love and shall vnto I dye:

we are, however, far from being convinced by this that "The King's Ballet" is the song referred to in the Complaynt.

[3] There is a song or poem in the Maitland MSS. (Pinkerton's Ancient Scotish Poems, vol. ii., p. 205) entitled "The Murning Maidin," which is supposed to be the piece referred to. It is a poem of eighteen stanzas, of nine lines each, descriptive of a neglected damsel mourning the loss of her swain in the woods. She is overheard by the poet, who makes love to her and is accepted.

INTRODUCTION.

Cou thou me the raschis grene.[1]
Allace I vyit your twa fayr ene.
Gode you gude day vil boy.
King Villyamis Note.[2]
The lang, nouno non.[3]
The Cheapel-valk.[4]
Faytht is there none.
Skald a bellis nou.[5]
The Abirdenis nou.[6]
Brume, brume on hil.[7]
Allone I veip in grit distress.
Trolee lollee lemmendou.[8]
Bille, vil thou cum by a lute and belt thee in Sanct Francis cord,[9]
The frog cam' to the myl dur,[10]
The sang of Gilquhiskar
Rycht soirly musing in my mynde,
God sen the Duc, hed byddin in France,
And Delabaute had neuyr cum hame,[11] }

---

[1] There is an old English song of which "Colle to me the ryshes grene" is the chorus.

[2] This is supposed to be the song sung by Hendy Nicholas, in Chaucer's Miller's Tale.
"And after that he song the kingis note,
Ful often blessed was his mery throte."—*Ritson.*
Leyden in his introduction to the Complaynt considers this suggestion improbable.

[3] Probably a part of the chorus of a song. Mr. Robert Chambers seems to consider it equal to "Sing niddis, sing noddle, sing now, now, now."

[4] Supposed by Mr. Chambers to be identical with Henryson's poem of "The Abbey Walk."

[5, 6] Probably popular burdens to songs.

[7] This song is mentioned by Laneham, describing the literary collections of Captain Cox, the Mason of Coventry. And Mr. Ritson quotes from an old authority the following lines:—
"Brome, brume on hil,
The gentill brome on hil, hil,
Brume, brume on hline hil,
The gentill brome on hline hil,
The brume stands on hline hil."—*Leyden.*

[8] See note 7 page 5. Probably an old Chorus.

[9] In Constable's Cantus, it is stated by Leyden, two lines of this song are introduced in a piece—
Billie, will ye come by a lute,
And tuick it with your pin trow low.

[10] This is probably the beginning of a childish ballad. There is a ballad beginning—
There lived a puddy in a well,
And a merry mouse in a mill,
printed in the Ballad Book, 1824. And Leyden quotes one which he himself heard, beginning—
The frog sat in the mill door, spin, spin, spinning,
When by cam the little mouse, rin, rin, rinning.

[11] "John, Duke of Albany, regent during the minority of James V., being sent for into France, left in his place Sir Andrew D'Arcy, a Frenchman called the chevalier De la Beaute, who appears to have been a very gallant and amiable character, and was savagely murdered, near Dunbar, by the Laird of Wedderburn and others in 1517."—*Ritson.* The two lines quoted seem to be the beginning of a ballad on the event.

Al musing of mervellis a myshef I gon,[1]
Maistres fayr ye vil for foyr.
O hustye mayo vith Flora Queen.[2]
O mine hart, hay this is my sang.
The battel of the Hayrlau.[3]
The Huntlis of Chevet.[4]
Sal I go vitht you to Rumbelo fayr.
Grealt is my sorow.[5]
Turne the swelt ville to me.
My lufe is lyand seik.
  Send him loy, loy.
The Persee and the Mongumerye met
  That day, that gentil day.[6]
My luf is laid apon ane knycht.
Allace that samyn suet face.
In ane mirthful morow.
My hart is leinit on the land.

The author of the Complaynt also gives us the following list of Dances and Airs. All Christin Mennis Dance, The North of Scotland, Huntis Up, The Comont entray, Lang plat fut of Gariau; Robene Hude, Thom of Lyn, The Loch of Slene, The Gossip Dance, Leuis Grene, The Lemnes Wynd, Cum Kittil me nakyt wantounly, Baglap and al, Johne Ermestrangis dance, The bace of Voragon, Schaik a trot, &c.

Sir Richard Maitland, of Lethington, Lord Privy Seal, and Judge in the Court of Session (born 1496, died 1586), was one of the principal poets of the period, and is entitled to notice in this introduction on account of the manuscript collection of Scotch Poetry compiled by him, or under his auspices, about 1555. This collection, now in the Pepysian Library, Cambridge, contains pieces by Dunbar, Gawain Douglas, Schaw, Arbuthnot, and others, besides a large number of pieces by Maitland himself. Pinkerton, the celebrated antiquary, published a selection from the manuscript, with copious introductions and notes in

---

[1] Mr. Leyden discovered, what he considered a verse of this song, in Constable's Cantus—

  All musing of mervelles in the mid morne
  Through a slunk in a slaid, amlass have I gone;
  I heard a song me beside, that reft from me my sprite,
  But through my dreame, as I dream'd this was the effect.

[2] First printed in 1608, by Chepman and Myllar. It also appears in the Aberdeen Cantus, 1666. In the Bannatyne MS. it is ascribed to Alexander Scott. It will be found on page 6 of the present collection with its Orthography slightly altered.

[3] Supposed to be the still popular ballad of that name (see Ballad Minstrelsy of Scotland.)

[4] Supposed to be the old ballad entitled "Chevy Chace."

[5] See Ritson's Ancient Songs, page 93; where is printed a piece entitled "The Dying Malden's Complaint," supposed to be the song here mentioned.

[6] Probably a ballad on the battle of Otterbourne.

1786, and from this work we have extracted the following list of songs :—

    Wa worth Maryage.[1]
    Sang upon a maist melancholic aventure.[2]
    Sang on absence.[3]
    A welcum to eild.[4]
    The Lament of a pure courtman.[5]
    God gif I war wedo now.[6]
    The murning maidin.[7]
    The Bankis of Helicon.[8]
    Luve sang on houp.

---

[1] Attributed to ——Clapperton, a poet, of whose life we have no particulars, even his christian name being unknown. He is supposed to have been contemporary with Dunbar. The song, which Pinkerton praises very highly, details the woes of a damsel who, being married to "ane schrew," regrets her position. It is too long for insertion here.

[2] A Love Song in four stanzas, unfit for quotation. The author is unknown.

[3] A Song in thirteen stanzas, of 9 lines each.

[4] A not very contented welcome to age as may be gathered from a reading of the last stanza—

    My curland hair, my cristal ene,
    Are bald, and bleird, as all may se,
    My bak that sumtyme brent has bene
    Now crukis lyk ane camok tree,
    Be me your sampill ye may se,
    For so said wourthy Solomon,
    Elding is end of eriblis glie ;
    Walcum ulid, for youth is gone.

[5] The Lament of a courtier. He tells how his two brothers have occupied good positions, one being a "Preist of Pryis," and the other, having carried a pack, has attained great wealth ; while he, devoting his attention and talents to the service of the court, has been left in great poverty. Beyond exemplifying the "old saw" of "Put not your trust in princes," it is of little moment.

[6] The lament of a married man for the loss of his freedom.

[7] Alluded to before. Note 3 page 7.

[8] A piece of eleven stanzas in the style of "The Cherrie and the Slae," and supposed to be by Montgomery, the author of that poem. In Mr. Chambers's Songs of Scotland prior to Burns, 1862, the first two stanzas are given in a modernised form to an air composed by Andrew Blackhall, Minister of the parish of Inveresk, who died in 1609. We here give the first stanza as printed by Pinkerton, which will serve as a specimen of the poem :—

    Declair ye bankis of Helicon,
    Parnassus hills and daillis ilk one,
    And fontaine Caballein.
    Gif ony of your musis all
    Or nymphis, may be peregall
    Unto my ladye schein ?
    Or if the ladyis that did lave
    Their bodyis by your brim,
    So semlie war or [yit] sa fauve,
    So bewitful, or trim ?
    Contempill, exempill,
    Tak he hir propar port,
    Gif onye so bonye,
    Amang you did resort.

INTRODUCTION. xxxi

The faythful luifar.[1]
Constance the cure of absence.
On the New Yeir.[2]

[1] This is a very pretty little song, and well worth insertion here,—

Gif faithfulness ye find,
  And that your mynd content,
Ane band hairby I bind,
  Of firme fayth and fervant,
And to be permanent
  For ocht that may befall,
My hairt heir I present,
  In pledge perpetuall.

Quhilk simplie I resing,
  As hostage in your hand,
And willingle it bring,
  To bind it in sic band,
As pleises your command;
  To left, till I may leif,
Quhilk is the gadge and pand,
  Maist suir that I can geif.

Ressve it then, and treit it
  As treuth sall try my pairt,
Gif I be fals, forsit it,
  And let me suffer smairt.
Dalll efter my desert,
  Then dreid I no disdaine,
Bot hoap to half ane hairt
  In recompence again.

Gif loyaltie may lufe
  An recompence procure,
Or honest mening move
  Your favour to induire;
Gif lautie you allnire,
  Or constance mak yow kind,
Firme fayth sall me assuire,
  And treuth content your mynd.

[2] Ascribed in the manuscript to Sir Richard Maitland. In 1560 the Queen Dowager, who acted as Regent of Scotland, was besieged in Leith by the Lords of the Congregation. The Regent was assisted by a body of French troops, under the leadership of the Count de Martigues, while her opponents were assisted by English troops and money. This song is very interesting as one of the political pieces of the period,—

In this new yeir I sie bot weir,
  Na caus to sing,
In this new yeir I sie bot weir,
  Na caus thair is to sing.

I cannot sing for the vexatioun
Of Frenchmen, and the Congregatioun,
That hes maid troubil on the natioun,
And monye hair biggin
  In this new yeir, etc.

I have na will to sing or dans,
For fair of England and of France,
God send thame sorow and mischance,
In caus of their cuming
  In this new yeir, etc.

We ar as reulit, riche and puir,
That we wait not quhair to be suire,
The bordour as the Borrow muir,
Quhair sum perchance will ling
  In this new yeir, etc.

And yit I think it best that we,
Pluck up our hairt, and mirrie be;
For thoch we wald ly doun and die,
It will help us na thing
  In this new yeir, etc.

Let us pray God to stannch this weir,
That we may leif withouten feir,
In mirrines quhill we ar heir
And hevin at our ending.
  In this new yeir, etc.

In 1568, when Scotland was visited by the plague, a certain George Bannatyne retired to his house to escape infection, and employed his leisure time in compiling his celebrated collection of Scotch poetry, the most valuable in existence, it being the only medium by which many pieces of our best early Scotch poets have reached to our times. Of Bannatyne's personal life we know absolutely nothing; one of our antiquaries, who described him as a Canon of Moray, having evidently confounded him with Bellenden, an old Scotch poet, who held the position of Archdeacon of Moray and Canon of Ross.

To this collection we are indebted for the preservation of the following songs amongst others:—

Wooing of Jok and Jenny.[1]

---

[1] We have given a modernised version of this song in the present collection, page 7: we here give it as written in the manuscript in all its beauty of antique spelling.

THE WOWING OF JOK AND JYNNY.

Robeyns Jok come to wow our Jynny,
  On our feist evin quhen we wer fow;
Scho braklit fast, and made hir bony,
  And said, Jok, come ye for to wow?
Scho birneist hir baith breist and brow,
  And maid hir cheik as ony cick;
Than spak hir dame, and said, I trow,
  Ye come to wow our Jynny, Jok.

Jok said, forsuth, I yarn full fane,
  To lok my heid, and sit doun by yow,
Than spak hir modir, and said agane,
  My bairnis hes tocher gud to ge yow.
Te be, quoth Jynny, keik, keik, I se yow
  Mudar, yone man makis yow a mok,
I scho the, lyar! full loks me yow,
  I come to wow your Jynny, quoth Jok.

My berne, scho sayis, hes of hir awin,
  Ane guse, ane gryce, ane cok, ane hen,
Ane calf, ane hog, ane fute-braid sawin,
  Ane kirn, ane pin, that ye weill ken,
Ane pig, ane pot, ane raip thair ben,
  Ane fork, ane flaik, ane reill, ane rok,
Dischis and dublaris nyne or ten;
  Come ye to wow our Jynny, Jok?

Ane blankat, and ane wecht also,
  Ane schule, ane schelt, and ane lang flail,
Ane ark, ane almry, and laidillis two,
  Ane milk-syth, with ane swyne taill,
Ane rowsty quhittill to scheir the kaill,
  Ane quheill, ane mell the beir to knok,
Ane coig, ane caird wantand ane naill:
  Come ye to wow our Jynny, Jok?

Ane farme, ane furlet, ane pott, ane pek,
  Ane tub, ane barrow, with ane quheilband,
Ane turs, ane troch, and ane meil-sek,
  Ane spurtill braid and ane elwand.
Jok tuk Jynny be the hand,
  And cryd, ane feist; and slew ane cok,
And maid a brydell up alland:
  Now haif I gottin your Jynny, quoth Jok.

INTRODUCTION.

Ballat of evill Wyffis.[1]
Robyn and Makyn.[2]
Wife of Auchtermuchty.[3]
Twysbank.[4]

Besides a number of pieces by Montgomery, Scott, &c., a selection of which will be found in the present work.

Now, dame, I half your bairns markit;
Suppois ye mak it never an twche,
I lat yow wit schee nocht miskarsit,
It is weill kend I haif anewch;
Ane crukit gleyd fell our ane huch,
Ane speld, ane spell, ane spur, ane sok,
Without oxin I haif a pinche
To gang to gidder Jynny and Jok.

I half ane halter, ane ylk, ane hek,
Ane cord, ane creill, and als ane crall,
Fyve fidder of raggis to stuff ane jak,
Ane auld pannell of ane laid sadill,
Ane pepper-polk maid of a padill,
Ane spounge, spindill, wastand ane nok,
Twa lusty lippis to lik ane laiddill,
To gang to gidder Jynny and Jok.

Ane brechame, and twa brechis fyne,
Weill baklit with a byrdill renye,
Ane sark maid of the linkrege twyne,
Ane gay grene cloke that will nocht stayne,
And yit for mister I will nocht fenye,
Fyve hundreth findis now in a flok
Call ye nocht that ane joly menye,
To go to giddir Jynny and Jok.

Ane trene truncheour, ane ramshorn spone,
Twa bothis of barkit, bleasit ledder,
All graith that ganis to hobbill schone,
Ane thrawcruk to twyne ane tedder,
Ane brydill, ane girth, and ane swyne bledder,
Ane maskene-fatt, ane fetterit lok,
Ane schalp weill heipit fra ill wedder,
To gang to gidder, Jynny and Jok.

Tak thair for my parte of the feist;
It is weill knawin I am weill bodin;
Ye may nocht say my parte is leist,
The wyfe said, speid, the haill are soddin,
And als the laverock is fast and loddin;
Quhen ye half done tak hame the brok,
The rost wes twche, as wer thay bodin;
Syne gaid to gidder baytb Jynny and Jok.

[1] Ascribed in the MS. to Fleming, a poet, of whom nothing is known.

[2] By Robert Henryson, Schoolmaster of Dunfermline. This fine ballad is printed in Mr. Laing's valuable edition of Henryson's Poems, Edinb. 1865.

[3] Ascribed to Moffat, and presumed to be by Sir John Moffat, a priest. The poem is that on which the more modern John Grumlie is founded, the outline of the story being the same in both pieces.

[4] Mentioned in the "Complaynt."

We are indebted to rather a curious work for our next reliques of song.[1] About 1570, during the height of the progress of the Reformation in Scotland, there appeared in Edinburgh a curious work entitled "Ane Compendious buik of Godlie Psalmes and Spirituall Sangis, collectit furthe of sindrie partis of the Scripture, with diveris otheris Ballatis changeit out of prophane Sangis, in Godlie Sangis for auoyding of sin and harlotrie," &c. It is conjectured to have been principally the work of three brothers, James, John, and Robert Wedderburn, of Dundee, but unfortunately very little is known regarding their lives except the fact that they were staunch supporters of the Reformation. "It is generally admitted," says Mr. Laing,[2] "that this collection was not only popular, but had considerable influence on the minds of the common people, who could easily appreciate words sung to popular airs. The number of such satirical invectives against the corruptions and abuses which prevailed in the Romish Church, could not fail to enlighten the ignorant portion of the laity, and tend to facilitate the progress of the Reformed doctrines."

The air of a song, often the first line or the chorus, formed the burden for a "Godlie" piece; and however unharmonious the association may appear to a refined mind, still we cannot but acknowledge that the trick was certain to be successful and popular among the lower and less educated orders of society. Even in our own time the religious agitators have not overlooked this method of gaining possession of the popular mind, for it is no uncommon thing to find a street preacher leading the harmony of his audience by a hymn to the tune of Annie Laurie, Annot Lyle, Rule Britannia, Such a getting Upstairs, and many other of the popular songs of the day.

To this volume we are indebted for the following names:—

    Allone I veip in great distress.
    Rycht sorely musing in my mynde.
    O mine hart, hey this is my sang.
    Grouit is my sorow.
    Allace that samyn sueit face.
    Huntis up.
    In ane mirthful may morow.
    All Cristin mennis dance.[3]
    Hay let us sing and mak greit mirth.

---

[1] A very beautiful reprint of the earliest known edition of this work was published in 1868 at Edinburgh, under the editorial care of Mr. David Laing, who added a very valuable introduction and series of notes. Lord Hailes, in 1765, had issued a small volume of specimens, and in 1801 a reprint of another edition was published by Dalyell, under the title of "Scottish Poems of the sixteenth century," 2 vols. An interesting pamphlet intitled "The Wedderburns and their Work," published 1867, by Professor Mitchell, of St. Andrew's, also gives some valuable information regarding the work and the authors.

[2] Preface to Gude and Godlie Ballatis, 1868, p. xlvii.

[3] These eight songs are previously mentioned in the "Complaynt."

In Burgh and Land, east, west, north, south.
For lufe of one I mak my mone.[1]
O vho is at my windo? quho, quho?[2]
My lufe murnis for me.
Johne cum kiss me now[3]
Downe be sone River I ran.

---

[1] These three are the first lines of hymns, and appear to have originally belonged to profane songs.

[2] Songs beginning in this or similar manner, have always been popular in England as well as Scotland. We here give two verses of this piece as a specimen.

O vho is at my windo? quho, quho?
Go from my windo, go, go!
Quho callis thair so lyke a strangair,
Go from my windo, go!

Lord I am heir ane wretchit mortall
That for thy mercy dois cry and call
Unto the my lord celestiall,
Se quho is at my windo, quho.

How dar thow for mercy cry,
Sa lang in sin as thow dois ly?
Mercy to have thow art not worthy,
Go from my windo, go.

[3] There is a very old and popular English tune with this title, which has been traced to the time of Queen Elizabeth. Mr. Chappell has also found many allusions to the song in the works of the Dramatists. We cannot forbear quoting part of the version in the "Gude and Godlie Ballatis," as it shows to what an absurd extent this method of popularising religion may be carried :—

Johne, cum kiss me now,
Johne cum kiss me now;
Johne cum kiss me by and by
And mak no moir adow.
The Lord thy God I am
That Johne dois the call :
Johne representit man,
Be grace celestiall.
For Johne, Goddis grace it is
(Ladis flat till expone the same)
Och Johne, thow did arris,
Quhen that thow tuke this name.
Havin and eirth of nocht
I maid them for thy saik
For mair mair I socht
To my lyknes the mak.
In Paradise I plantit the
And made the Lord of all.
My creatures, not forbidding the
Na thing bot ane of all;
That wald thow not obey,
Nor sit follow to my will;
Bot did cast thyrsalf away,
And thy posteritie spill
My Justice contempnit tho
To everlasting paine,
Man culd find na remedie,
To bey man fre againe.
O pure lufe and meik mercy
Frome swit sone downe I send,
God become man for the
For thy sin his lyfe did spend.

> Hay now the day dallis ! [1]
> Till our gudeman, till our gudeman,
> Hay trix trim go trix, [2]
> Was not Solomon the king ? [3]
> All my lufe leif me not.
> O man ryse up, and be not sweir. [4]

---

[1] See p. 6, note 2. We quote the first two verses of the version in the "Ballatis"—

> Hay now the day dallis,
> Now Christ on vs callis,
> Now welth on our wallis,
>   Apperis anone.
> Now the word of God regnis,
> Quhilk is King of all kingis ;
> Now Christi's flock singis,
>   The nicht is neir gone.

> Wo be vnto now hypocritis,
> That on the Lord sa loudlie leis,
> And all for to fill zour foule bellais,
>   Ze ar nocht of Christis blude or bone.
> For ze preiche zour awin dremis,
> And sa the word of God blasphemis,
> God wat sa weill it semis,
>   The nicht is neir gone.

The fourth stanza is directed against the papal dignitaries—

> Wo be to zow Paip and Cardinall,
> I traist to God ze sall get ane fall,
> With Monkis, Freiris, and Freiris all,
>   That traistis nocht in God allone.
> For all zour greit pomp and pryde,
> The word of God ze sall nocht hyde,
> Nor zit till ve na mair be gyde,
>   The nicht is neir gone.

[2] This song begins—

> The paip, that pagan full of pryde,

and is a very vigorous exposure of the immoralities of the clergy.

[3] This shows the evils of being too much enamoured of the ladies. Mr. Laing notices that a piece similar in style, signed "Finis quod ane Inglisman," is in the Bannatyne MS., with the difference that in the MS. King Solomon is held up as a pattern to lovers, while in the ballads he acts as a warning.

[4] Begins—

> O man ryse vp and be not sweir,
> Prephir aganis this gude new seir,
> My new zeir gift thow lies in stoir,
> Sen I am he that coft the deir
> Gif me thy hart, I ask no muir,

This is probably, as Mr. Chambers has remarked, based upon a silly rhyme sung by children about the new year time, to assist them in opening the hearts of the neighbours at that merry-making period, so as to enable them to amuse themselves in their own fashion. Mr. Chambers has heard the boys sing in Peebles—

> Get up gudewife, and binna sweir,
> And deal your breid to them thats here,
> For the time will come when ye'll be deid,
> And then ye'll neither need yill nor breid.

In Edinburgh and Glasgow it is different from this, but the import is the same—

> Get up gudewife and shake your feathers,
> Dinna ye think that we are beggars,
> For we are bairns come out to play,—
> Rise up an gies our hogmanay.

We are indebted for our next song to a very curious and unlikely source. In 1568, a "Psalme Buike" was printed at Edinburgh, and at the end was printed what has been described as "ane baudy sang," called—

Welcome Fortunes.

A very romantic story quoted by Ritson from "Verstegans Restitution of Decayed Intelligence," printed in 1605, introduces us to another song. "So it fell out of late years, that an English gentleman, travelling in Palestine, not far from Jerusalem, as he passed thorow a country town, he heard by chance a woman sitting at her door dandling her child, to sing 'Bothwel Bank, thou blumest fayre;' the gentleman hereat exceedingly wondered, and forthwith in English saluted the woman, who joyfully answered him, and said, 'she was right glad to see a gentleman of our isle,' and told him 'she was a Scotish woman, and came first from Scotland to Venice, and from Venice thither, where her fortune was to be the wife of an officer under the Turk, who being at that instant absent and very soon to return, she entreated the gentleman to stay there till his return; the which he did, and she for country sake, to show herself the more kind and bountiful unto him, told her husband at his home coming that the gentleman was her kinsman, whereupon her husband entertained him very friendly, and at his departure gave him divers things of good value."[1]

Between 1615 and 1620, a manuscript collection of music was compiled by a member of the family of Skene, and generally supposed to have been John Skene of Hallyards, son of Sir John Skene, Clerk Register of Scotland. He appears to have been born about 1578, and his death is known to have taken place in 1644. The manuscript was bequeathed by one of his descendants to the Library of the Faculty of Advocates, Edinburgh; and in 1838, Mr. Dauney printed it with a valuable Introduction and series of notes,[2] and to this work we are indebted for the following summary of the contents of the collection. The space at our disposal for this essay will not allow us to enumerate all the airs in the MS. We will therefore content ourselves with naming only the principal, referring the reader who wishes to follow the subject more fully to Mr. Dauney's very interesting and valuable work.

[1] In Pinkerton's Select Scotish Ballads, vol. ii., a song is given (see also in the present collection, page 149) purporting to be the original ballad sung in Palestine, as narrated in the quotation. Ritson, in his Scotish Songs, characterizes this version with his usual asperity as "a despicable forgery," and subsequent revelations showed that his assertion was quite right, and that the author of the song was his rival antiquary.

[2] Ancient Scotish Melodies from a manuscript of the reign of King James VI., with an introductory inquiry, illustrative of the History of the Music of Scotland, by William Dauney, Esq., F.S.A. Scot. 4to, Edinburgh, 1838.

xxxviii   INTRODUCTION.

Allace yat I cam oer the muir and left my love behind me.[1]
Peggie is over ye sea wi ye souldier.
To dance about the Bailzeis Dubb.
Lady Rothemayis Lilt.[2]
I love my love for love again.[3]
Blew Ribbenn at the Bound Rod.[4]
Johne Andersonne my Jo.[5]
My dearest musts is fardest fra me.
Prettie well begunn, man.
Long are onie old man.[6]
Kilt thy coat, Maggie.[7]
Allace this night yat we suld sinder.
The Flowers of the Forest.
Ostend.[8]
Good night, and God be wi' yow.[9]
My love shoe winns not her away.
Jenny drinks na water.
Remember me at evenings.
I cannot live and want thee.[10]
Adew, Dundee.[11]
Allace, I lie my lon; I'm lik to die awld.[12]

---

[1] Afterwards corrupted to "The last time I cam ower the muir," as a song with that title is given in a Manuscript dated 1692; and Ramsay, who seems to have been acquainted with the first line, if not with the whole of the old version, composed a song so beginning. No other vestige of the old words is now extant.

[2] Supposed to apply to the words of the old Ballad of "The Burning of the Castle of Frendraught," (see Ballad Minstrelsy of Scotland.)

[3] An early version of the air of Jenny Nettles.

[4] The Blew Ribbon probably refers to the National Colour of Scotland, and the Bound Rod, a road to a place so called at Berwick-on-Tweed. It was in all likelihood an old gathering song.

[5] This is the earliest time to which we can trace the air of this ever popular tune. Its popularity does not seem to have been confined to Scotland, for it is similar to an old English dance tune called "Paul's Steeple" (Hawkins's History of Music, vol. v. p. 469), and there is an old Swedish air still extant to which it bears great resemblance.

[6] The air is similar to that of My Jo Janet.

[7] At the trial of John Douglas, "and eight women (belonging to Tranent), for witchcraft, on 3rd May, 1659, where the panels confessed, among other things, that they had had several merry meetings with the Devil, at which they were entertained with music, John Douglas being their piper; and that two of the tunes to which they danced were Kilt thy coat, Maggie, and Come this way with me. Dauney's Ancient Scotish Melodies, p. 262.

[8] Probably the title of a popular song on the capture of Ostend in 1604.

[9] The origin of the favourite Gude Nicht, and Joy be wi' you, of our song writers.

[10] Similar to the air of Dainty Davy, as given in Durfey's collection, 1700.

[11] The town of Dundee has always been a favourite spot with our Scotish Minstrels: many old scraps of song relating to it are extant.

[12] Probably the lament of some aged maiden for having lost all chance of securing that great prize of all maidens, old or young, a gudeman! The air is similar to that of—O a' the Airts the Wind can Blaw.

Lady Cassellis lilt.[1]
Three sheeps skinns.[2]
My mistres' blush is bonie.
Bonie Jean maks meikle o' me.
The lass o' Glasgowe.
Doun in yon banks.
Sa mirrie as we has been.
Keitie Bairdie.[3]
I serve a worthie ladie.[4]
Omnia Vincit Amor.
Marie me, marie me, quoth the bonie lass.
Pitt on your shirt on Monday.[5]
Froggie Galziard.[6]
The nightarale.
O, sillie soul, Allace.
Scerdustia.[7]

We again become indebted to a collection of music for our next insight into these forgotten songs. A manuscript cantus of about the beginning of the seventeenth century, which belonged to Mr. Constable, the celebrated Edinburgh publisher, gives us a few scraps, from which we select the following:—

"Come all your old malt to me
Come all your old malt to me,
And ye sall have the draff again
Though all our deukes should die."[8]

Johne Robinson, Johne Robinson,
That fair young man, Johne Robinson.

I biggit a bouir to my lemmane
In land is none so fair.

---

[1] This air is almost the same as that of the ballad of Johnnie Faa, the Gipsie Laddie, on which the well-known beautiful air of Glen's equally beautiful song of Wass me for Prince Charlie is founded. The story of Lady Cassellis will be found entered fully into in the companion volume to this work, *The Ballad Minstrelsy of Scotland*.

[2] A similar air to that of Clout the Caldron.

[3] This seems to have been a very popular air, and Kitty is still celebrated amongst us in the form of a nursery rhyme. King James VI, in Scott's Fortunes of Nigel, is made to say that "a man may lawfully dance Chrichty Bairdie, or any other dance in a tavern, but not *inter parietes ecclesiæ.*"

[4] The air is that of the more modern song of Dumbarton's Drums.

[5] Mr. Dauney is careful to point out that this is not to be taken literally, that is, in terms of reminder that a clean shirt is essential at least once a week, but that it is a gathering cry to be ready for action by putting on their armour, Monday being generally the day on which the weapon schaws were held.

[6] Supposed to be the song mentioned in the Complaynt, as "The frog cam' to the myl dur."

[7] Probably a corruption of the old name of Surdastruma, drum. The air is similar to that of "Steer her up and haud her gaun."

[8] See p. 56 of the present collection.

> The Hemlock is the best o' seed
> That any man may sow,
> When bairnies greet after breid
> Give them a horne to blow.
>
> Come reke me to the Rowan tree.
>
> Come row me round about, bony dowie.
>
> I and my cumner, my cumner and I
> Shall never part with our mouth so dry.
>
> All the mane that I make says the guidman;
> Who's to have my wife, daid when I am?
> Care for thy winding sheet, false hurdun,
> For I shall get ane other when thow art gone.[1]

We have now exhausted the majority of the early sources of fragments of our songs, and will conclude this essay by a glance at our principal printed collections. It cannot but be painful to any literary antiquary to contemplate the baldness of these early remains, and to reflect that the songs prior to the middle of the seventeenth century, which delighted our ancestors and assisted them in their merry-meetings, and emboldened them in love or war, have with few exceptions passed away with them, leaving only the titles of a small number, to register, like tombstones in an auld kirk-yard, that such things were. No one can fully appreciate the amount of knowledge of the daily life of the singers, their little troubles and doings, the appearance of their homes, their dress, sentiments, education, and other objects far beneath the dignity of history to chronicle which have thus been lost to us, never to be recovered! The fragments we have only enable us to see that the song was a favourite species of literature, that the airs which were current were often of the most beautiful description, and to surmise that the words to which they were allied were often equal to the beauty of the tune, and that is all.

The Aberdeen Cantus published at the city of Bonaccord in 1666, contains about fifty songs with their tunes, of which only some half-a-dozen are Scotish, and these of the most dubious description: amongst others, Alexander Scot's O Lusty Maye, with Flora Queen, is there set to music.

Watson's collection of Scots poems published at Edinburgh in 1706, 1709, and 1711, is the first collection of Scotish poetry we have, and is supposed to have been compiled by John Spottiswood, editor of Hope's Minor Practicks. It contains for the first time, "Fy let us a' to the Bridal," the version of Old Long Syne, attributed to Ayton; several pieces by the Marquis of Montrose, etc.

---

[1] A complete list of the scraps in this cantus will be found in the introduction to Mr. Chambers's Scotish Songs, 1829, vol. I.

The first of our collections of songs is the Tea Table Miscellany of Allan Ramsay, the first volume of which appeared in 1724. Scotish music had become fashionable about that time, and Allan Ramsay the bookseller, considered a collection of the Songs of his country would answer as a publishing speculation, while his own talents as a poet and those of his friends, would assist him in making a respectable-sized volume. The work has been a perfect mine to all future collectors and editors of song, and its extent may be learned from the fact that it gives us upwards of twenty presumably old songs, upwards of a dozen old songs altered, and about one hundred by Allan himself, Crawford, Hamilton, and others; we also have a great number of names of old airs to which the new songs were directed to be sung, and a host of the popular English songs of the day. As an editor, Ramsay has been much blamed by antiquaries for preferring to give his own songs rather than the old versions on which he based some of his pieces, but surely these gentlemen do not reflect sufficiently on the character of a great majority of these old songs. When Ramsay set about collecting, he had a task before him at once delicate and dangerous. He required to prune the old songs of indelicacies before submitting them to the taste of

"Ilka lovely British lass,
Frae ladies Charlotte, Ann, and Jean,
Down to ilk bonnie singing lass,
Wha dances barefoot on the green."

He dared not present any thing which would be flouted as immoral at the rigidly righteous tea-meetings which then abounded, and as a poet he exerted his skill in covering over these blemishes,[1] in providing new verses to fill up obvious gaps, and to furnish totally new songs in place of old ones at once worthless and wicked. A trenchant editor, certainly, for the antiquary; but no lover of poetry can regret the cause which drew so many fine songs from the best Scotch poets of the time. Hamilton, Crawford, and Ramsay himself, gave not a bad exchange, for songs in all likelihood trashy and licentious, and we have sufficient confidence in Ramsay's judgment to believe, that no piece at all worthy of preservation which came under his notice in its entirety was not duly preserved.

Herd's Collection, issued in 1770, and afterwards with additions in 1776, attends more to the taste of the antiquary. Very little is known of the life of Honest David, and even the editorship of the two celebrated volumes cannot with certainty be given to him. All that is known is that he was a native of

---

[1] Since Ramsay's time public refinement has so far advanced, that no editor would dare to print in a popular work a great number of the songs given in the Tea Table Miscellany, a fact which may be confirmative that Ramsay did not use too much liberty with the old pieces—certainly no more than what made them presentable.

St. Cyrus, in Kincardineshire, that he was for many years a clerk
to an accountant in Edinburgh, and died in June, 1810, aged
78 years. A notice of his death appeared in the Scots Magazine
for July, 1810, and included the following sketch:—"He was a
most active investigator of Scottish Literature and Antiquities,
and enjoyed the friendship of nearly all the eminent artists and
men of letters who have flourished in Edinburgh within these
fifty years. Runciman, the painter, was one of his most intimate
friends; and with Ruddiman, Gilbert Stuart, Fergusson, and
Robert Burns, he was well acquainted. His information regarding the History of Scotland was extensive. Many of his remarks
have appeared in periodical publications; and the notes appended
to several popular works are enriched by materials of his own
collecting. He was a man truly of the old school, inoffensive,
modest, and unambitious, and in an extraordinary degree forming
in all these respects a very striking contrast to the forward puff-
ing and ostentatious disposition of the present age." Sir Walter
Scott informs us that "His hardy and antique mould of coun-
tenance and his venerable grizzled locks procured him, amongst
his acquaintances, the name of Groysteil." George Paton, who
appears to have been co-editor of the Collection, was in the Cus-
tom-house. He carried on a most extensive correspondence
with many of the most celebrated antiquarians of his time,
amongst others Bishop Percy, Gough, and Joseph Ritson.[1] Herd's
Collection, as it is commonly called, was arranged in several
divisions according to the subject of the pieces, and a glance at
the pages of the present volume will show how much old Scotish
Song has been indebted to it for preservation. Herd and Paton,
so far as we know, were model editors for antiquarians: Scraps
and Fragments were printed exactly as they found them, as
well as complete songs, without the slightest regard to rhyme
or metre, decency or beauty.[2]

What must always be esteemed as the most valuable collection of the early Songs and Music of Scotland, "Johnson's Scots
Musical Museum," was begun at Edinburgh in 1786. James
Johnson was a Music Seller and Engraver in Edinburgh, and
was the first who used Pewter plates for engraving music. The
work seems to have been projected by William Tytler, of Wood-
houselee, the celebrated antiquary (whose "Dissertation on
Scotish Song and Music" was long the standard authority on
the subject, though now but of little use), Dr. Blacklock, and

---

[1] A Selection of Letters received by Paton from Percy, Herd, and Callender of
Craigforth, were published by Mr. Maidment, at Edinburgh, in 1830, and forms one
of the most valuable contributions which that zealous antiquary has given to
Scotish Literature.

[2] Herd's Collection was reprinted twice during 1869, one at Edinburgh being
produced under the editorial care of Mr. Sidney Gilpin, while the other, published
in Glasgow, is a mere reprint.

INTRODUCTION. xliii

Samuel Clark who appears to have acted as musical editor. From the note addressed "To the True Lovers of Caledonian Music and Song," prefixed to the first volume, we find that the work originated from "A just and general complaint, that among all the music books of Scots Songs which have been hitherto offered to the public, not even altogether can be said to have merited the name of what may be called a complete collection; having been published in detached pieces and parcels; amounting however on the whole to more than twice the price of this publication; attended moreover with this further disadvantage, that they have been printed in such large unportable sizes that they could by no means answer the purpose of being pocket-companions, which is no small encumbrance, especially to the admirers of social music." Each volume was to contain one hundred songs with music, &c. In the second volume, the authors' names so far as known were given, and several of the old pieces marked as such. The work would probably not have reached a third volume had not Robert Burns entered into the scheme. Burns had been introduced to Johnson in Edinburgh, and contributed two original songs to the first volume. To the second volume he contributed largely, and continued to furnish the publisher with songs original, or collected, or half of each. He informed a friend that he had "collected, begged, borrowed, and stolen, all the songs" he had met with, and this enthusiasm continued to the last. Without his aid in rousing contributors, finding material, old or new, the Scots Musical Museum would have been on a level with Thomson's Orpheus Caledonius, instead of occupying the important position it now enjoys in the literature of our song. The work finished with the sixth volume. One thing was wanted, as Johnson left it, to make it complete, and that was, a series of good and trustworthy notes. This was undertaken by William Stenhouse, an accountant in Edinburgh who died in 1827, leaving his task unfinished. Mr. David Laing next took up the work, and with the assistance of Mr. Charles Kirkpatrick Sharpe, gave a series of additional notes illustrative and corrective of those of Stenhouse, added prefaces and indexes, and in 1853 gave all lovers of Scotish Song an edition of Johnson, the value of which is immeasurable. To it we gratefully acknowledge our obligations for much and valuable information.

In 1794 the celebrated antiquary, Joseph Ritson, published a collection of Scotish Songs with the music in two volumes. The collection itself so far as the songs were concerned, was of little consequence, the Scotch words being very incorrectly printed, and the music in a great number of instances being left blank. Its principal value lies in the Introductory Essay, the first dissertation on our Songs and Music written in a fitting manner, and to it the student is indebted for a careful investigation into the early remains of our Song. There are of course many things in it now allowed to be incorrect, and at least one of his critical opinions will be laughed at; but in spite of this Ritson's Essay at once occupied and still holds the position of being the best historical sketch we have of our early songs. To its pages every succeeding writer and editor has been largely indebted, and we have also to award it our homage.

Thomson's Select Melodies of Scotland has been characterised in this work as "a sort of drawing-room edition," of the Scots Musical Museum. Its publication was begun in 1793, by Mr. George Thomson, Clerk to the Board of Trustees, Edinburgh. Mr. Thomson's idea was to give the favourite airs accompanied where possible by the words. When, from their character, these were unfitted for the perusal of ladies he proposed to print original verses. He also gave symphonies and accompaniments to the airs by the best composers of his time, as Haydn, Beethoven, and Pleyel; and, greatest of all, he secured for the literary portion the services of Robert Burns, who entered into the spirit of the work with the greatest enthusiasm and enriched it with a great number of original songs, many of them being the best that came from his pen, and given to Thomson without fee or reward. Sir Walter Scott, Sir Alexander Boswell, Johanna Baillie, Thomas Campbell, and many others contributed to the work, and as it also contained a selection of the best of the old songs, with the music carefully given, the work was altogether a noble undertaking, well planned and carried out.

In 1829, Mr. Robert Chambers published his collection of Scotish songs in two volumes, with an Introductory Essay. It is needless at the present time to reiterate Mr. Chambers's numerous services to the literature and antiquities of Scotland. On the subject of songs and ballads, Mr. Chambers has always been considered, and justly so, as one of our foremost critics, while in the "Book of Days," "Popular Annals of Scotland," and his Histories of the Rebellions, he has made a name for himself in the popular elucidation of our History and Antiquities. Mr. Chambers in his essay on Scotish Song principally follows the authority of Ritson, adding much valuable information resulting from his own inquiries. The songs are well selected, but printed without any attempt at arrangement, a fact which we cannot too deeply deplore. In the notes affixed to the songs, Mr. Chambers adds greatly to our knowledge of their history, and we have to acknowledge with pleasure the obligations we are under to them. In a few instances we have had to dissent from several of Mr. Chambers's speculations, but we have done

---

[1] We allude to the passage where he says of Burns, that "he does not appear to his usual advantage in song."

so only after very careful consideration and with very great regret.'

A few words on a peculiar branch of our subject, and we conclude. Scotch Music became very popular in England about the middle of the seventeenth century, and in 1719 Thomas D'Urfey issued his celebrated "Pills to purge Melancholy," a Collection of Songs, &c., containing a great number of Scotch airs and imitations, with *Scotch* words specially written for the collection by D'Urfey, and his Grub-street compeers. Why the Scotch words were rejected we cannot say, certainly it was not on grounds of morality, for a more filthy series of volumes could hardly have been issued; nor on grounds of *poetry*, for we might as well compare Boucicault to Shakspere, as the Songs in D'Urfey's collection to their Scotish Models. But it is certain that the work was highly popular in England, and is now one of the rarest gems in the Ballad Collector's Library.

Nothing can be more distasteful to any lover of the ring of

---

[1] It may increase the usefulness of this work to give a list of some of the minor collections and works illustrative of the subject which have appeared.

Thomson's Orpheus Caledonius, 1725 folio, and 2 vols. 8vo, 1733, is the first collection of Scotch Music styled such. It is of but little importance now, and only prized by collectors. The Charmer, "a collection of songs chiefly such as are eminent for poetical merit; among which are many originals and others that were never before printed in a song book," 2 vols., Edinburgh, 1752; "The Lark," Edinburgh, 1740. Sir Walter Scott's Minstrelsy of the Scotish Border, though principally treating of Ballads, contained a number of songs. Jamieson's Popular Ballads and Songs, 2 vols, Edinburgh, 1806; Cromek's Select Scotish Songs, ancient and modern, with Critical and Biographical Notes by Robert Burns, 2 vols., London, 1810; Gilchrist's Select Scotish Ballads, Tales and Songs, with explanatory notes and observations, 2 vols., Edinburgh, 1815; Campbell's Albyn's Anthology, Edinburgh, 1816. Hogg's Jacobite Relics of Scotland, 2 vols., Edinburgh, 1819-21, deals as its title imports exclusively with the songs relating to the Rebellions, and, in place of a better, must rank as the best collection. Struthers's Harp of Caledonia, 3 vols., Glasgow, 1819; Smith's Modern Scotish Minstrel, 6 vols., Edinburgh, 1820-24, a fine collection, the music given with much care and taste, as would be expected from the composer of the air of "Jessie the flower o' Dumblane." C. K. Sharpe's "Ballad Book," a tiny volume of which only thirty copies were printed in 1824, contains a few traditionary scraps of song, as does also Maidment's North Countrie Garland, the impression of which was also limited to thirty copies issued in the same year. Allan Cunningham's Songs of Scotland, 4 vols., 1825, was a most ambitious performance, but of little use. In 1835, Peter Cunningham edited a small volume of songs which gave the public, for the first time, the pieces arranged in the only satisfactory manner—according to their age. It is one of the best of the minor collections. Mr. George F. Graham edited "The Songs of Scotland," adapted to their appropriate melodies, in three volumes 1854-6. This work is undoubtedly the most popular drawing-room edition of the songs, and deservedly so. In 1845, Mr. William Whitelaw edited "The Book of Scotish Song," a work which aimed at comprehensiveness in the early and latter period. Original songs were freely admitted, and the consequence is that we have a pretty full collection of early song printed side by side with the effusions of every petty pastaster; in short, the editor's boast that his work comprised upwards of twelve hundred original songs, seems to us the greatest blemish of the work. To do Mr. Whitelaw every justice, his notes displayed great research, and his pieces are, as a rule, correctly printed, but we have them without any arrangement, a vast heterogeneous mass. The modern Scotish Minstrel, edited by Dr. Charles Rogers in 1856, is a valuable contribution, dealing as it does with the poets of the first half of the present century and containing memoirs of many minor poets. We have to acknowledge our indebtedness to it for much information for the later part of our work.

our old Songs than to read these poor rhymes, and yet for a long time they passed current in England, if not to a great extent among the educated Scotchmen of their time as veritable Scotish productions: Ramsay's Tea TableMiscellany, Herd's Collection, and Johnson's Museum, will be found to contain a large number of them.

In later times several southern writers have "tried their hands," and succeeded so well that it was with great regret that the plan of the present collection could not allow the Editor to include a number in it. But from the outset, the plan was to give only veritable native productions, and we have now to be content with drawing attention to the names of two of these writers. Richard Hewit, a native of Cumberland, who was for some time Secretary to Dr. Blacklock, the admirer of Burns, wrote the following beautiful song [1]:—

ROSLIN CASTLE.

'Twas in that season of the year,
When all things gay and sweet appear,
That Colin with the morning ray,
Arose and sung his rural lay,
Of Nanny's charms the shepherd sung,
The hills and dales with Nanny rung,
While Roslin Castle heard the swain,
And echoed back the cheerful strain.

Awake sweet muse! the breathing spring
With rapture warms; awake and sing!
Awake and join the vocal throng,
Who hail the morning with a song,
To Nanny raise the cheerful lay,
O! bid her haste and come away,
In sweetest smiles herself adorn,
And add new graces to the morn.

O hark, my love, on ev'ry spray
Each feather'd warbler tunes his lay;
'Tis beauty fires the ravish'd throng,
And love inspires the melting song.
Then let my raptur'd notes arise,
For beauty darts from Nanny's eyes,
And love my rising bosom warms,
And fills my soul with sweet alarms.

O come, my love! thy Colin's lay,
With rapture calls, O come away,
Come while the muse this wreath shall twine,
Around that modest brow of thine,
O hither haste, and with thee bring,
That beauty blooming like the spring,
Those graces that divinely shine
And charm this ravish'd breast of mine!

---

[1] From Johnson' Museum.

Miss Susanna Blamire, another native of Cumberland (died 1795), wrote a number of Scotch Songs of which the following is at once the best and most popular:—

THE SILLER CROUN.

And ye sall walk in silk attire,
  And siller hae to spare,
Gin ye'll consent to be his bride
  Nor think o' Donald mair.
Oh! wha wad buy a silken goun
  Wi' a puir broken heart;
Or what's to me a siller croun,
  Gin frae my love I part?

The mind wha's every wish is pure
  Far dearer is to me,
And ere I'm forced to break my faith,
  I'll lay me down and die;
For I hae pledged my virgin troth
  Brave Donald's fate to share,
And he has gi'en to me his heart,
  Wi' a' its virtues rare.

His gentle manners wan my heart,
  He gratefu' took the gift,
Could I but think to seek it back
  It wad be waur than theft;
For langest life can ne'er repay
  The love he bears to me,
And ere I'm forced to break my troth
  I'll lay me down and dee.

Towards the conclusion of his Essay on Scotish Song, Ritson indulges in the following literary prophecy:—"The era of Scotish Music and Scotish Song is now passed. The pastoral simplicity and natural genius of former ages no longer exist; a total change of manners has taken place in all parts of the country, and servile imitation usurped the place of original invention. All, therefore, which now remains to be wished is, that industry should exert itself to retrieve and illustrate the relics of departed genius." Never was judgment more erroneously pronounced, or prophecy more easily shown to be false, so far as the Songs are concerned, than this. On the contrary, the brightest period in this branch of our literature is that of Ritson's own time, or immediately after, as the names of Robert Burns, Lady Nairne, Lady Ann Barnard, Hector Macneill, and Robert Tannahill, as the authors of some of our finest and most popular pieces sufficiently prove. And though the singers have not been so great as the past merges nearer the present, still we can point to more than sufficient to show that the grand roll of our lyric bards is not yet at an end. Boswell, Hogg, Scott, Johanna Baillie, Allan Cunningham, Riddell, and Motherwell, have all contributed to our treasures, what we would not willingly let die; and their successors, our own contemporaries, have given us many proofs that the harp will not rest even in our day, but that the Halls and Villages, Hills and Rivers, Lads and Lasses, will still continue to be celebrated, rousing depths of love and passion hitherto unknown, and fanning patriotism into a still purer and brighter flame.

GLASGOW, *November*, 1870.

THE SONGS OF SCOTLAND

CHRONOLOGICALLY ARRANGED.

PART I.

From James V. *to the* Union, 1702.

THE GABERLUNZIE MAN.

Attributed to King James V., and supposed to be an account of one of his exploits while amusing himself by travelling in disguise among the country folks. It appears in the *Tea Table Miscellany*.

The pawkie auld carle came o'er the lea,
Wi' mony gude e'ens and days to me,
Saying, Gudewife, for your courtesie,
  Will you lodge a silly poor man?
The nicht was cauld, the carle was wat,
And down ayont the ingle he sat;
My daughter's shouthers he 'gan to clap,
  And cadgily ranted and sang.

O wow! quo' he, were I as free,
As first when I saw this countrie,
How blythe and merry wad I be!
  And I wad never think lang.
He grew canty, and she grew fain;
But little did her auld minny ken
What thir slie twa together were say'ng,
  When wooing they were sae thrang.

And O! quo' he, an' ye were as black
As e'er the crown of my daddy's hat,
'Tis I wad lay thee by my back,
  And awa' wi' me thou should gang.
And O! quo' she, an' I were as white,
As e'er the snaw lay on the dike,
I'd cleed me braw and lady like,
  And awa' wi' thee I would gang.

Between the twa was made a plot;
They raise a wee before the cock,
And wilily they shot the lock,
   And fast to the bent are they gane.
Up in the morn the auld wife raise,
And at her leisure pat on her claise;
Syne to the servant's bed she gaes,
   To speer for the silly poor man.

She gaed to the bed where the beggar lay,
The strae was cauld, he was away,
She clapt her hands, cry'd, Waladay!
   For some of our gear will be gane.
Some ran to coffer, and some to kist,
But nought was stown that cou'd be mist,
She danc'd her lane, cry'd, Praise be blest!
   I have lodg'd a leal poor man.

Since naething's awa', as we can learn,
The kirn's to kirn, and milk to earn,
Gae butt the house, lass, and waken my bairn,
   And bid her come quickly ben.
The servant gade where the daughter lay,
The sheets were cauld, she was away,
And fast to the gudewife 'gan say,
   She's aff wi' the gaberlunzie man.

O fy gar ride, and fy gar rin,
And haste ye find these traytors again;
For she's be burnt, and he's be slain,
   The wearifu' gaberlunzie man.
Some rade upo' horse, some ran a fit,
The wife was wud, and out o' her wit;
She cou'd na gang, nor yet cou'd she sit,
   But aye she curs'd and she ban'd.

Mean time far hind out o'er the lee,
Fu' snug in a glen, where nane could see,
The twa wi' kindly sport and glee,
   Cut frae a new cheese a whang:
The priving was good, it pleas'd them baith,
To lo'e her for aye, he ga'e her his aith,
Quo' she, To leave thee I will be laith,
   My winsome gaberlunzie man.

O kend my minny I were wi' you,
Ill-far'dly wad she crook her mou',
Sic a poor man she'd never trow,
   After the gaberlunzie man.

My dear, quo' he, ye're yet o'er young,
And ha'e nae learn'd the beggar's tongue,
To follow me frae town to town,
And carry the gaberlunzie on.

Wi' cauk and keel I'll win your bread,
And spindles and whorles for them wha need,
Whilk is a gentle trade indeed,
To carry the gaberlunzie on.

I'll bow my leg, and crook my knee,
And draw a black clout o'er my e'e,
A cripple or blind they will ca' me,
While we shall be merry and sing.

HEY NOW THE DAY DAWIS.

CAPTAIN ALEXANDER MONTGOMERY, *Author of the "Cherrie and the Slae."*

Like many other of our old Scots poets littile is known of the events of his life. The date of his birth has not been proved, but it is supposed to have been about the middle of the Sixteenth Century. He enjoyed a pension from King James VI, with whom he seems to have been a favourite. In his latter years he shared the usual fate of poets—want and bitterness. His pension was stopped, and he appears even to have been the inmate of a prison on account of poverty. His death is supposed to have taken place between 1597 and 1615. His poems have been collected and published under the able Editorship of Mr. David Laing.

HAY! nou the day dawis;
The jolie cok crauis,
Nou shrouds the shauis
    Throu natur anone.
The Thrisell-cok cryis
On louers wha lyis,
Nou skaillis the skyis;
    The nicht is neir gone.

The fields ou'rflouis
With gouans that grouis;
Quhair lilios lyk lou is,
    Als rid als the rone:
The Turtill that treu is,
With nots that reneuis
Hir pairtie perscuis,
    The nicht is neir gone.

Nou Hairts with Hynds,
Conforme to thair kynds,
Hie tursis thair tynds,
    On grund vhair they grone.

Nou Hurchonie, with Hairs,
Ay passis in pairs;
Quhilk dewly declars
　The nicht is neir gone.

The sesone excellis
Thrugh suestness that smellis,
Nou Cupid compells
　Our hairts echone.
On Venus vha vaiks
To muse on our maiks,
Syn sing for thair saiks,
　The nicht is neir gone.

All curageous knichts
Aganis the day dichts,
The breist-plate, that bright is,
　To feght with thair sone.
The stoned stampis
Throu curage and crampis,
Syn on the land lampis,
　The nicht is neir gono.

The freiks on Feildis
That wicht wapins wieldes,
With shyning bright shields
　At Titan in trone.
Stiff speirs in roists
Ouer cursors crists,
Ar brok on their breists,
　The night is neir gone.

So hard ar thair bittis,
Some sueyis, some sittis,
And some perforce flittis
　On grund vhill they grone.
Syn grooms that gay is,
On blonks that brayis
With suords assayis,
　The nicht is noir gone.

FIENT A CRUM OF THEE SHE FAWS.

ALEXANDER SCOTT.

One of our minor poets of the reign of Queen Mary. Of his life nothing is known, and it is to the Bannatyne manuscript that we are indebted for the few poems we have of this "Scottish Anacreon." His best pieces are those of an amatory cast, his muse getting jaded when instructing Queen Mary in a "New Year's Gift, when sche came first hame, 1562," and his "Justing betwixt Adamsone and Sym," serves only to make us admire its model, "Christ's Kirk on the Green," the more. For his love "ballats," however, he well merits the title which his admirers have bestowed upon him.

RETURN thee hameward, heart, again,
  And bide where thou was wont to bo;
Thou art ane fule, to suffer pain
  For luve of her that luves not thee:
My heart, let be sic fantasie,
  Luve nane but as they mnk theo cause;
And let her seek ane heart for thee;
  For fient a crum of thee she faws.

To what effect should thou be thrall
  But thank, sin' thou has thy free will?
My heart be not ane beatial,
  But knaw wha does thee guid or ill.
Remain with me and tarry still,
  And see wha playis best their pawe,
And let fillock gae fling her fill,
  For fient a crum of thee she faws.

Though thou be fair, I will not fonzie
  She is the kind of othere mae;
For why? thore is a fellow Menzie
  That seemis guid and are not aae.
My heart, tak nowthir pain nor wae,
  For Meg, for Marjorie, or yet Mauso,
But be thou glad and let her gae;
  For fient a crum of thee she faws.

Because I find she took in ill,
  At her departing thou mak nae care;
But all beguiled go where she will,
  Ashrew the heart that mane maks mair!
My heart be merry late and air,
  This is the final end and clause;
And let her fallow ane filly fair,
  For fient a crum of thee she faws.

A RONDEL OF LOVE.
ALEXANDER SCOTT.

Lo, what it is to lufe,
Lerne ye that list to prufe,
Be me I say, that no wayis may,
The grund of greif remufe;
Bot still decay, both nicht and day;
  Lo what it is to lufe.

Lufe is ane fervent fyre,
Kendillit without desyre;
Schort plesour, lang displesour,
Repentance is the hyre;
Ane pure tressour, without mesour;
  Lufe is ane fervent fyre.

To lufe and to be wyiss,
To rege with gude adwyiss;
Now thus, now than, so gois the game,
Incertane is the dyiss,
Thair is no man, I say, that can
  Both lufe and to be wyiss.

Fle alwayis frome the snair,
Lerne at me to be waro;
It is ane pane, and dowbill trane,
Of endless wo and cair;
For to refrane, that denger plane,
  Fle alwayis frome the snair.

O LUSTIE MAY.

ALEXANDER SCOTT. (?)

From the *Aberdeen Cantus*, 1666. It also appears in the Bannatyne manuscript.

O lustie May, with Flora quene,
The balmy drops from Phœbus sheene
  Prelucent beam before the day;
By thee Diana groweth green,
  Through gladness of this lusty May.

Then Aurora that is so bright
To woful hearts she casts great light,
  Right pleasantly before the day,
And shows and sheds forth of that light,
  Through gladness of this lusty May.

Birds on the boughs, of every sort,
Send forth their notes, and make great mirth
  On banks that bloom, and every brae;
And fare and flee ower every firth,
  Through gladness of this lusty May.

And lovers all that are in care
To their ladies they do repair,
  In fresh morning before the day;
And are in mirth aye mair and mair,
  Through gladness of this lusty May.

Of everie moneth in the year
To mirthful May there is no peer;
Her glistering garments are so gay;
You lovers all make merry cheer
Through gladness of this lusty May.

WOOING OF JOCK AND JENNY.

The Bannatyne manuscript contains a version of this in an older style, which will be found in the introduction to this work, we here give the more modernised version adopted by Ramsay (and except in a very few instances by Herd). The principal merit of the song lies in the comprehensive inventory it presents of the worldly "guids and gear" of a Scottish farmer of the time.

Rob's Jock cam' to woo our Jenny,
 On ae feast day when we were fou;
She brankit fast, and made her bonnie,
 And said Jock, come ye here to woo?
She burnist her, baith breast and brou,
 And made her clear as ony clock;
Then spak' her dame, and said, I trou
 Ye come to woo our Jenny, Jock.

Jock said, Forsuith, I yearn fu' fain,
 To luk my head, and sit down by you:
Then spak' her minny, and said again,
 My bairn has tocher enough to gi'e you,
Tehie! quo' Jenny; Keik, keik, I see you;
 Minny, yon man makes but a mock,
Deil hae the liers, fu leis me o' you,
 I come to woo your Jenny, quo' Jock.

My bairn has tocher of her ain;
 A guse, a gryce, a cock and hen,
A stirk, a staig, an acre sawin,
 A bake-bread, and a bannock-stane,
A pig, a pot, and a kirn there ben,
 A kame but and a kaming stock;
With cogs and luggies nine or ten:
 Come ye to woo our Jenny, Jock?

A wecht, a peat-creel, and a cradle,
 A pair of clips, a graip, a flail,
An ark, an ambry, and a laidle,
 A milsie, and a sowen-pail,
A rousty whittle to shear the kail,
 And a timber-mell the bear to knock,
Twa shelfs made of an auld fir-dale;
 Come ye to woo our Jenny, Jock?

A furm, a furlet, and a peck,
　A rock, a reel, and a wheel-band,
A tub, a barrow, and a seck,
　A spurtle-braid, and an elwand.
Then Jock took Jenny by the hand,
And cry'd, A feast! and slew a cock,
　And made a bridal upo' land,
Now I ha'e got your Jenny, quo' Jock,

Now dame, I have your dochter married,
　And tho' ye mak' it ne'er sae tough,
I let you wit she's nae miscarried,
　It's well kend I ha'e gear enough;
An auld gawd gloyd fell owre a heugh,
A spade, a spoot, a spur, a sock:
　Withouten owsen I have a pleugh:
May that no ser your Jenny, quo' Jock?

A t'reen truncher, a ram-horn spoon,
　Twa bits of barket blasint leather,
A graith that ganes to coble shoon,
　And a thrawcruck to twyne a teather,
Twa crocks that moup amang the heather,
A pair of branks and a letter lock,
　A tough purse made of a swine's blether,
To haud your tocher, Jenny, quo' Jock.

Good elding for our winter fire,
　A cod of caff wad fill a cradle,
A rake of iron to claut the byre,
　A douk about the dubs to paddle;
The pannel of an auld led-saddle,
And Rob my eem hecht me a stock,
　Twa lusty lips to lick a laiddle,
May this no gane your Jenny, quo' Jock?

A pair of hems and brechom fine,
　And without bitts a bridle renzie,
A sark made of the linkome-twine,
　A grey green cloke that will not stenzie;
Mair yet in store—I needna fenzie,
Five hundred flaes, a fendy flock;
　And are not thae a wakrife menzie,
To gae to bed with Jenny and Jock?

Tak' thir for my part of the feast,
　It is well knawin I am weel bodin:
Ye needna say my part is least,
　Were they as meikle as they're lodin'.

The wife speer'd gin the kail was sodin,
When we have done, tak' hame the brok,
The roast was tough as raploch hodin,
With which they feasted Jenny and Jock.

MUIRLAND WILLIE.

TEA TABLE MISCELLANY.—"It is certainly a composition of considerable antiquity, probably from style and structure of verse by the author of the 'Gaberlunzie Man.'"—*Robert Chambers.*

HARKEN, and I will tell you how
Young Muirland Willie came to woo,
Tho' he could neither say nor do;
   The truth I tell to you.
But ay he crys, whate'er betide,
Maggy I'se ha'e to be my bride,
   With a fal, dal, &c.

On his gray yade as he did ride,
With durk and pistol by his side,
He prick'd her on wi' meikle pride,
   Wi' meikle mirth and glee;
Out o'er yon moss, out o'er yon muir,
Till he came to her dady's door,
   With a fal, dal, &c.

Goodman, quoth he, be ye within,
I'm come your doughter's love to win;
I care no for making meikle din,
   What answer gi' ye me?
Now, wooer, quoth he, wou'd ye light down,
I'll gie ye my doughter's love to win,
   With a fal, dal, &c.

Now, wooer, sin ye are lighted down,
Where do ye win, or in what town?
I think my doughter winna gloom
   On sic a lad as ye.
The wooer he step'd up the house,
And wow but he was wond'rous crouse,
   With a fal, dal, &c.

I have three owsen in a plough,
Twa good ga'en yads, and gear enough,
The place they ca' it Cadeneugh;
   I scorn to tell a lie:
Besides, I had frae the great laird
A peat pat, and a lang-kail-yard,
   With a fal, dal, &c.

The maid put on her kirtle brown,
She was the brawest in a' the town;
I wat on him she did na gloom,
   But blinkit bonnilie.
The lover he stended up in haste,
And gript her hard about the waist,
   With a fal, dal, &c.

To win your love, maid, I'm come here,
I'm young, and hae enough o' gear,
And for myseell you need na fear,
   Troth try me whan ye like.
He took aff his bonnet, and spat in his chew,
He dighted his gab, and he pri'd her mou',
   With a fal, dal, &c.

The maiden blush'd and bing'd fu law,
She had na will to say him na,
But to her dady she left it a',
   As they twa cou'd agree.
The lover he ga'e her the tither kiss,
Syne ran to her dady, and tell'd him this,
   With a fal, dal, &c.

Your doughter wad na say me na,
But to yoursell she has left it a',
As we cou'd gree between us twa;
   Say what'll ye gi' me wi' her?
Now, wooer, quo' he, I ha'e no meikle,
But sic's I ha'e ye's get a pickle,
   With a fal, dal, &c.

A kilnfu of corn I'll gi'e to thee,
Three soums of sheep, twa good milk ky,
Ye's ha'e the wadding dinner free;
   Troth I dow do no mair.
Content, quo' he, a hargain be't;
I'm far frae hame, make haste, let's do't,
   With a fal, dal, &c.

The bridal day it came to pass,
With mony a blythsome lad and lass;
But sicken a day there never was,
   Sic mirth was never seen.
This winsome couple straked hands,
Mess John ty'd up the marriage bands,
   With a fal, dal, &c.

And our bride's maidens were na few,
Wi' tap-knots, lug-knots, a' in blew,
Frae tap to tae they were braw new,
   And blinkit bonnilie;

Their toys and mutches were sae clean,
They glanc'd in our ladses' e'en,
 With a fal, dal, &c.

Sic birdum, dirdum, and sic din,
Wi' he o'er her, and she o'er him;
The minstrels they did never blin,
 Wi' meikle mirth and glee.
And ay they bobit, and ay they beckt,
And ay their lips together met,
 With a fal, dal, &c.

INCONSTANCY REPROVED.
SIR ROBERT AYTOUN.

Born at Kinaldie in Fife, in 1570. He was brought under the notice of James VI. by a Latin poem on that monarch's accession to the English Throne; and entering the Royal Household, became Private Secretary to the Queen, &c. He was the personal friend of many literary personages, and amongst others of Ben Jonson, Hobbes, Sir James Balfour, Earl of Stirling, Drummond of Hawthornden, &c. · He died in 1638, and was buried in Westminster Abbey. His poetical works were collected and published in 1844. The song is here given from Watson's collection, 1711. Burns wrote a version, but without his usual success.

I do confess thou'rt smooth and fair,
 And I might have gone near to love thee,
Had I not found the slightest pray'r
 That lips could speak, had pow'r to move thee;
  But I can let thee now alone
  As worthy to be loved by none.

I do confess thou'rt sweet, yet find
 Thee such an unthrift of thy sweets,
Thy favours are but like the wind,
 Which kisseth everything it meets;
  And since thou can'st love more than one
  Thou'rt worthy to be kissed by none.

The morning rose, that untouch'd stands,
 Arm'd with her briars, how sweet she smells!
But pluck'd, and strain'd through ruder hands,
 Her sweets no longer with her dwells;
  But scent and beauty both are gone,
  And leaves fall from her one by one.

Such fate ere long will thee betide,
 When thou hast handled been awhile,
Like fair flow'rs to be thrown aside,
And thou shalt sigh, when I shall smile
  To see thy love to every one,
  Hath brought thee to be lov'd by none.

TO AN INCONSTANT MISTRESS.

SIR ROBERT AYTOUN.

I loved thee once, I'll love no more,
   Thine be the grief, as is the blame,
Thou art not what thou wast before,
   What reason I should be the same?
He that can love unlov'd again,
Hath better store of love than brain;
God send me love my debts to pay,
While unthrifts fool their love away.

Nothing could have my love o'erthrown,
   If thou had still continued mine,
Nay, if thou had remain'd thine own,
   I might perchance have yet been thine.
But thou thy freedom did recall,
That it thou might elsewhere enthrall;
And, then, how could I but disdain
A captive's captive to remain.

What new desires have conquer'd thee,
   And chang'd the object of thy will,
It had been lethargy in me,
   Not constancy, to love thee still.
Yea it had been a sin to go
And prostitute affection so,
Since we are taught no pray'rs to say,
To such as must to others pray.

Yet do thou glory in thy choice—
   Thy choice, of his good fortune boast,
I'll neither grieve, nor yet rejoice,
   To see him gain what I have lost.
The height of my disdain shall be
To laugh at him, to blush for thee;
To love thee still, but go no more
A begging at a beggar's door.

OLD LONG SYNE.

ASCRIBED TO SIR ROBERT AYTOUN.

From Watson's Collection of Scottish Poems, part 3, but has been traced in Broadsides prior to the close of the seventeenth century (Chambers); it has also been ascribed to Francis Semple of Beltrees. This song is curious, apart from its own merits, as showing that the phrase "Auld Lang Syne" was current as early as the time of Charles I., and as the earliest known attempt to turn it into song. Allan Ramsay wrote a song under this title, and with the same sentiment, but his version, like the present, only leads us to admire more highly that of Robert Burns.

PART FIRST.

SHOULD old acquaintance be forgot,
 And never thought upon,
The flames of love extinguished,
 And freely past and gone?
Is thy kind heart now grown so cold
 In that loving breast of thine,
That thou canst never once reflect
 On old long syne?

Where are thy protestations,
 Thy vows, and oaths, my dear,
Thou mad'st to me and I to thee,
 In register yet clear?
Is faith and truth so violate
 To th' immortal gods divine,
That thou canst never once reflect
 On old long syne?

Is't Cupid's fears, or frosty cares,
 That makes thy spirits decay?
Or is't some object of more worth
 That's stolen thy heart away?
Or some desert makes thee neglect
 Him, so much once was thine,
That thou canst never once reflect
 On old long syne?

Is't worldly cares, so desperate,
 That makes thee to despair?
Is't that makes thee exasperate,
 And makes thee to forbear?
If thou of that were free as I,
 Thou surely should be mine;
If this were true, we should renew
 Kind old long syne.

But since that nothing can prevail,
 And all hope is in vain,
From these dejected eyes of mine
 Still showers of tears shall rain:
And though thou hast me now forgot,
 Yet I'll continue thine,
And ne'er forget for to reflect
 On old long syne.

If e'er I have a house, my dear,
  That truly is call'd mine,
And can afford but country cheer,
  Or ought that's good therein;
Though thou wert rebel to the king,
  And beat with wind and rain,
Assure thyself of welcome, love,
  For old long syne.

PART SECOND.

My soul is ravish'd with delight
  When you I think upon;
All griefs and sorrows take their flight,
  And hastily are gone;
The fair resemblance of your face
  So fills this breast of mine,
No fate nor force can it displace,
  For old long syne.

Since thoughts of you do banish grief,
  When I'm from you removed;
And if in them I find relief,
  When with sad cares I'm moved,
How doth your presence me affect
  With ecstasies divine,
Especially when I reflect
  On old long syne.

Since thou hast robb'd me of my heart,
  By those resistless powers
Which Madam Nature doth impart
  To those fair eyes of yours,
With honour it doth not consist
  To hold a slave in pyne;
Pray let your rigour, then, desist,
  For old long syne.

'Tis not my freedom I do crave,
  By deprecating pains;
Sure, liberty he would not have
  Who glories in his chains:
But this I wish—the gods would move
  That noble soul of thine
To pity, if thou canst not love,
  For old long syne.

SCORNFU NANCY.

Ramsay's TEA TABLE MISCELLANY.—Where it is marked as of unknown age. It is considered by Mr. Stenhouse to be as early as the union of the Crowns in 1603. The tune was selected by Gay for one of the songs in his Opera of " Achilles," performed in 1733.

NANCY'S to the greenwood gane,
  To hear the gowdspink chatt'ring,
And Willie he has follow'd her,
  To gain her love by flatt'ring:
But a' that he could say or do,
  She geck'd and scorned at him;
And aye when he began to woo,
  She bade him mind wha gat him.

What ails ye at my dad, quoth he,
  My minny, or my auntie?
With crowdy-mowdy they fed me,
  Langkale and ranty-tanty:
With bannocks of good barley-meal,
  Of thae there was right plenty,
With chapped stocks fu' butter'd weel;
  And was not that right dainty?

Although my father was nae laird,
  ('Tis daffin to be vaunty,)
He keepit aye a good kale yard,
  A ha'-house, and a pantry;
A guid blue-bonnet on his head,
  An o'erlay 'bout his craigie;
And aye until the day he died
  He rade on guid shanks-naigie.

Now wae and wonder on your snout,
  Wad ye ha'e bonnie Nancy,
Wad ye compare yoursel' to me,
  A docken to a tansie?
I have a wooer o' my ain,
  They ca' him souple Sandy,
And weel I wat his bonnie mou'
  Is sweet like sugar-candy.

Wow, Nancy, what needs a' this din?
  Do I no ken this Sandy?
I'm sure the chief o' a' his kin
  Was Rab the beggar randy;
His minny Meg upo' her back
  Bare baith him and his billy;
Will ye compare a nasty pack
  To me your winsome Willie?

My gutcher left a good braidsword,
  Though it be auld and rusty,
Yet ye may tak' it on my word,
  It is baith stout and trusty;
And if I can but get it drawn,
  Which will be right uneasy,
I shall lay baith my lugs in pawn,
  That he shall get a heezy.

Then Nancy turn'd her round about,
  And said, Did Sandy hear ye,
Ye widna miss to get a clout,
  I ken he disna fear you:
Sae haud ye'r tongue and say nae mair,
  Set somewhere else your fancy;
For as lang's Sandy's to the fore,
  Ye never shall get Nancy.

TAK' YOUR AULD CLOAK ABOUT YE.

One of our earliest and most popular songs. The fourth stanza is sung by Iago in Shakspere's Othello (1611), where, however, the name of the monarch is changed from the Scottish *Robert* to the English Stephen. A version in a more English dress than the one here given is in Percy's folio manuscript. Amongst other variations we have "King Harry" in place of "King Robert,—the Threlly year is changed into Four and Forty, and an extra stanza is given.* Neither Dr. Percy, nor the later Editors of the manuscript, however, dispute the nationality of the song. The version here given is from the Tea Table Miscellany, collated with that given in Herd.

In winter, when the rain rain'd cauld,
  And frost and snaw on ilka hill,
And Boreas, wi' his blasts sae bauld,
  Was threat'nin a' our kye to kill:
Then Bell, my wife, wha lo'es nae strife,
  She said to me richt hastilie,
Get up, gudeman, save Crummie's life,
  And tak' your auld cloak about ye.

---

* This Stanza, the second in the manuscript version, is as follows:—

"O Bell, my wiffe! why dost thou flyte?
  Thou kens my cloake is verry thin;
It is soe sore ower worne,
  A cricke theron cannot runn.
I'll goe find the court within,
  He noe longer lend nor borrow,
Ile goe find the court within,
  For Ile have a new cloake about me."

Percy MS., vol. 2, p. 322.

My Crummie is a usefu' cow,
 And she is come of a good kin';
Aft has she wet the bairns's mou',
 And I am laith that she should tyne;
Get up, gudeman, it is fu' time,
 The sun shines i' the lift sae hie;
Sloth never made a gracious end;
 Gae tak' your auld cloak about ye.

My cloak was ance a gude gray cloak,
 When it was fitting for my wear;
But now it's scantly worth a groat,
 For I have worn't this thretty year;
Let's spend the gear that we ha'e won,
 We little ken the day we'll die;
Then I'll be proud, since I have sworn
 To ha'e a new cloak about me.

In days when our King Robert rang,
 His trews they cost but half a croun;
He said they were a groat ower dear,
 And ca'd the tailor thief and loon;
He was the king that wore a croun,
 And thou'rt a man of laigh degree:
It's pride puts a' the country doun;
 Sae tak' your auld cloak about ye.

Ilka land has its ain lauch,
 Ilk kind o' corn has its ain hool;
I think the world is a' gane wrang,
 When ilka wife her man wad rule;
Do ye no see Rob, Jock, and Hab,
 As they are girded gallantlie,
While I sit burklin i' the ase?—
 I'll ha'e a new cloak about me.

Gudeman, I wat 'tis thretty year
 Sin' we did ane anither ken;
And we ha'e had atween us twa
 Of lads and bonnie lasses ten:
Now they are women grown and men,
 I wish and pray weel may they be;
If you would prove a gude husband,
 E'en tak' your auld cloak about ye.

Bell, my wife, she lo'es nae strife,
 But she would guide me if she can;
And to maintain an easy life,
 I aft maun yield, though I'm gudeman:

Nought's to be gain'd at woman's hand,
Unless ye gi'e her a' the plea;
Then I'll leave aff where I began,
And tak' my auld cloak about me.

WILLIE WINKIE'S TESTAMENT.

Thomson's ORPHEUS CALEDONIUS 1725. This undoubtedly early song seems to have escaped the notice of Ramsay. Its catalogue of "Guids and Gear" is interesting and amusing, and forms a good supplement to that given in the "Wooin of Jock and Jenny," from the popularity of which it, in all likelihood, had its origin.

My daddy left me gear enough:
A couter, and an auld beam-plough,
A nebbed staff, a nutting-tyne,
A fishing-wand with hook and line;
With twa auld stools, and a dirt-house,
A jerkenet, scarce worth a louse,
An auld pat, that wants the lug,
A spurtle and a sowen mug.

A hempen heckle, and a mell,
A tar-horn, and a weather's bell,
A muck-fork, and an auld peak-creel,
The spakes of our auld spinning-wheel;
A pair of branks, yea, and a saddle,
With our auld brunt and broken laddle,
A whang-bit and a sniffle-bit:
Cheer up, my bairns, and dance a fit.

A flailing-staff, a timmer-spit,
An auld kirn and a hole in it,
Yarn-winnles, and a reel,
A fetter-lock, a trump of steel,
A whistle, and a tup-horn spoon,
Wi' an auld pair o' clouted shoon,
A timmer spade, and a gleg shear,
A bonnet for my bairns to wear.

A timmer tong, a broken cradle,
The pinion of an auld car-saddle,
A gullie-knife, and a horse-wand,
A mitten for the left hand,
With an auld broken pan of brass,
With an auld hyeuk for cutting grass,
An auld band, and a hoodling-how,
I hope, my bairns, ye're a' weel now.

Aft have I borne ye on my back,
With a' this riff-raff in my pack;
And it was a' for want of gear,
That gart me steal Mess John's grey mare;
But now, my bairns, what ails ye now,
For ye ha'e naigs enough to plow;
And hose and shoon fit for your feet,
Cheer up, my bairns, and dinna greet.

Then with mysel' I did advise,
My daddie's gear for to comprise;
Some noighbours I ca'd in to see
What gear my daddy left to me.
They sat three-quarters of a year,
Comprising of my daddy's gear;
And when they had gi'en a' their votes,
'Twas scarcely a' worth four pounds Scots.

WHERE HELEN LIES.

PENNANT (Tour in Scotland, V. 2, 101) describes the tradition on which this song is founded, as follows:—

"In the burying-ground of Kirkconnel is the grave of the fair Ellen Irvine, and that of her lover: she was daughter of the house of Kirkconnel, and was beloved by two gentlemen at the same time; the one vowed to sacrifice the successful rival to his resentment, and watched an opportunily while the happy pair were sitting on the banks of the Kirtle, that washes these grounds. Ellen perceived the desperate lover on the opposite side, and fondly thinking to save her favourite, interposed; and receiving the wound intended for her beloved, fell, and expired in his arms. He instantly revenged her death; then fled into Spain, and served for some time against the infidels; on his return he visited the grave of his unfortunate mistress, stretched himself on it, and expiring on the spot, was interred by her side. A sword and a cross are engraven on the tombstone, with *Hic jacet Adam Fleming*: the only memorial of this unhappy gentleman, except an ancient ballad of no great merit, which records the tragical event." "Which," he adds in a note, "happened either the latter end of the reign of James V., or the beginning of that of Mary."

Other traditions vary in minute particulars—for instance, the heroine is sometimes described as Helen Bell—the mortal combat between the rivals takes place in Syria, &c.

There are numerous versions of the song, the first here given is from Ritson's Scots Songs, the second is that adopted by Mr. Robert Chambers, and is "chiefly from the traditionary copy preserved by Mr. Charles K. Sharpe, as he had been accustomed to hear it sung in Annandale in his childhood."

I wish I were where Helen lies!
Where day and night she on me cries!
I wish I were where Helen lies,
        On fair Kirkonnell leo!

Oh Helen fair! Oh Helen chaste!
Were I with thee I would be blest!
Where thou liest low, and at thy rest,
    On fair Kirkonnell lee.

I wish my grave were growing green!
My winding sheet put o'er my e'en!
I wish my grave were growing green,
    On fair Kirkonnell lee!

Where Helen lies! where Helen lies!
I wish I were where Helen lies!
Soon may I be where Helen lies!
    Who died for luve of me.

SECOND VERSION.

I wish I were where Helen lies,
For night and day on me she cries,
I wish I were where Helen lies,
    On fair Kirkconnell lee.

Curst be the hand that shot the shot,
Likewise the gun that ga'e the crack,
Into my arms Burd Helen lap,
    And died for love o' me.

Oh, think na ye my heart was sair,
To see her lie and speak nae mair!
There did she swoon wi' mickle care,
    On fair Kirkconnell lee.

I loutit down, my sword did draw,
I cuttit him in pieces sma',
I cuttit him in pieces sma',
    On fair Kirkconnell lee.

Oh, Helen fair, without compare,
I'll mak a garland o' thy hair,
And wear the same for evermair,
    Until the day I dee.

I wish my grave were growing green,
A winding-sheet put ower my een,
And I in Helen's arms lying,
    On fair Kirkconnell lee.

Oh Helen chaste, thou were modest;
Were I with thee I wad be blest,
Where thou lies low and takes thy rest,
    On fair Kirkconnell lee.

I wish I were where Helen lies,
For night and day on me she cries;
I wish I were where Helen lies,
    On fair Kirkconnell lee.

MY DEAR AND ONLY LOVE.
JAMES, FIRST MARQUIS OF MONTROSE,

Born in 1612. His short but glorious career is well known to every reader of Scottish History. Beginning his public life on the side of the Covenant, he in 1642 left their camp, and joined the standard of Charles I. His victories, talent, courage and fidelity in the Royal cause gained him the title of Great. Defeated at length, he took refuge in Assint, but was betrayed and delivered up to the Scottish Parliament. After undergoing a form of trial at Edinburgh, he was executed there in 1650.

Seven poems by this nobleman appeared in the third part of Watson's choice collection of Scotch Poems, 1711, and these were probably but reprinted from Broadsides. The song here given is the first and finest of the whole. It is supposed to have been modelled on an early English song, and to be addressed by the author to his country instead of a mistress in real life, and this latter supposition will be allowed as correct if we consider the deep metaphorical cloud under which the poets of the period clothed their fancies.

My dear and only love, I pray
  That little world of thee
Be govern'd by no other sway,
  But purest monarchy;
For if confusion have a part,
  Which virtuous souls abhor,
I'll call a synod in my heart
  And never love thee more.

As Alexander I will reign,
  And I will reign alone,
My thoughts did evermore disdain
  A rival on my throne.
He either fears his fate too much,
  Or his deserts are small,
Who dares not put it to the touch,
  To gain or lose it all.

But I will reign, and govern still,
  And always give the law,
And have each subject at my will,
  And all to stand in awe:
But 'gainst my batt'ries if I find
  Thou storm or vex me sore,
As if thou set me as a blind,
  I'll never love thee more.

And in the empire of thy heart,
  Where I should solely be,
If others should pretend a part,
  Or dare to share with me;

Or committees if thou erect,
  Or go on such a score,
I'll smiling mock at thy neglect,
  And never love thee more.

But if no faithless action stain
  Thy love and constant word,
I'll make thee famous by my pen,
  And glorious by my sword.
I'll serve thee in such noble ways,
  As ne'er were known before;
I'll deck and crown my head with bays,
  And love thee evermore.

CLOUT THE CALDRON.

Ramsay's TEA TABLE MISCELLANY.—Printed without any mark. Burns mentions a tradition that an old song, probably an older version of the words here given, was composed by a member of the Kenmure family alluding to one of his amours. The air is sometimes styled "The Blacksmith and his apron."

HAVE ye any pots or pans,
  Or any broken chandlers?
I am a tinker to my trade,
  And newly come frae Flanders,
As scant of siller as of grace;
  Disbanded, we've a bad run;
Gar tell the lady of the place,
  I'm come to clout her caldron,
    Fa, adrie, diddle, diddle, &c.

Madam, if you have wark for me,
  I'll do't to your contentment;
And dinna care a single flie
  For any man's resentment;
For, lady fair, though I appear
  To every ane a tinker,
Yet to yoursell I'm bauld to tell,
  I am a gentle jinker.

Love Jupiter into a swan
  Turn'd for his loved Leda;
He like a bull ower meadows ran,
  To carry off Europa.
Then may not I, as well as he,
  To cheat your Argus blinker,
And win your love like mighty Jove,
  Thus hide me in a tinker?

Sir, ye appear a cunning man;
  But this fine plot you'll fail in;
For there is neither pot nor pan,
  Of mine, you'll drive a nail in.
Then bind your budget on your back,
  And nails up in your apron;
For I've a tinker under tack,
  That's used to clout my ca'dron.

FARE YE WELL MY AULD WIFE.

A Fragment preserved in Herd's Collection.

AND fare ye weel, my auld wife;
  Sing bum, bee, berry, bum;
Fare ye weel, my auld wife;
  Sing bum, bum, bum.
Fare ye weel, my auld wife,
The steerer up o' sturt and strife,
The maut 's abune the meal the nicht,
  Wi' some, some, some.

And fare ye weel, my pike-staff;
  Sing bum, bee, berry, bum;
Fare ye weel, my pike-staff;
  Sing bum, bum, bum.
Fare ye weel, my pike staff,
Wi' you nae mair my wife I'll baff;
The maut 's abune the meal the nicht,
  Wi' some, some, some.

GALA WATER.

From Herd's COLLECTION, slightly collated with other copies. The earliest version extant of this celebrated song.

BRAW, braw lads of Gala Water,
  O! braw lads of Gala Water;
I'll kilt my coats aboon my knee,
  And follow my love through the water.

Sae fair her hair, sae brent her brow,
  Sae bonnie blue her een, and cheerie,
Sae white her teeth, sae sweet her mou',
  I aften kiss her till I'm wearie.

Ower yon bank, and ower yon brae,
  Ower yon moss amang the heather,
I'll kilt my coats aboon my knee,
  And follow my love through the water.

Down amang the broom, the broom,
Down amang the broom sae drearie,
The lassie lost her silken snood
That gart her greet till she was wearie.

BONNIE ROBIN.

HERD'S COLLECTION. Mr. Chambers (Scottish Songs, Vol. 1. p. 97, 1829) conjectures this song to have been written about 1641. In 1622 "the Old Bridge of Tay at Perth, built by Robert Bruce, gave way and was not built again till 1772. The mending or re-erection of the Bridge of Tay was a matter of agitation during the reign of Charles I., and that Sovereign when in Scotland in 1641, subscribed a hundred pounds for the purpose."

GUDE day now, bonnie Robin,
How lang ha'e ye been here?
I've been a bird about this bush
This mair than twenty year.

But now I am the sickest bird
That ever sat on brier;
And I wad mak my testament,
Gudeman, if ye wad hear.

Gar' tak' this bonnie neb o' mine,
That picks upon the corn,
And gie't to the duke o' Hamilton,
To be a hunting-horn.

Gar tak' these bonnie feathers o' mine,
The feathers o' my neb,
And gi'e to the lady 'o Hamilton,
To fill a feather bed.

Gar tak' this gude richt leg o' mine,
And mend the brig o' Tay,
It will be a post and pillar gude,
It will neither bow nor [gae.]

And tak' this other leg of mine,
And mend the brig o' Weir;
It will be a post and pillar gude,
It will neither bow nor steer.

Gar tak' thae bonnie feathers o' mine,
The feathers o' my tail,
And gi'e to the lads o' Hamilton
To be a barn-flail.

And tak' thae bonnie feathers o' mine,
The feathers o' my breast,
And gi'e them to the bonnie lad,
Will bring to me a priest.

Now in there cam' my lady wren,
Wi' mony a sigh and groan,
O what care I for a' the lads,
If my wee lad be gane!

Then Robin turn'd him round about,
E'en like a little king;
Gae pack ye out at my chamber-door,
Ye little cutty-quean.

GENERAL LESLIE'S MARCH.

TEA TABLE MISCELLANY.—"It seems to have been written by some sneering cavalier as a quiz upon the Scottish army, which marched to join the English parliamentary forces, 1644, in terms of the Solemn League and Covenant, and which was so instrumental in winning for that party the decisive battle of Longmarston Moor."—(*Chambers Scottish Songs, vol. 1, p. 173.*)

MARCH, march, why the deil do ye na march?
Stand to your arms, my lads,
Fight in good order;
Front about, ye musketeers all,
Till ye come to the English border.
Stand till't, and fight like men,
True gospel to maintain;
The Parliament['s] blyth to see us a coming.
When to the kirk we come,
We'll purge it ilka room,
Frae Popish relicks, and a' sic innovations,
That all the warld may see,
There's nane i' the right, but we
Of the auld Scottish nation.
Jenny shall wear the hood,
Jocky the sark of God;
And the kist fou of whistles,
That make sic a cleiro,
Our pipers braw
Shall hae them a'
Whate'er come on it.
Busk up your plaids, my lads,
Cock up your bonnets.
    March, march, &c.

BLINK O'ER THE BURN SWEET BETTY.

"Blink o'er the bourn, sweet Bettie, to me," is the beginning of a fragment quoted in King Lear, (Act iii. Sc. 6.) The expression has also been traced by Dr. Rimbault as far back as the reign of Henry VIII. None of the fragments, however, bear any resemblance to either of the versions here given, the first from Herd's Collection, 1776 (also adopted by Ritson), and the second from Stenhouse's Illustrations, and stated there to have been written previous to 1684.

I.

In summer I mawed my meadow,
In harvest I shure my corn,
In winter I married a widow,
I wish I was free the morn!
Blink over the burn, sweet Betty,
Blink over the burn to me:
O, it is a thousand pities
But I was a widow for thee!

II.

Blink o'er the burn, sweet Betty,
It is a cauld winter night;
It rains, it hails, and it thunders,
The moon she gi'es nae light:
It's a' for the sake o' sweet Betty,
That ever I tint my way;
O lassie let me creep ayont thee,
Until it be break o' day.

III.

O Betty shall bake my bread,
And Betty shall brew my ale,
And Betty shall be my love,
When I come over the dale;
Blink o'er the burn, sweet Betty,
Blink o'er the burn to me:
And while I ha'e life, my dear lassie,
My ain sweet Betty thou's be.

THE WREN.

An old Nursery song, from Herd's Collection.

The wren scho lyes in care's bed,
In care's bed, in care's bed;
The wren scho lyes in care's bed,
In meikle dule and pyne, O.
When in cam' Robin Redbriest,
Redbriest, Redbriest;
When in cam' Robin Redbriest
Wi' succar-saps and wine, O.

Now, maiden, will ye taste o' this,
　Taste o' this, taste o' this;
Now, maiden, will ye taste o' this?
　It's succar-saps and wine, O.
Na, ne'er a drap, Robin,
　Robin, Robin;
Na, ne'er a drap, Robin,
　Gin it was ne'er sae fine, O.

　　* * * * * *

And where's the ring that I gied ye,
　That I gied ye, that I gied ye;
And where's the ring that I gied ye,
　Ye little cutty-quean, O?
I gied it till a soger,
　A soger, a soger;
I gied it till a soger,
　A true sweetheart o' mine, O.

WE'RE A' NODDIN.

In Percy's Reliques, we are presented with an early version of "John Anderson My Joe," very much after the style of that here given. The Air seems to have been always very popular, and Percy's surmise is likely correct, that his version has a political meaning, and originated solely in consequence of the popularity of the Air assisting the Reformers in venting a quiet sarcasm against their enemies. The version here given is from the Additional Note to Stenhouse's Illustrations, part 8, and were communicated by Mr. C. K. Sharpe.

Hoo are ye, Kimmer,
　An' hoo do ye thrive?
Hoo mony bairns hae ye?
　Kimmer, I hae five.

　　An we're a' noddin,
　　Nid, nid, noddin,
　　An we're a' noddin
　　At our house at hame.

Are they a' Johnnie's bairns?
　Na, Kimmer, na!
For three o' them were gotten
　When Johnie was awa!

　　An we're a' noddin, &c.

Cats like milk,
　And dogs like broo;
Lads like Lassies,
　And Lassies Lads too.

　　An we're a' noddin, &c.

GET UP, GUDE WIFE.

From Ritson's Scots Songs, taken by him from a manuscript of the time of Charles I, in the British Museum.

Get up, gudewife, don on your claise,
   And to the market mak' you boune:
'Tis lang time sin' your neebors rase;
   They're weel nigh gotten into the toune.
See ye don on your better goune,
And gar the lasse big on the fyre.
   Dame, do not look as ye wad frowne,
But doe the thing whilk I desyre.

I spier what haste ye hae, gudeman!
   Your mother staid till ye war born;
Wad ye be at the tother can,
   To scoure your throat sae sune this morn?
Gude faith, I haud it but a scorne,
That ye suld with my rising mell;
   For when ye have baith said and sworne,
I'll do but what I like mysel'.

Gudewife, we maun needs have a care,
   Sae lang's we wonne in neebor's rawe,
O' neeborheid to tak' a share,
   And rise up when the cock does crawe;
For I have heard an auld said sawe,
"They that rise last big on the fyre,"
   What wind or weather so ever blaw,
Dame, do the thing whilk I desyre.

Nay, what do ye talk of neeborheid?
   Gif I lig in my bed till noone,
By nae man's shine I bake my breid,
   And ye need not reck what I have done.
Nay, look to the clooting o' your shoone,
And with my rising do not mell:
   For, gin ye lig baith sheets abune,
I'll do but what I will mysel'.

Gudewife, ye maun needs tak' a care
   To save the geare that we ha'e won:
Or lye away baith plow and car,
   And hang up Ring when a' is done.
Then may our bairns a-begging run,
To seek their mister in the myre.
   Sae fair a thread as we ha'e won!
Dame, do the thing whilk I require.

Gudeman, ye may weel a-begging gang,
  Ye seem sae weel to bear the pocke;
Ye may as weel gang sune as syne,
  To seek your meat amang gude folke.
In ilka house ye'll get a locke,
  When ye come whar your gossips dwell.
Nay, lo you luik sae like a gowke,
  I'll do but what I list mysel'.

Gudewife, you promised, when we were wed,
  That ye wad me truly obey;
Moss John can witness what you said,
  And I'll go fetch him in this day;
And, gif that haly man will say,
  Ye's do the thing that I desyre,
Then sall we sune end up this fray,
  And ye sall do what I require.

I nowther care for John nor Jacke—
  I'll tak' my pleasure at my ease;
I care not what you say a placke—
  Ye may go fetch him gin ye please.
And, gin ye want ane of a mease,
  Ye may e'en gae fetch the deil frae helle;
I wad you wad let your japin cease,
  For I'll do but what I like mysel'.

Woll, sin' it will nae better bee,
  I'll tak' my share or a' bee gane:
The warst card in my hand sall flee,
  And i' faith, I wait I can shifte for ane.
I'll sell the plow, and lay to wadd the waine,
  And the greatest spender sall beare the bell:
And then, when all the gudes are gane,
  Dame, do the thing ye list yoursel'.

MY JO JANET.

TEA TABLE MISCELLANY.—The air is of considerable antiquity, being found under the title of "Long or any old Man" in the Skene MS., 1630.

Sweet sir, for your courtesie,
  When ye come by the Bass, then,
For the love ye bear to me,
  Buy me a keekin' glass, then.
Keek into the draw-well,
  Janet, Janet;
There ye'll see your bonnie sell,
  My jo Janet.

Keekin' in the draw-well clear,
  What if I fa' in, sir?
Then a' my kin' will say and swear
  I droun'd mysell for sin, sir.
Haud the better by the brae,
  Janet, Janet;
Haud the better by the brae,
  My jo Janet.

Gude sir, for your courtesie,
  Comin' through Aberdeen, then,
For the love ye bear to me,
  Buy me a pair o' sheen, then.
Clout the auld—the new are dear,
  Janet, Janet;
Ae pair may gain ye hauf a year,
  My jo Janet.

But, what if, dancin' on the green,
  And skippin' like a maukin,
They should see my clouted sheen,
  Of me they will be taukin.
Dance aye laigh, and late at e'en,
  Janet, Janet;
Syne a' their fauts will no be seen,
  My jo Janet.

Kind sir, for your courtesie,
  When ye gae to the cross, then,
For the love ye bear to me,
  Buy me a pacin' horse, then.
Pace upon your spinnin' wheel,
  Janet, Janet;
Pace upon your spinnin' wheel,
  My jo Janet.

My spinnin' wheel is auld and stiff,
  The rock o't winna stand, sir;
To keep the temper-pin in tiff
  Employs richt aft my hand, sir.
Mak' the best o't that ye can,
  Janet, Janet;
But like it never wale a man,
  My jo Janet.

FY, LET US ALL TO THE BRIDAL.

FRANCIS SEMPLE, OF BELTREES.

WHO died about 1682, the last of a family of poets; one of whom wrote the "Packman's Paternoster," and another immortalised Habbie Simpson, the Town Piper of Kilbarchan. The authorship of this song has also been claimed for Sir William Scott, of Thirlestane. It first appeared in Watson's Collection, 1706; the version here given has been altered a little.

Fy, let us a' to the bridal,
   For there'll be liltin' there;
For Jock's to be married to Maggie,
   The lass wi' the gowden hair.
And there'll be lang kale and parridge,
   And bannocks o' barley meal;
And there'll be guid saut herrin'
   To relish a cog o' guid ale.
        Fy, let us a', &c.

And there'll be Sandie the souter,
   And Will wi' the mickle mou';
And there'll be Tam the bluter,
   And Andrew the tinkler, I trow.
And there'll be bow-leggit Robbie,
   Wi' thumless Katie's gudeman;
And there'll be blue-cheekit Dobbie,
   And Lawrie, the laird o' the land.

And there'll be sow-libber Patie,
   And plookie-fac'd Wat o' the mill;
Capper-nosed Francie, and Gibbie,
   That wins in the howe o' the hill.
And there'll be Alaster Sibbie,
   That in wi' black Bessie did mool;
Wi' sneevlin' Lillie, and Tibbie,
   The lass that sits aft on the stool.

And there'll be Judan Maclowrie,
   And blinkin' daft Barbara Macleg;
Wi' flae-luggit shairnie-faced Lawrie,
   And shangie-mou'd halnket Meg.
And there'll be happer-hipp'd Nancie,
   And fairy-faced Flowrie by name,
Muck Maudie, and fat-luggit Grizzie,
   The lass wi' the gowden wame.

And there'll be Girnagain Gibbie,
   And his glaikit wife Jenny Doll;
And misle-shinn'd Mungo Macapie,
   The lad that was skipper himsell.

There lads and lasses in pearlings
  Will feast in the heart o' the ha',
On sybows, and reefarts, and carlins,
  That are baith sodden and raw.

And there'll be fadges and brachen,
  And fouth o' gude gabbocks o' skate,
Powsoudie, and drammock, and crowdie,
  And caller nowt-feet on a plate:
And there'll be partens and buckies,
  And whytens and speldins enew,
And singit sheep-heads and a haggis,
  And scadlips to sup till ye spew.

And there'll be gude lapper-milk kebbucks,
  And sowens, and farles, and baps,
Wi' swats and weel-scraped painches,
  And brandy in stoups and in caups;
And there'll be meal-kail and kustocks,
  Wi' skink to sup till ye rive;
And roasts to roast on a brander,
  Of flouks that were taken alive.

Scrapped haddocks, wilks, dulse, and tangle,
  And a mill o' good sneeshin' to prie;
When weary wi' eatin' and drinkin',
  We'll rise up and dance till we dee.
Fy, let us a'-to the bridal,
  For there'll be liltin' there;
For Jock's to be married to Maggie,
  The lass wi' the gowden hair.

MAGGIE LAUDER.

FRANCIS SEMPLE OF BELTREES. (?)

The Authorship of this piece has been hotly disputed by several critics "learned in ballad lore," but on very flimsy grounds. Mr. Chambers thinks it smacks of the pen which produced "Wanton Willie."

Wha wadna be in love
  Wi' bonnie Maggie Lauder?
A piper met her gaun to Fife,
  And speir'd what was't they ca'd her;—
Right scornfully she answer'd him,
  Begone you hallanshaker!
Jog on your gate, you bladderskate,
  My name is Maggie Lauder.

Maggie quo' he, and by my bags,
　I'm fidgin' fain to see thee;
Sit down by me, my bonnie bird,
　In troth I winna steer thee:
For I'm a piper to my trade,
　My name is Rob the Ranter;
The lasses loup as they were daft,
　When I blaw up my chanter.

Piper, quo' Meg, ha'e ye your bags?
　Or is your drone in order?
If ye be Rob, I've heard of you,
　Live you upo' the border?
The lasses a', baith far and near,
　Have heard o' Rob the Ranter;
I'll shake my foot wi' right gude will,
　Gif you'll blaw up your chanter.

Then to his bags he flew wi' speed,
　About the drone he twisted;
Meg up and wallop'd o'er the green,
　For brawly could she frisk it.
Weel done! quo' he—play up! quo' she;
　Weel bobbed! quo' Rob the Ranter;
'Tis worth my while to play indeed,
　When I ha'e sic a dancer.

Weel ha'e you play'd your part, quo' Meg,
　Your cheeks are like the crimson;
There's nane in Scotland plays sae weel,
　Since we lost Habbie Simpson.
I've lived in Fife, baith maid and wife,
　These ten years and a quarter;
Gin' ye should come to Anster fair,
　Speir ye for Maggie Lauder.

LEADER HAUGHS AND YARROW.

In the Roxburghe Ballads this song is signed "The words of Burne the Violer," and supposed by Mr. Chambers to be Nicol Burne, a wandering minstrel of the seventeenth century. It also appeared in the Tea Table Miscellany.

"This song," says Mr. Chambers, "is little better than a string of names of places, yet there is something so pleasing in it, especially to the ear of a 'South country man,' that it has long maintained its place in our collections."

When Phœbus bright the azure skies
　With golden rays enlight'neth,
He makes all nature's beauties rise,
　Herbs, trees, and flowers he quick'neth:

Amongst all those he makes his choice,
  And with delight goes thorow,
With radiant beams, the silver streams
  Of Leader Haughs and Yarrow.

When Aries the day and night
  In equal length divideth,
And frosty Saturn takes his flight,
  Nae langer he abideth;
Then Flora queen, with mantle green,
  Casts off her former sorrow,
And vows to dwell with Ceres' sel',
  In Leader Haughs and Yarrow.

Pan, playing on his aiten reed,
  And shepherds, him attending,
Do here resort, their flocks to feed,
  The hills and haughs commending
With cur and kent, upon the bent,
  Sing to the sun, Good-morrow,
And swear nae fields mair pleasures yield,
  Than Leader Haughs and Yarrow.

A house there stands on Leader side,
  Surmounting my descriving,
With rooms sae rare, and windows fair,
  Like Daedalus' contriving:
Men passing by do aften cry,
  In sooth it hath no marrow;
It stands as fair on Leader side,
  As Newark does on Yarrow.

A mile below, who lists to ride,
  Will hear the mavis singing;
Into St. Leonard's banks she bides,
  Sweet birks her head owerhinging.
The lint-white loud, and Progne proud,
  With tuneful throats and narrow,
Into St. Leonard's banks they sing,
  As sweetly as in Yarrow.

The lapwing lilteth ower the lea,
  With nimble wing she sporteth;
But vows she'll flee far from the tree
  Where Philomel resorteth:
By break of day the lark can say,
  I'll bid you a good morrow;
I'll stretch my wing, and mounting sing
  O'er Leader Haughs and Yarrow.

Park, Wanton-wa's, and Wooden-cleuch,
   The East and Wester Mainses,
The wood of Lauder's fair eneuch,
   The corns are good in the Blainslies:
There sits are fine, and said by kind,
   That if ye search all thorough
Mearns, Buchan, Marr, nane better are
   Than Leader Haughs and Yarrow.

In Burn-mill-bog and Whitslaid Shaws,
   The fearful hare she haunteth;
Brig-haugh and Braidwoodsheil she knaws,
   And Chapel-wood frequenteth:
Yet when she irks, to Kaidslie birks
   She rins, and sighs for sorrow,
That she should leave sweet Leader Haughs
   And cannot win to Yarrow.

What sweeter musick wad ye hear,
   Than hounds and beigles crying?
The started hare rins hard with fear,
   Upon her speed relying:
But yet her strength it fails at length,
   Nae bielding can she borrow,
In Sorrel's fields, Cleckman, or Hags,
   And sighs to be in Yarrow.

For Rockwood, Ringwood, Spoty, Shag,
   With sight and scent pursue her,
Till, ah! her pith begins to flag,
   Nae cunning can rescue her:
O'er dub and dyke, o'er seugh and syke,
   She'll rin the fields all thorow,
Till fail'd she fa's in Leader Haughs,
   And bids farewell to Yarrow.

Sing Erslington and Cowdenknows,
   Where Homes had ance commanding;
And Drygrange with the milk-white ews,
   'Twixt Tweed and Leader standing:
The bird that flees through Reedpath trees,
   And Gledswood banks ilk morrow,
May chant and sing sweet Leader Haughs,
   And bonny howms of Yarrow.

But Minstrel-Burne cannot assuage
   His grief while life endureth,
To see the changes of this age,
   That fleeting time procureth:

For mony a place stands in hard case,
Where blyth fowk kend nae sorrow,
With Homes that dwelt on Leader-side,
And Scots that dwell on Yarrow.

OMNIA VINCIT AMOR.

TEA TABLE MISCELLANY, 1724.—A copy is also in the Roxburghe Collection, from a broadside of the period. Mr. Chambers considers it a composition of Minstrel Burne.

As I went forth to view the spring,
 Which Flora had adornèd
In gorgeous raiment, everything
 The rage of winter scornèd,
I cast mine eye, and did espy
 A youth that made great clamour,
And, drawing nigh, I heard him cry,
 Ah, Omnia vincit amor!

Upon his breast he lay along,
 Hard by a murm'ring river,
And mournfully his doleful song
 With sighs he did deliver;
Ah! Jeany's face was comely grace,
 Her locks that shine like lammer,
With burning rays have cut my days;
 For Omnia vincit amor.

Her glancy een like comets' sheen,
 The morning sun outshining,
Have caught my heart in Cupid's net,
 And makes me die with pining.
Durst I complain, nature's to blame,
 So curiously to frame her,
Whose beauties rare make me with care
 Cry, Omnia vincit amor.

Ye crystal streams that swiftly glide,
 Be partners of my mourning,
Ye fragrant fields and meadows wide,
 Condemn her for her scorning;
Let every tree a witness be,
 How justly I may blame her;
Ye chanting birds, note these my words,
 Ah! Omnia vincit amor.

Had she been kind as she was fair,
 She long had been admired,
And been ador'd for virtues rare,
 Wh' of life now makes me tired.

Thus said, his breath began to fail,
　He could not speak, but stammer;
　He sigh'd full sore, and said no more,
　　But Omnia vincit amor.

When I observ'd him near to death,
　I run in haste to save him,
But quickly he resign'd his breath,
　So deep the wound love gave him.
Now for her sake this vow I'll make,
　My tongue shall aye defame her,
While on his hearse I'll write this verse,
　Ah! Omnia vincit amor.

Straight I consider'd in my mind
　Upon the matter rightly,
And found, though Cupid he be blind,
　He proves in pith most mighty.
For warlike Mars, and thund'ring Jove,
　And Vulcan with his hammer,
Did ever prove the slaves of love;
　For Omnia vincit amor.

Hence we may see the effects of love,
　Which gods and men keep under,
That nothing can his bounds remove,
　Or torments break asunder;
Nor wise, nor fool, need go to school
　To learn this from his grammar:
His heart's the book where he's to look
　For Omnia vincit amor.

BARBARA ALLAN.

TEA TABLE MISCELLANY.—"I remember," says Mr. C. Kirkpatrick Sharpe, "that the peasantry of Annandale sang many more verses of this ballad than have appeared in print, but they were of no merit—containing numerous magnificent offers from the lover to his mistress—and, amongst others some ships, in sight, which may strengthen the belief that this song was composed near the shores of the Solway."—*Additional Illustrations to Stenhouse*, p. 800.

It was in and about the Martinmas time,
　When the green leaves were a-falling,
That Sir John Graham, in the west countrie,
　Fell in love wi' Barbara Allan.

He sent his man down through the town,
　To the place where she was dwallin'.
Oh, haste and come to my master dear,
　Gin ye be Barbara Allan.

Oh, hooly, hooly, rase she up
  To the place where he was lyin',
And when she drew the curtain by,
  Young man, I think ye're dyin'.

It's oh, I'm sick, I'm very very sick,
  And its a' for Barbara Allan.
Oh, the better for me yo'se never be,
  Though your heart's bluid were a-spillin.'

Oh, dinna ye mind, young man, she said,
  When ye was in the tavern a-drinkin',
That ye made the healths gae round and round,
  And slichtit Barbara Allan?

He turned his face unto the wa',
  And death was with him dealin':
Adieu, adieu, my dear friends a',
  And be kind to Barbara Allan.

And slowly, slowly rase she up,
  And slowly, slowly left him,
And sighin', said, she could not stay,
  Since death of life had reft him.

She hadna gane a mile but twa,
  When she heard the deid-bell ringin',
And every jow that the deid-bell gied,
  It cried, Woe to Barbara Allan.

Oh, mother, mother, mak' my bed,
  And mak it saft and narrow,
Since my love died for me to-day,
  I'll die for him to-morrow.

CROMLET'S LILT.

The tradition on which this song is based is as follows:—Helen, daughter of William Stirling (of the family of Ardoch), was beloved by Sir James Chisholm of Cromlet, who, having to visit France, arranged with a friend to convey his letters to his mistress. This individual in the course of his missions to the young lady, fell in love with her himself, and, by dint of well-plied stories reflecting on Chisholm's conduct, and by withholding his letters, caused her to renounce her absent lover, and consent to become his own wife. The song here given is said to have been composed by Chisholm at this period. The tradition winds up in the good old style. On the marriage evening, while the dance went through the ha', Chisholm entered the house, killed his rival, cleared his own good name, and in due time married the lady.

Mr. Maidment questions the supposition of the song being written by Sir James, and probably with reason. The song appears with music in Thomson's Orpheus Caledonius, and it is generally agreed that both words and music are very ancient, and probably of the reign of James VI.

    SINCE all thy vows, false maid,
      Are blown to air,
    And my poor heart betray'd
      To sad despair;
    Into some wilderness
    My grief I will express,
    And thy hard-heartedness,
      Oh, cruel fair!

    Have I not graven our loves
      On every tree
    In yonder spreading grove,
      Though false thou be?
    Was not a solemn oath
    Plighted betwixt us both,
    Thou thy faith, I my troth,
      Constant to be?

    Some gloomy place I'll find,
      Some doleful shade,
    Where neither sun nor wind
      E'er entrance had.
    Into that hollow cave
    There will I sigh and rave,
    Because thou dost behave
      So faithlessly.

    Wild fruit shall be my meat,
      I'll drink the spring;
    Cold earth shall be my seat;
      For covering,
    I'll have the starry sky
    My head to canopy,
    Until my soul on high
      Shall spread its wing.

    I'll have no funeral fire,
      No tears nor sighs;
    No grave do I require,
      Nor obsequies:
    The courteous red-breast, he
    With leaves will cover me,
    And sing my elegy
      With doleful voice.

And when a ghost I am,
  I'll visit thee,
Oh, thou deceitful dame,
  Whose cruelty
Has kill'd the kindest heart
That e'er felt Cupid's dart,
And never can desert
  From loving thee!

JOHN HAY'S BONNIE LASSIE,

Said to have been written in honour of the Lady Margaret, eldest daughter of the First Marquis of Tweedale. This Lady became the wife of the Third Earl of Roxburghe. It is supposed to have been composed about 1670. Her husband was drowned in 1682, she survived till 1758, when she died at Broomlands, near Kelso, at the ripe age of 96. The authorship of this piece was long ascribed in literary circles to Allan Ramsay (in whose Tea Table Miscellany it first appeared), and in the traditions of Tweedside to a working Joiner, who is supposed to have loved the lass without daring to "discover his pain."

By smooth-winding Tay a swain was reclining,
Aft cried he, Oh, hey! maun I still live pining
Mysel' thus away, and daurna discover
To my bonnie Hay, that I am her lover?

Nae mair it will hide; the flame waxes stranger;
If she's not my bride, my days are nae langer:
Then I'll take a heart, and try at a venture;
May be, ere we part, my vows may content her.

She's fresh as the spring, and sweet as Aurora,
When birds mount and sing, bidding day a good morrow:
The sward of the mead, enamell'd with daisies,
Looks wither'd and dead, when twined of her graces.

But if she appear where verdure invite her,
The fountains run clear, and the flowers smell the sweeter.
'Tis heaven to be by, when her wit is a-flowing;
Her smiles and bright eyes set my spirits a-glowing.

The mair that I gaze, the deeper I'm wounded;
Struck dumb with amaze my mind is confounded:
I'm all in a fire, dear maid, to caress ye;
For a' my desires is John Hay's bonnie lassie.

O, WALY, WALY!

TEA TABLE MISCELLANY, where it is marked as old. Nothing definite is known as to the age or personages of this song. Mr. Stenhouse and others considered it to belong to the age of Queen Mary, and to refer to some affair of the court; while Mr. Robert Chambers considers it to refer to Lady Barbara Erskine, wife of John 2nd Marquis of Douglas. The lady was married in 1670, and " owing, there can be little doubt, to his lordship's unworthy conduct, the alliance was productive of misery to the lady. She had even to bewail that her own honour was brought into question, chiefly, it would appear, through the influence of a chamberlain over her husband's mind. At length, a separation, with a suitable provision, left her in the worst kind of widowhood, after she had brought the marquis one son (subsequently first commander of the Cameronian regiment, and who fell at the battle of Steenkirk)."—*Songs of Scotland prior to Burns*, p. 280.

O waly, waly up the bank,
   And waly, waly down the brae,
And waly, waly yon burnside,
   Where I and my love wont to gae.
I lean'd my back unto an aik,
   I thought it was a trusty tree,
But first it bow'd, and syne it brak,
   Sae my true love did lightly me.

O waly, waly, but love be bonny
   A little time, while it is new;
But when 'tis auld it waxeth cauld,
   And fades away like the morning dew.
O wherefore shou'd I busk my head?
   Or wherefore shou'd I kame my hair?
For my true love has me forsook,
   And says he'll never love me mair.

Now Arthur Seat shall be my bed,
   The sheets shall ne'er be fyl'd by me:
Saint Anton's well shall be my drink,
   Since my true love's forsaken me.
Martinmas wind, when wilt thou blaw,
   And shake the green leaves off the tree?
O gentle death, when wilt thou come?
   For of my life I am weary.

'Tis not the frost that freezes fell,
   Nor blawing snaw's inclemency;
'Tis not sic cauld that makes me cry,
   But my love's heart grown cauld to me.
When we came in by Glasgow town,
   We were a comely sight to see;
My love was clad in the black velvet,
   And I mysel' in cramasie.

But had I wist, before I kiss'd,
　That love had been sae ill to win,
I'd lock'd my heart in a case of gold,
　And pinn'd it wi' a siller pin.
Oh, oh, if my young babe were born,
　And set upon the nurse's knee,
And I mysel' were dead and gane,
　For a maid again I never shall be.

KATH'RINE OGIE.

TEA TABLE MISCELLANY.—Collated with a copy in Stenhouse's Illustrations to Johnson's Museum. This song can be traced to the time of Charles II., when it was sung by John Abell, a musical favourite of the Merry monarch. Several broadsides have been found, published with the air about 1680. Gay wrote a song for the air for one of his operas, and a miserable parody of the words may be found in Durfey's "Pills to Purge Melancholy." Mr. Robert Chambers considers this an Anglo-Scottish production, like "'Twas within a mile o' Edinburgh Town;" but we cannot think that he has satisfactorily made out a case. Burns's "Highland Mary" is to the same tune.

As walking forth to view the plain,
　Upon a morning early,
While May's sweet scent did cheer my brain,
　From flowers which grew so rarely,
I chanc'd to meet a pretty maid,
　She shin'd tho' it was foggie:
I ask'd her name: Kind sir, she said,
　My name is Kath'rine Ogie.

I stood a while, and did admire,
　To see a nymph so stately:
So brisk an air there did appear
　In a country maid so neatly:
Such nat'ral sweetness she display'd,
　Like a lily in a bogie;
Diana's self was ne'er array'd
　Like this same Kath'rine Ogie.

Thou flow'r of females, beauty's queen,
　Who sees thee sure must prize thee;
Though thou art drest in robes but mean,
　Yet these cannot disguise thee;
Thy mind sure, as thine eyes do look,
　Above each clownish rogie;
Thou'rt match for laird, or lord, or duke,
　My bonnie Kath'rine Ogie.

O! if I were some shepherd swain,
  To feed my flock beside thee;
And gang with thee alang the plain,
  At buchtin to abide thee.
More rich and happy I could be
  Wi' Kate, and crook, and dogie,
Than he that does his thousands see,
  My winsome Kath'rine Ogie.

Then I'd despise th' imperial throne,
  And statesmen's dang'rous stations,
I'd be no king, I'd wear no crown,
  I'd smile at conqu'ring nations,
Might I caress, and still possess
  This lass of whom I'm vogie,
For they're but toys, and still look less,
  Compar'd with Kath'rine Ogie.

I fear for me is not decreed
  So fair, so fine a creature,
Whose beauty rare makes her exceed
  All other works of nature.
Clouds of despair surround my love,
  That are both dark, and foggie;
Pity my case, ye Powers above!
  I die for Kath'rine Ogie.

SILLY AULD MAN.

HERD'S COLLECTION.—Mr. Robert Chambers (Scottish Songs, vol. I, p. 134) makes this song to belong to the reign of Charles II., and gives it as the composition of one of the Covenanting clergy, who, to deceive a body of military who were in pursuit of him, assumed the dress and air of an idiotic beggar, and after a due amount of dancing and capering in the midst of the soldiers, treated them to these verses composed "on the spur of the moment." This versatile gentleman succeeded in effecting his escape. What truth there be in this legend we know not, but the generality of the preachers of the Covenant are generally depicted as men of a different stamp. However, the song, as we have it, bears evident marks of antiquity.

I AM a pair silly auld man,
  And hirplin' ower a tree;
Yet fain, fain kiss wad I,
  Gin the kirk wad let me be.

Gin a' my duds were aff,
  And guid halll claes put on,
O, I could kiss a young lass
  As weel as ony man.

THE BRIDE CAM' OUT O' THE BYRE.

Herd's Collection—although of much older date, being current in the border long before the time of Ramsay. (See Stenhouse's Illustrations.) The air has always been popular, and numerous versions of the song have been written.

The bride cam' out o' the byre,
  And, O, as she dighted her cheeks!
Sirs, I'm to be married the night,
  And have neither blankets nor sheets;
Have neither blankets nor sheets,
  Nor scarce a coverlet too;
The bride that has a' to borrow,
  Has e'en right muckle ado.
    Woo'd, and married, and a',
    Married, and woo'd, and a'!
    And was she nae very weel off,
    That was woo'd, and married, and a'?

Out spake the bride's father,
  As he cam' in frae the pleugh,
O, haud your tongue, my dochter,
  And ye'se get gear eneugh;
The stirk stands i' th' tether,
  And our bra' bawsint yade,
Will carry ye hame your corn—
  What wad ye be at, ye jade?

Out spake the bride's mither,
  What deil needs a' this pride?
I had nae a plack in my pouch
  That night I was a bride;
My gown was linsy-woolsy,
  And ne'er a sark ava;
And ye ha'e ribbons and buskins,
  Mae than ane or twa.

What's the matter, quo' Willie;
  Though we be scant o' claes,
We'll creep the closer thegither,
  And we'll smoor a' the fleas;
Simmer is coming on,
  And we'll get taits o' woo;
And we'll get a lass o' our ain,
  And she'll spin claiths anew.

Out spake the bride's brither,
  As he came in wi' the kie;
Poor Willie had ne'er a' ta'en ye,
  Had he kent ye as weel as I;

For you're baith proud and saucy,
    And no for a poor man's wife;
Gin I canna get a better,
    Ise never tak ane i' my life.
Out spake the bride's sister,
    As she came in frae the byre;
O gin I were but married,
    It's a' that I desire:
But we poor fo'k maun live single,
    And do the best we can;
I dinna care what I shou'd want,
    If I could but get a man.

ANNIE LAURIE.
DOUGLASS OF FINGLAND,

COMPOSED, it is said, upon one of the daughters of Sir Robert Laurie, of Maxwelton (1685), who, however, was not sufficiently charmed by the song to become his wife. First printed by Mr. C. K. Sharpe in 1824.

Maxweltown banks are bonnie,
    Where early fa's the dew;
Where me and Annie Laurie
    Made up the promise true;
Made up the promise true,
    And never forget will I;
And for bonnie Annie Laurie
    I'll lay me down and die.

She's backit like the peacock,
    She's breistit like the swan,
She's jimp about the middle,
    Her waist ye weel micht span;
Her waist ye weel micht span,
    And she has a rolling eye;
And for bonnie Annie Laurie
    I'll lay me down and die.

A COUNTRY LASS.

TEA TABLE MISCELLANY, where it is marked as an old song. It first appears in Durfey's "Pills to Purge Melancholy," published at London about 1700, where it is directed to be sung to the tune of "Cold and Raw." Ramsay, however, refers it to "its ain tune."

Although I be but a country lass,
    Yet a lofty mind I bear, O;
And think mysel' as rich as those
    That rich apparel wear, O;

Although my gown be hame-spun grey,
  My skin it is as saft, O,
As theirs that satin weeds do wear,
  And carry their heads aloft, O.

What though I keep my father's sheep,
  The thing that maun be done, O;
With garlands o' the finest flowers,
  To shade me frae the sun, O?
When they are feeding pleasantly,
  Where grass and flowers do spring, O;
Then, on a flowery bank, at noon,
  I set me down and sing, O.

My Paisley piggy, corked with sage,
  Contains my drink but thin, O;
No wines did e'er my brains engage,
  To tempt my mind to sin, O.
My country curds and wooden spoon,
  I think them unco fine, O;
And on a flowery bank, at noon,
  I set me down and dine, O.

Although my parents cannot raise
  Great bags of shining gold, O,
Like them whase daughters, now a-days,
  Like swine, are bought and sold, O;
Yet my fair body it shall keep
  An honest heart within, O;
And for twice fifty thousand crowns,
  I value not a prin, O.

I use nae gums upon my hair,
  Nor chains about my neck, O,
Nor shining rings upon my hands,
  My fingers straight to deck, O.
But for that lad to me shall fa',
  And I have grace to wed, O,
I'll keep a braw that's worth them a';
  I mean my silken snood, O.

If cannie fortune give to me
  The man I dearly love, O,
Though he want gear, I dinna care,
  My hands I can improve, O;
Expecting for a blessing still
  Descending from above, O;
Then we'll embrace, and sweetly kiss,
  Repeating tales of love, O.

THE AULD GOODMAN.

THE TABLE MISCELLANY, where it is initialed as an old song. It also appears with music in Thomson's Orpheus Caledonius, 1725. The woman's comparison between her auld guidman (first husband) and her now, is very amusing, and edifying to any man about to take up the same position.

LATE in an evening forth I went,
 A little before the sun gade down,
And there I chanc'd by accident
 To light on a battle new begun.
A man and his wife was fa'in' in a strife,
 I canna well tell ye how it began;
But aye she wail'd her wretched life,
 And cry'd over, Alake my auld goodman!

HE.

Thy auld goodman that thou tells of,
 The country kens where he was born,
Was but a silly poor vagabond,
 And ilka ane lough him to scorn;
For he did spend, and make an end
 Of gear that his fore-fathers wan,
He gart the poor stand frae the door,
 Sae tell nae mair of thy auld goodman.

SHE.

My heart, alake, is liken to break,
 When I think on my winsome John:
His blinkan eye, and gate sae free,
 Was naething like thee, thou dosend drone;
His rosie face, and flaxen hair,
 And a skin as white as ony swan,
Was large and tall, and comely withall,
 And thou'lt never be like my auld goodman.

HE.

Why dost thou pleen? I thee maintain,
 For meal and mawt thou disna want;
But thy wild boes I canna please,
 Now when our gear 'gins to grow scant.
Of household stuff thou hast enough,
 Thou wants for neither pot nor pan;
Of siclike ware he left thee bare,
 Sae tell nae mair of thy auld goodman.

SHE.

Yes, I may tell, and fret mysell,
 To think on these blyth days I had,
When he and I together lay
 In arms into a well-made bed.

But now I sigh, and may be sad,
  Thy courage is cauld, thy colour wan,
Thou falds thy feet, and fa's asleep,
  And thou'lt ne'er be like my auld goodman.
Then coming was the night sae dark,
  And gane was a' the light of day;
The carle was fear'd to miss his mark,
  And therefore wad nae langer stay:
Then up he gat, and he ran his way,
  I trowe the wife the day she wan,
And ay the o'erword of the fray
  Was ever, Alake my auld goodman!

AULD ROB MORRIS.

Tea Table Miscellany, 1724, where it is marked as an old song, with additions. The air has been found in an old MS. collection, dated 1692.

MOTHER.
Auld Rob Morris that wons in yon glen,
He's the king o' guid fallows, and wale o' auld men;
He has fourscore o' black sheep, and fourscore too;
Auld Rob Morris is the man ye maun lo'e.

DAUGHTER.
Haud your tongue, mother, and let that abee;
For his eild and my eild can never agree:
They'll never agree, and that will be seen;
For he is fourscore, and I'm but fifteen.

MOTHER.
Haud your tongue, dochter, and lay by your pride,
For he is the bridegroom, and ye'se be the bride;
He shall lie by your side, and kiss you too;
Auld Rob Morris is the man ye maun lo'e.

DAUGHTER.
Auld Rob Morris, I ken him fu' weel,
His back sticks out like ony peat-creel;
He's out-shinn'd, in-kneed, and ringle-eyed too;
Auld Rob Morris is the man I'll ne'er lo'e.

MOTHER.
Though auld Rob Morris be an elderly man,
Yet his auld brass will buy you a new pan;
Then, dochter, ye should na be sae ill to shoo,
For auld Rob Morris is the man ye maun lo'e.

DAUGHTER.
But auld Rob Morris I never will ha'e,
His back is so stiff, and his beard is grown gray;
I had rather die than live wi' him a year;
Sae mair o' Rob Morris I never will hear.

JOCKY SAID TO JENNY.

TEA TABLE MISCELLANY, where it is marked as an old song.

Jocky said to Jenny, Jenny wilt thou do't?
Ne'er a fit, quo' Jenny, for my tocher-gude;
For my tocher-gude, I winna marry thee.
E'en 's ye like, quo' Johnnie; ye may let it be!
I ha'e gowd and gear; I ha'e land eneuch;
I ha'e seven good owsen gangin' in a pleuch;
Gangin' in a pleuch, and linkin' ower the lea:
And gin ye winna tak' me, I can let ye be.

I ha'e a gude ha' house, a barn, and a byre,
A stack afore the door; I'll mak' a rantin fire:
I'll mak' a rantin fire, and merry shall we be:
And, gin ye winna tak' me, I can let ye be.

Jenny said to Jocky, Gin ye winna tell,
Ye shall be the lad; I'll be the lass mysell:
Ye're a bonnie lad, and I'm a lassie free;
Ye're welcomer to tak' me than to let me be.

TODLIN' HAME.

TEA TABLE MISCELLANY.

When I ha'e a saxpence under my thoom,
Then I get credit in ilka toun;
But aye when I'm puir they bid me gang by:
Oh, poverty parts gude company!
   Todlin' hame, todlin' hame,
   Couldna my loove come todlin' hame.

Fair fa' the gudewife, and send her gude sale!
She gi'es us white bannocks to rolish her alo;
Syne, if that her tippeny chance to be sma',
We tak' a gude scour o't, and ca't awa'.
   Todlin' hame, todlin' hame,
   As round as a neep come todlin' hame.

My kimmer and I lay down to sleep,
Wi' twa pint stoups at our bed's feet;
And aye when we waken'd we drank them dry:—
What think ye o' my wee kimmer and I?
   Todlin' butt, and todlin ben,
   Sae round as my loove comes todlin' hame.

Leeze me on liquor, my todlin' dow,
Ye're aye sae gude-humour'd when weetin' your mou'!
When sober sae sour, ye'll fecht wi' a flea,
That 'tis a blythe nicht to the bairns and me,
   When todlin' hame, todlin' hame,
   When, round as a neep, ye come todlin' hame.

JENNY'S BAWBEE.

HERD'S COLLECTION.

And a' that e'er my Jenny had,
My Jenny had, my Jenny had;
And a' that e'er my Jenny had,
Was ae bawbee.

There's your plack, and my plack
And your plack, and my plack,
And my plack, and your plack,
And Jenny's bawbee.

We'll put it in the pint-stoup,
The pint-stoup, the pint-stoup,
We'll put it in the pint-stoup,
And birle 't a' three.

MAGGIE'S TOCHER.

TEA TABLE MISCELLANY, where it is marked as of unknown antiquity.

The meal was dear short syne,
  We buckled us a' thegither;
And Maggie was in her prime,
  When Willie made courtship till her.
Twa pistols charg'd by guess,
  To gi'e the courting shot;
And syne came ben the lass,
  Wi' swats drawn frae the butt.
He first speir'd at the gudeman,
  And syne at Giles the mither,
An' ye wad gie's a bit land,
  We'd buckle us e'en thegither.
My dochter ye shall ha'e,
  I'll gi'e you her by the hand;
But I'll part wi' my wife, by my fac,
  Or I part wi' my land.
Your tocher it s'all be good,
  There's nane s'all ha'e its maik,
The lass bound in her snood,
  And Crummie wha kens her stake:
Wi' an auld bedding o' claes,
  Was left me by my mither,
They're jet black o'er wi' flaes,
  Ye may cuddle in them thegither.
Ye speak right weel, gudeman,
  But ye maun mend your hand,
And think o' modesty,
  Gin ye'll no quit your land.

We are but young, ye ken,
  And now we're gaun thegither,
A house is but and ben,
  And Crummie will want her fother.
The bairns are coming on,
  And they'll cry, O their mither!
We've neither pat nor pan,
  But four bare logs thegither.

Your tocher's be good enough,
  For that ye needna fear,
Twa good stilts to the pleugh,
  And ye yoursel' maun steer:
Ye s'all ha'e twa guid pocks
  That anes were o' the tweel,
The tane to haud the groats,
  The tither to haud the meal:
Wi' an auld kist made o' wands,
  And that sall be your coffer,
Wi' aiken woody bands,
  And that may haud your tocher.

Consider weel, gudeman,
  We ha'e but barrow'd gear,
The horse that I ride on
  Is Sandy Wilson's mare;
The saddle's nane o' my ain,
  And thae's but borrow'd boots,
And when that I gae hame,
  I maun tak' to my coots;
The cloak is Geordy Watt's,
  That gars me look sae crouse;
Come, fill us a cogue o' awats,
  We'll mak' nae mair toom roose.

I like you weel, young lad,
  For telling me sae plain,
I married whan little I had
  O' gear that was my ain.
But sin' that things are sae,
  The bride she maun come forth,
Tho' a' the gear she'll ha'e
  'Twill be but little worth.
A bargain it maun be,
  Fye cry on Giles the mither;
Content am I, quo' she,
  E'en gar the hizzie come hither.

The bride she gaed to her bed,
   The bridegroom he came till her,
The fiddler crap in at the fit,
   And they cuddl'd it a' thegither.

THE PLOUGHMAN.

Herd's Collection. It appears also in Johnson's Museum, re-touched by Burns.

The ploughman he's a bonnie lad,
   And a' his wark's at leisure,
And when that he comes hame at e'en,
   He kisses me wi' pleasure.
     Then up wi't now, my ploughman lad,
       And hey, my merry ploughman;
     Of a' the lads that I do fee,
       Commend me to the ploughman.

Now the blooming Spring comes on,
   He takes his yoking early,
And whistling o'er the furrowed land,
   He goes to fallow clearly.
     Then up wi't now, &c.

When my ploughman comes hame at e'en,
   He's aften wat and weary;
Cast aff the wat, put on the dry,
   And gae to bed, my dearie.
     Then up wi't now, &c.

I will wash my ploughman's hose,
   And I will wash his o'erlay:
I will mak' my ploughman's bed,
   And cheer him late and early.
     Merry butt, and merry ben,
       Merry is my ploughman,
     Of a' the trades that I do ken,
       Commend me to the ploughman.

Plough yon hill, and plough yon dale,
   Plough your faugh and fallow,
Wha winna drink the ploughman's health,
   Is but a dirty fellow.
     Merry butt, and &c.

O GIN MY LOVE WERE YON RED ROSE.

FROM HERD'S MS.

O gin my love were yon red rose,
  That grows upon the castle wa',
And I mysel' a drap of dew,
  Down on that red rose I would fa'.
O my love's bonnie, bonnie, bonnie;
  My love's bonnie and fair to see:
Whene'er I look on her weel-far'd face,
  She looks and smiles again to me.

O gin my love were a pickle of wheat,
  And growing upon yon lily lea,
And I mysel' a bonnie wee bird,
  Awa' wi' that pickle o' wheat I wad flee.
    O my love's bonnie, &c.

O gin my love were a coffer o' gowd,
  And I the keeper of the key,
I wad open the kist whene'er I list,
  And in that coffer I wad be.
    O my love's bonnie, &c.

THE EWE-BUCHTS, MARION.

TEA TABLE MISCELLANY. Dr. Percy inserted it in his Reliques.

WILL ye gae to the ewe-buchts, Marion,
  And wear in the sheep wi' me?
The sun shines sweet, my Marion,
  But nae half so sweet as thee.

O, Marion's a bonnie lass,
  And the blythe blink 's in her e'e;
And fain wad I marry Marion,
  Gin Marion wad marry me.

There's gowd in your garters, Marion,
  And silk on your white hause-bane;
Fu' fain wad I kiss my Marion,
  At e'en, when I come hame.

There's braw lads in Earnslaw, Marion,
  Wha gape, and glower wi' their e'e,
At kirk when they see my Marion,
  But nane o' them lo'es like me.

I've nine milk-ewes, my Marion,
  A cow and a brawny quey;
I'll gi'e them a' to my Marion,
  Just on her bridal-day.

And ye'se get a green sey apron,
And waistcoat o' London broun;
And wow but ye'se be vap'rin'
Whene'er ye gang to the toun.

I'm young and stout, my Marion;
Nane dances like me on the green:
And, gin ye forsake me, Marion,
I'll e'en gae draw up wi' Jean.

Sae put on your pearlins, Marion,
And kirtle o' cramasie;
And, as sune as my chin has nae hair on,
I will come west, and see ye.

I'LL GAR OUR GUDEMAN TROW.

An early song, given by Mr. Charles Kirkpatrick Sharpe, in his Ballad Book, 1824.

I'LL gar our gudeman trow
 I'll sell the ladle,
If he winna buy to me
 A bonnie side-saddle,
To ride to kirk and bridal,
 And round about the town;
Stand about, ye fisher jauds,
 And gi'e my gown room!

I'll gar our gudeman trow
 I'll tak' the fling-strings,
If he winna buy to me
 Twal bonnie gowd rings;
Ane for ilka finger,
 And twa for ilka thoom;
Stand about, ye fisher jauds,
 And gi'e my gown room!

I'll gar our gudeman trow
 That I'm gaun to die,
If he winna fee to me
 Valets twa or three,
To bear my train up frae the dirt,
 And ush me through the town;
Stand about ye fisher jauds,
 And gi'e my gown room!

DUMBARTON'S DRUMS.

TEA TABLE MISCELLANY. "Dumbarton's Drums" were the drums belonging to a British regiment, which took its name from the officer who first commanded it, to wit, the Earl of Dumbarton. This nobleman was a cadet of the family of Douglas, and being commander of the Royal Forces in Scotland, during the reigns of Charles II. and James II., he bears a distinguished figure in the dark and blood-stained history of Scotland during that period.—*Chambers.*

DUMBARTON'S drums beat bonnie, O,
When they mind me of my dear Johnnie, O;
   How happie am I
   When my soldier is by,
While he kisses and blesses his Annie, O!
'Tis a soldier alone can delight me, O,
For his graceful looks do invite me, O;
   While guarded in his arms,
   I'll fear no war's alarms,
Neither danger nor death shall e'er fright me, O.

My love is a handsome laddie, O,
Genteel, but ne'er foppish nor gaudy, O.
   Though commissions are dear,
   Yet I'll buy him one this year;
For he'll serve no longer a cadie, O.
A soldier has honour and bravery, O;
Unacquainted with rogues and their knavery, O,
   He minds no other thing
   But the ladies or the king;
For every other care is but slavery, O.

Then I'll be the captain's lady, O,
Farewell all my friends and my daddy, O;
   I'll wait no more at home,
   But I'll follow with the drum,
And whene'er that beats I'll be ready, O.
Dumbarton's drums sound bonnie, O,
They are sprightly like my dear Johnnie, O;
   How happy shall I be
   When on my soldier's knee,
And he kisses and blesses his Annie, O.

BRING A' YOUR MAUT.

CHAMBERS' SCOTTISH SONGS, 1829. Sung to Mr. Robert Chambers by a friend. The chorus is as old as the seventeenth century, as it appears in a manuscript of that period, formerly in the possession of Mr. Constable, publisher. A song, entitled *The Mautman*, similar to this, is given by Ramsay in his Tea Table Miscellany.

SOME say that kissing 's a sin,
   But I think it's nane ava,
For kissing has wonn'd in this warld,
   Since ever that there was twa.
O, if it waana lawfu',
   Lawyers wadna allow it;
If it waana holy,
   Ministers wadna do it.
If it waana modest,
   Maidens wadna tak' it;
If it waana plenty,
   Puir folk wadna get it!
Bring a' your maut to me,
   Bring a' your maut to me;
My draff ye'se get for ae pund ane,
   Though a' my deukies should dee.

TWEEDSIDE.
LORD YESTER,

BORN 1645, a distinguished Statesman of his time, being one of the most active promoters of the Union in 1702. He became Marquis of Tweeddale in 1697, and died in 1713. The song first appears in Herd's Collection, 1776. The air is very beautiful, and is traditionally ascribed to the unfortunate David Rizzio.

WHEN Maggy and me were acquaint,
   I carried my noddle fu' hie,
Nae lintwhite in a' the gay plain,
   Nae gowdspink sae bonnie as she!
I whistled, I piped, and I sang;
   I woo'd, but I cam' nae great speed;
Therefore I maun wander abroad,
   And lay my banes far frae the Tweed.

To Maggy my love I did tell;
   My tears did my passion express:
Alas! for I lo'ed her ower weel,
   And the women lo'e sic a man less.
Her heart it was frozen and cauld;
   Her pride had my ruin decreed;
Therefore I maun wander abroad,
   And lay my banes far frae the Tweed.

WERE NA MY HEART LICHT.
LADY GRIZZEL BAILLIE.

BORN 1665, daughter of Sir Patrick Home, Earl of Marchmont, and married in 1692, to George Baillie of Jerviswood. Her devotion to her father and her husband when both were outlawed and hunted down by King James II., gives us a picture which has not been surpassed even in romance. She died in London in 1746, at the ripe age of eighty-one. The song here given (from the Tea Table Miscellany), and the following are the only songs of this lady which have been published—though several others are said to be extant in a manuscript volume.

There was anes a maid, and she loo'd na men;
She biggit her bonnie bower down i' yon glen,
But now she cries dool, and well-a-day:
Come down the green gate, and come here away.
    But now she, &c.

When bonnie young Johnnie cam' ower the sea,
He said he saw naething sae lovely as me;
He hecht me baith rings an monie braw things;
And were na my heart licht I wad dee.
    He hecht me, &c.

He had a wee titty that loo'd na me,
Because I was twice as bonnie as she;
She rais'd such a pother 'twixt him and his mother,
That were na my heart licht I wad dee.
    She rais'd, &c.

The day it was set, and the bridal to be:
The wife took a dwam, and lay down to dee.
She main'd and she graned, out o' dolour and pain,
Till he vow'd he never wad see me again.
    She main'd, &c.

His kin was for ane of a higher degree,
Said, What had he to do wi' the like of me?
Albeit I was bonnie, I was na for Johnnie:
And were na my heart licht I wad dee.
    Albeit I was bonnie, &c.

They said I had neither cow nor calf,
Nor dribbles o' drink rins through the draff,
Nor pickles o' meal rins through the mill-e'e;
And were na my heart licht I wad dee.
    Nor pickles, &c.

His titty she was baith wylie and slee,
She spied me as I cam' ower the lea;
And then she ran in, and made a loud din;
Believe your ain een an ye trow na me.
    And then she ran in, &c.

His bonnet stood aye fu' round on his brow;
His auld ane look'd aye as weel as some's new;
But now he lets 't wear ony gait it will hing,
And casts himself dowie upon the corn-bing.
    But now he, &c.

And now he gaes daundrin' about the dykes,
And a' he dow do is to hund the tykes;
The live-lang nicht he ne'er steeks his e'e;
And were na my heart licht I wad dee.
    The live-lang nicht, &c.

Were I young for thee as I ha'e been,
We should ha'e been gallopin' down on yon green,
And linkin' it on yon lilie-white lea;
And wow! gin I were but young for thee!
    And linkin' it, &c.

O, THE EWE-BUCHTIN'S BONNIE.
LADY GRIZZEL BAILLIE.

AN air for this song was composed by Mr. Sharpe of Hoddam (father of the celebrated Antiquary), at the very early age of seven years.

O, the ewe-buchtin's bonnie, baith e'ening and morn,
When our blithe shepherds play on the bog-reed and horn;
While we're milking, they're lilting, baith pleasant and clear—
But my heart's like to break when I think on my dear.

O the shepherds take pleasure to blow on the horn,
To raise up their flocks o' sheep soon i' the morn;
On the bonnie green banks they feed pleasant and free,
But, alas, my dear heart, all my sighing's for thee!

HERE AWA', THERE AWA'.
HERD'S COLLECTION.

HERE awa', there awa', here awa', Willie!
  Here awa', there awa', haud awa' hame!
Lang have I sought thee, dear have I bought thee;
  Now I have gotten my Willie again.

Through the lang muir I have followed my Willie;
  Through the lang muir I have followed him hame
Whatever betide us, nought shall divide us;
  Love now rewards all my sorrow and pain.

Here awa', there awa', here awa', Willie!
  Here awa', there awa', haud awa' hame!
Come, love, believe me, nothing can grieve me,
  Ilka thing pleases, when Willie's at hame.

YELLOW-HAIR'D LADDIE.

TEA TABLE MISCELLANY—the air was published in 1709. Ramsay, who seems to have been fond of the air, composed two songs to it.

The yellow-hair'd laddie sat doun on yon brae,
Cried, Milk the yowes, lassie, let nane o' them gae;
And aye as she milkit, she merrily sang,
The yellow-hair'd laddie shall be my gudeman.
And aye as she milkit, she merrily sang,
The yellow-hair'd laddie shall be my gudeman.

The weather is cauld, and my claithing is thin,
The yowes are new clipt, and they winna bucht in;
They winna bucht in, although I should dee:
Oh, yellow-hair'd laddie, be kind unto me.

The gudewife cries butt the house, Jennie, come ben;
The cheese is to mak', and the butter's to kirn.
Though butter, and cheese, and a' should gang sour,
I'll crack and I'll kiss wi' my love ae half hour.
It's ae lang half hour, and we'll e'en mak' it three,
For the yellow-hair'd laddie my husbman shall be.

A COCK-LAIRD.

APPEARED in a more licentious form in Thomson's ORPHEUS CALEDONIUS. The version here given has been altered a little, and we must say for the better. Its authorship has often been given to Ramsay, but seemingly without foundation.

A COCK-LAIRD, fu' cadgie,
 Wi' Jennie did meet;
He hawsed, he kiss'd her,
 And ca'd her his sweet.
Wilt thou gae alang wi' me,
 Jennie, Jennie?
Thou'se be my ain lemmane,
 Jo Jennie, quo' he.

If I gae alang wi' thee,
 Ye maunna fail
To feast me wi' caddels
 And guid hackit kail.
What needs a' this vanity,
 Jennie? quo' he;
Is na bannocks and dribly-beards
 Guid meat for thee?

Gin I gang alang wi' you,
  I maun ha'e a silk hood,
A kirtle-sark, wyliecoat,
  And a silk snood,
To tie up my hair in
  A cockernonie.
Hout awa', thou's gane wud, I trow,
  Jennie! quo' he.

Gin ye'd ha'e me look bonnie,
  And shine like the moon,
I maun ha'e katlets and patlets,
  And cam'rel-heel'd shoon;
Wi' craig-claiths and lug-babs,
  And rings twa or three.
Hout the deil's in your vanity,
  Jennie! quo' he.

And I maun ha'e pinners,
  With pearlins set roun',
A skirt o' the paudy,
  And a waistcoat o' brown.
Awa' wi' sic vanities,
  Jennie, quo' he,
For curches and kirtles
  Are fitter for thee.

My lairdship can yield me
  As muckle a-year,
As haud us in pottage
  And guid knockit bear;
But, havin' nae tenants,
  Oh, Jennie, Jennie,
To buy ought I ne'er have
  A penny, quo' he.

The Borrowstown merchants
  Will sell ye on tick;
For we maun ha'e braw things,
  Although they should break:
When broken, frae care
  The fools are set free,
When we mak' them lairds
  In the Abbey, quo' she.

THE GEAR AND THE BLATHRIE O'T.

A PROVERB—" Shame fall the gear and the blathrie o't" is given in Kelly's PROVERBS, 1721 as the burden of an old Scottish song. We have one or two other versions of this song, but the one here given appears to be accepted as the oldest.

When I think on this warld's pelf,
And the little wee share I ha'e o't to mysclf,
And how the lass that wants it is by the lads forgot,
May the shame fa' the gear and the blathrie o't!
Jockie was the laddie that held the pleugh,
But now he's got gowd and gear enough;
He thinks nae mair o' me that wears the plaiden coat :—
May the shame fa' the gear and the blathrie o't!
Jenny was the lassie that mucked the byre,
But now she is clad in her silken attire;
And Jockie says he lo'es her, and swears he's me forgot :—
May the shame fa' the gear and the blathrie o't!
But all this shall never daunton me,
Sae lang as I keep my fancy free;
For the lad that's sae inconstant he is not worth a groat :—
May the shame fa' the gear and the blathrie o't!

SAW YE NAE MY PEGGY.

HERD'S COLLECTION. The air is given in Thomson's ORPHEUS CALEDONIUS, 1725.

  Saw ye nae my Peggy,
  Saw ye nae my Peggy,
  Saw ye nae my Peggy,
   Coming ower the lea?
  Sure a finer creature
  Ne'er was formed by Nature,
  So complete each feature,
   So divine is she!

  O! how Peggy charms me;
  Every look still warms me;
  Every thought alarms me;
   Lest she lo'e nae mo.
  Peggy doth discover
  Nought but charms all over:
  Nature bids me love her;
   That's a law to me.

  Who would leave a lover,
  To become a rover?
  No, I'll ne'er give over,
   Till I happy be.

For since love inspires me,
As her beauty fires me,
And her absence tires me,
  Nought can please but she.

When I hope to gain her,
Fate seems to detain her;
Could I but obtain her,
  Happy would I be!
I'll lie down before her,
Bless, sigh, and adore her,
With faint looks implore her,
  Till she pity me.

SAW YE JOHNNY COMIN'?

SUPPOSED to be prior to the days of Ramsay, although we can find no trace of its author or precise age. The air was much admired by Burns, who heard it played in Dumfries by Mr. Thomas Fraser, oboist in the theatre there, and composed a song for it.

Saw ye Johnny comin', quo' she,
  Saw ye Johnny comin';
Saw ye Johnny comin', quo' she,
  Saw ye Johnny comin';
Saw ye Johnny comin', quo' she,
  Saw ye Johnny comin';
Wi' his blue bonnet on his head,
  And his doggie rinnin', quo' she,
  And his doggie rinnin'?

Fee him, father, fee him, quo' she,
  Fee him, father, fee him;
Fee him, father, fee him, quo' she,
  Fee him, father, fee him;
For he is a gallant lad,
  And a weel-doin';
And a' the wark about the house,
  Gaes wi' me when I see him, quo' she,
  Wi' me when I see him.

What will I do wi' him, quo' he,
  What will I do wi' him?
He's ne'er a sark upon his back,
  And I hae nane to gi'e him.
I hae twa sarks into my kist,
  And ane o' them I'll gi'e him;
And for a merk o' mair fee,
  Dinna stand wi' him, quo' she,
  Dinna stand wi' him.

For weel do I lo'e him, quo' she,
  Weel do I lo'e him;
For weel do I lo'e him, quo' she,
  Weel do I lo'e him.
O, fee him, father, fee him, quo' she,
  Fee him, father, fee him;
He'll haud the pleugh, thrash in the barn,
  And crack wi' me at e'on, quo' she,
  And crack wi' me at e'en.

ETTRICK BANKS.

THOMSON'S ORPHEUS CALEDONIUS, 1725.

On Ettrick banks, ae simmer's night,
  At gloamin', when the sheep drave hame,
I met my lassie, braw and tight,
  Come wading barefoot a' her lane.
My heart grew light;—I ran, I flang
  My arms about her lily neck,
And kiss'd and clapp'd her there fu' lang,
  My words they were na monie feck.

I said, My lassie, will ye gang
  To the Highland hills, the Erse to learn?
I'll gi'e thee baith a cow and ewe,
  When ye come to the brig o' Earn:
At Leith auld meal comes in, ne'er fash,
  And herrings at the Broomielaw;
Cheer up your heart, my bonnie lass,
  There's gear to win ye never saw.

A' day when we ha'e wrought eneugh,
  When winter frosts and snaw begin,
Soon as the sun gaes west the loch,
  At night when ye sit down to spin,
I'll screw my pipes, and play a spring:
  And thus the weary night will end,
Till the tender kid and lamb-time bring
  Our pleasant simmer back again.

Syne, when the trees are in their bloom,
  And gowans glent o'er ilka fiel',
I'll meet my lass amang the broom,
  And lead you to my simmer shiel.
Then, far frae a' their scornfu' din,
  That mak' the kindly heart their sport,
We'll laugh, and kiss, and dance, and sing,
  And gar the langest day seem short.

PART II.

From the UNION *to* 1776.

THE AULD WIFE AYONT THE FIRE.

TEA TABLE MISCELLANY. Marked as an old song with additions. Worthy of preservation for the moral contained in the last stanza.

There was a wife wonn'd in a glen,
And she had dochters nine or ten,
That sought the house baith butt and ben
  To find their mam a snishing.
    The auld wife ayont the fire,
    The auld wife aniest the fire,
    The auld wife aboon the fire,
      She died for lack of snishing.

Her mill into some hole had fawn,
What recks, quoth she, let it be gawn,
For I maun ha'e a young gudeman,
  Shall furnish me wi' snishing.
    The auld wife, &c.

Her eldest dochter said right bauld,
Fy, mother, mind that now ye're auld,
And if you wi' a younker wald,
  He'll waste away your snishing.
    The auld wife, &c.

The youngest dochter ga'e a shout,
O mother dear! your teeth's a' out,
Besides half blind, ye ha'e the gout,
  Your mill can haud nae snishing.
    The auld wife, &c.

Ye lie, ye limmers, cries auld mump,
For I hae baith a tooth and stump,
And will nae langer live in dump,
  By wanting of my snishing.
    The auld wife, &c.

Thole ye, says Peg, that pauky slut,
Mother, if ye can crack a nut,
Then we will a' consent to it,
  That ye shall have a snishing.
    The auld wife, &c.

The auld ane did agree to that,
And they a pistol-bullet gat:
She powerfully began to crack,
  To win hersel' a snishing.
    The auld wife, &c.

Braw sport it was to see her chow 't,
And 'tween her gums sae squeeze and row 't,
While frae her jaws the slaver flow'd,
  And aye she curst poor stumpy.
    The auld wife, &c.

At last she ga'e a desperate squeeze,
Which brak the lang tooth by the nooze,
And syne poor stumpy was at ease,
  But she tint hopes of snishing.
    The auld wife, &c.

She of the task began to tire,
And frae her dochters did retire,
Syne loan'd her down ayont the fire,
  And died for lack o' snishing.
    The auld wife, &c.

Ye auld wives, notice weel this truth,
As soon as ye're past mark o' mouth,
Ne'er do what's only fit for youth,
  And leave aff thoughts o' snishing.
    Else, like this wife ayont the fire,
    Your bairns against you will conspire;
    Nor will you get, unless you hire,
      A young man with your snishing.

JOCKEY FOU, JENNY FAIN.

TEA TABLE MISCELLANY—where it is marked as an old song, with additions.

Jockey fou, Jenny fain;
Jenny was na ill to gain;
She was couthie, he was kind;
And thus the wooer tell'd his mind:

Jenny, I'll nae mair be nice;
Gi'e me love at ony price:
I winna prig for red or white,
Love alane can gi'e delyte.

Others seek they kenna what,
In looks, in carriage, and a' that;
Gi'e me love for her I court:
Love in love makes a' the sport.

Colours mingled unco fine,
Common notions lang sinsyne,
Never can engage my love,
Until my fancy first approve.
It is nae meat, but appetite,
That makes our eating a delyte;
Beauty is at best deceit;
Fancy only kens nae cheat.

HAUD AWA'.

TEA TABLE MISCELLANY—where it is marked as an old song, with additions; probably by Ramsay himself. The air is very old (being found in Playford's "DANCING MASTER," 1657), and has always been very popular, numerous songs to it being extant.

DONALD.

O, come awa', come awa',
    Come awa' wi' me, Jenny!
Sic frowns I canna bear frae ane,
    Whase smiles ance ravish'd me, Jenny.
If you'll be kind, you'll never find
    That ought shall alter me, Jenny;
For ye're the mistress of my mind,
    Whate'er ye think of me, Jenny!

First when your sweets enslaved my heart,
    Ye seem'd to favour me, Jenny;
But now, alas! you act a part
    That speaks inconstancie, Jenny.
Inconstancie is sic a vice,
    It's not befitting thee, Jenny;
It suits not with your virtue nice,
    To carry ane to me, Jenny.

JENNY.

O, haud awa', bide awa',
    Haud awa' frae me, Donald!
Your heart is made ower large for ane—
    It is not meet for me, Donald.
Some fickle mistress you may find
    Will jilt as fast as thee, Donald;
To ilka swain she will prove kind,
    And nae less kind to thee, Donald:

But I've a heart that's naething such;
    'Tis filled wi' honestie, Donald.
I'll ne'er love mony; I'll love much;
    I hate all levitie, Donald.

Therefore nae mair, wi' art, pretend
  Your heart is chain'd to mine, Donald;
For words of falsehood ill defend
  A roving love like thine, Donald.

First when ye courted, I must own,
  I frankly favour'd you, Donald;
Apparent worth, and fair renown,
  Made me believe you true, Donald:
Ilk virtue then seem'd to adorn
  The man esteem'd by me, Donald;
But now the mask's faun aff, I scorn
  To ware a thocht on thee, Donald.

And now for ever haud awa',
  Haud awa' frae me, Donald!
Sae, seek a heart that's like your ain,
  And come nae mair to me, Donald:
For I'll reserve mysel' for ane,
  For ane that's liker me, Donald.
If sic a ane I canna find,
  I'll ne'er lo'e man, nor thee, Donald.

DONALD.

Then I'm the man, and fause report
  Has only tauld a lie, Jenny;
To try thy truth, and make us sport,
  The tale was raised by me, Jenny.

JENNY.

When this ye prove, and still can love,
  Then come awa' to me, Donald!
I'm weel content ne'er to repent
  That I ha'e smiled on thee, Donald!

MERRY MAY THE MAID BE.
SIR JOHN CLERK, BART.,

Born about 1680. He was appointed in 1708 one of the Barons of Exchequer in Scotland, which post he held till his death in 1755. Sir John was a profound antiquarian, and he carried on a long and learned correspondence with Roger Gale, the celebrated English antiquary. The song here given appeared first in THE CHARMER, 1751, minus the last stanza, which was afterwards added by the author. The first stanza belongs to an old song.

MERRY may the maid be
  That marries the miller,
For foul day or fair day
  He's aye bringing till her;

Has aye a penny in his purse
  For dinner and for supper;
And gin she please, a good fat cheese,
  And lumps o' yellow butter.

When Jamie first did woo me,
  I spier'd what was his calling:
Fair maid, says he, O come and see,
  Ye're welcome to my dwelling.
Though I was shy, yet I cou'd spy
  The truth of what he told me,
And that his house was warm and couth,
  And room in it to hold me.

Behind the door a bag o' meal,
  And in the kist was plenty
O' good hard cakes his mither bakes,
  And bannocks were na scanty;
A good fat sow, a sleeky cow
  Was standin' in the byre;
Whilst lazy puss with mealy mou's
  Was playing at the fire.

Good signs are these, my mither says,
  And bids me tak the miller;
For foul day and fair day
  He's aye bringing till her;
For meal and maut he does na want,
  Nor ony thing that's dainty;
And now then a keckling hen
  To lay her eggs in plenty.

In winter when the wind and rain
  Blaws o'er the house and byre,
He sits beside a clean hearth stane
  Before a rousing fire;
With nut-brown ale he tells his tale,
  Which rows him o'er fu' nappy:
Who'd be a king—a petty thing,
  When a miller lives so happy?

THE AULD MAN'S MEAR'S DEAD.

PATRICK BIRNIE,

A well-known piper of his day. He flourished about the beginning of the eighteenth century. Allan Ramsay, in 1721, published an "Elegie on Patie Birnie," one of the stanzas of which is as follows:—

"This sang he made frae his ain head,
And eke 'The auld man's mare's dead—
The peats and turfs and a's to lead;'
O fy upon her!
A bonny auld thing this indeed,
An't like your honour."

THE auld man's mear's dead;
The puir body's mear's dead;
The auld man's mear's dead,
A mile aboon Dundee.

There was hay to ca', and lint to lead,
A hunder hotts o' muck to spread,
And peats and truffs and a' to lead—
And yet the jaud to dee!

She had the fiercie and the fleuk,
The wheezloch and the wanton yeuk;
On ilka knee she had a breuk—
What ail'd the beast to dee?

She was lang-tooth'd and blench-lippit,
Heam-hough'd and haggis-fittit,
Lang-neckit, chandler-chaftit,
And yet the jaud to dee!

EDINBURGH KATIE.

ALLAN RAMSAY,

Often styled "The restorer of Scottish Poetry," was born at Leadhills, in Lanarkshire, 15th October, 1686. His father, who was manager of Lord Hopetonn's mines, at Leadhills, died shortly after his birth, and his mother then became the wife of a petty landholder in the same district. In his fifteenth year he was sent to Edinburgh, and apprenticed by his stepfather to a wigmaker. He pursued this calling till 1716, when, encouraged by the success of a few fugitive pieces of poetry, he began business as a bookseller, in the High Street of Edinburgh. In 1721, he published a volume of his poems, and realised a very handsome profit on its sale. In 1724, the first volume of the TEA TABLE MISCELLANY (so often referred to in the course of this work) was published, and its success warranted its being succeeded by the remaining three volumes. In this publication he was assisted by Hamilton of Bangour, Mallet, Crawford, and many others. In 1724, also, he published "THE EVERGREEN," our second collection of early Scots poetry. His masterpiece, "The Gentle Shepherd," appeared in 1725, and established his fame as a writer, not only in Scotland but in England, where Pope, Gay, and other critics, applauded and studied it. He carried on his business as a bookseller and publisher till about 1745, when he retired. He died in 1758, and was interred in the Greyfriars Churchyard, Edinburgh.

He married Christian Ross, and had a large family. His son, Allan, rose to great eminence as a painter, holding the post of "Portrait Painter to His Majesty" from 1767. He died in 1784.

Allan Ramsay's fame as a song writer has faded since the time of Burns; but we must not forget that no small share of Burns's inspiration, and love of Scottish song, was fostered by admiration for Ramsay and his works; and that the TEA TABLE MISCELLANY, gathered by him, has been the means of preserving many an early gem, which, but for his care, might have been lost. As an editor, he has been blamed for tampering with the original versions, but this was generally done to cover some loose and immoral language; and no one who is at all acquainted with the originals of some of our most popular songs will be inclined to concur in this censure, when they recollect that the TEA TABLE MISCELLANY was dedicated to the ladies of Great Britain. Whatever loose expressions are now to be found in it were not considered as such in the times of "Honest Allan."

 Now wat ye wha I met yestreen,
  Coming down the street, my joe?
 My mistress, in her tartan screen,
  Fu' bonnie, braw, and sweet, my joe!
 My dear, quoth I, thanks to the nicht
  That never wish'd a lover ill,
 Sin' ye're out o' your mither's sicht,
  Let's tak' a walk up to the hill.

 Oh, Katie, wilt thou gang wi' me,
  And leave the dinsome toun a while?
 The blossom's sprouting frae the tree,
  And a' the simmer's gaun to smile.
 The mavis, nichtingale, and lark,
  The bleeting lambs and whistling hynd,
 In ilka dale, green, shaw and park,
  Will nourish health, and glad your mind.

 Sune as the clear gudeman o' day
  Does bend his morning draught o' dew,
 We'll gae to some burn-side and play,
  And gather flouirs to busk your brow.
 We'll pou the daisies on the green,
  The lucken-gowans frae the bog;
 Between hands, now and then, we'll lean
  And sport upon the velvet fog.

 There's, up into a pleasant glen,
  A wee piece frae my father's tower,
 A canny, saft, and flowery den,
  Which circling birks have form'd a bower.

Whene'or the sun grows high and warm,
We'll to the caller shade remove;
There will I lock thee in my arm,
And love and kiss, and kiss and love.

KATIE'S ANSWER.
ALLAN RAMSAY.

My mither's aye glowrin' ower me,
Though she did the same before me;
  I canna get leave
  To look at my love,
Or else she'd be like to devour me.

Right fain wad I tak' your offer,
Sweet sir—but I'll tyne my tocher;
  Then, Sandy, ye'll fret,
  And wyte your puir Kate,
Whene'er ye keek in your toom coffer.

For though my father has plenty
Of silver, and plenishing dainty,
  Yet he's unco sweir
  To twine wi' his gear;
And sae we had need to be tenty.

Tutor my parents wi' caution,
Be wylie in ilka motion;
  Brag weel o' your land,
  And there's my leal hand,
Win them, I'll be at your devotion.

BONNIE CHIRSTY.
ALLAN RAMSAY.

How sweetly smells the simmer green;
  Sweet taste the peach and cherry;
Painting and order please our een,
  And claret makes us merry:
But finest colours, fruits and flowers,
  And wine, though I be thirsty,
Lose a' their charms, and weaker powers,
  Compar'd wi' those of Chirsty.

When wandring o'er the flow'ry park,
  No natural beauty wanting;
How lightsome is't to hear the lark
  And birds in concert chanting!

But if my Chirsty tunes her voice,
  I'm rapt in admiration;
My thoughts wi' ecstasies rejoice,
  And drap the haill creation.

Whene'er she smiles a kindly glance,
  I take the happy omen,
And aften mint to make advance,
  Hoping she'll prove a woman:
But, dubious o' my ain desert,
  My sentiments I smother;
Wi' secret sighs I vex my heart,
  For fear she love another.

Thus sang blate Edie by a burn,
  His Chirsty did o'er-hear him;
She doughtna let her lover mourn,
  But, ere he wist, drew near him.
She spak' her favour wi' a look,
  Which left nae room to doubt her:
He wisely this white minute took,
  And flang his arms about her.

My Chirsty! witness, bonny stream,
  Sic joys frae tears arising!
I wish this may na be a dream
  O love thou maist surprising!
Time was too precious now for tauk,
  This point of a' his wishes
He wadna wi' set speeches bauk,
  But wair'd it a' on kisses.

OLD LONGSYNE.
ALLAN RAMSAY.

Should auld acquaintance be forgot,
  Though they return with scars?
These are the noble hero's lot,
  Obtain'd in glorious wars:
Welcome, my Varo, to my breast,
  Thy arms about me twine,
And make me once again as blest,
  As I was lang syne.

Methinks around us on each bough,
  A thousand Cupids play,
Whilst through the groves I walk with you,
  Each object makes me gay.

Since your return the sun and moon
  With brighter beams do shine,
Streams murmur soft notes while they run,
  As they did lang syne.

Despise the court and din of state;
  Let that to their share fall,
Who can esteem such slavery great,
  While bounded like a ball:
But sunk in love, upon my arms
  Let your brave head recline;
We'll please ourselves with mutual charms,
  As we did lang syne.

O'er moor and dale, with your gay friend,
  You may pursue the chace,
And, after a blythe bottle, end
  All cares in my embrace:
And in a vacant rainy day
  You shall be wholly mine;
We'll make the hours run smooth away,
  And laugh at lang syne.

The hero, pleased with the sweet air,
  And signs of generous love,
Which had been utter'd by the fair,
  Bow'd to the powers above.
Next day, with consent and glad haste,
  They approach'd the sacred shrine,
Where the good priest the couple blest,
  And put them out of pine.

THE COLLIER'S BONNIE LASSIE.
ALLAN RAMSAY.

The collier has a daughter,
  And, O! she's wondrous bonnie.
A laird he was that sought her,
  Rich baith in lands and money.
The tutors watched the motion
  Of this young honest lover:
But love is like the ocean;
  Wha can its depths discover!

He had the art to please ye,
  And was by a' respected;
His airs sat round him easy,
  Genteel but unaffected.

The collier's bonnie lassie,
  Fair as the new-blown lilie,
Aye sweet, and never saucy,
  Secured the heart o' Willie.
He loved, beyond expression,
  The charms that were about her,
And panted for possession;
  His life was dull without her.
After mature resolving,
  Close to his breast he held her;
In saftest flames dissolving,
  He tenderly thus telled her:

My bonnie collier's daughter,
  Let naething discompose ye;
It's no your scanty tocher,
  Shall ever gar me lose ye:
For I have gear in plenty;
  And love says, it's my duty
To ware what heaven has lent me
  Upon your wit and beauty.

GI'E ME A LASS WI' A LUMP O' LAND.
ALLAN RAMSAY.

GI'E me a lass with a lump o' land,
  And we for life shall gang thegither;
Tho' daft or wise, I'll ne'er demand,
  Or black or fair, it maksna whether.
I'm aff wi' wit, and beauty will fade,
  And blood alane 's nae worth a shilling;
But she that's rich, her market's made,
  For ilka charm about her's killing.

Gi'e me a lass with a lump o' land,
  And in my bosom I'll hug my treasure;
Gin I had ance her gear in my hand,
  Should love turn dowf, it will find pleasure.
Laugh on wha likes; but there's my hand,
  I hate with poortith, though bonnie, to meddle:
Unless they bring cash, or a lump o' land,
  They'se ne'er get me to dance to their fiddle.

There's meikle gude love in bands and bags;
  And siller and gowd's a sweet complexion;
But beauty and wit and virtue, in rags,
  Have tint the art of gaining affection.

Love tips his arrows with woods and parks,
And castles, and riggs, and muirs, and meadows;
And naething can catch our modern sparks,
But weel-tocher'd lasses, or jointur'd widows.

AN THOU WERT MY AIN THING.

TEA TABLE MISCELLANY (with the exception of the first verse), marked Q, signifying that it is a modern song by an unknown author. The air has been traced as far back as 1657. The present version of the words are doubtless of Ramsay's own time, if not by himself.

An thou were my ain thing,
 I would lo'e thee, I would lo'e thee;
An thou were my ain thing,
 How dearly would I lo'e thee!

I would clasp thee in my arms,
I'd secure thee from all harms;
For above mortal thou hast charms:
 How dearly do I lo'e thee!
  An thou were, &c.

Of race divine thou needs must be,
Since nothing earthly equals thee,
So I must still presumptuous be,
 To show how much I lo'e thee.
  An thou were, &c.

The gods one thing peculiar have,
To ruin none whom they can save;
O, for their sake, support a slave,
 Who only lives to lo'e thee.
  An thou were, &c.

To merit I no claim can make,
But that I lo'e, and, for your sake,
What man can more, I'll undertake,
 So dearly do I lo'e thee.
  An thou were, &c.

My passion, constant as the sun,
Flames stronger still, will ne'er have done,
Till fates my thread of life have spun,
 Which breathing out, I'll lo'e thee.
  An thou were, &c.

AN THOU WERE MY AIN THING.
ALLAN RAMSAY.
Written as a continuation of the song already given.

Like bees that suck the morning dew,
Frae flowers of sweetest scent and hue,
Sae wad I dwell upo' thy mou',
   And gar the gods envy me.
     An thou were, &c.

Sae lang's I had the use of light,
I'd on thy beauties feast my sight,
Syne in saft whispers through the night,
   I'd tell how much I loo'd thee.
     An thou were, &c.

How fair and ruddy is my Jean,
She moves a goddess o'er the green;
Were I a king, thou should be queen,
   Nane but mysel' aboon thee.
     An thou were, &c.

I'd grasp thee to this breast of mine,
Whilst thou, like ivy, or the vine,
Around my stronger limbs should twine,
   Form'd hardy to defend thee.
     An thou were, &c.

Time's on the wing, and will not stay,
In shining youth let's make our hay,
Since love admits of nae delay,
   O let nae scorn undo thee.
     An thou were, &c.

While love does at his altar stand,
Ha's there's my heart, gi'e me thy hand,
And with ilk smile thou shalt command
   The will of him wha loves thee.
     An thou were, &c.

POLWARTH, ON THE GREEN.
ALLAN RAMSAY.

At Polwarth, on the green,
  If you'll meet me the morn,
Where lads and lasses do convene
  To dance around the thorn;
A kindly welcome you shall meet
  Fra her, wha likes to view
A lover and a lad complete,
  The lad and lover you.

Let dorty dames say Na,
 As lang as e'er they please,
Seem caulder than the sna',
 While inwardly they bleeze;
But I will frankly shaw my mind,
 And yield my heart to thee—
Be ever to the captive kind,
 That langs na to be free.

At Polwarth, on the green,
 Amang the new-mawn hay,
With sangs and dancing keen
 We'll pass the live-lang day.
At nicht, if beds be ower thrang laid,
 And thou be twined of thine,
Thou shalt be welcome, my dear lad,
 To take a part of mine.

LOCHABER NO MORE.
ALLAN RAMSAY.

FAREWELL to Lochaber, farewell to my Jean,
Where heartsome wi' thee I ha'e mony a day been;
To Lochaber no more, to Lochaber no more,
We'll may be return to Lochaber no more.
These tears that I shed, they're a' for my dear,
And no for the dangers attending on weir;
Though borne on rough seas to a far bloody shore,
Maybe to return to Lochaber no more.

Though hurricanes rise, though rise every wind,
No tempest can equal the storm in my mind;
Though loudest of thunders on louder waves roar,
There's naething like leavin' my love on the shore.
To leave thee behind me my heart is sair pain'd;
But by ease that's inglorious no fame can be gain'd:
And beauty and love's the reward of the brave;
And I maun deserve it before I can crave.

Then glory, my Jeanie, maun plead my excuse;
Since honour commands me, how can I refuse?
Without it, I ne'er can have merit for thee;
And losing thy favour I'd better not be.
I gae then, my lass, to win honour and fame;
And if I should chance to come glorious hame,
I'll bring a heart to thee with love running o'er,
And then I'll leave thee and Lochaber no more.

THIS IS NO MINE AIN HOUSE.
ALLAN RAMSAY.

This is no mine ain house,
  I ken by the rigging o't;
Since with my love I've changed vows,
  I dinna like the bigging o't.
For now that I'm young Robie's bride,
And mistress of his fire-side,
Mine ain house I'll like to guide,
  And please me with the trigging o't.

Then fareweel to my father's house,
  I gang whare love invites me;
The strictest duty this allows,
  When love with honour meets me.
When Hymen moulds us into ane,
My Robbie's nearer than my kin,
And to refuse him were a sin,
  Sae lang's he kindly treats me.

When I'm in my ain house,
  True love shall be at hand aye,
To make me still a prudent spouse,
  And let my man command aye;
Avoiding ilka cause of strife,
The common pest of married life,
That mak's ane wearied of his wife,
  And breaks the kindly band aye.

GIN YE MEET A BONNIE LASSIE.
ALLAN RAMSAY.

Gin ye meet a bonnie lassie,
  Gi'e her a kiss and let her gae;
But if ye meet a dirty hizzie,
  Fye, gar rub her ower wi' strae.
Be sure ye dinna quit the grip
  Of ilka joy when ye are young,
Before auld age your vitals nip,
  And lay ye twa-fauld ower a rung.

Sweet youth's a blythe and heartsome time:
  Then, lads and lasses, while it's May,
Gae pou the gowan in its prime,
  Before it wither and decay.
Watch the saft minutes o' delight,
  When Jenny speaks beneath her breath,
And kisses, layin' a' the wyte
  On you if she kep ony skaith.

Faith, ye're ill-bred, she'll smilin' say,
　Ye'll worry me, ye greedy rook;
Syne frae your arms she'll rin away,
　And hide hersel' in some dark neuk.
Her lauch will lead ye to the place,
　Where lies the happiness ye want;
And plainly tell ye to your face,
　Nineteen nay-says are hauf a grant.

Now to her heavin' bosom cling,
　And sweitly tuilyie for a kiss;
Frae her fair finger whup a ring,
　As taiken o' a future bliss.
These benisons, I'm very sure,
　Are of kind heaven's indulgent grant;
Then, surly carles, wheesht, forbear
　To plague us wi' your whinin' cant!

THE WIDOW CAN BAKE.
ALLAN RAMSAY.

The widow can bake, an' the widow can brew,
The widow can shape, an' the widow can sew,
An' mony braw things the widow can do;
　Then have at the widow, my laddie.
With courage attack her, baith early and late,
To kiss her an' clap her ye maunna be blate:
Speak well, an' do better; for that's the best gate
　To win a young widow, my laddie.

The widow she's youthfu', and never ae hair
The waur of the wearing, and has a good shair
Of every thing lovely; she's witty and fair,
　An' has a rich jointure, my laddie.
What could ye wish better, your pleasure to crown,
Than a widow, the bonniest toast in the town,
With, naething but—draw in your stool and sit down,
　And sport with the widow, my laddie!

Then till her, and kill her with courtesie dead,
Though stark love and kindness be all you can plead;
Be heartsome and airy, and hope to succeed
　With the bonnie gay widow, my laddie.
Strike iron while 'ts het, if ye'd have it to wald;
For fortune aye favours the active and bauld,
But ruins the wooer that's thowless and cauld,
　Unfit for the widow, my laddie.

BESSIE BELL, AND MARY GRAY.
ALLAN RAMSAY.

O, Bessie Bell, and Mary Gray,
  They were twa bonnie lasses;
They biggit a bower on yon burn-brae,
  And theekit it ower wi' rashes.
Fair Bessie Bell I lo'ed yestreen,
  And thocht I ne'er could alter;
But Mary Gray's twa pawky een
  Gar'd a' my fancy falter.

Bessie's hair's like a lint-tap,
  She smiles like a May mornin',
When Phœbus starts frae Thetis' lap,
  The hills with rays adornin';
White is her neck, saft is her hand,
  Her waist and feet fu' genty,
With ilka grace she can command:
  Her lips, O, wow! they're denty.

An' Mary's locks are like the craw,
  Her een like diamonds glances;
She's aye sae clean, redd-up, and braw;
  She kills whene'er she dances.
Blythe as a kid, wi' wit at will,
  She blooming, tight, and tall is,
And guides her airs sae gracefu' still;
  O, Jove, she's like thy Pallas!

Dear Bessie Bell, and Mary Gray,
  Ye unco sair oppress us;
Our fancies jee between ye twa,
  Ye are sic bonnie lasses.
Wae's me! for baith I canna get;
  To ane by law we're stentit;
Then I'll draw cuts, and tak' my fate,
  And be wi' ane contentit.

THE YELLOW-HAIR'D LADDIE.
ALLAN RAMSAY.

In April, when primroses paint the sweet plain,
And summer approaching rejoiceth the swain,
The yellow-hair'd laddie would oftentimes go
To woods and deep glens where the hawthorn trees grow.

There, under the shade of an old sacred thorn,
With freedom he sung his loves, evening and morn:
He sung with so soft and enchanting a sound,
That sylvans and fairies, unseen, danced around.

The shepherd thus sung: "Though young Maya be fair,
Her beauty is dash'd with a scornful proud air;
But Susie was handsome, and sweetly could sing;
Her breath's like the breezes perfumed in the spring.

"That Madie, in all the gay bloom of her youth,
Like the moon, was inconstant, and never spoke truth;
But Susie was faithful, good-humour'd, and free,
And fair as the goddess that sprung from the sea.

"That mamma's fine daughter, with all her great dower,
Was awkwardly airy, and frequently sour."
Then sighing, he wish'd, would but parents agree,
The witty sweet Susie his mistress might be.

HAP ME WI' THY PETTICOAT.
ALLAN RAMSAY.

O BELL, thy looks ha'e kill'd my heart,
   I pass the day in pain;
When night returns, I feel the smart,
   And wish for thee in vain.
I'm starving cold, while thou art warm;
   Have pity and incline,
And grant me for a hap that charm-
   ing petticoat of thine.

My ravish'd fancy in amaze
   Still wanders o'er thy charms,
Delusive dreams ten thousand ways
   Present thee to my arms.
But waking, think what I endure,
   While cruel thou decline
Those pleasures, which alone can cure
   This panting breast of mine.

I faint, I fall, and wildly rove,
   Because you still deny
The just reward that's due to love,
   And let true passion die.
Oh! turn, and let compassion seize
   That lovely breast of thine;
Thy petticoat could give me ease,
   If thou and it were mine.

Sure heaven has fitted for delight
That beauteous form of thine,
And thou'rt too good its law to slight,
By hind'ring the design.
May all the powers of love agree,
At length to make thee mine;
Or loose my chains and set me free
From every charm of thine.

HIGHLAND LADDIE.
ALLAN RAMSAY.

The Lawland lads think they are fine,
  But O! they're vain and idly gaudy;
How much unlike the gracefu' mien
  And manly looks of my Highland laddie.
    O my bonnie Highland laddie,
    My handsome, charming, Highland laddie;
    May heaven still guard, and love reward,
    The Lawland lass and her Highland laddie.

If I were free at will to choose,
  To be the wealthiest Lawland lady,
I'd tak' young Donald without trews,
  With bonnet blue and belted plaidie.
    O my bonnie, &c.

The brawest beau in burrows town,
  In a' his airs, wi' art made ready,
Compared to him, he's but a clown,
  He's finer far in 's tartan plaidie.
    O my bonnie, &c.

O'er benty hill wi' him I'll run,
  And leave my Lawland kin and daddie;
Frae winter's cauld and summer's sun,
  He'll screen me wi' his Highland plaidie.
    O my bonnie, &c.

A painted room, and silken bed,
  May please a Lawland laird and lady;
But I can kiss and be as glad
  Behind a bush in 's Highland plaidie.
    O my bonnie, &c.

Few compliments between us pass;
  I ca' him my dear Highland laddie,
And he ca's me his Lawland lass,
  Syne rows me in beneath his plaidie.
    O my bonnie, &c.

Nae greater joy I'll e'er pretend,
  Than that his love prove true and steady,
Like mine to him, which ne'er shall end,
  While heaven preserves my Highland laddie.
    O my bonnie, &c.

UP IN THE AIR.
ALLAN RAMSAY.

Now the sun's gaen out o' sight,
Beat the ingle, and snuff the light:
In glens the fairies skip and dance,
And witches wallop o'er to France.
    Up in the air
      On my bonny grey mare,
And I see her yet, and I see her yet.
    Up in, &c.

The wind's drifting hail and sna',
O'er frozen hags like a foot-ba';
Nae starns keek through the azure slit,
'Tis cauld and mirk as ony pit.
    The man i' the moon
      Is carousing aboon,
D'ye see, d'ye see, d'ye see him yet.
    The man, &c.

Tak' your glass to clear your een,
'Tis the elixir heals the spleen,
Baith wit and mirth it will inspire,
And gently puffs the lover's fire.
    Up in the air,
      It drives away care,
Ha'e wi' ye, ha'e wi' ye, and ha'e wi' ye, lads, yet.
    Up in, &c.

Steek the doors, keep out the frost,
Come, Willy, gi'es about yo'r toast,
Till't lads, and lilt it out,
And let us ha'e a blythsome bowt.
    Up wi't, there, there,
      Dinna cheat, but drink fair,
Huzza, huzza, and huzza lads, yet.
    Up wi't, &c.

I WILL AWA' WI' MY LOVE.

ALLAN RAMSAY.

I will awa' wi' my love,
  I will awa' wi' her,
Though a' my kin had sworn and said,
  I'll ower Bogie wi' her.
If I can get but her consent,
  I dinna care a strae;
Though ilka ane be discontent,
  Awa' wi' her I'll gae.

For now she's mistress o' my heart,
  And wordy o' my hand;
And, weel I wat, we shanna part
  For siller or for land.
Let rakes delight to swear and drink,
  And beaux admire fine lace;
But my chief pleasure is to blink
  On Betty's bonnie face.

There a' the beauties do combine,
  Of colour, treats, and air;
The saul that sparkles in her een
  Makes her a jewel rare;
Her flowin' wit gives shining life
  To a' her other charms;
How blest I'll be when she's my wife,
  And lock'd up in my arms!

There blythely will I rant and sing,
  While o'er her sweets I'll range;
I'll cry, Your humble servant, king,
  Shame fa' them that wad change.
A kiss of Betty, and a smile
  A boit ye wad lay down,
The right ye hae to Britain's Isle,
  And offer me yer crown.

BONNIE SCOT-MAN.

ALLAN RAMSAY.

Ye gales, that gently wave the sea,
  And please the canny boat-man,
Bear me frae hence, or bring to me
  My brave, my bonnie Scot-man.
In haly bands we joined our hands,
  Yet may not this discover,
While parents rate a large estate
  Before a faithfu' lover.

But I loor chuse, in Highland glens
 To herd the kid and goat, man,
Ere I could for sic little ends,
 Refuse my bonnie Scot-man.
Wae worth the man, wha first began
 The base ungenerous fashion,
Frae greedy views love's art to use,
 While strangers to its passion!

Frae foreign fields, my lovely youth,
 Haste to thy longing lassie,
Who pants to press thy balmy mouth,
 And in her bosom hause thee.
Love gi'es the word; then, haste on board;
 Fair winds and tenty boat-man,
Waft o'er, waft o'er, frae yonder shore,
 My blythe, my bonnie Scot-man.

BRAES OF BRANKSOME.
ALLAN RAMSAY.

As I cam' in by Teviot side,
 And by the braes of Branksome,
There first I saw my bonnie bride,
 Young, smiling, sweet, and handsome.
Her skin was safter than the down,
 And white as alabaster;
Her hair, a shining, waving brown;
 In straightness nane surpass'd her.

Life glow'd upon her lip and cheek,
 Her clear een were surprising,
And beautifully turn'd her neck,
 Her little breasts just rising:
Nae silken hose with gushats fine,
 Or shoon with glancing laces,
On her bare leg, forbad to shine
 Wool-shapen native graces.

Ae little coat and bodice white
 Was sum o' a' her claithing;
E'en these o'er muckle;—mair delight
 She'd given clad wi' naething.
We lean'd upon a flowery brae,
 By which a burnie trotted;
On her I glowr'd my soul away,
 While on her sweets I doated.

A thousand beauties of desert
Before had scarce alarm'd me,
Till this dear artless struck my heart,
And, bot designing, charm'd me.
Hurried by love, close to my breast
I clasp'd this fund of blisses,—
Wha smiled, and said, Without a priest,
Sir, hope for nocht but kisses.

I had nae heart to do her harm,
And yet I couldna want her;
What she demanded, ilka charm
O' hers pled I should grant her.
Since heaven had dealt to me a routh,
Straight to the kirk I led her;
There plighted her my faith and trouth,
And a young lady made her.

THE LAST TIME I CAM' OWRE THE MUIR.
ALLAN RAMSAY.

The last time I cam' owre the muir,
I left my love behind me:
Ye powers, what pains do I endure
When soft ideas mind me!
Soon as the ruddy morn display'd
The beaming day ensuing,
I met betimes my lovely maid,
In fit retreats for wooing.

We stray'd beside yon wand'ring stream,
And talk'd with hearts o'erflowing;
Until the sun's last setting beam
Was in the ocean glowing.
I pitied all beneath the skies,
Even kings, when she was nigh me;
In raptures I beheld her eyes,
Which could but ill deny me.

Should I be call'd where cannons roar,
Where mortal steel may wound me,
Or cast upon some foreign shore,
Where dangers may surround me;
Yet hopes again to see my love,
To feast on glowing kisses,
Shall make my cares at distance move,
In prospect of such blisses.

In all my soul there's not one place
  To let a rival enter:
Since she excels in ev'ry grace,
  In her my love shall centre.
Sooner the seas shall cease to flow,
  Their waves the Alps shall cover,
On Greenland ice shall roses grow,
  Before I cease to love her.

The neist time I gang ower the muir,
  She shall a lover find me;
And that my faith is firm and pure,
  Though I left her behind me;
Then Hymen's sacred bonds shall chain
  My heart to her fair bosom;
There, while my being does remain,
  My love more fresh shall blossom.

LOVE INVITING REASON.
ALLAN RAMSAY.

When innocent pastime our pleasures did crown,
  Upon a green meadow, or under a tree,
Ere Annie became a fine lady in town,
  How lovely, and loving, and bonnie was she!
Rouse up thy reason, my beautiful Annie,
  Let ne'er a new whim ding thy fancy ajee;
Oh! as thou art bonnie, be faithfu' and cannie,
  And favour thy Jamie wha doats upon thee.

Does the death of a lintwhite give Annie the spleen?
  Can tyning of trifles be uneasy to thee?
Can lap-dogs and monkeys draw tears frae these een
  That look with indifference on poor dying me?
Rouse up thy reason, my beautiful Annie,
  And dinna prefer a paroquet to me:
Oh! as thou art bonnie, be prudent and cannie,
  And think on thy Jamie wha doats upon thee.

Ah! should a new manteau or Flanders lace head,
  Or yet a wee coatie, though never so fine,
Gar thee grow forgetfu', and let his heart bleed,
  That ance had some hope of purchasing thine?
Rouse up thy reason, my beautiful Annie,
  And dinna prefer your flageeries to me;
Oh! as thou art bonnie, be solid and cannie,
  And tent a true lover that doats upon thee.

Shall a Paris edition of newfangled Sawney,
　Though gilt o'er wi' laces and fringes he be,
By adoring himself, be adored by fair Annie,
　And aim at those bonisons promised to me?
Rouse up thy reason, my beautiful Annie,
　And never prefer a light dancer to me;
Oh! as thou art bonnie, be prudent and cannie;
　Love only thy Jamie wha doats upon thee.

Oh! think, my dear charmer, on ilka sweet hour,
　That slade away saftly between thee and me,
Ere squirrels, or beaux, or foppery, had power
　To rival my love and impose upon thee.
Rouse up thy reason, my beautiful Annie,
　And let thy desires a' be centred in me;
Oh! as thou art bonnie, be faithfu' and cannie,
　And love ane wha lang has been loving to thee.

MARY SCOTT THE FLOWER OF YARROW.
ALLAN RAMSAY.

Happy's the love which meets return,
When in soft flames souls equal burn;
But words are wanting to discover
The torments of a hopeless lover.
Ye registers of heaven, relate,
If looking o'er the rolls of fate,
Did you there see me mark'd to marrow
Mary Scott the flower of Yarrow?

Ah no! her form's too heavenly fair,
Her love the gods above must share;
While mortals with despair explore her,
And at distance due adore her.
O lovely maid! my doubts beguile,
Revive and bless me with a smile;
Alas! if not, you'll soon debar a
Sighing swain the banks of Yarrow.

Be hush'd, ye fears, I'll not despair,
My Mary's tender as she's fair;
Then I'll go tell her all mine anguish,
She is too good to let me languish.
With success crown'd I'll not envy
The folks who dwell above the sky:
When Mary Scott's become my marrow,
We'll make a paradise on Yarrow.

JEAN.
ALLAN RAMSAY.

Love's goddess, in a myrtle grove,
  Said, Cupid, bend thy bow with speed,
Nor let thy shaft at random rove,
  For Jeany's haughty heart maun bleed.
The smiling boy with art divine,
  From Paphos shot an arrow keen,
Which flew, unerring, to the heart,
  And kill'd the pride of bonnie Jean.

Nae mair the nymph, wi' haughty air,
  Refuses Willie's kind address;
Her yielding blushes show nae care,
  But too much fondness to suppress.
Nae mair the youth is sullen now,
  But looks the gayest on the green,
Whilst ev'ry day he spies some new
  Surprising charms in bonnie Jean.

A thousand transports crowd his breast,
  He moves as light as fleeting wind;
His former sorrows seem a jest,
  Now when his Jeany is turn'd kind:
Riches he looks on wi' disdain;
  The glorious fields of war look mean;
The cheerful hound and horn give pain,
  If absent from his bonnie Jean.

The day he spends in amorous gaze,
  Which ev'n in summer shorten'd seems;
When sunk in downs, wi' glad amaze,
  He wonders at her in his dreams.
A' charms disclos'd, she looks more bright
  Than Troy's fair prize, the Spartan queen;
Wi' breaking day he lifts his sight,
  And pants to be wi' bonnie Jean.

THROUGH THE WOOD.
ALLAN RAMSAY.

O, Sandy, why leave thou thy Nelly to mourn?
  Thy presence could ease me,
  When naething can please me;
Now dowie I sigh on the banks of the burn,
Or through the wood, laddie, until thou return.

Though woods now are bonnie, and mornings are clear,
    While lav'rocks are singing,
    And primroses springing;
Yet nane o' them pleases my eye or my ear,
When through the wood, laddie, ye dinna appear.

That I am forsaken, some spare not to tell;
    I'm fash'd wi' their scornin'
    Baith e'enin' and mornin';
Their jeering gaes aft to my heart wi' a knell,
When through the wood, laddie, I wander mysel'.

Then stay, my dear Sandy, nae langer away;
    But, quick as an arrow,
    Haste here to thy marrow,
Wha's living in languor till that happy day,
When through the wood, laddie, we'll dance, sing and play.

TIBBIE HAS A STORE O' CHARMS.
ALLAN RAMSAY.

Tibby has a store o' charms
Her genty shape our fancy warms;
How strangely can her sma' white arms
    Fetter the lad who looks but at her;
Fra'er ancle to her slender waste,
    These sweets conceal'd invite to dawt her;
Her rosy cheek, and rising breast,
    Gar ane's mouth gush bowt fu' o' water.

Nelly's gawsy, saft and gay,
Fresh as the lucken flowers in May;
Ilk ane that sees her, cries, Ah hey,
    She's bonny! O I wonder at her.
The dimples of her chin and cheek,
    And limbs sae plump invite to dawt her;
Her lips sae sweet, and skin sae sleek,
    Gar mony mouths beside mine water.

Now strike my finger in a bore,
My wyson with the maiden shore,
Gin I can tell whilk I am for,
    When these twa stars appear thegither.
O love! why does thou gi'e thy fires
    Sae large, while we're oblig'd to neither?
Our spacious sauls immense desires,
    And aye be in a hankerin' swither.

Tibby's shape and airs are fine,
And Nelly's beauties are divine:
But since they canna baith be mine,
  Ye gods, give ear to my petition:
Provide a good lad for the tane,
  But let it be with this provision,
I get the other to my lane,
  In prospect *plano* and fruition.

FAIR WIDOW ARE YE WAKIN'.
ALLAN RAMSAY.

O wha's that at my chamber-door?
  "Fair widow, are ye waking?"
Auld carle, your suit give o'er,
  Your love lyes a' in tawking.
Gi'e me the lad that's young and tight,
  Sweet like an April meadow;
'Tis sic as he can bless the sight,
  And bosom of a widow.
"O widow, wilt thou let me in?
  I'm pawky, wise and thrifty,
And come of a right gentle kin;
  I'm little more than fifty."
Daft carle, dit your mouth,
  What signifies how pawky,
Or gentle born ye be,—bot youth,
  In love you're but a gawky.
"Then, widow, let these guineas speak,
  That powerfully plead clinkan,
And if they fail my mouth I'll steek,
  And nae mair love will think on."
These court indeed, I maun confess,
  I think they make you young, sir,
And ten times better can express
  Affection, than your tongue, sir.

I'LL OWRE THE MUIR TO MAGGY.
ALLAN RAMSAY.

AND I'll owre the muir to Maggy,
  Her wit and sweetness call me;
There to my fair I'll show my mind,
  Whatever may befall me:
If she loves mirth, I'll learn to sing
  Or likes the Nine to follow,
I'll lay my lugs in Pindus' spring,
  And invocate Apollo.

If she admire a martial mind,
  I'll sheathe my limbs in armour;
If to the softer dance inclined,
  With gayest airs I'll charm her;
If she love grandeur, day and night
  I'll plot my nation's glory,
Find favour in my prince's sight,
  And shine in future story.

Beauty can wonders work with ease,
  Where wit is corresponding,
And bravest men know best to please,
  With complaisance abounding.
My bonnie Maggie's love can turn
  Me to what shape she pleases,
If in her breast that flame shall burn,
  Which in my bosom bleezes.

WOE'S MY HEART THAT WE SHOULD SUNDER.
ALLAN RAMSAY.

With broken words, and downcast eyes,
  Poor Colin spoke his passion tender;
And, parting with his Grisy, cries,
  Ah! woe's my heart that we should sunder.
To others I am cold as snow,
  But kindle with thine eyes like tinder:
From thee with pain I'm forced to go;
  It breaks my heart that we should sunder.

Chain'd to thy charms, I cannot range,
  No beauty new my love shall hinder,
Nor time nor place shall ever change
  My vows, though we're obliged to sunder.
The image of thy graceful air,
  And beauties which invite our wonder,
Thy lively wit and prudence rare,
  Shall still be present though we sunder.

Dear nymph, believe thy swain in this,
  You'll ne'er engage a heart that's kinder;
Then seal a promise with a kiss,
  Always to love me though we sunder.
Ye gods! take care of my dear lass,
  That as I leave her I may find her;
When that blest time shall come to pass,
  We'll meet again and never sunder.

THERE'S MY THUMB, I'LL NE'ER BEGUILE THEE.
ALLAN RAMSAY.

My sweetest May, let love incline thee
T' accept a heart which he designs thee;
And as your constant slave regard it,
Syne for its faithfulness reward it.
'Tis proof a-shot to birth or money,
But yields to what is sweet and bonnie;
Receive it, then, with a kiss and smily;
There's my thumb, it will ne'er beguile ye.

How tempting sweet these lips of thine are!
Thy bosom white, and legs sae fine are,
That, when in pools I see thee clean 'em,
They carry away my heart between 'em.
I wish, and I wish, while it gaes duntin',
O gin I had thee on a mountain!
Though kith and kin and a' should revile thee,
There's my thumb, I'll ne'er beguile thee.

Alane through flow'ry howes I daunder,
Tenting my flocks, lest they should wander;
Gin thou'll gae alang, I'll daute thee gaylie,
And gi'e my thumb, I'll ne'er beguile thee.
O my dear lassie, it is but daffin',
To haud thy wooer up niff-naffin':
That Na, na, na, I hate it most vilely;
O say, Yes, and I'll ne'er beguile thee.

YE WATCHFUL GUARDIANS.
ALLAN RAMSAY.

Ye watchful guardians of the fair,
Who skiff on wings of ambient air,
Of my dear Delia take a care,
　And represent her lover
With all the gaiety of youth,
With honour, justice, love, and truth;
Till I return, her passions soothe,
　For me in whispers move her.

Be careful no base sordid slave,
With soul sunk in a golden grave,
Who knows no virtue but to save,
　With glaring gold bewitch her.
Tell her, for me she was design'd,
For me who knew how to be kind,
And have mair plenty in my mind,
　Than ane who's ten times richer.

Let all the world turn upside down,
And fools rin an eternal round,
In quest of what can ne'er be found,
  To please their vain ambition;
Let little minds great charms espy,
In shadows which at distance lie,
Whose hop'd-for pleasure when come nigh,
  Proves nothing in fruition:

But cast into a mould divine,
Fair Delia does with lustre shine,
Her virtuous soul's an ample mine,
  Which yields a constant treasure.
Let poets in sublimest lays,
Employ their skill her fame to raise;
Let sons of music pass whole days,
  With well-tuned reeds to please her.

THE LASS O' PATIE'S MILL.
ALLAN RAMSAY.

The lass o' Patie's Mill,
  Sae bonnie, blythe, and gay,
In spite of a' my skill,
  She stole my heart away.
When teddin' out the hay,
  Bareheaded on the green,
Love mid her locks did play,
  And wanton'd in her een.

Without the help of art,
  Like flowers that grace the wild,
She did her sweets impart,
  Whene'er she spak' or smiled:
Her looks they were so mild,
  Free from affected pride,
She me to love beguiled;
  I wish'd her for my bride.

Oh! had I a' the wealth
  Hopetoun's high mountains fill,
Insured lang life and health,
  And pleasure at my will;
I'd promise, and fulfil,
  That nane but bonnie she,
The lass o' Patie's Mill,
  Should share the same wi' me.

DEAR ROGER, IF YOUR JENNY GECK.
ALLAN RAMSAY.

Dear Roger, if your Jonny geck,
  And answer kindness with a slight,
Seem unconcern'd at her neglect,
  For women in our vows delight;
But them despise wha're soon defeat,
  And with a simple face give way
To a repulse; then be not blate,
  Push bauldly on and win the day.

These maidens, innocently young,
  Say aften what they never mean;
Ne'er mind their pretty lying tongue,
  But tent the language of their uen;
If these agree, and she persist
  To answer all your love with hate,
Seek elsewhere to be better blest,
  And let her sigh when 'tis too late.

PEGGY AND PATIE.
ALLAN RAMSAY.

PEGGY.

When first my dear laddie gaed to the green hill,
And I at ewe-milking first seyed my young skill,
To bear the milk bowie nae pain was to me,
When I at the bughting forgather'd with thee.

PATIE.

When corn-riggs waved yellow, and blue heather-bells
Bloom'd bonnie on moorland and sweet rising fells,
Nae birns, brier, or bracken, gave trouble to me,
If I found but the berries right ripened for thee.

PEGGY.

When thou ran, or wrestled, or putted the stane,
And cam' aff the victor, my heart was aye fain:
Thy ilka sport manly gave pleasure to me,
For nane can put, wrestle, or run swift as thee.

PATIE.

Our Jenny sings saftly the "Cowden Broom-knowes,"
And Rosie lilts sweetly the "Milking the Ewes,"
There's few "Jenny Nettles" like Nancy can sing;
With, "Through the wood, Laddie," Bess gars our lugs ring.
But when my dear Peggy sings, with better skill,
The "Boatman," "Tweedside," or the "Lass of the Mill,"
'Tis many times sweeter and pleasing to me,
For though they sing nicely, they cannot like thee.

PEGGY.
How easy can lasses trow what they desire,
With praises sae kindly increasing love's fire!
Give me still this pleasure, my study shall be
To make myself better and sweeter for thee.

CORN-RIGS ARE BONNY.
ALLAN RAMSAY.

My Patie is a lover gay;
  His mind is never muddy;
His breath is sweeter than new hay;
  His face is fair and ruddy.
His shape is handsome middle size;
  He's stately in his walking;
The shining of his een surprise;
  'Tis heaven to hear him talking.

Last night I met him on a bauk,
  Where yellow corn was growing;
There mony a kindly word he spake,
  That set my heart a-glowing.
He kiss'd, and vow'd he wad be mine,
  And lo'ed me best of ony;
That gars me like to sing sinsyne,
  O corn-rigs are bonny.

Let maidens of a silly mind
  Refuse what maist they're wanting;
Since we for yielding are design'd,
  We chastely should be granting.
Then I'll comply and marry Pate;
  And syne my cockernony
He's free to touzle air or late,
  When corn-rigs are bonny.

THE WAUKING O' THE FAULD.
ALLAN RAMSAY.

My Peggie is a young thing,
  Just enter'd in her teens,
Fair as the day, and sweet as May,
Fair as the day, and always gay:
  My Peggy is a young thing,
  And I'm nae very auld,
Yet weel I like to meet her at
  The wauking o' the fauld.

My Peggy speaks sae sweetly
  Whene'er we meet alane,
I wish nae mair to lay my care,
I wish nae mair o' a' that's rare:
  My Peggy speaks sae sweetly,
    To a' the lave I'm cauld;
  But she gars a' my spirits glow
    At wauking o' the fauld.

My Peggy smiles sae kindly
  Whene'er I whisper love,
That I look down on a' the town,
That I look down upon a crown:
  My Peggy smiles sae kindly,
    It makes me blythe and bauld,
  And naething gi'es me sic delight,
    As wauking o' the fauld.

My Peggy sings sae saftly,
  When on my pipe I play;
By a' the rest it is confest,
By a' the rest that she sings best:
  My Peggy sings sae saftly,
    And in her sangs are tauld,
  Wi' innocence the wale o' sense,
    At wauking o' the fauld.

AT SETTING DAY.
ALLAN RAMSAY.

At setting day and rising morn,
  With soul that still shall love thee,
I'll ask of heaven thy safe return,
  With all that can improve thee.
I'll visit oft the birken bush,
  Where first thou kindly told me
Sweet tales of love, and hid my blush,
  Whilst round thou didst enfold me.

To all our haunts I will repair,
  By greenwood, shaw, or fountain;
Or where the summer day I'd share
  With thee upon yon mountain.
There will I tell the trees and flowers,
  From thoughts unfeign'd and tender,
By vows you're mine, by love is yours
  A heart which cannot wander.

WILLIE WAS A WANTON WAG.

ASCRIBED TO WILLIAM HAMILTON OF GILBERTFIELD,

This Translator into "Modern Scots" of Blind Harry's Wallace. It appears in the TEA TABLE MISCELLANY, with the initials W. W., which Mr. David Laing considers to refer to Hamilton's sobriquet of Wanton Willie. Hamilton died in 1751. He contributed several pieces to Watson's collection of Scots Poems, 1706, and his rhyming epistles to Allan Ramsay are well known to every reader of Honest Allan's works. The song has also been ascribed to William Walkinshaw of Walkinshaw, but without any foundation.

WILLIE was a wanton wag,
  The blythest lad that e'er I saw,
At bridals still he bore the brag,
  An' carried aye the gree awa'.
His doublet was of Zetland shag,
  And wow! but Willie he was braw,
And at his shoulder hang a tag,
  That pleas'd the lasses best of a'.

He was a man without a clag,
  His heart was frank without a flaw;
And aye whatever Willie said,
  It still was hauden as a law.
His boots they were made of the jag,
  When he went to the weaponschaw,
Upon the green nane durst him brag,
  The feind a ane amang them a'.

And was na Willie weel worth gowd?
  He wan the love o' great and sma';
For after he the bride had kiss'd,
  He kiss'd the lasses hale-sale a'.
Sae merrily round the ring they row'd,
  When by the hand he led them a',
And smack on smack on them bestow'd,
  By virtue of a standing law.

And was nae Willie a great loun,
  As shyre a lick as e'er was seen;
When he danc'd wi' the lasses round.
  The bridegroom speir'd where he had been,
Quoth Willie, I've been at the ring,
  Wi' bobbing, baith my shanks are sair;
Gae ca' your bride and maidens in,
  For Willie he dow do nae mair.

Then rest ye. Willie, I'll gae out,
  And for a wee fill up the ring.
But, shame lit on his souple snout,
  He wanted Willie's wanton fling.

Then straught he to the bride did fare,
  Says, Weels me on your bonnie face;
Wi' bobbing Willie's shanks are sair,
  And I'm come out to fill his place.

Bridegroom, she says, ye'll spoil the dance,
  And at the ring ye'll aye be lag,
Unless like Willie ye advance:
  O! Willie has a wanton leg;
For wi't he learns us a' to steer,
  And foremost aye bears up the ring;
We will find nae sic dancing here,
  If we want Willie's wanton fling.

MACPHERSON'S RANT.

HERD's COLLECTION.—Said to have been composed by James Macpherson, a notorious freebooter, while under sentence of death. though probably it is as genuine a piece of prison poetry as were the "last dying speeches and confessions," specimens of gallows prose. Macpherson was tried at Banff, and was executed there November 16, 1700. He appears to have been, according to tradition, an outlaw of the Robin Hood sort—robbing the rich and giving to the poor, and deterring his followers from all violent and cruel acts. He was betrayed by one of his band, who took that way of revenging a reprimand he received from his chief. Burns's celebrated "Macpherson's Rant" refers to the same personage.

I've spent my time in rioting,
  Debauch'd my health and strength;
I've pillaged, plunder'd, murdered,
  But now, alas, at length,
I'm brought to punishment direct;
  Pale death draws near to me;
This end I never did project,
  To hang upon a tree.

To hang upon a tree, a tree!
  That cursed unhappy death!
Like to a wolf, to worried be,
  And choaked in the breath.
My very heart wad surely break
  When this I think upon,
Did not my courage singular
  Did pensive thoughts begone.

No man on earth that draweth breath,
  More courage had than I;
I dared my foes unto their face,
  And would not from them fly.

This grandeur stout I did keep out,
  Like Hector, manfully;
Then wonder one like me so stout
  Should hang upon a tree.

The Egyptian band I did command,
  With courage more by far,
Than ever did a general
  His soldiers in the war.
Being fear'd by all, both great and small,
  I lived most joyfullie :
Oh, curse upon this fate of mine,
  To hang upon a tree!

As for my life I do not care,
  If justice would take place,
And bring my fellow-plunderers
  Unto the same disgrace.
But Peter Brown, that notour loon,
  Escaped, and was made free :
Oh, curse upon this fate of mine,
  To hang upon a tree!

Both law and justice buried aro,
  And fraud and guile succeed;
The guilty pass unpunished,
  If money intercede.
The Laird of Grant, that Highland saunt,
  His mighty majestie,
He pleads the cause of Peter Brown,
  And lets Macpherson die.

The destiny of my life, contrived
  By those whom I obliged,
Rewarded me much ill for good,
  And left me no refuge.
But Braco Duff, in rage enough,
  He first laid hands on me;
And if that death would not prevent,
  Avenged would I be.

As for my life, it is but short,
  When I shall be no more;
To part with life I am content,
  As any heretofore.
Therefore, good people all, take heed,
  This warning take by me,
According to the lives you lead,
  Rewarded you shall be.

TWEEDSIDE.

ROBERT CRAWFORD,

A CADET of the house of Drumsoy in Renfrewshire. Very little is known of the events of his life. He is supposed to have been born about the year 1695, to have spent the greater part of his life abroad, and to have died in 1732 on his passage to this country from France.

The whole of the poems here given appeared in the TEA TABLE MISCELLANY. He had probably become acquainted with William Hamilton, of Bangour, during his sojourn on the Continent, for one of his songs, "Look where dear Hamilla smiles," is addressed to Mrs. Hamilton, a relation of the poet's; and it was probably through Hamilton's influence that he contributed to Ramsay's work.

WHAT beauties does Flora disclose!
  How sweet are her smiles upon Tweed!
Yet Mary's still sweeter than those,
  Both nature and fancy exceed.
No daisy, nor sweet blushing rose,
  Not all the gay flowers of the field,
Not Tweed, gliding gently through those,
  Such beauty and pleasure does yield.

The warblers are heard in the grove,
  The linnet, the lark, and the thrush;
The blackbird, and sweet cooing dove,
  With music enchant ev'ry bush.
Come, let us go forth to the mead;
  Let us see how the primroses spring;
We'll lodge in some village on Tweed,
  And love while the feather'd folk sing.

How does my love pass the long day?
  Does Mary not tend a few sheep?
Do they never carelessly stray
  While happily she lies asleep?
Should Tweed's murmurs lull her to rest,
  Kind nature indulgin' my bliss,
To ease the soft pains of my breast,
  I'd steal an ambrosial kiss.

'Tis she does the virgins excel;
  No beauty with her may compare;
Love's graces around her do dwell;
  She's fairest where thousands are fair.
Say, charmer, where do thy flocks stray?
  Oh, tell me at morn where they feed?
Shall I seek them on sweet-winding Tay?
  Or the pleasanter banks of the Tweed?

BUSH ABOON TRAQUAIR.
ROBERT CRAWFORD.

Hear me, ye nymphs, and ev'ry swain,
  I'll tell how Peggy grieves me;
Though thus I languish and complain,
  Alas! she ne'er believes me.
My vows and sighs, like silent air,
  Unheeded, never move her;
At the bonnie bush aboon Traquair,
  'Twas there I first did love her.

That day she smil'd, and made me glad,
  No maid seem'd ever kinder;
I thought myself the luckiest lad,
  So sweetly there to find her.
I tried to soothe my am'rous flame;
  In words that I thought tender:
If more there pass'd, I'm not to blame;
  I meant not to offend her.

Yet now she scornful flies the plain,
  The fields we then frequented;
If e'er we meet she shows disdain,
  She looks as ne'er acquainted.
The bonnie bush bloom'd fair in May;
  Its sweets I'll aye remember;
But now her frowns make it decay;
  It fades as in December.

Ye rural pow'rs who hear my strains,
  Why thus should Peggy grieve me?
Oh! make her partner in my pains;
  Then let her smiles relieve me.
If not, my love will turn despair;
  My passion no more tender;
I'll leave the bush aboon Traquair;
  To lonely wilds I'll wander.

LEADER HAUGHS AND YARROW.
ROBERT CRAWFORD.

The morn was fair, saft was the air,
  All nature's sweets were springing;
The buds did bow with silver dew,
  Ten thousand birds were singing;
When on the bent with blythe content,
  Young Jamie sang his marrow,
Nae bonnier lass e'er trod the grass,
  On Leader Haughs and Yarrow.

How sweet her face, with ev'ry grace
  In heav'nly beauty planted!
Her smiling een, and comely mien,
  That nae perfection wanted.
I'll never fret, nor ban my fate,
  But bless my bonnie marrow:
If her dear smile my doubts beguile,
  My mind shall ken nae sorrow.

Yet though she's fair, and has full share
  Of every charm enchanting,
Each good turns ill, and soon will kill
  Poor me, if love be wanting.
O, bonnie lass! have but the grace
  To think ere ye gae further,
Your joys maun flit, if you commit
  The crying sin of murder.

My wand'ring ghaist will ne'er get rest,
  And day and night affright ye;
But if ye're kind, with joyful mind,
  I'll study to delight ye.
Our years around, with love thus crown'd,
  From all things joy shall borrow:
Thus none shall be more blest than we,
  On Leader Haughs and Yarrow.

O sweetest Sue! 'tis only you
  Can make life worth my wishes,
If equal love your mind can move,
  To grant this best of blisses.
Thou art my sun, and thy least frown
  Would blast me in the blossom:
But if thou shine, and make me thine,
  I'll flourish in thy bosom.

MY DEARIE IF THOU DEE.
ROBERT CRAWFORD.

LOVE never more shall give me pain,
  My fancy's fix'd on thee;
Nor ever maid my heart shall gain,
  My Peggie, if thou dee.
Thy beauties did such pleasure give,
  Thy love's so true to me;
Without thee I shall never live,
  My dearie, if thou dee.

If fate shall tear thee from my breast,
  How shall I lonely stray!
In dreary dreams the night I'll waste,
  In sighs the silent day.
I ne'er can so much virtue find,
  Nor such perfection see:
Then I'll renounce all womankind,
  My Peggie, after thee.

No new-blown beauty fires my heart,
  With Cupid's raving rage;
But thine, which can such sweets impart,
  Must all the world engage.
'Twas this that like the morning sun,
  Gave joy and life to me;
And, when its destin'd day is done,
  With Peggy let me dee.

Ye powers that smile on virtuous love,
  And in such pleasures share,
Ye who its faithful flames approve,
  With pity view the fair:
Restore my Peggie's wonted charms,
  Those charms so dear to me;
Oh, never rob them from those arms—
  I'm lost if Peggy dee.

PEGGY, I MUST LOVE THEE.

ROBERT CRAWFORD.

Beneath a beech's grateful shade,
  Young Colin lay complaining;
He sigh'd and seem'd to love a maid,
  Without hopes of obtaining:
For thus the swain indulg'd his grief,
  Though pity cannot move thee,
Though thy hard heart gives no relief,
  Yet, Peggy, I must love thee.

Say, Peggy, what has Colin done,
  That thus you cruelly use him?
If love's a fault, 'tis that alone,
  For which you should excuse him:
'Twas thy dear self first rais'd this flame,
  This fire by which I languish;
'Tis thou alone can quench the same,
  And cool its scorching anguish.

For thee I leave the sportive plain,
  Where every maid invites me;
For thee, sole cause of all my pain,
  For thee that only alights me:
This love that fires my faithful heart
  By all but thee's commended.
Oh! would thou act so good a part,
  My grief might soon be ended.

That beauteous breast, so soft to feel,
  Seem'd tenderness all over,
Yet it defends thy heart like steel,
  'Gainst thy despairing lover.
Alas! tho' it should ne'er relent,
  Nor Colin's care e'er move thee,
Yet till life's latest breath is spent,
  My Peggy, I must love thee.

FAIREST MAID! I OWN THY POWER.
ROBERT CRAWFORD.

Look where my dear Hamilla smiles,
  Hamilla! heavenly charmer;
See how wi' a' their arts and wiles
  The loves and graces arm her.
A blush dwells glowing on her cheeks,
  Fair feats of youthful pleasures,
There love in smiling language speaks,
  There spreads his rosy treasures.

O fairest maid! I own thy power,
  I gaze, I sigh, and languish,
Yet ever, ever will adore,
  And triumph in my anguish.
But ease, O charmer! ease my care,
  And let my torments move thee;
As thou art fairest of the fair.
  So I the dearest love thee.

ONE DAY I HEARD MARY SAY.
ROBERT CRAWFORD.

One day I heard Mary say,
  How shall I leave thee?
Stay, dearest Adonis, stay;
  Why wilt thou grieve me?
Alas! my fond heart will break,
  If thou should leave me:
I'll live and die for thy sake,
  Yet never leave thee.

Say, lovely Adonis, say,
  Has Mary deceived thee?
Did o'er her young heart betray
  New love, that has grieved thee?
My constant mind ne'er shall stray;
  Thou may believe me.
I'll love thee, lad, night and day,
  And never leave thee.

Adonis, my charming youth,
  What can relieve thee?
Can Mary thy anguish soothe?
  This breast shall receive thee.
My passion can ne'er decay,
  Never deceive thee;
Delight shall drive pain away,
  Pleasure revive thee.

But leave thee, leave thee, lad,
  How shall I leave thee?
Oh! that thought makes me sad;
  I'll never leave thee!
Where would my Adonis fly?
  Why does he grieve me?
Alas! my poor heart would die,
  If I should leave thee.

DOWN THE BURN.
ROBERT CRAWFORD.

The third stanza is given as altered by Burns.

When trees did bud, and fields were green,
  And broom bloom'd fair to see;
When Mary was complete fifteen,
  And love laugh'd in her e'e;
Blythe Davie's blinks her heart did move
  To speak her mind thus free;
Gang down the burn, Davie, love,
  And I will follow thee.

Now Davie did each lad surpass
  That dwelt on this burnside;
And Mary was the bonniest lass,
  Just meet to be a bride:
Her cheeks were rosie, red and white;
  Her een were bonnie blue;
Her looks were like Aurora bright,
  Her lips like dropping dew.

As down the burn they took their way,
  And through the flow'ry dale;
His cheek to hers he aft did lay,
  And love was aye the tale.
With, Mary, when shall we return,
  Sic pleasure to renew?
Quoth Mary, Love, I like the burn,
  And aye will follow you.

UNGRATEFUL NANNY.

LORD BINNING,

ELDEST son of Thomas—sixth Earl of Haddington—was born in the year 1696, and died at Naples in 1732.

DID ever swain a nymph adore
  As I ungrateful Nannie do?
Was ever shepherd's heart so sore?
  Was ever broken heart so true?
My cheeks are swell'd with tears; but she
Has never shed a tear for me.

If Nannie call'd, did Robin stay,
  Or linger when she bade me run?
She only had a word to say,
  And all she ask'd was quickly done.
I always thought on her; but she
Would ne'er bestow a thought on me.

To let her cows my clover taste,
  Have I not rose by break of day?
When did her heifers ever fast,
  If Robin in his yard had hay?
Though to my fields they welcome were,
I never welcome was to her.

If Nannie ever lost a sheep,
  I cheerfully did give her two;
Did not her lambs in safety sleep
  Within my folds, in frost and snow?
Have they not there from cold been free?
But Nannie still is cold to me.

Whene'er I climb'd our orchard trees,
  The ripest fruit was kept for Nan:
Oh, how these hands that drown'd her bees
  Were stung! I'll ne'er forget the pain:
Sweet were the combs as sweet could be;
But Nannie ne'er look'd sweet on me.

If Nannie to the well did come,
  'Twas I that did her pitchers fill;
Full as they were, I brought them home;
  Her corn I carried to the mill:
My back did bear her sacks: but she
Could never bear the sight o' me.

To Nannie's poultry oats I gave;
  I'm sure they always had the best;
Within this week her pigeons have
  Eat up a peck of peas at least.
Her little pigeons kiss; but she
Would never take a kiss from me.

Must Robin always Nannie woo?
  And Nannie still on Robin frown?
Alas, poor wretch! what shall I do,
  If Nannie does not love me soon?
If no relief to me she'll bring,
I'll hang me in her apron string.

LUCKY NANCY.

HON. DUNCAN FORBES,

LORD PRESIDENT of the Court of Session, died 1747. An adaptation of an earlier song. It first appears in Ramsay's TEA TABLE MISCELLANY (marked as an old song with additions), where it is given to the tune of Dainty Davie.

While fops, in saft Italian verse,
Ilk fair ane's een and breist rehearse
While sangs abound, and wit is scarce,
  These lines I have indited.

But neither darts nor arrows, here,
Venus nor Cupid, shall appear;
Although with these fine sounds, I swear,
  The maidens are delighted.
    I was aye telling you,
      Lucky Nancy, Lucky Nancy,
    Auld springs wad ding the new,
      But ye wad never trow me.

Nor snaw with crimson will I mix,
To spread upon my lassie's cheeks;
And syne the unmeaning name prefix,
  Miranda, Cloe, Phillis;
I'll fetch nae simile frae Jove,
My height of ecstasy to prove,
Nor sighing—thus—present my love
  With roses eek and lilies.

But, stay—I had amaist forgot
My mistress, and my sang to boot,
And that's an unco faut, I wot;
  But, Nancy, 'tis nae matter:
Ye see I clink my verse wi' rhyme,
And ken ye that atones the crime;
Forbye, how sweet my numbers chime,
  And glide away like water!

Now ken, my reverend sonsy fair,
Thy runkled cheeks, and lyart hair,
Thy half-shut een, and hoddling air,
  Are a' my passion's fuel;
Nae skyring gowk, my dear, can see,
Or love, or grace, or heaven in thee;
Yet thou hast charms enew for me;
  Then smile, and be na cruel.

  Leeze me on thy snawy pow,
    Lucky Nancy, Lucky Nancy;
  Dryest wood will eitheat low,
    And, Nancy, sae will ye now.

Troth, I have sung the sang to you,
Which ne'er anither bard wad do;
Hear, then, my charitable vow,
  Dear venerable Nancy:
But, if the world my passion wrang,
And say ye only live in sang,
Ken, I despise a slandering tongue,
  And sing to please my fancy
    Leeze me on, &c.

THE BRAES OF YARROW.
WILLIAM HAMILTON OF BANGOUR,

ONE of the most refined poets of his day, was born in 1704. He was the second son of James Hamilton, of Bangour. He was educated, it is supposed, at the University of Edinburgh, for the bar, but does not seem to have entered into practice. In fact, his last biographer, Mr. James Paterson, is unable often to speak very decisively on many points of the greatest importance, his connection with the Jacobite Rebellion of 1745, for example; he seems, however, if not to have carried arms in favour of the Young Chevalier, to have given all his influence and talent to his service; and, after the fatal battle of Culloden, had to skulk about the Highlands in disguise for awhile, till he escaped to France. He returned after the country had quieted down, in 1749, and in the following year, through the death of his elder brother, he succeeded to the Bangour estate. He died at Lyons, in 1754, his remains being brought to Scotland and interred in Holyrood Abbey.

His poetry, though modelled upon the smooth affected style of his own age, is often natural and pleasing: he nowhere shows a straining after ideas, nor attempts the sensational in description, but as has been remarked, "his thoughts are always elegant and just; his figures bold and animated; his colouring warm and true." His principal defect, as a song writer, lies in his perpetual introduction in his songs of the heroes and heroines of mythology. It is not possible to make an Englishman or Scotchman accustomed to John Bull and his Sister Peg, and Jocky and Jenny, feel at all sentimental about Venus, Cupid, Pallas, or Minerva.

A. "Busk ye, busk ye, my bonnie, bonnie bride!
    Busk ye, busk ye, my winsome marrow!
    Busk ye, busk ye, my bonnie, bonnie bride,
    And think nae mair of the braes of Yarrow."

B. "Where gat ye that bonnie, bonnie bride?
    Where gat ye that winsome marrow?"
A. "I gat her whare I daurna weel be seen,
    Puing the birks on the braes of Yarrow.

    Weip not, weip not, my bonnie, bonnie bride,
    Weip not, weip not, my winsome marrow!
    Nor let thy heart lament to loive
    Pu'ing the birks on the braes of Yarrow."

B. "Why does she weip, thy bonnie, bonnie bride?
    Why does she weip thy winsome marrow?
    And why daur ye nae mair weel be seen,
    Puing the birks on the braes of Yarrow?"

A. "Lang maun she weip, lang maun she, maun she weip,
    Lang maun she weip wi' dule and sorrow,
    And lang maun I nae mair weel be seen,
    Puing the birks on the braes of Yarrow.

    For she has tint her luver, luver deir,
    Her luver deir, the cause of sorrow;
    And I ha'e slain the comeliest swain
    That e'er pu'd birks on the braes of Yarrow.

    Why runs thy stream, O Yarrow, Yarrow, red?
    Why on thy braes heard the voice of sorrow?
    And why yon melancholious weids,
    Hung on the bonnie birks of Yarrow?

    What's yonder floats on the rueful, rueful flude?
    What's yonder floats?—Oh, dule and sorrow!
    'Tis he the comely swain I slew
    Upon the dulefu' braes of Yarrow.

    Wash, oh wash his wounds, his wounds in tears,
    His wounds in tears o' dule and sorrow;
    And wrap his limbs in mourning weids,
    And lay him on the banks of Yarrow!

Then build, then build, ye sisters, sisters, sad,
  Ye sisters sad, his tomb wi' sorrow;
And welp around in waeful wise,
  His hapless fate on the braes of Yarrow!

Curse ye, curse ye, his useless, useless shield,
  The arm that wrocht the deed of sorrow,
The fatal speir that pierced his briest,
  His comely briest on the braes of Yarrow!

Did I not warn thee not to, not to love,
  And warn from fight? But, to my sorrow,
Too rashly bold, a stronger arm thou met'st,
  Thou met'st, and fell on the braes of Yarrow!

Sweit smells the birk; green grows, green grows the grass;
  Yellow on Yarrow's braes the gowan;
Fair hangs the apple frae the rock;
  Sweit the wave of Yarrow flowen!

Flows Yarrow sweit? as sweit, as sweit flows Tweed;
  As green its grass; its gowan as yellow;
As sweit smells on its braes the birk;
  The apple from its rocks as mellow!

Fair was thy love, fair, fair, indeed, thy love!
  In flowery bands thou didst him fetter;
Though he was fair, and well beloved again,
  Than me he never loved thee better.

Busk ye, then, busk, my bonnie, bonnie bride!
  Busk ye, busk ye, my winsome marrow!
Busk ye, and lo'e me on the banks of Twoed,
  And think nae mair on the braes of Yarrow."

C. "How can I busk a bonnie, bonnie bride?
  How can I busk a winsome marrow?
How can I lo'e him on the banks o' Tweed,
  That slew my love on the braes of Yarrow?

Oh, Yarrow fields, may never, never rain,
  Nor dew thy tender blossoms cover!
For there was basely slain my love,
  My love, as he had not been a lover.

The boy put on his robes, his robes of green,
  His purple vest—'twas my ain sewing;
Ah, wretched me! I little, little kenned,
  He was, in these, to meet his ruin.

The boy took out his milk-white, milk-white steed,
  Unmindful of my dule and sorrow:
But, ere the too-fa' of the night,
  He lay a corpse on the banks of Yarrow.

Much I rejoiced, that waefu', waefu' day;
  I sang, my voice the woods returning;
But, lang ere nicht, the spear was flown,
  That slew my love, and left me mourning.
What can my barbarous, barbarous father do,
  But with his cruel rage pursue me?
My luver's blude is on thy spear—
  How canst thou, barbarous man, then, woo me?

My happy sisters may be, may be proud,
  With cruel and ungentle scoffing—
May bid me seek, on Yarrow braes,
  My luver nailed in his coffin.
My brother Douglas may upbraid,
  And strive, with threat'ning words, to muve me;
My luver's blude is on thy spear—
  How canst thou ever bid me luve thee?

Yes, yes, prepare the bed, the bed of luve!
  With bridal-sheets my body cover!
Unbar, ye bridal-maids, the door!
  Let in th' expected husband-lover!
But who the expected husband, husband is?
  His hands, methinks, are bathed in slaughter!
Ah, me! what ghastly spectre's yon,
  Comes, in his pale shroud, bleeding, after?

Pale as he is, here lay him, lay him down;
  O lay his cold head on my pillow!
Take off, take off these bridal weids,
  And crown my careful head with willow.
Pale though thou art, yet best, yet best beloved,
  Oh, could my warmth to life restore thee!
Yet lie all night between my briests,—
  No youth lay ever there before thee!

Pale, pale, indeed, oh lovely, lovely youth,
  Forgive, forgive so foul a slaughter,
And lie all night between my briests,
  No youth shall ever lie there after!"

A. "Return, return, O mournful, mournful bride!
  Return and dry thy useless sorrow!
Thy luver heids nocht of thy sighs;
  He lies a corpse on the braes of Yarrow."

YE SHEPHERDS AND NYMPHS.
WILLIAM HAMILTON OF BANGOUR.

Ye shepherds and nymphs that adorn the gay plain,
Approach from your sports, and attend to my strain;
Amongst all your number a lover so true
Was ne'er so undone, with such bliss in his view.

Was ever a nymph so hard-hearted as mine?
She knows me sincere, and she sees how I pine;
She does not disdain me, nor frown in her wrath,
But calmly and mildly resigns me to death.

She calls me her friend, but her lover denies:
She smiles when I'm cheerful, but hears not my sighs,
A bosom so flinty, so gentle an air,
Inspires me with hope, and yet bids me despair!

I fall at her feet, and implore her with tears:
Her answer confounds, while her manner endears;
When softly she tells me to hope no relief,
My trembling lips bless her in spite of my grief.

By night, while I slumber, still haunted with care,
I start up in anguish, and sigh for the fair:
The fair sleeps in peace,—may she ever do so!
And only when dreaming imagine my woe.

Then gaze at a distance, nor farther aspire;
Nor think she should love whom she cannot admire:
Hush all thy complaining, and dying her slave,
Commend her to heaven, and thyself to the grave.

YE GODS! WAS STREPHON'S PICTURE BLEST?
WILLIAM HAMILTON OF BANGOUR.

Ye gods! was Strephon's picture blest
With the fair heaven of Chloe's breast?
Move softer, thou fond fluttering heart,
Oh gently throb,—too fierce thou art.
Tell me, thou brightest of thy kind,
For Strephon was the bliss design'd?
For Strephon's sake, dear charming maid,
Did'st thou prefer his wand'ring shade?

And thou, blest shade, that sweetly art
Lodged so near my Chloe's heart,
For me the tender hour improve,
And softly tell how dear I love.
Ungrateful thing! It scorns to hear
Its wretched master's ardent pray'r,
Engrossing all that beauteous heaven,
That Chloe, lavish maid, has given.

I cannot blame thee : were I lord
Of all the wealth those breasts afford,
I'd be a miser too, nor give
An alms to keep a god alive.
Oh smile not thus, my lovely fair,
On these cold looks, that lifeless air,
Prize him whose bosom glows with fire,
With eager love and soft desire.

'Tis true thy charms, O powerful maid,
To life can bring the silent shade :
Thou canst surpass the painter's art,
And real warmth and flames impart.
But oh ! it ne'er can love like me,
I've ever lov'd, and lov'd but thee :
Then, charmer, grant my fond request,
Say thou canst love, and make me blest.

WHY HANGS THAT CLOUD UPON THY BROW?
WILLIAM HAMILTON OF BANGOUR.

Why hangs that cloud upon thy brow,
  That beauteous heav'n erewhile serene?
Whence do these storms and tempests blow?
  Or what this gust of passion mean?
And must then mankind lose that light
  Which in thine eyes was wont to shine,
And lie obscur'd in endless night,
  For each poor silly speech of mine?

Dear child, how could I wrong thy name?
  Thy form so fair and faultless stands,
That could ill tongues abuse thy fame,
  Thy beauty would make large amends !
Or if I durst profanely try
  Thy beauty's powerful charms t' upbraid,
Thy virtue well might give the lie,
  Nor call thy beauty to its aid.

For Venus ev'ry heart t' ensnare,
  With all her charms has deck'd thy face,
And Pallas with unusual care,
  Bids wisdom heighten every grace.
Who can the double pain endure?
  Or who must not resign the field
To thee, celestial maid, secure
  With Cupid's bow and Pallas' shield?

If then to thee such power is giv'n,
  Let not a wretch in torment live,
But smile, and learn to copy heav'n,
  Since we must sin ere it forgive.
Yet pitying heav'n not only does
  Forgive th' offender and th' offence,
But even itself appeas'd bestows
  As the reward of penitence.

AH! THE POOR SHEPHERD'S MOURNFUL FATE.
WILLIAM HAMILTON OF BANGOUR.

Ah, the poor shepherd's mournful fate,
  When doom'd to love and doom'd to languish,
To bear the scornful fair one's hate,
  Nor dare disclose his anguish!
Yet eager looks and dying sighs
  My secret soul discover,
While rapture, trembling through mine eyes,
  Reveals how much I love her.
The tender glance, the reddening cheek,
  O'erspread with rising blushes,
A thousand various ways they speak
  A thousand various wishes.

For, oh! that form so heavenly fair,
  Those languid eyes so sweetly smiling,
That artless blush and modest air
  So fatally beguiling;
Thy every look, and every grace,
  So charm, whene'er I view thee,
Till death o'ertake me in the chase
  Still will my hopes pursue thee.
Then, when my tedious hours are past,
  Be this last blessing given,
Low at thy feet to breathe my last,
  And die in sight of heaven.

BROOM OF COWDENKNOWS.

TEA TABLE MISCELLANY, where it is printed with the initials, S. R., supposed by Mr. Chambers and others to refer to some personage of Ramsay's own time, and to whose position the authorship of a song would have been derogatory. The second set is by Crawford, a song writer, whose other productions are given in their proper place. The first set is undoubtedly founded upon an older song,* and the tune, which is certainly old, is

---

* A song, or ballad, "The Broom of the Cowdenknowes"—probably of a very early date—is printed in "Scott's Minstrelsy of the Scottish Border."

surmised to be representative of the "Brume, Brume on Hil," mentioned in the "Complaynt of Scotland," 1548. Mr. Chappell, as usual, claims it as of English origin.

The Cowdenknows are two hills at Lauderdale, Berwickshire.

How blythe ilk morn was I to see
  The swain come o'er the hill!
He skipt the burn, and flew to me,
  I met him wi' good will.

  O, the broom, the bonnie, bonnie broom,
    The broom of the Cowdenknows!
  I wish I were wi' my dear swain,
    Wi' his pipe, and my ewes.

I neither wanted ewe nor lamb,
  While his flocks near me lay;
He gather'd in my sheep at night,
  And cheer'd me a' the day,
    O, the broom, &c.

He tuned his pipe and reed sae sweet,
  The birds stood list'ning by;
Ev'n the dull cattle stood and gazed,
  Charm'd wi' his melody.
    O, the broom, &c.

While thus we spent our time by turns,
  Betwixt our flocks and play,
I envied not the fairest dame,
  Though e'er so rich and gay.
    O, the broom, &c.

Hard fate! that I should banish'd be,
  Gang heavily, and mourn,
Because I loved the kindest swain
  That ever yet was born.
    O, the broom, &c.

He did oblige me every hour;
  Could I but faithfu' be?
He staw my heart; could I refuse
  Whate'er he ask'd of me?
    O, the broom, &c.

My doggie, and my little kit,
  That held my wee soup whey,
My plaidie, broach, and crooked stick,
  Maun now lie useless by.
    O, the broom, &c.

Adieu, ye Cowdenknows, adieu!
Farewell a' pleasures there!
Ye gods, restore me to my swain,
It's a' I crave or care.
 O, the broom, &c.

SECOND SET.

When summer comes, the swains on Tweed
Sing their successful loves,
Around the ewes and lambkins feed,
And music fills the groves.

But my loved song is then the broom
So fair on Cowdenknows;
For sure, so sweet, so soft a bloom,
Elsewhere there never grows.

There Colin tuned his oaten reed,
And won my yielding heart;
No shepherd e'er that dwelt on Tweed,
Could play with half such art.

He sung of Tay, of Forth, and Clyde,
The hills and dales all round,
Of Leader-haughs, and Leader-side,
Oh! how I bless'd the sound.

Yet more delightful is the broom
So fair on Cowdenknows;
For sure, so fresh, so bright a bloom,
Elsewhere there never grows.

Not Tiviot braes, so green and gay,
May with this broom compare;
Not Yarrow banks in flowery May,
Nor the bush aboon Traquair.

More pleasing far are Cowdenknows,
My peaceful happy home,
Where I was wont to milk my ewes,
At e'en amang the broom.

Ye powers that haunt the woods and plains
Where Tweed and Tiviot flows,
Convey me to the best of swains,
And my loved Cowdenknows.

WILLIE'S RARE.

Tea Table Miscellany, where it is printed without any mark.

Willie's rare, and Willie's fair,
  And Willie's wondrous bonny,
And Willie hecht to marry me,
  Gin e'er he married ony.

Yestreen I made my bed fu' braid,
  This night I'll make it narrow;
For a' the live-lang winter-night
  I'll ly twin'd o' my marrow.

O came you by yon water side?
  Pu'd you the rose or lily?
Or came you by yon meadow green?
  Or saw ye my sweet Willie?

She sought him east, she sought him west,
  She sought him braid and narrow;
Syne in the cleaving of a craig,
  She found him drown'd in Yarrow.

TARRY WOO.

Tea Table Miscellany, probably written about that time on the remains of an older song. Mr. Chambers states that Sir Walter Scott, when at the Social Board, used to meet his turn for a song by giving a verse of "Tarry Woo." The tune is old, and the well-known air Lewie Gordon is adapted from it.

Tarry woo, tarry woo,
  Tarry woo is ill to spin;
Card it weil, card it weil,
  Card it weil, ere ye begin.
When it's cardit, row'd, and spun,
Then the work is haflins done;
But, when woven, dress'd, and clean,
It may be cleadin' for a queen.

Sing my bonnie harmless sheep,
That feed upon the mountains steep,
Bleating sweetly, as ye go
Through the winter's frost and snow.
Hart, and hynd, and fallow-deer,
No by half sae useful are;
Frae kings, to him that hauds the plou',
All are obliged to tarry woo.

Up, ye shepherds, dance and skip;
Ower the hills and valleys trip;
Sing up the praise of tarry woo;
Sing the flocks that bear it too:

Harmless creatures, without blame,
That clead the back, and cram the wame;
Keep us warm and hearty fou—
Leeze me on the tarry woo.

How happy is a shepherd's life,
Far frae courts and free of strife!
While the gimmers bleat and bae,
And the lambkins answer mae;
No such music to his ear!
Of thief or fox he has no fear:
Sturdy kent, and collie true,
Weil defend the tarry woo.

He lives content, and envies none:
Not even a monarch on his throne,
Though he the royal sceptre sways,
Has such pleasant holidays.
Who'd be king, can only tell,
When a shepherd sings sae well?
Sings sae well, and pays his due
With honest heart and tarry woo.

I WAS ONCE A WEEL-TOCHER'D LASS.

TEA TABLE MISCELLANY.

I was once a weel-tocher'd lass,
  My mither left dollars to me;
But now I'm brought to a poor pass,
  My step-dame has gart them a' flee.
My father, he's aften frae hame,
  And she plays the deil with his gear;
She neither has lawtith nor shame,
  And keeps the haill house in a steer.

She's barmy-faced, thriftless, and bauld,
  And gars me aft fret and repine;
While hungry, half-naked, and cauld,
  I see her destroy what's mine.
But soon I might hope a revenge,
  And soon of my sorrows be free;
My poortith to plenty wad change,
  If she were hung up on a tree.

Quoth Ringan, wha lang time had loo'd
  This bonnie lass tenderlie,
I'll tak' thee, sweet May, in thy snood,
  Gif thou wilt gae hame with me.

'Tis only yoursel' that I want;
  Your kindness is better to me
Than a' that your stepmother, scant
  Of grace, now has taken frae thee.
I'm but a young farmer, it's true,
  And ye are the sprout of a laird;
But I have milk-cattle enow,
  And ruth of good rucks in my yard.
Ye shall have naething to fash ye,
  Sax servants shall jouk to thee:
Then kilt up thy coats, my lassie,
  And gae thy ways hame with me.

The maiden her reason employ'd,
  Not thinking the offer amiss,
Consented, while Ringan, o'erjoy'd,
  Received her with mony a kiss.
And now she sits blythely singin',
  And joking her drunken stepdame,
Delighted with her dear Ringan,
  That makes her goodwife at hame.

ANDRO WI' HIS CUTTY GUN.

Tea Table Miscellany, where it is printed without any mark.

Blythe, blythe, and merry was she,
  Blythe was she but and ben;
And weel she loo'd a Hawick gill,
  And leugh to see a tappit hen.

She took me in, and set me down,
  And hecht to keep me lawing-free;
But, cunning carline that she was,
  She gart me birl my bawbee.

We loo'd the liquor well enough;
  But waes my heart my cash was done,
Before that I had quench'd my drouth,
  And laith I was to pawn my shoon.

When we had three times toom'd our stoup,
  And the neist chappin new begun,
Wha started in, to heeze our hope,
  But Andro wi' his cutty gun.

The carline brought her kebbuck ben,
  With girdle-cakes weel toasted brown,
Weel does the canny kimmer ken
  They gar the swats gae glibber down.

We ca'd the bicker aft about;
　Till dawning we ne'er jeed our bum,
And aye the cleanest drinker out,
　Was Andro wi' his cutty gun.
He did like ony mavis sing,
　And as I in his oxter sat,
He ca'd me aye his bonnie thing,
　And mony a sappy kiss I gat.
I ha'e been east, I ha'e been west,
　I ha'e been far ayont the sun;
But the blythest lad that e'er I saw,
　Was Andro wi' his cutty gun.

WHEN SPRING TIME RETURNS.
DR. A. WEBSTER,

ONE of the ministers of Edinburgh. He was born at Edinburgh in 1707, and died there in 1784.

The spring-time returns, and clothes the green plains,
　And Alloa shines more cheerful and gay;
The lark tunes his throat, and the neighbouring swains,
　Sing merrily round me wherever I stray:
But Sandy nae mair returns to my view;
　Nae spring-time me cheers, nae music can charm;
He's gane! and, I fear me, for ever: adieu!
　Adieu every pleasure this bosom can warm!

O Alloa house! how much art thou chang'd!
　How silent, how dull to me is each grove!
Alane I here wander where once we both rang'd,
　Alas! where to please me my Sandy ance strove!
Here, Sandy, I heard the tales that you tauld,
　Here list'ned too fond whenever you sung;
Am I grown less fair then, that you are turn'd cauld?
　Or, foolish, believ'd a false flattering tongue?

So spoke the fair maid, when sorrow's keen pain,
　And shame, her last fault'ring accents supprest;
For fate, at that moment, brought back her dear swain,
　Who heard, and with rapture his Nelly addrest:
My Nelly! my fair, I come; O my love!
　Nae power shall thee tear again from my arms,
And, Nelly! nae mair thy fond shepherd reprove,
　Who knows thy fair worth, and adores a' thy charms.

She heard; and new joy shot thro' her saft frame;
　And will you, my love! be true? she replied:
And live I to meet my fond shepherd the same?
　Or dream I that Sandy will make me his bride?

O Nelly! I live to find thee still kind:
　Still true to thy swain, and lovely as true:
Then adieu to a' sorrow; what soul is so blind,
　As not to live happy for ever with you?

OH! HOW COULD I VENTURE.
DR. A. WEBSTER.

Oh, how could I venture to love one like thee,
And you not despise a poor conquest like me,
On lords, thy admirers, could look wi' disdain,
And knew I was naething, yet pitied my pain?
You said, while they teased you with nonsense and dress,
When real the passion, the vanity's less;
You saw through that silence which others despise,
And, while beaux were a-talking, read love in my eyes.

Oh, how shall I fauld thee, and kiss a' thy charms,
Till, fainting wi' pleasure, I die in your arms;
Through all the wild transports of ecstasy tost,
Till, sinking together, together we're lost!
Oh, where is the maid that like thee ne'er can cloy,
Whose wit can enliven each doll pause of joy;
And when the short raptures are all at an end,
From beautiful mistress turn sensible friend?

In vain do I praise thee, or strive to reveal,
(Too nice for expression,) what only we feel:
In a' that ye do, in each look and each mien,
The graces in waiting adorn you unseen.
When I see you, I love you; when hearing, adore;
I wonder and think you a woman no more:
Till, mad wi' admiring, I canna contain,
And, kissing your lips, you turn woman again.

With thee in my bosom how can I despair?
I'll gaze on thy beauties, and look awa' care;
I'll ask thy advice, when with troubles opprest,
Which never displeases, but always is best.
In all that I write I'll thy judgment require;
Thy wit shall correct what thy charms did inspire:
I'll kiss thee and press thee till youth is all o'er,
And then live in friendship, when passion's no more.

I'VE SEEN THE SMILING.
MRS. COCKBURN,

DAUGHTER of Robert Rutherford of Fernylee, in Selkirkshire. She was born about 1712, and married in 1731, to Patrick Cockburn, a son of Cockburn of Ormiston, Lord Justice Clerk of Scotland. She survived her husband more than forty years. Sir Walter Scott has given us a very genial description of Mrs. Cockburn, as he saw her and heard about her in her later years. "Mrs. Cockburn," says he, "was one of those persons whose talents for conversation made a stronger impression on her contemporaries than her writings can be expected to produce. In person and features she somewhat resembled Queen Elizabeth, but the nose was rather more aquiline. She was proud of her auburn hair, which remained unbleached by time, even when she was upwards of eighty years old. She maintained the rank in the society of Edinburgh which French women of talent usually do in that of Paris, and her little parlour used to assemble a very distinguished and accomplished circle, among whom David Hume, John Home, Lord Monboddo, and many other men of name were frequently to be found." This song (referring to commercial instead of warlike disasters among the men of the forest) appears in the LARK, 1765, and in HERD'S COLLECTION,—from which collection we take the copy here printed.

> I'VE seen the smiling
> Of Fortune beguiling;
> I've felt all its favours, and found its decay:
> Sweet was its blessing,
> Kind its caressing;
> But now 'tis fled—fled fur away.
>
> I've seen the forest
> Adorned the foremost
> With flowers of the fairest, most pleasant and gay;
> Sae bonnie was their blooming!
> Their scent the air perfuming!
> But now they are wither'd and weeded away.
>
> I've seen the morning
> With gold the hills adorning,
> And loud tempest storming before the mid-day.
> I've seen Tweed's silver streams,
> Shining in the sunny beams,
> Grow drumly and dark as he row'd on his way.
>
> Oh, fickle Fortune,
> Why this cruel sporting?
> Oh, why still perplex us, poor sons of a day?
> Nae mair your smiles can cheer me,
> Nae mair your frowns can fear me;
> For the Flowers of the Forest are a' wede away.

THE BIRKS OF INVERMAY.
DAVID MALLET,
or MALLOCH, a favourite poet of his time, born 1714; died 1765.

The smiling morn, the breathing spring,
Invite the tunefu' birds to sing;
And, while they warble from the spray,
Love melts the universal lay.
Let us, Amanda, timely wise,
Like them, improve the hour that flies;
And in soft raptures waste the day,
Among the birks of Invermay.

For soon the winter of the year,
And age, life's winter, will appear;
At this thy living bloom will fade,
As that will strip the verdant shade.
Our taste of pleasure then is o'er,
The feathered songsters are no more;
And when they drop, and we decay,
Adieu the birks of Invermay!

THE LAWLANDS OF HOLLAND.

Given from the copy in Johnson's Museum, omitting the spurious third verse there given, and adding the last which was omitted. Mr. Stenhouse was informed that it was composed by a young widow in Galloway, whose husband was drowned on a voyage to Holland. There is a fragment of the song given in Herd's Collection, and we may consider it to belong to the first half of the eighteenth century. The air was always very popular, and on it is founded Marshall's tune "Miss Admiral Gordon's Strathspey," to which Burns's beautiful song "Of a' the airts the win' can blaw" was written.

The luve that I had chosen,
I'll therewith be content,
The saut sea will be frozen
Before that I repent;
Repent it will I never
Until the day I dee,
Tho' the lawlands o' Holland
Ha'e twined my luve and me.

My luve lies in the salt sea,
And I am on the side,
Enough to break a young thing's heart
Wha lately was a bride;
Wha lately was a bonnie bride,
And pleasure in her e'e;
But the lawlands o' Holland
Ha'e twined my luve and me.

My luve he built a bonnie ship,
　And sent her to the sea,
Wi' seven score brave mariners
　To bear her companie;
Threescore gaed to the bottom,
　And threescore died at sea,
And the lawlands o' Holland
　Ha'e twined my luve and me.
My luve has built anither ship,
　And sent her to the main,
He had but twenty mariners,
　And a' to bring her hame;
The stormy clouds did roar again,
　The raging waves did rout,
And my luve, and his bonnie ship,
　Turn'd widdershins about!
There shall nae mantle cross my back,
　Nae comb come in my hair,
Neither shall coal or candle light
　Shine in my bowit mair;
Nor shall I ha'e anither luve,
　Until the day I dee,
I never lo'ed a luve but ane,
　And he's drown'd in the sea.
O, haud your tongue, my daughter dear,
　Be still and be content,
There are mair lads in Galloway,
　Ye need nae sair lament.
O! there is nane in Galloway,
　There 's nane at a' for me,
For I never lov'd a lad but ane,
　And he 's drown'd in the sea.

ROSLIN CASTLE.

HERD'S COLLECTION—probably written shortly after the time of Ramsay, as the stilted style of the love-lorn maid's address smacks of the affected manner then in vogue. The air, which is very beautiful, was published in "McGibbon's Collection of Scots Tunes."

From Roslin castle's echoing walls
Resound my shepherd's ardent calls,
My Colin bids me come away,
And love demands I should obey.
His melting strain and tuneful lay,
So much the charms of love display,
I yield—nor longer can refrain
To own my love, and bless my swain.

No longer can my heart conceal
The painful pleasing flame I feel,
My soul retorts the am'rous strain,
And echoes back in love again;
Where lurks my songster? from what grove
Does Colin pour his notes of love?
O bring me to the happy bow'r,
Where mutual love may bliss secure.

Ye vocal hills that catch the song,
Repeating, as it flies along,
To Colin's ear my strain convey,
And say, I haste to come away.
Ye zephyrs soft that fan the gale,
Waft to my love the soothing tale;
In whispers all my soul express,
And tell, I haste his arms to bless.

MY LOVE WAS ONCE A BONNIE LAD.

SUPPOSED to have been written about the middle of the eighteenth century, but by whom it is impossible to say. The air, the well-known "Flowers of Edinburgh," appears in "Oswald's Caledonian Pocket Companion," 1742, but is probably of a much earlier date.

My love was once a bonnie lad,
  He was the flower of a' his kin,
The absence of his bonnie face
  Has rent my tender heart in twain.
I day or night find no delight;
  In silent tears I still complain;
And exclaim 'gainst those my rival foes,
  That ha'e ta'en from me my darling swain.

Despair and anguish fill my breast,
  Since I have lost my blooming rose;
I sigh and moan while others rest;
  His absence yields me no repose.
To seek my love I'll range and rove,
  Through every grove and distant plain;
Thus I'll ne'er cease, but spend my days,
  To hear tidings from my darling swain.

There's naething strange in nature's change,
  Since parents show such cruelty;
They caused my love from me to range,
  And know not to what destiny.
The pretty kids and tender lambs
  May cease to sport upon the plain;
But I'll mourn and lament in deep discontent
  For the absence of my darling swain.

Kind Neptune, let me thee entreat,
  To send a fair and pleasant gale;
Ye dolphins sweet, upon me wait,
  And convey me upon your tail;
Heaven bless my voyage with success,
  While crossing of the raging main,
And send me safe o'er to a distant shore,
  To meet my lovely darling swain.

All joy and mirth at our return
  Shall then abound from Tweed to Tay;
The bells shall ring and sweet birds sing,
  To grace and crown our nuptial day.
Thus bless'd wi' charms in my love's arms,
  My heart once more I will regain;
Then I'll range no more to a distant shore,
  But in love will enjoy my darling swain.

ARGYLL IS MY NAME.

SAID to have been written by John, Duke of Argyll (1678-1743), by one tradition; by another, the authorship is given to the celebrated James Boswell. Whoever may have written the song, and we cannot think that either of the parties was likely to have written it, there can be no doubt as to its referring to the Duke of Argyll, one of the principal characters in the "Heart of Midlothian." Tune—"Bannocks o' barley meal."

ARGYLL is my name, and you may think it strange,
To live at a court, yet never to change;
A' falsehood and flattery I do disdain,
In my secret thoughts nae guile does remain.
My king and my country's foes I have faced,
In city or battle I ne'er was disgraced;
I do every thing for my country's weal,
And feast upon bannocks o' barley meal.

Adieu to the courtie of London town,
For to my ain countrie I will gang down;
At the sight of Kirkaldy ance again,
I'll cock up my bonnet, and march amain.
O, the muckle deil tak' a' your noise and strife:
I'm fully resolved for a country life,
Where a' the braw lasses, wha ken me weel,
Will feed me wi' bannocks o' barley meal.

I will quickly lay down my sword and my gun,
And put my blue bonnet and my plaidie on;
With my silk tartan hose, and leather-heel'd shoon,
And then I will look like a sprightly loon.

And when I'm sae dress'd frae tap to tae,
To meet my dear Maggie I vow I will gae,
Wi' target and hanger hung down to my heel;
And I'll feast upon bannocks o' barley meal.

I'll buy a rich garment to gi'e to my dear,
A ribbon o' green for Maggie to wear;
And mony thing brawer than that I declare,
Gin she will gang wi' me to Paisley fair.
And when we are married, I'll keep her a cow,
And Maggie will milk when I gae to plow;
We'll live a' the winter on beef and lang kail,
And feast upon bannocks o' barley meal.

Gin Maggie should chance to bring me a son,
He'll fight for his king, as his daddy has done;
He'll hie him to Flanders, some breeding to learn,
And then hame to Scotland, and get him a farm.
And there we will live by our industry,
And wha'll be sae happy as Maggie and me?
We'll a' grow as fat as a Norway seal,
Wi' our feasting on bannocks o' barley meal.

Then fare ye weel, citizens, noisy men,
Wha jolt in your coaches to Drury Lane;
Ye bucks o' Bear-garden, I bid you adieu,
For drinking and swearing, I leave it to you.
I'm fairly resolved for a country life,
And nae langer will live in hurry and strife;
I'll aff to the Highlands as hard's I can reel,
And whang at the bannocks o' barley meal.

IN THE GARB OF OLD GAUL.
SIR H. ERSKINE, BART., M.P.

Born about 1720. Son of Sir John Erskine, of Alva, Bart. He became commander of the "Royal Scots" Regiment in 1762, and died at York in 1765.

The tune was composed by General Reid, Colonel of the 88th Regiment, whose love for music led him to found the much-abused Chair of Music in the University of Edinburgh.

In the garb of old Gaul, with the fire of old Rome,
From the heath-cover'd mountains of Scotia we come;
Where the Romans endeavour'd our country to gain,
But our ancestors fought, and they fought not in vain.

Such is our love of liberty, our country, and our laws,
That, like our ancestors of old, we'll stand in freedom's cause:
We'll bravely fight, like heroes bold, for honour and applause,
And defy the French, with all their art, to alter our laws.

No effeminate customs our sinews unbrace;
No luxurious tables enervate our race;
Our loud sounding pipe breathes the true martial strain,
And our hearts still the old Scottish valour retain.
    Such is our love, &c.

We're tall as the oak on the mount of the vale,
And swift as the roe which the hound doth assail;
As the full moon in autumn our shields do appear;
Ev'n Minerva would dread to encounter our spear.
    Such is our love, &c.

As a storm in the ocean, when Boreas blows,
So are we enrag'd when we rush on our foes;
We sons of the mountains tremendous as rocks,
Dash the force of our foes with our thundering strokes.
    Such is our love, &c.

Quebec and Cape Breton, the pride of old France,
In their numbers fondly boasted, till we did advance;
But when our claymores they saw us produce,
Their courage did fail, and they sued for a truce.
    Such is our love, &c.

In our realm may the fury of faction long cease,
May our councils be wise, and our commerce increase,
And in Scotia's cold climate may each of us find,
That our friends still prove true, and our beauties prove kind.

Then we'll defend our liberty, our country, and our laws,
And teach our late posterity to fight in freedom's cause;
That they, like their ancestors bold, for honour and applause,
May defy the French, with all their arts, to alter our laws.

CAULD KAIL IN ABERDEEN.

We give two versions here of this popular old song, the first appears in Herd's Collection, and is probably the oldest set of the words extant. We are unable to state the precise age of the second version, but it is mentioned by Burns as an old song.

I.

Cauld kail in Aberdeen,
    And castocks in Strathbogie,
But yet I fear they'll cook o'er soon,
    And never warm the cogie.
The lasses about Bogie gicht,
Their limbs they are sae clean and tight,
That if they were but girded right,
    They'll dance the reel o' Bogie.

K

Wow, Aberdeen, what did you mean,
  Sae young a maid to woo, sir?
I'm sure it was nae joke to her,
  Whate'er it was to you, sir.
For lasses now are no sae blate
But they ken auld folk's out o' date,
And better playfare can they get
  Than custocks in Strathbogie.

II.

There's cauld kail in Aberdeen,
  And custocks in Stra'bogie,
Where ilka lad maun ha'e his lass,
  But I maun ha'e my cogie.
    For I maun ha'e my cogie, sirs,
      I canna want my cogie;
    I widna gi'e my three-gir'd cog
      For a' the wives in Bogie.

Johnny Smith has got a wife
  Wha scrimps him o' his cogie:
But were she mine, upon my life,
  I'd dook her in a bogie.
    For I maun ha'e my cogie, sirs,
      I canna want my cogie;
    I wadna gi'e my three-gir'd cog
      For a' the wives in Bogie.

Twa three todlin' weans they ha'e,
  The pride o' a' Stra'bogie;
Whene'er the totums cry for meat,
  She curses aye his cogie;
    Crying, Wae betide the three-gir'd cog!
      Oh, wae betide the cogie!
    It does mair skaith than a' the ills
      That happen in Stra'bogie.

She fand him once at Willie Sharp's;
  And, what the maist did laugh at,
She brak the bicker, spilt the drink,
  And tightly gouff'd his baffet,
    Crying, Wae betide the three-gir'd cog!
      Oh, wae betide the cogie,
    It does mair skaith than a' the ills
      That happen in Stra'bogie.

Yet here's to ilka honest soul
Wha'll drink wi' me a cogie,
And for ilk silly whinging fool,
We'll dook him in a bogie.
For I maun ha'e my cogie, sirs,
I canna want my cogie;
I wadna gi'e my three gir'd cog
For a' the queans in Bogie.

LOGIE O' BUCHAN.
DISPUTED.

LADY Ann Barnard (authoress of Auld Robin Gray), and George Halket, of Aberdeen (author of "Whirry, Whigs, awa, &c.), have been given as the authors of this favourite song; and from the evidence which has been brought forward we think the claims of Halket must be admitted. He was schoolmaster at Rathen, in Aberdeenshire, and Mr. Peter Buchan considers the song to have been written by him in 1736. Halket was a Jacobite of the most intense description, and the sum of one hundred pounds was offered for his arrest by the Duke of Cumberland, in consequence of a pasquil he had written on George II. Halket died in 1756. The song first appeared in Johnson's Museum, along with its tune.

O Logie o' Buchan, O Logie the laird,
They ha'e ta'en awa' Jamie, that delved in the yard,
Wha play'd on the pipe, and the viol sae sma';
They ha'e ta'en awa' Jamie, the flower o' them a'.
    He said, Think na lang lassie, tho' I gang awa';
    He said, Think na lang lassie, tho' I gang awa';
    The simmer is come, and the winter's awa',
    And I'll come and see thee in spite o' them a'.

Tho' Sandy has owsen, and siller, and kye;
A house and a hadden, and a' things forbye:
Yet I'd tak' mine ain lad, wi' his staff in his hand,
Before I'd ha'e him, wi' the houses and land.
    He said, Think nao lang, &c.

My daddie looks sulky, my minnie looks sour,
They frown upon Jamie because he is poor:
But daddie and minnie altho' that they be,
There's nane o' them a' like my Jamie to me.
    He said, Think nao lang, &c.

I sit on my creepie, I spin at my wheel,
And think on my Jamie that lo'es me sae weel;
He had but ae saxpence, he brak it in twa,
And gi'ed me the hauf o't when he gade awa'.
    Then haste ye back, Jamie, and bide na awn',
    Then haste ye back, Jamie, and bide na awa',
    The simmer is come, and the winter's awa',
    And ye'll come and see me in spite o' them a'.

HEY BONNIE LASSIE, BLINK OVER THE BURN.
REV. JAMES HONEYMAN.

"THIS popular song has hitherto appeared in all the collections as an anonymous production, but we have the authority of a highly esteemed correspondent for saying that it was written by the Rev. James Honeyman, minister of Kinneff, in Kincardineshire, who died at an advanced age, in or about the year 1779. Mr. Honeyman wrote other poetical pieces, but none of them came before the public except this song."—*Blackie's Book of Scottish Song.*

HIE, bonnie lassie, blink over the burn,
And if your sheep wander I'll gi'o them a turn;
Sae happy as we'll be on yonder green shade,
If ye'll be my dawtie, and sit in my plaid.

A yowe and twa lammies are a' my haill stock,
But I'll sell a lammie out of my wee flock,
To buy the a head-piece, sae bonnie and braid,
If ye'll be my dawtie, and sit in my plaid.

I ha'e a wee whittle made me a trout creel,
And, oh, that wee whittle I likit it weel;
But I'll gi'e't to my lassie, and mair if I had,
If she'll be my dawtie, and sit in my plaid.

I ha'e little silver, but ae hauf-year's fee,
But if ye will tak' it, I'll gi'e't a' to thee;
And then we'll be married, and lie in ae bed,
If ye'll be my dawtie, and sit in my plaid.

TA HIGHLAND SHENTLEMAN.
DOUGALD GRAHAM,

WAS born about the year 1724. He was long the public bellman of Glasgow and wrote a history of the Rebellion of 1745 in Verse, a work of little merit, but highly prized by the book collector on account of its scarcity. Dougald died in 1779. The song appears in Herd's Collection, 1776, where the old air Clout the Candron is named as its tune. We do not know what authority there is for assigning the song to Graham.

HERSELL pe Highland shentleman,
Pe auld as Pothwell Prig, man;
And many alterations seen
Amang te Lawland Whig, man.
Fa a dra, diddle diddle dee, &c.

First when she to te Lawlands cam'
Nainsell was driving cows, man,
There was nae laws about him's nerse,
About te precks or trews, man.

Nainsell did wear te philabeg,
    Te plaid prick'd on her shouder;
Te gude claymore hung py her pelt;
    Her pistol sharged with powder.

But for whereas these cursed preeks,
    Wherewith her legs pe lockit;
Ohon that ere she saw the day!
    For a' her houghs pe prokit.

Every thing in te Highlands now
    Pe turn'd to alteration;
Te sodger dwall at our door cheek,
    And tat pe great vexation.

Scotland be turn'd a Ningland now,
    The laws pring in te caudger;
Nainsell wad dirk him for his deeds,
    But, och she fears te sodger.

Anither law came after tat,
    Mo never saw the like, man,
They mak' a lang road on te crund,
    And ca' him Turnimspike, man!

And wow she pe a ponny road,
    Like Loudon corn riggs, man,
Where twa carts may gang on her,
    And no preak ither's legs, man.

They charge a penny for ilka horse,
    In troth she'll no be shcaper,
For nought but gaun upon the ground,
    And they gi'e her a paper.

They tak' the horse then py te head,
    And there they make him stand, man;
She tell them she had seen the day
    They had nae sic command, man.

Nae doubt nainsell maun draw her purse;
    And pay him what him like, man,
She'll see a shudgement on his toor,
    That filthy turnimspike, man.

But she'll awa' to ta Highland hills,
    Where deil a ane dare turn her,
And no come near te turnimspike,
    Unless it pe to purn her.

FOR LACK OF GOLD.

DR. AUSTIN.

BORN about 1726, a celebrated physician of his time, in Edinburgh. The song was composed upon Miss Jean Drummond, to whom he was engaged to be married. The lady, however, having attracted the attention of the Duke of Athol, jilted her first love and in 1749 became Duchess of Athol. Dr. Austin does not seem to have always remained in the disconsolate state depicted in the song, for, in 1754 he married Ann Sempill, sister of Lord John Sempill. He died in 1774 leaving a large family. The air has been traced to 1692, and the song appears in "The Charmer," 1751.

> For lack of gold she has left me, O,
> And of all that's dear she's bereft me, O;
> She me forsook for Athole's duke,
>   And to endless woe she has left me, O.
> A star and garter have more art
> Than youth, a true and faithful heart;
> For empty titles we must part—
>   For glittering show she has left me, O.
>
> No cruel fair shall ever move
> My injured heart again to love;
> Through distant climates I must rove,
>   Since Jeany she has left me, O.
> Ye powers above, I to your care
> Resign my faithless, lovely fair;
> Your choicest blessing be her share,
>   Though she has ever left me, O.

FLOWERS OF THE FOREST.

MISS JANE ELLIOT.

DAUGHTER of Sir Gilbert Elliot, of Minto. She was born in 1727. The song here given was written about 1755, and long passed as an old ballad. Sir Walter Scott, in including it in his Minstrelsy, says, "The following well-known and beautiful stanzas, were composed, many years ago, by a lady of family in Roxburghshire. The manner of the ancient minstrels is so happily imitated, that it required the most positive evidence to convince the editor that the song was of modern date." Miss Elliot died at Mount Teviot, Roxburghshire, in 1805.

> I'VE heard the lilting, at our yowe-milking,
>   Lasses a-lilting, before the dawn o' day;
> But now they are moaning, on ilka green loaning;
>   The Flowers of the Forest are a' wede away.
>
> At buchts, in the morning, nae blythe lads are scorning,
>   The lasses are lonely, and dowie, and wae;
> Nae daffin', nae gabbin', but sighing and sabbing,
>   Ilk ane lifts her leglin and hies her away.

In hairst, at the shearing, nae youths now are jeering,
   The bandsters are runkled, and lyart and grey;
At fair, or at preaching, nae wooing, nae fleeching—
   The Flowers of the Forest are a' wede away.

At e'en, at the gloaming, nae swankies are roaming,
   'Bout stacks wi' the lasses at bogle to play;
But ilk ane sits drearie, lamenting her dearie—
   The Flowers of the Forest are a' wede away.

Dule and wae to the order sent our lads to the border!
   The English, for ance, by guile wan the day;
The Flowers of the Forest, that foucht aye the foremost,
   The prime o' our land, are cauld in the clay.

We hear nae mair lilting at our yowe-milking,
   Women and bairns are heartless and wae;
Sighing and moaning on ilka green loaning—
   The Flowers of the Forest are a' wede away.

MY SHEEP I NEGLECTED.
SIR GILBERT ELLIOT, BART.,

BORN 1729. He was educated for the Scottish Bar, was elected Member of Parliament for Roxburghshire, and became Treasurer of the Navy. His private character has been highly extolled by his friends; and in connection with his Parliamentary business, he showed himself to be highly accomplished, expert, and sagacious. He died in 1777.

  Sir Gilbert belonged to an extraordinary family. His father was a poet; his sister, Miss Jean Elliot, has immortalised herself in the annals of Scottish song as authoress of "The Flowers of the Forest," and his son was made Governor-General of India, and became Earl of Minto.

This song first appeared in the "Charmer," 1749.

My sheep I neglected—I lost my sheep-hook,
   And all the gay haunts of my youth I forsook;
No more for Amynta fresh garlands I wove;
   For ambition, I said, would soon cure me of love.
     Oh, what had my youth with ambition to do?
     Why left I Amynta? Why broke I my vow?
     Oh, give me my sheep, and my sheep-hook restore,
     And I'll wander from love and Amynta no more.

Through regions remote in vain do I rove,
And bid the wide ocean secure me from love!
Oh, fool! to imagine that aught could subdue
A love so well founded, a passion so true!
   Oh, what, &c.

Alas! 'tis too late at thy fate to repine;
Poor shepherd, Amynta can never be thine:
Thy tears are all fruitless, thy wishes are vain,
The moments neglected return not again.
   Oh, what, &c.

THE SMILING PLAINS.
WILLIAM FALCONER,

AUTHOR of "The Shipwreck." Born at Edinburgh in 1730. He served his apprenticeship to the seafaring profession on board a Leith vessel. He early gave evidence of his genius as a poet, and attracting the patronage of the Duke of York, was appointed purser to the "Royal George," one of the finest ships in the Navy. In 1769 he was appointed to the "Aurora" frigate bound for India. The "Aurora" arrived in safety at the Cape of Good Hope, but after leaving there, was never afterwards seen or heard of.

THE smiling plains, profusely gay,
Are dress'd in all the pride of May;
The birds on every spray above,
To rapture wake the vocal grove.
But, ah! Miranda, without thee,
Nor spring nor summer smiles on me,
All lonely in the secret shade,
I mourn thy absence, charming maid.

O soft as love! as honour fair!
Serenely sweet as vernal air!
Come to my arms; for you alone
Can all my absence past atone.
O come! and to my bleeding heart
The sovereign balm of love impart;
Thy presence lasting joy shall bring,
And give the year eternal spring.

THE RUN-AWAY BRIDE.
FROM THE "CHARMER," 1751.

A LADDIE and a lassie fair
  Lived in the south countrie;
They ha'e coost their claes thegither,
  And wedded wad they be:
On Tuesday to the bridal feast
  Cam fiddlers flocking free—
But hey play up the rinaway bride,
  For she has ta'en the gee.

She had nae run a mile or mair,
  Till she 'gan to consider
The angering of her father dear,
  The vexing of her mither;
The slighting of the silly bridegroom,
  The warst of a' the three—
Then hey play up the rinaway bride,
  For she has ta'en the gee.

Her father and her mither baith
  Ran after her wi' speed;
And aye they ran and cried, How, Ann!
  Till they came to the Tweed:
Saw ye a lass, a lovesome lass,
  That weel a queen might be?
O that's the bride, the rinaway bride,
  The bride that's ta'en the gee.

And when they came to Kelso town,
  They gaur'd the clap gang through;
Saw ye a lass wi' a hood and mantle,
  The face o't lined up wi' blue?
The face o't lined up wi' blue,
  Aud the tail turn'd up wi' green;
Saw ye a lass wi' a hood and mantle,
  Should ha'e been married on Tuesday 't e'en?

O at the saft and silly bridegroom
  The bridemaids a' were laughin';
When up there spake the bridegroom's man,
  Now what means a' this daffin'?
For woman's love's a wilfu' thing,
  And fancy flies fu' free;
Then hey play up the rinaway bride,
  For she has ta'en the gee.

HOOLY AND FAIRLY.

THE CHARMER. Edinburgh, 1751.

Doun in yon meadow a couple did tarry:
The gudewife she drank naething but sack and canary;
The gudeman complain'd to her friends richt sairly—
Oh, gin my wife wad drink hooly and fairly!
  Hooly and fairly, hooly and fairly,
  Oh! gin my wife wad drink hooly and fairly!

First she drank Crummie, and syne she drank Gairie,
And syne she drank my bonnie gray marie,
That carried me through a' the dubs and the glairie—
Oh, gin my wife wad drink hooly and fairly!

She drank her hose, she drank her shoon,
And syne she drank her bonnie new goun;
She drank her sark that cover'd her rarely—
Oh, gin my wife wad drink hooly and fairly!

Wad she drink but her ain things, I wadna care,
But she drinks my claes that I canna weel spare;
When I'm wi' my gossips it angers me sairly—
Oh! gin my wife wad drink hooly and fairly!

My Sunday's coat she's laid it in wad,
And the best blue bonnet e'er was on my head;
At kirk or at mercat I'm cover'd but barely—
Oh! gin my wife wad drink hooly and fairly!

My bonnie white mittens I wore on my hands,
Wi' her neibour's wife she laid them in pawns;
My bane-headed staff that I looed sae dearly—
Oh, gin my wife wad drink hooly and fairly!

I never was for wranglin' nor strife,
Nor did I deny her the comforts o' life;
For when there's a war, I'm aye for a parley—
Oh, gin my wife wad drink hooly and fairly!

When there's ony money she maun keep the purse;
If I seek but a bawbee she'll scold and she'll curse;
She lives like a queen—I but scrimpit and sparely—
Oh! gin my wife wad drink hooly and fairly!

A pint wi' her cummers I wad her allow;
But when she sits down, she gets hersel' fou,
And when she is fou she is unco camstarie—
Oh, gin my wife wad drink hooly and fairly!

When she comes to the street she roars and she rants,
Has nae fear o' her neibours, nor minds the house wants;
She rants up some fule-sang, like, Up your heart, Charlie—
Oh, gin my wife wad drink hooly and fairly!

When she comes hame she lays on the lads,
The lasses she ca's baith bitches and jauds,
And ca's mysell an auld cuckle-carlie—
Oh, gin my wife wad drink hooly and fairly!

NAE DOMINIES FOR ME LADDIE.
REV. NATHANIEL MACKAY,

MINISTER of Crossmichael, Kirkcudbright, where he died in 1781. It has also been attributed to the Rev. John Forbes, minister of Deer, Aberdeenshire, who died in 1769. We are unable to decide as to the merits of the candidates. Dr. Laing seems to favour the claim of Mr. Forbes, while Mr. Robert Chambers, and Mr. Stenhouse, prefer that of Mr Mackay.

I chanc'd to meet an airy blade,
  A new-made pulpiteer, laddie,
With cock'd up hat and powder'd wig,
  Black coat and cuffs fu' clear, laddie:
A long cravat at him did wag,
  And buckles at his knee, laddie
Says he, My heart, by Cupid's dart,
  Is captivate to thee, lassie.

I'll rather chuse to thole grim death;
  So cease and let mo be, laddie :
For what? says he. Good troth, says I,
  No dominies for me, laddie :
Ministers' stipends are uncertain rents
  For ladies' conjunct-fee laddio :
When books and gowns are all cried down,
  No dominies for me, laddie.
But for your sake I'll fleece the flock,
  Grow rich as I grow auld, lassie ;
If I be spar'd I'll be a laird,
  And thou's be Madam call'd, lassie.
But what if ye shou'd chance to die,
  Leave bairns, ane or twa, laddie?
Naething wad be reserv'd for them
  But hair-mould books to gnaw, laddie.
At this he angry was, I wat,
  He gloom'd and look'd fu' high, laddie :
When I perceived this, in haste
  I left my dominie, laddie.
Fare ye well, my charming maid,
  This lesson learn of me, lassie,
At the next offer hold him fast,
  That first makes love to thee, lassie.
Then I returning hame again,
  And coming down the town, laddie,
By my good luck I chanc'd to meet
  A gentleman dragoon, laddie ;
And he took me by baith the hands,
  'Twas help in time of need, laddie :
Fools on ceremonies stand,
  At twa words we agreed, laddie.
He led me to his quarter-house,
  Where we exchang'd a word, laddie :
We had nae use for black gowns there,
  We married o'er the sword, laddie.
Martial drums is music fine,
  Compar'd wi' tinkling bells, laddie ;
Gold, red and blue, is more divine
  Than black, the hue of hell, laddie.
Kings, queens, and princes, crave the aid
  Of my brave stout dragoon, laddie ;
While dominies are much employ'd
  'Bout whores and sackcloth-gowns, laddie :
Away wi' a' these whining loons,
  They look like Let me be, laddie ;
I've more delight in roaring guns ;
  No dominies for me, laddie.

SYMON BRODIE.
HERD'S COLLECTION.

Symon Brodie had a cow:
  The cow was lost, and he couldna find her:
When he had done what man could do,
  The cow cam' hame, and her tail behind her.
    Honest auld Symon Brodie,
    Stupid auld doitit bodie!
      I'll awa' to the north countrie,
    And see my ain dear Symon Brodie.

Symon Brodie had a wife,
  And, wow! but she was braw and bonnie.
She took the dish-clout aff the buik,
  And preen'd it to her cockernonie.
    Honest auld Symon Brodie, &c.

TIBBIE FOWLER.

JOHNSON'S MUSEUM, 1787. A fragment appearing previously however in Herd's Collection, 1776, enables us to trace the song to an earlier time. It probably belongs to the middle of the eighteenth century, though Mr. Robert Chambers, from finding that a certain Isabella Fowler was married to a son of Logan of Restalrig in the sixteenth century, concludes thereby that it must refer to her, and dates accordingly.

Tibbie Fowler o' the Glen,
  There's ower mony wooing at her;
Tibbie Fowler o' the Glen,
  There's ower mony wooing at her.
    Wooin' at her, pu'in' at her,
      Courtin' her, and canna get her;
    Filthy elf, it's for her pelf
      That a' the lads are wooin' at her.

Ten cam' east, and ten cam' west;
  Ten cam' rowin' ower the water;
Twa cam' down the lang dyke-side:
  There's twa-and-thirty wooin' at her.
There's seven but, and seven ben,
  Seven in the pantry wi' her;
Twenty head about the door:
  There's ane-and-forty wooin' at her.

She's got pendles in her lugs;
  Cockle-shells wad set her better!
High-heel'd shoon, and siller tags,
  And a' the lads are wooin' at her.

Be a lassie e'er sae black,
  Gin she ha'e the name o' siller,
Set her up on Tintock tap,
  The wind will blaw a man till her.
Be a lassie e'er so fair,
  An' she want the penny siller,
A flie may fell her i' the air,
  Before a man be even'd till her.

BESS THE GAWKIE.
REV. JAMES MUIRHEAD, D.D.,

BORN 1742. He was educated at the University of Edinburgh for the ministry, and in 1770 was ordained minister of Urr, in Galloway; he died in 1808, in his sixty-eighth year. The song here given first appeared in Herd's Collection.

BLYTHE young Bess to Jean did say,
  Will ye gang to yon sunny brae,
Whare flocks do feed, and herds do stray,
  And sport awhile wi' Jamie?
Ah, na, lass! I'll no gang there,
Nor about Jamie tak' a care,
Nor about Jamie tak' a care,
  For he's ta'en up wi' Maggie.

For hark, and I will tell you, lass,
Did I not see young Jamie pass,
Wi' meikle blytheness in his face
  Out owre the muir to Maggie?
I wat he ga'e her monie a kiss,
And Maggie took them nae amiss:
'Tween ilka smack pleas'd her wi' this,
  "That Bess was but a gawkie.

"For when a civil kiss I seek,
She turns her head and thraws her cheek,
And for an hour she'll hardly speak;
  Wha'd no ca' her a gawkie?
But sure my Maggie has mair sense,
She'll gi'e a score without offence;
Now gi'e me ane into the mense,
  And ye shall be my dawtie."

'O Jamie, ye ha'e monie ta'en,
But I will never stand for ane
Or twa when we do meet again,
  So ne'er think me a gawkie.'
"Ah, na, lass, that canna be;
Sic thoughts as thae are far frae me,
Or onie thy sweet face that see,
  E'er to think thee a gawkie."

But, whisht, nae mair o' this we'll speak,
For yonder Jamie does us meet:
Instead o' Meg he kiss'd sae sweet,
  I trow he likes the gawkie.
"O dear Bess, I hardly knew,
When I cam' by your gown sae new;
I think you've got it wet wi' dew."
  Quoth she, 'that's like a gawkie;
'It's wat wi' dew, and 'twill get rain,
And I'll got gowns when it is gane;
Sae ye may gang the gate ye came
  And tell it to your dawtie.'
The guilt appear'd in Jamie's cheek:
He cried, "O cruel maid, but sweet,
If I should gang anither gate,
  I ne'er could meet my dawtie."

The lasses fast frae him they flew,
And left poor Jamie sair to rue,
That ever Maggie's face he knew,
  Or yet ca'd Bess a gawkie.
As they gade owre the muir they sang,
The hills and dales wi' echo rang,
The hills and dales wi' echo rang,
  "Gang o'er the muir to Maggie."

PINKIE HOUSE.
JOHN MITCHELL,

BORN 1749; a poet of some eminence of his time, but now forgotten. He was a great favourite of Sir Robert Walpole, the celebrated Whig Statesman. He died in 1738. Air—"Rothes' Lament."

By Pinkie House oft let me walk,
  And muse o'er Nelly's charms!
Her placid air, her winning talk,
  Even envy's self disarms.
O let me, ever fond, behold
  Those graces void of art—
Those cheerful smiles that sweetly hold,
  In willing chains, my heart!

O come, my love! and bring anew
  That gentle turn of mind;
That gracefulness of air in you
  By nature's hand designed.
These, lovely as the blushing rose,
  First lighted up this flame,
Which, like the sun, for ever glows
  Within my breast the same.

Ye light coquettes! ye airy things!
How vain is all your art!
How seldom it a lover brings!
How rarely keeps a heart!
O gather from my Nelly's charms
That sweet, that graceful ease,
That blushing modesty that warms,
That native art to please!

Come then, my love! O, come along!
And feed me with thy charms;
Come, fair inspirer of my song!
Oh, fill my longing arms!
A flame like mine can never die,
While charms so bright as thine,
So heavenly fair, both please the eye,
And fill the soul divine!

THE ESK.

REV. JOHN LOGAN,

Born 1749. Was for some time one of the ministers of Leith, and afterward a literary hack in London. He died in 1788. His poems have been collected along with his tragedy of Runnymede, and published in one volume.

While frequent on Tweed and on Tay,
Their harps all the muses have strung,
Should a river more limpid than they,
The wood-fringed Esk flow unsung?
While Nelly and Nancy inspire
The poet with pastoral strains,
Why silent the voice of the lyre
On Mary, the pride of the plains?

O nature's most beautiful bloom
May flourish unseen and unknown;
And the shadows of solitude gloom
A form that might shine on a throne.
Through the wilderness blossoms the rose,
In sweetness retired from the sight;
And Philomel warbles her woes
Alone to the ear of the night.

How often the beauty is hid
Amid shades that her triumphs deny!
How often the hero forbid
From the path that conducts to the sky!

A Helen has pined in the grove;
   A Homer has wanted his name;
Unseen in the circle of love,
   Unknown to the temple of fame.

Yet let us walk forth to the stream,
   Where poet ne'er wander'd before;
Enamour'd of Mary's sweet name,
   How the echoes will spread to the shore!
If the voice of the muse be divine,
   Thy beauties shall live in my lay;
While reflecting the forest so fine,
   Sweet Esk o'er the valleys shall stray.

MARY'S DREAM.
JOHN LOWE.

BORN in 1750 at Kenmure, in Galloway, where his father was gardener. Showing, we suppose, superior talents in his youth, he was educated for the church. He became tutor in the family of Mr. M'Ghie of Airds, "wha had mony bonnie dochters;" one of whom captivated the tutor's fancy. The beautiful song here given was written at this period. A Mr. Miller, who was engaged to be married to one of the young ladies, was drowned at sea, an event which would now have been forgotten but for the exquisitely tender and pathetic song of Mary's Dream, which has given to it immortality. Lowe's life was unfortunate; giving up his love at Airds, he emigrated to America. He opened a school in Fredericksburgh, in Virginia, and afterwards took orders in the Church of England. He married a lady whose conduct, joined to other misfortunes, brought him to his grave in 1798, in his 48th year. Lowe wrote a number of other pieces, but none of them of any extra degree of merit. Like the author of the "Burial of Sir John Moore," his fame depends on one poem.

THE moon had climb'd the highest hill,
   Which rises o'er the source of Dee,
And from the eastern summit shed
   Her silver light on tower and tree;
When Mary laid her down to sleep,
   Her thoughts on Sandy far at sea;
When soft and low, a voice was heard,
   Saying, "Mary, weep no more for me!"

She from her pillow gently raised
   Her head, to ask who there might be,
And saw young Sandy shivering stand,
   With visage pale, and hollow e'e.
"O Mary dear, cold is my clay;
   It lies beneath a stormy sea.
Far, far from thee, I sleep in death;
   So, Mary, weep no more for me!

"Three stormy nights and stormy days,
  We tossed upon the raging main;
And long we strove our bark to save,
  But all our striving was in vain.
Even then, when horror chilled my blood,
  My heart was filled with love for thee:
The storm is past, and I at rest;
  So, Mary, weep no more for me!

"O maiden dear, thysel' prepare;
  We soon shall meet upon that shore,
Where love is free from doubt and care,
  And thou and I shall part no more!"
Loud crowed the cock, the shadow fled:
  No more of Sandy could she see.
But soft the passing spirit said,
  "Sweet Mary, weep no more for me!"

MY DADDIE IS A CANKERT CARLE.

From "The Lark," Edin., 1765. It has been ascribed to Carnegie, of Balnamoon, Esq., but the sole authority for this statement was "a garrulous old fellow," who had no doubt about it. (See Struthers' Harp of Caledonia.)

My daddie is a cankert carle,
  He'll no twine wi' his gear;
My minnie she's a scauldin' wife,
  Hauds a' the house asteer;
    But let them say, or let them do,
      It's a' ane to me,
    For he's low doun, he's in the brume,
      That's waitin' on me:
    Waiting on me, my love,
      He's waiting on me;
    For he's low doun, he's in the brume,
      That's waitin' on me.

My auntie Kate sits at her wheel,
  And sair she lightlies me;
But weel ken I it's a' envy,
  For ne'er a joe has she;
    But let them say, &c.

My cousin Kate was sair beguiled
  Wi' Johnnie o' the Glen;
And aye sinsyne she cries, Beware
  O' fause deluding men;
    But let them say, &c.

Gleed Sandy, he cam' wast yestreen,
  And speir'd when I saw Pate;
And aye sinsyne the neebors round
  They jeer me air and late;
    But let them say, &c.

HALLOW FAIR.
ROBERT FERGUSSON.

THE predecessor of Burns, whose wayward life, and bitter end, is well known to every reader in Scotch Literature. He was born at Edinburgh in 1750, and after studying at the University of St. Andrew's for a short time, he changed his views as to his occupation, and returned to Edinburgh, where he was employed in a Lawyer's office. Poor Fergusson soon became mixed in all the wild life of the Metropolis, and the end of a short career of debauchery and excess was a mad-house, where he died at the early age of twenty-four. He was buried in the Canongate Churchyard, and one of the most affecting incidents in the life of Robert Burns is, that when he acquired a little money and fame, he hastened to erect a simple stone over the ashes of his "elder brother in misfortune." Fergusson's Poems have frequently been published in various forms.

THERE's fouth o' braw Jockies and Jennies
  Comes weel-buskit into the fair,
With ribbons on their cockernonies,
  And fouth o' fine flour on their hair.
Maggie she was sae weel buskit,
  That Willie was tied to his bride;
The pownie was ne'er better whisket
  Wi' cudgel that hang frae his side.

But Maggie was wond'rous jealous,
  To see Willie buskit sae braw;
And Sandy he sat in the alehouse,
  And hard at the liquor did ca'.
There was Geordie, that weel looed his lassie,
  He took the pint-stoup in his arms,
And hugged it, and said, Trouth they're saucie,
  That loes na a guid-father's bairn.

There was Wattie, the muirland laddie,
  That rides on the bonnie grey cowt,
With sword by his side like a cadie
  To drive in the sheep and the nowt.
His doublet sae weel it did fit him,
  It scarcely cam' down to mid-thio,
With hair pouthered, hat, and a feather,
  And hausing at curpen and tee.

But Bruckie played boo to Bessie,
  And aff scoured the cout like the wind;
Puir Wattie he fell on the caussey,
  And birzed a' the banes in his skin.
His pistols fell out o' the hulstera,
  And were a' bedanbed wi' dirt,
The folk they cam' round him in clusters;
  Some leuch, and cried, Lad, was ye hurt?
But cout wad let naebody steer him,
  He aye was sae wanton and skeigh;
Tho packmon's stands he overturned them,
  And garred a' the Jocks stand abeigh;
Wi' sneerin' behind and before him,
  For sic is the mettle o' brutes,
Puir Wattie, and wae's me for him,
  Was fain to gang hame in his boots.

Now it was late in the e'ening,
  And boughting-time was drawing near;
The lasses had stanched their greening
  Wi' fouth o' braw apples and beer:
There was Lillie, and Tibbie, and Sibbie,
  And Ceicy on the spindle could spin,
Stood glowrin' at signs and glass winnocks,
  But deil a ane bade them come in.

Gude guide us! saw ye e'er the like o't?
  See, yonder's a bonnie black swan;
It glow'rs as it wad fain be at us;
  What's yon that it hauds in its hand?
Awa', daft gowk, cries Wattie,
  They're a' but a ruckle o' sticks;
See, there is Bill-Jock and auld Hawkie,
  And yonder's Mess John and auld Nick.

Quoth Maggie, Come buy ns our fairin';
  And Wattie richt sleely could tell,
I think thou'rt the flower o' the clachan,—
  In trowth, now, I'se gi'e thee mysell.
But wha wad ha' e'er thocht it o' him,
  That e'er he had rippled the lint?
Sae proud was he o' his Maggie,
  Though she was baith scaulie and squint.

THE LEE RIG.
ROBERT FERGUSSON.

With the exception of the third, fourth, and fifth stanzas, which were added by William Reid, a bookseller in Glasgow, a notice of whom is given elsewhere.

Will ye gang o'er the lea rig,
　My ain kind dearie, O;
And cuddle there fu' kindly,
　Wi' me, my kind dearie, O!
At thorny bush, or birken tree,
　We'll daff, and never weary, O;
They'll scug ill een frae you and me,
　My ain kind dearie, O.

Nae herds wi' kent or colly there,
　Shall ever come to fear ye, O;
But laverocks whistling in the air
　Shall woo, like me, their dearie, O.
While ithers herd their lambs and ewes,
　And toil for warld's gear, my jo,
Upon the lee my pleasure grows
　Wi' thee, my kind dearie, O.

At gloamin', if my lane I be,
　Oh, but I'm wondous eerie, O:
And mony a heavy sigh I gi'e,
　When absent frae my dearie, O;
But seated 'neath the milk-white thorn,
　In ev'ning fair and clearie, O,
Enraptur'd, a' my cares I scorn,
　When wi' my kind dearie, O.

Whare through the birks the burnie rows,
　Aft ha'e I sat fu' cheerie, O,
Upon the bonnie greensward howes,
　Wi' thee, my kind dearie, O,
I've courted till I've heard the craw
　Of honest Chanticleerie, O,
Yet never miss'd my sleep ava,
　When wi' my kind dearie, O.

For though the night were ne'er sae dark,
　And I were ne'er sae weary, O,
I'd meet thee on the lea rig,
　My ain kind dearie, O,
While in this weary warld of wae,
　This wilderness sae dreary, O,
What makes me blythe, and keeps me sae?
　'Tis thee, my kind dearie, O.

THE BANKS OF THE DEE.

GENERALLY ascribed to John Home, author of Douglas. The editor of *Blackie's Book of Scottish Song*, however, states it to have been written by John Tait, a writer to the Signet in Edinburgh, and to have been written in 1775 on the occasion of a friend leaving Scotland, to join the forces in North America. Tune *Langolee*.

'Twas summer, and softly the breezes were blowing,
  And sweetly the nightingale sung from the tree;
At the foot of a rock, where the river was flowing,
  I sat myself down on the banks of the Dee.
Flow on, lovely Dee, flow on, thou sweet river,
  Thy banks, purest stream, shall be dear to me ever:
For there first I gain'd the affection and favour
  Of Jamie, the glory and pride of the Dee.

But now he's gone from me, and left me thus mourning,
  To quell the proud rebels—for valiant is he;
And ah! there's no hope of his speedy returning,
  To wander again on the banks of the Dee.
He's gone, hapless youth, o'er the loud roaring billows,
  The kindest and sweetest of all the gay fellows,
And left me to stray 'mongst the once loved willows,
  The loneliest maid on the banks of the Dee.

But time and my prayers may perhaps yet restore him,
  Blest peace may restore my dear shepherd to me;
And when he returns, with such care I'll watch o'er him,
  He never shall leave the sweet banks of the Dee.
The Dee then shall flow, all its beauties displaying,
The lambs on its banks shall again be seen playing,
While I with my Jamie am carelessly straying,
  And tasting again all the sweets of the Dee.

BOTHWELL BANK.

JOHN PINKERTON,

This distinguished Antiquary. He was born at Edinburgh in 1758, and died at Paris in 1825. His works are numerous and important, more especially in the department of Scottish poetry, in which he laboured long and well. Though terrible, however, in his denunciations of others for anything like dishonesty in literature, he could not resist passing a few of his own pieces into the midst of his collections of early poems; and the song here given first appeared in his Select Scottish Ballads, 1773, as the old words of the beautiful and ancient air of "Bothwell Bank." The trick, however, was too palpable to escape detection, and has fatally injured his position in the History of Antiquarianism.

On the blyth Beltane, as I went
Be mysel' attour the green bet,
Wharby the crystal waves of Clyde,
Throch saughs and hanging hazels glyde;
There, sadly sitting on a brae,
I heard a damsel speak her wae.

"Oh, Bothwell Bank, thou blumest fair,
But, ah, thou mak'st my heart fou' sair!
For a' beneath thy holts sae grene
My luve and I wad sit at ene;
While primroses and daisies, mixt
Wi blue bells, in my loks he fixt.

"But he left me ae droarie day,
And haplie now sleeps in the clay,
Without ae sich his dethe to roun',
Without ae flouir his grave to croun!
Oh, Bothwell Bank, thou blumest fair,
But, ah, thou mak'st my heart fou' sair."

THE WAYWARD WIFE.
MISS JENNY GRAHAM,

A MAIDEN lady, who died at an advanced age at Dumfries, towards the middle of the last century.

ALAS! my son, you little know
The sorrows that from wedlock flow.
Farewell to every day of ease,
When you have gotten a wife to please.
    Sae bide you yet, and bide you yet,
    Ye little ken what's to betide you yet;
    The half of that will gane you yet,
    If a wayward wife obtain you yet.

[Your experience is but small,
As yet you've met with little thrall:]
The black cow on your foot ne'er trod,
Which gars you sing alang the road.
    Sae bide you yet, &c.

Sometimes the rock, sometimes the reel,
Or some piece of the spinning-wheel,
She will drive at you wi' good will,
And then she'll send you to the de'il,
    Sae bide you yet, &c.

When I like you was young and free,
I valued not the proudest she;
Like you I vainly boasted then,
That men alone were born to reign.
   But bide you yet, &c.

Great Hercules, and Samson too,
Were stronger men than I or you,
Yet they were baffled by their dears,
And felt the distaff and the sheers.
   Sae bide you yet, &c.

Stout gates of brass, and well-built walls,
Are proof 'gainst swords and cannon-balls,
But nought is found, by sea or land,
That can a wayward wife withstand.
   Sae bide you yet, &c.

OUR GOODMAN CAM' HAME AT E'EN.

Herd's Collection. An English version was recovered in Yorkshire by Mr. J. H. Dixon.

Our goodman came hame at e'en,
   And hame came he;
And there he saw a saddle horse,
   Where nae horse should be.

How came this horse here?
   How can this be?
How came this horse here
   Without the leave o' me?

A horse! quo' she:
   Ay, a horse, quo' he.
Ye auld blind dotard carle,
   Blind mat ye be,
'Tis naething but a bonny milk cow,
   My minny sent to me.

A milk cow! quo' he:
   Ay, a milk cow, quo' she.
Far hae I ridden,
   And meikle hae I seen,
But a saddle on a cow's back
   Saw I never nane.

Our goodman came hame at e'en,
   And hame came he;
He spy'd a pair of jackboots,
   Where nae boots should be.

What's this now, goodwife?
  What's this I see?
How came these boots there
  Without the leave o' me?

  Boots! quo' she:
    Ay, boots, quo' he.
Shame fa' your cuckold face,
  And ill mat ye see,
It's but a pair of water stoups
  The cooper sent to me.

  Water stoups! quo' he:
    Ay, water stoups, quo' she.
Far hae I ridden,
  And farer hae I gane,
But siller spurs on water stoups
  Saw I never nane.

Our goodman came hame at e'en,
  And hame came he;
And then he saw a [siller] sword,
  Where a sword should nae be:

What's this now, goodwife?
  What's this I see?
O how came this sword here
  Without the leave o' me?

  A sword! quo' she:
    Ay, a sword, quo' he.
Shame fa' your cuckold face,
  And ill mat ye see,
It's but a parridge spurtle
  My minnie sent to me.

  A parridge spurtle! quo' he:
    Ay, a parridge spurtle, quo' she.
Weil, far hae I ridden,
  And muckle hae I seen;
But siller-handed spurtles
  Saw I never nane.

Our goodman came hame at e'en,
  And hame came he;
There he spy'd a powder'd wig,
  Where nae wig should be.

What's this now, goodwife?
  What's this I see?
How came this wig here
  Without the leave o' me?

A wig! quo' she:
　Ay, a wig, quo' he.
Shame fa' your cuckold face,
　And ill mat you see,
'Tis naething but a clocken hen
　My minnie sent to me.
　　[A] clocken hen! quo' he:
　　Ay, [a] clocken hen, quo' she.
Far hae I ridden,
　And muckle hae I seen,
But powder on a clocken-hen
　Saw I never nane.
Our goodman came hame at e'en,
　And hame came he;
And there he saw a muckle coat,
　Where nae coat shou'd be.
O how came this coat here?
　How can this be?
How came this coat here
　Without the leave o' me?
　　A coat! quo' she:
　　Ay, a coat, quo' he.
Ye auld blind dotard carle,
　Blind mat ye be,
It's but a pair of blankets
　My minnie sent to me.
　　Blankets! quo' he:
　　Ay, blankets, quo' she.
Far hae I ridden,
　And muckle hae I seen,
But buttons upon blankets
　Saw I never nane.
Ben went our goodman,
　And ben went he;
And there he spy'd a sturdy man,
　Where nae man should be.
How came this man here?
　How can this be?
How came this man here
　Without the leave o' me?
　　A man! quo' she:
　　Ay, a man, quo' he.
Poor blind body,
　And blinder mat ye be,
It's a new milking maid,
　My mither sent to me.

A maid! quo' he:
  Ay, a maid, quo' she.
Far hae I ridden,
  And muckle hae I seen,
But lang-bearded maidens
  I saw never nane.

PATIE'S WEDDIN'.

HERD'S COLLECTION. No trace of author or era can be found, but it is probably of an earlier date than the publication of Herd.

As Patie cam' up frae the glen,
  Drivin' his wedders before him,
He met bonnie Meg ganging hame—
  Her beauty was like for to smoore him.
O Maggie, lass, dinna ye ken
  That you and I 's gaun to be married?
I had rather had broken my leg,
  Before sic a bargain miscarried.

O Patie, lad, wha tell'd ye that?
  I think o' news they've been scanty:
I'm nae to be married the year,
  Though I should be courted by twenty!
Now, Maggie, what gars ye to taunt?
  Is 't 'cause that I ha'ena a mailen?
The lad that has gear needna want
  For neither a half nor a haill ane.

My dad has a gude grey meare,
  And yours has twa cows and a filly;
And that will be plenty o' gear:
  Sae, Maggie, be na sae ill-willy.
Weel, Patie, lad, I dinna ken;
  But first ye maun speir at my daddie;
You're quite as weel born as Ben,
  And I canna say but I'm ready.

We ha'e walth o' yarn in clews,
  To mak' me a coat and a jimpey,
And plaidin' eneuch to be trews—
  Gif I get ye, I shanna scrimp ye!
Now fair fa' ye, my bonnie Meg!
  I'se e'en let a smackie fa' on yo:
May my neck be as lang as my leg,
  If I be an ill husband unto ye!

She gang your ways hame e'en now;
  Mak' ready gin this day fifteen days,
And tell your father fra me,
  I'll be his gude-son in great kindness.

Maggie's as blythe as a wran,
　　Bodin' the blast o' ill weather,
And a' the gaite singin' she ran,
　　To tell the news to her father.

But aye the auld man cried out,
　　He'll no be o' that mind on Sunday.
There's nae fear o' that quo' Meg;
　　For I gat a kiss on the bounty.
And what was the matter o' that?
　　It was naething out o' his pocket,
I wish the news were true,
　　And we had him fairly bookit.

A very wee while after that,
　　Wha cam' to our biggin but Patie?
Dress'd up in a braw new coat,
　　And wow but he thocht himsel' pretty!
His bonnet was little frae new,
　　And in it a loop and a slittie,
To draw in a ribbon sae blue,
　　To bab at the neck o' his coatie.

Then Patie cam' in wi' a stend;
　　Cried, Peace be under the biggin!
You're welcome, quo' William, Come ben,
　　Or I wish it may rive frae the riggin'!
Now draw in your seat, and sit doun,
　　And tell's a' your news in a hurry:
And haste ye, Meg, and be dune,
　　And hing on the pan wi' the berry.

Quoth Patie, My news is nae thrang;
　　Yestreen I was wi' his honour;
I've ta'en three rigs o' braw land,
　　And bound myself under a bonour;
And, now, my errand to you,
　　Is for Maggie to help me to labour;
But I'm fear'd we'll need your best cow,
　　Because that our haddin's but sober.

Quoth William, To harl ye through,
　　I'll be at the cost o' the bridal,
I'se cut the craig o' the ewe,
　　That had amaist dee'd o' the side-ill:
And that'll be plenty o' bree,
　　Sae lang as our well is na reested,
To a' the neebours and you;
　　Sae I think we'll be nae that ill feasted.

Quoth Patie, O that'll do well,
And I'll gie you your brose i' the mornin',
O' kail that was made yestreen,
For I like them best i' the forenoon.
Sae Tam, the piper, did play;
And ilka ane danced that was willin';
And a' the lave they rankit through;
And they held the wee stoupie aye fillin'.
The auld wives sat and they chew'd;
And when that the carles grew nappy,
They danced as well as they dow'd
Wi' a crack o' their thooms and a happie.
The lad that wore the white band,
I think they ca'd him Jamie Mather,
He took the bride by the hand,
And cried to play up Maggie Lauder.

BANKS OF FORTH.
HERD'S COLLECTION.

AWAKE, my love! with genial ray,
The sun returning glads the day.
Awake! the balmy zephyr blows,
The hawthorn blooms, the daisy glows,
The trees regain their verdant pride,
The turtle woos his tender bride;
To love each warbler tunes the song,
And Forth in dimples glides along.
Oh, more than blooming daisies fair!
More fragrant than the vernal air!
More gentle than the turtle dove,
Or streams that murmur through the grove!
Bethink thee all is on the wing,
These pleasures wait on wasting spring;
Then come, the transient bliss enjoy,
Nor fear what fleets so fast will cloy.

THE HUMBLE BEGGAR.
HERD'S COLLECTION.

IN Scotland there lived a humble beggar,
He had neither house, nor hald, nor hame,
But he was weel liked by ilka bodie,
And they gu'e him sunkets to rax his wame.

A nivefu' of meal, a handfu' of groats,
A daad of bannock, or herring brie,
Cauld parridge, or the lickings of plates,
Wad mak' him as blythe as a beggar could be.

This beggar he was a humble beggar,
　The feint a bit of pride had he,
He wad a ta'en his a'ms in a bikker,
　Frae gentleman, or poor bodie.
His wallets ahint and afore did hang,
　In as good order as wallets could be:
And a lang kail-gooly hang down by his side,
　And a meikle nowt-horn to rout on had he.
It happen'd ill, it happen'd warse,
　It happen'd sae that he did die;
And wha do you think was at his late-wake,
　But lads and lasses of a high degree.
Some were blythe and some were sad,
　And some they play'd at Blind Harrie;
But suddenly up-started the auld carle,
　I redd ye, good folks, tak' tent o' me.
Up gat Kate that sat i' the nook,
　Vow kimmer, and how do ye?
Up he gat, and ca't her limmer,
　And ruggit and tuggit her cockernonie.
They houkit his grave in Duket's kirk-yard,
　E'en far frae the companie:
But when they were gaun to lay him i' the yird,
　The feint a dead nor dead was he.
And when they brought him to Duket's kirk-yard,
　He dunted on the kist, the boards did flee:
And when they were gaun to put him i' the yird,
　In fell the kist, and out lap he.
He cried, I'm cauld, I'm unco cauld;
　Fu' fast ran the fock, and fu' fast ran he:
But he was first hame at his ain ingle side,
　And he helped to drink his ain dirgie.

THE DECEIVER.

HERD'S COLLECTION.

With tuneful pipe and hearty glee,
　Young Watty wan my heart;
A blyther lad ye couldna see,
　All beauty without art.
　　His winning tale
　　Did soon prevail
　To gain my fond belief;
　　But soon the swain
　　Gangs o'er the plain,
And leaves me full, and leaves me full,
　And leaves me full of grief.

Though Colin courts with tuneful sang,
　Yet few regard his mane;
The lasses a' round Watty thrang,
　While Colin's left alane:
　　In Aberdeen
　　Was never seen
　A lad that gave sic pain;
　　He daily wooes,
　　And still pursues,
Till he does all, till he does all,
　Till he does all obtain.

But soon as he has gain'd the bliss,
　Away then does he run,
And hardly will afford a kiss,
　To silly me undone:
　　Bonnie Katy,
　　Maggy, Beaty,
　Avoid the roving swain,
　　His wyly tongue
　　Be sure to shun,
Or you like me, or you like me,
　Like me will be undone.

GET UP AND BAR THE DOOR.
HERD'S COLLECTION.

It fell about the Martinmas time,
　And a gay time it was than,
When our gudewife got puddings to mak',
　And she boil'd them in the pan.

The wind sae cauld blew south and north,
　And blew into the floor:
Quoth our gudeman to our gudewife,
　"Gae out and bar the door."

"My hand is in my hussy'f skap,
　Gudeman, as ye may see,
An' it shou'd nae be barr'd this hundred year,
　It's no be barr'd for me."

They made a paction 'tween them twa,
　They made it firm and sure;
That the first word whase'er shou'd speak,
　Shou'd rise and bar the door.

Then by there came twa gentlemen,
　At twelve o'clock at night,
And they could neither see house nor hall,
　Nor coal nor candle light.

Now, whether is this a rich man's house,
  Or whether is it a poor?
But never a word wad ane o' them speak,
  For barring o' the door.

And first they ate the white puddings,
  And then they ate the black,
Tho' muckle thought the gudewife to hersel',
  Yet ne'er a word she spak'.

Then said the one unto the other,
  "Here, man, tak' ye my knife,
Do ye tak' aff the auld man's beard,
  And I'll kiss the gudewife."

"But there's nae water in the house,
  And what shall we do than?"
"What ails you at the puddin' broo,
  That boils into the pan?"

O up then started our gudeman,
  And an angry man was he;
"Will ye kiss my wife before my een,
  And scad me wi' pudding bree?"

Then up and started our gudewife,
  Gied three skips on the floor:
"Gudeman, ye've spoken the foremost word,
  Get up and bar the door."

AS I WAS A-WALKING.

HERD'S COLLECTION.

As I was a walking ae May morning,
  The fiddlers an' youngsters were making their game,
And there I saw my faithless lover,
  And a' my sorrows return'd again.
Well since he is gane, joy gang wi' him;
  It's ne'er be he shall gar me complain:
I'll cheer up my heart, and I will get anither;
  I'll never lay a' my love upon ane.

I could na get sleeping yestreen for weeping,
  The tears ran down like showers o' rain;
An' had na I got greiting my heart wad a broken;
  And O! but love's a tormenting pain.
But since he is gane, may joy gae wi' him;
  It's never be he that shall gar me complain;
I'll cheer up my heart, and I will get anither;
  I'll never lay a' my love upon ane.

When I gade into my mither's new house,
  I took my wheel and sat down to spin,
'Twas there I first began my thrift;
  And a' the wooers came linking in.
It was gear he was seeking, but gear he'll na get;
  And its never be he that shall gar me complain:
For I'll cheer up my heart, and I'll soon get anither;
  I'll never lay a' my love upon ane.

WANDERING WILLIE.
HERD'S COLLECTION.

Here awa', there awa', wandering Willie,
  Here awa', there awa', here awa' hame!
Lang have I sought thee, dear have I bought thee,
  Now I have gotten my Willie again!

Through the lang muir I have followed my Willie;
  Through the lang muir I have followed him hame:
Whatever betide us, nought shall divide us;
  Love now rewards all my sorrow and pain.

Here awa', there awa', wandering Willie,
  Here awa', there awa', here awa' hame!
Come, love, believe me, nothing can grieve me,
  Ilka thing pleases while Willie's at hame.

JOCKY HE CAME HERE TO WOO.
HERD'S COLLECTION. Two verses have necessarily been omitted.

Jocky he came here to woo,
  On ae feast-day when we were fu';
And Jenny pat on her best array,
  When she heard Jocky was come that way.

Jenny she gaed up the stair,
  Sae privily to change her smock;
And ay sae loud as her mother did rair,
  Hey, Jenny, come down to Jock.

Jenny she came down the stair,
  And she came bobbin and bakin ben;
Her stays they were lac'd, and her waist it was jimp,
  And a bra' new-made manco gown.

Jocky took her by the hand,
  O Jenny, can ye fancy me?
My father is dead, and he 'as left me some land,
  And bra' houses twa or three.

And I will gi'e them a' to thee,
   A haith, quo' Jenny, I fear you mock!
Then foul fa' me gin I scorn thee;
   If ye'll be my Jenny, I'll be your Jock.

Jenny lookit, and syne she leugh,
   Ye first maun get my mither's consent.
A weel, goodwife, and what say ye?
   Quo' she, Jocky, I'm weel content.

Jenny to her mither did say,
   O mither fetch us some good meat,
A piece o' the butter was kirn'd the day,
   That Jocky and I thegither may eat.

Jocky unto Jenny did say,
   Jenny, my dear, I want nae meat;
It was nae for meat that I came here,
   But a' for the love of you, Jenny, my dear.

Jenny she gaed up the gait
   Wi' a green gown as syde as her smock,
And sy sae loud as her mither did rair,
   Vow, sirs, has nae Jenny seen Jock.

A CANTY SANG.

HERD'S COLLECTION.

GIN I had a wee house and a cantie wee fire,
A bonnie wee wifie to praise and admire,
A bonnie wee yardie beside a wee burn,
Fareweel to the bodies that yammer and mourn.
   And bide ye yet, and bide ye yet,
   Ye little ken what may betide me yet;
   Some bonnie wee bodie may be my lot,
   And I'll aye be cantie wi' thinking o't.

When I gang afield and come hame at e'en,
I'll get my wee wifie fu' neat and fu' clean;
And a bonnie wee bairnie upon her knee,
That'll cry papa, or daddie, to me.

And if there ever should happen to be
A difference atween my wee wifie and me;
In hearty good-humour, although she be teased,
I'll kiss her and clap her until she be pleased.

SAE MERRY AS WE TWA HA'E BEEN.

HERD'S COLLECTION. One of the tunes in the Skene Manuscript (1630), is titled, "Sae merry as we ha's been," which seems to indicate that the refrain is of a very early period, though we cannot class the song earlier than the time of Herd.

A LASS that was laden'd with care,
  Sat heavily under yon thorn;
I listen'd a while for to hear,
  When thus she began for to mourn.
Whene'er my dear shepherd was there,
  The birds did melodiously sing,
And cold nipping winter did wear
  A face that resembled the spring.
    Sae merry as we twa ha'e been,
    Sae merry as we twa ha'e been,
    My heart it is like for to break
    When I think on the days we ha'e seen.

Our flocks feeding close by his side,
  He gently pressing my hand,
I view'd the wide world in its pride,
  And laugh'd at the pomp of command!
My dear, he would oft to me say,
  What makes you hard-hearted to me?
Oh! why do you thus turn away
  From him who is dying for thee?

But now he is far from my sight,
  Perhaps a deceiver may prove,
Which makes me lament day and night,
  That ever I granted my love.
At eve, when the rest of the folk
  Are merrily seated to spin,
I set myself under an oak,
  And heavily sighed for him.

THERE'S NAE LUCK ABOUT THE HOUSE,
DISPUTED.

WAS sung as a street ballad about 1772. A copy of it was found among the papers of William Julius Mickle, the celebrated translator of the Lusiad, and his admirers have since claimed the song as his. It has also been said, with more plausibility, to have been the production of Mrs. Jean Adams, a schoolmistress at Crawford's Dyke, near Greenock. While, however, we consider the claim of Mrs. Adams to be the preferable one, it is but fair to state that the evidence is not much to the point on either side, and that a satisfactory solution of the question is in all likelihood utterly impossible.

It appeared in Herd's Collection: the version here given has been much altered and improved, the sixth stanza, for instance (so much admired by Burns), having been added by Dr. Beattie, the author of "The Minstrel."

AND are you sure the news is true?
  And are you sure he's weel?
Is this a time to think o' wark?
  Ye jauds, fling bye your wheel.
Is this a time to think o' wark,
  When Colin's at the door?
Rax me my cloak,—I'll to the quay,
  And see him come ashore.
    For there's nae luck about the house,
      There's nae luck at a';
    There's little pleasure in the house
      When our gudeman's awa'.

And gie to me my bigonet,
  My bishop's satin gown,
For I maun tell the bailie's wife
  That Colin's come to town.
My turkey slippers maun gae on,
  My hose o' pearl blue;
'Tis a' to please my ain gudeman,
  For he's baith leal and true.
    For there's nae luck, &c.

Rise up and mak' a clean fireside;
  Put on the muckle pot;
Gi'e little Kate her button gown,
  And Jock his Sunday coat;
And mak' their shoon as black as slaes,
  Their hose as white as snaw;
It's a' to please my ain gudeman,
  For he's been lang awa'.
    For there's nae luck, &c.

There's twa fat hens upon the bauk,
  They've fed this month and mair;
Mak' haste and thraw their necks about,
  That Colin weel may fare;
And spread the table neat and clean,
  Gar ilka thing look braw;
For wha can tell how Colin fared,
  When he was far awa'.
    For there's nae luck, &c.

Sae true his heart, sae smooth his speech,
  His breath like caller air;
His very foot has music in't,
  As he comes up the stair.
And will I see his face again?
  And will I hear him speak?
I'm downright dizzy wi' the thought,—
  In troth, I'm like to greet.
    For there's nae luck, &c.

The cauld blasts o' the winter wind,
  That thirl'd through my heart,
They're a' blawn by, I ha'e him safe,
  Till death we'll never part:
But what puts parting in my head?
  It may be far awa';
The present moment is our ain,
  The neist we never saw.
    For there's nae luck, &c.

Since Colin's weal, I'm weel content,
  I ha'e nae mair to crave;
Could I but live to mak' him blest,
  I'm blest aboon the lave.
And will I see his face again?
  And will I hear him speak?
I'm downright dizzy wi' the thought,—
  In troth, I'm like to greet.
    For there's nae luck, &c.

MY WIFE'S A WANTON WEE THING.

THE first two verses appeared in Herd's Collection, the rest appears in Johnson's Museum.

My wife's a wanton wee thing,
My wife's a wanton wee thing,
My wife's a wanton wee thing;
  She winna be guided by me.

She play'd the loon ere she was married,
She play'd the loon ere she was married,
She play'd the loon ere she was married;
  She'll do't again ere she die!

She sell'd her coat, and she drank it,
She sell'd her coat, and she drank it,
She row'd hersel in a blanket;
  She winna be guided by me.

She mind't na when I forbade her,
She mind't na when I forbade her;
I took a rung and I claw'd her,
 And a braw guid bairn was she!

ROBIN IS MY ONLY JO.

Herd's Collection, based upon a very old and licentious ditty.

Robin is my only jo,
Robin has the art to lo'e,
So to his suit I mean to bow,
 Because I ken he lo'es me.
Happy, happy was the shower,
That led me to his birken bower,
Whare first of love I fand the power,
 And kend that Robin loe'd me.

They speak of napkins, speak of rings,
Speak of gloves and kissing strings,
And name a thousand bonnie things,
 And ca' them signs he lo'es me.
But I prefer a smack of Rob,
Sporting on the velvet fog,
To gifts as lang's a plaiden wob,
 Because I ken he lo'es me.

He's tall and sonsy, frank and free,
Lo'ed by a', and dear to me,
Wi' him I'd live, wi' him I'd die,
 Because my Robin lo'es me.
My titty, Mary, said to me,
Our courtship but a joke wad be,
And I or lang be made to see,
 That Robin did na lo'e me.

But little kens she what has been,
Me and my honest Rob between,
And in his wooing, O sae keen
 Kind Robin is that lo'es me.
Then fly, ye lazy hours away,
And hasten on the happy day,
When "join your hands," Mess John shall say,
 And mak' him mine that lo'es me.

Till then, let every chance unite,
To weigh our love, and fix delight,
And I'll look down on such wi' spite,
 Who doubt that Robin lo'es me.
O hey, Robin, quo' she,
O hey, Robin, quo' she,
O hey, Robin, quo' she,
 Kind Robin lo'es me.

THERE CAM' A YOUNG MAN.

Herd's Collection. Nothing is known as to its authorship. The air is called in old collections "Bung your eye in the morning."

There cam' a young man to my daddie's door,
My daddie's door, my daddie's door;
There cam' a young man to my daddie's door,
  Cam' seeking me to woo.
    And wow! but he was a braw young lad,
    A brisk young lad, and a braw young lad,
    And wow! but he was a braw young lad,
      Cam' seeking me to woo.

But I was baking when he came,
When he came, when he came;
I took him in and gied him a scone,
  To thowe his frozen mou'.

I set him in aside the bink;
I ga'e him bread and ale to drink;
But ne'er a blythe styme wad he blink,
  Until his wame was fu',

Gae, get you gone, you cauldrife wooer,
Ye sour-looking, cauldrife wooer!
I straightway show'd him to the door,
  Saying, Come nae mair to woo.

There lay a deuk-dub before the door,
Before the door, before the door;
There lay a deuk-dub before the door,
  And there fell he, I trow!

Out cam' the gudeman, and high he shouted;
Out cam' the guidwife, and laigh she louted;
And a' the toun-neebors were gather'd about it;
  And there lay he I trow!

Then out cam' I, and sneer'd and smil'd;
Ye cam' to woo, but ye're a' bofyled;
Ye've fa'en i' the dirt, and ye're a' beguiled;
  We'll ha'e nae mair o' you!

O SAW YE MY FAITHER.

Herd's Collection. Mr. Chappell (Music of the Olden time), from finding an English version in an earlier collection, has sprung to the conclusion that it is of English origin,—a conclusion which he does not satisfactorily prove.

O saw ye my father, or saw ye my mither,
  Or saw ye my true love John?
I saw nae your father, I saw nae your mither,
  But I saw your true love John.

It's now ten at night, and the stars gi'e nae light,
   And the bells they ring ding dang,
He's met wi' some delay that causes him to stay,
   But he will be here ere lang.

The surly auld carle did naething but snarl,
   And Johnny's face it grew red,
Yet tho' he often sigh'd he ne'er a word replied,
   Till a' were asleep in bed.

Then up Johnny rose, and to the door he goes,
   And gently tirled at the pin,
The lassie taking tent unto the door she went,
   And she open'd and lat him in.

And are ye come at last! and do I hold you fast!
   And is my Johnny true?
I have nae time to tell, but sae lang's I like mysel',
   Sae lang sall I like you.

Flee up, flee up, my bonnie grey cock,
   And craw when it is day;
And your neck shall be like the bonnie beaten gold,
   And your wings of the silver grey.

The cock proved false, and untrue he was,
   For he crew an hour owre soon:
The lassie thought it day when she sent her love away,
   And it was but a blink of the moon.

THE LOVE O' SILLER.

HERD'S COLLECTION.

'Tis no very lang sinsyne,
   That I had a lad o' my ain;
But now he's awn' to anither,
   And left me a' my lane.
The lass he is courting has siller,
   And I ha'e nane at a',
And 'tis nought but the love o' the tocher
   That's tane my lad awa'.

But I'm blythe that my heart's my ain,
   And I'll keep it a' my life,
Until that I meet wi' a lad,
   Wha has sense to wale a good wife.
For though I say't mysel',
   That should nae say't, 'tis true,
The lad that gets me for a wife
   He'll ne'er ha'e occasion to rue.

I gang aye fu' clean and fu' tosh,
  As a' the neighbours can tell,
Though I've seldom a gown on my back,
  But sic as I spin mysel';
And when I'm clad in my curtsey,
  I think mysel' as braw
As Susie, wi' her pearling,
  That's tane my lad awa'.

But I wish they were buckl'd thegither,
  And may they live happy for life;
Though Willie now slights me, an's left me,
  The chiel he deserves a gude wife.
But, O! I am blythe that I miss'd him,
  As blythe as I weel can be;
For ane that's sae keen o' the siller,
  Would never agree wi' me.

But the truth is, I am aye hearty,
  I hate to be scrimpit or scant;
The wee thing I ha'e I'll mak use o't,
  And there's nane about me shall want:
For I'm a gude guide o' the warld,
  I ken when to haud and to gi'e;
But whinging and cringing for siller
  Would never agree wi' me.

Contentment is better than riches,
  And he wha has that has enough;
The master is seldom sae happy
  As Robin that drives the plough.
But if a young lad wad cast up,
  To mak' me his partner for life,
If the chiel has the sense to be happy,
  He'll fa' on his feet for a wife.

SOUTHLAND JENNY.
HERD'S COLLECTION.

A SOUTHLAND JENNY, that was right bonnie,
Had for a suitor a Norland Johnnie;
But he was sicken a bashful wooer,
That he could scarcely speak unto her;
Till blinks o' her beauty, and hopes o' her siller,
Forced him at last to tell his mind till her.
My dear, quoth he, we'll nae langer tarry,
Gin ye can loo me, let's o'er the muir and marry.

She

Come, come awa' then, my Norland laddie,
Though we gang neatly, some are mair gawdy;
And albeit I have neither gowd nor money,
Come, and I'll ware my beauty on thee.

He

Ye lasses o' the south, ye're a' for dressing;
Lasses o' the north mind milking and threshing;
My minnie wad be angry, and sae wad my daddy,
Should I marry ane as dink as a lady;
For I maun ha'e a wife that will rise i' the morning,
Crudle a' the milk, and keep the house a' scolding,
Toolie wi' her nei'bours, and learn at my minny,
A Norland Jocky maun ha'e a Norland Jenny.

She

My father's only daughter, and twenty thousand pound,
Shall never be bestow'd on sic a silly clown:
For a' that I said was to try what was in ye;
Ga'e hame, ye Norland Jock, and court your Norland Jenny.

HEY, HOW, JOHNNIE LAD.

HERD'S COLLECTION. We have, however, given the song with a few variations from the first version, by Allan Cunningham, and which are necessary to fit the song for "ears polite."

HEY, how, Johnnie lad,
  Ye're no sae kind's ye sud ha'e been,
For gin your voice I had na kent,
  I'm sure I couldna trust my een;
Sae weel's ye might ha'e courted me,
  And sweetly pree'd my mou' bedeen:
Hey, how, my Johnnie lad,
  Ye're no sae kind's ye sud ha'e been.

My father, he was at the pleugh,
  My mither, she was at the mill;
My billie, he was at the moss,
  And no ane near our sport to spile:
The feint a body was therein,
  Ye need na fley'd for being seen:
Hey, how, my Johnnie lad,
  Ye're no sae kind's ye sud ha'e been.

But I maun hae anither joe,
  Whase love gangs never out o' mind,
And winna let the moment pass
  When to a lass he can be kind.

Then ye may woo wi' blinkin' Bess—
  For you nae mair I'll sigh and green:
Hey, how, my Johnnie lad,
  Ye're no sae kind's ye sud ha'e been.

MY WIFE HAD TA'EN THE GEE.
HERD'S COLLECTION.

A FRIEND of mine came here yestreen,
  And he would ha'e me down
To drink a bottle of ale wi' him
  In the neist burrows town.
But, O! indeed it was, Sir,
  Sae far the waur for me;
For lang or e'er that I came hame
  My wife had ta'en the gee.

We sat sae late, and drank sae stout,
  The truth I'll tell to you,
That ere the middle o' the night,
  We were a' roaring fou.
My wife sits at the fire-side,
  And the tears blind aye her e'e,
The ne'er a bed' will she gae to,
  But sit and tak' the gee.

In the morning soon, when I came down,
  The ne'er a word she spake,
But monie a sad and sour look,
  And aye her head she'd shake.
My dear, quoth I, what aileth thee,
  To look sae sour on me?
I'll never do the like again;
  If ye'll ne'er tak' the gee.

When that she heard, she ran, she flang
  Her arms about my neck;
And twenty kisses in a crack,
  And, poor wee thing, she grat.
If ye'll ne'er do the like again,
  But bide at hame wi' me,
I'll lay my life I'se be the wife
  That's never tak' the gee.

IF MY DEAR WIFE.

FROM Maidment's North Country Garland, 1824; recovered from oral tradition.

If my dear wife should chance to gang,
  Wi' me, to Edinburgh toun,
Into a shop I will her tak',
  And buy her a new goun.
But if my dear wife should hain the charge,
  As I expect she will,
And if she says, The auld will do,
  By my word she shall ha'e her will.

If my dear wife should wish to gang,
  To see a neebor or friend,
A horse or a chair I will provide,
  And a servant to attend.
But if my dear wife shall hain the charge,
  As I expect she will,
And if she says, I'll walk on foot,
  By my word she shall ha'e her will.

If my dear wife shall bring me a son,
  As I expect she will,
Cake and wine I will provide,
  And a nurse to nurse the child.
But if my dear wife shall hain the charge,
  As I expect she will,
And if she says, She'll nurs't hersel',
  By my word she shall ha'e her will.

THE SPINNIN' O'T.
ALEXANDER ROSS,

AUTHOR of "Helenore," or the "Fortunate Shepherdess." He was for upwards of fifty years schoolmaster of Lochlee, in Forfarshire. He died in 1783, at the advanced age of 83.

THERE was an auld wife had a wee pickle tow,
  And she wad gae try the spinnin' o't;
She louted her doun, and her rock took a-low,
  And that was a bad beginnin' o't.
She sat and she grat, and she flat and she flang,
  And she threw and she blew, and she wriggled and wrang,
And she chokit and boakit, and cried like to mang,
  Alas, for the dreary beginnin' o't.

I've wanted a sark for these aught years and ten,
  And this was to be the beginnin' o't;
But I vow I shall want it for as lang again,
  Or ever I try the spinnin' o't.

For never since ever they ca'd as they ca' me,
Did sic a mishap and mischanter befa' me;
But ye shall hae leave baith to hang and to draw me,
The neist time I try the spinnin' o't.

I hae keepit my house now these threescore years,
  And aye I kept frae the spinnin' o't;
But how I was sarkit, foul fa' them that speirs,
  For it minds me upo' the beginnin' o't.
But our women are now-a-days a' grown sae braw,
That ilk ane maun hae a sark, and some ha'e twa—
The warlds were better where ne'er ane ava
Had a rag, but ane at the beginnin' o't.

In the days they ca' yore, gin auld fouks had but won
  To a surcoat, hough-syde, for the winnin' o't,
Of coal-raips weel cut by the cast o' their bum,
  They never socht mair o' the spinnin' o't.
A pair o' grey hoggers weel cluikit benew,
Of nae ither lit but the hue of the ewe,
With a pair o' rough mullions to scuff through the dew,
  Was the fee they socht at the beginning o't.

But we maun ha'e linen, and that maun ha's we,
  And how get we that but by spinnin' o't?
How can we hae face for to seek a great fee,
  Except we can help at the winnin' o't?
And we maun ha'e pearlins, and mabbies, and cocks,
And some other things that the ladies ca' smocks;
And how get we that, gin we tak' na our rocks,
  And pow what we can at the spinnin' o't?

'Tis needless for us to mak' our remarks,
  Frae our mither's miscookin' the spinnin' o't.
She never kenn'd ocht o' the guid o' the sarks,
  Frae this aback to the beginnin' o't.
Twa-three ell o' plaiden was a' that was socht
By our auld-warld bodies, and that bude be bought;
For in ilka town siccan things wasna wrocht—
  Sae little they kenn'd o' the spinnin' o't!

THE BRIDAL.
ALEXANDER ROSS.

They say that Jockey'll speed weel o't,
  They say that Jockey'll speed weel o't,
For he grows brawer ilka day;
  I hope we'll ha'e a bridal o't:
For yesternight, nae farther gane,
  The back-house at the side-wa' o't,
He there wi' Meg was mirdin' seen;
  I hope we'll ha'e a bridal o't.

An we had but a bridal o't,
  An we had but a bridal o't,
We'd leave the rest unto good luck,
  Although there might betide ill o't.
For bridal days are merry times,
  And young folk like the coming o't,
And scribblers they bang up their rhymes,
  And pipers play the bumming o't.

The lasses like a bridal o't,
  The lasses like a bridal o't,
Their braws maun be in rank and file,
  Although that they should guide ill o't.
The boddom o' the kist is then
  Turn'd up into the inmost o't;
The end that held the keeks sae clean,
  Is now become the teemest o't.

The bangster at the threshing o't,
  The bangster at the threshing o't,
Afore it comes is fidgin fain,
  And ilka day's a clashing o't:
He'll sell his jerkin for a groat,
  His linder for another o't,
And ere he want to clear his shot,
  His sark'll pay the tother o't.

The pipers and the fiddlers o't,
  The pipers and the fiddlers o't,
Can smell a bridal unco far,
  And like to be the middlers o't:
Fan thick and three-fauld they convene
  Ilka ane envies the tother o't,
And wishes nane but him alane
  May ever see another o't.

Fan they ha'e done wi' eating o't,
  Fan they ha'e done wi' eating o't,
For dancing they gae to the green,
  And aiblins to the beatin o't:
He dances best that dances fast,
  And loups at ilka reesing o't,
And claps his hands frae hough to hough,
  And furls about the feezings o't.

ABSENCE.

DR. BLACKLOCK,

THE author of the celebrated letter to Burns, which overthrew the poet's Jamaica scheme, and turned his steps to Edinburgh. Blacklock was born at Annan in 1721. He lost his sight when very young, and though he studied for the Church, and was duly licensed, his infirmity prevented him from receiving any appointment. He latterly kept a select boarding-house in Edinburgh, devoting himself, however, principally to literary pursuits. He died in 1791.

YE rivers so limpid and clear,
  Who reflect, as in cadence you flow,
All the beauties that vary the year,
  All the flow'rs on your margins that grow!
How blest on your banks could I dwell,
  Were Marg'ret the pleasure to share,
And teach your sweet echoes to tell
  With what fondness I doat on the fair!

Ye harvests, that wave in the breeze
  As far as the view can extend!
Ye mountains, umbrageous with trees,
  Whose tops so majestic ascend!
Your landscape what joy to survey,
  Were Marg'ret with me to admire!
Then the harvest would glitter, how gay,
  How majestic the mountains aspire.

In pensive regret whilst I rove,
  The fragrance of flow'rs to inhale;
Or catch as it swells from the grove,
  The music that floats on the gale:
Alas! the delusion how vain!
  Nor odours nor harmony please
A heart agonizing with pain,
  Which tries ev'ry posture for ease.

If anxious to flatter my woes,
  Or the languor of absence to cheer,
Her breath I would catch in the rose,
  Or her voice in the nightingale hear.
To cheat my despair of its prey,
  What object her charms can assume!
How harsh is the nightingale's lay,
  How insipid the rose's perfume!

Ye zephyrs that visit my fair,
  Ye sunbeams around her that play,
Does her sympathy dwell on my care?
  Does she number the hours of my stay?

First perish ambition and wealth,
  First perish all else that is dear,
Ere one sigh should escape her by stealth,
  Ere my absence should cost her one tear.

When, when shall her beauties once more
  This desolate bosom surprise?
Ye fates! the blest moments restore
  When I bask'd in the beams of her eyes;
When with sweet emulation of heart,
  Our kindness we struggled to show;
But the more that we strove to impart
  We felt it more ardently glow.

THE BRAES OF BALLENDINE.
DR. BLACKLOCK.

BENEATH a green shade, a lovely young swain
Ae evening reclined to discover his pain;
So sad, yet so sweetly, he warbled his woe,
The winds ceased to breathe, and the fountain to flow;
Rude winds wi' compassion could hear him complain,
Yet Chloe, less gentle, was deaf to his strain.

How happy, he cried, my moments once flew,
Ere Chloe's bright charms first flash'd in my view!
Those eyes then wi' pleasure the dawn could survey;
Nor smiled the fair morning mair cheerful than they.
Now scenes of distress please only my sight;
I'm tortured in pleasure, and languish in light.

Through changes in vain relief I pursue,
All, all but conspire my griefs to renew;
From sunshine to zephyrs and shades we repair—
To sunshine we fly from too piercing an air;
But love's ardent fire burns always the same,
No winter can cool it, no summer inflame.

But see the pale moon, all clouded, retires;
The breezes grow cool, not Strephon's desires:
I fly from the dangers of tempest and wind,
Yet nourish the madness that preys on my mind.
Ah, wretch! how can life be worthy thy care?
To lengthen its moments, but lengthens despair.

THE WEDDING DAY.
DR. BLACKLOCK.

One night as young Colin lay musing in bed,
With a heart full of love and a vapourish head;
To wing the dull hours, and his sorrows allay,
Thus sweetly he sang of his wedding day:
 "What would I give for a wedding day!
 Who would not wish for a wedding day!
 Wealth and ambition, I'd toss ye away,
 With all ye can boast, for a wedding day.
Should heaven bid my wishes with freedom implore
One bliss for the anguish I suffered before,
For Jessy, dear Jessy, alone I would pray,
And grasp my whole wish on my wedding day!
 Blessed be the approach of my wedding day!
 Hail, my dear nymph and my wedding day!
 Earth smile more verdant, and heaven shine more gay!
 For happiness dawns with my wedding day."
But Luna, who equally sovereign presides
O'er the hearts of the ladies and flow of the tides,
Unhappily changing, soon changed his wife's mind:
O fate, could a wife prove so constant and kind!
 "Why was I born to a wedding day!
 Cursed, ever cursed be my wedding day."
 Colin, poor Colin thus changes his lay,
 And dates all his plagues from his wedding day.
Ye bachelors, warned by the shepherd's distress,
Be taught from your freedom to measure your bliss,
Nor fall to the witchcraft of beauty a prey,
And blast all your joys on your wedding day.
 Horns are the gift of a wedding day;
 Want and a scold crown a wedding day;
 Happy and gallant, who, wise when he may
 Prefers a stout rope to a wedding day!

ALL LOVELY ON THE SULTRY BEACH.
WILLIAM WALLACE,

Of Cairnhill, Ayrshire. Born 1712, died 1763. Air—The Gordons ha'e the guiding o't.

 All lovely, on the sultry beach,
  Expiring Strephon lay;
 No hand the cordial draught to reach,
  Nor cheer the gloomy way.
 Ill-fated youth! no parent nigh
  To catch thy fleeting breath,
 No bride to fix thy swimming eye,
  Or smooth the face of death.

Far distant from the mournful scene,
  Thy parents sit at ease;
Thy Lydia rifles all the plain,
  And all the spring to please.
Ill-fated youth! by fault of friend,
  Not force of foe depress'd,
Thou fall'st, alas! thyself, thy kind,
  Thy country, unredress'd.

TULLOCHGORUM.

REV. JOHN SKINNER,

Was born at Balfour, in the parish of Birse, Aberdeenshire, in 1721. In 1742 he settled at Longside, near Peterhead, as Pastor of the Episcopal Church. He ministered there till his death, which took place in 1807.

No one was a greater admirer of Skinner's genius as a song writer than Robert Burns, who styled "'Tullochgorum' the best Scotch Song Scotland ever saw."

Come, gi'e's a sang Montgomery cried,
And lay your disputes all aside,
What signifies't for folks to chide
  For what's been done before them?
Let Whig and Tory all agree,
Whig and Tory, Whig and Tory,
Let Whig and Tory all agree,
  To drop their Whig-mig-morum;
Let Whig and Tory all agree,
To spend the night in mirth and glee,
And cheerfu' sing alang wi' me
  The reel of Tullochgorum.

O, Tullochgorum's my delight,
It gars us a' in ane unite,
And ony sumph that keeps up spite,
  In conscience I abhor him.
For blythe and cheerie we's be a',
Blythe and cheerie, blythe and cheerie,
Blythe and cheerie we's be a',
  And mak' a happy quorum.
For blythe and cheerie we's be a',
As lang as we ha'e breath to draw,
And dance, till we be like to fa',
  The reel of Tullochgorum.

There needs na' be sae great a phraise,
Wi' dringing dull Italian lays,
I wadna gi'e our ain strathspeys,
  For half a hundred score o' 'em.

N

They're douff and dowie at the best,
Douff and dowie, douff and dowie,
They're douff and dowie at the best,
　Wi' a' their variorum:
They're douff and dowie at the best,
Their allegros, and a' the rest,
They canna please a Scottish taste,
　Compar'd wi' Tullochgorum.

Let warldly minds themselves oppress
Wi' fears of want, and double cess,
And sullen sots themselves distress
　Wi' keeping up decorum:
Shall we sae sour and sulky sit,
Sour and sulky, sour and sulky,
Shall we sae sour and sulky sit,
　Like auld Philosophorum?
Shall we sae sour and sulky sit,
Wi' neither sense, nor mirth, nor wit,
Nor ever rise to shake a fit
　To the reel of Tullochgorum?

May choicest blessings still attend
Each honest open-hearted friend,
And calm and quiet be his end,
　And a' that's good watch o'er him!
May peace and plenty be his lot,
Peace and plenty, peace and plenty,
May peace and plenty be his lot,
　And dainties a great store o' em:
May peace and plenty be his lot,
Unstain'd by any vicious spot!
And may he never want a groat
　That's fond of Tullochgorum.

But for the dirty, fawning fool,
Who wants to be oppression's tool,
May envy gnaw his rotten soul,
　And discontent devour him!
May dool and sorrow be his chance,
Dool and sorrow, dool and sorrow,
May dool and sorrow be his chance,
　And nane say, Wae's me for 'im!
May dool and sorrow be his chance,
Wi' a' the ills that come frae France,
Whae'er he be, that winna dance
　The reel of Tullochgorum!

A SONG ON THE TIMES.
REV. JOHN SKINNER.

When I began the world first,
It was not as 'tis now,
For all was plain and simple then,
And friends were kind and true.
    O! the times, the weary, weary times,
    The times that I now see,
    I think the world's all gone wrong,
    From what it used to be.

There were not then high capering heads,
Prick'd up from ear to ear,
And cloak, and caps were rarities
For gentle folks to wear.
    O! the times, &c.

There's not an upstart mushroom now,
But what sets up for taste,
And not a lass in all the land
But must be lady-drest.
    O! the times, &c.

Our young men married then for love,
So did our lasses too,
And children loved their parents dear
As children ought to do.
    O! the times, &c.

For O! the times are sadly chang'd,
A heavy change indeed!
For truth and friendship are no more,
And honesty is fled.
    O! the times, &c.

There's nothing now prevails but pride
Among both high and low,
And strife, and greed, and vanity,
Is all that's minded now.
    O! the times, &c.

When I looked through the world wide,
How times and fashions go,
It draws the tears from both my eyes,
And fills my heart with woe.
    O! the times, the weary, weary times,
    The times that I now see,
    I wish the world were at an end,
    For it will not mend for me.

THE EWIE WI' CROOKIT HORN.
REV. JOHN SKINNER.

O, WERE I able to rehearse,
My ewie's praise in proper verse,
I'd sound it out as loud and fierce
   As ever piper's drone could blaw.
My ewie wi' the crookit horn!
A' that kenn'd her would ha'e sworn,
Sic a ewie ne'er was born,
   Hereabouts nor far awa'.

She neither needed tar nor keel,
To mark her upon hip or heel;
Her crookit hornie did as weel
   To ken her by amang them a'.

She never threaten'd scab nor rot,
But keepit aye her ain jog-trot;
Baith to the fauld and to the cot,
   Was never sweir to lead nor ca'.

A better nor a thriftier beast,
Nae honest man need e'er ha'e wish'd;
For, silly thing, she never miss'd
   To ha'e ilk year a lamb or twa.

The first she had I ga'e to Jock,
To be to him a kind o' stock;
And now the laddie has a flock
   Of mair than thretty head and twa.

The neist I ga'e to Jean; and now
The bairn's sae braw, has faulds sae fu',
That lads sae thick come her to woo,
   They're fain to sleep on hay or straw.

Cauld nor hunger never dang her,
Wind or rain could never wrang her;
Ance she lay au ouk and langer
   Forth aneath a wreath o' snaw.

When other ewies lap the dyke,
And ate the kale for a' the tyke,
My ewie never play'd the like,
   But teazed about the barn wa'.

I lookit aye at even for her,
Lest mishanter should come ower her,
Or the foumart micht devour her,
   Gin the beastie baide awa'.

Yet, last ouk, for a' my keeping,
(Wha can tell o't without greeting?)
A villain cam', when I was sleeping,
   Staw my ewie, horn and a'.

I socht her sair upon the morn,
And down aneath a bush o' thorn,
There I fand her crookit horn,
   But my ewie was awa'.

But gin I had the loon that did it,
I ha'e sworn as weel as said it,
Although the laird himsell forbid it,
   I sall gi'e his neck a thraw.

I never met wi' sic a turn:
At e'en I had baith ewe and horn,
Safe steekit up; but, 'gain the morn,
   Baith ewe and horn were stown awa'.

A' the claes that we ha'e worn,
Frae her and hers sae aft was shorn;
The loss o' her we could ha'e borne,
   Had fair-strae death ta'en her awa'.

O, had she died o' croup or cauld,
As ewies die when they grow auld,
It hadna been, by mony fauld,
   Sae sair a heart to ane o' us a'.

But thus, puir thing, to lose her life,
Beneath a bluidy villain's knife;
In troth, I fear that our gudewife
   Will never get abune 't ava.

O, all ye bards benorth Kinghorn,
Call up your muses, let them mourn
Our ewie wi' the crookit horn,
   Frae us stown, and fell'd and a'!

JOHN O' BADENYON.
REV. JOHN SKINNER.

WHEN first I came to be a man, of twenty years, or so,
I thought myself a handsome youth, and fain the world would
   know;
In best attire I stept abroad, with spirits brisk and gay;
And here, and there, and every where, was like a morn in May.
No care I had, no fear of want, but rambled up and down;
And for a beau I might have pass'd in country or in town:
I still was pleased where'er I went; and, when I was alone,
I tuned my pipe, and pleased myself wi' John o' Badenyon.

Now in the days of youthful prime, a mistress I must find;
For love, they say, gives one an air, and ev'n improves the mind:
On Phillis fair, above the rest, kind fortune fix'd mine eyes;
Her piercing beauty struck my heart and she became my choice.

To Cupid, now, with hearty prayer, I offer'd many a vow,
And danced and sung, and sigh'd and swore, as other lovers do;
But when at last I breathed my flame, I found her cold as stone—
I left the girl, and tuned my pipe to John o' Badenyon.

When love had thus my heart beguiled with foolish hopes and vain,
To friendship's port I steer'd my course, and laugh'd at lovers' pain;
A friend I got by lucky chance—'twas something like divine;
An honest friend's a precious gift, and such a gift was mine.
And now, whatever may betide, a happy man was I,
In any strait I knew to whom I freely might apply.
A strait soon came; my friend I tried—he laugh'd, and spurn'd my moan;
I hied me home, and tuned my pipe to John o' Badenyon.

I thought I should be wiser next, and would a patriot turn,
Began to doat on Johnie Wilkes, and cry'd up parson Horne;
Their noble spirit I admir'd, and praised their noble zeal,
Who had, with flaming tongue and pen, maintain'd the public weal.
But, e'er a month or two had pass'd, I found myself betray'd;
'Twas Self and Party, after all, for all the stir they made.
At last I saw these factious knaves insult the very throne;
I cursed them all, and tuned my pipe to John o' Badenyon.

What next to do I mused a while, still hoping to succeed;
I pitch'd on books for company, and gravely tried to read:
I bought and borrowed every where, and studied night and day,
Nor miss'd what dean or doctor wrote, that happen'd in my way.
Philosophy I now esteem'd the ornament of youth,
And carefully, through many a page, I hunted after truth:
A thousand various schemes I tried, and yet was pleased with none;
I threw them by, and tuned my pipe to John o' Badenyon.

And now, ye youngsters everywhere, who wish to make a show,
Take heed in time, nor vainly hope for happiness below;
What you may fancy pleasure here is but an empty name;
And girls, and friends, and books also, you'll find them all the same.
Then be advised, and warning take from such a man as me;
I'm neither pope nor cardinal, nor one of high degree;
You'll meet displeasure every where; then do as I have done—
E'en tune your pipe, and please yourself with John o' Badenyon.

THE MARQUIS'S REEL.
REV. JOHN SKINNER.

Tune your fiddles, tune them sweetly,
Play the marquis' reel discreetly,
Here we are a band completely
    Fitted to be jolly.
Come, my boys, blythe and gawcie,
Every youngster choose his lassie,
Dance wi' life and be not saucy,
    Shy nor melancholy.
  Come, my boys, &c.

Lay aside your sour grimaces,
Clouded brows and drumlie faces,
Look about and see their Graces,
    How they smile delighted:
Now's the season to be merry,
Hang the thoughts of Charon's ferry,
Time enough to come camsterry,
    When we're auld and doited.
  Now's the season, &c.

Butler, put about the claret,
Through us a' divide and share it,
Gordon Castle weel can spare it,
    It has claret plenty:
Wine's the true inspiring liquor,
Draffy drink may please the vicar,
When he grasps the foaming bicker,
    Vicars are not dainty.
  Wine's the true inspiring liquor, &c.

We'll extol our noble master,
Sprung from many a brave ancestor,—
Heaven preserve him from disaster,
    So we pray in duty.
Prosper, too, our pretty duchess,
Safe from all distressful touches,
Keep her out of Pluto's clutches,
    Long in health and beauty.
  Prosper, too, our pretty duchess, &c.

Angels guard their gallant boy,
Make him long his father's joy,
Sturdy, like the heir of Troy,
    Stout and brisk and healthy.
Pallas grant him every blessing,
Wit and strength, and size increasing,
Plutus, what's in thy possessing,
    Make him rich and wealthy.
  Pallas grant him every blessing, &c.

Youth, solace him with thy pleasure,
In refined and worthy measure:
Merit gain him choicest treasure,
  From the Royal donor:
Famous may he be in story,
Full of days and full of glory;
To the grave, when old and hoary,
  May he go with honour!
 Famous may he be in story, &c.

Gordons, join our hearty praises,
Honest, though in homely phrases,
Love our cheerful spirit raises,
  Lofty as the lark is:
Echo, waft our wishes daily,
Through the grove and through the alley
Sound o'er every hill and valley,
  Blessings on our Marquis.
 Echo, waft our wishes, &c.

OLD AGE.
REV. JOHN SKINNER.

O! why should old age so much wound us, O?
There is nothing in't all to confound us, O?
 For how happy now am I,
 With my old wife sitting by,
And our bairns and our oyes all around us, O.
We began in the world wi' naething, O,
And we've jogged on and toiled for the ae thing, O;
 We made use of what we had,
 And our thankfu' hearts were glad,
When we got the bit meat and the claithing, O.

We have lived all our lifetime contented, O,
Since the day we became first acquainted, O;
 It's true we've been but poor,
 And we are so to this hour,
Yet we never pined nor lamented, O.
We ne'er thought o' schemes to be wealthy, O,
By ways that were cunning or stealthie, O;
 But we always had the bliss—
 And what farther could we wiss?—
To be pleased wi' ourselves and be healthy, O.

What though we canna boast of our guineas, O,
We have plenty of Jockies and Jeanies, O;
 And these, I'm certain, are
 More desirable by far,
Than a pock full of poor yellow steenies, O.

We have seen many a wonder and ferlie, O,
Of changes that almost are yearlie, O,
   Among rich folks up and down,
   Both in country and in town,
Who now live but scrimply and barely, O.

Then why should people brag of prosperity, O?
A straitened life, we see, is no rarity, O;
   Indeed, we've been in want,
   And our living been but scant,
Yet we never were reduced to need charity, O.
In this house we first came together, O,
Where we've long been a father and mother, O;
   And though not of stone and lime,
   It will last us a' our time;
And I hope we shall never need anither, O.

And when we leave this poor habitation, O,
We'll depart with a good commendation, O;
   We'll go hand in hand, I wiss,
   To a better house than this,
To make room for the next generation, O.
Then why should old age so much wound us, O?
There is nothing in't all to confound us, O?
   For how happy now am I,
   With my auld wife sitting by,
And our bairns and our oyes all around us, O!

THERE LIVES A LASSIE ON THE BRAE.
REV. JOHN SKINNER.

ANOTHER version is given in the collected volume of the Author's poems, 1809.

   THERE lives a lassie on the brae,
    O! but she's a bonnie creature;
   They ca' her Lizy Liberty,
    And monie ane's wooing at her.
      Wooing at her, fain wad ha'e her,
      Courting at, but canna get her;
      Bonnie Lizy Liberty,
      There's o'er mony wooing at her.

   Her mither wears a plettit mutch;
    Her father is an honest dyker,
   An' she hersel's a daintie quean,
    Ye winna shaw me monie like her,
      Wooing at her, &c.

A pleasant lass she's kent to be,
  Wi' fouth o' sense an' smeddum in her;
There's no a swankie far or near,
  But tries wi' a' his might to win her.
    Wooing at her, &c.

But sweet and pleasant as she is,
  She winna thole the marriage tether,
But likes to rove and rant about,
  Like highland couts amang the heather.
    Wooing at her, &c.

It's seven years and somewhat mair,
  Sin' Matthew Dutch made courtship till her,
A merchant bluff, ayont the burn,
  Wi' heaps o' breeks an' bags o' siller.
    Wooing at her, &c.

The next to him was Baltic John,
  Stept up the brae and kesket at her,
Syne turn'd as great a fool's he came,
  And in a day or twa forgat her.
    Wooing at her, &c.

Now Lawrie French has ta'en the whim,
  To toss his airs, and frisk about her,
And Malcolm Fleming puffs and swears
  He disna value life without her.
    Wooing at her, &c.

They've casten out wi' a' their kin,
  Thinking that wad gar them get her;
Yet after a' the fash they've ta'en,
  They maybe winna be the better.
    Wooing at her, &c.

But Donald Scot's the happy lad,
  Wha seems to be the coshest wi' her;
He never fails to get a kiss,
  As aften as he likes to see her.
    Wooing at her, &c.

But Donald, tak' a friend's advice,
  Although I kon ye fain wad ha'e her,
E'en just be doing as ye are,
  And haud wi' what ye're getting frae her.
    Wooing at her, &c.

Ye're weel, and wats nae, as we say,
　In getting leave to dwell beside her;
And gin ye had her mair your ain,
　Ye'd maybe find it waur to guide her.
　　Wooing at her, &c.

Ah! Lawrie, ye've debauch'd the lass,
　Wi' vile new-fangled tricks ye've play'd her;
Depraved her morals;—like an ass,
　Ye've courted her, and syne betray'd her.
　　Wi' hanging of her, burning of her,
　　Cutting, hacking, slashing at her;
　　Bonnie Lizy Liberty,
　　May ban the day ye ettled at her.

WHEN I UPON THY BOSOM LEAN.
JOHN LAPRAIK.

A SMALL Ayrshire Laird, who was ruined by the bursting of "that villanous bubble, the Ayr Bank." He was born at Dalfram, near Muirkirk, in 1727, and died at Muirkirk, where he kept the Post-office, in 1807. He was intimately acquainted with Burns, who describes him as "a very worthy facetious old fellow." The song here given, addressed to his wife, is said to have been written when he was a prisoner for debt in Ayr gaol.

When I upon thy bosom lean,
　Enraptured do I call thee mine,
I glory in the sacred ties
　That made us ane, wha ance were twain.
A mutual flame inspires us baith,
　The tender look, the meltin' kiss:
Even years shall ne'er destroy our love,
　But only gi'e us change o' bliss.

Ha'e I a wish? it's a' for thee!
　I ken thy wish is me to please.
Our moments pass sae smooth away,
　That numbers on us look and gaze;
Weel pleased they see our happy days,
　Nor envy's sel' finds aught to blame;
And aye, when weary cares arise,
　Thy bosom still shall be my hame.

I'll lay me there and tak' my rest;
　And, if that aught disturb my dear,
I'll bid her laugh her cares away,
　And beg her not to drop a tear.
Ha'e I a joy? it's a' her ain!
　United still her heart and mine;
They're like the woodbine round the tree,
　That's twined till death shall them disjoin.

MY AULD MAN.

Ritson's Scottish Songs, 1794.

In the land of Fife there lived a wicked wife,
  And in the town of Cupar then,
Who sorely did lament, and made her complaint,
  Oh when will ye die, my auld man?

In cam her cousin Kate, when it was growing late,
  She said, What's guid for an auld man?
O wheit-breid and wine, and a kinnen new slain;
  That's guid for an auld man.

Cam ye in to jeer, or cam ye in to scorn,
  And what for cam ye in?
For bear-bread and water, I'm sure, is much better—
  It's ower guid for an auld man.

Now the auld man's deid, and, without remeid,
  Into his cauld grave he's gane:
Lie still wi' my blessing! of thee I hae nae missing;
  I'll ne'er mourn for an auld man.

Within a little mair than three-quarters of a year,
  She was married to a young man then,
Who drank at the wine, and tippled at the beer,
  And spent mair gear than he wan.

O black grew her brows, and howe grew her een,
  And cauld grew her pat and her pan:
And now she sighs, and aye she says,
  I wish I had my silly auld man!

THE SCOTTISH KAIL BROSE.

Ascribed, says Mr. Robert Chambers, to "—— Shariff, an Aberdeenshire poet," a contemporary of Burns. Mr. Peter Buchan ascribes a somewhat similar song to Alex. Watson, at one time tailor in Aberdeen, and states that it was composed during the American War of Independence.

When our ancient forefathers agreed wi' the laird,
  For a wee piece grund to be a kail-yard,
It was to the brose that they paid their regard;
    O! the kail brose of auld Scotland;
    And O! for the Scottish kail brose.

When Fergus, the first of our kings I suppose,
At the head of his nobles had vanquish'd our foes,
Just before they began they 'd been feastin' on brose.
    O! the kail brose, &c.

Our sodgers were drest in their kilts and short hose,
With bonnet and belt which their dross did compose,
With a bag of oatmeal on their back to be brose.
    O! the kail brose, &c.

At our annual election of bailies or mayor,
Nae kickshaws or puddings or tarts were seen there,
But a cog o' guid brose was the favourite fare.
   O! the kail brose, &c.

But when we remember the English, our foes,
Our ancestors beat them wi' very few blows;
John Bull oft cried, O! let us rin—they've got brose;
   O! the kail brose, &c.

But, now that the thistle is joined to the rose,
And the English nae langer are counted our foes,
We've lost a good deal of our relish for brose;
   O! the kail brose, &c.

Yet each true-hearted Scotchman by nature jocose,
Likes always to feast on a cog o' guid brose,
And thanks be to Heaven we've plenty of those.
   O! the kail brose, &c.

CA' THE YOWES.
ATTRIBUTED TO ISABELLA PAGAN,

A CONTEMPORARY of Burns. A strange compound of woman and devil. She lived at Muirkirk, Ayrshire, where she subsisted partly by charity, but principally by selling whisky (without a licence) to drouthy neighbours and visitors. She sang well, had great and ready wit, and could be sociable when she pleased, but generally her temper was furious, her manner cruel, her habits dissolute, and her wit biting and sarcastic. She died in 1821, in her eightieth year. A curious account of her is given in Mr. Paterson's contemporaries of Burns.

   CA' the yowes to the knowes,
   Ca' them whare the heather grows,
   Ca' them whare the burnie rows,
     My bonnie dearie.

   As I gaed down the water side,
   There I met my shepherd lad,
   He row'd me sweetly in his plaid,
     And ca'd me his dearie.
     Ca' the ewes, &c.

   Will ye gang down the water side,
   And see the waves sae sweetly glide,
   Beneath the hazels spreading wide,
     The moon it shines fu' clearly.
     Ca' the yowes, &c.

   I was bred up at nae sic school,
   My shepherd lad, to play the fool;
   And a' the day to sit in dool,
     And nae body to see me.
     Ca' the yowes, &c.

Ye shall get gowns and ribbons meet,
Cauf leather shoon upon your feet,
And in my arms ye'se lie and sleep,
And ye shall be my dearie.
    Ca' the yowes, &c.

If ye'll but stand to what ye've said,
I'se gang wi' you, my shepherd lad;
And ye may row me in your plaid,
And I shall be your dearie.
    Ca' the yowes, &c.

While waters wimple to the sea,
While day blinks in the lift sae hie,
Till clay-cauld death shall blin' my e'e,
Ye aye shall be my dearie.
    Ca' the yowes, &c.

IF DOUGHTY DEEDS MY LADY PLEASE.
ROBERT GRAHAM OF GARTMORE.
Born 1750, died 1797.

If doughty deeds my lady please,
  Right soon I'll mount my steed:
And strong his arm, and fast his seat,
  That bears frae me the meed.
I'll wear thy colours in my cap,
  Thy picture in my heart;
And he that bends not to thine eye,
  Shall rue it to his smart.
    Then tell me how to woo thee, love,
      O tell me how to woo thee!
    For thy dear sake, nae care I'll take,
      Though ne'er another trow me.

If gay attire delight thine eye,
  I'll dight me in array;
I'll tend thy chamber door all night,
  And squire thee all the day.
If sweetest sounds can win thine ear,
  These sounds I'll strive to catch;
Thy voice I'll steal to woo thysell,
  That voice that nane can match.

But if fond love thy heart can gain,
  I never broke a vow;
Nae maiden lays her skaith to me;
  I never loved but you.
For you alone I ride the ring,
  For you I wear the blue;
For you alone I strive to sing—
  O tell me how to woo!

O'ER THE MUIR.

JEAN GLOVER,

A STROLLING Player. She was born at Kilmarnock in the year 1758, and at a comparatively early age eloped with an actor, and in her future life had a full share of the usual lot of strollers—almost constant poverty, vice, and riot. Burns, to whom we are indebted for the preservation of this song, took it down from her singing. She died suddenly at Letterkenny in Ireland, in 1801.

  Comin' through the craigs o' Kyle,
   Amang the bonnie bloomin' heather,
  There I met a bonnie lassie,
   Keepin' a' her flocks thegither.
    Ower the muir amang the heather,
    Ower the muir amang the heather,
    There I met a bonnie lassie,
    Keepin' a' her flocks thegither.

  Says I, My dear, where is thy hame?
   In muir or dale, pray tell me whether?
  Says she, I tent the fleecy flocks
   That feed amang the bloomin' heather.

  We laid us down upon a bank,
   Sae warm and sunnie was the weather;
  She left her flocks at large to rove
   Amang the bonnie bloomin' heather.

  She charm'd my heart, and aye sinsyne
   I could nae think on ony ither:
  By sea and sky ! she shall be mine,
   The bonnie lass amang the heather.

PART III.

From BURNS *to* MOTHERWELL.

THERE WAS A LAD.

ROBERT BURNS,

WAS born on the 25th January, 1759, in a small roadside cottage about two miles southward from Ayr, and in the immediate vicinity of "Alloway's Auld Haunted Kirk," &c. His father at the time was acting as overseer to Mr. Fergusson of Doonholm, from whom he leased a few acres of ground, whereby he added to his income by acting as Nurseryman and Market Gardener. In 1776 he entered upon a lease of the farm of Mount Oliphant, with a view of bettering his position, and above all a wish of personally superintending the education and employment of his children. From that moment began the hard grim battle which William Burness fought with fortune, and from which he only retired when despair and poverty fairly mastered him. He died of consumption in 1784.

In his sixth year Robert was sent to a small village school; afterwards his education was completed by William Murdoch, a young man engaged by William Burness and several of his neighbours to act as teacher, at a small salary, he lodging and boarding in their houses by turns. So far as the rudiments of learning were concerned Robert received a larger share than generally fell to the lot of children of his class. While pursuing his education, however, his help had to be given to the working of the farm. His brother Gilbert has recorded: "To the buffetings of fortune, we could only oppose hard labour and the most rigid economy. We lived very sparing. For several years butchers' meat was a stranger in the house, while all the members of the family exerted themselves to the utmost of their strength, and rather beyond it in the labours of the farm. My brother at the age of thirteen assisted in threshing the crop of corn, and at fifteen was the principal labourer on the farm, for we had no hired servant, male or female."

Some short while before the death of their father, observing that affairs were drawing to a crisis, Robert and Gilbert had taken a lease of another farm, and stocked it as well as their means would allow, so as to form a shelter for the family, when the crash came. Mossgiel, as the farm was called, did not however, prove a profitable speculation: the soil was poor and damp, and the crops were constantly turning out failures. Other and foreign troubles now came upon him. He entered with avidity into the miserable theological disputes which then agitated Ayrshire. Auld Light and New Light was the cry of the disputants, and Burns having thrown himself with all his power on the side of the New Lights, succeeded in bringing upon himself all the wrath and bitterness of religious animosity. He struck out vigorously, however, and the Twa Herds, Holy Fair, and above all Holy Willie's prayer, fell with terrific power into the midst of the Auld Lights, accompanied by the laughter and derision of the New. Burns' best friends advised him against continuing the warfare, but his blood was up and he continued the assault, leaving himself as a mark for all the bigots of the country. No fault, however trifling, could be committed by him without being loudly proclaimed from the housetops. Every form of meanness was resorted to, to punish the satirist, and this retaliation pursued him to the grave, and, it is with shame we record it, his memory even to our own time.

Another trouble. He had met with Jean Armour at a penny wedding in Mauchline, and a mutual passion seems to have sprung up between the two. Promise of marriage doubtless followed, but its consummation was prevented by the failure of his farming speculations. In 1786 he learned that Jean was about to become a mother, and that, irritated at his daughter's treatment, her father had debarred any further correspondence between them. A letter was immediately sent by the poet to Jean acknowledging her as his wife, (constituting a legal marriage under the Scotch Law.) This letter was destroyed by Mr. Armour. "Burns's feelings at this crisis," says Mr. Alexander Smith, "may be imagined. Pride, love, anger, despair, strove for mastery in his heart. Weary of his existence, and seeing ruin staring him in the face at Mossgiel, he resolved to seek better fortune and solace for a lacerated heart in exile." An engagement was secured by him to go to Jamaica and act as book-keeper on an estate there. In order to raise sufficient funds to defray his passage, he was advised to print a volume of his poems by subscription. The idea, once started, was soon worked out, and Johnny Wilson of Kilmarnock commenced printing.

About this time occurs the celebrated episode of Highland Mary, a love passage involved in considerable mystery. The general opinion now is, that, disgusted with the Armours, and bitter at Jean for giving way to her father, he met with Mary Campbell, a servant girl, and fell in love with her with all the ardour and force of his nature. Their marriage was arranged, and Mary gave up her situation, and proceeded to visit her friends in the West Highlands. She died suddenly in Greenock and was buried there. Word was brought to Burns, and its reception was perhaps the deepest grief he ever bore. How he loved her his own words tell, and how he still mourned for her when many years had passed, and other ties had woven round his heart, his beautiful and impassioned lines sufficiently testify. "To Mary in Heaven" is one of the finest laments in the whole realm of poetry.

Jean had become the mother of twins, and her father proceeded to put in execution his right to prosecute Burns for their support, and threatened him with jail till he could find suitable security for the same. Burns was unable to pay, and a jail would only finally ruin him. He therefore skulked about, stealing into Kilmarnock at times to correct his proofs. The volume appeared in July, 1786, and his prospects immediately brightened. "I threw off six hundred copies," he tells, "for which I got subscriptions for three hundred and fifty. My vanity was gratified by the reception I got from the public, and besides I pocketed, all expenses deducted, nearly twenty pounds. * * * As soon as I was master of nine guineas the price of wafting me to the torrid zone, I took a steerage passage in the first ship that was to sail from the Clyde. * * * I had taken the last farewell of my few friends. My chest was on the way to Greenock. I had composed the last song I should ever measure in Caledonia.—"The gloomy night is gathering fast," when a letter from Dr. Blacklock to a friend of mine, overthrew all my schemes by opening new prospects to my poetic ambition."

This letter which exercised so powerful an influence on his career was expressive of the writer's deepest admiration, and counselling a visit to Edinburgh, with the view of producing a second and larger edition. Golden words too poured in from all quarters. Professor Dugald Stewart, Dr. Blair, and others, expressed the warmest approbation of the poems, and instead of sailing down the Clyde a desolate and ruined man, he turned to Edinburgh to become the gaze and glory of a fashionable season.

The visit to Edinburgh is the greatest episode in his career: courted, petted, and caressed for a while, the public soon tired of its darling and sought for newer attractions. He did not leave the town, however, without a good slice of the solid pudding which was so necessary to him. The second edition of his poems appeared in 1787, under the auspices of the Caledonian Hunt, and his profits amounted to upwards of £400. From this sum he advanced £200 to his brother Gilbert, who still struggled at Mossgiel. This fact is not very prominently remembered by the maligners of his character, but we cannot help thinking that, even in a Christian land, one man, as soon as he has earned a few hundred pounds, giving one half of it to assist a struggling brother is an action seldom heard of. With the rest of the money he leased and stocked the farm of Ellisland, in Dumfriesshire; and having, on the 24th March, 1788, atoned to Jean Armour by making her his wife, he settled down industriously as a farmer.

For a few months all went well. The farm worked pretty fairly, and between his duties in connection with it during the day, and his reading and composing at night, the time passed on, probably the happiest in his life. Johnson's Museum was in course of publication, and for it, as all the world knows, he worked heartily and well. Songs, snatches, and hints were duly posted to Johnson in Edinburgh, and but for his aid that glorious work would have died an untimely death with the first volume.

His family now began to increase, and he found that the farm did not pay extra well. He obtained an appointment in the Excise at a salary of fifty pounds per annum, and as his duties in connection with this office were great, the farm was not properly attended to. Troubles again thickened around him, and disease too, began to add its terrors. After a short struggle he sold his farming stock, and receiving an appointment in the Dumfries division of Excise, at a salary of seventy pounds per annum, he removed to that town in November.

And now begins the most melancholy part of his career. He could not hide from himself that his worldly prospects were dimmed, and his pride waxed stronger. He raved about independence, hurrahed the French Revolutionists, sent them presents of guns, &c., and, above all, entered deeply into the convivial pleasures of which the little country town was full. His duties were regularly performed, but the open garment of republicanism he wore, brought down upon him the resentment of his superiors. He was severely reprimanded for his rashness, but the reprimand only served to make him fairly lose heart, and to hurl him deeper into the mire of dissipation, to hide if possible his position from himself.

His literary work in Dumfries consisted of his contributions to Thomson's Melodies, a sort of Drawing-room Edition of the Songs of Scotland. He had joined the Dumfries Volunteers, and "Does Haughty Gaul invasion threat" inspired his comrades with additional valour and determination to defend their country. The end, however, was fast approaching. In January, 1796, he was seized with a rheumatic fever, and when almost recovered, his own imprudence brought on a relapse. His frame fairly broke down. Sea-bathing was tried without success, and the hand of death pressed heavily upon him: remorse, grief, and debt added their terrors, till on the 21st July, 1796, he passed beyond their pale.

There was a lad was born in Kyle,
But whatna day o' whatna style,
I doubt it's hardly worth the while
  To be sae nice wi' Robin.
Robin was a rovin' boy,
  Rantin' rovin', rantin' rovin;
Robin was a rovin' boy,
  Rantin' rovin' Robin.

Our monarch's hindmost year but ane
Was five-and-twenty days begun,
'Twas then a blast o' Janwar' win'
  Blew hansel in on Robin.

The gossip keekit in his loof,
Quo' she, Wha lives will see the proof,
This waly boy will be na coof;
  I think we'll ca' him Robin.

He'll ha'e misfortunes great and sma',
But aye a heart aboon them a';
He'll be a credit to us a'—
  We'll a' be proud o' Robin.

But sure as three times three mak' nine,
I see by ilka score and line,
This chap will dearly like our kin',
  So leeze me on thee, Robin.

ONCE I LOVED A BONNIE LASS.
ROBERT BURNS.

Oh once I lov'd a bonnie lass,
  Ay, and I love her still;
An' whilst that honour warms my breast
  I'll love my handsome Nell.

As bonnie lasses I ha'e seen,
  An mony full as braw;
But for a modest, gracefu' mien,
  The like I never saw.

A bonnie lass I will confess,
  Is pleasant to the ee,
But without some better qualities,
  She's no the lass for me.

But Nelly's looks are blythe and sweet,
  An', what is best of a',
Her reputation is complete,
  An' fair without a flaw.

She dresses aye sae clean and neat,
  Both decent and genteel:
An' then there's something in her gait
  Gars onie dress look weel.

A gaudy dress and gentle air
  May slightly touch the heart;
But it's innocence and modesty
  That polishes the dart.

'Tis this in Nelly pleases me,
  'Tis this enchants my soul;
For absolutely in my breast
  She reigns without control.

I DREAMED I LAY.
ROBERT BURNS.

I DREAM'D I lay where flowers were springing
  Gaily in the sunny beam,
List'ning to the wild birds singing,
  By a falling, crystal stream:
Straight the sky grew black and daring;
Thro' the woods the whirlwinds rave;
Trees with aged arms were warring,
  O'er the swelling drumlie wave.

Such was my life's deceitful morning,
  Such the pleasure I enjoyed;
But lang or noon, loud tempests storming,
  A' my flowery bliss destroy'd.
Tho' fickle fortune has deceiv'd me,
  She promis'd fair, and perform'd but ill;
Of mony a joy and hope bereav'd me,
  I bear a heart shall support me still.

ON CESSNOCK BANKS.
ROBERT BURNS.

ON Cessnock banks there lives a lass,
  Could I describe her shape an' mien;
The graces of her weel-faur'd face,
  An' the glancin' of her sparklin' een!
She's fresher than the morning dawn
  When rising Phœbus first is seen,
When dew-drops twinkle o'er the lawn;
  An' she's twa glancin' sparklin' een.

She's stately like yon youthful ash,
  That grows the cowslip braes between,
An' shoots its head above each bush;
  An' she's twa glancin' sparklin' een.

She's spotless as the flow'ring thorn,
　With flowers so white an' leaves so green,
When purest in the dewy morn;
　An' she's twa glancin' sparklin een.
Her looks are like the sportive lamb,
　When flow'ry May adorns the scene,
That wantons round its bleating dam;
　An' she's twa glancin' sparklin' een.
Her hair is like the curling mist
　That shades the mountain-side at e'en,
When flow'r reviving rains are past;
　An' she's twa glancin' sparklin' een.
Her forehead's like the show'ry bow,
　When shining sunbeams intervene,
An' gild the distant mountain's brow:
　An' she's twa glancin' sparklin een.
Her voice is like the evening thrush
　That sings in Cessnock banks unseen,
While his mate sits nestling in the bush;
　An' she's twa glancin' sparklin' een.
Her lips are like the cherrie ripe
　That sunny walls from Boreas screen—
They tempt the taste an' charm the sight;
　An she's twa glancin' sparklin een.
Her teeth are like a flock of sheep,
　With fleeces newly washen clean,
That slowly mount the rising steep;
　An' she's twa glancin' sparklin' een.
Her breath is like the fragrant breeze
　That gently stirs the blossom'd bean,
When Phœbus sinks beneath the seas;
　An' she's twa glancin' sparklin' een.
But it's not her air, her form, her face,
　Tho' matching beauty's fabled queen,
But the mind that shines in ev'ry grace,
　An' chiefly in her sparklin' een.

MARY MORISON.
ROBERT BURNS.

Oh Mary, at thy window be,
　It is the wish'd, the trysted hour!
Those smiles an' glances let me see,
　That make the miser's treasure poor;
How blythely wad I bide the stoure,
　A weary slave frae sun to sun,
Could I the rich reward secure,
　The lovely Mary Morison.

Yestreen when to the trembling string,
　The dance gaed thro' the lighted ha',
To thee my fancy took its wing,
　I sat, but neither heard nor saw.
Tho' this was fair, an' that was braw,
　An' yon the toast of a' the town,
I sigh'd, an' said amang them a',
　"Ye are na Mary Morison."

Oh Mary, canst thou wreck his peace,
　Wha for thy sake wad gladly die?
Or canst thou break that heart of his,
　Whase only faut is loving thee?
If love for love thou wilt nae gie,
　At least be pity on me shown;
A thought ungentle canna be
　The thought o' Mary Morison.

MY FATHER WAS A FARMER.
ROBERT BURNS.

My father was a farmer upon the Carrick border, O,
And carefully he bred me in decency and order, O;
He bade me act a manly part, though I had ne'er a farthing, O;
For without an honest manly heart, no man was worth regarding, O.

Then out into the world my course I did determine, O;
Tho' to be rich was not my wish, yet to be great was charming, O;
My talents they were not the worst, nor yet my education, O;
Resolv'd was I at least to try to mend my situation, O.

In many a way, and vain essay, I courted fortune's favour, O;
Some cause unseen still stopt between to frustrate each endeavour, O.
Sometimes by foes I was o'erpower'd; sometimes by friends
　　forsaken, O:
And when my hope was at the top I still was worst mistaken, O.

Then sore harass'd, and tir'd at last with fortune's vain delusion, O,
I dropt my schemes like idle dreams, and came to this conclusion, O;
The past was bad, and the future hid; its good or ill untried, O;
But the present hour was in my pow'r, and so I would enjoy it, O.

No help, nor hope, nor view had I, nor person to befriend me, O;
So I must toil, and sweat and broil, and labour to sustain me, O;
To plough and sow, to reap and mow, my father bred me early, O;
For one, he said, to labour bred, was a match for fortune fairly, O.

Thus all obscure, unknown, and poor, thro' life I'm doom'd to
　　wander, O,
Till down my weary bones I lay in everlasting slumber, O.
No view nor care, but shun whate'er might breed me pain or
　　sorrow, O!
I live to-day, as well's I may, regardless of to-morrow, O.

But cheerful still, I am as well as a monarch in a palace, O,
Tho' fortune's frown still hunts me down, with all her wonted malice, O;
I make indeed my daily bread, but ne'er can make it farther, O;
But, as daily bread is all I need, I do not much regard her, O.

When sometimes by my labour I earn a little money, O,
Some unforeseen misfortune comes gen'rally upon me, O:
Mischance, mistake, or by neglect, or my good-natur'd folly, O;
But come what will, I've sworn it still, I'll ne'er be melancholy, O.

All you who follow wealth and power with unremitting ardour, O,
The more in this you look for bliss, you leave your view the farther, O:
Had you the wealth Potosi boasts, or nations to adore you, O,
A cheerful, honest-hearted clown I will prefer before you, O.

NANNIE O.
ROBERT BURNS.

Behind yon hills where Lugar flows,
  'Mang moors an' mosses many, O,
The wintry sun the day has clos'd,
  An' I'll awa' to Nannie, O.

The westlin wind blaws loud an' shill;
  The night's baith mirk an' rainy, O;
But I'll get my plaid, an' out I'll steal,
  An' owre the hills to Nannie, O.

My Nannie's charming, sweet, an' young;
  Nae artfu' wiles to win ye, O;
May ill befa' the flattering tongue
  That wad beguile my Nannie, O.

Her face is fair, her heart is true,
  As spotless as she's bonnie, O:
The op'ning gowan, wat wi' dew,
  Nae purer is than Nannie, O.

A country lad is my degree,
  An' few there be that ken me, O;
But what care I how few they be?
  I'm welcome aye to Nannie, O.

My riches a's my penny-fee,
  An' I maun guide it cannie, O;
But warl's gear ne'er troubles me,
  My thoughts are a' my Nannie, O.

Our auld gudeman delights to view
His sheep an' kye thrive bonnie, O;
But I'm as blythe that hauds his pleugh,
And has nae care but Nannie, O.

Come weel, come woe, I care na by,
I'll tak' what Heav'n will sen' me, O;
Nae ither care in life ha'e I,
But live, an' love my Nannie, O.

CORN RIGS.
ROBERT BURNS.

It was upon a Lammas night,
When corn rigs are bonnie,
Beneath the moon's unclouded light,
I held awa' to Annie:
The time flew by wi' tentless heed,
Till 'tween the late and early,
Wi' sma' persuasion she agreed
To see me thro' the barley.
   Corn rigs, and barley rigs,
     And corn rigs are bonnie:
   I'll ne'er forget that happy night
     Amang the rigs wi' Annie.

The sky was blue, the wind was still,
The moon was shining clearly;
I set her down wi' right good will
Amang the rigs o' barley;
I ken't her heart was a' my ain;
I lov'd her most sincerely;
I kissed her owre and owre again,
Amang the rigs o' barley.

I lock'd her in my fond embrace;
Her heart was beating rarely:
My blessings on that happy place,
Amang the rigs o' barley;
But by the moon and stars so bright,
That shone that hour so clearly!
She aye shall bless that happy night,
Amang the rigs o' barley.

I ha'e been blythe wi' comrades dear:
I ha'e been merry drinkin';
I ha'e been joyfu' gath'rin' gear;
I ha'e been happy thinkin':

But a' the pleasures e'er I saw,
Tho' three times doubl'd fairly,
That happy night was worth them a',
Amang the rigs o' barley.

GREEN GROW THE RASHES.
ROBERT BURNS.

There's nought but care on ev'ry han',
In every hour that passes, O:
What signifies the life o' man,
An 'twere na for the lasses, O.
   Green grow the rashes, O!
   Green grow the rashes, O!
   The sweetest hours that e'er I spend
   Are spent amang the lasses, O.

The war'ly race may riches chase,
An' riches still may fly them, O;
An' tho' at last they catch them fast,
Their hearts can ne'er enjoy them, O.

But gi'e me a canny hour at e'en,
My arms about my dearie, O;
An' warly cares, an' warly men,
May a' gae tapsalteerie, O.

For you sae douce, ye sneer at this,
Ye're nought but senseless asses, O;
The wisest man the warl' e'er saw,
He dearly lov'd the lasses, O.

Auld Nature swears, the lovely dears
Her noblest work she classes, O:
Her 'prentice han' she tried on man,
An' then she made the lasses, O.

FLOW GENTLY, SWEET AFTON.
ROBERT BURNS.

Flow gently, sweet Afton, amang thy green braes,
Flow gently, I'll sing thee a song in thy praise;
My Mary's asleep by thy murmuring stream,
Flow gently, sweet Afton, disturb not her dream.

Thou stock-dove whose echo resounds thro' the glen,
Ye wild whistling blackbirds in yon thorny den,
Thou green-crested lapwing thy screaming forbear,
I charge you disturb not my slumbering fair.

How lofty, sweet Afton, thy neighbouring hills,
Far mark'd with the courses of clear winding rills;
There daily I wander as noon rises high,
My flocks and my Mary's sweet cot in my eye.

How pleasant thy banks and green valleys below,
Where wild in the woodlands the primroses blow;
There oft as mild evening weeps over the lea,
The sweet-scented birk shades my Mary and me.

Thy crystal stream, Afton, how lovely it glides,
And winds by the cot where my Mary resides;
How wanton thy waters her snowy feet lave,
As gathering sweet flow'rets she stems thy clear wave.

Flow gently, sweet Afton, among thy green braes,
Flow gently, sweet river, the theme of my lays;
My Mary's asleep by thy murmuring stream,
Flow gently, sweet Afton, disturb not her dream.

WILL YE GO TO THE INDIES?
ROBERT BURNS.

Will ye go to the Indies, my Mary,
  And leave auld Scotia's shore?
Will ye go to the Indies, my Mary,
  Across the Atlantic's roar?

Oh sweet grow the lime and the orange,
  And the apple on the pine;
But a' the charms o' the Indies
  Can never equal thine.

I ha'e sworn by the heavens to my Mary,
  I ha'e sworn by the heavens to be true;
And sae may the heavens forget me,
  When I forget my vow!

O plight me your faith, my Mary,
  And plight me your lily-white hand;
Oh plight me your faith, my Mary,
  Before I leave Scotia's strand.

We ha'e plighted our truth, my Mary,
  In mutual affection to join,
And curst be the cause that shall part us!
  The hour and the moment o' time!

HIGHLAND LASSIE.
ROBERT BURNS.

Nae gentle dames, tho' e'er sae fair,
Shall ever be my muse's care:
Their titles a' are empty show;
Gi'e me my Highland lassie, O.
    Within the glen sae bushy, O,
    Aboon the plains sae rushy, O,
    I set me down wi' right good will,
    To sing my Highland lassie, O.

Oh, were yon hills an' valleys mine,
Yon palace an' yon gardens fine!
The world then the love should know
I bear my Highland lassie, O.

But fickle fortune frowns on me,
An' I maun cross the raging sea;
But while my crimson currents flow,
I'll love my Highland lassie, O.

Altho' thro' foreign climes I range,
I know her heart will never change,
For her bosom burns with honour's glow,
My faithful Highland lassie, O.

For her I'll dare the billows' roar,
For her I'll trace a distant shore,
That Indian wealth may lustre throw
Around my Highland lassie, O.

She has my heart, she has my hand,
By sacred truth an' honour's band!
Till the mortal stroke shall lay me low,
I'm thine, my Highland lassie, O.
    Farewell the glen sae bushy, O!
    Farewell the plain sae rushy, O!
    To other lands I now must go,
    To sing my Highland lassie, O.

POWERS CELESTIAL.
ROBERT BURNS.

Powers celestial! whose protection
  Ever guards the virtuous fair,
While to distant climes I wander,
  Let my Mary be your care:
Let her form sae fair and faultless,
  Fair and faultless as your own,
Let my Mary's kindred spirit
  Draw your choicest influence down.

Make the gales you waft around her
  Soft and peaceful as her breast,
Breathing in the breeze that fans her,
  Soothe her bosom into rest:
Guardian angels! oh protect her,
  When in distant lands I roam;
To realms unknown while fate exiles me,
  Make her bosom still my home.

HIGHLAND MARY.
ROBERT BURNS.

Ye banks, and braes, and streams around
  The castle o' Montgomery,
Green be your woods, and fair your flowers,
  Your waters never drumlie!
There simmer first unfauld her robes,
  An' there the langest tarry;
For there I took the last fareweel
  O' my sweet Highland Mary.

How sweetly bloom'd the gay green birk,
  How rich the hawthorn's blossom,
As underneath their fragrant shade,
  I clasp'd her to my bosom!
The golden hours, on angel wings,
  Flew o'er me and my deary;
For dear to me as light and life,
  Was my sweet Highland Mary.

Wi' mony a vow, and lock'd embrace,
  Our parting was fu' tender;
And pledging aft to meet again,
  We tore oursel's asunder;
But, Oh! fell death's untimely frost,
  That nipt my flower sae early!
Now green's the sod, and cauld's the clay,
  That wraps my Highland Mary!

Oh pale, pale, now, those rosy lips,
  I aft ha'e kiss'd sae fondly!
An' clos'd for aye the sparkling glance
  That dwelt on me sae kindly;
And mouldering now in silent dust
  That heart that lov'd me dearly!
But still within my bosom's core
  Shall live my Highland Mary.

TO MARY IN HEAVEN.
ROBERT BURNS.

Thou ling'ring star, with less'ning ray,
  That lov'st to greet the early morn,
Again thou usher'st in the day
  My Mary from my soul was torn.
Oh Mary! dear departed shade!
  Where is thy place of blissful rest?
See'st thou thy lover lowly laid?
  Hear'st thou the groans that rend his breast?

That sacred hour can I forget;
  Can I forget the hallowed grove,
Where by the winding Ayr we met,
  To live one day of parting love!
Eternity will not efface
  Those records dear of transports past—
Thy image at our last embrace;
  Ah! little thought we 'twas our last!

Ayr, gurgling, kiss'd his pebbl'd shore,
  O'erhung with wild woods, thick'ning green;
The fragrant birch, and hawthorn hoar,
  Twin'd amorous round the raptur'd scene;
The flow'rs sprang wanton to be prest,
  The birds sang love on every spray—
Till too, too soon, the glowing west
  Proclaim'd the speed of winged day.

Still o'er these scenes my mem'ry wakes,
  And fondly broods with miser care!
Time but th' impression stronger makes,
  As streams their channels deeper wear,
My Mary, dear departed shade!
  Where is thy place of blissful rest?
See'st thou thy lover lowly laid?
  Hear'st thou the groans that rend his breast?

TURN AGAIN.
ROBERT BURNS.

Turn again, thou fair Eliza,
  Ae kind blink before we part,
Rue on thy despairing lover!
  Canst thou break his faithful heart?
Turn again, thou fair Eliza;
  If to love thy heart denies,
For pity hide the cruel sentence
  Under friendship's kind disguise!

Thee, dear maid, ha'e I offended?
　　The offence is loving thee:
Canst thou wreck his peace for ever,
　　Wha for thine wad gladly die?
While the life beats in my bosom,
　　Thou shalt mix in ilka throe;
Turn again, thou lovely maiden,
　　Ae sweet smile on me bestow.

Not the bee upon the blossom,
　　In the pride o' sunny noon;
Not the little sporting fairy,
　　All beneath the simmer moon;
Not the poet in the moment
　　Fancy lightens on his e'e,
Kens the pleasure, feels the rapture
　　That thy presence gi'es to me.

FROM THEE ELIZA.
ROBERT BURNS.

From thee, Eliza, I must go,
　　And from my native shore,
The cruel Fates between us throw
　　A boundless ocean's roar:
But boundless oceans, roaring wide,
　　Between my love and me,
They never, never can divide
　　My heart and soul from thee!

Farewell, farewell, Eliza dear,
　　The maid that I adore!
A boding voice is in mine ear,
　　We part to meet no more!
The latest throb that leaves my heart,
　　While death stands victor by,
That throb, Eliza, is thy part,
　　And thine that latest sigh!

THE BRAES O' BALLOCHMYLE.
ROBERT BURNS.

The Catrine woods were yellow seen,
　　The flowers decay'd on Catrine lea,
Nae lav'rock sang on hillock green,
　　But nature sicken'd on the e'e.
Thro' faded groves Maria sang,
　　Hersel' in beauty's bloom the while,
And aye the wild-wood echoes rang,
　　Fareweel the braes o' Ballochmyle!

Low in your wintry beds, ye flowers,
　Again ye'll flourish fresh and fair;
Ye birdies dumb, in withering bowers,
　Again ye'll charm the vocal air.
But here, alas! for me nae mair
　Shall birdie charm, or flow'ret smile;
Fareweel the bonnie banks of Ayr,
　Fareweel, fareweel! sweet Ballochmyle.

THE LASS O' BALLOCHMYLE.

ROBERT BURNS.

'Twas even—the dewy fields were green,
　On every blade the pearls hang,
The zephyr wanton'd round the bean,
　An' bore its fragrant sweets alang:
In ev'ry glen the mavis sang,
　All nature list'ning seem'd the while,
Except where greenwood echoes rang,
　Amang the braes o' Ballochmyle.

With careless step I onward stray'd,
　My heart rejoic'd in nature's joy,
When, musing in a lonely glade,
　A maiden fair I chanc'd to spy;
Her look was like the morning's eye,
　Her air like nature's vernal smile,
Perfection whisper'd, passing by,
　Behold the lass o' Ballochmyle!

Fair is the morn in flow'ry May,
　And sweet is night in autumn mild;
When roving thro' the garden gay,
　Or wand'ring in the lonely wild:
But woman, nature's darling child!
　There all her charms she does compile;
Ev'n there her other works are foil'd
　By the bonnie lass o' Ballochmyle.

Oh, had she been a country maid,
　And I the happy country swain,
Tho' shelter'd in the lowest shed
　That ever rose on Scotland's plain,
Thro' weary winter's wind and rain,
　With joy, with rapture, I would toil;
And nightly to my bosom strain
　The bonnie lass o' Ballochmyle!

Then pride might climb the slipp'ry steep,
  Where fame and honours lofty shine;
And thirst of gold might tempt the deep,
  Or downward seek the Indian mine;
Give me the cot below the pine,
  To tend the flocks, or till the soil,
And every day have joys divine
  With the bonnie lass o' Ballochmyle.

YE BANKS AN' BRAES.
ROBERT BURNS.

YE banks an' braes o' bonnie Doon,
  How can ye bloom sae fresh an' fair;
How can ye chant, ye little birds,
  An' I sae weary fu' o' care!
Thou'lt break my heart, thou warbling bird,
  That wantons thro' the flowering thorn:
Thou minds me o' departed joys,
  Departed—never to return!
Aft ha'e I roved by bonnie Doon,
  To see the rose an' woodbine twine;
An' ilka bird sang o' its luve,
  An' fondly sae did I o' mine.
Wi' lightsome heart I pu'd a rose,
  Fu' sweet upon its thorny tree;
An' my fause luver stole my rose,
  But, ah! he left the thorn wi' me.

FAREWELL.
ROBERT BURNS.

THE gloomy night is gath'ring fast,
Loud roars the wild inconstant blast;
Yon murky cloud is foul with rain,
I see it driving o'er the plain;
The hunter now has left the moor,
The scatter'd coveys meet secure;
While here I wander prest with care,
Along the lonely banks of Ayr.

The autumn mourns her rip'ning corn,
By early winter's ravage torn;
Across her placid, azure sky,
She sees the scowling tempest fly:
Chill runs my blood to hear it rave—
I think upon the stormy wave,
Where many a danger I must dare,
Far from the bonnie banks of Ayr.

'Tis not the surging billows roar,
'Tis not that fatal deadly shore:
Tho' death in every shape appear,
The wretched have no more to fear!
But round my heart the ties are bound,
That heart transpierc'd with many a wound;
These bleed afresh, those ties I tear,
To leave the bonnie banks of Ayr.

Farewell old Coila's hills and dales,
Her heathy moors and winding vales;
The scenes where wretched fancy roves,
Pursuing past, unhappy loves!
Farewell, my friends! farewell, my foes!
My peace with these, my love with those—
The bursting tears my heart declare;
Farewell the bonnie banks of Ayr!

OF A' THE AIRTS.
ROBERT BURNS.

Of a' the airts the wind can blaw,
 I dearly like the west,
For there the bonnie lassie lives,
 The lassie I lo'e best:
There wild woods grow, an' rivers row,
 An' mony a hill between;
But day an' night my fancy's flight
 Is ever wi' my Jean.

I see her in the dewy flow'rs,
 I see her sweet an' fair:
I hear her in the tunefu' birds,
 I hear her charm the air:
There's not a bonnie flow'r that springs
 By fountain, shaw, or green,
There's not a bonnie bird that sings,
 But minds me o' my Jean.

THE WEAVER.
ROBERT BURNS.

Where Cart rins rowin' to the sea,
By mony a flow'r and spreading tree,
There lives a lad, the lad for me,
 He is a gallant weaver.
Oh, I had wooers aucht or nine,
They gi'ed me rings and ribbons fine,
An' I was fear'd my heart would tine,
 An' I gi'ed it to the weaver.

My daddie sign'd my tocher-band,
  To gi'e the lad that has the land;
But to my heart I'll add my hand,
  An' gi'e it to the weaver.
While birds rejoice in leafy bowers;
While bees delight in op'ning flowers;
While corn grows green in simmer showers,
  I'll love my gallant weaver.

THEIR GROVES OF SWEET MYRTLE.
ROBERT BURNS.

Their groves o' sweet myrtle let foreign lands reckon,
  Where bright-beaming summers exalt the perfume;
Far dearer to me yon lone glen o' green breckan,
  Wi' the burn stealing under the lang yellow broom.
Far dearer to me are yon humble broom bowers,
  Where the blue-bell an' gowan lurk lowly unseen;
For there, lightly tripping amang the wild flowers,
  A-listening the linnet, aft wanders my Jean.
Tho' rich is the breeze in their gay sunny valleys,
  An' cauld Caledonia's blast on the wave;
Their sweet scented woodlands that skirt the proud palace,
  What are they?—the haunt of the tyrant and slave!
The slave's spicy forests, and gold-bubbling fountains,
  The brave Caledonian views wi' disdain;
He wanders as free as the winds of his mountains,
  Save love's willing fetters—the chains o' his Jean!

I'LL AYE CA' IN BY YON TOWN.
ROBERT BURNS.

I'll aye ca' in by yon town,
  And by yon garden green, again;
I'll aye ca' in by yon town,
  And see my bonnie Jean, again.
There's nane sall ken, there's nane sall guess,
  What brings me back the gate again,
But she, my fairest, faithfu' lass,
  And stowlins we sall meet again.
She'll wander by the aiken tree,
  When trystin-time draws near again;
And when her lovely form I see,
  Oh, haith, she's doubly dear again!
I'll aye ca' in by yon town,
  And by yon garden green again;
I'll aye ca' in by yon town,
  And see my bonnie Jean again.

I HA'E A WIFE O' MY AIN.
ROBERT BURNS.

I ha'e a wife o' my ain—
  I'll partake wi' naebody;
I'll tak' cuckold frae nane,
  I'll gi'e cuckold to naebody.
I ha'e a penny to spend,
  There—thanks to naebody;
I ha'e naething to lend,
  I'll borrow frae naebody.

I am naebody's lord—
  I'll be slave to naebody;
I ha'e a gude braid sword,
  I'll tak' dunts frae naebody.
I'll be merry an' free,
  I'll be sad for naebody;
If naebody care for me,
  I'll care for naebody.

THE WINSOME WEE THING.
ROBERT BURNS.

She is a winsome wee thing,
She is a handsome wee thing,
She is a bonnie wee thing,
This sweet wee wife o' mine.

I never saw a fairer,
I never lo'ed a dearer;
And neist my heart I'll wear her,
For fear my jewel tine.

Oh leeze me on my wee thing,
My bonnie, blythesome wee thing;
Sae lang's I ha'e my wee thing,
I'll think my lot divine.

Tho' warld's care we share o't,
And may see meikle mair o't;
Wi' her I'll blythely bear it,
And ne'er a word repine.

AE FOND KISS.
ROBERT BURNS.

Ae fond kiss, and then we sever;
Ae fareweel, alas! for ever!
Deep in heart-wrung tears I'll pledge thee,
Warring sighs and groans I'll wage thee.

Who shall say that fortune grieves him,
While the star of hope she leaves him?
Me, nae cheerfu' twinkle lights me;
Dark despair around benights me.

I'll ne'er blame my partial fancy,
Naething could resist my Nancy;
But to see her was to love her;
Love but her, and love for ever.
Had we never lov'd sae kindly,
Had we never lov'd sae blindly,
Never met—or never parted,
We had ne'er been broken-hearted.

Fare thee weel, thou first and fairest;
Fare thee weel, thou best and dearest!
Thine be ilka joy and treasure,
Peace, enjoyment, love, and pleasure!
Ae fond kiss, and then we sever;
Ae fareweel, alas! for ever!
Deep in heart-wrung tears I'll pledge thee,
Warring sighs and groans I'll wage thee.

A ROSE-BUD BY MY EARLY WALK.
ROBERT BURNS.

A rose-bud by my early walk,
Adown a corn-enclosed bawk,
Sae gently bent its thorny stalk,
   All on a dewy morning.
Ere twice the shades o' dawn are fled,
In a' its crimson glory spread,
An' drooping rich the dewy head,
   It scents the early morning.

Within the bush, her covert nest,
A little linnet fondly prest,
The dew sat chilly on her breast
   Sae early in the morning.
She soon shall see her tender brood,
The pride, the pleasure o' the wood,
Amang the fresh green leaves bedew'd,
   Awake the early morning.

So thou, dear bird, young Jeanie fair!
On trembling string or vocal air,
Shall sweetly pay the tender care
   That tends thy early morning.
So thou, sweet rose-bud, young an' gay,
Shall beauteous blaze upon the day,
An' bless the parent's evening ray
   That watch'd thy early morning.

GO FETCH TO ME A PINT O' WINE.
ROBERT BURNS.

Go fetch to me a pint o' wine,
  And fill it in a silver tassie;
That I may drink before I go,
  A service to my bonnie lassie:
The boat rocks at the pier o' Leith,
  Fu' loud the wind blaws frae the ferry;
The ship rides by the Berwick-law,
  And I maun leave my bonnie Mary.

The trumpets sound, the banners fly,
  The glittering spears are ranked ready;
The shouts o' war are heard afar,
  The battle closes thick and bloody;
But it's not the roar o' sea or shore
  Wad make me langer wish to tarry;
Nor shouts o' war that's heard afar—
  It's leaving thee, my bonnie Mary.

LOGAN'S BRAES.
ROBERT BURNS.

Oh Logan, sweetly didst thou glide
That day I was my Willie's bride;
An' years sinsyne ha'e o'er us run,
Like Logan to the simmer sun.
But now thy flow'ry banks appear
Like drumlie winter, dark and drear,
While my dear lad maun face his faes,
Far, far frae me an' Logan braes.

Again the merry month o' May
Has made our hills an' valleys gay;
The birds rejoice in leafy bowers,
The bees hum round the breathing flowers;
Blythe morning lifts his rosy eye,
An' evening's tears are tears of joy:
My soul, delightless, a' surveys,
While Willie's far frae Logan braes.

Within yon milk-white hawthorn bush,
Amang her nestlings sits the thrush;
Her faithfu' mate will share her toil,
Or wi' his songs her cares beguile;
But I wi' my sweet nurslings here,
Nae mate to help, nae mate to cheer,
Pass widow'd nights an' joyless days,
While Willie's far frae Logan braes.

Oh, wae upon you, men o' state,
That brethren rouse to deadly hate!
As ye make many a fond heart mourn,
See may it on your heads return!
How can your flinty hearts enjoy
The widow's tear, the orphan's cry?
But soon may peace bring happy days,
An' Willie hame to Logan braes!

YOUNG PEGGIE.
ROBERT BURNS.

Young Peggy blooms our bonniest lass,
　Her blush is like the morning,
The rosy dawn the springing grass,
　With early gems adorning:
Her eyes outshine the radiant beams
　That gild the passing shower,
And glitter o'er the crystal streams,
　And cheer each fresh'ning flower.

Her lips, more than the cherries bright,
　A richer dye has graced them;
They charm th' admiring gazer's sight,
　And sweetly tempt to taste them:
Her smile is, as the evening, mild,
　When feather'd tribes are courting,
And little lambkins wanton wild,
　In playful bands disporting.

Were fortune lovely Peggy's foe,
　Such sweetness would relent her,
As blooming spring unbends the brow
　Of surly, savage winter.
Detraction's eye no aim can gain,
　Her winning powers to lessen;
And fretful envy grins in vain
　The poison'd tooth to fasten.

Ye powers of honour, love, and truth,
　From every ill defend her;
Inspire the highly-favour'd youth,
　The destinies intend her:
Still fan the sweet connubial flame
　Responsive in each bosom,
And bless the dear parental name
　With many a filial blossom.

SAE FLAXEN WERE HER RINGLETS.
ROBERT BURNS.

Sae flaxen were her ringlets,
  Her eyebrows of a darker hue,
Bewitchingly, o'er-arching
  Twa laughing een o' bonnie blue,
Her smiling, sae wiling,
  Wad make a wretch forget his woe;
What pleasure, what treasure,
  Unto those rosy lips to grow;
Such was my Chloris' bonnie face,
  When first her bonnie face I saw,
An' aye my Chloris' dearest charm,
  She says she lo'es me best of a'.

Like harmony her motion;
  Her pretty ankle is a spy
Betraying fair proportion,
  Wad make a saint forget the sky.
Sae warming, sae charming,
  Her faultless form and graceful air;
Ilk feature—auld nature
  Declared that she could do nae mair.
Hers are the willing chains o' love,
  By conquering beauty's sovereign law;
An' aye my Chloris' dearest charm,
  She says she lo'es me best of a'.

Let others love the city,
  And gaudy show at sunny noon;
Gi'e me the lonely valley,
  The dewy eve, and rising moon
Fair beaming, and streaming,
  Her silver light the boughs amang;
While falling, recalling,
  The amorous thrush concludes his sang:
There, dearest Chloris, wilt thou rove
  By wimpling burn and leafy shaw,
An' hear my vows o' truth and love,
  An' say thou lo'es me best of a'.

THERE WAS A LASS.
ROBERT BURNS.

There was a lass, they ca'd her Meg,
  An' she held owre the moors to spin;
There was a lad that follow'd her,
  They ca'd him Duncan Davison.

The moor was driegh, an' Meg was skiegh,
  Her favour Duncan could na win;
For wi' the rock she wad him knock,
  An' aye she shook the temper-pin.
As o'er the moor they lightly foor,
  A burn was clear, a glen was green,
Upon the banks they eas'd their shanks,
  An' aye she set the wheel between:
But Duncan swore a haly aith
  That Meg should be a bride the morn,
Then Meg took up her spinnin' graith,
  An' flang them a' out owre the burn.

We'll big a house—a wee, wee house,
  An' we will live like king an' queen,
Sae blythe an' merry we will be
  When ye sit by the wheel at e'en.
A man may drink an' no be drunk;
A man may fight an' no be slain;
A man may kiss a bonnie lass,
  An' aye be welcome back again.

GUDEWIFE COUNT THE LAWIN.
ROBERT BURNS.

GANE is the day, an' mirk's the night,
But we'll ne'er stray for fau't o' light,
For ale an' brandy's stars an' moon,
An' bluid-red wine's the rising sun.
  Then gudewife, count the lawin,
    The lawin, the lawin;
  Then gudewife, count the lawin,
    An' bring a coggie mair.

There's wealth an' ease for gentlemen,
An' semple folk maun fecht an' fen;
But here we're a' in ae accord,
For ilka man that's drunk 's a lord.

My coggie is a haly pool,
That heals the wounds o' care an' dool;
An' pleasure is a wanton trout,
An ye drink but deep ye'll find him out.

A BIG-BELLIED BOTTLE.
ROBERT BURNS.

No churchman am I for to rail and to write,
No statesman or soldier to plot or to fight,
No sly man of business contriving a snare—
For a big-bellied bottle's the whole of my care.

The peer I don't envy, I give him his bow;
I scorn not the peasant, tho' ever so low:
But a club of good fellows, like those that are here,
And a bottle like this, are my glory and care.

Here passes the squire on his brother—his horse:
There centum per centum, the cit with his purse;
But see you the Crown, how it waves in the air!
There a big-bellied bottle still eases my care.

The wife of my bosom, alas! she did die;
For sweet consolation to church I did fly;
I found that old Solomon proved it fair,
That a big-bellied bottle's a cure for all care.

I once was persuaded a venture to make;
A letter inform'd me that all was to wreck;—
But the pursy old landlord just waddled up stairs,
With a glorious bottle that ended my cares.

"Life's cares they are comforts"—a maxim laid down
By the bard, what d'ye call him, that wore the black gown;
An' faith, I agree with th' old prig to a hair;
For a big-bellied bottle's a heav'n of care.

STANZA ADDED IN A MASON'S LODGE.

Then fill up a bumper an' make it o'erflow,
An' honours masonic prepare for to throw;
May every true brother of the compass an' square,
Have a big-bellied bottle when harass'd with care!

OH! TIBBIE, I HA'E SEEN THE DAY.
ROBERT BURNS.

Oh Tibbie, I ha'e seen the day
  Ye wad na been sae shy;
For lack o' gear ye lightly me,
  But, trowth, I care na by.

Yestreen I met you on the moor,
Ye spak na but gaed bye like stoure;
Ye geck at me because I'm poor,
  But fient a hair care I.

I doubt na, lass, but ye may think,
Because ye ha'e the name o' clink,
That ye can please me at a wink,
   Whene'er ye like to try.

But sorrow tak' him that's sae mean,
Altho' his pouch o' coin were clean,
Wha follows ony saucy quean,
   That looks sae proud and high.

Altho' a lad were e'er sae smart,
If that he want the yellow dirt,
Ye'll cast your head anither airt,
   An' answer him fu' dry.

But if he ha'e the name o' gear,
Ye'll fasten to him like a brier,
Tho' hardly he, for sense or lear,
   Be better than the kye.

But, Tibbie, lass, tak' my advice,
Your daddie's gear mak's you sae nice;
The de'il a ane wad spier your price,
   Were ye as poor as I.

There lives a lass in yonder park,
I wad na gi'e her in her sark,
For thee, wi' a' thy thousan' mark;
   Ye need na look sae high.

MY LUVE IS LIKE A RED, RED ROSE.
ROBERT BURNS.

Oh, my luve's like a red, red rose,
   That's newly sprung in June:
Oh, my luve's like the melodie,
   That's sweetly played in tune.
As fair art thou, my bonnie lass,
   So deep in luve am I;
And I will luve thee still, my dear,
   Till a' the seas gang dry.

Till a' the seas gang dry, my dear,
   And the rocks melt wi' the sun;
I will love thee still, my dear,
   While the sands o' life shall run.
And fare thee weel, my only luve!
   And fare thee weel a while!
And I will come again, my luve,
   Tho' it were ten thousand mile.

SOMEBODY.
ROBERT BURNS.

My heart is sair—I dare na tell—
My heart is sair for somebody;
I could wake a winter night
For the sake of somebody.
  Oh-hon, for somebody!
  Oh-hey, for somebody!
I could range the world around,
For the sake o' somebody!

Ye powers that smile on virtuous love,
Oh, sweetly smile on somebody!
Frae ilka danger keep him free,
And send me safe my somebody.
  Oh-hon, for somebody!
  Oh-hey, for somebody!
I wad do—what wad I not!
For the sake of somebody!

GALA WATER.
ROBERT BURNS.

There's braw, braw lads on Yarrow braes,
That wander thro' the blooming heather;
But Yarrow braes, nor Ettrick shaws,
Can match the lads o' Gala Water.

But there is ane, a secret ane,
Aboon them a' I lo'e him better;
And I'll be his and he'll be mine,
The bonnie lad o' Gala Water.

Altho' his daddie was nae laird,
And tho' I ha'e na meikle tocher;
Yet rich in kindest, truest love,
We'll tent our flocks by Gala Water.

It ne'er was wealth, it ne'er was wealth,
That coft contentment, peace, or pleasure:
The bands and bliss o' mutual love,
Oh that's the chiefest warld's treasure.

CONTENTED WI' LITTLE.
ROBERT BURNS.

Contented wi' little, an' cantie wi' mair,
Whene'er I forgather wi' sorrow an' care,
I gi'e them a skelp as they're creepin' alang,
Wi' a cog o' guid swats, an' an auld Scottish sang.

I whiles claw the elbow o' troublesome thought;
But man is a sodger, an' life is a faught:
My mirth an' good humour are coin in my pouch,
An' my freedom's my lairdship nae monarch dare touch.

A towmond o' trouble, should that be my fa',
A night o' gude fellowship sowthers it a':
When at the blythe end of our journey at last,
Wha the de'il ever thinks o' the road he has past?

Blind chance, let her snapper an' stoyte on her way;
Be't to me, be't frae me, e'en let the jade gae;
Come ease, or come travail; come pleasure, or pain,
My warst word is—" Welcome, an' welcome again!"

OH! WERE I ON PARNASSUS' HILL.
ROBERT BURNS.

Oh, were I on Parnassus' hill!
Or had of Helicon my fill;
That I might catch poetic skill,
  To sing how dear I love thee.
But Nith maun be my muse's well,
My muse maun be thy bonnie sel';
On Corsincon I'll glow'r an' spell,
  An' write how dear I love thee.

Then come, sweet muse, inspire my lay!
For a' the lee-lang simmer's day
I couldna sing, I couldna say,
  How much, how dear I love thee.
I see thee dancing o'er the green,
Thy waist sae jimp, thy limbs sae clean,
Thy tempting lips, thy roguish een—
  By heaven an' earth I love thee!

By night, by day, a-field, at hame,
The thoughts o' thee my breast inflame;
An' aye I muse an' sing thy name—
  I only live to love thee.
Tho' I were doom'd to wander on
Beyond the sea, beyond the sun,
Till my last weary sand was run;
  Till then—and then I love thee.

OH POORTITH CAULD.
ROBERT BURNS.

Oh poortith cauld, and restless love,
  Ye wreck my peace between ye;
Yet poortith a' I could forgive,
  An 'twere na for my Jeanie.
    Oh why should fate sic pleasure have,
      Life's dearest bands untwining?
    Or why sae sweet a flower as love,
      Depend on Fortune's shining?

This warld's wealth when I think on,
  Its pride and a' the lave o't;
Fie, fie on silly coward man,
  That he should be the slave o't.
    Oh why, &c.

Her een sae bonnie blue betray
  How she repays my passion;
But prudence is her o'erword aye,
  She talks of rank and fashion.
    Oh why, &c.

Oh wha can prudence think upon,
  And sic a lassie by him?
Oh wha can prudence think upon,
  And sae in love as I am?
    Oh why, &c.

How blest the humble cottar's fate!
  He woos his simple dearie;
The silly bogles, wealth and state,
  Can never make them eerie.
    Oh why, &c.

STRATHALLAN'S LAMENT.
ROBERT BURNS.

Thickest night, o'erhang my dwelling!
  Howling tempests o'er me rave!
Turbid torrents, wintry swelling,
  Still surround my lonely cave!

Crystal streamlets gently flowing,
  Busy haunts of base mankind,
Western breezes softly blowing,
  Suit not my distracted mind.

In the cause of right engaged,
　Wrongs injurious to redress,
Honour's war we strongly waged,
　But the heavens denied success.

Ruin's wheel has driven o'er us,
　Not a hope that dare attend:
The wide world is all before us—
　But a world without a friend.

I'M OWRE YOUNG TO MARRY YET.
ROBERT BURNS.

I'm owre young to marry yet;
　I'm owre young to marry yet;
　I'm owre young—'twad be a sin
　　To tak' me frae my mammy yet.

I am my mammy's ae bairn,
　Wi' unco folk I weary, Sir;
An' if I gang to your house,
　I'm fley'd 'twill make me eerie, Sir.

Hallowmas is come an' gane,
　The nights are lang in winter, Sir;
An' you an' I in ae bed,
　In trouth I dare na venture, Sir.

Fu' loud an' shrill the frosty wind
　Blaws through the leafless timmer, Sir;
But if ye come this gate again,
　I'll aulder be gin simmer, Sir.

OWER THE HILLS AND FAR AWA'.
ROBERT BURNS.

On how can I be blythe and glad,
　Or how can I gang brisk and braw,
When the bonnie lad that I lo'e best
　Is ower the hills and far awa'?
　　When the bonnie lad that I lo'e best
　　　Is ower the hills and far awa'?

It's no the frosty winter wind,
　It's no the driving drift an' snaw;
But aye the tear comes in my e'e,
　To think on him that's far awa'.
　　But aye the tear come in my e'e,
　　　To think on him that's far awa'.

My father pat me frae his door,
　My friends they ha'e disown'd me a',
But I ha'e ane will tak' my part,
　The bonnie lad that's far awa'.
　　But I ha'e ane will tak' my part,
　　The bonnie lad that's far awa'.

A pair o' gloves he ga'e to me,
　An' silken snoods he ga'e me twa,
An' I will wear them for his sake,
　The bonnie lad that's far awa'.
　　An' I will wear them for his sake,
　　The bonnie lad that's far awa'.

THE RED RED ROSE.
ROBERT BURNS.

The blude-red rose at Yule may blaw,
The simmer lilies bloom in snaw,
The frost may freeze the deepest sea;
But an auld man shall never daunton me.
　To daunton me, an' me so young,
　Wi' his fause heart an' flatt'ring tongue,
　That is the thing you ne'er shall see;
　For an auld man shall never daunton me.

For a' his meal an' a' his maut,
For a' his fresh beef an' his saut,
For a' his gold an' white monie,
An auld man shall never daunton ma.

His gear may buy him kye an' yowes,
His gear may buy him gleus an' knowes;
But me he shall not buy nor fee,
For an auld man shall never daunton me.

He hirples twa-faule as he dow,
Wi' his teethless gab an' his auld beld pow,
An' the rain rains down frae his red bleer'd e'e—
That auld man shall never daunton me.

LAY THY LOOF IN MINE.
ROBERT BURNS.

Oh lay thy loof in mine, lass,
　In mine, lass, in mine, lass;
And swear on thy white hand, lass,
　That thou wilt be my ain.

A slave to love's unbounded sway,
He aft has wrought me meikle wae;
But now he is my deadly fae,
  Unless thou be me ain.

There's mony a lass has broke my rest,
That for a blink I ha'e lo'ed best;
But thou art Queen within my breast,
  For ever to remain.
    Oh lay thy loof in mine, lass,
    In mine, lass, in mine, lass,
    And swear on thy white hand, lass,
That thou wilt be my ain.

OH! OPEN THE DOOR.
ROBERT BURNS.

"Oh! open the door, some pity to show,
  Oh! open the door to me, oh!
Tho' thou hast been false, I'll ever prove true,
  Oh! open the door to me, oh!

"Cauld is the blast upon my pale cheek,
  But caulder thy love for me, oh!
The frost that freezes the life at my heart,
  Is nought to my pains frae thee, oh!

"The wan moon is setting behind the white wave,
  An' time is setting with me, oh!
False friends, false love, farewell! for mair
  I'll ne'er trouble them nor thee, oh!"

She has open'd the door, she has open'd it wide;
  She sees his pale corse on the plain, oh!
"My true love!" she cried, an' sank down by his side,
  Never to rise again, oh!

THE JOYFUL WIDOWER.
ROBERT BURNS.

I married with a scolding wife
  The fourteenth of November;
She made me weary of my life,
  By one unruly member.
Long did I bear the heavy yoke,
  And many griefs attended;
But to my comfort be it spoke,
  Now, now her life is ended.

We lived full one and twenty years,
 A man and wife together;
At length from me her course she steer'd,
 And gone I know not whither:
Would I could guess, I do profess,
 I speak and do not flatter,
Of all the women in the world,
 I never could come at her.

Her body is bestowed well,
 A handsome grave does hide her;
But sure her soul is not in hell,
 The de'il would ne'er abide her;
I rather think she is aloft,
 And imitating thunder;
For why?—methinks I hear her voice
 Tearing the clouds asunder!

TAM GLEN.
ROBERT BURNS.

My heart is a-breaking, dear tittie!
 Some counsel unto me come len',
To anger them a' is a pity,
 But what will I do wi' Tam Glen?

I'm thinking wi' sic a braw fellow
 In poortith I might make a fen';
What care I in riches to wallow,
 If I maunna marry Tam Glen?

There's Lowrie, the laird o' Dromeller,
 "Guid day, to you, brute!" he comes ben
He brags and he blaws o' his siller,
 But when will he dance like Tam Glen?

My minnie does constantly deave me,
 And bids me beware o' young men;
They flatter, she says, to deceive me,
 But wha can think sae o' Tam Glen?

My daddie says, gin I'll forsake him,
 He'll gi'e me guid hunder marks ten:
But if it's ordain'd I maun tak' him,
 O wha will I get but Tam Glen?

Yestreen at the valentine's dealing,
 My heart to my mou' gi'ed a sten;
For thrice I drew ane without failing,
 And thrice it was written—Tam Glen.

The last Halloween I was waukin'
My droukit sark sleeve, as ye ken;
His likeness cam' up the house staukin',
And the very gray breeks o' Tam Glen!

Come counsel, dear tittie! don't tarry—
I'll gi'e you my bonnie black hen,
Gif ye will advise me to marry
The lad I lo'e dearly, Tam Glen.

OH WHISTLE AN' I'LL COME TO YOU.

ROBERT BURNS.

Oh whistle an' I'll come to you, my lad,
Oh whistle an' I'll come to you, my lad;
Tho' father an' mither an' a' should gae mad,
Oh whistle an' I'll come to you, my lad.

But warily tent, when ye come to court me,
An' come na unless the back yett be a-jee;
Syne up the back stile, an' let naebody see,
An' come as ye were na comin' to me.
    An' come, &c.

At kirk, or at market, whene'er ye meet me,
Gang by me as tho' that ye car'd nae a flie;
But steal me a blink o' your bonnie black e'e,
Yet look as ye were na lookin' at me.
    Yet look, &c.

Aye vow an' protest that ye care na for me,
An' whiles ye may lightly my beauty a wee;
But court na anither, tho' jokin' ye be,
For fear that she wile your fancy frae me.
    For fear, &c.

DAINTY DAVIE.

ROBERT BURNS.

Now rosy May comes in wi' flowers,
To deck her gay, green spreading bowers;
An' now come in my happy hours,
    To wander wi' my Davie.

CHORUS.

Meet me on the warlock knowe,
    Dainty Davie, dainty Davie;
There I'll spend the day wi' you,
    My ain dear dainty Davie.

The crystal waters round us fa',
The merry birds are lovers a',
The scented breezes round us blaw,
A wandering wi' my Davie.

When purple morning starts the hare,
To steal upon her early fare,
Then thro' the dews I will repair,
To meet my faithfu' Davie.

When day, expiring in the west,
The curtain draws o' nature's rest,
I flee to his arms I lo'e best,
An' that's my ain dear Davie.

THOU HAST LEFT ME EVER.
ROBERT BURNS.

Thou hast left me ever, Jamie, thou hast left me ever;
Thou hast left me ever, Jamie, thou hast left me ever;
Aften hast thou vow'd that death only should us sever,
Now thou'st left thy lass for aye—I maun see thee never, Jamie,
I'll see thee never.

Thou hast me forsaken, Jamie, thou hast me forsaken;
Thou hast me forsaken, Jamie, thou hast me forsaken;
Thou canst love anither jo, while my heart is breaking:
Soon my weary een I'll close—never mair to waken, Jamie,
Ne'er mair to waken.

WHAT CAN A YOUNG LASSIE.
ROBERT BURNS.

What can a young lassie, what shall a young lassie,
  What can a young lassie do wi' an' auld man?
Bad luck on the penny that tempted my minnie
  To sell her poor Jenny for siller an' lan'!
    Bad luck on the penny that tempted my minnie
      To sell her poor Jenny for siller an' lan'!

He's always compleenin' frae morning to e'ening',
  He hoasts an' he hirples the weary day lang;
He's doylt an' he's dozin', his bluid it is frozen,
  Oh, dreary's the night wi' a crazy auld man!
    He's doylt an' he's dozin', his bluid it is frozen,
      Oh, dreary's the night wi' a crazy auld man!

He hums an' he hankers, he frets an' he cankers,
I never can please him, do a' that I can;
He's peevish an' jealous of a' the young fellows:
Oh, dool on the day I met wi' an auld man!
He's peevish an' jealous of a' the young fellows:
Oh, dool on the day I met wi' an auld man!

My auld auntie Katie upon me tak's pity,
I'll do my endeavour to follow her plan;
I'll cross him, an' wrack him, until I heart-break him,
An' then his auld brass will buy me a new pan.
I'll cross him, an' wrack him, until I heart-break him,
An' then his auld brass will buy me a new pan.

LEEZE ME ON MY SPINNIN' WHEEL.
ROBERT BURNS.

Oh leeze me on my spinnin' wheel,
Oh leeze me on my rock an' reel;
Frae tap to tae that cleeds me bien,
An' haps me fiel an' warm at e'en!
I'll sit me down an' sing an' spin,
While laigh descends the simmer sun,
Blest wi' content, an' milk an' meal—
Oh leeze me on my spinnin' wheel!

On ilka hand the burnies trot,
An' meet below my theekit cot;
The scented birk an' hawthorn white,
Across the pool their arms unite,
Alike to screen the birdie's nest,
An' little fishes' caller rest:
The sun blinks kindly in the biel',
Where blythe I turn my spinnin' wheel.

On lofty aiks the cushats wail,
An' echo cons the dolefu' tale;
The lintwhites in the hazel braes,
Delighted, rival ither's lays:
The craik amang the clover hay,
The paitrick whirrin' o'er the ley,
The swallow jinkin' round my shiel,
Amuse me at my spinnin' wheel.

Wi' sma' to sell, an' loss to buy,
Aboon distress, below envy,
Oh wha wad leave this humble state,
For a' the pride of a' the great?
Amid their flarin', idle toys,
Amid their cumbrous, dinsome joys,
Can they the peace and pleasure feel
Of Bessy at her spinnin' wheel?

HEY FOR A LASS WI' A TOCHER.
ROBERT BURNS.

Awa' wi' your witchcraft o' beauty's alarms,
The slender bit beauty you grasp in your arms:
Oh, gi'e me the lass that has acres o' charms,
Oh, gi'e me the lass wi' the weel-stockit farms.

CHORUS.

Then hey for a lass wi' a tocher, then hey for a lass with a tocher.
Then hey for a lass wi' a tocher—the nice yellow guineas for me.

Your beauty's a flower, in the morning that blows,
And withers the faster, the faster it grows;
But the rapturous charm o' the bonnie green knowes,
Ilk spring they're new deckit wi' bonnie white yowes.

And e'en when this beauty your bosom has blest,
The brightest o' beauty may cloy when possest;
But the sweet yellow darlings wi' Geordie imprest,
The langer ye ha'e them, the mair they're carest.

MEIKLE THINKS MY LOVE.
ROBERT BURNS.

Oh meikle thinks my luve o' my beauty,
An' meikle thinks my luve o' my kin;
But little thinks my luve I ken brawly
My tocher's the jewel has charms for him.
It's a' for the apple he'll nourish the tree;
It's a' for the hiney he'll cherish the bee;
My laddie's sae meikle in luve wi' the siller,
He canna ha'e luve to spare for me.

Your proffer o' luve's an arle-penny,
My tocher's the bargain ye wad buy;
But an ye be crafty, I am cunnin',
Sae ye wi' another your fortune maun try.
Ye're like to the timmer o' yon rotten wood,
Ye're like to the bark o' yon rotten tree;
Ye'll slip frae me like a knotless thread,
An' ye'll crack your credit wi' man nor me.

OH! FOR ANE-AND-TWENTY, TAM.
ROBERT BURNS.

And oh, for ane-and-twenty, Tam,
  And hey, sweet ane-and-twenty, Tam,
I'll learn my kin a rattlin' sang,
  An I saw ane-and-twenty, Tam.

They snool me sair, and haud me down,
  And gar me look like bluntie, Tam!
But three short years will soon wheel roun'—
  And then comes ane-and-twenty, Tam.

A gleib o' lan', a claut o' gear,
  Was left me by my auntie, Tam;
At kith or kin I need na spier,
  An I saw ane-and-twenty, Tam.

They'll ha'e me wed a wealthy coof,
  Tho' I mysel' ha'e plenty, Tam;
But hear'st thou, laddie—there's my loof—
  I'm thine at ane-and-twenty, Tam.

UP IN THE MORNING.
ROBERT BURNS.
CHORUS.

Up in the morning's no for me,
  Up in the morning early;
When a' the hills are cover'd wi' snaw,
  I'm sure it's winter fairly.

Cauld blaws the wind frae east to west,
  The drift is driving sairly;
Sae loud and shrill I hear the blast,
  I'm sure it's winter fairly.

The birds sit chittering in the thorn,
  A' day they fare but sparely;
And lang's the night frae e'en to morn—
  I'm sure it's winter fairly.

THIS IS NO MY AIN LASSIE.
ROBERT BURNS.
CHORUS.

Oh this is no my ain lassie,
  Fair tho' the lassie be;
Oh weel ken I my ain lassie,
  Kind love is in her e'e.

I see a form, I see a face
Ye weel may wi' the fairest place;
It wants to me the witching grace,
    The kind love that's in her e'e.

She's bonnie, blooming, straight, and tall,
And lang has had my heart in thrall;
And aye it charms my very saul,
    The kind love that's in her o'e.

A thief sae paukie is my Jean,
To steal a blink, by a' unseen;
But gleg as light are lovers' een,
    When kind love is in her e'e.

It may escape the courtly sparks,
It may escape the learned clerks;
But weel the watching lover marks
    The kind love that's in her e'e.

MY NANNIE'S AWA'.
ROBERT BURNS.

Now in her green mantle blythe nature arrays,
An' listens the lambkins that bleat o'er the braes,
While birds warble welcome in ilka green shaw;
But to me it's delightless—my Nannie's awa'.

The snaw-drap an' primrose our woodlands adorn,
An' violets bathe in the weet o' the morn;
They pain my sad bosom, sae sweetly they blaw,
They mind me o' Nannie—an' Nannie's awa'.

Thou lav'rock that springs frae the dews of the lawn,
The shepherd to warn o' the gray-breaking dawn,
An' thou mellow mavis that hails the night-fa',
Give over for pity—my Nannie's awa'.

Come, autumn, sae pensive, in yellow an' gray,
An' soothe me wi' tidings o' nature's decay;
The dark, dreary winter, an' wild-driving snaw,
Alane can delight me—now Nannie's awa'.

LAST MAY A BRAW WOOER.
ROBERT BURNS.

Last May a braw wooer cam' down the lang glen,
And sair wi' his love he did deave me;
I said there was naething I hated like men—
    The deuce gae wi'm to believe me, believe me,
    The deuce gae wi'm to believe me.

He spak' o' the darts o' my bonnie black een,
  And vow'd for my love he was dying;
I said he might die when he liked for Jean—
  The Lord forgi'e me for lying, for lying,
  The Lord forgi'e me for lying!

A weel-stockit mailen, himsel' for the laird,
  And marriage aff-hand, were his proffers;
I never loot on that I kenn'd it, or car'd,
  But thought I might ha'e waur offers, waur offers,
  But thought I might ha'e waur offers.

But what wad ye think? in a fortnight or less—
  The de'il tak' his taste to gae near her!
He up the lang loan to my black cousin Bess,
  Guess ye how, the jad! I could bear her, could bear her.
  Guess ye how, the jad! I could bear her.

But a' the neist week as I fretted wi' care,
  I gaed to the tryste o' Dalgarnock,
An' wha but my fine fickle lover was there!
  I glowr'd as I'd seen a warlock, a warlock,
  I glowr'd as I'd seen a warlock.

But owre my left shouther I ga'e him a blink,
  Lest neibors might say I was saucy;
My wooer he caper'd as he'd been in drink,
  And vow'd I was his dear lassie, dear lassie,
  And vow'd I was his dear lassie.

I spier'd for my cousin fu' couthy and sweet,
  Gin she had recover'd her hearin',
And how her new shoon fit her auld shachl't feet,
  But, heavens! how he fell a-swearin', a-swearin',
  But, heavens! how he fell a-swearin'.

He begg'd, for guidsake, I wad be his wife,
  Or else I wad kill him wi' sorrow:
So e'en to preserve the puir body in life,
  I think I maun wed him to-morrow, to-morrow,
  I think I maun wed him to-morrow.

MY LOVE SHE'S BUT A LASSIE YET.
ROBERT BURNS.

My love she's but a lassie yet,
  My love she's but a lassie yet,
We'll let her stand a year or two,
  She'll no be half sae saucy yet.
I rue the day I sought her, O,
  I rue the day I sought her, O,
Wha gets her needs na say she's woo'd,
  But he may say he's bought her, O!

Come, draw a drap o' the best o't yet,
 Come draw a drap o' the best o't yet;
Gae seek for pleasure where ye will,
 But here I never miss'd it yet.
We're a' dry wi' drinking o't;
 We're a' dry wi' drinking o't;
The minister kiss'd the fiddler's wife,
 An' could na preach for thinking o't.

BIRKS OF ABERFELDY.
ROBERT BURNS.
CHORUS.

Bonnie lassie, will ye go,
 Will ye go, will ye go;
Bonnie lassie, will ye go,
 To the birks of Aberfeldy?

Now simmer blinks on flowery braes,
And o'er the crystal streamlet plays;
Come, let us spend the lightsome days
 In the birks of Aberfeldy.

The little birdies blythely sing,
While o'er their heads the hazels hing,
O'er lightly flit on wanton wing
 In the birks of Aberfeldy.

The braes ascend, like lofty wa's,
The foamy stream deep-roaring fa's,
O'erhung wi' fragrant spreading shaws,
 The birks of Aberfeldy.

The hoary cliffs are crown'd wi' flowers,
White o'er the linns the burnie pours,
An' rising, weets wi' misty showers
 The birks of Aberfeldy.

Let fortune's gifts at random flee,
They ne'er shall draw a wish frae me,
Supremely blest wi' love an' thee,
 In the birks of Aberfeldy.

JOHN ANDERSON, MY JO.
ROBERT BURNS.

John Anderson, my jo, John,
 When we were first acquant,
Your locks were like the raven,
 Your bonnie brow was brent;

But now your brow is beld John,
  Your locks are like the snaw;
But blessings on your frosty pow,
  John Anderson, my jo.

John Anderson, my jo, John,
  We clamb the hill thegither,
An' mony a canty day, John,
  We've had wi' ane anither;
Now we maun totter down, John,
  But hand in hand we'll go,
An' sleep thegither at the foot,
  John Anderson, my jo.

OH WILLIE BREW'D A PECK O' MAUT.
ROBERT BURNS.

Oh, Willie brew'd a peck o' maut,
  An' Rob an' Allan cam' to pree:
Three blyther hearts that lee-lang night,
  Ye wad na find in Christendie.
We are na fou', we're nae that fou',
  But just a drappie in our e'e;
The cock may craw, the day may daw,
  And aye we'll taste the barley bree.

Here are we met, three merry boys,
  Three merry boys, I trow, are we;
An' mony a night we've merry been,
  And mony mae we hope to be!

It is the moon, I ken her horn,
  That's blinkin' in the lift sae hie;
She shines sae bright to wile us hame,
  But, by my sooth, she'll wait a wee!

Wha first shall rise to gang awa',
  A cuckold, coward loon is he!
Wha last beside his chair shall fa',
  He is the king amang us three!

OH! LUVE WILL VENTURE IN.
ROBERT BURNS.

Oh luve will venture in where it daurna weel be seen;
Oh luve will venture in where wisdom ance has been;
But I will down yon river rove, among the wood sae green—
  An' a' to pu' a posie to my ain dear May.

The primrose I will pu', the firstling o' the year,
An' I will pu' the pink, the emblem o' my dear;
For she's the pink o' womankind, and blooms without a peer—
An' a' to be a posie to my ain dear May.

I'll pu' the budding rose, when Phœbus peeps in view,
For it's like a baumy kiss o' her sweet bonnie mou';
The hyacinth for constancy, wi' its unchanging blue—
An' a' to be a posie to my ain dear May.

The lily it is pure, an' the lily it is fair,
An' in her lovely bosom I'll place the lily there;
The daisy's for simplicity, an' unaffected air—
An' a' to be a posie to my ain kind May.

The hawthorn I will pu' wi' its locks o' siller gray,
Where, like an aged man, it stands at break of day;
But the songster's nest within the bush I winna tak' away—
An' a' to be a posie to my ain dear May.

The woodbine I will pu' when the e'ening star is near,
And the diamond drops o' dew shall be hore e'en sae clear;
The violets for modesty which weel she fa's to wear,
And a' to be a posie to my ain dear May.

I'll tie a posie round wi' the silken band o' luve,
And I'll place it in her breast, and I'll swear by a' above,
That to my latest draught o' life the band shall ne'er remove,
And this will be a posie to my ain dear May.

THE SOLDIER'S RETURN.
ROBERT BURNS.

When wild war's deadly blast was blawn,
  An' gentle peace returning,
Wi' mony a sweet babe fatherless,
  An' mony a widow mourning,
I left the lines an' tented field,
  Where lang I'd been a lodger,
My humble knapsack a' my wealth,
  A poor but honest sodger.

A leal, light heart was in my breast,
  My hand unstain'd wi' plunder;
An' for fair Scotia, hame again,
  I cheery on did wander.
I thought upon the banks o' Coil,
  I thought upon my Nancy;
I thought upon the witching smile
  That caught my youthful fancy.

At length I reach'd the bonnie glen
  Where early life I sported;
I pass'd the mill, an' trysting thorn,
  Where Nancy aft I courted:

Wha spied I but my ain dear maid
 Down by her mother's dwelling!
An turn'd me round to hide the flood
 That in my een was swelling.

Wi' alter'd voice, quoth I, "Sweet lass,
 Sweet as yon hawthorn's blossom,
Oh! happy happy may he be,
 That's dearest to thy bosom!
My purse is light, I've far to gang,
 An' fain wad be thy lodger;
I've serv'd my king an' country lang—
 Take pity on a sodger!"

Sae wistfully she gazed on me,
 An' lovelier was than ever;
Quo' she, "A sodger ance I lo'ed,
 Forget him shall I never:
Our humble cot an' hamely fare
 Ye freely shall partake o't;
That gallant badge, the dear cockade,
 Ye're welcome for the sake o't."

She gaz'd—she redden'd like a rose—
 Syne pale like ony lily;
She sank within my arms, an' cried,
 "Art thou my ain dear Willie?"
"By him who made yon sun and sky,
 By whom true love's regarded,
I am the man; an' thus may still
 True lovers be rewarded.

"The wars are o'er, an' I'm come hame,
 An' find thee still true-hearted!
Tho' poor in gear we're rich in love,
 An' mair we'se ne'er be parted."
Quo' she, "My grandsire left me gowd,
 A mailen plenish'd fairly;
An' come, my faithfu' sodger lad,
 Thou'rt welcome to it dearly."

For gold the merchant ploughs the main,
 The farmer ploughs the manor;
But glory is the sodger's prize,
 The sodger's wealth is honour.
The brave poor sodger ne'er despise,
 Nor count him as a stranger;
Remember he's his country's stay
 In day an' hour of danger.

FOR A' THAT.
ROBERT BURNS.

Is there for honest poverty
  That hangs his head, an' a' that?
The coward slave we pass him by,
  We dare be poor for a' that!
For a' that, an' a' that,
  Our toils obscure, an' a' that,
The rank is but the guinea's stamp,
  The man's the gowd for a' that.

What though on hamely fare we dine,
  Wear hoddin gray, an' a' that!
Gi'e fools their silks, an' knaves their wine,
  A man's a man for a' that;
For a' that, an' a' that,
  Their tinsel show an' a' that;
The honest man, though e'er sae poor,
  Is king o' men for a' that.

Ye see yon birkie, ca'd a lord,
  Wha struts, an' stares, an' a' that;
Tho' hundreds worship at his word,
  He's but a coof for a' that:
For a' that, an' a' that,
  His riband, star, an' a' that,
The man of independent mind,
  He looks an' laughs at a' that.

A prince can mak' a belted knight,
  A marquis, duke, an' a' that;
But an honest man's aboon his might,
  Gude faith he manna fa' that.
For a' that, an' a' that,
  Their dignities, an' a' that,
The pith o' sense, an' pride o' worth,
  Are higher ranks than a' that.

Then let us pray that come it may,
  As come it will for a' that,
That sense an' worth, o'er a' the earth,
  May bear the gree an' a' that.
For a' that, an' a' that,
  It's coming yet, for a' that,
That man to man, the warld o'er,
  Shall brothers be for a' that.

SUCH A PARCEL OF ROGUES.
ROBERT BURNS.

Fareweel to a' our Scottish fame,
  Fareweel our ancient glory,
Fareweel even to the Scottish name,
  Sae fam'd in martial story.
Now Sark rins o'er the Solway sands,
  And Tweed rins to the ocean,
To mark where England's province stands—
  Such a parcel of rogues in a nation.

What force or guile could not subdue,
  Thro' many warlike ages,
Is wrought now by a coward few,
  For hireling traitors' wages.
The English steel we could disdain,
  Secure in valour's station;
But English gold has been our bane—
  Such a parcel of rogues in a nation.

Oh would, or I had seen the day
  That treason thus could sell us,
My auld gray head had lein in clay,
  Wi' Bruce an' loyal Wallace!
But pith an' power, till my last hour,
  I'll make this declaration;
We're bought and sold for English gold—
  Such a parcel of rogues in a nation.

SCOTS WHA HA'E.
ROBERT BURNS.

Scots, wha ha'e wi' Wallace bled,
Scots, wham Bruce has afton led;
Welcome to your gory bed,
  Or to victorie!

Now's the day, and now's the hour;
See the front o' battle lour;
See approach prond Edward's power—
  Chains and Slavery!

Wha will be a traitor knave?
Wha can fill a coward's grave?
Wha sae base as be a slave?
  Let him turn and flee!

Wha for Scotland's king and law
Freedom's sword will strongly draw
Freeman stand, or freeman fa',
  Let him follow me!

By oppression's woes and pains!
By your sons in servile chains!
We will drain our dearest veins,
But they shall be free!
Lay the proud usurpers low!
Tyrants fall in every foe!
Liberty's in every blow!—
Let us do, or die!

DOES HAUGHTY GAUL.
ROBERT BURNS.

Does haughty Gaul invasion threat?
  Then let the loons beware, Sir;
There's wooden walls upon our seas,
  An' volunteers on shore, Sir.
The Nith shall run to Corsincon,
  An' Criffel sink in Solway,
Ere we permit a foreign foe
  On British ground to rally!
    Fall de rall, &c.

Oh, let us not, like snarling tykes,
  In wrangling be divided;
Till, slap, come in an unco loon,
  An' wi' a rung decide it.
Be Britain still to Britain true,
  Among oursel's united:
For never but by British hands
  Maun British wrangs be righted.
    Fall de rall, &c.

The kettle o' the kirk an' state,
  Perhaps a clout may fail in't;
But de'il a foreign tinkler loon
  Shall ever ca' a nail in't.
Our fathers' bluid the kettle bought,
  An' wha wad dare to spoil it,
By heaven, the sacrilegious dog
  Shall fuel be to boil it.
    Fall de rall, &c.

The wretch that wad a tyrant own,
  An' the wretch, his true-born brother,
Who would set the *mob* aboon the *throne*,
  May they be damned together!
Who will not sing, "God save the King,"
  Will hang as high's the steeple;
But while we sing, "God save the King,"
  We'll ne'er forget the People.

AULD LANG SYNE.
ROBERT BURNS.

Should auld acquaintance be forgot,
  An' never brought to mind?
Should auld acquaintance be forgot,
  An' days o' auld lang syne?

CHORUS.
For auld lang syne, my dear,
  For auld lang syne,
We'll tak' a cup o' kindness yet,
  For auld lang syne.

We twa ha'e ran about the braes,
  An' pu'd the gowans fine;
But we've wandered mony a weary foot,
  Sin' auld lang syne.

We twa ha'e paidl't i' the burn,
  Frae mornin' sun till dine;
But seas between us braid ha'e roar'd
  Sin auld lang syne.

An' here's a hand, my trusty fiere,
  An' gi'e's a hand o' thine;
An' we'll tak' a right guid willie-waught,
  For auld lang syne.

An' surely you'll be your pint-stoup,
  An' surely I'll be mine;
An' we'll tak' a cup o' kindness yet
  For auld lang syne.

WILLIE WASTLE.
ROBERT BURNS.

Willie Wastle dwalt on Tweed,
  The spot they called it Linkum-doddie;
Willie was a wabster gude,
  Could stown a clew wi' ony body.
He had a wife was dour an' din,
  Oh Tinkler Madgie was her mither;
Sic a wife as Willie had,
  I wad na gi'e a button for her.

She has an e'e—she has but ane,
  The cat has twa the very colour;
Five rusty teeth, forbye a stump,
  A clapper tongue wad deave a miller

A whiskin' beard about her mou',
　Her nose an' chin they threaten ither—
Sic a wife as Willie had,
　I wad na gi'e a button for her.

She's bough-hough'd, she's hein-shinn'd,
　Ae limpin' leg, a hand-breed shorter;
She's twisted right, she's twisted left,
　To balance fair in ilka quarter;
She has a hump upon her breast,
　The twin o' that upon her shouther;
Sic a wife as Willie had,
　I wad na gi'e a button for her.

Auld baudrons by the ingle sits,
　An' wi' her loof her face a washin';
But Willie's wife is na sae trig,
　She dights her grunzie wi' a hushion;
Her walie nieves like midden-creels,
　Her face wad fyle the Logan Water;
Sic a wife as Willie had,
　I wad na gi'e a button for her.

I GAED A WAEFU GATE YESTREEN.
ROBERT BURNS.

I GAED a waefu' gate yestreen,
　A gate, I fear, I'll dearly rue;
I gat my death frae twa sweet een,
　Twa lovely een o' bonnie blue.
'Twas not her golden ringlets bright;
　Her lips like roses wat wi' dew,
Her heaving bosom, lily-white—
　It was her een sae bonnie blue.

She talk'd, she smil'd, my heart she wil'd;
　She charm'd my soul—I wist na how;
An' aye the stound, the deadly wound,
　Cam' frae her een sae bonnie blue.
But spare to speak, and spare to speed;
　She'll aiblins listen to my vow;
Should she refuse, I'll lay my dead
　To her twa een sae bonnie blue.

MY SPOUSE, NANCY.
ROBERT BURNS.

"HUSBAND, husband, cease your strife,
　Nor longer idly rave, sir;
Tho' I am your wedded wife,
　Yet I am not your slave, sir."

R

"One of two must still obey,
 Nancy, Nancy;
Is it man, or woman, say,
 My spouse, Nancy?"

"If 'tis still the lordly word,
 Service and obedience;
I'll desert my sov'reign lord,
 And so good-bye allegiance!"

"Sad will I be, so bereft,
 Nancy, Nancy,
Yet I'll try to make a shift,
 My spouse, Nancy."

"My poor heart then break it must,
 My last hour I'm near it:
When you lay me in the dust,
 Think, think how you will bear it."

"I will hope and trust in heaven,
 Nancy, Nancy,
Strength to bear it will be given,
 My spouse, Nancy."

"Well, sir, from the silent dead,
 Still I'll try to daunt you;
Ever round your midnight bed
 Horrid sprites shall haunt you."

"I'll wed another like my dear,
 Nancy, Nancy;
Then all hell will fly for fear,
 My spouse, Nancy."

LASSIE WI' THE LINT-WHITE LOCKS.
ROBERT BURNS.
CHORUS.

Lassie wi' the lint-white locks,
 Bonnie lassie, artless lassie,
Wilt thou wi' me tent the flocks,
 Wilt thou be my dearie, O?

Now Nature cleeds the flowery lea,
An' a' is young an' sweet like thee:
Oh, wilt thou share its joys wi' me,
 An' say thou'lt be my dearie, O?
An' when the welcome simmer shower
Has cheer'd ilk drooping little flower,
We'll to the breathing woodbine bower
 At sultry noon, my dearie, O.

When Cynthia lights, wi' silver ray,
The weary shearer's hameward way,
Thro' yellow waving fields we'll stray,
 An' talk o' love, my dearie, O.
An' when the howling wintry blast
Disturbs my lassie's midnight rest,
Enclasped to my faithful breast,
 I'll comfort thee, my dearie, O.

MY AIN KIND DEARIE, O.
ROBERT BURNS.

When o'er the hill the eastern star
 Tells bughtin' time is near, my jo;
An' owsen frae the furrow'd field
 Return sae dowf an' weary, O;
Down by the burn, where scented birks
 Wi' dew are hanging clear, my jo,
I'll meet thee on the lea rig,
 My ain kind dearie, O.

In mirkest glen, at midnight hour,
 I'd rove, an' ne'er be earie, O,
If thro' that glen I gaed to thee,
 My ain kind dearie, O.
Altho' the night was ne'er sae wild,
 An' I were ne'er sae wearie, O,
I'd meet thee on the lea rig,
 My ain kind dearie, O.

The hunter lo'es the morning sun,
 To rouse the mountain deer, my jo:
At noon the fisher seeks the glen,
 Along the burn to steer, my jo;
Gi'e me the hour o' gloamin' gray,
 It mak's my heart sae cheery, O,
To meet thee on the lea rig,
 My ain kind dearie, O.

OH SAW YE BONNIE LESLIE.
ROBERT BURNS.

Oh saw ye bonnie Lesley,
 As she gaed owre the border?
She's gane, like Alexander,
 To spread her conquests farther.

To see her is to love her,
  An' love but her for ever;
For nature made her what she is,
  An' never made anither!

Thou art a queen, fair Lesley,
  Thy subjects we, before thee;
Thou art divine, fair Lesley,
  The hearts o' men adore thee.

The de'il he could na scaith thee,
  Or aught that wad belang thee;
He'd look into thy bonnie face,
  An' say, "I canna wrang thee!"

The powers aboon will tent thee;
  Misfortune sha' na steer thee;
Thou'rt like themselves sae lovely,
  That ill they'll ne'er let near thee.

Return again, fair Lesley,
  Return to Caledonie!
That we may brag, we ha'e a lass
  There's nane again sae bonnie.

MENIE.
ROBERT BURNS.

AGAIN rejoicing nature sees,
  Her robe assume its vernal hues,
Her leafy locks wave in the breeze,
  All freshly steep'd in morning dews.
    An' maun I still on Menie doat,
      An' bear the scorn that's in her e'e?
    For it's jet, jet black, an' like a hawk,
      An' winna let a body be.

In vain to me the cowslips blaw,
  In vain to me the vi'lots spring;
In vain to me, in glen or shaw,
  The mavis an' the lintwhite sing.

The merry ploughboy cheers his team,
  Wi' joy the tentie seedsman stalks;
But life to me's a weary dream,
  A dream of ane that never wauks.

The wanton coot the water skims,
  Amang the reeds the duckling cry,
The stately swan majestic swims,
  An' every thing is blest but I.

The shepherd sleeks his faulding slap,
    An' owre the moorland whistles shrill;
Wi' wild unequal, waud'ring step,
    I meet him on the dewy hill.

An' when the lark, 'tween light an' dark,
    Blythe waukens by the daisy's side,
An' mounts an' sings on flittering wings,
    A woe-worn ghaist I hameward glide.

Come, Winter, with thine angry howl,
    An' raging bend the naked tree:
Thy gloom will soothe my cheerless soul,
    When nature all is sad like me!

THE DE'IL'S AWA' WI' THE EXCISEMAN.
ROBERT BURNS.

The de'il cam' fiddling through the town,
    An' danced awa' wi' the Exciseman,
And ilka wife cries—" Auld Mahoun,
    I wish you luck o' the prize, man!"
    The de'il's awa', the de'il's awa',
        The de'il's awa' wi' the Exciseman;
    He's danc'd awa', he's danc'd awa',
        He's danc'd awa' wi' the Exciseman!

We'll mak' our maut, we'll brew our drink,
    We'll dance, an' sing, an' rejoice, man;
And mony braw thanks to the meikle black de'il
    That danc'd awa' wi' the Exciseman.
    The de'il's awa', the de'il's awa',
        The de'il's awa' wi' the Exciseman;
    He's danc'd awa', he's danc'd awa',
        He's danc'd awa' wi' the Exciseman.

There's threesome reels, there's foursome reels,
    There's hornpipes and strathspeys, man;
But the ae best dance e'er cam' to the land
    Was—the de'il's awa' wi' the Exciseman,
    The de'il's awa', the de'il's awa',
        The de'il's awa' wi' the Exciseman;
    He's danc'd awa', he's danc'd awa,
        He's danc'd awa' wi' the Exciseman.

THE DEVON.
ROBERT BURNS.

How pleasant the banks of the clear winding Devon,
  With green spreading bushes, and flowers blooming fair;
But the bonniest flower on the banks of the Devon
  Was once a sweet bud on the braes of the Ayr.
Mild be the sun on this sweet blushing flower,
  In the gay rosy morn as it bathes in the dew;
And gentle the fall of the soft vernal shower,
  That steals on the evening each leaf to renew.

Oh spare the dear blossom, ye orient breezes,
  With chill hoary wing, as ye usher the dawn;
And far be thou distant, thou reptile that seizes
  The verdure and pride of the garden and lawn!
Let Bourbon exult in his gay gilded Lilies,
  And England, triumphant, display her proud Rose;
A fairer than either adorns the green valleys,
  Where Devon, sweet Devon, meandering flows.

MALLY'S MEEK.
ROBERT BURNS.

Oh Mally's meek, Mally's sweet,
  Mally's modest and discreet,
Mally's rare, Mally's fair,
  Mally's every way complete.

As I was walking up the street,
  A barefit maid I chanc'd to meet;
But oh the road was very hard
  For that fair maiden's tender feet.

It were mair meet that those fine feet
  Were weel lac'd up in silken shoon,
An' 'twere more fit that she should sit
  Within yon chariot gilt aboon.

Her yellow hair, beyond compare,
  Comes trinkling down her swan-white neck:
An' her two eyes, like stars in skies,
  Would keep a sinking ship frae wreck.

BONNIE WEE THING.
ROBERT BURNS.

Bonnie wee thing, cannie wee thing,
  Lovely wee thing, wert thou mine,
I wad wear thee in my bosom,
  Lest my jewel I should tine.

Wishfully I look an' languish
 In that bonnie face of thine;
An' my heart it stounds wi' anguish,
 Lest my wee thing be na mine.
Wit, an' grace, an' love, an' beauty,
 In ae constellation shine;
To adore thee is my duty,
 Goddess o' this soul o' mine!
Bonnie wee thing, cannie wee thing,
 Lovely wee thing, wert thou mine,
I wad wear thee in my bosom,
 Lest my jewel I should tine!

'TWAS NA HER BONNIE BLUE E'E.
ROBERT BURNS.

'Twas na her bonnie blue e'e was my ruin;
Fair tho' she be, that was ne'er my undoing;
'Twas the dear smile when naebody did mind us,
'Twas the bewitching, sweet, stown glance o' kindness.

Sair do I fear that to hope is denied me,
Sair do I fear that despair maun abide me;
But tho' fell fortune should fate us to sever,
Queen shall she be in my bosom for ever.

Mary, I'm thine wi' a passion sincerest,
And thou hast plighted me love o' the dearest!
And thou'rt the angel that never can alter,
Sooner the sun in his motion would falter.

NITH.
ROBERT BURNS.

The Thames flows proudly to the sea,
 Where royal cities stately stand;
But sweeter flows the Nith, to me,
 Where Cummins ance had high command:
When shall I see that honour'd land,
 That winding stream I love so dear!
Must wayward fortune's adverse hand
 For ever, ever keep me here?

How lovely, Nith, thy fruitful vales,
 Where spreading hawthorn's gaily bloom!
How sweetly wind thy sloping dales,
 Where lambkins wanton thro' the broom!
Tho' wandering, now, must be my doom,
 Far frae thy bonnie banks and braes,
May there my latest hours consume,
 Amang the friends of early days!

MARK YONDER POMP.
ROBERT BURNS.

Mark yonder pomp of costly fashion,
  Round the wealthy, titled bride:
But when compar'd with real passion,
  Poor is all that princely pride.
    What are the showy treasures?
    What are the noisy pleasures?
The gay gaudy glare of vanity and art:
    The polish'd jewel's blaze
    May draw the wond'ring gaze,
    And courtly grandeur bright
    The fancy may delight,
But never, never can come near the heart.

But did you see my dearest Chloris,
  In simplicity's array;
Lovely as yonder sweet op'ning flower is,
  Shrinking from the gaze of day.
    Oh then the heart alarming,
    And all resistless charming,
In Love's delightful fetters she chains the willing soul!
    Ambition would disown
    The world's imperial crown,
    Even Avarice would deny
    His worshipp'd deity,
And feel thro' ev'ry vein Love's raptures roll.

WHISTLE O'ER THE LAVE O'T.
ROBERT BURNS.

First when Maggy was my care,
Heaven I thought was in her air;
Now we're married—spier nae mair—
    Whistle o'er the lave o't.
Meg was meek, an' Meg was mild,
Bonnie Meg was nature's child;
Wiser men than me's beguil'd—
    Whistle o'er the lave o't.

How we live, my Meg an' me,
How we love, an' how we 'gree,
I care na by how few may see—
    Whistle o'er the lave o't.
Wha I wish were maggots' meat,
Dish'd up in her winding sheet,
I could write—but Meg maun see't—
    Whistle o'er the lave o't.

DEATH SONG.
ROBERT BURNS.

Scene.—A field of battle.—Time of the day, evening.—The wounded and dying of the victorious army are supposed to join in the following song:—

FAREWELL, thou fair day, thou green earth, and ye skies,
  Now gay with the bright setting sun;
Farewell loves and friendships, ye dear tender ties—
  Our race of existence is run!

Thou grim king of terrors, thou life's gloomy foe!
  Go, frighten the coward and slave;
Go, teach them to tremble, fell tyrant! but know,
  No terrors hast thou to the brave!

Thou strik'st the dull peasant—he sinks in the dark,
  Nor saves e'en the wreck of a name;
Thou strik'st the young hero—a glorious mark!
  He falls in the blaze of his fame!

In the field of proud honour—our swords in our hands,
  Our king and our country to save—
While victory shines on life's last ebbing sands,
  Oh! who would not die with the brave!

BLYTHE, BLYTHE AND MERRY WAS SHE.
ROBERT BURNS.

CHORUS.

BLYTHE, blythe and merry was she,
  Blythe was she butt and ben;
Blythe by the banks of Ern,
  An' blythe in Glenturit glen.

By Auchtertyre grows the aik,
  On Yarrow banks the birken shaw;
But Phemie was a bonnier lass
  Than braes o' Yarrow ever saw.

Her looks were like a flow'r in May,
  Her smile was like a simmer morn:
She tripped by the banks o' Ern,
  As light's a bird upon a thorn.

Her bonnie face it was as meek
  As ony lamb upon a lea;
The evening sun was ne'er sae sweet
  As was the blink o' Phemie's e'e.

The Highland hills I've wander'd wide,
  An' o'er the lowlands I ha'e been;
But Phemie was the blythest lass
  That ever trod the dewy green.

THE DAY RETURNS.
ROBERT BURNS.

The day returns, my bosom burns,
  The blissful day we twa did meet,
Tho' winter wild in tempest toil'd,
  No'er summer sun was half so sweet.
Than a' the pride that loads the tide,
  An' crosses o'er the sultry line;
Than kingly robes, than crowns an' globes,
  Heav'n gave me more—it made thee mine

While day an' night can bring delight,
  Or nature aught of pleasure give,
While joys above my mind can move,
  For thee, an' thee alone, I live.
When that grim foe of life below
  Comes in between to make us part,
The iron hand that breaks our band,
  It breaks my bliss—it breaks my heart!

AYE WAUKIN', O.
ROBERT BURNS.

Simmer's a pleasant time,
  Flowers of every colour;
The water rins o'er the heugh,
  An' I long for my true lover.

  Aye waukin', O,
    Waukin' still an' wearie;
  Sleep I can get nane
    For thinking on my dearie.

When I sleep I dream,
  When I wauk I'm eerie:
Sleep I can get nane
  For thinkin' on my dearie.

Lanely night comes on,
  A' the lave are sleepin';
I think on my bonnie lad,
  An' bleer my een wi' greetin'.

SWEET FA'S THE EVE.
ROBERT BURNS.

Sweet fa's the eve on Craigieburn,
  An' blythe awakes the morrow;
But a' the pride o' spring's return
  Can yield me nocht but sorrow.

I see the flowers an' spreading trees,
  I hear the wild birds singing;
But what a weary wight can please,
  An' care his bosom wringing?

Fain, fain would I my griefs impart,
  Yet dare na for your anger;
But secret love will break my heart,
  If I conceal it langer.
If thou refuse to pity me,
  If thou shalt love anither,
When yon green leaves fade frae the tree,
  Around my grave they'll wither.

OH AYE MY WIFE SHE DANG ME.
ROBERT BURNS.

Oh aye my wife she dang me,
An' aft my wife did bang me,
If ye gi'e a woman a' her will,
Gude faith, she'll soon o'ergang ye.
On peace an' rest my mind was bent,
  An' fool I was, I married;
But never honest man's intent
  As cursedly miscarried.

Some sair o' comfort still at last,
  When a' my days are done, man;
My pains o' hell on earth are past,
  I'm sure o' bliss aboon, man.
Oh aye my wife she dang me,
An' aft my wife did bang me,
If ye gi'e a woman a' her will,
Gude faith, she'll soon o'ergang ye.

LORD GREGORY.
ROBERT BURNS.

Oh mirk, mirk is this midnight hour,
  An' loud the tempest's roar;
A waefu' wanderer seeks thy tower,
  Lord Gregory, ope thy door.

An' exile frae her father's ha',
  An' a' for loving thee;
At least some *pity* on me shaw,
  If *love* it may na be.

Lord Gregory, mind'st thou not the grove,
  By bonnie Irwine side,
Where first I own'd that virgin love
  I lang, lang had denied?
How aften didst thou pledge an' vow
  Thou wad for aye be mine;
And my fond heart, itsel' sae true,
  It ne'er mistrusted thine.

Hard is thy heart, Lord Gregory,
  An' flinty is thy breast:
Thou dart of heaven that flashest by,
  Oh wilt thou give me rest!
Ye mustering thunders from above
  Your willing victim see!
But spare an' pardon my fause love,
  His wrangs to Heaven an' me!

HEY, THE DUSTY MILLER.
ROBERT BURNS.

Hey, the dusty miller,
  And his dusty coat;
He will win a shilling,
  Or he spend a groat.
    Dusty was the coat,
      Dusty was the colour,
    Dusty was the kiss
      That I got frae the miller.

Hey, the dusty miller,
  And his dusty sack:
Leeze me on the calling
  Fills the dusty peck—
    Fills the dusty peck,
      Brings the dusty siller;
    I wad gi'e my coatie
      For the dusty miller.

DUNCAN GRAY.
ROBERT BURNS.

Duncan Gray cam' here to woo,
  Ha, ha, the wooing o't,
On blythe Yule night when we were fu',
  Ha, ha, the wooing o't.

Maggie coost her head fu' high,
Look'd asklent an' unco skeigh,
Gart poor Duncan stand abeigh;
    Ha, ha, the wooing o't.
Duncan fleech'd an' Duncan pray'd,
    Ha, ha, the wooing o't;
Meg was deaf as Ailsa Craig,
    Ha, ha, the wooing o't.
Duncan sigh'd baith out an' in,
Grat his een baith bleert an' blin',
Spak' o' lowpin owre a linn;
    Ha, ha, the wooing o't.

Time an' chance are but a tide,
    Ha, ha, the wooing o't;
Slighted love is sair to bide,
    Ha, ha, the wooing o't.
Shall I, like a fool, quoth he,
For a haughty hizzie die?
She may gae to—France for me!
    Ha, ha, the wooing o't.

How it comes let doctors tell,
    Ha, ha, the wooing o't;
Meg grew sick—as he grew hale,
    Ha, ha, the wooing o't.
Something in her bosom wrings,
For relief a sigh she brings;
An' oh, her een, they speak sic things!
    Ha, ha, the wooing o't.

Duncan was a lad o' grace,
    Ha, ha, the wooing o't.
Maggie's was a piteous case,
    Ha, ha, the wooing o't.
Duncan could na be her death,
Swelling pity smoor'd his wrath;
Now they're crouse an' canty baith;
    Ha, ha, the wooing o't.

AULD ROB MORRIS.
ROBERT BURNS.

There's auld Rob Morris that wons in yon glen,
He's the king o' gude fellows an' wale o' auld men
He has gowd in his coffers, he has owsen an' kine,
An' ae bonnie lassie, his darling an' mine.

She's fresh as the morning, the fairest in May;
She's sweet as the ev'ning among the new hay;
As blythe and as artless as the lambs on the lea,
An' dear to my heart as the light to my e'e.

But, oh! she's an heiress, auld Robin's a laird,
An' my daddie has naught but a cot-house an' yard;
A wooer like me maunna hope to come speed,
The wounds I must hide that will soon be my dead.

The day comes to me, but delight brings me nane;
The night comes to me, but my rest it is gane:
I wander my lane like a night-troubled ghaist,
And I sigh as my heart it wad burst in my breast.

Oh had she but been of a lower degree,
I then might ha'e hop'd she wad smil'd upon me!
Oh, how past describing had then been my bliss,
As now my distraction no words can express!

AND OH! MY EPPIE.
ROBERT BURNS.

And oh! my Eppie,
My jewel, my Eppie!
Wha wadna be happy
  Wi' Eppie Adair!
By love, and by beauty,
By law, and by duty,
I swear to be true to
  My Eppie Adair!

And oh! my Eppie,
My jewel, my Eppie,
Wha wadna be happy
  Wi' Eppie Adair?
A' pleasure exile me,
Dishonour defile me,
If e'er I beguile thee,
  My Eppie Adair?

HAD I A CAVE.
ROBERT BURNS.

Had I a cave on some wild distant shore,
Where the winds howl to the waves' dashing roar
  There would I weep my woes,
  There seek my lost repose,
  Till grief my eyes should close,
    Ne'er to wake more!

Falsest of womankind, canst thou declare,
All thy fond plighted vows—fleeting as air!
  To thy new lover hie,
  Laugh o'er thy perjury;
  Then in thy bosom try
    What peace is there!

MACPHERSON'S FAREWELL.
ROBERT BURNS.

FAREWELL, ye dungeons dark and strong,
  The wretch's destinie!
Macpherson's time will not be long
  On yonder gallows-tree.
    Sae rantingly, sae wantonly,
      Sae dauntingly gaed he;
    He play'd a spring, and danc'd it round,
      Below the gallows-tree.

Oh, what is death but parting breath!—
  On mony a bloody plain
I've dar'd his face, and in this place
  I scorn him yet again!

Untie these bands from off my hands,
  And bring to me my sword:
And there's no a man in all Scotland,
  But I'll brave him at a word.

I've liv'd a life of sturt and strife;
  I die by treacherie:
It burns my heart I must depart,
  And not avenged be.

Now farewell light—thou sunshine bright,
  And all beneath the sky!
May coward shame distain his name,
  The wretch that dares not die!

BONNIE ANN.
ROBERT BURNS.

YE gallants bright, I rede ye right,
  Beware o' bonnie Ann;
Her comely face sae fu' o' grace,
  Your heart she will trepan.
Her een sae bright, like stars by night,
  Her skin is like the swan;
Sae jimply lac'd her genty waist,
  That sweetly ye might span.

Youth, grace, an' love attendant move,
  An' pleasure leads the van:
In a' their charms, an' conquering arms,
  They wait on bonnie Ann.
The captive bands may chain the hands,
  But love enslaves the man;
Ye gallants braw, I rede you a',
  Beware o' bonnie Ann!

HIGHLAND HARRY.
ROBERT BURNS.

My Harry was a gallant gay,
  Fu' stately strode he on the plain:
But now he's banish'd far away,
  I'll never see him back again.
    Oh for him back again!
    Oh for him back again!
  I wad gi'e a' Knockhaspie's land
    For Highland Harry back again.

When a' the lave gae to their bed,
  I wander dowie up the glen;
I set me down and greet my fill,
  And aye I wish him back again.

Oh were some villains hangit high,
  And ilka body had their ain!
Then I might see the joyful sight,
  My Highland Harry back again.

SHE'S FAIR AND FAUSE.
ROBERT BURNS.

She's fair and fause that causes my smart,
  I lo'ed her meikle an' lang;
She's broken her vow, she's broken my heart,
  And I may e'en gae hang.
A coof cam' in wi' routh o' gear,
  And I ha'e tint my dearest dear;
But woman is but warld's gear,
  Sae let the bonnie lass gang.

Whae'er ye be that woman love,
  To this be never blind,
Nae ferlie 'tis tho' fickle she prove,
  A woman has't by kind.

Oh woman, lovely woman fair!
An angel form's fa'n to thy share,
'Twad been ower meikle to gi'en thee mair—
I mean an angel mind.

ROBIN SHURE IN HAIRST.
ROBERT BURNS.

CHORUS.

Robin shure in hairst,
  I shure wi' him;
Fient a heuk had I,
  Yet I stack by him.

I gaed up to Dunse,
  To warp a wab o' plaiden;
At his daddie's yett,
  Wha met me but Robin?

Was na Robin bauld,
  Though I was a cottar,
Play'd me sic a trick,
  And me the eller's dochter?

Robin promis'd me
  A' my winter vittle;
Fient haet he had but three
  Goose feathers and a whittle.

MY HEART'S IN THE HIGHLANDS.
ROBERT BURNS.

My heart's in the Highlands, my heart is not here;
My heart's in the Highlands, a-chasing the deer;
Chasing the wild deer, and following the roe—
My heart's in the Highlands wherever I go.
Farewell to the Highlands, farewell to the North,
The birth-place of valour, the country of worth;
Wherever I wander, wherever I rove,
The hills of the Highlands for ever I love.

Farewell to the mountains high cover'd with snow;
Farewell to the straths and green valleys below:
Farewell to the forests and wild-hanging woods;
Farewell to the torrents and loud-pouring floods.
My heart's in the Highlands, my heart is not here;
My heart's in the Highlands, a-chasing the deer:
Chasing the wild deer, and following the roe—
My heart's in the Highlands wherever I go.

TIBBIE DUNBAR.
ROBERT BURNS.

O wilt thou go wi' me, sweet Tibbie Dunbar?
O wilt thou go wi' me, sweet Tibbie Dunbar?
Wilt thou ride on a horse or be drawn in a car,
Or walk by my side, sweet Tibbie Dunbar?

I carena thy daddie, his lands and his money,
I carena thy kin, sae high and sae lordly;
But sae thou wilt ha'e me, for better for waur,
An' come in thy coatie, sweet Tibbie Dunbar!

HAPPY WE'VE BEEN A' THEGITHER.
ATTRIBUTED to ROBERT BURNS.

Here around the ingle bleezin',
  Wha sae happy and sae free?
Tho' the northern wind blaws freezin',
  Frien'ship warms baith you an' me.
    Happy we are a' thegither,
    Happy we'll be ane an' a';
    Time shall see us a' the blyther
    Ere we rise to gang awa'.

See the miser o'er his treasure
  Gloating wi' a greedy e'e!
Can he feel the glow o' pleasure
  That around us here we see?

Can the peer in silk and ermine,
  Ca' his conscience half his own?
His claes are spun an' edged wi' vermin
  Tho' he stan' afore a throne!

Thus then let us a' be tassing
  All our stoups o' gen'rous flame;
An' while roun' the board 'tis passing,
  Raise a sang in frien'ship's name.

Frien'ship mak's us a' mair happy,
  Frien'ship gi'es us a' delight;
Frien'ship consecrates the drappie,
  Frien'ship brings us here to night.
    Happy we've been a' thegither,
    Happy we've been ane an' a';
    Time shall find us a' the blyther
    When we rise to gang awa'.

WHEN SHE CAM BEN SHE BOBBIT FU' LAW.

JOHNSON'S MUSEUM. Altered by Burns from an old and licentious ditty.

O WHEN she cam ben she bobbit fu' law,
O when she cam ben she bobbit fu' law,
And when she cam ben she kissed Cockpen,
And syne she denied that she did it at a'.

And wasna Cockpen richt saucy witha',
And wasna Cockpen richt saucy witha',
In leaving the dochter of a lord,
And kissing a collier lassie an a'?

O never look doun, my lassie at a',
O never look doun, my lassie, at a';
Thy lips are as sweet, and thy figure complete,
As the finest dame in castle or ha'.

Though thou hae nae silk and holland sae sma',
Though thou hae nae silk and holland sae sma',
Thy coat and thy sark are thy ain handywark,
And Lady Jean was never sae braw.

LIZZY LINDSAY.

JOHNSON'S MUSEUM. Adapted by Burns from an earlier song. Air, "The Ewe Buchts."

WILL ye gang wi' me, Lizzy Lindsay,
 Will ye gang to the Highlands wi' me?
Will ye gang wi' me, Lizzy Lindsay,
 My bride and my darling to be?

To gang to the Highlands wi' you, sir,
 I dinna ken how that may be;
For I ken nae the land that ye live in,
 Nor ken I the lad I'm gaun wi'.

O Lizzy, lass, ye maun ken little,
 If sae ye dinna ken me;
For my name is Lord Ronald MacDonald,
 A chieftain o' high degree.

She has kilted her coats o' green satin,
 She has kilted them up to the knee,
And she's off wi' Lord Ronald MacDonald,
 His bride and his darling to be.

THE CAMPBELLS ARE COMING.

Johnson's Museum.

The Campbells are coming, O-ho, O-ho!
  The Campbells are coming, O-ho!
The Campbells are coming to bonnie Lochleven!
  The Campbells are coming, O-ho, O-ho!

Upon the Lomonds I lay, I lay;
  Upon the Lomonds I lay;
I lookit doun to bonnie Lochleven,
  And saw three perches play.
    The Campbells are coming, &c.

Great Argyle he goes before
He makes the cannons and guns to roar;
With sound of trumpet, pipe, and drum;
  The Campbells are coming, O-ho, O-ho!

The Campbells they are a' in arms,
  Their loyal faith and truth to show,
With banners rattling in the wind;
  The Campbells are coming, O-ho, O-ho!

DUNCAN GRAY.

Johnson's Museum. The old version, communicated by Burns and slightly altered by him.

Weary fa' you, Duncan Gray,
  Ha, ha, the girdin' o't;
Wae gae by you, Duncan Gray,
  Ha, ha, the girdin' o't;
When a' the lave gae to their play,
Then I maun sit the lee-lang day,
An' jeeg the cradle wi' my tae,
  An' a' for the girdin' o't.

Bonnie was the Lammas moon,
  Ha, ha, the girdin' o't,
Glowrin' a' the hills aboon,
  Ha, ha, the girdin' o't;
The girdin' brak', the beast cam' down,
I tint my curch an' baith my shoon;
An', Duncan, ye're an unco loon,
  Wae on the bad girdin' o't.

But, Duncan, gin ye'll keep your aith,
  Ha, ha, the girdin' o't,
I'll bless you wi' my hindmost breath,
  Ha, ha, the girdin' o't.
Duncan, gin ye'll keep your aith,
The beast again can bear us baith,
An' auld Mess John will mend the skaith,
  An' clout the bad girdin' o't.

JAMIE O' THE GLEN.

Johnson's Museum.

Auld Rob, the laird o' muckle land,
  To woo me was na very blate,
But spite o' a' his gear he fand
  He came to woo a day owre late.
    A lad sae blythe, sae fu' o' glee,
      My heart did never ken,
    And nane can gi'e sic joy to me
      As Jamie o' the glen.

My minnie grat like daft, and rair'd,
  To gar me wi' her will comply,
But still I wadna ha'e the laird,
  Wi' a' his ousen, sheep, and kye.
    A lad sae blythe, &c.

Ah, what are silks and satins braw?
  What's a' his warldly gear to me?
They're daft that cast themsel's awa',
  Where nae content or love can be.
    A lad sae blythe, &c.

I cou'dna bide the silly clash
  Came hourly frae the gawky laird!
And sae, to stop his gab and fash,
  Wi' Jamie to the kirk repair'd.
    A lad sae blythe, &c.

Now ilka summer's day sae lang,
  And winter's clad wi' frost and snaw,
A tunefu' lilt and bonnie sang
  Aye keep dull care and strife awa'.
    A lad sae blythe, &c.

THE BREIST KNOTS.

Johnson's Museum. But considerably abridged.

Hey the bonnie, how the bonnie,
  Hey the bonnie breist-knots!
Tight and bonnie were they a',
  When they got on their breist-knots.

There was a bridal in this town,
And till't the lasses a' were boun',
Wi' mankie facings on their gowns,
  And some o' them had breist-knots.

At nine o'clock the lads convene,
Some clad in blue, some clad in green,
Wi' glancin' buckles in their shoon,
    And flowers upon their waistcoats.

Forth cam' the wives a' wi' a phrase,
And wished the lassie happy days;
And meikle thocht they o' her claes,
    And 'specially the breist-knots.

MY LADDIE IS GANE.

Johnson's Museum.

My laddie is gane far away o'er the plain,
While in sorrow behind I am forc'd to remain,
Though blue-bells and violets the hedges adorn,
Though trees are in blossom and sweet blows the thorn.
No pleasure they give me, in vain they look gay,
There's nothing can please me now Jockie's away;
Forlorn I sit singing, and this is my strain—
Haste, haste, my dear Jockie, to me back again.

When lads and their lassies are on the green met,
They dance and they sing, and they laugh and they chat,
Contented and happy, with hearts full of glee,
I can't without envy their merriment see.
Those pleasures offend me, my Shepherd's not there,
No pleasure I relish that Jockie don't share;
It makes me to sigh, I from tears scarce refrain,
I wish my dear Jockie returned back again.

But hope shall sustain me, nor will I deplore,
He promised he would in a fortnight be here;
On fond expectation my wishes I'll feast,
For love my dear Jockie to Jenny will haste.
Then farewell each care, and adieu each vain sigh,
Who'll then be so blest or so happy as I?
I'll sing on the meadows and alter my strain,
When Jockie returns to my arms back again.

MARY.

Johnson's Museum.

Thou art gane awa', thou art gane awa',
    Thou art gane awa' frae me, Mary!
Nor friends nor I could make thee stay—
    Thou hast cheated them and me, Mary!

Until this hour I never thought
  That aught could alter thee, Mary;
Thou'rt still the mistress of my heart,
  Think what you will of me, Mary.

Whate'er he said or might pretend,
  That stole the heart of thine, Mary,
True love, I'm sure, was ne'er his end,
  Or nae sic love as mine, Mary.
I spoke sincere, nor flattered much,
  Had no unworthy thoughts, Mary;
Ambition, wealth, nor naething such;
  No, I loved only thee, Mary.

Though you've been false, yet while I live,
  I'll lo'e nae maid but thee, Mary;
Let friends forget, as I forgive,
  Thy wrongs to them and me, Mary.
So then farewell! of this be sure,
  Since you've been false to me, Mary;
For all the world I'd not endure
  Half what I've done for thee, Mary.

THE COLLIER LADDIE.

JOHNSON'S MUSEUM.

Whare live ye, my bonnie lass,
  And tell me what they ca' ye?
My name, she says, is Mistress Jean,
  And I follow the collier laddie.

See ye not yon hills and dales,
  The sun shines on sae brawlie!
They a' are mine, and they shall be thine,
  Gin ye'll leave your collier laddie.

Ye shall gang in gay attire,
  Weel buskit up sae gawdy:
And ane to wait on every hand,
  Gin ye'll leave your collier laddie.

Though ye had a' the sun shines on,
  And the earth conceals sae lowly,
I wad turn my back on you and it a',
  And embrace my collier laddie.

I can win my five-pennies in a day,
  And spen't at night fu' brawlie:
And make my bed in the collier's neuk,
  And lie down wi' my collier laddie.

Love for love is the bargain for me,
Tho' the wee cot-house should haud me,
And the warld before me to win my bread,
And fair fa' my collier laddie.

HEY DONALD, HOWE DONALD.

JOHNSON'S MUSEUM. The air has been traced as far back as the seventeenth century.

Hey, Donald, howe Donald,
 Hey Donald Couper!
He's gane awa' to seek a wife,
 And he's come hame without her.

O Donald Couper and his man
 Held to a Highland fair, man;
And a' to seek a bonnie lass—
 But fient a ane was there, man.

At length he got a carlin gray,
 And she's come hirplin' hame, man;
And she's fawn ower the buffet stool,
 And brak' her rumple-bane, man.

NURSERY SONG.

JOHNSON'S MUSEUM.

O can ye sew cushions,
 Or can ye sew sheets,
Or can ye sing Ba-loo-loo,
 When the bairnie greets?
And hee and ba-birdie,
 And hee and ba-lamb,
And hee and ba-birdie,
 My bonnie wee lamb.
  Hee-o, wee-o, what would I do wi' you?
  Black's the life that I lead wi' you.
  O'er mony o' you, little for to gi'e you,
  Hee-o, wee-o, what would I do wi' you?

I've placed my cradle
 On yon holly top,
And aye, as the wind blew,
 My cradle did rock.
And hush-a-ba, baby,
 O ba-lilly-loo,
And hee and ba-birdie,
 My bonnie wee doo!
  Hee-o, wee-o, what would I do wi' you? &c.

O, AN YE WERE DEAD GUIDMAN.

JOHNSON'S MUSEUM.

O, an ye were dead, guidman,
O, an ye were dead, guidman,
That I might wair my widowheid
Upon a ranting Highlandman.

There's six eggs in the pan, guidman,
There's six eggs in the pan, guidman;
There's ane to you and twa to me,
And three to our John Highlandman.

There's beef into the pot, guidman,
There's beef into the pot, guidman;
The banes to you, the broe to me,
And the beef for our John Highlandman.

There's sax horse in the sta', guidman,
There's sax horse in the sta', guidman;
There's ane to you, and twa to me,
And three to our John Highlandman.

There's sax kye in the byre, guidman,
There's sax kye in the byre, guidman;
There's nane o' them yours, but twa o' them mine,
And the lave is our John Highlandman's.

A COGIE O' YILL.

ANDREW SHERIFF,

Editor of the Aberdeen Chronicle. He published in 1787, a Scottish Pastoral entitled "Jamie and Bess."

A cogie o' yill,
And a pickle aitmeal,
And a dainty wee drappie o' whisky,
Was our forefathers' dose,
For to sweel down their brose,
And keep them aye cheery and frisky.

Then hey for the whisky, and hey for the meal,
And hey for the cogie, and hey for the yill,
Gin ye steer a' thegither they'll do unco weel,
To keep a chiel cheery and brisk aye.

When I see our Scots lads,
Wi' their kilts and cockauds,
That sae aften ha'e lounder'd our foes, man;
I think to mysel',
On the meal and the yill,
And the fruits o' our Scottish kail brose, man,
Then hey, &c.

When our brave Highland blades,
　Wi' their claymores and plaids,
In the field drove like sheep a' our foes, man;
　Their courage and pow'r—
　Spring frae this to be sure,
They're the noble effects o' the brose, man.
　　Then hey, &c.

But your spyndle-shank'd sparks,
　Wha sae ill fill their sarks,
Your pale-visaged milksops and beaux, man;
　I think when I see them,
　'Twere kindness to gi'e them—
A cogie o' yill or o' brose, man.
　　Then hey, &c.

What John Bull despises,
　Our better sense prizes,
He denies eatin' blanter ava, man;
　But by eatin' o' blanter,
　His mare's grown, I'll warrant her,
The manliest brute o' the twa, man.
　　Then hey, &c.

THE BLACK EAGLE.

JAMES FORDYCE, D.D.,

At one time Minister of Brechin, afterwards Minister of a Presbyterian Church in London. He published a volume of poems in 1786, in which is the following song, intended for a pathetic air of that name ("The Black Eagle") in Oswald's Collection of Scotch Tunes. He died in 1796, in his 76th year.

Hark! yonder eagle lonely wails,
His faithful bosom grief assails;
Last night I heard him in my dream,
When death and woe were all the theme.
Like that poor bird I make my moan,
I grieve for dearest Delia gone;
With him to gloomy rocks I fly,
He mourns for love and so do I.

'Twas mighty love that tamed his breast,
'Tis tender grief that breaks his rest;
He droops his wings, he hangs his head,
Since she he fondly loved was dead.
With Delia's breath my joy expired,
'Twas Delia's smiles my fancy fired;
Like that poor bird I pine, and prove
Nought can supply the place of love.

Dark as his feathers was the fate
That robb'd him of his darling mate;
Dimm'd is the lustre of his eye,
That wont to gaze the sun-bright sky.
To him is now for ever lost,
The heartfelt bliss he once could boast;
Thy sorrows, hapless bird, display,
An image of my soul's dismay.

THE TOOM MEAL POCK.

JOHN ROBERTSON,

WRITTEN about the year 1793.

Preserve us a'! what shall we do,
 Thir dark unhallowed times?
We're surely dreeing penance now,
 For some most awfu' crimes.
Sedition daurna now appear,
 In reality or joke,
For ilka chiel maun mourn wi' me,
 O' a hinging toom meal pock.
       And sing, Oh waes me!

When lasses braw gaed out at e'en,
 For sport and pastime free,
I seem'd like ane in paradise,
 The moments quick did flee.
Like Venuses they a' appeared,
 Weel pouthered was their locks,
'Twas easy dune, when at their hame,
 Wi' the shaking o' their pocks.
       And sing, O waes me!

How happy past my former days,
 Wi' merry heartsome glee,
When smiling fortune held the cup,
 And peace sat on my knee;
Nae wants had I but were supplied,
 My heart wi' joy did knock,
When in the neuk I smiling saw
 A gaucie weel fill'd pock.
       And sing, Oh waes me!

Speak no ae word about reform,
 Nor petition Parliament,
A wiser scheme I'll now propose,
 I'm sure ye'll gi'e consent—

Send up a chiel or twa like me,
  As a sample o' the flock,
Whase hollow cheeks will be sure proof,
  O' a hinging toom meal pock.
      And sing, Oh waes me!

And should a sicht sae ghastly like,
  Wi' rags, and banes, and skin,
Ha'e na impression on yon folks,
  But tell ye'll stand ahin:
O what a contrast will ye shaw,
  To the glowrin' Lunnun folk,
When in St. James' ye tak' your stand,
  Wi' a hinging toom meal pock.
      And sing, Oh waes me!

Then rear your hand, and glowr, and stare,
  Before yon bills o' beef,
Tell them ye are frae Scotland come,
  For Scotia's relief;
Tell them ye are the vera best,
  Wal'd frae the fattest flock,
Then raise your arms, and Oh! display
  A hinging toom meal pock.
      And sing, Oh waes me!

Tell them ye're wearied o' the chain
  That hauds the state thegither,
For Scotland wishes just to tak'
  Gude nicht wi' ane anither.
We canna thole, we canna bide,
  This hard unwieldy yoke,
For wark and want but ill agree,
  Wi' a hinging toom meal pock.
      And sing, Oh waes me!

THE WEE WIFUKIE.
DR. A. GEDDES,

Born at Banff in 1737, a Clergyman of the Roman Catholic Church. He died at London in 1802. His works, which are numerous, are chiefly of a Theological cast, and include a translation of the Sacred Scriptures.

THERE was a wee bit wifukie, was comin' frae the fair,
Had got a wee bit drappukie, that bred her meikle care,
It gaed about the wifie's heart, and she began to spew,
O! quo' the wee wifukie, I wish I binna fou.
  I wish I binna fou, quo' she, I wish I binna fou,
  Oh! quo' the wee wifukie, I wish I binna fou.

If Johnnie find me barley-sick, I'm sure he'll claw my skin;
But I'll lie down and tak' a nap before that I gae in.
Sitting at the dyke-side, and taking o' her nap,
By came a packman laddie wi' a little pack,
  Wi' a little pack, quo' she, wi' a little pack,
By came a packman laddie wi' a little pack.

He's clippit a' her gowden locks sae bonnie and sae lang;
He's ta'en her purse and a' her placks, and fast awa' he ran:
And when the wifie waken'd, her head was like a bee,
Oh! quo' the wee wifukie, this is nae me,
  This is nae me, quo' she, this is nae me,
Somebody has been felling me, and this is nae me.

I met with kindly company, and birl'd my bawbee!
And still, if this be Bessukie, three placks remain wi' me:
But I will look the pursie nooks, see gin the cunyie be:—
There's neither purse nor plack about me!—this is nae me.
  This is nae mo, &c.

I have a little housukie, but and a kindly man;
A dog, they ca' him Doussickie; if this be me he'll fawn;
And Johnnie, he'll come to the door, and kindly welcome gi'e,
And a' the bairns on the floor-head will dance if this be me.
  This is nae me, &c.

The night was late, and dang out weet, and oh but it was dark,
The doggie heard a body's foot, and he began to bark,
Oh when she heard the doggie bark, and keenin' it was he,
Oh weel ken ye, Doussie, quo' she, this is nae me.
  This is nae me, &c.

When Johnnie heard his Bessie's word, fast to the door he ran;
Is that you Bessukie?—Wow na, man!
He kind to the bairns a', and weel mat ye be;
And fareweel, Johnnie, quo' she, this is nae me!
  This is nae me, &c.

John ran to the minister, his hair stood a' on end,
I've gotten sic a fright, Sir, I fear I'll never mend:
My wife's come hame without a head, crying out most piteously,
Oh fareweel, Johnnie, quo' she, this is nae me!
  This is nae me, &c.

The tale you tell, the parson said, is wonderful to me,
How that a wife without a head could speak, or hear, or see!
But things that happen hereabout, so strangely alter'd be,
That I could maist wi' Bessie say, 'tis neither you nor she;
  Neither you nor she, quo' he, neither you nor she,
Wow na, Johnnie man, 'tis neither you nor she.

Now Johnnie he cam' hame again, and oh! but he was fain,
To see his little Bessukie come to hersel' again.
Ho got her sittin on a stool, wi' Tibbuck on her knee :
Oh, come awa', Johnnie, quo' she, come awa' to me,
For I've got a nap wi' Tibbuckie, and this is now me.
  This is now me, quo' she, this is now me,
  I've got a nap wi' Tibbuckie, and this is now me.

AULD ROBIN GRAY.

LADY ANN BARNARD,

DAUGHTER of James, Earl of Balcarres, was born in 1750. She married in 1793, Sir Andrew Barnard, librarian to George III. He died in 1807. Lady Ann survived to 1825, when she died at her house in London.

The song was originally written to a very old air, "The bridegroom grat when the sun gaed down." The old air, however, is now discarded for the very beautiful one composed by the Reverend William Leeves, rector of Wrington, in Somersetshire.

When the sheep are in the fauld, and the kye a' at hame,
When a' the weary world to sleep are gane,
The waes o' my heart fa' in showers frae my e'e,
While my gudeman lies sound by me.

Young Jamie lo'ed me weel, and sought me for his bride;
But saving a crown he had naething else beside.
To make the crown a pound, my Jamie gaed to sea;
And the crown and the pound, they were baith for me!

He hadna been awa' a week but only twa,
When my mither she fell sick, and the cow was stown awa;
My father brak his arm—my Jamie at the sea—
And Auld Robin Gray came a-courting me.

My father couldna work—my mither couldna spin;
I toil'd day and night, but their bread I couldna win;
Auld Rob maintain'd them baith, and, wi' tears in his e'e,
Said, "Jenny, for their sakes, will you marry me?"

My heart it said na, and I look'd for Jamie back;
But hard blew the winds, and his ship was a wrack:
His ship it was a wrack! Why didna Jenny dee?
And wherefore was I spar'd to cry, Wae is me!

My father argued sair—my mither didna speak,
But she look'd in my face till my heart was like to break;
They gied him my hand, but my heart was in the sea;
And so Auld Robin Gray, he was gudeman to me.

I hadna been his wife, a week but only four,
When mournfu' as I sat on the stane at the door,
I saw my Jamie's ghaist—I couldna think it he,
Till he said, "I'm come hame, my love, to marry thee!"

O sair, sair did we greet, and mickle did we say:
Ae kiss we took—nae mair—I bade him gang away.
I wish that I were dead, but I'm no like to dee;
And why do I live to say, Wae is me!

I gang like a ghaist, and I carena to spin;
I darena think o' Jamie, for that wad be a sin.
But I will do my best a gude wife to be,
For Auld Robin Gray, he is kind to me.

MY ONLY JO AND DEARIE, O.

RICHARD GALL,

A NATIVE of Linkhouse, near Dunbar, where he was born in 1776. He served his apprenticeship as compositor in the office of the *Edinburgh Evening Courant*, and continued in that office for some time after his apprenticeship was completed. He died in 1801, at the early age of twenty-five. His poems were published shortly after his death.

Thy cheek is o' the rose's hue,
  My only jo and dearie, O;
Thy neck is o' the siller dew
  Upon the bank sae brierie, O.
Thy teeth are o' the ivory;
O sweet's the twinkle o' thine ee:
Nae joy, nae pleasure, blinks on me,
  My only jo and dearie, O.

The birdie sings upon the thorn
  Its sang o' joy, fu' cheerie, O,
Rejoicing in the simmer morn,
  Nae care to mak' it eerie, O;
Ah! little kens the sangster sweet
Aught o' the care I ha'e to meet,
That gars my restless bosom beat,
  My only jo and dearie, O.

When we were bairnies on yon brae,
  And youth was blinkin' bonnie, O,
Aft we wad daff the lee-lang day,
  Our joys fu' sweet and monie, O.
Aft I wad chase thee o'er the lee,
And round about the thorny tree;
Or pu' the wild flowers a' for thee,
  My only jo and dearie, O.

I ha'e a wish I canna tine,
  'Mang a' the cares that grieve me, O,
A wish that thou wert ever mine,
  And never mair to leave me, O;
Then I would dawt thee night and day,
Nae ither warldly care I'd ha'e,
Till life's warm stream forgat to play,
  My only jo and dearie, O.

ON BURNS.

RICHARD GALL.

There's waefu' news in yon town,
  As e'er the warld heard ava;
There's dolefu' news in yon town,
  For Robbie's gane an' left them a'.

How blythe it was to see his face
  Come keeking by the hallan wa'!
He ne'er was sweir to say the grace,
  But now he's gane an' left them a'.

He was the lad wha made them glad,
  Whanever he the reed did blaw:
The lasses there may drap a tear,
  Their funny friend is now awa'.

Nae daffin now in yon town;
  The browster-wife gets leave to draw
An' drink hersel', in yon town,
  Sin' Robbie gaed an' left them a'.

The lawin's canny counted now,
  The bell that tinkled ne'er will draw,
The king will never get his due,
  Sin' Robbie gaed and left them a'.

The squads o' chiels that lo'ed a splore
  On winter e'enings, never ca';
Their blythesome moments a' are o'er,
  Sin' Robbie's gane an' left them a'.

Frae a' the een in yon town
  I see the tears o' sorrow fa',
An' weel they may, in yon town,
  Nae canty sang they hear ava.

Their e'ening sky begins to lour,
  The murky clouds thegither draw;
'Twas but a blink afore a shower,
  Ere Robbie gaed and left them a'.

The landwart hizzie winna speak;
  Ye'll see her sitting like a craw
Amang the reek, while rattons squeak—
  Her dawtit bard is now awa'.

But could I lay my hand upon
  His whistle, keenly wad I blaw,
An' screw about the auld drone,
  An' lilt a lightsome spring or twa.

If it were sweetest aye whan wat,
  Then wad I ripe my pouch, an' draw,
An' steep it weel amang the maut,
  As lang's I'd saxpence at my ca'.

For warld's gear I dinna care,
  My stock o' that is unco sma',
Come, friend, we'll pree the barley-bree
  To his braid fame that's now awa'.

THE WAITS.
RICHARD GALL.

Wha's this, wi' voice o' music sweet,
  Sae early wakes the weary wight?
O weel I ken them by their sough,
  The wand'ring minstrels o' the night.
O weel I ken their bonnie lilts,
  Their sweetest notes o' melody,
Fu' aft they've thrill'd out through my saul,
  And gart the tear fill ilka e'e.

O, sweetest minstrels! weet your pipe,
  A tender soothin' note to blaw;
Syne souf the "Broom o' Cowdenknowes,"
  Or "Roslin Castle's" ruined wa'.
They bring to mind the happy days,
  Fu' aft I've spent wi' Jenny dear:—
Ah! now ye touch the very note,
  That gars me sigh, and drap a tear.

Your fremit lilts I downa bide,
  They never yield a charm for me:
Unlike our ain, by nature made,
  Unlike the saft delight they gi'e;
For weel I ween they warm the breast,
  Though sair oppress'd wi' poortith cauld;
An' sae an auld man's heart they cheer,
  He tines the thought that he is auld.

O, sweetest minstrels! halt a wee,
  Anither lilt afore ye gang;
An' syne I'll close my waukrife e'e,
  Enraptured wi' your bonnie sang.
They're gane! the moon begins to dawn;
  They're weary paidlin' through the weel;
They're gane! but on my ravished ear,
  The dying sounds yet thrill fu' sweet.

THE HAZLEWOOD WITCH.
RICHARD GALL.

For mony lang year I ha'e heard frae my grannie,
  Of brownies an' bogles by yon castle wa',
Of auld wither'd hags, that were never thought cannie,
  An' fairies that danced till they heard the cock craw,
I leugh at her tales; an' last owk, i' the gloamin',
  I dander'd, alane, down the Hazlewood green:
Alas! I was reckless, an' rue sair my roaming,
  For I met a young witch wi' twa bonnie black een.

I thought o' the starns in a frosty night glancing,
  Whan a' the lift round them is cloudless and blue;
I look'd again, an' my heart fell a dancing;
  Whan I wad ha'e spoken, she glamour'd my mou'.
O wae to her cantraips! for dumpish I wander;
  At kirk or at market there's nought to be seen;
For she dances afore me wherever I dander,
  The Hazlewood Witch wi' the bonnie black een.

I WINNA GANG BACK.
RICHARD GALL.

I winna gang back to my mammy again,
I'll never gae back to my mammy again,
I've held by her apron these aught years an' ten,
But I'll never gang back to my mammy again.
  I've held by her apron, &c.

Young Johnnie cam' down i' the gloamin' to woo,
Wi' plaidie sae bonnie, an' bannet sae blue:
"O come awa', lassie, ne'er let mammy ken;"
An' I flew wi' my laddie o'er meadow an' glen.
  O come awa', lassie, &c.

He ca'd me his dawtie, his dearie, his dow,
An' press'd hame his words wi' a smack o' my mou';
While I fell on his bosom, heart-flichtered an' fain,
An' sigh'd out, "O Johnnie, I'll aye be your ain!"
  While I fell on his bosom, &c.

Some lasses will talk to the lads wi' their e'e,
Yet hanker to tell what their hearts really dree;
Wi' Johnnie I stood upon nae stappin'-stane,
Sae I'll never gang back to my mammy again.
  Wi' Johnnie I stood, &c.

For mony lang year sin' I play'd on the lea,
My mammy was kind as a mither could be;
I've hold by her apron these aught years and ten,
But I'll never gang back to my mammy again.
  I've held by her apron, &c.

GLENDOCHART VALE.
RICHARD GALL.

As I came through Glendochart vale,
 Whare mists o'ertap the mountains grey,
A wee bit lassie met my view,
 As cantily she held her way:
But O sic love each feature bore,
 She made my saul wi' rapture glow!
An' aye she spake sae kind and sweet,
 I couldna keep my heart in tow.
  O speak na o' your courtly queans!
   My wee bit lassie fools them a':
  The little cuttie's done me skaith,
   She's stown my thoughtless heart awa'.

Her smile was like the grey-e'ed morn,
 Whan spreading on the mountain-green;
Her voice saft as the mavis' sang;
 An' sweet the twinkle o' her een:
Aboon her brow, sae bonnie brent,
 Her raven locks waved o'er her e'e;
An' ilka slee bewitching glance
 Conveyed a dart o' love to me.
  O speak na o' your courtly queans, &c.

The lasses fair in Scotia's isle,
 Their beauties a' what tongue can tell?
But o'er the fairest o' them a'
 My wee bit lassie bears the bell.
O had I never mark'd her smile,
 Nor seen the twinkle o' her e'e!
It might na been my lot the day,
 A waefu' lade o' care to dree.
  O speak na o' your courtly queans, &c.

AULD LANG SYNE.

LADY NAIRNE,

Was born at the house of Gask, in Perthshire, on the 16th July, 1766. Her father, Laurence Oliphant of Gask, was one of the staunchest Jacobites, had followed Prince Charlie through the '45, and never spoke of King George otherwise than as the Elector of Hanover.

She married in 1806 Captain W. N. Nairne, a second cousin, and son of one of the unfortunate adherents of the young chevalier. He was the representative of the attainted title of Lord Nairne, in the honours of which, however, he was reinstated in 1824. He died in 1830. Lady Nairne survived him till 1845, when she died in the house of Gask in her seventy-ninth year. To Dr. Rogers, the lovers of Scottish song are indebted for a collected edition of her songs, accompanied by a full and interesting biography. (London, 1869.)

No one was more frightened of a literary reputation than Lady Nairne. Her best songs appeared first in print in Smith's "Scottish Minstrel," 1824, under the assumed initials of B. B., and so close was her secret guarded that even the publisher and editor of that work were unaware of the name and position of their contributor. Her best songs have been admitted into all collections of our National Minstrelsy since that time without any hint as to the author. This, however, is now changed, and Lady Nairne has taken her place as a song writer beside Burns, Hogg, and Tannahill.

> WHAT gude the present day can gi'e,
> May that be yours an' mine;
> But beams o' fancy sweetest rest
> On auld lang syne.
>
> On auld lang syne, my dear,
> On auld lang syne,
> The bluid is cauld that winna warm
> At thoughts o' lang syne.
>
> We twa hae seen the simmer sun,
> And thought it aye would shine;
> But mony a cloud has come between,
> Sin auld lang syne.
>
> Sin auld lang syne, &c.
>
> But still my heart beats warm to thee,
> And sae to me does thine,
> Blest be the pow'r that still has left
> The frien's o' lang sang.
>
> O' auld lang syne, &c.

CALLER HERRIN.
LADY NAIRNE.

WHA'LL buy my caller herrin'?
They're bonnie fish and dainty fairin',
Wha'll buy my caller herrin'?
New drawn frae the Forth.

When ye were sleepin' on your pillows,
Dream'd ye aught o' our puir fellows,
Darkling as they fac'd the billows,
A' to fill the woven willows?
    Buy my caller herrin',
    New drawn frae the Forth.

Wha'll buy my caller herrin'?
They're no brought here without brave daring,
Buy my caller herrin',
Haul'd thro' wind and rain.
    Wha'll buy my caller herrin', &c.?

Wha'll buy my caller herrin'?
Ye may ca' them vulgar fairin',
Wives and mithers maist despairin'
Ca' them lives o' men.
    Wha'll buy, my caller herrin', &c.?

When the creel o' herrin passes,
Ladies clad in silks and laces,
Gather in their braw pelisses,
Cast their necks and screw their faces.
    Wha'll buy my caller herrin', &c.?

Caller herrin's no got lightlie,
Ye can trip the spring fu' tightlie,
Spite o' tauntin', flauntin', flingin',
Gow has set you a' a-singin'.
    Wha'll buy my caller herrin', &c.?

Neighbour wives, now tent my tellin',
When the bonnie fish ye're sellin',
At ae word be in ye're dealin',
Truth will stand when a' thing's failin'.
    Wha'll buy my caller herrin', &c.?

THE VOICE OF SPRING.
LADY NAIRNE.

O, say is there ane wha does not rejoice,
  To hear the first note o' the wee' birdie's voice,
When in the grey mornin' o' cauld early spring,
  The snaw draps appear an' the wee birdies sing.
The voice o' the spring, O, how does it cheer !
  The winter's awa, the summer is near.

In your mantle o' green, we see thee, fair spring,
  O'er our banks, an' our braes, the wild flowers ye fling ;
The crocus sae gay, in her rich gowden hue ;
  The sweet violets hid 'mang the moss an' the dew ;
The bonnie white gowan, an' oh ! the white brier,
  A' tell it is spring, an' the summer is near.

An' they wha' in sorrow or sickness do pine,
  Feel blythe wi' the flowers an' sunshine o' spring ;
Tho' aft in dear Scotia, the cauld wind will blaw,
  An' cow'r a' the blossoms wi' frost and wi' snaw,
Yet the cloud it will pass, the sky it will clear,
  An' the birdies will sing, the summer is near.

JOHN TOD.
LADY NAIRNE.

He's a terrible man, John Tod, John Tod,
  He's a terrible man, John Tod ;
He scolds in the house, he scolds at the door,
  He scolds in the very hie road, John Tod,
  He scolds in the very hie road.

The weans a' fear John Tod, John Tod,
  The weans a' fear John Tod ;
When he's passing by, the mothers will cry,
  Here's an ill wean, John Tod, John Tod,
  Here's an ill wean, John Tod.

The callants a' fear John Tod, John Tod,
  The callants a' fear John Tod ;
If they steal but a neep, the laddie he'll whip,
  And it's unco weel done o' John Tod, John Tod,
  And it's unco weel done o' John Tod.

And saw ye nae little John Tod, John Tod ?
  O saw ye nae little John Tod ?
His shoon they were re'in, and his feet they were seen,
  But stout does he gang on the road, John Tod,
  But stout does he gang on the road.

How is he fendin', John Tod, John Tod?
How is he wendin', John Tod?
He is scourin' the land wi' his rung in his hand,
And the French wadna frighten John Tod, John Tod,
And the French wadna frighten John Tod.

Ye're sun-burnt and batter'd, John Tod, John Tod,
Ye'er tautit and tatter'd John Tod;
Wi' your auld strippit cowl ye look maist like a fule;
But there's nouse in the linin', John Tod, John Tod,
But there's nouse in the linin', John Tod.

He's weel respeckit, John Tod, John Tod,
He's weel respeckit, John Tod;
Though a terrible man, we'd a' gang wrang,
If e'er he should leave us, John Tod, John Tod,
If he should leave us, John Tod.

THE TWA DOOS.
LADY NAIRNE.

There were twa doos sat in a dookit,
Twa wise-like birds, and round they lookit,
An' says the ane unto the ither,
What do you see, my gude brither?

I see some pickles o' gude strae,
An' wheat some fule has thrown away;
For a rainy day they should be boukit,
Sae down they flew frae aff their dookit.

The snaw will come, an' cour the grund,
Nae grains o' wheat will then be fund,
They picket a' up an a' were boukit,
Then roun' an' roun' again they lookit.

O lang he thocht an' lang he lookit,
An' aye his wise-like head he shook it,
I see, I see, what ne'er should be,
I see what's seen by mair than me.

Wae's me there's thochtless lang Tam Gray,
Aye spendin' what he's no to pay;
In wedlock, to a taupie hookit,
He's ta'en a doo, but has nae dookit.

When we were young, it was nae sae;
Nae rummulgumshion folk now hae:
What gude for them can ere be lookit,
When folk tak doos that has nae dookit.

THE LAIRD O' COCKPEN.

LADY NAIRNE.

The two last stanzas were added by Miss Ferrier, authoress of "Marriage," &c.

The Laird o' Cockpen, he's proud and he's great;
His mind is ta'en up wi' the things o' the state:
He wanted a wife his braw house to keep;
But favour wi' wooin' was fashious to seek.

Doun by the dyke-side a lady did dwell,
At his table-head he thought she'd look well;
M'Clish's ae daughter o' Claverse-ha' Lee—
A pennyless lass wi' a lang pedigree.

His wig was weel pouther'd, as guid as when new,
His waistcoat was white, his coat it was blue:
He put on a ring, a sword, and cock'd hat—
And wha could refuse the Laird wi' a' that?

He took the grey mare, and rade cannilie—
And rapped at the yett o' Claverse-ha' Lee;
"Gae tell mistress Jean to come speedily ben;
She's wanted to speak wi' the Laird o' Cockpen."

Mistress Jean she was makin' the elder-flower wine;
"And what brings the Laird at sic a like time?"
She put aff her apron, and on her silk gown,
Her mutch wi' red ribbons, and gaed awa' down.

And when she cam' ben, he boued fu' low;
And what was his errand he soon let her know,
Amazed was the Laird when the lady said, Na,
And wi' a laigh curtsie she turned awa'.

Dumfounder'd he was, but nae sigh did he gi'e;
He mounted his mare, and rade cannilie;
And aften he thought, as he gaed through the glen,
"She's daft to refuse the Laird o' Cockpen."

And now that the Laird his exit had made,
Mistress Jean she reflected on what she had said;
"Oh! for ane I'll get better, it's waur I'll get ten—
I was daft to refuse the Laird o' Cockpen."

Neist time that the Laird and the Lady were seen,
They were gaun arm and arm to the kirk on the green;
Now she sits in the ha' like a weel-tappit hen,
But as yet there's nae chickens appear'd at Cockpen.

I'M WEARING AWA' JOHN.
LADY NAIRNE.

I'm wearing awa', John,
Like snaw wreaths in thaw, John,
I'm wearing awa',
   To the land o' the leal.
There's nae sorrow there, John,
There's neither cauld nor care, John,
The day is aye fair,
   In the land o' the leal.

Our bonnie bairn's there, John,
She was baith gude and fair, John,
And we grudged her right sair
   To the land o' the leal.
But sorrow's sel' wears past, John,
And joy's a'-comin' fast, John,
In joy that aye to last,
   In the land o' the leal.

Sae dear that joy was bought, John,
Sae free the battle fought, John,
That sinfu' man e'er brought
   To the land o' the leal.
Then dry that tearfu' e'e, John,
My soul langs to be free, John,
And angels wait on me
   To the land o' the leal.

Oh! haud ye leal and true, John,
Your day it's wearin' through, John,
And I'll welcome you
   To the land o' the leal.
Now, fare ye weel, my ain John,
This warld's care is vain, John,
We'll meet and aye be fain
   In the land o' the leal.

THE AULD HOUSE.
LADY NAIRNE.

Oh! the auld house, the auld house,
What tho' the rooms were wee!
Oh! kind hearts were dwellin' there,
And bairnies fu' o' glee:
The wild rose and the jessamine,
Still hang upon the wa',
How many cherished memories
Do they, sweet flowers, reca'.

Oh, the auld laird, the auld laird,
Sae canty, kind, and crouse,
How mony did he welcome to
His ain wee dear auld house?
And the leddy too sae genty,
There shelter'd Scotland's heir,
And clipt a lock wi' her ain hand
Frae his lang genty hair.

The mavis still doth sweetly sing,
The blue bells sweetly blaw,
The bonny Earn's clear winding still,
But the auld house is awa'.
The auld house, the auld house,
Deserted tho' ye be,
There ne'er can be a new house
Will seem sae fair to me.

Still flourishing the auld pear tree
The bairnies liked to see,
And oh! how aften did they spier
When ripe they a' wad be?
The voices sweet, the wee bit feet
Aye rinning here and there,
The merry shout, oh! whiles we greet
To think we'll hear nae mair.

For they are a' wide scattered now,
Some to the Indies gane,
And ane alas! to her lang hame;
Not her we'll meet again.
The kirkyard, the kirkyard!
Wi' flowers o' every hue,
Shelter'd by the holly's shade
An' the dark sombre yew.

The setting sun, the setting sun!
How glorious it gaed doon;
The cloudy splendour raised our hearts,
To cloudless skies aboon!
The auld dial, the auld dial!
It tauld how time did pass;
The wintry winds hae dung it doon,
Now hid 'mang trees and grass.

THE LASS O' GOWRIE.
LADY NAIRNE.

'Twas on a summer's afternoon,
  A wee afore the sun gaed down,
A lassie wi' a braw new goun
  Cam' ower the hills to Gowrie.
The rosebud wash'd in summer's shower,
  Bloom'd fresh within the sunny bower;
But Kitty was the fairest flower
  That e'er was seen in Gowrie.

To see her cousin she cam' there,
  And oh! the scene was passin' fair,
For what in Scotland can compare
  Wi' the Carse o' Gowrie?
The sun was settin' on the Tay,
  The blue hills meltin' into grey,
The mavis and the blackbird's lay
  Were sweetly heard in Gowrie.

O lang the lassie I had woo'd,
  An' truth an' constancy had vow'd,
But cam' nae speed wi' her I lo'ed
  Until she saw fair Gowrie.
I pointed to my faither's ha',
  Yon bonnie bield ayont the shaw,
Sae loun' that there nae blast could blaw,
  Wad she no bide in Gowrie?

Her faither was baith glad and wae;
  Her mither she wad naething say;
The bairnies thocht they wad get play
  If Kitty gaed to Gowrie.
She whiles did smile, she whiles did greet,
  The blush and tear were on her cheek;
She naething said, but hung her head,
  But now she's Leddy Gowrie.

THE ROWAN TREE.
LADY NAIRNE.

OH, Rowan tree! Oh, Rowan tree! thou'lt aye be dear to me,
Intwined thou art wi' mony ties o' hame and infancy;
Thy leaves were aye the first o' spring, thy flow'rs the simmer's pride;
There was nae sic a bonnie tree, in a' the country side.
  Oh, Rowan tree!

How fair wert thou in simmer time, wi' a' thy clusters white,
How rich and gay thy autumn dress, wi' berries red and bright,
We sat aneath thy spreading shade, the bairnies round thee ran;
They pu'd thy bonnie berries red, and necklaces they strang.
         Oh, Rowan tree!

On thy fair stem were mony names, which now nae mair I see,
But they're engraven on my heart, forgot they ne'er can be;
My mother! oh! I see her still, she smil'd our sports to see;
Wi' little Jeanie on her lap, wi' Jamie at her knee!
         Oh, Rowan tree!

Oh! there arose my father's prayer, in holy evening's calm,
How sweet was then my mother's voice, in the Martyr's psalm;
Now a' are gane! we meet nae mair aneath the Rowan tree,
But hallowed thoughts around thee twine o' hame and infancy.
         Oh, Rowan tree!

O WEEL MAY THE BOATIE ROW.

JOHN EWEN,

A native of Montrose, where he was born in 1741. In 1760 he went to Aberdeen, where he began business as a dealer in hardware goods. By dint of frugality, if not parsimony, and aided greatly by that amiable provision for the deserving poor, a rich wife, he amassed a considerable fortune, and at his death, which took place in 1821, bequeathed the bulk of it to trustees for the purpose of founding an hospital at Montrose, for the board and education of poor boys. His will, however, was challenged by his daughter, his only child, who appears to have been overlooked in that document, and was settled in her favour by the House of Lords.

    O weel may the boatie row,
      And better may she speed!
    And weel may the boatie row,
      That wins the bairns' bread!
    The boatie rows, the boatie rows,
      The boatie rows indeed;
    And happy be the lot of a'
      That wishes her to speed!

    I cuist my line in Largo Bay,
      And fishes I caught nine;
    There's three to boil, and three to fry,
      And three to bait the line.
    The boatie rows, the boatie rows,
      The boatie rows indeed;
    And happy be the lot of a'
      That wishes her to speed!

O weel may the boatie row,
  That fills a heavy creel,
And cleads us a' frae head to feet,
  And buys our parritch meal.
The boatie rows, the boatie rows,
  The boatie rows indeed;
And happy be the lot of a'
  That wish the boatie speed.

When Jamie vow'd he would be mine,
  And wan frae me my heart,
O muckle lighter grew my creel!
  He swore we'd never part.
The boatie rows, the boatie rows,
  The boatie rows fu' weel;
And muckle lighter is the lade,
  When love bears up the creel.

My kurtch I put upon my head,
  And dress'd mysel' fu' braw;
I trow my heart was dowf and woe,
  When Jamie gaed awa:
But weel may the boatie row,
  And lucky be her part;
And lightsome be the lassie's care
  That yields an honest heart!

When Sawnie, Jock, and Janetie,
  Are up, and gotten lear,
They'll help to gar the boatie row,
  And lighten a' our care.
The boatie rows, the boatie rows,
  The boatie rows fu' weel;
And lightsome be her heart that bears
  The murlain and the creel!

And when wi' age we are worn down,
  And hirpling round the door,
They'll row to keep us hale and warm
  As we did them before:
Then, weel may the boatie row,
  That wins the bairns' bread;
And happy be the lot of a'
  That wish the boat to speed!

THE BONNIE BRUCKET LASSIE.

JAMES TYTLER;

Born in 1747, was the son of a clergyman in the north of Scotland. "A clever but eccentric character," says Mr. Stenhouse, "commonly called Balloon Tytler, from the circumstance of his being the first person who projected and ascended from Edinburgh in one of these aerial machines." He edited the second and third editions of the "Encyclopædia Britannica." He ultimately got mixed up in some of the political squabbles of his time, and had to emigrate to America, where he died in 1805.

THE bonnie brucket lassie,
   She's blue beneath the een ;
She was the fairest lassie
   That danced on the green,
A lad he loo'd her dearly ;
   She did his love return :
But he his vows has broken,
   And left her for to mourn.

My shape, she says, was handsome,
   My face was fair and clean ;
But now I'm bonnie brucket,
   And blue beneath the een.
My eyes were bright and sparkling,
   Before that they turned blue ;
But now they're dull with weeping,
   And a', my love, for you.

My person it was comely ;
   My shape, they said, was neat ;
But now I am quite changed ;
   My stays they winna meet.
A' nicht I sleeped soundly ;
   My mind was never sad ;
But now my rest is broken
   Wi' thinking o' my lad.

O could I live in darkness,
   Or hide me in the sea,
Since my love is unfaithful,
   And has forsaken me ;
No other love I suffered
   Within my breast to dwell,
In nought I have offended,
   But loving him too well.

Her lover heard her mourning,
   As by he chanced to pass :
And pressed unto his bosom
   The lovely brucket lass.

My dear, he said, cease grieving;
 Since that you lo'ed so true,
My bonnie bruckel lassie,
 I'll faithful prove to you.

I HAE LAID A HERRING IN SAUT.
JAMES TYTLER.

Based upon a very old song.

I HAE laid a herring in saut—
 Lass, gin ye lo'e me, tell me now;
I hae brew'd a forpit o' maut,
 And I canna come ilka day to woo:
I hae a calf that will soon be a cow—
 Lass, gin ye lo'e me, tell me now;
I hae a stook, and I'll soon hae a mowe,
 And I canna come ilka day to woo:

I hae a house upon yon moor—
 Lass, gin ye lo'e me, tell me now;
Three sparrows may dance upon the floor,
 And I canna come ilka day to woo:
I hae a but, and I hae a ben—
 Lass, gin ye lo'e me, tell me now;
A penny to keep, and a penny to spen',
 And I canna come ilka day to woo:

I hae a hen wi' a happitie-leg—
 Lass, gin ye lo'e me, tell me now;
That ilka day lays me an egg,
 And I canna come ilka day to woo:
I hae a cheese upon my shelf—
 Lass, gin ye lo'e me, tell me now—
And soon wi' mites 'twill rin itself,
 And I canna come ilka day to woo.

LOCH-ERROCH SIDE.
ASCRIBED TO JAMES TYTLER.

As I cam' by Loch-Erroch side,
 The lofty hills surveying,
The water clear, the heather blooms,
 Their fragrance sweet conveying;
I met, unsought, my lovely maid,
 I found her like May morning;
With graces sweet, and charms so rare,
 Her person all adorning.

How kind her looks, how blest was I,
  While in my arms I prest her!
And she her wishes scarce conceal'd,
  As fondly I caress'd her:
She said, If that your heart be true,
  If constantly you'll love me,
I heed not care nor fortune's frowns,
  For nought but death shall move me.

But faithful, loving, true, and kind,
  For ever thou shalt find me;
And of our meeting here so sweet,
  Loch-Erroch sweet shall mind me.
Enraptured then, My lovely lass,
  I cried, no more we'll tarry!
We'll leave the fair Loch-Erroch side,
  For lovers soon should marry.

WE'LL HAP AND ROW.

WILLIAM CREECH,

A CELEBRATED Publisher in Edinburgh. Born 1745, died 1815. The first Edinburgh edition of Burns' Poems was issued by him, and every reader of Burns is aware of the respect the poet had for his publisher.

WE'LL hap and row, we'll hap and row,
  We'll hap and row the feetie o't;
It is a wee bit weary thing:
  I downa bide the greetie o't.

And we pat on the wee bit pan,
  To boil the lick o' meatie o't;
A cinder fell and spoil'd the plan,
  And burnt a' the feetie o't.

Fu' sair it grat, the puir wee brat,
  And aye it kick'd the footie o't,
Till, puir wee elf, it tired itself;
  And then began the sleepie o't.

The skirlin' brat nae parritch gat,
  When it gaed to the sleepie o't;
It's waesome true, instead o' 'ts mou',
  They're round about the feetie o't.

A' BODY'S LIKE TO BE MARRIED BUT ME.
ANONYMOUS.

From The Scots Magazine, July, 1802.

As Jenny sat down wi' her wheel by the fire,
An' thought o' the time that was fast fleein' by'er,
She said to hersel' wi' a heavy hoch hie,
Oh! a' body's like to be married but me.

My youthfu' companions are a' worn awa',
And though I've had wooers mysel' ane or twa,
Yet a lad to my mind I ne'er could yet see,
Oh! a' body's like to be married but me.

There's Lowrie, the lawyer, would ha'e me fu' fain
Who has baith a house an' a yard o' his ain:
But before I'd gang to it I rather wad die,
A wee stumpin' body! he'll never get me.

There's Dickey, my cousin, frae Lunnun cam' down,
Wi' fine yellow buskins that dazzled the town;
But, puir deevil, he got ne'er a blink o' my e'e,
Oh! a' body's like to be married but me.

But I saw a lad by yon saughie burn side,
Wha weel wad deserve ony queen for his bride,
Gin I had my will soon his ain I would be,
Oh! a' body's like to be married but me.

I gied him a look, as a kind lassie should,
My frien's, if they kenn'd it, would surely run wud;
For tho' bonnie and guid, he's no worth a bawbee,
Oh! a' body's like to be married but me.

'Tis hard to tak' shelter behint a laigh dyke,
'Tis hard for to tak' ane we never can like,
'Tis hard for to leave ane we fain wad be wi',
Yet it's harder that a' should be married but me.

WHAT AILS YOU NOW.
ALEXANDER DOUGLAS,

A WEAVER in Pathhead, in Fifeshire. He was born at Strathmiglo in 1771. and died in 1824. He published a volume of poems in 1806, which was favourably received.

What ails you now, my daintie Pate,
 Ye winna wed an' a' that?
Say, are ye flay'd, or are ye blate,
 To tell your love an' a' that?
  To kiss an' clap, an' a' that?
  O fy for shame, an' a' that,
  To spend your life without a wife;
   'Tis no the gate ava that.

Ere lang you will grow auld and frail,
  Your haffets white an' a' that;
An whare's the Meg, the Kate, or Nell,
  Will ha'e you syne wi' a' that?
    Runkled brow an' a' that;
    Wizzen'd face an' a' that;
  Wi' beard sae grey, there's nane will ha'e
  A kiss frae you, an' a' that.

O stand na up wi' whore an' bow,
  Wi' ifs an' buts an' a' that,
Wi' feckless scruples not a few:
  Pu' up your heart an' a' that.
    Crousely crack an' a' that;
    Come try your luck an' a' that:
  The hiney-moon will ne'er gang done,
  If guidit weel an' a' that.

There's monie lass baith douce an' fair,
  Fu' sonsy, fier, an' a' that,
Wad suit you to a very hair,
  Sae clever they're an' a' that;
    Handsome, young, an' a' that,
    Sae complaisant an' a' that;
  Sae sweet an' braw, and gude an' a';
  What ails the chield at a' that?

Come, look about, an' wale a wife,
  Like honest fouk an' a' that;
An' lead a cheerfu' virtuous life;
  Ha'e plenty, peace, an' a' that;
    A thrifty wife an' a' that,
    An' bonnie bairns an' a' that,
  Syne in your ha' shall pleasures a'
  Smile ilka day an' a' that.

LOGAN'S BRAES.
JOHN MAYNE,

Author of "The Siller Gun," &c. He was born in Dumfries, in 1759. His parents removed in 1782 when he began his apprenticeship as compositor to the celebrated Glasgow printers, Messrs. Foulis. He afterwards went to London, where he became editor and part proprietor of "The Star," newspaper. He died in 1836.

  The last three stanzas of this song have been attributed to another writer. They are certainly much inferior in style.

    "By Logan's streams that rin sae deep,
    Fu' aft wi' glee I've herded sheep;
    Herded sheep, or gathered slaes,
    Wi' my dear lad, on Logan braes.

But wae's my heart! thae days are gane,
And I, wi' grief, may herd alane;
While my dear lad maun face his faes,
Far, far frae me, and Logan braes.

"Nae mair at Logan Kirk will he
Atween the preachings meet wi' me;
Meet wi me, or when it's mirk,
Convoy me hame from Logan kirk.
I weel may sing thae days are gane—
Frae kirk an' fair I come alane,
While my dear lad maun face his faes,
Far, far frae me, and Logan braes!

"At e'en, when hope amaist is gane,
I dauner out, or sit alane,
Sit alane beneath the tree
Where aft he kept his tryst wi' me.
O! cou'd I see thae days again,
My lover skaithless, an' my ain!
Belov'd by frien's, rever'd by faes,
We'd live in bliss on Logan braes."

While for her love she thus did sigh,
She saw a sodger passing by,
Passing by wi' scarlet claes,
While sair she grat on Logan braes.
Says he, "What gars thee greet sae sair,
What fills thy heart sae fu' o' care?
Thae sporting lambs hae blithesome days,
An' playfu' skip on Logan braes?"

"What can I do but weep and mourn?
I fear my lad will ne'er return,
Ne'er return to ease my waes,
Will ne'er come hame to Logan braes."
Wi' that he clasp'd her in his arms,
And said, "I'm free from war's alarms,
I now hae conquer'd a' my faes,
We'll happy live on Logan braes."

Then straight to Logan kirk they went,
And join'd their hands wi' one consent,
Wi' one consent to end their days,
An' live in bliss on Logan braes.
An' now she sings, "thae days are gane,
When I wi' grief did herd alane,
While my dear lad did fight his faes,
Far, far frae me and Logan braes."

THE WINTER SAT LANG.
JOHN MAYNE.

The winter sat lang on the spring o' the year,
Our seedtime was late, and our mailing was dear;
My mither tint her heart when she look'd on us a',
And we thought upon them that were farest awa';
O! were they but here that are farest awa';
O! were they but here that are dear to us a'!
Our cares would seem light and our sorrows but sma',
If they were but here that are far frae us a'!

Last week, when our hopes were o'erclouded wi' fear,
And nae ane at hame the dull prospect to cheer,
Our Johnnie has written, frae far awa' parts,
A letter that lightens and hauds up our hearts:
He says, "My dear mither, though I be awa',
In love and affection I'm still wi' ye a';
While I hae a being, ye'se aye hae a ha',
Wi' plenty to keep out the frost and the snaw."

My mither, o'erjoy'd at this change in her state,
By the bairn that she doated on early and late,
Gi'es thanks, night and day, to the Giver of a',
There's been naething unworthy o' him that's awa'!
Then, here is to them that are far frae us a',
The friend that ne'er fail'd us, though farest awa'!
Health, peace, and prosperity, wait on us a'!
And a blythe comin' hame to the friend that's awa'!

HIS AIN KIND DEARIE YET.
JOHN MAYNE.

Jenny's heart was frank and free,
  And wooers she had mony, yet
Her sang was aye, Of a' I see,
  Commend me to my Johnnie yet.
For, ear' and late, he has sic gate
  To mak' a body cheerie, that
I wish to be, before I die,
  His ain kind dearie yet.

Now Jenny's face was fu' o' grace,
  Her shape was sma' and genty-like,
And few or nane in a' the place
  Had gowd and gear more plenty, yet
Though war's alarms, and Johnnie's charms,
  Had gart her aft look eerie, yet
She sung wi' glee, I hope to be
  My Johnnie's ain dearie yet.

What tho' he's now gaen far awa',
  Where guns and cannons rattle, yet
Unless my Johnnie chance to fa'
  In some uncanny battle, yet
Till he return, my breast will burn
  Wi' love that weel may cheer me yet,
For I hope to see, before I die,
  His bairns to him endear me yet.

A WAR SONG.
ANDREW SCOTT.

WRITTEN in 1803. Scott was "minister's man" to the parish minister of Bowden, Roxburghshire. He died in 1839, aged 83. He published several volumes of poetry during his lifetime.

  SURROUNDED wi' bent and wi' heather,
    Where muircocks and plovers were rife,
  For mony a lang towmond together,
    There lived an auld man and his wife;
  About the affairs o' the nation
    The twasome they seldom were mute;
  Bonaparte, the French, and invasion,
    Did sa'ur in their wizzins like soot.

  In winter, when deep were the gutters,
    And nicht's gloomy canopy spread,
  Auld Symon sat luntin' his cuttie,
    And lowsin' his buttons for bed;
  Auld Janet, his wife, out a-gazing,
    To lock in the door was her care;
  She, seeing her signals a-blazing,
    Came rinnin' in ryving her hair:

  O, Symon, the Frenchies are landit!
    Gae look man, and slip on your shoon;
  Our signals I see them extendit,
    Like red risin' rays frae the moon.
  What a plague! the French landit! quo' Symon,
    And clash gaed his pipe to the wa':
  Faith, then, there's be loadin' and primin',
    Quo' he, if they're landit ava.

  Our youngest son's in the militia,
    Our eldest grandson's volunteer:
  O' the French to be fu' o' the flesh o',
    I too i' the ranks shall appear.
  His waistcoat-pouch fill'd he wi' pouther,
    And bang'd down his rusty auld gun;
  His bullets he pat in the other,
    That he for the purpose had run.

Then humpled he out in a hurry,
  While Janet his courage bewails,
And cried out, Dear Symon, be wary!
  And teuchly she hung by his tails.
Let be wi' your kindness, cried Symon,
  Nor vex me wi' tears and your cares;
For, now to be ruled by a woman,
  Nae laurels shall crown my grey hairs.

Then hear me, quo' Janet, I pray thee,
  I'll tend thee, love, livin' or deid,
And if thou should fa', I'll dee wi' thee,
  Or tie up thy wounds if thou bleed.
Quo' Janet, O, keep frae the riot!
  Last nicht, man, I dreamt ye was daid:
This aught days I tentit a pyot
  Sit chatt'rin' upon the house-heid.

As yesterday, workin' my stockin',
  And you wi' the sheep on the hill,
A muckle black corbie sat croaking;
  I kenn'd it forebodit some ill.
Hout, cheer up, dear Janet, be hearty;
  For, ere the neist sun may gae down,
Wha kens but I'll shoot Bonaparte,
  And end my auld days in renown.

Syne off in a hurry he stumpled,
  Wi' bullets, and pouther, and gun;
At's curpin auld Janet, too, humpled
  Awa' to the neist neebour-toun:
There footmen and yeomen paradin',
  To scour off in dirdum were seen;
And wives and young lasses a' sheddin'
  The briny saut tears frae their een.

Then aff wi' his bonnet got Symie,
  And to the commander he gaes,
Quo' he, Sir, I mean to gae wi' ye,
  And help ye to lounder our faes:
I'm auld, yet I'm teuch as the wiro,
  Sae we'll at the rogues ha'e a dash,
And fegs, if my gun winna fire,
  I'll turn her but-end and I'll thrash.

Well spoken, my hearty old hero!
  The captain did smilin' reply;
But begg'd he wad stay till to-morrow,
  Till day-licht should glent in the sky.

Whatreck, a' the stoure cam' to naething,
 Sae Symon, and Janet his dame,
Halescart, frae the wars, without skaithing,
 Gaed, bannin' the French, away hame.

THE GUID FARMER.

ANDREW SCOTT.

I'm now a gude farmer, I've acres o' land,
 An' my heart aye loups light when I'm viewin' o't,
An' I ha'e servants at my command,
 An' twa dainty cowts for the plowin' o't.
My farm is a snug ane, lies high on a muir,
The muir-cocks an' plivers aft skirl at my door,
An' whan the sky low'rs I'm aye sure o' a show'r,
 To moisten my land for the plowin' o't.

Leeze me on the mailin that's fa'n to my share,
 It taks sax muckle bowes for the sawin' o't;
I've sax braid acres for pasture, an' mair,
 And a dainty bit bog for the mawin' o't.
A spence an' a kitchen my mansion-house gi'es,
I've a cantie wee wife to daut when I please,
Twa bairnies, twa callans, that skelp ower the leas,
 An' they'll soon can assist at the plowin' o't.

My biggan stands sweet on this south slopin' hill,
 An' the sun shines sae bonnily beamin' on't,
An' past my door trots a clear prattlin' rill,
 Frae the loch, where the wild ducks are swimmin' on't:
An' on its green banks, on the gay summer days,
My wifie trips barefoot, a-bleaching her claes,
An' on the dear creatnre wi' rapture I gaze,
 While I whistle and sing at the plowin' o't.

To rank amang farmers I ha'e muckle pride,
 But I mauna speak high when I'm tellin' o't,
How brawlie I strut on my sheltie to ride,
 Wi' a sample to show for the sellin' o't.
In blue worset boots that my auld mither span,
I've aft been fu' vanty sin' I was a man,
But now they're flung by, an' I've bought cordivan,
 And my wifie ne'er grudg'd me a shillin' o't.

See now, whan tae kirk or tae market I gae,
 My weelfare, what need I be hidin' o't?
In braw leather boots, shining black as the slae,
 I dink me to try the ridin' o't.

Last towmond I sell'd off four bowes o' gude bere,
An' thankfu' I was, for the victual was dear.
An' I came hame wi' spurs on my heels shinin' clear,
I had sic good luck at the sellin' o't.

Now hairst time is owre, an' a fig for the laird,
My rent's now secure for the toilin' o't;
My fields are a' bare, and my crap's in the yard,
An' I'm nae mair in doubts o' the spoilin' o't.
Now welcome gude weather, or wind, or come weet,
Or bauld ragin' winter, wi' hail, snaw, or sleet,
Nae mair can he draigle my crap 'mang his feet,
Nor wraik his mischief, an' be spoilin' o't.

An' on the dowf days, whan loud hurricanes blaw,
Fu' snug i' the spence I'll be viewin' o't,
An' jink the rude blast in my rush-theekit ha',
Whan fields are seal'd up frae the plowin' o't.
My bonnie wee wifie, the bairnies, an' me,
The peat-stack, and turf-stack, our Phœbus shall be,
Till day close the scoul o' its angry e'e,
An' we'll rest in gude hopes o' the plowin' o't.

HALUCKET MEG.

REV. JAMES NICHOL,

A NATIVE of Innerleithen, in Peebleshire, where he was born in 1793. He studied at the University of Edinburgh for the ministry, and for a long time was minister of Traquair. He died in 1819. Besides publishing two volumes of poetry, Mr. Nichol was a valued contributor to the Edinburgh Encyclopædia, &c.

MEG, muckin' at Geordie's byre,
  Wrought as gin her judgment was wrang:
Ilk daud o' the scartle strake fire,
  While, loud as a lavrock, she sang!
Her Geordie had promised to marrie,
  An' Meg, a sworn fae to despair,
Not dreamin' the job could miscarrie,
  Already seem'd mistress an' mair!

My neebours, she sang, aften jeer me,
  An' ca' me, daft, halucket Meg,
An' say, they expect soon to hear me
  I' the kirk, for my fun, get a flag!
An' now, 'bout my marriage they clatter,
  An' Geordie, poor fallow! they ca'
An' auld doitet hav'rel!—Nae matter,
  He'll keep me aye brankin' an' braw!

I grant ye, his face is kenspeckle,
　That the white o' his e'e is turn'd out,
That his black beard is rough as a heckle,
　That his mou to his lug's rax'd about;
But they needna let on that he's crazie,
　His pike-staff wull ne'er let him fa';
Nor that his hair's white as a daisie,
　For, fient a hair has he ava!

But a weel-plenish'd mailin has Geordie,
　An' routh o' gude goud in his kist,
An' if siller comes at my wordie,
　His beauty, I never wull miss't!
Daft gouks, wha catch fire like tinder,
　Think love-raptures over will burn!
But wi' poortith, hearts het as a cinder,
　Wull cauld as an iceshogle turn!

There'll just be ae bar to my pleasure,
　A bar that's aft fill'd me wi' fear,
He's aic a hard, ne'er-be-gawn miser,
　He likes his saul less than his gear!
But though I now flatter his failin',
　An' swear nought wi' goud can compare,
Gude sooth! it sall soon get a scailin'!
　His bags sall be mouldie nae mair!

I dream't that I rode in a chariot,
　A flunkie ahint me in green;
While Geordie cried out, he was harriet,
　An' the saut teer was blindin' his een;
But though 'gainst my spendin' he swear aye,
　I'll ha'e frae him what ser'e my turn;
Let him slip awa' whan he grows wearie,
　Shame fa' me! gin lang I wad mourn!

But Geordie, while Mog was haranguin',
　Was cloutin' his breeks i' the bauks,
An' when a' his failins she brang in,
　His strang, hazle pike-staff he taks:
Designin' to rax her a lounder,
　He chanced on the lather to shift,
An' down frae the bauks, flat's a flounder,
　Flew, like a shot-starn frae the lift!

But Meg, wi' the sight, was quite haster'd,
　An' nae doubt, was bannin' ill luck;
While the face o' poor Geordie was plaster'd,
　And his mou' was fill'd fu' wi' the muck!

Confound ye! cried Geordie, an' spat out
　The glaur that adown his beard ran;—
Preserve us! quo' Meg, as she gat out
　The door,—an' thus lost a gudeman!

MY DEAR LITTLE LASSIE.
REV. JAMES NICHOL.

My dear little lassie, why, what's a' the matter?
　My heart it gangs pittypat—winna lie still;
I've waited, and waited, an' a' to grow better,
　Yet, lassie, believe me, I'm aye growing ill:
My head 's a turn'd quite dizzy, an' aft, when I'm speaking,
　I sigh, an' am breathless, an' fearfu' to speak;
I gaze aye for something I fain wad be seeking,
　Yet, lassie, I kenna weel what I wad seek.

Thy praise, bonnie lassie, I ever could hear of,
　And yet whan to ruse ye the neebour lads try,
Though it's a' true they tell ye, yet never see far off,
　I could see 'em ilk ane, an' I canna tell why.
When we tedded the hayfield, I raked ilka rig o't,
　And never grew wearie the lang simmer day;
The rucks that ye wrought at were easiest biggit,
　And I fand sweeter scented aroun' ye the hay.

In har'st, whan the kirn-supper joys mak' us cheerie,
　'Mang the lave of the lasses I pried yere sweet mou';
Dear save us! how queer I felt whan I cam' near ye,
　My breast thrill'd in rapture, I couldna tell how.
Whan we dance at the gloamin' it's you I aye pitch on,
　And gin ye gang by me how dowie I be;
There's something, dear lassie, about ye bewitching,
　That tells me my happiness centres in thee.

WHERE QUAIR RINS SWEET.
REV. JAMES NICHOL.

Where Quair rins sweet amang the flowers,
　Down by yon woody glen, lassie,
My cottage stands—it shall be yours,
　Gin ye will be my ain, lassie.

I'll watch ye wi' a lover's care,
　And wi' a lover's e'e, lassie;
I'll weary heaven wi' mony a prayer,
　And ilka prayer for thee, lassie.

Tis true I ha'e na mickle gear;
　My stock it's unco sma, lassie;
Nae fine-spun foreign claes I wear,
　Nor servants tend my ca', lassie.

But had I heir'd the British crown,
　And thou o' low degree, lassie,
A rustic lad I wad ha'e grown,
　Or shared that crown wi' thee, lassie.

Whenever absent frae thy sight,
　Nae pleasure smiles on me, lassie;
I climb the mountain's towering height,
　And cast a look to thee, lassie.

I blame the blast blaws on thy cheek;
　The flower that decks thy hair, lassie,
The gales that steal thy breath sae sweet,
　My love and envy share, lassie.

If for a heart that glows for thee,
　Thou wilt thy heart resign, lassie,
Then come, my Nancy, come to me—
　That glowing heart is mine, lassie.

Where Quair rins sweet amang the flowers,
　Down by yon woody glen, lassie,
My cottage stands—it shall be yours,
　Gin ye will be my ain, lassie.

I HEARD THE EVENING LINNET'S VOICE.

JOHN FINLAY,

A Native of Glasgow, author of "Wallace or the Vale of Ellerslie and other poems," and editor of two volumes of Scottish Ballads. He died in 1810, in his twenty-eighth year.

I heard the evening linnet's voice the woodland tufts among,
Yet sweeter were the tender notes of Isabella's song!
So soft into the ear they steal, so soft into the soul,
The deep'ning pain of love they soothe, and sorrow's pang control.

I looked upon the pure brook that murmur'd through the glade,
And mingled in the melody that Isabella made;
Yet purer was the residence of Isabella's heart!
Above the reach of pride and guile, above the reach of art.

I look'd upon the azure of the deep unclouded sky,
Yet clearer was the blue serene of Isabella's eye!
Ne'er softer fell the rain drop of the first relenting year,
Than falls from Isabella's eye the pity-melted tear.

All this my fancy prompted, ere a sigh of sorrow prov'd
How hopelessly, yet faithfully, and tenderly I lov'd;
Yet though bereft of hope I love, still will I love the more,
As distance binds the exile's heart to his dear native shore.

THE SOMERVILLE TESTAMENT.

ROBERT LOCHORE,

A Native of Strathaven in Lanarkshire, where he was born in 1762. He carried on business in Glasgow as a Bootmaker, and occupied several prominent positions in the government of the city. He died in 1852.

Now, Jenny lass, my bonnie bird,
  My daddy's dead, an' a' that;
He's snugly laid aneath the yird,
  And I'm his heir, an' a' that.
    I'm now a laird, an' a' that;
    I'm now a laird, an' a' that;
  His gear an' land's at my command,
    And muckle mair than a' that.

He left me wi' his deein' breath
  A dwallin' house, an' a' that;
A barn, a byre, an' wabs o' claith—
  A big peat-stack, an' a' that.
    A mare, a foal, an' a' that,
    A mare, a foal, an' a' that,
  Sax guid fat kye, a cauf forby,
    An' twa pet ewes, an' a' that.

A yard, a meadow, lang braid leas,
  An' stacks o' corn an' a' that—
Enclosed weel wi' thorns an' trees;
  An' carts, an' cars, an' a' that.
    A pleugh, an' graith, an' a' that,
    A pleugh, an' graith, an' a' that;
  Guid harrows twa, cock, hens, an' a'—
    A gricie too, an' a' that.

I've heaps o' claes for ilka days,
  For Sundays too, an' a' that;
I've bills an' bonds, on lairds an' lands,
  An' siller, gowd, an' a' that.
    What think ye, lass, o' a' that?
    What think ye, lass, o' a' that?
  What want I noo, my dainty doo,
    But just a wife to a' that!

Now, Jenny dear, my errand here,
  Is to seek ye to a' that;
My heart's a' loupin' while I speer
  Gin ye'll tak' me, wi' a' that.
    Mysel', my gear, an' a' that,
    Mysel', my gear, an' a' that;
  Come, gie's your loof to be a proof
    Ye'll be a wife to a' that.

Syne Jenny laid her neive in his,
  Said, she'd tak' him wi' a' that;
An' he gied her a hearty kiss,
  An' dauted her, an' a' that.
    They set a day, an' a' that,
    They set a day, an' a' that;
  Whan she'd gang hame to be his dame,
    An' haud a rant, an' a' that.

MARRIAGE AND THE CARE O'T.
ROBERT LOCHORE.

Quoth Rab to Kate, My sonsy dear,
I've woo'd ye mair than ha'e a-year,
An' if ye'd wed me ne'er cou'd speer,
  Wi' blatencss, an' the care o't.
Now to the point: sincere I'm wi't:
Will ye be my ha'f-marrow, sweet?
Shake han's, and say a bargain be't,
  An' ne'er think on the care o't.

Na, na, quo' Kate, I winna wed,
O' sic a snare I'll aye be rede;
How mony, thochtless, are misled
  By marriage, an' the care o't!
A single life's a life o' glee,
A wife ne'er think to mak' o' me,
Frae toil an' sorrow I'll keep free,
  An' a' the dool an' care o't.

Weel, weel, said Robin, in reply,
Ye ne'er again shall me deny,
Ye may a toothless maiden die
  For me, I'll tak' nae care o't.
Fareweel for ever!—aff I hie:—
Sae took his leave without a sigh;
Oh! stop, quo' Kate, I'm yours, I'll try
  The married life, an' care o't.

Rab wheel't about, to Kate cam' back,
An' ga'e her mou' a hearty smack,
Syne lengthen'd out a lovin' crack
  'Bout marriage an' the care o't.
Though as she thocht she didna speak,
An' lookit unco mim an' meek,
Yet blythe was she wi' Rab to cleek
  In marriage, wi' the care o't.

ROY'S WIFE OF ALDIVALLOCH.

MRS. GRANT, OF CARRON,

BORN at Aberlour, Banffshire, in 1745; died at Bath about 1814.

Roy's wife of Aldivalloch,
Roy's wife of Aldivalloch,
Wat ye how she cheated me,
  As I cam' o'er the braes o' Balloch.

She vow'd, she swore, she wad be mine,
  She said she lo'ed me best of ony;
But oh! the fickle, faithless quean,
  She's ta'en the carle, and left her Johnnie.
    Roy's wife of Aldivalloch, &c.

O, she was a canty quean,
  Weel could she dance the Highland walloch;
How happy I had she been mine,
  Or I been Roy of Aldivalloch!
    Roy's wife of Aldivalloch, &c.

Her face sae fair, her een sae clear,
  Her wee bit mou' sae sweet and bonnie;
To me she ever will be dear,
  Though she's for ever left her Johnnie.
    Roy's wife of Aldivalloch, &c.

SAW YE MY WEE THING.

HECTOR MACNEILL,

Was born at Rosn Bank, near Edinburgh, 1746. He early began to weave his fancies into rhyme, and when comparatively young was well known amongst his acquaintances as a poet. His principal poems are "Scotland's Scaith; or, the History of Will and Jean," "The Harp," and "The Waes o' War." It is, however, on his songs that his fame principally depends. Macneill spent the greater part of his life abroad, holding positions at various times in Guadaloupe, Grenada, and Jamaica. He also served for some time in the navy as assistant Secretary to Admiral Geary, and afterwards to Admiral Sir Richard Bickerton. He finally returned to Scotland in 1800, and took up his residence in Edinburgh, where he closed a life of much vicissitude and suffering in 1818.

 O saw ye my woe thing? Saw ye my ain thing?
  Saw ye my true love down on yon lea?
 Cross'd she the meadow yestreen at the gloamin'?
  Sought she the burnie whar flow'rs the haw tree?
 Her hair it is lint-white; her skin it is milk white;
  Dark is the blue o' her saft rolling e'e;
 Red, red her ripe lips, and sweeter than roses:—
  Whar could my wee thing wander frae me?

 I saw na your woe thing, I saw na your ain thing,
  Nor saw I your true love down on yon lea;
 But I met my bonnie thing late in the gloamin',
  Down by the burnie whar flow'rs the haw tree.
 Her hair it was lint-white; her skin it was milk-white;
  Dark was the blue o' her saft rolling e'e;
 Red were her ripe lips, and sweeter than roses:
  Sweet were the kisses that she ga'e to me.

 It was na my woe thing, it was na my ain thing,
  It was na my true love ye met by the tree:
 Proud is her leal heart! modest her nature!
  She never lo'ed onie, till ance she lo'ed me.
 Her name it is Mary; she's frae Castle-Cary:
  Aft has she sat, when a bairn, on my knee:—
 Fair as your face is, war't fifty times fairer,
  Young bragger, she ne'er would gi'e kisses to thee.

 It was then your Mary; she's frae Castle-Cary;
  It was then your true love I met by the tree;
 Proud as her heart is, and modest her nature,
  Sweet were the kisses that she ga'e to me.
 Sair gloom'd his dark brow, blood-red his cheek grew,
  Wild flash'd the fire frae his red rolling e'e!—
 Ye's rue sair this morning your boasts and your scorning:
  Defend ye, fause traitor! fu' loudly ye lie.

Awa' wi' beguiling, cried the youth, smiling :—
Aff went the bonnet; the lint-white locks flee;
The belted plaid fa'ing, her white bosom shawing,
Fair stood the lov'd maid wi' the dark rolling e'e!
Is it my wee thing! is it my ain thing!
Is it my true love here that I see!
O Jamie forgi'e me; your heart's constant to me;
I'll never mair wander, dear laddie, frae thee!

DINNA THINK, BONNIE LASSIE.
HECTOR MACNEILL.
The last verse was added by Mr. John Hamilton.

O dinna think, bonnie lassie, I'm gaun to leave thee;
Dinna think, bonnie lassie, I'm gaun to leave thee;
Dinna think, bonnie lassie, I'm gaun to leave thee;
I'll tak' a stick into my hand, and come again and see thee.

Far's the gate ye ha'e to gang; dark's the night and eerie;
Far's the gate ye ha'e to gang; dark's the night and eerie;
Far's the gate ye ha'e to gang; dark's the night and eerie;
O stay this night wi' your love, and dinna gang and leave me.

It's but a night and hauf a day that I'll leave my dearie;
But a night and hauf a day that I'll leave my dearie;
But a night and hauf a day that I'll leave my dearie;
Whene'er the sun gaes west the loch, I'll come again and see thee.

Dinna gang, my bonnie lad, dinna gang and leave me;
Dinna gang, my bonnie lad, dinna gang and leave me;
When a' the lave are sound asleep, I am dull and eerie;
And a' the lee-lang night I'm sad, wi' thinking on my dearie.

O dinna think, bonnie lassie, I'm gaun to leave thee;
Dinna think, bonnie lassie, I'm gaun to leave thee;
Dinna think, bonnie lassie, I'm gaun to leave thee;
Whene'er the sun gaes out o' sight, I'll come again and see thee.

Waves are rising o'er the sea; winds blaw loud and fear me;
Waves are rising o'er the sea; winds blaw loud and fear me;
While the wind and waves do roar, I am wae and drearie,
And gin ye lo'e me as ye say, ye winna gang and leave me.

O never mair, bonnie lassie, will I gang and leave thee;
Never mair, bonnie lassie, will I gang and leave thee;
Never mair, bonnie lassie, will I gang and leave thee;
E'en let the world gang as it will, I'll stay at hame and cheer thee.

Frae his hand he coost his stick; I winna gang and leave thee;
Threw his plaid into the neuk; never can I grieve thee;
Drew his boots, and flang them by; cried, my lass, be cheerie;
I'll kiss the tear frae aff thy cheek, and never leave my dearie.

JEANIE'S BLACK E'E.
HECTOR MACNEILL.

The sun raise sae rosy, the grey hills adorning;
  Light sprang the laverock and mounted sae hie;
When true to the tryst o' blythe May's dewy morning,
  My Jeanie cam' linking out owre the green lea.
To mark her impatience I crap 'mang the brakens:
Aft, aft to the kent gate she turn'd her black e'e;
Then lying down dowylie, sigh'd by the willow tree,
  "Ha me mohatel na dousku me."[1]

Saft through the green birks I sta' to my jewel,
  Streik'd on spring's carpet aneath the saugh tree;
Think na, dear lassie, thy Willie's been cruel,—
  "Ha me mohatel na dousku me."
Wi' love's warm sensations I've mark'd your impatience,
  Lang hid 'mang the brakens I watch'd your black e'e.—
You're no sleeping, pawkie Jean; open thae lovely een;—
  "Ha me mohatel na dousku me."

Bright is the whin's bloom ilk green knowe adorning;
  Sweet is the primrose bespangled wi' dew;
Yonder comes Peggy to welcome May morning;
  Dark waves her baffet locks owre her white brow;
O! light, light she's dancing keen on the smooth gowany green,
Barefit and kilted half up to the knee;
While Jeanie is sleeping still, I'll rin and sport my fill,—
  "I was asleep, and ye've waken'd me!"

I'll rin and whirl her round; Jeanie is sleeping sonnd;
  Kiss her frae lug to lug—nae ane can see;
Sweet, sweet's her hinny mou.—"Will, I'm no sleeping now;
  I was asleep, but ye've waken'd me."
Laughing till like to drap, swith to my Jean I lap,
Kiss'd her ripe roses, and blest her black e'o;
And aye since, whane'er we meet, sing, for the sound is sweet,
  "Ha me mohatel na dousku me."

MY LUVE'S IN GERMANIE.
HECTOR MACNEILL.

My luve's in Germanie;
  Send him hame, send him hame;
My luve's in Germanie;
  Send him hame.

---

[1] "I am asleep, do not waken me," a Gaelic chorus pronounced according to the present orthography.

My luve's in Germanie,
Fighting brave for royalty;
He may ne'er his Jeanie see;
 Send him hame, send him hame;
He may ne'er his Jeanie see;
 Send him hame.

He's as brave as brave can be;
 Send him hame, send him hame;
Our faes are ten to three;
 Send him hame.
Our faes are ten to three;
He maun either fa' or flee,
In the cause of loyalty;
 Send him hame, send him hame;
In the cause of loyalty;
 Send him hame.

Your love ne'er learnt to flee,
 Bonnie dame, winsome dame;
Your luve ne'er learnt to flee,
 Winsome dame.
Your luve ne'er learnt to flee,
But he fell in Germanie,
Fighting brave for loyalty
 Mournfu' dame, mournfu' dame;
Fighting brave for loyalty,
 Mournfu' dame.

He'll ne'er come ower the sea;
 Willie's slain, Willie's slain;
He'll ne'er come ower the sea;
 Willie's gane!
He will ne'er come ower the sea,
To his luve and ain countrie:
This warld's nae mair for me;
 Willie's gane, Willie's gane;
This warld's nae mair for me:
 Willie's gane!

THE WAY TO WOO.
HECTOR MACNEILL.

Oh tell me, oh tell me, bonnie young lassie,
 Oh tell me, young lassie, how for to woo?
Oh tell me, oh tell me, bonnie sweet lassie,
 Oh tell me, sweet lassie, how for to woo?

Say, maun I roose your cheeks like the morning?
 Lips like the roses fresh moisten'd wi' dew?
Say maun I roose your een's pawkie scorning?
 Oh tell me, oh tell me, how for to woo!

Far ha'e I wander'd to see thee, dear lassie!
 Far ha'e I ventured across the saut sea!
Far ha'e I ventured ower muirland and mountain,
 Houseless and weary, slept cauld on the lea?
Ne'er ha'e I tried yet to mak' luve to ony,
 For ne'er loved I ony till ance I loved you;
Now we're alane in the green wood sae bonnie,
 Oh tell me, oh tell me, how for to woo!

What care I for your wand'ring, young laddie!
 What care I for your crossing the sea!
It was nae for naething ye left puir young Peggy!
 It was for my tochor ye cam' to court me.
Say ha'e ye gowd to busk me aye gaudy?
 Ribbons, and pearlins, and breist-knots enew?
A house that is cantie, wi' walth in't, my laddie?
 Without this ye never need try for to woo!

I ha'e nae gowd to busk ye aye gaudy!
 I canna buy pearlins and ribbons enew!
I've naething to brag o' house or o' plenty!
 I've little to gi'e but a heart that is true.
I cam' na for tocher—I ne'er heard o' ony;
 I never loved Peggy, nor e'er brak my vow:
I've wander'd, puir fule, for a face fause as bonnie!
 I little thocht this was the way for to woo!

Ha'e na ye roosed my cheeks like the morning?
 Ha'e na ye roosed my cherry-red mou?
Ha'e na ye come ower sea, muir, and mountain?
 What mair, my dear Johnnie, need ye for to woo?
Far ha'e ye wander'd, I ken, my dear laddie!
 Now that ye've found me, there's nae cause to rue;
Wi' health we'll ha'e plenty—I'll never gang gaudy:
 I ne'er wish'd for mair than a heart that is true.

She hid her fair face in her true lover's bosom;
 The saft tear of transport, fill'd ilk lover's e'e;
The burnie ran sweet by their side as they sabbit,
 And sweet sang the mavis abune on the tree.
He clasp'd her, he press'd her, he ca'd her his hinnie,
 And aften he tasted her hinnie-sweet mou';
And aye, 'tween ilk kiss, she sigh'd to her Johnnie—
 Oh laddie! oh laddie! weel weel can ye woo!

MY BOY, TAMMIE.
HECTOR MACNEILL.

Whar ha'e ye been a' day,
    My boy, Tammy?
I've been by burn and flow'ry brae,
Meadow green and mountain grey,
Courting o' this young thing,
    Just come frae her mammy.

And whar gat ye that young thing,
    My boy, Tammy?
I got her down in yonder howe,
Smiling on a bonnie knowe,
Herding ae wee lamb and ewe,
    For her poor mammy.

What said ye to the bonnie bairn,
    My boy, Tammy?
I praised her een, sae lovely blue,
Her dimpled cheek and cherry mou';—
I pree'd it aft, as ye may trow!—
    She said she'd tell her mammy.

I held her to my beating heart,
    My young, my smiling lammie!
I ha'e a house, it cost me dear,
I've wealth o' plenishen and gear;
Ye'se get it a', wore't ten times mair,
    Gin ye will leave your mammy.

The smile gaed aff her bonnie face—
    I maunna leave my mammy.
She's gien me meat, she's gien me claes,
She's been my comfort a' my days:—
My father's death brought monie waes—
    I canna leave my mammy.

We'll tak' her hame and mak' her fain,
    My ain kind-hearted lammie.
We'll gi'e her meat, we'll gie her claise,
We'll be her comfort a' her days,
The woe thing gi'es her hand, and says—
    There! gang and ask my mammy.

Has she been to the kirk wi' thee,
    My boy, Tammy?
She has been to the kirk wi' me,
And the tear was in her e'e;
For O! she's but a young thing,
    Just come frae her mammy.

COME UNDER MY PLAIDIE.
HECTOR MACNEILL.

Come under my plaidie; the night's gaun to fa';
Come in frae the cauld blast, the drift, and the snaw;
Come under my plaidie, and sit down beside me;
There's room in't, dear lassie, believe me, for twa.
Come under my plaidie, and sit down beside me;
I'll hap ye frae every cauld blast that can blaw:
Come under my plaidie, and sit down beside me;
There's room in't, dear lassie, believe me, for twa.

Gae 'wa wi' your plaidie! auld Donald, gae 'wa,
I fear na the cauld blast, the drift, nor the snaw!
Gae 'wa wi' your plaidie! I'll no sit beside ye;
Ye micht be my gutcher! auld Donald, gae 'wa.
I'm gaun to meet Johnnie—he's young and he's bonnie;
He's been at Meg's bridal, fu' trig and fu' braw!
Nane dances sae lichtly, sae gracefu', or tichtly,
His cheek's like the new rose, his brow's like the snaw!

Dear Marion, let that flee stick fast to the wa';
Your Jock's but a gowk, and has naething ava;
The haill o' his pack he has now on his back;
He's thretty, and I am but threescore and twa.
Be frank now and kindly—I'll busk ye aye finely;
To kirk or to market there'll few gang sae braw;
A bein house to bide in, a chaise for to ride in,
And flunkies to 'tend ye as aft as ye ca'.

My father aye tauld me, my mother and a',
Ye'd mak' a gude husband, and keep me aye braw;
It's true, I lo'e Johnnie; he's young and he's bonnie;
But, wae's me! I ken he has naething ava!
I ha'e little tocher; ye've made a gude offer;
I'm now mair than twenty; my time is but sma'!
Sae gi'e me your plaidie; I'll creep in beside ye;
I thocht ye'd been aulder than three score and twa!

She crap in ayont him, beside the stane wa',
Whare Johnnie was listnin', and heard her tell a':
The day was appointed!—his proud heart it dunted,
And struck 'gainst his side, as if burstin' in twa.
He wander'd hame wearie, the nicht it was drearie,
And, thowless, he tint his gate 'mang the deep snaw:
The howlet was screaming, while Johnnie cried, Women
Wad marry auld Nick, if he'd keep them aye braw.

O, the deil's in the lasses! they gang now sae braw,
They'll lie down wi' auld men o' four score and twa:
The haill o' their marriage is gowd and a carriage;
Plain love is the cauldest blast now that can blaw.

Auld dotards, be wary! tak' tent wha you marry;
Young wives, wi' their coaches, they'll whip and they'll ca',
Till they meet wi' some Johnnie that's youthfu' and bonnie,
And they'll gi'e ye horns on ilk haffet to claw.

I NE'ER LO'ED A LADDIE BUT ANE.
HECTOR MACNEILL.

WITH the exception of the first eight lines which formed part of a song, written by Rev. John Clunie of Borthwick.

I LO'ED ne'er a laddie but ane;
  He lo'ed ne'er a lassie but me;
He's willing to mak' me his ain;
  And his ain I am willing to be.
He has coft me a rockelay o' blue,
  And a pair o' mittens o' green;
The price was a kiss o' my mou';
  And I paid him the debt yestreen.

Let ithers brag weel o' their gear,
  Their land, and their lordly degree;
I carena for aught but my dear,
  For he's ilka thing lordly to me:
His words are sae sugar'd, sae sweet!
  His sense drives ilk fear far awa'!
I listen, poor fool! and I greet;
  Yet how sweet are the tears as they fa'!

Dear lassie, he cries wi' a jeer,
  Ne'er heed what the auld anes will say;
Though we've little to brag o'—ne'er fear;
  What's gowd to a heart that is wae?
Our laird has baith honours and wealth,
  Yet see how he's dwining wi' care;
Now we, though we've naething but health,
  Are cantie and leal overmair.

O Marion! the heart that is true,
  Has something mair costly than gear;
Ilk e'en it has naething to rue—
  Ilk morn it has naething to fear.
Ye warldlings, ga'e hoard up your store,
  And tremble for fear ought you tyne;
Guard your treasures wi' lock, bar, and door,
  While here in my arms I lock mine!

He ends wi' a kiss and a smile—
  Wae's me, can I tak' it amiss!
My laddie's unpractised in guile,
  He's free aye to daut and to kiss!

Ye lasses wha lo'e to torment
Your wooers wi' fause scorn and strife,
Play your pranks—I ha'e gi'en my consent,
And this night I am Jamie's for life.

THE FLOWER O' DUNBLANE.

ROBERT TANNAHILL,

THE greatest of Paisley's Poets was born on the 3rd of June, 1774. His parents were poor and unable to give Robert, one of a family of seven, more than the merest rudiments of education, and at a very early age he was apprenticed a weaver, at that time one of the most lucrative, and numbering among its ranks the most intelligent, trades in Scotland.

He worked at his trade in Paisley till the year 1800, when he removed to Bolton in Lancashire, where he worked for about two years. He then, on receiving intelligence of his father's approaching death, returned to his native town.

He had been known for some time past among his townsmen as a Rhymster; he now began to be appreciated as a Poet. "Blythe was the time," "Keen blaws the wind," and other songs were floating about Paisley in manuscript, and one of them being sung in presence of R. A. Smith, the composer, he earnestly desired an introduction to the Poet. This was effected, and they became firm friends. Smith composed airs for many of his friend's songs, and they became so popular that in 1807 Tannahill ventured to publish a small volume of his poems. It was a great success, the impression being sold off in a few weeks.

His fame was now firmly established, and of course he became one of the lions of his neighbourhood. He was largely sought after to enter into the life of a provincial town and merry-meetings. Taverns, and occasional bursts of sheer debauchery tended to make him miserable, and his misery was deepened by the rejection of several of his songs by Mr. George Thomson, and the refusal of Constable, the publisher, to risk a new issue of his poems.

In the early part of 1810, he received a visit from James Hogg,—the Ettrick Shepherd, who visited Paisley for the express purpose of seeing him. "They spent one night in each other's company," says Mr. Ramsay (to whose biography of the Poet we are indebted for the particulars in this sketch), "and, ere they parted, Tannahill convoyed the Shepherd on foot, halfway to Glasgow. It was a melancholy adieu our author gave him. He grasped his hand, and with tears in his eyes said, "Farewell, we shall never meet again,—Farewell, I shall never see you more!"—a prediction which was too soon to be verified. In a letter to one of his friends he noticed this meeting with manifest pride.

The gloom, dispelled for a while by this incident, seems to have closed over him again darker than ever. His health failed, and even his mind at times seems to have been affected. He visited a friend in Glasgow, who considered his mental and physical condition such as induced him to personally attend him back to Paisley. On the night of his return he retired to rest more tranquil than usual; about an hour afterwards it was discovered that he had stolen from the house; a search was instantly begun, but it was not till the morning that his coat was found lying by the side of a deep pond from which his body was soon afterwards recovered.

And thus, on the 17th of May, 1810, was a poet lost to Scotland, who ranks second only to Burns as a song-writer. His genius never seems to have been properly developed, and the consequence is, that a more unequal production than the volume containing his poems is not to be found. Between "Jessie, the Flower o' Dunblane," and the song beginning "From the rude bustling camp," there is a wide difference; but, if we compare one of his best songs with any of his poems, the difference is still wider. It is as a song-writer that he will be loved and remembered, and principally for the songs in praise of the scenery and objects surrounding his native town.

  The sun has gane down o'er the lofty Ben Lomond,
   And left the red clouds to preside o'er the scene,
  While lonely I stray, in the calm simmer gloamin',
   To muse on sweet Jessie, the flower o' Dunblane.
  How sweet is the brier, wi' its saft fauldin' blossom!
   And sweet is the birk, wi' its mantle o' green;
  Yet sweeter and fairer, and dear to this bosom,
   Is lovely young Jessie, the flower o' Dunblane.

  She's modest as onie, and blythe as she's bonnie;
   For guileless simplicity marks her its ain;
  And far be the villain, divested o' feeling,
   Wha'd blight in its bloom the sweet flower o' Dunblane.
  Sing on, thou sweet mavis, thy hymn to the e'ening,
   Thou'rt dear to the echoes of Calderwood glen;
  Sae dear to this bosom, sae artless and winning,
   Is charming young Jessie, the flower of Dunblane.

  How lost were my days till I met wi' my Jessie!
   The sports o' the city seemed foolish and vain;
  I ne'er saw a nymph I could ca' my dear lassie,
   Till charm'd wi' sweet Jessie, the flower o' Dunblane.
  Though mine were the station o' loftiest grandeur,
   Amidst its profusion I'd languish in pain,
  And reckon as naething the height o' its splendour,
   If wanting sweet Jessie, the flower o' Dunblane.

WALLACE.
TANNAHILL.

Thou dark winding Carron once pleasing to see,
 To me thou can'st never give pleasure again,
My brave Caledonians lie low on the lea,
 And thy streams are deep ting'd with the blood of the slain.
'Twas base-hearted treach'ry that doom'd our undoing,—
 My poor bleeding country, what more can I do?
Even valour looks pale o'er the red field of ruin,
 And freedom beholds her best warriors laid low.

Farewell, ye dear partners of peril! farewell!
Tho' buried ye lie in one wide bloody grave,
Your deeds shall ennoble the place where ye fell,
And your names be enroll'd with the sons of the brave.
But I, a poor outcast, in exile must wander,
Perhaps, like a traitor ignobly must die!
On thy wrongs, O my country! indignant I ponder—
Ah! woe to the hour when thy Wallace must fly!

LOUDON'S BONNIE WOODS AND BRAES.
ROBERT TANNAHILL.

Loudon's bonnie woods and braes,
  I maun leave them a', lassie;
Wha can thole when Britain's faes
  Would gi'e to Britons law, lassie?
Wha would shun the field o' danger?
Wha to fame would live a stranger?
Now when Freedom bids avenge her,
  Wha would shun her ca', lassie?
Loudon's bonnie woods and braes,
Ha'e seen our happy bridal days,
And gentle hope shall soothe thy waes,
  When I am far awa', lassie.

Hark! the swelling bugle rings,
  Yielding joy to thee, laddie;
But the dolefu' bugle brings
  Waefu' thochts to me, laddie.
Lanely I may climb the mountain,
Lanely stray beside the fountain,
Still the weary moments counting,
  Far frae love and thee, laddie.
Ower the gory fields o' war,
Where Vengeance drives his crimson car,
Thou'lt may be fa' frae me afar,
  And nane to close thy e'e, laddie.

Oh, resume thy wonted smile,
  Oh, suppress thy fears, lassie;
Glorious honour crowns the toil
  That the soldier shares, lassie:
Heaven will shield thy faithful lover,
Till the vengeful strife is over;
Then we'll meet, nae mair to sever,
  Till the day we dee, lassie:
Midst our bonnie woods and braes,
We'll spend our peaceful happy days,
As blythe's yon lichtsome lamb that plays
  On Loudon's flowery lea, lassie.

THE BRAES O' GLENIFFER.
ROBERT TANNAHILL.

Keen blaws the wind o'er the braes o' Gleniffer,
   The auld castle turrets are covered wi' snaw,
How changed frae the time when I met wi' my lover,
   Amang the broom bushes by Stanley green shaw.
The wild flowers o' simmer were spread a' sae bonnie,
   The mavis sang sweet frae the green birken tree;
But far to the camp they ha'e march'd my dear Johnnie,
   And now it is winter wi' nature and me.

Then ilk thing around us was blythesome and cheerie,
   Then ilk thing around us was bonnie and braw;
Now naething is heard but the wind whistling drearie,
   And naething is seen but the wide-spreading snaw.
The trees are a' bare, and the birds mute and dowie,
   They shake the cauld drift frae their wings as they flee:
And chirp out their plaints, seeming wae for my Johnnie;
   'Tis winter wi' them and 'tis winter wi' me.

Yon cauld sleety cloud skiffs along the bleak mountain,
   And shakes the dark firs on the stey rocky brae,
While down the deep glen brawls the snaw-flooded fountain,
   That murmur'd sae sweet to my laddie and me.
It's no its loud roar on the wintry winds swollin',
   It's no the cauld blast brings the tear to my e'e;
For, O! gin I saw but my bonnie Scots callan,
   The dark days o' winter were simmer to me.

THE BRAES O' BALQUHITHER.
ROBERT TANNAHILL.

Let us go, lassie, go,
   To the braes o' Balquhither,
Where the blae-berries grow
   'Mang the bonny Highland heather;
Where the deer and the rae,
   Lightly bounding together,
Sport the lang simmer day
   On the braes o' Balquhither.

I will twine thee a bower,
   By the clear siller fountain,
And I'll cover it o'er
   Wi' the flowers o' the mountain;
I will range through the wilds,
   And the deep glens sae dreary,
And return wi' their spoils
   To the bower o' my deary.

When the rude wintry win'
 Idly raves round our dwelling,
And the roar of the linn
 On the night breeze is swelling,
So merrily we'll sing,
 As the storm rattles o'er us,
'Till the dear shieling ring
 Wi' the light lilting chorus.

Now the simmer is in prime,
 Wi' the flowers richly blooming,
And the wild mountain thyme,
 A' the moorlands perfuming;
To our dear native scenes,
 Let us journey together,
Where glad innocence reigns,
 'Mang the braes o' Dalquhither.

CROCKSTON CASTLE.
ROBERT TANNAHILL.

Through Crockston Castle's lanely wa's,
 The wintry wind howls wild and dreary;
Though mirk the cheerful e'ening fa's,
 Yet I ha'e vow'd to meet my Mary.
Yes, Mary, though the winds should rave
 Wi' jealous spite to keep me frae thee,
The darkest stormy night I'd brave,
 For ae sweet secret moment wi' thee.

Loud o'er Cardonald's rocky steep,
 Rude Cartha pours in boundless measure,
But I will ford the whirling deep,
 That roars between me and my treasure.
Yes, Mary, though the torrent rave
 With jealous spite to keep me frae thee,
Its deepest floods I'd bauldly brave,
 For ae sweet secret moment wi' thee.

The watch-dog's howling loads the blast,
 And makes the nightly wand'rer eerie,
But when the lonesome way is past,
 I'll to this bosom clasp my Mary.
Yes, Mary, though stern Winter rave,
 With a' his storms, to keep me frae thee,
The wildest dreary night I'd brave,
 For ae sweet secret moment wi' thee.

O, ARE YE SLEEPIN', MAGGIE?
ROBERT TANNAHILL.

O, are ye sleepin', Maggie?
 O, are ye sleepin', Maggie?
Let me in, for loud the linn
 Is roarin' o'er the warlock craigie!

Mirk and rainy is the night;
 No a starn in a' the carie;
Lightnings gleam athwart the lift,
 And winds drive on wi' winter's fury.

Fearfu' soughs the boor-tree bank;
 The rifted wood roars wild and drearie;
Loud the iron yett does clank;
 And cry o' howlets maks me eerie.

Aboon my breath I daurna speak,
 For fear I raise your waukrife daddy;
Cauld's the blast upon my cheek;
 O rise, rise, my bonnie lady!

She oped the door; she let him in;
 He cuist aside his droopin' plaidie;
Blaw your warst, ye rain and win',
 Since, Maggie, now I'm in beside ye!

Now, since ye're waukin', Maggie,
 Now, since ye're waukin', Maggie,
What care I for howlet's cry,
 For boor-tree bank and warlock craigie?

THE LASS O' ARRANTEENIE.
ROBERT TANNAHILL.

Far lone amang the Highland hills,
 Midst nature's wildest grandeur,
By rocky dens and woody glens,
 With weary steps I wander.
The langsome way, the darksome day,
 The mountain mist sae rainy,
Are naught to me, when gaun to thee,
 Sweet lass o' Arranteenie.

Yon mossy rose-bud down the howe,
 Just opening fresh and bonny,
It blinks beneath the hazel bough,
 And's scarcely seen by ony.
Sae sweet amidst her native hills,
 Obscurely blooms my Jeanie,
Mair fair and gay than rosy May,
 The flower o' Arranteenie.

Now from the mountain's lofty brow,
  I view the distant ocean,
There avarice guides the bounding prow,
  Ambition courts promotion,
Let fortune pour her golden store,
  Her laurell'd favours many,
Give me but this, my soul's first wish,
  The lass o' Arranteeuie.

GLOOMY WINTER'S NOW AWA'.
ROBERT TANNAHILL.

Gloomy winter's now awa,
Saft the westlin' breezes blaw:
'Mang the birks o' Stanley-shaw
  The mavis sings fu' cheerie, O.
Sweet the craw-flower's early bell
Decks Gleniffer's dewy dell,
Blooming like thy bonnie sel',
  My young, my artless dearie, O.

Come, my lassie, let us stray
O'er Glenkilloch's sunny brae,
Blithely spend the gowden day
  'Midst joys that never wearie O.
Towering o'er the Newton woods,
Laverocks fan the snaw-white clouds;
Siller saughs, wi' downie buds,
  Adorn the banks sae brierie, O.

Round the sylvan fairy nooks,
Feath'ry braikens fringe the rocks,
'Neath the brae the burnie jouks,
  And ilka thing is cheerie, O.
Trees may bud, and birds may sing,
Flowers may bloom, and verdure spring,
Joy to me they canna bring,
  Unless wi' thee, my dearie, O.

BONNIE WOOD OF CRAIGIE-LEA.
ROBERT TANNAHILL.

Thou bonnie wood of Craigie-lea,
  Thou bonnie wood of Craigie-lea,
Near thee I pass'd life's early day,
  And won my Mary's heart in thee.

The broom, the brier, the birken bush,
  Bloom bonnie o'er thy flowery lea,
An' a' the sweets that ane can wish
  Frae nature's hand are strew'd on thee.
    Thou bonnie wood, &c.

Far ben thy dark-green planting's shade,
  The cushat croodles am'rously,
The mavis, down thy buchted glade,
  Gars echo ring frae every tree.
    Thou bonnie wood, &c.

Awa', ye thoughtless, murd'ring gang,
  Wha tear the nestlings ere they flee!
They'll sing you yet a canty sang,
  Then, O in pity let them be!
    Thou bonnie wood, &c.

When winter blaws in sleety showers,
  Frae aff the Norlan' hills sae hie,
He lightly skiffs thy bonnie bowers,
  As laith to harm a flower in thee.
    Thou bonnie wood, &c.

Though fate should drag me south the line,
  Or o'er the wide Atlantic sea;
The happy hours I'll ever min'
  That I in youth ha'e spent in thee.
    Thou bonnie wood, &c.

LANGSYNE.

ROBERT TANNAHILL.

LANGSYNE, beside the woodland burn,
  Amang the broom sae yellow,
I lean'd me 'neath the milkwhite thorn,
  On nature's mossy pillow;
A' 'round my seat the flowers were strew'd,
That frae the wildwood I had pu'd,
To weave mysel' a simmer snood,
  To pleasure my dear fellow.

I twined the woodbine round the rose,
  Its richer hues to mellow,
Green sprigs of fragrant birk I chose,
  To busk the sedge sae yellow.
The craw-flower blue, and meadow-pink,
I wove in primrose-braided link,
But little, little did I think,
  I should have wove the willow.

My bonnie lad was forced afar,
　Toss'd on the raging billow,
Perhaps he's fa'n in bluidy war,
　Or wreck'd on rocky shallow;
Yet aye I hope for his return,
As round our wonted haunts I mourn,
And aften by the woodland burn,
　I pu' the weeping willow.

MARJORY MILLER.
ROBERT TANNAHILL.

LOUDER than the trump of fame
　Is the voice of Marjory Miller;
Time, the wildest beast can tame,
　She's eternally the same:
Loud the mill's incessant clack,
Loud the clank of Vulcan's hammer,
Loud the deep-mouth'd cataract,
But louder far her dinsome clamour!
　Nought on earth can equal be
　To the noise of Marjory.

Calm succeeds the tempest's roar,
　Peace does follow war's confusion,
Dogs do bark and soon give o'er,
But she barks for evermore:
Loud's the sounding bleachfield horn,
But her voice is ten times louder!
Red's the sun on winter morn,
But her face is ten times redder!
　She delights in endless strife,
　Lord preserve's from such a wife!.

YE WOOER LADS WHA GREET AN' GRANE.
ROBERT TANNAHILL.

YE wooer lads wha greet an' grane,
Wha preach an' flecch, an' mak' a moue,
An' pine yoursels to skin and bane,
　Come a' to Callum Brogach:
I'll learn you here the only art,
To win a bonnie lassie's heart—
Just tip wi' gowd Love's siller dart,
　Like dainty Callum Brogach.

I ca'd her aye my sonsie dow,
The fairest flower that e'er I knew;
Yet, like a souple spankie grew,
   She fled frae Callum Brogach:
But soon's she heard the guinea ring,
She turn'd as I had been a king,
Wi' "Tak' my hand, or ony thing,
   Dear, dainty Callum Brogach."

It's gowd can mak' the blind to see,
Can bring respect whare nane would be,
And Cupid ne'er shall want his fee
   Frae dainty Callum Brogach:
Nae mair wi' greetin' blind your een,
Nae mair wi' sichin' warm the win',
But hire the gettlin for your frien',
   Like dainty Callum Brogach.

YE ECHOES THAT RING.
ROBERT TANNAHILL.

YE echoes that ring round the woods of Bowgreen,
   Say, did ye e'er listen sae melting a strain,
When lovely young Jessie gaed wand'ring unseen,
   And sung of her laddie, the pride of the plain?
Aye she sung, "Willie, my bonny young Willie!
There's no a sweet flow'r on the mountain or valley,
Mild blue spreckl'd crawflow'r, nor wild woodland lily,
   But tines a' its sweets in my bonny young swain.
Thou goddess of love, keep him constant to me,
Else, with'ring in sorrow, poor Jessie shall die!"

Her laddie had stray'd through the dark leafy wood,
   His thoughts were a' fix'd on his dear lassie's charms,
He heard her sweet voice, all transported he stood,
   'Twas the soul of his wishes—he flew to her arms.
"No, my dear Jessie! my lovely young Jessie!
Through summer, through winter I'll daut and caress thee,
Thou'rt dearer than life! thou'rt my ae only lassie!
   Then, banish thy bosom these needless alarms;
Yon red setting sun sooner changeful shall be,
Ere wav'ring in falsehood I wander frae thee."

MY WINSOME MARY.
ROBERT TANNAHILL.

FORTUNE, frowning most severe,
Forced me from my native dwelling,
Parting with my friends so dear,
Cost me many a bitter tear:

But, like the clouds of early day,
Soon my sorrows fled away,
When blooming sweet, and smiling gay,
I met my winsome Mary.

Wha can sit with gloomy brow,
Blest with sic a charming lassie?
Native scenes, I think on you,
Yet the change I canna' rue:
Wand'ring many a weary mile,
Fortune seem'd to low'r, the while,
But now she's gi'en me, for the toil,
My bonnie winsome Mary.

Though our riches are but few,
Faithful love is aye a treasure—
Ever cheery, kind, and true,
Nane but her I e'er can lo'e.
Hear me, a' ye powers above!
Powers of sacred truth and love!
While I live I'll constant prove
To my dear winsome Mary.

YE DEAR ROMANTIC SHADES.
ROBERT TANNAHILL.

FAR from the giddy court of mirth,
  Where sick'ning follies reign,
By Levern banks I wander forth
  To hail each sylvan scene.
All hail! ye dear romantic shades!
Ye banks, ye woods, and sunny glades!
Here oft the musing poet treads
  In Nature's riches great;
Contrasts the country with the town,
Makes nature's beauties all his own,
And, borne on fancy's wings, looks down
  On empty pride and fate.

By dewy dawn, or sultry noon,
  Or sober evening gray,
I'll often quit the dinsome town,
  By Levern banks to stray;
Or from the upland's mossy brow,
Enjoy the fancy-pleasing view
Of streamlets, woods, and fields below,
  A sweetly varied scene!
Give riches to the miser's care,
Let folly shine in fashion's glare,
Give me the wealth of peace and health,
  With all their happy train.

Y

THE HIGHLANDER'S INVITATION.
ROBERT TANNAHILL.

WILL you come to the board I've prepared for you?
Your drink shall be good, of the true Highland blue;
Will you, Donald, will you, Callum, come to the board?
There each shall be great as her own native lord.

There'll be plenty of pipe, and a glorious supply
Of the good sneesh-te-bacht, and the fine cut-an-dry,
Will you, Donald, will you, Callum, come then at e'en?
There be some for the stranger, but more for the frien'.

There we'll drink foggy Care to his gloomy abodes,
And we'll smoke till we sit in the clouds like the gods;
Will you, Donald, will you, Callum, won't you do so?
'Tis the way that our forefathers did long ago.

And we'll drink to the Cameron, we'll drink to Lochiel,
And, for Charlie, we'll drink all the French to the de'il.
Will you, Donald, will you, Callum, drink there until
There be beads lie like peats if hersel' had her will!

There be groats on the land, there be fish in the sea,
And there's fouth in the coggie for friendship and me;
Come then, Donald, come then, Callum, come then to-night,
Sure the Highlander be first in the fuddle and the fight.

RAB RORYSON'S BONNET.
ROBERT TANNAHILL.

YE'LL a' hae heard tell o' Rab Roryson's bonnet,
Ye'll a' hae heard tell o' Rab Roryson's bonnet;
'Twas no for itsel', 'twas the head that was in it,
Gar'd a' bodies talk o' Rab Roryson's bonnet.

This bonnet, that theekit his wonderfu' head,
Was his shelter in winter, in summer his shade;
And, at kirk or at market, or bridals, I ween,
A braw gawcier bonnet there never was seen.

Wi' a round rosy tap, like a muckle blackboyd,
It was slouch'd just a kenning on either hand side:
Some maintain'd it was black, some maintain'd it was blue,
It had something o' baith as a body may trow.

But, in sooth, I assure you, for ought that I saw,
Still his bonnet had naething uncommon ava;
Tho' the haill parish talk'd o' Rab Roryson's bonnet,
'Twas a' for the marvellous head that was in it.

That head—let it rest—it is now in the mools,
Though in life a' the warld beside it were fools;
Yet o' what kind o' wisdom his head was possest,
Nane e'er kent but himsel', see there's nane that will miss't.

WHILE THE GRAY-PINIONED LARK.
ROBERT TANNAHILL.

While the gray-pinion'd lark early mounts to the skies,
 And cheerily hails the sweet dawn,
And the sun, newly risen, sheds the mist from his eyes,
 And smiles over mountain and lawn;
Delighted I stray by the fairy-wood side,
 Where the dew-drops the crowflowers adorn,
And Nature, array'd in her midsummer's pride,
 Sweetly smiles to the smile of the morn.

Ye dark waving plantings, ye green shady bowers,
 Your charms ever varying I view;
My soul's dearest transports, my happiest hours,
 Have owed half their pleasure to you.
Sweet Ferguslie, hail! thou'rt the dear sacred grove,
 Where first my young Muse spread her wing;
Here Nature first wak'd me to rapture and love,
 And taught me her beauties to sing.

THE WANDERING BARD.
ROBERT TANNAHILL.

Chill the wintry winds were blowing,
Foul the murky night was snowing,
Through the storm the minstrel, bowing,
 Sought the inn on yonder moor.
All within was warm and cheery,
All without was cold and dreary,
There the wanderer, old and weary,
 Thought to pass the night secure.

Softly rose his mournful ditty,
Suiting to his tale of pity;
But the master, scoffing, witty,
 Check'd his strain with scornful jeer;
"Hoary vagrant, frequent comer,
Canst thou guide thy gains of summer?—
No, thou old intruding thrummer,
 Thou canst have no lodging here."

Slow the bard departed, sighing;
Wounded worth forbade replying;
One last feeble effort trying,
  Faint he sunk no more to rise.
Through his harp the breeze sharp ringing,
Wild his dying dirge was singing,
While his soul, from insult springing,
  Sought its mansion in the skies.

Now, though wintry winds be blowing,
Night be foul, with raining, snowing,
Still the traveller, that way going,
  Shuns the inn upon the moor.
Though within 'tis warm and cheery,
Though without 'tis cold and dreary,
Still he minds the minstrel weary,
  Spurn'd from that unfriendly door.

FROM THE RUDE BUSTLING CAMP.
ROBERT TANNAHILL.

From the rude bustling camp, to the calm rural plain,
I'm come, my dear Jeanie, to bless thee again;
Still burning for honour our warriors may roam,
But the laurel I wish'd for I've won it at home;
All the glories of conquest no joy could impart,
When far from the kind little girl of my heart:
Now, safely return'd, I will leave thee no more,
But love my dear Jeanie till life's latest hour.

The sweets of retirement how pleasing to me!
Possessing all worth, my dear Jeanie, in thee!
Our flocks early bleating will make us to joy,
And our raptures exceed the warm tints in the sky;
In sweet rural pastimes our days still will glide,
Till Time, looking back, will admire at his speed!
Still blooming in virtue, though youth then be o'er,
I'll love my dear Jeanie till life's latest hour.

COGGIE, THOU HEALS ME.
ROBERT TANNAHILL.

Dorothy sits i' the cauld ingle neuk;
  Her red rosy neb's like a labster tae,
Wi' girning, her mou's like the gab o' the fleuk,
  Wi' smoking, her teeth's like the jet o' the slae.
And aye she sings "Weel's me!" aye she sing "Weel's me!
Coggie, thou heals me, coggie, thou heals me;
Aye my best friend, when there's ony thing ails me:
Ne'er shall we part till the day that I die."

Dorothy ance was a weel tocher'd lass,
  Had charms like her neighbours, and lovers enew,
But she spited them sae wi' her pride and her sauce,
  They left her for thretty lang simmers to rue.
Then aye she sang "Waes me!" aye she sang "Waes me!
O I'll turn crazy, O I'll turn crazy!
Naething in a' the wide world can ease me,
De'il take the wooers—O what shall I do!"

Dorothy, dozen'd wi' living her lane,
  Pu'd at her rock, wi' the tear in her e'e,
She thocht on the braw merry days that were gane,
  And coft a wee coggie for companie.
Now aye she sings "Weel's me!" aye she sings "Weel's me!
Coggie, thou heals me, coggie, thou heals me;
Aye my best friend, when there's ony thing ails me:
Ne'er shall we part till the day that I die."

O SAIR I RUE THE WITLESS WISH.
ROBERT TANNAHILL.

O SAIR I rue the witless wish,
  That gar'd me gang with you at e'en,
And sair I rue the birken bush,
  That screen'd us wi' its leaves sae green.
And though ye vow'd ye wad be mine,
  The tear o' grief aye dims my e'e,
For O! I'm fear'd that I may tine
  The love that ye ha'e promised me!

While ithers seek their e'ening sports,
  I wander, dowie, a' my lane,
For when I join their glad resorts,
  Their daffing gi'es me meikle pain,
Alas! it was na' sae shortsyne,
  When a' my nights were spent wi' glee;
But, O! I'm fear'd that I may tine
  The love that ye ha'e promis'd me.

Dear lassie, keep thy heart aboon,
  For I ha'e wair'd my winter's fee,
I've coft a bonnie silken gown,
  To be a bridal gift for thee.
And sooner shall the hills fa' down,
  And mountain-high shall stand the sea,
Ere I'd accept a gowden crown,
  To change that love I bear for thee.

FLY WE TO SOME DESERT ISLE.
ROBERT TANNAHILL.

Fly we to some desert isle,
   There we'll pass our days together,
Shun the world's derisive smile,
   Wandering tenants of the heather:
Shelter'd in some lonely glen,
Far removed from mortal ken,
Forget the selfish ways o' men,
   Nor feel a wish beyond each other.

Though my friends deride me still,
   Jamie, I'll disown thee never;
Let them scorn me as they will,
   I'll be thine—and thine for ever.
What are a' my kin to me,
A' their pride o' pedigree?
What were life if wanting thee,
   And what were death, if we maun sever!

I'LL HIE ME TO THE SHIELING HILL.
ROBERT TANNAHILL.

I'll hie me to the shieling hill,
And bide amang the braes, Callum,
Ere I gang to Crochan mill,
I'll live on hips and slaes, Callum.
Wealthy pride but ill can hide
Your runkl'd, mizzly shins, Callum,
Lyart pow, as white's the tow,
And beard as rough's the whins, Callum.

Wily woman aft deceives!
Sae ye'll think, I ween, Callum,
Trees may keep their wither'd leaves,
'Till ance they get the green, Callum.
Blithe young Donald's won my heart,
Has my willing vow, Callum,
Now, for a' your couthy art,
I winna marry you, Callum.

THE FLOWER ON LEVEN SIDE.
ROBERT TANNAHILL.

Ye sunny braes that skirt the Clyde
 Wi' simmer flowers sae braw,
There's ae sweet flower on Leven side,
 That's fairer than them a':
Yet aye it droops its head in wae,
 Regardless o' the sunny ray,
And wastes its sweets frae day to day,
 Beside the lonely shaw;
Wi' leaves a' steep'd in sorrow's dew,
 Fause, cruel man, it seems to rue,
Wha aft the sweetest flower will pu',
 Then rend its heart in twa.

Thou bonny flow'r on Leven side,
 O gin thou'lt be but mine;
I'll tend thee wi' a lover's pride,
 Wi' love that ne'er shall tine;
I'll take thee to my sheltering bower,
And shield thee frae the beating shower,
Unharm'd by ought thou'lt bloom secure
 Frae a' the blasts that blaw:
Thy charms surpass the crimson dye
That streaks the glowing western sky,
But here, unshaded, soon thou'lt die,
 And lone will be thy fa'.

OUR BONNIE SCOTS LADS.
ROBERT TANNAHILL.

Our bonnie Scots lads, in their green tartan plaids,
 Their blue-belted bonnets, and feathers sae braw,
Rank'd up on the green were fair to be seen,
 But my bonnie young laddie was fairest of a',
His cheeks were as red as the sweet heather-bell,
 Or the red western cloud looking down on the snaw,
His lang yellow hair o'er his braid shoulders fell,
 And the een o' the lasses were fix'd on him a'.

My heart sunk wi' wae on the wearifu' day,
 When torn frae my bosom they march'd him awa',
He bade me farewell, he cried, "O be leel,"
 And his red cheeks were wat wi' the tears that did fa'.
Ah! Harry, my love, though thou ne'er shoul'dst return,
 Till life's latest hour I thy absence will mourn,
And memory shall fade, like the leaf on the tree,
 Ere my heart spare ae thought on anither but thee.

MARY.

ROBERT TANNAHILL.

My Mary is a bonnie lassie,
   Sweet as the dewy morn,
When Fancy tunes her rural reed,
   Beside the upland thorn.
She lives ahint yon sunny knowe,
Whore flow'rs in wild profusion grow,
Where spreading birks and hazels throw
   Their shadows o'er the burn.

'Tis no the streamlet-skirted wood,
   Wi' a' its leafy bowers,
That gars me wait in solitude
   Among the wild-sprung flowers;
But aft I cast a langing e'e,
Down frae the bank out-owre the lea,
There haply I my lass may see,
   As through the broom she scours.

Yestreen I met my bonnie lassie
   Coming frae the town,
We raptured sunk in ither's arms
   And prest the breckans down;
The pairtrick sung his e'ening note,
The rye-craik rispt his clam'rous throat,
While there the heavenly vow I got,
   That erl'd her my own.

HIGHLAND LADDIE.

ROBERT TANNAHILL.

Blythe was the time when he fee'd wi' my father, O,
Happy were the days when we herded thegither, O,
Sweet were the hours when he row'd me in his pladdie, O,
And vow'd to be mine, my dear Highland laddie, O.

But, ah! waes me! wi' their sodgering sae gaudy, O,
The laird's wyl'd awa' my braw Highland laddie, O,
Misty are the glens and the dark hills sae cloudy, O,
That aye seem'd sae blythe wi' my dear Highland laddie, O.

The blae-berry banks now are lonesome and dreary, O,
Muddy are the streams that gush'd down sae clearly, O,
Silent are the rocks that echoed sae gladly, O,
The wild melting strains o' my dear Highland laddie, O.

He pu'd me the crawberry, ripe frae the boggy fen,
He pu'd me the strawberry, red frae the foggy glen,
He pu'd me the rowan frae the wild steep sae giddy, O,
Sae loving and kind was my dear Highland laddie, O.

Fareweel, my ewes, and fareweel, my doggie, O,
Fareweel, ye knowes, now sae cheerloss and scroggie, O,
Fareweel, Glenfeoch, my mammy and my daddie, O,
I will lea' you a' for my dear Highland laddie, O.

BARROCHAN JEAN.

ROBERT TANNAHILL.

'Tis hinna ye heard, man, o' Barrochan Jean?
 And hinna ye heard, man, o' Barrochan Jean!
How death and starvation came o'er the haill nation,
 She wrought sic mischief wi' her twa pawky een;
The lads and the lasses were dying in dizzens,
 The taen kill'd wi' love, and the tither wi' spleen,
The ploughing, the sawing, the shearing, the mawing,
 A' wark was forgotten for Barrochan Jean!

Frae the south and the north, o'er the Tweed and the Forth,
 Sic coming and ganging there never was seen,
The comers were cheery, the gangers were blearie,
 Despairing, or hoping for Barrochan Jean.
The carlins at hame were a' girning and graning,
 The bairns were a' greeting frae morning till e'en,
They gat naething for crowdy, but runts boil'd to sowdie,
 For naething gat growing for Barrochan Jean.

The doctors declar'd it was past their descriving,
 The ministers said 'twas a judgment for sin,
But they lookit sae blae, and their hearts were sae wae,
 I was sure they were dying for Barrochan Jean.
The burns on road-sides were a' dry wi' their drinking,
 Yet a' wadna sloken the drouth i' their skin;
A' around the peat-stacks, and alangst the dyke backs,
 E'en the winds were a' sighing, sweet Barrochan Jean.

The timmer ran done wi' the making o' coffins,
 Kirkyards o' their sward were a' howkit fu' clean,
Dead lovers were packit like herring in barrels,
 Sic thousands were dying for Barrochan Jean.
But mony braw thanks to the Laird o' Glen-Brodie,
 The grass owre their graffs is now bonnie and green,
He sta' the proud heart of our wanton young lady,
 And spoil'd a' the charms o' her twa pawky een.

THE COGIE.

ROBERT TANNAHILL.

When poortith cauld, and sour disdain,
 Hang o'er life's vale sae fogie,
The sun that brightens up the scene,
 Is friendship's kindly cogie.
  Then, O revere the cogie, sirs,
   The friendly, social cogie;
  It gars the wheels o' life rin light,
   Though e'er sae doilt and clogie.

Let pride in fortune's chariots fly,
 Sae empty, vain, and vogie;
The source of wit, the spring of joy,
 Lies in the social cogie.
  Then, O revere the cogie, sirs,
   The independent cogie;
  And never snool beneath the frown
   Of onie selfish rogie.

Poor modest worth, with heartless e'e,
 Sits burkling in the bogie,
Till she asserts her dignity,
 By virtue of the cogie.
  Then, O revere the cogie, sirs,
   The poor man's patron cogie;
  It warsals care, it lights life's faughts,
   And lifts him frae the bogie.

Gi'e feckless Spain her weak snail broo,
 Gi'e France her weel spic'd frogie,
Gi'e brither John his luncheon too,
 But gi's to us our cogie.
  Then, O revere the cogie, sirs,
   Our kind heart-warming cogie;
  We doubly feel the social tie,
   When just a wee thought grogie.

In days of yore our sturdy sires,
 Upon their hills sae scrogie,
Glow'd with true freedom's warmest fires,
 And fought to save their cogie.
  Then, O revere the cogie, sirs,
   Our brave forefathers' cogie;
  It rous'd them up to doughty deeds,
   O'er which we'll lang be vogie.

Then here's may Scotland ne'er fa' down,
 A cringing coward dogie,
But bauldly stand, and bang the loon,
 Wha'd reave her of her cogie.
  Then, O protect the cogie, sirs,
   Our good auld mither's cogie;
  Nor let her luggie e'er be drain'd
   By ony foreign rogie.

WE'LL MEET BESIDE THE DUSKY GLEN.
ROBERT TANNAHILL.

We'll meet beside the dusky glen, on yon burn-side,
Where the bushes form a cozie den, on yon burn-side:
 Though the broomy knowes be green,
 Yet there we may be seen;
But we'll meet—we'll meet at e'en, down by yon burn-side.

I'll lead thee to the birken bower on yon burn-side,
Sae sweetly wove wi' woodbine flower, on yon burn-side:
 There the busy prying eye
 Ne'er disturbs the lover's joy,
While in other's arms they lie, down by yon burn-side.

Awa', ye rude unfeelin' crew, frae yon burn-side!
Those fairy scenes are no for you, by yon burn-side:
 There fancy smooths her theme,
 By the sweetly murmurin' stream,
And the rock-lodged echoes skim, down by yon burn-side.

Now the plantin' taps are tinged wi' gowd on yon burn-side,
And gloamin' draws her foggie shroud o'er yon burn-side:
 Far frae the noisy scene,
 I'll through the fields alane;
There we'll meet, my ain dear Jean! down by yon burn-side.

NOW WINTER, WI' HIS CLOUDY BROW.
ROBERT TANNAHILL.

Now winter, wi' his cloudy brow,
 Is far ayont yon mountains,
And spring beholds her azure sky
 Reflected in the fountains.
Now, on the budding slaethorn bank,
 She spreads her early blossom,
And wooes the mirly-breasted birds
 To nestle in her bosom.
But lately a' was clad wi' snaw,
 Sae darksome, dull, and dreary,
Now lavrocks sing, to hail the spring,
 And nature all is cheery.

Then let us leave the town, my love,
  And seek our country dwelling,
Where waving woods, and spreading flow'rs,
  On every side are smiling.
We'll tread again the daisied green,
  Where first your beauty moved me;
We'll trace again the woodland scene,
  Where first ye own'd ye loved me.
We soon will view the roses blaw
  In a' the charms of fancy,
For doubly dear these pleasures a',
  When shared with thee, my Nancy.

THE MIDGES DANCE ABOON THE BURN.

ROBERT TANNAHILL.

The midges dance aboon the burn,
  The dews begin to fa',
The pairtricks down the rushy holm,
  Set up their e'ening ca'.
Now loud and clear the blackbird's sang
  Rings through the briery shaw,
While flitting, gay, the swallows play
  Around the castle wa'.

Beneath the golden gloaming sky,
  The mavis mends her lay,
The redbreast pours his sweetest strains,
  To charm the ling'ring day;
While weary yeldrins seem to wail
  Their little nestlings torn,
The merry wren, frae den to den,
  Gaes jinking through the thorn.

The roses fauld their silken leaves,
  The foxglove shuts its bell,
The honeysuckle, and the birk,
  Spread fragrance through the dell.
Let others crowd the giddy court
  Of mirth and revelry,
The simple joys that nature yields
  Are dearer far to me.

OCH, HEY! JOHNNIE LAD.
ROBERT TANNAHILL.

Och, hey! Johnnie lad,
 Ye're no sae kind's ye should ha'e been;
Och, hey! Johnnie lad,
 Ye didna keep your tryst yestreen.
I waited lang beside the wood,
 Sae was and weary a' my lane,
Och, hey! Johnnie lad,
 Ye're no sae kind's ye should ha'e been.

I looked by the whinny knowe,
 I looked by the firs sae green,
I looked owre the spunkie howe,
 And aye I thought ye wad ha'e been.
The ne'er a supper cross'd my craig,
 The ne'er a sleep has closed my een,
Och, hey! Johnnie lad,
 Ye're no sae kind's ye should ha'e been.

Gin ye were waiting by the wood,
 Then I was waiting by the thorn,
I thought it was the place we set,
 And waited maist till dawning morn.
Sae be na vex'd, my bonnie lassie,
 Let my waiting stand for thine,
We'll awa' to Craigton shaw,
 And seek the joys we tint yestreen.

CLEAN PEASE STRAE.
ROBERT TANNAHILL.

When John and me were married,
 Our hadding was but sma',
For my minnie, canker'd carline,
 Wad gi'e us nocht ava.
I wair't my fee wi' cannie care,
 As far as it wad gae;
But, weel I wat, our bridal bed
 Was clean pease strae.

Wi' working late and early,
 We're come to what you see;
For fortune thrave aneath our hands,
 Sae eydent aye were we.
The lowe o' love made labour light;
 I'm sure you'll find it sae,
When kind ye cuddle down at e'en
 'Mang clean pease strae.

The rose blooms gay on cairny brae
　As weel's in birken shaw,
And love will live in cottage low,
　As weel's in lofty ha',
Sae, lassie, tak' the lad ye like,
　Whate'er your minnie say,
Though ye should mak' your bridal bed
　O' clean pease strae.

I MARK'D A GEM OF PEARLY DEW.
ROBERT TANNAHILL.

I MARK'D a gem of pearly dew,
　While wand'ring near yon misty mountain,
Which bore the tender flow'r so low,
　It dropp'd it off into the fountain.
So thou hast wrung this gentle heart,
　Which in its core was proud to wear thee,
Till drooping sick beneath thy art,
　It sighing found it could not bear thee.

Adieu, thou faithless fair! unkind!
　Thy falsehood dooms that we must sever;
Thy vows were as the passing wind,
　That fans the flow'r, then dies for ever.
And think not that this gentle heart,
　Though in its core 'twas proud to wear thee,
Shall longer droop beneath thy art;—
　No, cruel fair, it cannot bear thee.

WITH WAEFU' HEART.
ROBERT TANNAHILL.

WITH waefu' heart, and sorrowing e'e,
　I saw my Jamie sail awa';
O 'twas a fatal day to me,
　That day he pass'd the Berwick Law:
How joyless now seem'd all behind!
　I lingering stray'd along the shore;
Dark boding fears hung on my mind
　That I might never see him more.

The night came on with heavy rain,
　Loud, fierce, and wild, the tempest blew;
In mountains roll'd the awful main—
　Ah, hapless maid! my fears how true!
The landsmen heard their drowning cries,
　The wreck was seen with dawning day;
My love was found, and now he lies
　Low in the isle of gloomy May.

O boatman, kindly waft me o'er!
　The cavern'd rock shall be my home;
'Twill ease my burden'd heart to pour
　Its sorrows o'er his grassy tomb.
With sweetest flowers I'll deck his grave,
　And tend them through the langsome year;
I'll water them ilk morn and eve,
　With deepest sorrow's warmest tear.

MARY, WHY WASTE?
ROBERT TANNAHILL.

"MARY, why thus waste thy youth-time in sorrow?
　See, a' around you the flowers sweetly blaw;
Blythe sets the sun o'er the wild cliffs of Jura,
　Blythe sings the mavis in ilka green shaw."
"How can this heart ever mair think of pleasure?
　Summer may smile, but delight I ha'e nane;
Cauld in the grave lies my heart's only treasure,
　Nature seems dead since my Jamie is gane.

"This 'kerchief he gave me, a true lover's token,
　Dear, dear to me was the gift for his sake!
I wear't near my heart, but this poor heart is broken,
　Hope died with Jamie, and left it to break;
Sighing for him, I lie down in the e'ening,
　Sighing for him, I awake in the morn;
Spent are my days a' in secret repining,
　Peace to this bosom can never return.

"Oft have we wander'd in sweetest retirement,
　Telling our loves 'neath the moon's silent beam,
Sweet were our meetings of tender endearment,
　But fled are these joys like a fleet-passing dream.
Cruel remembrance, in pity forsake me,
　Brooding o'er joys that for ever are flown!
Cruel remembrance, in pity forsake me,
　Flee to some bosom where grief is unknown!"

HARPER OF MULL.
ROBERT TANNAHILL.

WHEN Rosie was faithful, how happy was I!
Still gladsome as summer the time glided by:
I play'd my heart cheery, while fondly I sang
Of the charms of my Rosie the winter nights lang:
But now I'm as waefu' as waefu' can be,
Come simmer, come winter, 'tis a' ane to me,
For the dark gloom of falsehood sae clouds my sad soul,
That cheerless for aye is the Harper of Mull.

I wander the glens and the wild woods alane,
In their deepest recesses I make my sad mane;
My harp's mournful melody joins in the strain,
While sadly I sing of the days that are gane.
Though Rosie is faithless, she's no the less fair,
And the thoughts of her beauty but feed my despair;
With painful remembrance my bosom is full,
And weary of life is the Harper of Mull.

As slumb'ring I lay by the dark mountain stream,
My lovely young Rosie appear'd in my dream;
I thought her still kind, and I ne'er was sae blest,
As in fancy I clasp'd the dear nymph to my breast:
Thou false fleeting vision, too soon thou wert o'er,
Thou wak'dst me to tortures unequall'd before;
But death's silent slumbers my griefs soon shall lull,
And the green grass wave over the Harper of Mull.

ACCUSE ME NOT, INCONSTANT FAIR.

ROBERT TANNAHILL.

Accuse me not, inconstant fair,
  Of being false to thee,
For I was true, would still been so,
  Had'st thou been true to me:
But when I knew thy plighted lips
  Once to a rival's prest,
Love-smother'd independence rose,
  And spurn'd thee from my breast.

The fairest flow'r in nature's field
  Conceals the rankling thorn;
So thou, sweet flower! as false as fair,
  This once kind heart hast torn:
'Twas mine to prove the follest pangs
  That slighted love can feel;
'Tis thine to weep that one rash act,
  Which bids this long farewell.

HEY DONALD! HOWE DONALD!
ROBERT TANNAHILL.

The second, third, and fifth stanzas were written by Mr. Gibson, Greenock. The fourth is by William Motherwell.

Tho' simmer smiles on bank and brae,
An' nature bids the heart be gay;
Yet a' the joys o' flow'ry May,
  Wi' pleasure ne'er can move me.
    Hey Donald! howe Donald!
    Think upon your vow, Donald!
    Mind the heathery knowe, Donald,
    Whare ye vow'd to lo'e me.

When first ye climb'd the heath'ry steep,
Wi' me to wear my father's sheep,
The vows ye made ye said ye'd keep,
  The vows ye made to lo'e me.
    Hey Donald, &c.

But love is but a weary dream,
Its joys are like the summer scene,
Whose beauty is the sunny beam,
  That dazzles to deceive me.
    Hey Donald, &c.

I downa look on bank or brae,
I downa greet where a' are gay;
But, oh! my heart will break wi' wae,
  Gin Donald cease to lo'e me.
    Hey Donald, &c.

My father has a haddin braw,
His setting sun's just gaun to fa',
And Donald thou sall get it a',
  My Donald gin ye'll lo'e me.
    Hey Donald, &c.

GLOOMY FEBER'WAR.

The first stanza is by Tannahill, the others by Dr. Patrick Buchan.

Thou cauld gloomy Feber'war,
  Oh! gin thou wert awa'!
I'm wae to hear thy soughin' winds,
  I'm wae to see thy snaw;
For my bonnie braw young Hielandman,
  The lad I lo'e sae dear,
Has vow'd to come and see me,
  In the spring time o' the year.

A silken ban' he gae me,
  To bin' my gowden hair;
A siller brooch and tartan plaid,
  A' for his sake to wear:
And oh! my heart was like to break,
  (For partin' sorrows sair,)
As he vow'd to come and see me,
  In the spring time o' the year.

Aft, aft as gloaming dims the sky,
  I wander out alane,
Whare buds the bonnie yellow whins,
  Around the trystin' stane:
'Twas there he press'd me to his heart,
  And kiss'd awa' the tear,
As he vow'd to come and see me,
  In the spring time o' the year

Ye gentle breezes saftly blaw,
  And cleed anew the wuds:
Ye lav'rocks lilt your cheery sangs,
  Amang the fleecy cluds;
Till Febar'war and a' his train,
  Affrighted disappear—
I'll hail wi' you the blythsome change,
  The spring time o' the year.

THE LASSES A' LEUGH.

THE first stanza is by Tannahill, the others were added by Alexander Rodger.

The lasses a' leugh, and the carlin flate,
But Maggie was sitting fu' ourie and blate,
The auld silly gawkie, she couldna contain,
How brawly she was kiss'd yestreen;
  Kiss'd yestreen, kiss'd yestreen,
  How brawly she was kiss'd yestreen;
She blethered it round to her fae an' her freen,
  How brawly she was kiss'd yestreen.

She loosed the white napkin frae 'bout her dun neck,
An' cried, The big sorrow tak' lang Geordie Fleck!
D'ye see what a scart I gat frae a preen,
By his tousling an' kissing at me yestreen;
  At me yestreen, at me yestreen,
  By his tousling an' kissing at me yestreen;
I canna conceive what the fallow could mean,
  By his kissing sae meikle at me yestreen.

Then she pu'd up her sleeve an' shawed a blue mark,
Quo' she, I gat that frae young Davy our clark,
But the creature had surely forgat himsel' clean,
Whon he nipt me sae hard for a kiss yestreen,
　For a kiss yestreen, for a kiss yestreen,
Whon he nipt me sae hard for a kiss yestreen;
I wonder what keepit my nails frae his een,
　When he nipt me sae hard for a kiss yestreen.

Then she held up her cheek, an' cried, Foul fa' the laird,
Just leuk what I gat with his black birsie beard,
The vile filthy body! was e'er the like seen?
To rub me sae sair for a kiss yestreen;
　For a kiss yestreen, for a kiss yestreen;
To rub me sae sair for a kiss yestreen,
I'm sure that nae woman o' judgment need green
　To be rubbit, like me, for a kiss yestreen.

Syne she tald what grand offers she aften had had,
But wad she tak' a man?—na, she wasna sae mad;
For the hale o' the sex she cared na a preen,
An' she hated the way she was kiss'd yestreen;
　Kiss'd yestreen, kiss'd yestreen,
She hated the way she was kiss'd yestreen;
'Twas a mercy that naething mair serious had been,
　For it's dangerous whiles to be kiss'd at e'en.

THE NE'ER-DO-WEEL.

The first stanza is by Tannahill, the others were afterwards written by Alexander Rodger.

Come hame to your lingels, ye ne'er-do-weel loon,
You're the king o' the dyvours, the talk o' the town,
Sae soon as the Munonday morning comes in,
Your wearifu' daidling again maun begin.
Gudewife, you're a skillet, your tongue's just a bell,
To the peace o' gude fallows it rings the death-knell,
But clack till ye deafen auld Barnaby's mill,
The souter shall aye ha'e his Munonday's yill.

Come hame to your lap-stane, come hame to your last,
It's a bonnie affair that your family maun fast,
While you and your crew here a-guzzling maun sit,
Ye daised drunken gude-for-nocht heir of the pit;
Just leuk, how I'm gaun without stocking or shoe,
Your bairns a' in tatters, an' fotherless too,
An' yet, quite content, like a sot, ye'll sit still,
Till your kyte's like to crack, wi' your Munonday's yill.

I tell you, gudewife, gin you haud na your clack,
I'll lend you a reestle wi' this owre your back;
Mann we be abused an' affronted by you,
Wi' siccan foul names as "loon," "dyvour," an' "crew?"
Come hame to your lingals, this instant come hame,
Or I'll redden your face, gin ye've yet ony shame,
For I'll bring a' the bairns, an' we'll just ha'e our fill,
As weel as yoursel', o' your Munonday's yill.

Gin that be the gate o't, sirs, come, let us stir,
What need we sit here to be pestered by her?
For she'll plague an' affront us as far as she can;
Did ever a woman sae bother a man?
Frae yill house to yill house she'll after us rin,
An' raise the hale town wi' her yelpin' and din;
Come, ca' the gudewife, bid her bring in her bill,
I see I maun quat takin' Munonday's yill.

UP AMANG YON CLIFFY ROCKS.
WILLIAM DUDGEON,

A NATIVE of Tyninghame in East Lothian, where he was born about 1758. He died at his farm of Primrose Hill, near Dunse, in 1813.

Up amang yon cliffy rocks,
  Sweetly rings the rising echo,
To the maid that tends the goats,
  Lilting o'er her native notes.
    Hark, she sings, "Young Sandy's kind,
      An' he's promis'd aye to lo'e me;
    Here's a broach I ne'er shall tine,
      Till he's fairly married to me;
Drive away, ye drone, Time,
An' bring about our bridal day.

Sandy herds a flock o' sheep,
  Aften does he blaw the whistle,
In a strain sae saftly sweet,
  Lammies list'ning daurna bleat.
    He's as fleet's the mountain roe,
      Hardy as the highland heather,
    Wading through the winter snow,
      Keeping aye his flock together;
But a plaid, wi' bare houghs,
He braves the bleakest norlan' blast.

Brawly can he dance and sing,
  Canty glee or highland cronach;
  Nane can ever match his fling,
At a reel, or round a ring;

Wightly can he wield a rung,
  In a brawl he's aye the bangster;
A' his praise can ne'er be sung
  By the langest-winded sangster,
Sangs that sing o' Sandy
Seem short, tho' they were e'er sae lang.

DARK LOWERS THE NIGHT.
ALEXANDER WILSON,

THE American Ornithologist, was born at Paisley in 1766. He was by trade a weaver, but afterwards left that occupation and shouldered a pack, selling his wares throughout the country. His principal poem is "Watty and Meg," which, as a picture of "low life" in Scotland, is unsurpassed. Wilson emigrated to America in 1794, and there devoted his whole attention to the study of Natural History. His great Work—American Ornithology, has ever been the delight of naturalists, and has made his name famous amongst a very different class from the purchasers of the halfpenny chap-book containing "Watty and Meg." He died at Philadelphia in 1813.

DARK lowers the night o'er the wide stormy main,
Till mild rosy morning rise cheerful again;
Alas! morn returns to revisit the shore;
But Connel returns to his Flora no more.

For see, on yon mountain, the dark cloud of death,
O'er Connel's lone cottage, lies low on the heath;
While bloody and pale, on a far distant shore,
He lies to return to his Flora no more.

Ye light floating spirits that glide o'er the steep,
O would you but waft me across the wild deep!
There fearless I'd mix in the battle's loud roar,
I'd die with my Connel, and leave him no more.

OLD AUCHTERTOOL.
ALEXANDER WILSON.

FROM the village of Lesly with a heart full of glee,
And my pack on my shoulders, I rambled out free,
Resolved that same evening, as Luna was full,
To lodge ten miles distant, in old Auchtertool.

Through many a lone cottage and farm-house I steer'd,
Took their money, and off with my budget I sheer'd;
The road I explored out, without form or rule,
Still asking the nearest to old Auchtertool.

A clown I accosted, inquiring the road,
He stared like an idiot, then roar'd out, "Gude G-d!
Gin ye're ga'n there for quarters, ye're surely a fool,
For there's nought but starvation in auld Auchtertool!"

Unminding his nonsense, my march I pursued,
Till I came to a hill top, where joyful I view'd,
Surrounded with mountains, and many a white pool,
The small smoky village of old Auchtertool.

At length I arrived at the edge of the town,
As Phœbus behind a high mountain went down;
The clouds gather'd dreary, and weather blew foul,
And I hugg'd myself safe now in old Auchtortool.

An inn I inquired out, a lodging desired,
But the landlady's pertness seem'd instantly fired;
For she saucy replied, as she sat carding wool,
"I ne'er kept sic lodgers in auld Auchtertool."

With scorn I soon left her to live on her pride;
But, asking, was told, there was none else beside,
Except an old Weaver, who now kept a school,
And these were the whole that were in Auchtertool.

To his mansion I scamper'd, and rapt at the door,
He op'd, but as soon as I dared to implore,
He shut it like thunder, and utter'd a howl,
That rung thro' each corner of old Auchtertool.

Provoked now to fury, the Dominie I curst,
And offer'd to cudgel the wretch, if he durst;
But the door he fast bolted, tho' Boreas blew cool,
And left me all friendless in old Auchtertool.

Deprived of all shelter, through darkness I trod,
Till I came to a ruin'd old house by the road;
Here the night I will spend, and, inspired by the owl,
I'll send up some prayers for old Auchtertool.

THE RANTIN HIGHLANDMAN.

JOHN HAMILTON,
A music-seller in Edinburgh, where he died in 1814, aged 58 years.

AE morn, last ouk, as I gaed out
  To flit a tether'd yowe and lamb,
I met, as skiffing ower the green,
  A jolly rantin' Highlandman.
His shape was neat, wi' feature sweet,
  And ilka smile my favour wan;
I ne'er had seen ane braw a lad,
  As this young rantin' Highlandman.

He said, My dear, ye're sune asteer;
　　Cam' ye to hear the laverock's sang?
O' wad ye gang and wed wi' me,
　　And wed a rantin' Highlandman?
In summer days, on flowery braes,
　　When frisky is the ewe and lamb,
I'se row ye in my tartan plaid,
　　And be your rantin' Highlandman.

With heather bells, that sweetly smells,
　　I'll deck your hair sae fair and lang,
If ye'll consent to scour the bent
　　Wi' me, a rantin' Highlandman.
We'll big a cot, and buy a stock,
　　Syne do the best that e'er we can:
Then come, my dear, ye needna fear
　　To trust a rantin' Highlandman.

His words sae sweet gaed to my heart,
　　And fain I wad ha'e gi'en my han',
Yet duratna, lest my mother should
　　Dislike a rantin' Highlandman.
But I expect he will come back;
　　Then, though my kin' should scould and ban,
I'll ower the hill, or where he will,
　　Wi' my young rantin' Highlandman.

UP IN THE MORNIN'.

JOHN HAMILTON.

CAULD blaws the wind frae north to south;
　　The drift is drifting sairly;
The sheep are cowrin' in the heuch,
　　O! sirs, it's winter fairly.
Now up in the mornin's no for me,
　　Up in the mornin' early;
I'd rather gae supperless to my bed,
　　Than rise in the morning early.

Loud roars the blast amang the woods,
　　And tirls the branches barely;
On hill and house hear how it thuds!
　　The frost is nipping sairly.
Now up in the mornin's no for me,
　　Up in the morning early,
To sit a' nicht wad better agree,
　　Than rise in the mornin' early.

The sun peeps owre yon southland hills,
  Like ony timorous carlie,
Just blinks a wee, then sinks again;
  And that we find severely.
Now up in the mornin's no for me,
  Up in the mornin' early;
When snaw blaws in at the chimley cheek,
  Wha'd rise in the mornin' early?

Nae linties lilt on hedge or bush:
  Poor things, they suffer sairly;
In cauldrife quarters a' the nicht;
  A' day they feed but sparely.
Now up in the mornin's no for me,
  Up in the mornin' early;
A pennyless purse I wad rather dree
  Than rise in the mornin' early.

A cosie house and canty wife,
  Aye keep a body cheerly;
And pantries stowed wi' meat and drink,
  They answer unco rarely.
But up the mornin'—na, na, na!
  Up in the mornin' early!
The gowans maun glent on bank and brae,
  When I rise in the mornin' early.

GO TO BERWICK, JOHNNIE.

JOHN HAMILTON.

Go to Berwick, Johnnie;
  Bring her frae the Border;
Yon sweet bonnie lassie,
  Let her ga'e nae farther.
English loons will twine ye
  O' the lovely treasure;
But we'll let them ken,
  A sword wi' them we'll measure.

Go to Berwick, Johnnie,
  And regain your honour;
Drive them ower the Tweed,
  And show our Scottish banner.
I am Rob the king,
  And ye are Jock, my brither;
But, before we lose her,
  We'll a' there thegither.

THE MAID OF ISLAY.

REV. WILLIAM DUNBAR, D.D.,

Minister of Applegarth, in the beginning of the present century. He was born at Dumfries in 1780, and died at Applegarth in 1861.

    Rising o'er the heaving billow,
      Evening gilds the ocean's swell,
    While with thee, on grassy pillow,
      Solitude! I love to dwell.
    Lonely to the sea breeze blowing,
      Oft I chaunt my love-lorn strain,
    To the streamlet sweetly flowing,
      Murmur oft a lover's pain.

    'Twas for her, the Maid of Islay,
      Time flew o'er me wing'd with joy;
    'Twas for her, the cheering smile aye
      Beam'd with rapture in my eye.
    Not the tempest raving round me,
      Lightning's flash, or thunder's roll,
    Not the ocean's rage could wound me,
      While her image fill'd my soul.

    Farewell, days of purest pleasure,
      Long your loss my heart shall mourn!
    Farewell, hours of bliss the measure,
      Bliss that never can return.
    Cheerless o'er the wild heath wandering,
      Cheerless o'er the wave-worn shore,
    On the past with sadness pondering,
      Hope's fair visions charm no more.

CORUNNA.

ANDREW SHARPE,

A JOURNEYMAN shoemaker. He died at Perth in 1815, aged 35.

Do you weep for the woes of poor wandering Nelly?
  I love you for that, but of love now no more,
All I had long ago lies entomb'd with my Billy,
  Whose grave rises green on Corunna's lone shore.
Oh! they tell me my Billy looked lovely when dying,
  That round him, the boldest in battle stood crying,
While from his deep wound life's red floods fast were drying,
  At evening's pale close on Corunna's lone shore.

That night Billy died as I lean'd on my pillow,
  I thrice was alarm'd with a knock at my door,
Thrice my name it was call'd with a voice soft and mellow,
  And thrice did I dream of Corunna's lone shore.

Methought Billy stood on the beach where the billow
Boom'd over his head, breaking loud, long and hollow;
In his hand he held waving a flag of green willow;
 Save me, God! he exclaimed, on Corunna's lone shore.

And now when I mind on't, my dear Billy told me,
 While tears wet his eyes, but those tears are no more,
At our parting, he never again would behold me;
 'Twas strange then I thought on Corunna's lone shore.
But shall I ne'er see him when drowsy-eyed night falls,
When thro' the dark arch Luna's tremulous light falls,
As o'er his new grave, slow the glow-worm of night crawls,
 And ghosts of the slain foot Corunna's lone shore.

Yes, yes, on this spot shall these arms infold him,
 For here hath he kiss'd me a thousand times o'er;
How bewilder'd's my brain, now methinks I behold him,
 All bloody and pale on Corunna's lone shore.
Come away, my beloved, come in haste, my dear Billy,
On the wind's wafting wing to thy languishing Nelly,
I've got kisses in store, I've got secrets to tell thee,
 Come, ghost of my love, from Corunna's lone shore.

Oh! I'm told that my blue eyes have lost all their splendour,
 That my locks, once so yellow, now wave thin and hoar,
'Tis, they tell me, because I'm so restless to wander,
 And in thinking so much on Corunna's lone shore.
But, God help me, where can I go to forget him;
If to father's at home, in each corner I meet him,
The sofa, alas! where he us'd aye to seat him,
 Says, Think, Nelly, think on Corunna's lone shore.

And here as I travel all tatter'd and torn,
 By bramble and brier, over mountain and moor,
Not a bird bounds aloft to salute the new morn,
 But warbles aloud, O Corunna's lone shore!
It is heard in the blast when the tempest is blowing,
It is heard on the white broken waterfall flowing,
It is heard in the songs of the reaping and mowing,—
 Oh, my poor bleeding heart! Oh, Corunna's lone shore!

OCTOBER WINDS.

JAMES SCADLOCK,

An intimate friend of Tannahill. He was a native of Renfrewshire, and while pursuing his trade of copperplate engraving, he devoted a part of his time to the service of the muses. He died in 1818. A volume of his poems was published shortly after his death.

October winds, wi' biting breath,
  Now nip the leaves that's yellow fading;
Nae gowans glint upon the green,
  Alas! they're co'er'd wi' winter's cleading.
As through the woods I musing gang,
  Nae birdies cheer me frae the bushes,
Save little Robin's lonely sang,
  Wild warbling where the burnie gushes.

The sun is jogging down the brae,
  Dimly through the mist he's shining,
And cranroogh hoar creeps o'er the grass,
  As day resigns his throne to e'ening.
Oft let me walk at twilight gray,
  To view the face of dying nature,
Till spring again wi' mantle green,
  Delights the heart o' ilka creature.

CAULD KAIL IN ABERDEEN.

ALEXANDER, FOURTH DUKE OF GORDON,

Born in 1743, died, 1827. Mr. Chambers surmises that the expression "Cauld Kail in Aberdeen," does not refer to any "mess connected with the ancient city, but a metaphorical allusion to the faded love-fervours of an aged nobleman who, in spite of years, was presuming to pay his addresses to a young lady."

There's cauld kail in Aberdeen,
  And castocks in Stra'bogie,
Gin I ha'e but a bonnie lass,
  Ye're welcome to your cogie.
And ye may sit up a' the night,
  And drink till it be braid day-light:
Gi'e me a lass baith clean and tight,
  To dance the reel o' Bogie.

In cotillions the French excel,
  John Bull loves country dances;
The Spaniards dance fandangoes well;
  Mynheer an allemande prances:
In foursome reels the Scots delight,
  At threesome's they dance wondrous light,
But twasome's ding a' out o' sight,
  Danc'd to the reel o' Bogie.

Come, lads, and view your partners weel,
  Wale each a blythesome rogie:
I'll tak' this lassie to mysel',
  She looks sae clean and vogie:

Now, piper lad, bang up the spring;
  The country fashion is the thing,
To prie their mou's ere we begin
  To dance the reel o' Bogie.

Now ilka lad has got a lass,
  Save yon auld doited fogie,
And ta'en a fling upon the grass,
  As they do in Stra'bogie;
But a' the lassies look sae fain,
We canna think oursel's to hain;
For they maun ha'e their come-again
  To dance the reel o' Bogie.

Now a' the lads ha'e done their best,
  Like true men o' Stra'bogie;
We'll stop a-while and tak' a rest,
  And tipple out a cogie.
Come now, my lads, and tak' your glass,
And try ilk other to surpass,
In wishing health to ev'ry lass,
  To dance the reel o' Bogie.

OH WHERE, TELL ME WHERE.

MRS. GRANT, OF LAGGAN,

Born at Glasgow in 1755. In 1779 she married the Rev. James Grant, afterwards Minister of Laggan in Inverness-shire. He died in 1801, leaving her a widow with eight children to support. In 1825 she received a pension of £50 per annum from the government, which, with the profits gained from her published writings, gave her sufficient means to support herself in comfort. She died at Edinburgh in 1838.

O where, tell me where, is your Highland laddie gone?
O where, tell me where, is your Highland laddie gone?
He's gone with streaming banners, where noble deeds are done,
And my sad heart will tremble till he come safely home.

O where, tell me where, did your Highland laddie stay?
O where, tell me where, did your Highland laddie stay?
He dwelt beneath the holly trees, beside the rapid Spey,
And many a blessing follow'd him, the day he went away.

O what, tell me what, does your Highland laddie wear?
O what, tell me what, does your Highland laddie wear?
A bonnet with a lofty plume, the gallant badge of war,
And a plaid across the manly breast that yet shall wear a star.

Suppose, ah suppose, that some cruel, cruel wound
Should pierce your Highland laddie, and all your hopes confound!
The pipe would play a cheering march, the banners round him by,
The spirit of a Highland chief would lighten in his eye.

But I will hope to see him yet in Scotland's bonnie bounds,
But I will hope to see him yet in Scotland's bonnie bounds,
His native land of liberty shall nurse his glorious wounds,
While wide through all our Highland hills his warlike name resounds.

BLYTHE ARE WE SET.

EBENEZER PICKEN.

A NATIVE of Paisley, where he was born in 1769. He attended the University of Glasgow for several sessions, intending to devote himself to the Ministry. In 1791, however, he became a teacher at Falkirk, and after many ups and downs died at Edinburgh in 1816, in rather reduced circumstances. He published two volumes of poetry in 1813.

BLYTHE are we set wi' ither:
  Fling care ayont the moon;
Nae sae aft we meet thegither!
  Wha wad think o' parting soon?
Though snaw bends down the forest trees,
  And burn and river cease to flow;
Though nature's tide has shor'd to freeze,
  And winter nithers a' below.
    Blythe are we, &c.

Now, round the ingle cheerly met,
  We'll scog the blast and dread nae harm,
Wi' jaws o' toddy reeking het,
  We'll keep the genial current warm.
The friendly crack, the cheerfu' sang,
  Shall cheat the happy hours awa'.
Gar pleasure reign the e'ening lang,
  And laugh at biting frost and snaw.
    Blythe are we, &c.

The cares that cluster round the heart,
  And gar the bosom stound wi' pain,
Shall get a fright afore we part,
  Will gar them fear to come again.
Then, fill about, my winsome chiels,
  The sparkling glass will banish pine:
Nae pain the happy bosom feels,
  Sae free o' care as yours and mine.
    Blythe are we, &c.

TODLIN' HAME.

JOHANNA BAILLIE,

DAUGHTER of Dr. James Baillie, minister of Bothwell. She was born at the manse there in 1762.

There are very few incidents in her quiet life which can be recorded. She early devoted herself to literature. In her twenty-eighth year she published a volume of poems, and in 1798 published the first volume of her "Plays," which at once gave her a high position in the literary world. She died at Hampstead in 1851, at the mature age of eighty-nine.

No one had a higher regard for her talents than Sir Walter Scott, who dedicated one of his poems to her.

WHEN white was my o'erlay as foam o' the linn,
And siller was clinkin' my pouches within;
When my lambkins were bleating on meadow and brae;
As I gaed to my love in new cleeding sae gay,
  Kind was she, and my friends were free,
  But poverty parts gude companie.

How swift pass'd the minutes and hours of delight!
The piper play'd cheerly, the crusie burn'd bright;
And link'd in my hand was the maiden sae dear,
As she footed the floor in her holiday gear.
  Woe is me, and can it then be,
  That poverty parts sic companie!

We met at the fair, we met at the kirk,
We met in the sunshine, and met in the mirk,
And the sounds of her voice, and the blinks of her een,
The cheering and life of my bosom have been.
  Leaves frae the tree at Martinmas flee;
  And poverty parts sweet companie.

At bridal and infare I've braced me wi' pride;
The *bruse* I ha'e won, and a kiss o' the bride;
And loud was the laughter gay fellows among,
When I utter'd my banter and chorus'd my song.
  Dowie to dree are jesting and glee,
  When poverty parts gude companie.

Wherever I gaed the blythe lasses smiled sweet,
And mithers and aunties were mair than discreet,
While kebbuck and bicker were set on the board;
But now they pass by me, and never a word.
  So let it be, for the worldly and slie
  Wi' poverty keep nae companie.

THE SHEPHERD'S SONG.

JOHANNA BAILLIE.

THE gowan glitters on the sward,
  The lav'rock's in the sky,
And Collie on my plaid keeps ward,
  And time is passing by.
    Oh, no! sad an' slow!
    I hear nae welcome sound;
  The shadow of our trystin' bush,
    It wears sae slowly round!

My sheep-bell tinkles frae the west,
  My lambs are bleating near,
But still the sound that I lo'e best,
  Alack! I canna hear.
    Oh, no! sad an' slow!
    The shadow lingers still;
  And like a lanely ghaist I stand,
    And croon upon the hill.

I hear below the water roar,
  The mill wi' clackin' din;
  And Lucky scolding frae her door,
    To bring the bairnies in.
    Oh, no! sad an' slow!
    These are nae sounds for me;
  The shadow of our trystin' bush,
    It creeps sae drearily.

I coft yestreen frae chapman Tam,
  A snood of bonnie blue,
And promised, when our trystin' cam',
  To tie it round her brow.
    Oh, no! sad an' slow!
    The time it winna pass;
  The shadow of that weary thorn
    Is tether'd on the grass.

O now I see her on the way,
  She's past the witches' knowe;
She's climbin' up the brownie's brae—
  My heart is in a lowe.
    Oh, no! 'tis na so!
    'Tis glaumrie I ha'e seen:
  The shadow of that hawthorn bush
    Will move nae mair till e'en.

My book of grace I'll try to read,
   Though conn'd wi' little skill;
When Collie barks I'll raise my head,
   And find her on the hill.
      Oh, no! sad an' slow!
      The time will ne'er be gane;
      The shadow of the tryatin' bush
      Is fix'd like ony stane.

WOO'D AND MARRIED AND A'.
JOHANNA BAILLIE.

THE bride she is winsome and bonnie,
   Her hair it is snooded sae sleek,
And faithful and kind is her Johnnie,
   Yet fast fa' the tears on her cheek.
New pearlings are cause o' her sorrow,
   New pearlings and plenishing too;
The bride that has a' to borrow,
   Has e'en right meikle ado.
      Woo'd and married and a',
      Woo'd and married and a',
      And is na she very weel aff
      To be woo'd and married and a'?

Her mother then hastily spak';
   "The lassie is glaiket wi' pride;
In my pouches I hadna a plack
   The day that I was a bride.
E'en tak' to your wheel and be clever,
   And draw out your thread in the sun,
The gear that is gifted, it never
   Will last like the gear that is won.
      Woo'd an' married an' a',
      Tocher and havings sae sma'
      I think ye are very weel aff,
      To be woo'd and married an' a'."

"Toot, toot!" quo' the gray-headed father,
   "She's less of a bride than a bairn;
She's ta'en like a cowt frae the heather,
   Wi' sense and discretion to learn.
Half husband, I trow, and half daddy,
   As humour inconstantly leans;
A chiel may be constant and steady
   That yokes wi' a mate in her teens.
      'Kerchief to cover sae neat,
      Locks the winds used to blaw,
      I'm baith like to laugh and to greet,
      When I think o' her married at a'."

Then out spak' the wily bridegroom,
　Weel waled were his wordies I ween ;
"I'm rich, though my coffer be toom,
　Wi' the blinks o' your bonnie blue een ;
I'm prouder o' thee by my side,
　Though thy ruffles or ribbons be few,
Than if Kate o' the craft were my bride,
　Wi' purples and pearlings enew.
　　Dear and dearest of ony,
　　Ye're woo'd and bookit and a',
　　And do ye think scorn o' your Johnnie,
　　And grieve to be married at a'."

She turn'd, and she blush'd, and she smil'd,
　And she lookit sae bashfully down ;
The pride o' her heart was beguil'd,
　And she play'd wi' the sleeve o' her gown ;
She twirl'd the tag o' her lace,
　And she nippet her boddice sae blue,
Syne blinket sae sweet in his face,
　And aff like a mawkin she flew.
　　Woo'd and married and a',
　　Married and carried awa',
　　She thinks hersel' very weel aff,
　　To be woo'd and married and a'.

IT FELL ON A MORNING.

JOHANNA BAILLIE.

It fell on a morning whan we were thrang,
　Our kirn was gaun, our cheese was making,
　And bannocks on the girdle baking,
That ane at the door chapt loud and lang.
But the auld gudewife and her Mays sae tight,
Of this stirring and din took sma' notice, I ween
　For a chap at the door, in braid day-light,
Is no like a chap when heard at e'en.

Then the clocksey auld laird of the warlock glen,
　Wha stood without, half cow'd, half cheerie,
　And yearn'd for a sight of his winsome dearie,
Raised up the latch and came crousely ben.
　His coat was new and his o'erlay was white,
And his hose and his mittens were coozy and bein ;
　But a wooer that comes in braid day-light,
Is no like a wooer that comes at e'en.

He greeted the carlin' and lasses sae braw,
And his bare lyart pow he smoothly straiket,
And looked about, like a body half glaiket,
On bonnie sweet Nanny the youngest of a'.
"Ha ha!" quo' the carlin, "and look ye that way?
Hoot! let na sic fancies bewilder ye clean:
An elderlin man i' the noon o' the day,
Should be wiser than youngsters that come at e'en."

"Na na!" quo' the pauky auld wife, "I trow,
You'll fash na' your head wi' a youthfu' gilly,
As wild and as skeigh as a muirland filly,
Black Madge is far better and fitter for you."
He hem'd and he haw'd and he screw'd in his mouth,
And he squeez'd his blue bonnet his twa hands between,
For wooers that come when the sun's in the south,
Are mair ankwart than wooers that come at e'en.

"Black Madge she is prudent."—"What's that to me?"
"She is cident and sober, has sense in her noddle,
Is douse and respeckit."—"I care na a boddle.
I'll baulk na' my luive, and my fancy's free."
Madge toss'd back her head wi' a saucy slight,
And Nanny ran laughing out to the green;
For wooers that come whan the sun shines bright,
Are na like the wooers that come at e'en.

Awa' flung the laird and loud mutter'd he;
"All the daughters of Eve, between Orkney and Tweed, O,
Black and fair, young and old, dame, damsel, and widow,
May gang wi' their pride to the deil for me!"
But the auld gudewife and her Mays sae tight,
For a' his loud banning cared little, I ween;
For a wooer that comes in braid day-light,
Is no like a wooer that comes at e'en.

HOOLY AND FAIRLY.
JOHANNA BAILLIE.

Oh, neighbours! what had I ado for to marry,
My wife she drinks possets and wine o' Canary,
And ca's me a niggardly, thraw-gabbit carly,
O gin my wife wad drink hooly and fairly!
    Hooly and fairly, &c.

She feasts wi' her kimmers on dainties enew,
Aye bowing and smirking and dighting her mou',
While I sit aside and am helpet but sparely,
O gin my wife wad feast hooly and fairly!
    Hooly and fairly, &c.

To fairs and to bridals and preachings and a',
She gangs sae light-hearted and busket sae braw,
It's ribbons and mantuas that gars me gae barely,
O gin my wife would spend hooly and fairly!
    Hooly and fairly, &c.

In the kirk sic commotion last Sabbath she made,
Wi' babs o' red roses and briest-knots o'erlaid,
The dominie sticket his psalm very nearly,
O gin my wife wad dress hooly and fairly!
    Hooly and fairly, &c.

She's warring and flyting frae morning till e'en,
And if ye gainsay her, her eye glowrs sae keen!
Then tongue, neive and cudgel, she'll lay on you sairly!
O gin my wife wad strike hooly and fairly!
    Hooly and fairly, &c.

When tired wi' her cantraps, she lies in her bed,
The wark a' neglecket, the house ill up-red,
When a' our guid neighbours are stirring right early,
O gin my wife wad sleep timely and fairly!
    Hooly and fairly, &c.

A word o' good counsel or grace she'll hear none,
She hardies the elders and mocks at mess John,
And back in his teeth his ain text she flings rarely!
O gin my wife wad speak hooly and fairly!
    Hooly and fairly, &c.

I wish I were single, I wish I were freed,
I wish I were doited, I wish I were dead;
Or she in the mools, to doment me nae mairlay;
What does't avail to cry hooly and fairly?
    Hooly and fairly, hooly and fairly,
    Wasting my breath to cry hooly and fairly!

NEIL GOW'S FAREWEEL.
MRS. LYON.

DAUGHTER of John R. L'Amy of Dunkenny, Forfarshire, was born at Dundee in 1762, and became the wife of Dr. Lyon, Minister of Glammis, to whom she was married in 1786: she died in 1840.

The song here given is stated to have been written by her at the request of the celebrated Neil Gow, to accompany a tune composed by him. It at once became very popular. In Dr. Rogers' "Modern Scottish Minstrel," a copy is printed varying slightly in the phraseology from that here given.

    You've surely heard o' famous Neil,
    The man that play'd the fiddle weel;
    I wat he was a canty chiel,
        And dearly lo'ed the whisky, O!

And, aye sin' he wore the tartan trews,
He dearly liket Athole brose;
And wae was he, you may suppose,
    To play fareweel to whisky, O.

Alake, quoth Neil, I'm frail and auld,
And find my blude grows unco cauld;
I think 'twad make me blythe and bauld,
    A wee drap Highland whisky, O.
Yet the doctors they do a' agree,
That whisky's no the drink for me.
Saul! quoth Neil, 'twill spoil my glee,
    Should they part me and whisky, O.

Though I can baith get wine and ale,
And find my head and fingers hale,
I'll be content, though legs should fail,
    To play fareweel to whisky, O.
But still I think on auld lang syne,
When Paradise our friends did tyne,
Because something ran in their mind—
    Forbid like Highland whisky, O.

Yet I'll tak' my fiddle in my hand,
And screw the pegs up while they'll stand,
To make a lamentation grand,
    On gude auld Highland whisky, O.
Come, a' ye powers o' music, come;
I find my heart grows unco glum;
My fiddle-strings will no play bum,
    To say, Fareweel to whisky, O.

FAIR MODEST FLOWER.

WILLIAM REID,

BORN at Glasgow in 1764. He carried on business as Bookseller and Publisher in Glasgow for twenty-seven years in company with Mr. James Brash. Reid wrote very few complete songs of any moment, his peculiar gift being the knack of adding verses, &c. to already popular songs. He died in 1831.

FAIR modest flower, of matchless worth!
    Thou sweet, enticing, bonnie gem,
Blest is the soil that gave thee birth,
    And blest thine honour'd parent stem.
But doubly blest shall be the youth,
    To whom thy heaving bosom warms;
Possess'd of beauty, love, and truth,
    He'll clasp an angel in his arms.

Though storms of life were blowing snell,
  And on his brow sat brooding care,
Thy seraph smile would quick dispel
  The darkest gloom of black despair.
Sure heaven hath granted thee to us,
  And chose thee from the dwellers there,
And sent thee from celestial bliss,
  To show what all the virtues are.

LASS O' GOWRIE.
WILLIAM REID.

When Katie was scarce out nineteen,
O but she had twa coal-black een;
A bonnier lass ye wadna seen,
  In a' the Carse o' Gowrie.
Quite tired o' livin' a' his lane,
Pate did to her his love explain,
And swore he'd be, were she his ain,
  The happiest lad in Gowrie.

Quo' she, I winna marry thee
For a' the gear that ye can gi'e;
Nor will I gang a step ajee,
  For a' the gowd in Gowrie.
My father will gi'e me twa kye;
My mother's gaun some yarn to dye;
I'll get a gown just like the sky,
  Gif I'll no gang to Gowrie.

Oh, my dear Katie, say na sae;
Ye little ken a heart that's wae;
Ha'e! there's my hand; hear me, I pray,
  Sin' thou'll no gang to Gowrie.
Since first I met thee at the sheil,
My saul to thee's been true and leal;
The darkest night I fear nae deil,
  Warlock, or witch, in Gowrie.

I fear nae want o' claes, nor nought;
Sic silly things my mind ne'er taught.
I dream a' nicht, and start about,
  And wish for thee in Gowrie.
I lo'e thee better, Kate, my dear,
Than a' my riggs and out-gaun gear;
Sit down by me till ance I swear,
  Thou'rt worth the Carse o' Gowrie.

Syne on her mouth sweet kisses laid,
Till blushes a' her cheeks o'erspread;
She sighed, and in soft whispers said,
    O Pate, tak' me to Gowrie!
Quo' he, let's to the auld fouk gang;
Say what they like, I'll bide their bang,
And bide a' nicht, though beds be thrang,
    But I'll ha'e thee to Gowrie.

The auld fouk syne baith gied consent:
The priest was ca'd: a' were content;
And Katie never did repent
    That she gaed hame to Gowrie.
For routh o' bonnie bairns had she;
Mair strappin' lads ye wadna see;
And her braw lasses bore the gree
    Frae a' the rest o' Gowrie.

THE LASS OF ISLA.

SIR ALEXANDER BOSWELL, BART.,

ELDEST son of the celebrated biographer of Dr. Johnson, was born in 1775. He succeeded to the Auchinleck Estate in 1795. Sir Alexander was a keen politician at a time when political feeling ran high in Scotland, and not unfrequently called in the aid of his pen to assist the Tory party. One of his poetic satires was levelled too openly at James Stuart, younger, of Dunearn, and a challenge was the result. The opponents met near the village of Auchtertool in Fife, on the 26th of March, 1822, and resulted in the death of Sir Alexander.

"An, Mary, sweetest Maid, farewell!
    My hopes are flown, for a's to wreck;
Heaven richly guard you, love, and heal
    Your heart, though mine, alas! maun break"—

"Dearest lad, what ills betide?
    Is Willie to his love untrue?
Engaged the morn to be his bride,
    Ah! ha'e ye, ha'e ye ta'en the rue?"

"Ye canna wear a ragged gown,
    Or beggar wed, wi' nought ava;
My kye are drown'd, my house is down,
    My best sheep lies aneath the snaw"—

"Tell na me o' storm or flood,
    Or sheep a' smoor'd ayont the hill,
For Willie's sake, I Willie lo'ed;
    Though poor, ye are my Willie still"—

"Ye canna thole the wind or rain,
  Or wander, friendless, far frae hame;
Cheer, cheer your heart, some other swain
  Will soon blot out lost Willie's name"—
"I'll tak' my bundle in my hand,
  An' wipe the dew-drop frae my e'e,
I'll wander wi' ye o'er the land,
  I'll venture wi' ye through the sea"—
"Forgi'e me, love, 'twas all a snare,
  My flocks are safe, we need na part,
I'd forfeit them, and ten times mair,
  To clasp thee, Mary, to my heart."
"How could ye wi' my feelings sport,
  Or doubt a heart sae warm and true?
I should wish mischief on you for't,
  But canna wish ought ill to you."

TASTE LIFE'S GLAD MOMENTS.

SIR ALEXANDER BOSWELL, BART.

Taste life's glad moments,
  Whilst the wasting taper glows;
Pluck, ere it withers,
  The quickly fading rose.

Man blindly follows grief and care,
He seeks for thorns and finds his share,
Whilst violets to the passing air
  Unheeded shed their blossoms.
    Taste life's, &c.

When tim'rous nature veils her form,
And rolling thunder spreads alarm,
Then, ah! how sweet when, lull'd the storm,
  The sun smiles forth at even.
    Taste life's, &c.

How spleen and envy anxious flies,
And meek content, in humble guise,
Improves the shrub, a tree shall rise,
  Which golden fruits shall yield him.
    Taste life's, &c.

Who fosters faith in upright breast,
And freely gives to the distress'd,
There sweet contentment builds her nest,
  And flutters round his bosom.
    Taste life's, &c.

And when life's path grows dark and strait,
And pressing ills on ills await,
Then friendship, sorrow to abate,
　　The helping hand will offer.
　　　　Taste life's, &c.

She dries his tears, she strews his ways,
E'en to the grave, with flow'rets gay;
Turns night to morn, and morn to day,
　　And pleasure still increases.
　　　　Taste life's, &c.

Of life she is the fairest band,
Joins brothers truly hand in hand;
Thus onward to a better land
　　Man journeys light and cheerly.
　　　　Taste life's, &c.

JENNY'S BAWBEE.

SIR ALEXANDER BOSWELL, BART.

I MET four chaps yon birks amang,
Wi' hinging lugs and faces lang;
I spiered at neebour Bauldy Strang,
　　Wha's they I see?
Quo' he, ilk cream-faced pawky chiel,
Thought he was cunning as the deil,
And here they cam', awa' to steal
　　Jenny's bawbee.

The first, a Captain to his trade,
Wi' skull ill-lined, but back weel-clad,
March'd round the barn, and by the shed,
　　And papped on his knee:
Quo' he, "My goddess, nymph, and queen,
Your beauty's dazzled baith my een!"
But deil a beauty he had seen
　　But—Jenny's bawbee.

A Lawyer neist, wi' blatherin' gab,
Wha speeches wove like ony wab,
In ilk ane's corn aye took a dab,
　　And a' for a fee.
Accounts he owed through a' the toun,
And tradesmen's tongues nae mair could drown,
But now he thocht to clout his goun
　　Wi' Jenny's bawbee.

A Norland Laird neist trotted up,
Wi' bawsand nag and siller whip,
Cried, "There's my beast, lad, haud the grup,
　　Or tie 't till a tree!
What's gowd to me?—I've walth o' lan'!
Bestow on ane o' worth your han'!"—
He thocht to pay what he was awn
　　Wi' Jenny's bawbee.

Drest up just like the knave o' clubs,
A THING came neist, (but life has rubs,)
Foul were the roads, and fu' the dubs,
　　And jaupit a' was he.
He danced up, squinting through a glass,
And grinn'd, "I' faith, a bonnie lass!"
He thought to win, wi' front o' brass,
　　Jenny's bawbee.

She bade the Laird gae kame his wig,
The Sodger no to strut sae big,
The Lawyer no to be a prig,
　　The Fool he cried, "Tehee!
I kenn'd that I could never fail!"
But she preen'd the dishclout to his tail,
And soused him in the water-pail,
　　And kept her bawbee.

Then Johnnie cam', a lad o' sense,
Although he had na mony pence;
And took young Jenny to the spence,
　　Wi' her to crack a wee.
Now Johnnie was a clever chiel,
And here his suit he press'd sae weel,
That Jenny's heart grew saft as jeel,
　　And she birled her bawbee.

JENNY DANG THE WEAVER.
SIR ALEXANDER BOSWELL, BART.

AT Willie's wedding on the green,
　　The lasses, bonnie witches,
Were a' dress'd out in aprons clean,
　　And braw white Sunday mutches;
Auld Maggie bade the lads tak' tent,
　　But Jock would not believe her;
But soon the fool his folly kent,
　　For Jenny dang the Weaver.
　　And Jenny dang, Jenny dang,
　　　　Jenny dang the Weaver;
　　But soon the fool his folly kent,
　　　　For Jenny dang the Weaver.

At ilka country dance or reel,
  Wi' her he would be bobbing;
When she sat down—he sat down,
  And to her would be gabbing;
Where'er she gaed baith butt and ben,
  The coof would never leave her;
Aye kecklin' like a clocking hen,
  But Jenny dang the Weaver.
    Jonny dang, &c.

Quo' he, My lass, to speak my mind,
  In troth I needna swither;
You've bonnie een, and if you're kind,
  I'll never seek anither;
He humm'd and haw'd, the lass cried Peugh!
  And bade the coof no deave her;
Syne snapt her fingers, lap and leugh,
  An'd dang the silly Weaver.
    And Jenny dang, Jenny dang,
      Jenny dang the Weaver;
    Syne snapt her fingers, lap and leugh,
      And dang the silly Weaver.

AULD GUDEMAN YE'RE A DRUCKEN CARLE.

SIR ALEXANDER BOSWELL.

AULD gudeman, ye're a drucken carle, drucken carle;
A' the lang day ye wink and drink, and gape and gaunt;
O' sottish loons ye're the pink and pearl, pink and pearl,
Ill-far'd, doited ne'er-do-weel.

Hech, gudewife! ye're a flyting body, flyting body;
Will ye ha'e; but, guid be praised, the *wit* ye want.
The puttin' cow should be aye a doddy, aye a doddy.
Mak' na sic an awsome reel.

  Ye're a sow, auld man:
  Ye got fou, auld man:
  Fye for shame, auld man;
  To your wame, auld man:
Pinch'd I win, wi' spinnin tow,
A plack to cleid your back and pow.
    It's a lie, gudewife,
    It's your tea, gudewife,
    Na, na, gudewife,
    Ye spend a', gudewife.
  Dinna fa' on me peil-mell,
  Ye like the drap fu' weel yoursel.

Ye's rue auld gowk, your jest and frolic, jest and frolic.
Dare ye say, goose, I ever liked to tak' a drappy?
An 'twerena just to cure the cholic, cure the cholic,
　Deil a drap wad weet my mou'.

Troth, gudewife, an' ye wadna swither, wadna swither,
Soon to tak' a cholic, when it brings a drap o' cappy.
But twascore years we ha'e fought thegither, fought thegither;
　Time it is to gree, I trow.

　　　I'm wrang, auld John,
　　　Ower lang, auld John,
　　　For nought, gude John,
　　　We ha'e fought, gude John;
　　Let's help to bear ilk ither's weight,
　　We're far ower feckless now to fight.
　　　Ye're richt, gude Kate;
　　　The nicht, gude Kate,
　　　Our cup, gude Kate,
　　　We'll sup, gude Kate;
　　Thegither frae this hour we'll draw,
　　And toom the stoup atween us twa.

SAE WILL WE YET.

WALTER WATSON,

A WEAVER at Chryston, in Stirlingshire. He published in 1808 a volume of poems, which was well received, and several of the songs there printed became very popular. In 1823 and 1846 he issued volumes, and in 1853 a selected edition of his best pieces was issued under the editorship of Mr. Hugh Macdonald. He died in 1854 in his seventy-fifth year.

SIT ye down here, my cronies, and gi'e us your crack,
Let the win' tak' the care o' this life on its back,
Our hearts to despondency we never will submit,
For we've aye been provided for, and sae will we yet.
　　And sae will we yet, &c.

Let the miser delight in the hoarding of pelf,
Since he has not the saul to enjoy it himself:
Since the bounty of providence is new every day,
As we journey through life, let us live by the way.
　　Let us live by the way, &c.

Then bring us a tankard o' nappy gude ale,
For to comfort our hearts and enliven the tale;
We'll aye be the merrier the langer we sit,
For we've drank thegither mony a time, and sae will we yet.
　　And sae will we yet, &c.

Success to the farmer, and prosper his plough,
Rewarding his eident toils a' the year through!
Our seed time and harvest we ever will get,
For we've lippen'd aye to Providence, and sae will we yet.
    And sae will we yet.

Long live the king, and happy may he be,
And success to his forces by land and by sea!
His enemies to triumph we never will permit,
Britons aye have been victorious, and sae will they yet.
    And sae will they yet, &c.

Let the glass keep its course, and go merrily roun',
For the sun has to rise, though the moon it goes down,
Till the house be rinnin' roun' about, it's time enough to flit;
When we fell, we aye got up again, and sae will we yet.
    And sae will we yet, &c.

THE BRAES O' BEDLAY.

WALTER WATSON.

When I think on the sweet smiles o' my lassie,
  My cares flee awa' like a thief frae the day;
My heart loups light, an' I join in a sang
  Amang the sweet birds on the braes o' Bedlay;
How sweet the embrace, yet how honest the wishes,
When luve fa's a-wooin', an' modesty blushes;
Whar Mary an' I meet amang the green bushes,
  That screen us sae weel on the braes o' Bedlay.

There's nane sae trig, or sae fair, as my lassie,
  An' mony a wooer she answers wi' Nay,
Wha fain wad ha'e her to lea'e me alane,
  An' meet me nae mair on the braes o' Bedlay.
I fearna, I carena, their braggin' o' siller,
Nor a' the fine things they can think on to tell her:
Nae vauntin' can buy her, nae threat'nin' can sell her,
  It's luve leads her out to the braes o' Bedlay.

We'll gang by the links o' the wild rowin' burnie,
  Whar aft in my mornin' o' life I did stray,
Whar luve was invited and care was beguil'd,
  By Mary an' me, on the braes o' Bedlay;
Sae lovin', sae movin', I'll tell her my story,
Unmix't wi' the deeds o' ambition for glory,
Whar wide spreadin' hawthorns, sae ancient and hoary,
  Enrich the sweet breeze on the braes o' Bedlay.

BOBBING JOHN.
ROBERT JAMIESON.

EDITOR of "Popular Ballads and Songs," 1806. A native of Moray, where he was born in 1780. He held for a long time the position of Assistant Deputy Clerk Register. He died in London in 1844.

HEY for bobbing John!
  Kittle up the chanter!
Bang up a strathspey,
  So fling wi' John the ranter.
Johnnie's stout an' bald,
  Ne'er could thole a banter;
Bein in byre and fauld,
  An', lasses, he's a wanter!

Back as braid's a door;
  Bowhought like a filly;
Thick about the brawns,
  An' o'er the breast and belly.
Hey for bobbing John!
  Kittle up the chanter!
Queans are a' gane gyte,
  To fling wi' John the ranter.

Bonnie's his black e'e,
  Blinkin', blythe, and vogie,
Wi' lassie on his knee,
  In his nieve a coggie;
Syne the lad will kiss,
  Sweetly kiss an' cuddle;
Cauld wad be her heart,
  That could wi' Johnnie widdle.

Sonsc fa' bobbing John;
  Want an' wae gae by him;
There's in town nor land
  Nae chiel disna envy him.
Flingin' to the pipe,
  Bobbing to the fiddle,
Kneif was ilka lass,
  That could wi' Johnnie meddle.

GO TO HIM.
ROBERT JAMIESON.

Go to him, then, if thou canst go;
  Waste not a thought on me;
My heart and mind are a' my store;—
  They ance were dear to thee.

But there is music in his gold,
  (I ne'er sae sweet could sing,)
That finds a chord in every breast,
  In unison to ring.
The modest virtues dread the spell;
  The honest loves retire;
The finer sympathies of soul
  Far other charms require.
The breathings of my plaintive reed
  Sink dying in despair;
The still small voice of gratitude,
  Even that is heard nae mair.

But, if thy heart can suffer thee,
  The powerful cause obey;
And mount the splendid bed that wealth
  And pride for thee display.
There gaily bid farewell to a'
  Love's trembling hopes and fears;
While I my lonely pillow, here,
  Wash with unceasing tears.

Yet, in the fremmit arms of him,
  That half thy worth ne'er knew,
O think na on my lang-tried love,
  How tender and how true!
For sure 'twould break thy tender heart,
  My breaking heart to see,
Wi' a' the wrangs and waes it tholed,
  And yet maun thole for thee.

THE QUERN LILT.

ROBERT JAMIESON.

The *cronach* stills the dowie heart,
  The *jurram* stills the bairnie;
The music for a hungry wame
  Is grinding o' the quernie.
    And loes me o' my little quernie!
    Grind the graddan, grind it:
    We'll a' get crowdie whan it's done
    And bannocks steeve to bind it.

The married man his joy may prize:
  The lover prize his arles;
But gin the quernie gangna round,
  They baith will soon be aareless.
    Sae loes me, &c.

The whisky gars the bark o' life
  Drive merrily and rarely;
But graddan is the ballast gars
  It steady gang and fairly.
    Then loes me, &c.

Though winter steeks the door wi' drift,
  And o'er the inglo hings us;
Let but the little quernie gae,
  We're blythe, whatever dings us.
    Then loes me, &c.

And how it cheers the herd at e'en,
  And sets his heart-strings dirlin',
When comin' frae the hungry hill,
  He hears the quernie birlin'!
    Then loes me, &c.

Though sturt and stride wi' young and auld,
  And flytin' butt and ben be;
Let but the quernie play, they'll soon
  A' lown and fidgin'-fain be.
    Then loes me, &c.

THE LANDART LAIRD.
FROM JAMIESON'S BALLADS.

THERE lives a landart laird in Fife,
And he has married a dandily wife;
She wadna shape, nor yet wad she sew,
But sit wi' her cummers, and fill hersel' fu'.
She wadna spin, nor yet wad she card;
But she wad sit and crack wi' the laird:
Sae he is donn to the sheep-fauld,
And cleekit a wother by the spauld.
He's whirled aff the gude wether's skin,
And wrapped the dandily lady therein.
"I downa pay you, for your gentle kin;
But weel may I skelp my wether's skin."

TRANENT WEDDING.
PETER FORBES,

A GARDENER at Dalkeith. He published a volume of poems in 1812.

IT was at a wedding near Tranent,
Where scores an' scores on fun were bent,
An' to ride the broose wi' full intent,
  Was either nine or ten, jo!
    Then aff they a' set galloping, galloping,
    Legs an' arms a walloping, walloping,
    Shame take the hindmost, quo' Duncan M'Callapin,
    Laird o' Tullyben, jo.

The souter he was fidgin' fain,
An' stuck like roset till the mane,
Till smash like auld boots in a drain,
　He nearly reach'd his end, jo!
　　Yet still they a' gade, &c.

The miller's mare flew o'er the souter,
An syne began to glow'r about her,
Cries Hab, I'll gi'e you double mouter,
　Gin ye'll ding Tullyben, jo.
　　Then still they a' gade, &c.

Now Will the weaver rode sae kittle,
Ye'd thought he was a flying shuttle,
His doup it daddet like a bittle,
　But wafted till the end, jo.
　　Yet still they a' gade, &c.

The tailor had an awkward beast,
It funket first an' syne did reest,
Then threw poor Snipe five ell at least,
　Like auld breeks, o'er the mane, jo.
　　Yet a' the rest gade, &c.

The blacksmith's beast was last of a',
Its sides like bellowses did blaw,
Till he an' it got sic a fa',
　An' bruises nine or ten, jo.
　　An' still the lave gade, &c.

Now Duncan's mare she flew like drift,
An' aye sae fast her feet did lift,
Between ilk stenn she ga'e a rift,
　Out frae her hinder end, jo.
　　Yet aff they a' gade, &c.

Now Duncan's mare did bang them a',
To rin wi' him they maunna fa',
Then up his gray mare he did draw,
　The broose it was his ain, jo.
　　Nae mair wi' him they'll gallop, they'll gallop,
　　Nae mair wi' him they'll wallop, they'll wallop,
　　Or they will chance to get some jallup,
　　Frae the laird o' Tullyben, jo.

ROW WEEL, MY BOATIE.
ANONYMOUS.

APPEARED in 1816. Air by R. A. Smith.

Row weel, my boatie, row weel,
 Row weel, my merry men a',
For there's dool and there's wae in Glenfiorich's bowers,
 And there's grief in my father's ha'.

And the skiff it danc'd light on the merry wee waves,
 And it flow ower the water sae blue,
And the wind it blew light, and the moon it shone bright,
 But the boatie ne'er reached Allandhu.

Ohon! for fair Ellen, ohon!
 Ohon! for the pride of Strathcoe—
In the deep, deep sea, in the salt, salt bree,
 Lord Reoch, thy Ellen lies low.

THE HILLS O' GALLOWA'.
THOMAS M. CUNNINGHAM,

BORN 1776, died at London in 1834. An elder brother of Allan Cunningham. He was principal clerk to Rennie the celebrated Engineer. His poems were principally contributed to "The Scots Magazine," and the "Edinburgh Magazine."

Amang the birks sae blythe an' gay,
 I met my Julia hameward gaun;
The linties chauntit on the spray,
 The lammies loupit on the lawn;
On ilka howm the sward was mawn,
 The braes wi' gowans buskit bra',
An' gloamin's plaid o' gray was thrawn
 Out owre the hills o' Gallowa'.

Wi' music wild the woodlands rang,
 An' fragrance wing'd alang the lea,
As down we sat the flowers amang,
 Upon the banks o' stately Dee;
My Julia's arms encircled me,
 An' saftly slade the hours awa',
Till dawin coost a glimmerin' e'e
 Upon the hills o' Gallowa'.

It isna owsen, sheep, and kye,
 It isna gowd, it isna gear,
This lifted e'e wad ha'e, quoth I,
 The warld's drumlie gloom to cheer.

2 B

But gi'e to me my Julia dear,
  Ye powers wha rowe this yirthen ba',
An' O! sae blythe through life I'll steer,
  Amang the hills o' Gallowa'.

Whan gloamin' dauners up the hill,
  An' our gudeman ca's hame the yowes,
Wi' her I'll trace the mossy rill
  That owre the muir meand'ring rowes;
Or tint amang the scroggy knowes,
  My birken pipe I'll sweetly blaw,
An' sing the streams, the straths, and howes,
  The hills an' dales o' Gallowa'.

An' whan auld Scotland's heathy hills,
  Her rural nymphs an' jovial swains,
Her flow'ry wilds an' wimpling rills,
  Awake nae mair my canty strains;
Whare friendship dwells an' freedom reigns,
  Whare heather blooms an' muircocks craw,
O! dig my grave, and hide my banes
  Amang the hills o' Gallowa'.

THE BRAES OF BALLAHUN.
THOMAS CUNNINGHAM.

Now smiling summer's balmy breeze,
Soft whispering, fans the leafy trees:
The linnet greets the rosy morn,
Sweet in yon fragrant flowery thorn;
The bee hums round the woodbine bower,
Collecting sweets from every flower;
And pure the crystal streamlets run
Amang the braes of Ballahun.

O blissful days, for ever fled,
When wand'ring wild as Fancy led,
I ranged the bushy bosom'd glen,
The scroggie shaw, the rugged linn,
And mark'd each blooming hawthorn bush,
Where nestling sat the speckled thrush;
Or careless roaming, wandered on,
Amang the braes of Ballahun.

Why starts the tear, why bursts the sigh,
When hills and dales rebound with joy?
The flowery glen, and lilied lea
In vain display their charms to me.

I joyless roam the heathy waste,
To soothe this sad, this troubled breast;
And seek the haunts of men to shun
Amang the braes of Ballahun.

The virgin blush of lovely youth,
The angel smile of artless truth,
This breast illum'd with heavenly joy,
Which lyart time can ne'er destroy:
O Julia dear!—the parting look,
The sad farewell we sorrowing took,
Still haunts me as I stray alone
Amang the braes of Ballahun.

ADVICE TO THE LASSIES.
J. BURT,

A NATIVE of Knockmarlock in Ayrshire, where he was born in 1790. He was bred a weaver and worked at that trade till 1807, when he was pressed on one of His Majesty's ships of war, *The Magnificent*, where he served for five years. On his return to Scotland, he worked again for a while at his trade, then he opened a small school in Kilmarnock. In 1816 he went to Paisley, still following his new profession of teacher, but not meeting with success, he emigrated in the following year to America, when he became a licentiate of the Presbyterian Church. He finally settled in Philadelphia as Pastor of a Presbyterian Church there. A life of adventure truly, with the golden ending so seldom allotted to poets.

LASSIES, lookna sourly meek,
  But laugh an' love in youth's gay morn:
If ance the bloom forsake your cheek,
  Fareweel your heuks, the hairst is shorn.

The secret favour that you meet,
  Or the favour ye return,
If vainly ye let ithers see't,
  Fareweel your heuks, the hairst is shorn.

Wi' care the tender moments grip,
  When your cautious lovers burn;
But if you let that moment slip,
  Fareweel your heuks, the hairst is shorn.

Be on your guard wi' Sir or Laird;
  A' ties but that o' marriage spurn;
For if ye grant what he may want,
  Fareweel your heuks, your hairst is shorn.

The lad that's wi your siller ta'en,
  Reject his vows wi' honest scorn;
For ance the glitterin' ore's his ain,
  Fareweel your heuks, the hairst is shorn.

Widows rest you as ye are—
Nae lover now dare crook his horn;
But mak' him master o' your gear—
Fareweel your heuks, the hairst is shorn.

Lassies that nae lads ha'e got,
But live in garrets lane and lorn,
Let ilk be carefu' o' her cat—
Ne'er think o' heuks—your hairst is shorn.

O'ER THE MIST-SHROUDED CLIFTS.
JOHN BURTT.

O'ER the mist-shrouded clifts of the gray mountain straying,
Where the wild winds of winter incessantly rave;
What woes wring my heart, while intently surveying
The storm's gloomy path on the breast of the wave.
Ye foam-crested billows allow me to wail,
Ere ye toss me afar from my loved native shore;
Where the flower which bloom'd sweetest in Coila's green vale,
The pride of my bosom, my Mary's no more!

No more by the banks of the streamlet we'll wander,
And smile at the moon's rimpled face in the wave;
No more shall my arms cling with fondness around her,
For the dew-drops of morning fall cold on her grave.
No more shall the soft thrill of love warm my breast,
I haste with the storm to a far distant shore,
Where unknown, unlamented, my ashes shall rest,
And joy shall revisit my bosom no more.

TO THINK O' THEE.
JOHN BURTT.

O LASSIE I lo'e dearest,
Mair fair to me than fairest,
Mair rare to me than rarest;
  How sweet to think o' thee!
When blythe the blue e'ed dawnin'
Steals saftly o'er the lawnin',
And furls night's sable awnin',
  I love to think o' thee.

An' while the honied dew-drap
Still trembles at the flower-tap,
The fairest bud I pu't up,
  An' kiss't for sake o' thee;

An' when by stream, or fountain,
In glen, or on the mountain,
The lingering moments counting,
  I pause an' think o' thee.

When the sun's red-rays are streamin',
Warm on the meadow beamin',
Or o'er the loch wild gleamin',
  My heart is fu' o' thee.
An' tardy-footed gloamin',
Out o'er the hills slow comin',
Still finds me lanely roamin',
  And thinkin' still o' thee.

When soughs the distant billow,
An' night blasts shake the willow,
Stretch'd on my lanely pillow
  My dreams are a' o' thee.
Then think when frien's caress thee,
O think when cares distress thee,
O think when pleasures bless thee,
  O' him that thinks o' thee!

AND CAN THY BOSOM BEAR THE THOUGHT?

JOHN GOLDIE,

Born at Ayr in 1793. He was for some time Editor of the Ayr Courier, but latterly conducted the Paisley Advertiser. He died suddenly in 1826.

And can thy bosom bear the thought,
  To part frae love and me, laddie?
Are all those plighted vows forgot,
  Sae fondly pledged by thee, laddie?
Can'st thou forget the midnight hour,
When in yon love-inspiring bower,
You vow'd by every heavenly power,
  You'd ne'er lo'e ane but me, laddie?
Wilt thou—wilt thou gang and leave me,
Win my heart, and then deceive me?
Oh! that heart will break, believe me,
  Gin ye part wi' me, laddie.

Aft ha'e ye roos'd my rosy cheek,
  Aft prais'd my sparkling e'e, laddie,
Aft said nae bliss on earth ye'd seek,
  But love and live wi' me, laddie.
But soon those cheeks will lose their red,
Those eyes in endless sleep be hid,

And 'neath the turf the heart be laid,
  That beats for love, and thee, laddie.
Wilt thou—wilt thou gang and leave me,
Win my heart and then deceive me?
Oh! that heart will break, believe me,
  Gin ye part frae me, laddie.

You'll meet a form mair sweet and fair,
  Where rarer beauties shine, laddie,
But oh! the heart can never bear,
  A love sae true as mine, laddie.
But when that heart is laid at rest,
That heart that lo'ed ye last and best,
Oh, then the pangs that rend thy breast,
  Will sharper be than mine, laddie.
Broken vows will vex and grieve me,
Till a broken heart relieve me,
Yet its latest thought, believe me,
  Will be love and thine, laddie.

SWEET'S THE DEW-DECK'D ROSE.
JOHN GOLDIE.

Sweet's the dew-deck't rose in June,
  And lily fair to see, Annie,
But there's ne'er a flower that blooms,
  Is half so fair as thee, Annie.
Beside those blooming cheeks o' thine,
The opening rose its beauties tine,
Thy lips the rubies far outshine;
  Love sparkles in thy e'e, Annie.

The snow that decks yon mountain top,
  Nae purer is than thee, Annie;
The haughty mien, and pridefu' look,
  Are banish'd far frae thee, Annie;
And in thy sweet angelic face,
Triumphant beams each modest grace,
" And ne'er did Grecian chisel trace,"
  A form sae bright as thine, Annie.

Wha could behold thy rosy cheek,
  And no feel love's sharp pang, Annie,
What heart could view thy smiling looks,
  And plot to do thee wrang, Annie.
Thy name in ilka sang I'll weave,
My heart, my soul wi' thee I'll leave,
And never, till I cease to breathe,
  I'll cease to think on thee, Annie.

VITTORIA.

WILLIAM GLEN.

A NATIVE of Glasgow. "He was, for some period of his life," says Mr. Whitelaw, "a manufacturer in his native city, but his latter days were marked by the poet's too frequent lot, poverty and misfortune." He died in 1826. A volume of "Poems," chiefly lyrical, was published by him in 1815.

Sing a' ye bards wi' loud acclaim,
High glory gi'e to gallant Grahame,
Heap laurels on our Marshal's fame,
    Wha conquer'd at Vittoria.
Triumphant freedom smiled on Spain,
An' raised her stately form again,
Whan the British Lion shook his mane
    On the mountains o' Vittoria.

Let blust'rin' Suchet crously crack,
Let Joseph tin the coward's track,
And Jourdan wish his baton back,
    He left upon Vittoria;
If e'er they meet their worthy king,
Let them dance roun' him in a ring,
An' some Scottish piper play the spring
    He blew them at Vittoria.

Gi'e truth an' honour to the Dane,
Gi'e German's monarch heart and brain;
But aye in such a cause as Spain,
    Gi'e Britons a Vittoria.
The English Rose was ne'er sae red,
The Shamrock waved whare glory led,
And the Scottish Thistle raised its head,
    An' smiled upon Vittoria.

Loud was the battle's stormy swell,
Whare thousands fought and mony fell;
But the Glasgow heroes bore the bell
    At the battle of Vittoria.
The Paris maids may ban them a',
Their lads are maistly wede awa',
An' cauld an' pale as wreaths o' snaw
    They lie upon Vittoria.

Wi' quakin' heart and tremblin' knees
The Eagle standard-bearer flees,
While the "meteor flag" floats to the breeze,
    An' wantons on Vittoria.
Britannia's glory there was shown,
By the undaunted Wellington,
An' the tyrant trembled on his throne,
    Whan hearin' o' Vittoria.

Peace to the spirits o' the brave,
Let a' their trophies for them wave,
An' green be our Cadogan's grave,
　Upon thy field, Vittoria!
There let eternal laurels bloom,
While maidens mourn his early doom,
An' deck his lowly honour'd tomb
　Wi' roses on Vittoria.

Ye Caledonian war-pipes play,
Barossa heard your Highlan' lay,
An' the gallant Scot show'd there that day,
　A prelude to Vittoria.
Shout to the heroes—swell ilk voice,
To them wha made poor Spain rejoice,
Shout Wellington an' Lynedoch, boys.
　Barossa an' Vittoria!

GLASGOW FAIR.

JOHN BRECKENRIDGE,

A COMPOSITOR in Glasgow about 1820.

O, THE sun frae the eastward was peeping,
　And braid through the winnocks did stare,
When Willie cried—Tam, are ye sleeping?
　Mak' haste, man, and rise to the fair;
For the lads and the lasses are thranging,
　And a' body's now in a steer;
Fye, haste ye, and let us be ganging,
　Or, faith, we'll be langsome I fear.
　　Lilt te turan an uran, &c.

Then Tam he got up in a hurry,
　And wow but he made himsel' snod,
And a pint o' milk brose he did worry,
　To mak him mair teugh for the road:
On his head his blue bonnet he slippet,
　His whip o'er his shouther he flang,
And a clumsy oak cudgel he grippet,
　On purpose the loons for to bang.
　　Lilt te turan an uran, &c.

Now Willock had trysted wi' Jenny,
　For she was a braw canty quean,
Word gade that she had a gay penny,
　For whilk Willie fondly did grean.

Now Tam he was blaming the liquor,
  Yes night he had got himsel' fou,
And trysted gleed Maggy MacVicar,
  And faith he thocht shame for to rue.
    Lilt te turan an uran, &c.

The carles, fu' cadgie, sat cocking
  Upon their white nags and their brown,
Wi' snuffing, and laughing, and joking,
  They soon cantered into the town;
'Twas there was the funning and sporting,
  Eh! lord what a swarm o' braw folk,
Rowly-powly, wild beasts, wheel o' fortune,
  Sweety stan's, Maister Punch, and black Jock.
    Lilt te turan an uran, &c.

Now Willock and Tam gayan bouzie,
  By this time had met wi' their joes,
Consented wi' Gibbie and Susy
  To gang awa' down to the shows;
'Twas there was the fiddling and drumming,
  Sic a crowd they could scarcely get through,
Fiddles, trumpets, and organs a bumming;
  O, Sirs, what a hully-baloo!
    Lilt te turan an uran, &c.

Then hie to the tents at the paling,
  Weel theeked wi' blankets and mats,
And deals seated round like a tap-room,
  Supported on stanes and on pats;
The whisky like water they're selling;
  And porter as sma' as their yill,—
And aye as you're pouring they're telling,
  "Troth, dear, it's just sixpence the gill!"
    Lilt te turan an uran, &c.

Says Meg—" See yon beast wi' the claes on't,
  Wi' the face o't as black as the soot,
Preserve's! it has fingers and taes on't—
  Eh, lass, it's an unco like brute!"
"O, woman, but ye are a gomeral,
  To mak' sic a won'er at that,
D'ye na ken, you daft gowk, that's a mongrel,
  That's bred 'twixt a dog and a cat."
    Lilt te turan an uran, &c.

"See yon sonple jaud how she's dancing,
  Wi' the white ruffled breeks and red shoon,
Frae the tap to the tae she's a' glancing
  Wi' gowd, and a feather aboon.—

My troth, she's a braw decent kimmer,
  As I have yet seen in the fair."
"Her decent!" quo' Meg, "she's a limmer,
  Or, faith, she would never be there."
    Lilt te turan an uran, &c.

Now Gibbie was wanting a toothfu',
  Says he, "I'm right tired o' the fun,
D'ye think we'd be the waur o' a mouthfu'
  O gude nappy yill and a bun?"
"Wi' a' my heart," Tam says, "I'm willing,—
  'Tis best for to water the corn;
By jing, I've a bonnie white shilling,
  And a saxpence that ne'er saw the morn."
    Lilt te turan an uran, &c.

Before they got out o' the bustle,
  Poor Tam got his fairing I trow,
For a stick at the ginge'bread play'd whistle,
  And knocked him down like a cow;
Says Tam, "Wha did that, deil confound him—
  Fair play, let me win at the loon,"
And he whirled his stick round and round him,
  And swore like a very dragoon.
    Lilt te turan an uran, &c.

Then next for a house they gaed glow'ring,
  Whare they might get wetting their mou'.
Says Meg, "Here's a house keeps a pouring,
  Wi' the sign o' the muckle black cow."
"A cow!" quo' Jenny, "ye gawky!
  Preserve us! but ye've little skill,
Did ye e'er see a hawky like that—
  Look again and ye'll see it's a *bill*."
    Lilt te turan an uran, &c.

But just as they darken'd the entry,
  Says Willie, "We're now far enough,
I see it's a house for the gentry—
  Let's gang to the sign o' the pleugh."
"Na faith," then says Gibbie, "we'se raither
  Gae dauner to auld Luckie Gunn's,
For there I'm to meet wi' my faither,
  And auld uncle John o' the Whins."
    Lilt te turan an uran, &c.

Now they a' in Luckie's had landed,
  Twa rounds at the bicker to try,
The whisky and yill round was handed
  And baps in great bourocks did lie.

Blind Aleck the fiddler was trysted,
And he was to handle the bow;
On a big barrel head he was hoisted,
To keep himsel' oot o' the row.
 Lilt te turan an uran, &c.

Had ye seen sic a din and guffawing,
Sic hooching and dancing was there,
Sic rugging, and riving, and drawing,
Was ne'er seen before in a fair.
For Tam, he wi' Maggy was wheeling,
And he gied sic a terrible loup,
That his head came a thump on the ceiling,
And he cam' down wi' a dump on his doup.
 Lilt te turan an uran, &c.

Now they ate and they drank till their bellies
Were bent like the head o' a drum,
Syne they raise, and they capered like fillies,
Whene'er that the fiddle played bum.
Wi' dancing they now were grown weary,
And scarcely were able to stan',
So they took to the road a' fu' cheery,
As day was beginning to dawn.
 Lilt te turan an uran, &c.

WOO'D AND MARRIED AND A'.
MRS. SCOTT,
Of Dumbartonshire. Written about 1810.

The grass had nae freedom o' growin'
As lang as she wasna awa',
Nor in the toun could there be stowin'
For wooers that wanted to ca'.
Sic boxin', sic brawlin', sic dancin',
Sic bowin' and shakin' a paw;
The toun was for ever in brulyies:
But now the lassie's awa'.
 Wooed, and married, and a',
 Married, and wooed, and a';
 The dandalie toast of the parish,
  She's wooed, and she's carried awa'.

But had he a' kenn'd her as I did,
His wooin' it wad ha'e been sma':
She kens neither bakin', nor brewin',
Nor cardin', nor spinnin' ava;

But a' her skill lies in her buskin':
　And, O, if her braws were awa',
She sune wad wear out o' fashion,
　And knit up her huggers wi' straw.

But yesterday I gaed to see her,
　And, O, she was bonnie and braw;
She cried on her gudeman to gi'e her
　An ell o' red ribbon or twa.
He took, and he set down beside her
　A wheel and a reel for to ca';
She cried, Was he that way to guide her?
　And out at the door and awa'.

The first road she gaed was her mither,
　Wha said, Lassie, how gaes a'?
Quo' she, Was it for nae ither
　That I was married awa',
But to be set down to a wheelie,
　And at it for ever to ca'?
And syne to hae't reel'd by a chieldie
　That's everly crying to draw.

Her mither said till her, Hech, lassie!
　He's wisest, I fear, o' the twa;
There'll be little to put in the tassie,
　Gif ye be sae backward to draw;
For now ye should work like a tiger,
　And at it baith wallop and ca',
Sae lang's ye ha'e youdith and vigour,
　And weanies and debt keep awa'.

Sae swift away hame to your haddin',
　The mair fule ye e'er came awa';
Ye maunna be ilka day gaddin',
　Nor gang sae white-finger'd and braw;
For now wi' a neebor ye're yokit,
　And wi' him should cannilie draw;
Or else ye deserve to be knockit—
　So that's an answer for a'.

Young Luckie thus fand hersell mither'd,
　And wish'd she had ne'er come awa';
At length wi' hersell she consider'd,
　That hameward 'twas better to draw,
And e'en tak' a chance o' the landin',
　However that matters might fa':
Folk maunna on freits aye be standin',
　That's wooed, and married, and a'.

THE FOLK AT LINDORES.

JAMES STIRLING,

A SCHOOLMASTER in Glasgow about 1820.

O WEEL may I mind on the folk at Lindores;
Though it's lang sin' I had onie troke at Lindores;
    For the blythe winter night
    Flew o'er us fu' light,
Wi' the sang, an' the crack, an' the joke at Lindores.

The auld wife an' the lasses would spin at Lindores;
An' the auld man to tales would begin at Lindores,
    How in days o' his youth
    The red rebels cam' south,
An' spulzied the feck o' his kin at Lindores.

An' he'd tell monie strange says and saws at Lindores;
How he hated the dominie's tawse at Lindores,
    How i' the lang-day
    The truan' he'd play,
An' set aff to herrie the craws at Lindores.

An' he'd sing monie an auld warld rhyme at Lindores;
An' tall o' the Covenant time at Lindores;
    How Clavers, fell chiel'!
    Was in league wi' the deil,
How a ball stottit ance aff his wame at Lindores.

They were kind to ilk body that came to Lindores,
To the puir, an' the blind, an' the lame at Lindores;
    Wi' handfuls o' meal,
    An' wi' platefuls o' kale,
An' the stranger was sure o' a hame at Lindores.

But the auld man's departed this life at Lindores;
An' a tear's in the e'e o' the wife at Lindores;
    I dinna weel ken
    Whan I'll be there again,
But sorrow, I'm fearin', is rife at Lindores.

JENNY'S DAWBEE.

FROM CHAMBERS'S SONGS.

"This song," says Mr. Chambers, "the composition as I have been informed of a clergyman in Galloway, was never before printed."

WHEN gloamin o'er the welkin steals,
And brings the ploughman frae the fiel's,
Oh, Jenny's cot, amang the shiels,
    Is aye the hame to me.

To meet wi' her my heart is fain,
And parting gi'es mo meikle pain;
A queen and throne I would disdain
    For Jenny's ae bawbee.

Tho' braws she has na mony feck,
Nae riches to command respec',
Her rosy lip and lily neck
    Mair pleasure gi'e to me.
I see her beauties, prize them a',
Wi' heart as pure as new-blawn snaw;
I'd prize her cot before a ha',
    Wi' Jenny's ae bawbee.

Nae daisy, wi' its lovely form,
Nor dew-drap shining frae the corn,
Nor echo frae the distant horn,
    Is half sae sweet to me!
And if the lassie were my ain,
For her I'd toil through wind and rain,
And gowd and siller I would gain
    Wi' Jenny's ae bawbee.

THE SOLDIER'S GRAVE.

JAMES FRASER.

AUTHOR of a volume of Poems published at Edinburgh in 1818.

DEAR land of my birth, of my friends, of my love,
    Shall I never again climb thy mountains;
Nor wander at eve through some lone leafy grove,
    To list to the dash of thy fountains?
Shall no hand that I love close my faint beaming eye,
    That darkens 'mid warfare and danger?
Ah, no! for I feel that my last heaving sigh
    Must fleet on the gale of the stranger.

Then farewell, ye valleys, ye fresh blooming bow'rs,
    Of childhood the once happy dwelling;
No more in your haunts shall I chase the gay hours,
    For death at my bosom is kneeling.
But proudly the lotus shall bloom o'er my grave,
    And mark where a freeman is sleeping,
And my dirge shall be heard in the Nile's dashing wave
    While the Arab his night watch is keeping.

'Twas a soldier who spoke—but his voice now is gone,
    And lowly the hero is lying;
No sound meets the ear, save the crocodile's moan,
    Or the breeze through the palm-tree sighing.

But lone though he rests where the camel is seen,
By the wilderness heavily pacing;
His grave in our bosoms shall ever be green,
And his monument ne'er know defacing.

NOW SPRING AGAIN.
JAMES FRASER.

WHEN gowans sprinkled a' the lea,
An' blossoms hung on ilka tree,
'Twas then my Jeanie's saft blue e'e
  Shot a' its witchery through me.
I felt—I wonder'd at the smart,
New wishes floated roun' my heart—
Ah! little kenn'd I 'twas a dart
  That's fated to undo me.

Through lanely glen and greenwood shaw
I stole frae heartless mirth awa',
Or wander'd heedless o' the snaw,
  That heap'd its wraiths around me;
But still I felt I kenn'd nae what,
Nor wist I what I would be at;
And aftentimes my cheek was wat,
  Though stars shone clear aboon me.

And when a sidelang stowan glance
I took, as if't might seem by chance,
My very bluid was in a dance—
  My heart lap sae within me.
Her voice was music in my ear—
Her lip I daur'd na touch for fear,
But O methought the hinny pear
  Less sweetness had to win me.

O Jeanie! dinna think I'm cauld,
When ither lads may be mair bauld;
True love like mine can ne'er be tauld—
  'Tis constancy maun prove me.
Your hair I'll braid wi' spring's young flow'rs,
I'll shade you cool in simmer bow'rs,
An' a' the winter's lang cauld hours
  Nae blast shall ever move ye.

WHEN LONELY THOU WANDEREST.

REV. DAVID ARNOT,

OF Dundee. He published a volume of Poems in 1825.

When lonely thou wanderest along by the wild wood
As twilight steals over the earth like a dream;
An' nature, all lovely as when in her childhood,
On thy heart and thine eye in beauty may beam.
When over the world the gray shades are returning,
And the star of the evening all silent is burning,
With splendour celestial the heavens adorning,
And thy soul is enraptured by ecstasy's gleam.

Then think of thy lover who sigheth in sadness,
When viewing that star as he wanders alone,
Which once to his soul was the emblem of gladness,
As thy faithful bosom he rested upon.
Oh! think of the woes on his heart that are preying,
And think of that love that can know no decaying,
And, oh! may that breast never dream of betraying
The youth it has blest in the days that are gone.

THE TEARS I SHED.

MRS. DUGALD STEWART,

Born in 1765. She was the daughter of the Honourable George Cranstoun, a son of the fifth Lord Cranstoun. She married in 1790 the celebrated Professor Dugald Stewart, and died at Edinburgh in 1838. The first four lines of the fifth stanza are by Burns.

The tears I shed must ever fall:
 I mourn not for an absent swain;
For thoughts may past delights recall,
 And parted lovers meet again.
I weep not for the silent dead:
 Their toils are past, their sorrows o'er;
And those they loved their steps shall tread,
 And death shall join to part no more.

Though boundless oceans roll between,
 If certain that his heart is near,
A conscious transport glads each scene,
 Soft is the sigh, and sweet the tear.
E'en when by death's cold hand removed,
 We mourn the tenant of the tomb:
To think that e'en in death he loved,
 Can gild the horrors of the gloom.

But bitter, bitter are the tears
  Of her who slighted love bewails;
No hope her dreary prospect cheers,
  No pleasing melancholy hails.
Hers are the pangs of wounded pride,
  Of blasted hope, of wither'd joy;
The flattering veil is rent aside,
  The flame of love burns to destroy.

In vain does memory renew
  The hours once tinged in transport's dye;
The sad reverse soon starts to view,
  And turns the past to agony.
E'en time itself despairs to cure
  Those pangs to ev'ry feeling due:
Ungenerous youth! thy boast how poor,
  To win a heart—and break it too.

No cold approach, or alter'd mien,
  Just what would make suspicion start;
No pause the dire extremes between
  He made me blest—and broke my heart.
From hope, the wretched's anchor, torn;
  Neglected and neglecting all;
Friendless, forsaken, and forlorn;
  The tear I shed must ever fall.

JOCK O' HAZELDEAN.
SIR WALTER SCOTT, BART.

The story of Sir Walter Scott's life is so familiar to every admirer of Scotch Literature that it is needless to enter into it here. Suffice it to state that he was born at Edinburgh on the 15th of August 1771; studied for the bar, to which he was called in 1792, and that though nominally following that profession during his whole life time, literature was his real pursuit. "The Minstrelsy of the Scottish Border," "The Lay of the Last Minstrel," "Marmion," and other Works, enchanted the reading public, and placed him for a time at the head of all contemporary poets. In 1814 he issued the first of that wonderful series of Romances—"The Waverley Novels." Sir Walter died at Abbotsford in 1832.

"Why weep ye by the tide, ladye—
  Why weep ye by the tide?
I'll wed ye to my youngest son,
  And ye sall be his bride;
And ye sall be his bride, ladye,
  Sae comely to be seen:"
But aye she loot the tears down fa',
  For Jock o' Hazeldean.

"Now let this wilful grief be done,
  And dry that cheek so pale;
Young Frank is chief of Errington,
  And lord of Langley dale;
His step is first in peaceful ha'
  His sword in battle keen;"
But aye she loot the tears down fa',
  For Jock o' Hazeldean.

"A chain o' gold ye sall not lack,
  Nor braid to bind your hair,
Nor mottled hound, nor managed hawk,
  Nor palfrey fresh and fair;
And you, the foremost o' them a',
  Sall ride our forest queen:"
But aye she loot the tears down fa',
  For Jock o' Hazeldean.

The kirk was deck'd at morning-tide,
  The tapers glimmer'd fair;
The priest and bridegroom wait the bride,
  And dame and knight were there;
They sought her baith by bower and ha';
  The ladye was not seen!—
She's o'er the border, and awa'
  Wi' Jock o' Hazeldean!

HE IS GONE ON THE MOUNTAIN.

SIR WALTER SCOTT, BART.

He is gone on the mountain,
  He is lost to the forest,
Like a summer-dried fountain,
  When our need was the sorest.
The font, re-appearing,
  From the rain-drops shall borrow,
But to us comes no cheering,
  To Duncan no morrow!

The hand of the reaper
  Takes the ears that are hoary,
But the voice of the weeper
  Wails manhood in glory.
The autumn winds rushing
  Waft the leaves that are searest,
But our flower was in flushing,
  When blighting was nearest.

  Fleet foot on the correi,
   Sage counsel in cumber,
  Red hand in the foray,
   How sound is thy slumber!
  Like the dew on the mountain,
   Like the foam on the river,
  Like the bubble on the fountain,
   Thou art gone, and for ever!

A WEARY LOT IS THINE.
SIR WALTER SCOTT, BART.

 "A WEARY lot is thine, fair maid,
  A weary lot is thine!
To pull the thorn thy brow to braid,
  And press the rue for wine.
A lightsome eye, a soldier's mien,
  A feather of the blue,
A doublet of the Lincoln green—
  No more of me you knew, love!
   No more of me you knew.

 "This morn is merry June, I trow,
  The rose is budding fain;
But it shall bloom in winter snow,
  Ere we two meet again."
He turn'd his charger as he spake,
  Upon the river shore;
He gave his bridle-reins a shake,
  Said, "Adieu for evermore, my love!
   And adieu for evermore."

ALLEN-A-DALE.
SIR WALTER SCOTT, BART.

ALLEN-A-DALE has no faggot for burning,
Allen-a-dale has no furrow for turning,
Allen-a-dale has no fleece for the spinning;
Yet Allen-a-dale has red gold for the winning.
Come read me my riddle, come hearken my tale,
And tell me the craft of bold Allen-a-Dale.

The baron of Ravensworth prances in pride,
And he views his domains upon Arkindale side,
The mere for his net, and the lamb for his game,
The chase for the wild, and the park for the tame;
Yet the fish of the lake, and the deer of the vale
Are less free to Lord Dacre than Allen-a-Dale.

Allen-a-Dale was ne'er belted a knight,
Tho' his spur be as sharp, and his blade be as bright;
Allen-a-Dale is no baron or lord,
Yet twenty tall yeomen will draw at his word;
And the best of our nobles his bonnet will veil;
Who at Rerecross on Stanmore meets Allen-a-Dale.

Allen-a-Dale to his wooing is come;
The mother she asked of his household and home;—
"Tho' the castle of Richmond stands fair on the hill,
My hall," quoth bold Allen, "shows gallanter still,
'Tis the blue vault of heaven, with its crescent so pale,
And with all its bright spangles!" said Allen-a-Dale.

The father was steel, and the mother was stone,
They lifted the latch and bade him be gone;
But loud on the morrow their wail and their cry—
He had laughed on the lass with his bonnie black eye;
And she fled to the forest to hear a love-tale,
And the youth it was told by was Allen-a-Dale.

SOLDIER, REST! THY WARFARE O'ER.
SIR WALTER SCOTT, BART.

SOLDIER, rest! thy warfare o'er,
  Sleep the sleep that knows not breaking;
Dream of battled fields no more,
  Days of danger, nights of waking,
In our isle's enchanted hall,
  Hands unseen thy couch are strewing,
Fairy strains of music fall,
  Every sense in slumber dewing,
    Soldier, rest! thy warfare o'er,
    Dream of fighting fields no more;
    Sleep the sleep that knows not breaking;
    Morn of toil, nor night of waking.

No rude sound shall reach thine ear;
  Armour's clang, or war-steed champing;
Trump nor pibroch summon here,
  Mustering clan, or squadron tramping,
Yet the lark's shrill fife may come,
  At the daybreak from the fallow,
And the bittern sound his drum,
  Booming from the sedgy shallow.
    Ruder sounds shall none be near,
    Guards nor warders challenge here;
    Here's no war steed's neigh and champing,
    Shouting clans, or squadrons tramping.

Huntsman, rest! thy chase is done;
   While our slumb'rous spells assail ye,
Dream not, with the rising sun,
   Bugles here shall sound reveillie.
Sleep!—the deer is in his den;
   Sleep!—thy hounds are by thee lying;
Sleep!—nor dream in yonder glen
   How thy gallant steed lay dying,
      Huntsman, rest! thy chase is done;
      Think not of the rising sun;
      For at dawning to assail ye,
      Here no bugles sound reveillie.

PIBROCH OF DONUIL DHU.
SIR WALTER SCOTT, BART.

PIBROCH of Donuil Dhu,
   Pibroch of Donuil,
Wake thy wild voice anew,
   Summon Clan Conuil.
Come away, come away,
   Hark to the summons;
Come in your war array,
   Gentles and commons!

Come from deep glen, and
   From mountain so rocky,
The war-pipe and pennon
   Are at Inverlochy.
Come every hill-plaid, and
   True heart that wears one;
Come every steel blade, and
   Strong hand that bears one!

Leave the deer, leave the steer,
   Leave nets and barges;
Come with your fighting gear,
   Broadswords and targes.
Leave untended the herd,
   The flock without shelter;
Leave the corpse uninterr'd,
   The bride at the altar.

Come as the winds come, when
   Forests are rended;
Come as the waves come, when
   Navies are stranded.

Faster come, faster come,
　Faster and faster:
Chief, vassal, page, and groom,
　Tenant and master.
Fast they come, fast they come;
　See how they gather!
Wide waves the eagle plume,
　Blended with heather.
Cast your plaids, draw your blades,
　Forward each man set;
Pibroch of Donuil Dhu,
　Now for the onset!

MARCH, MARCH, ETTRICK AND TEVIOTDALE.
SIR WALTER SCOTT, BART.

March, march, Ettrick and Teviotdale,
　Why, my lads, dinna ye march forward in order?
March, march, Eskdale and Liddesdale,
　All the blue bonnets are over the border.
Many a banner spread, flutters above your head,
　Many a crest that is famous in story,
Mount and make ready then, sons of the mountain glen,
　Fight for your Queen and the old Scottish glory.

Come from the hills where your hirsels are grazing,
　Come from the glen of the buck and the roe;
Come to the crag where the beacon is blazing;
　Come with the buckler, the lance, and the bow.
Trumpets are sounding, war-steeds are bounding;
　Stand to your arms, and march in good order:
England shall many a-day tell of the bloody fray,
　When the blue bonnets came over the border.

THE MACGREGOR'S GATHERING.
SIR WALTER SCOTT, BART.

The moon's on the lake, and the mist's on the brae,
And the clan has a name that is nameless by day—
　Then gather, gather, gather, Grigalach!

Our signal for fight, which from monarchs we drew,
Must be heard but by night, in our vengeful halloo—
　Then halloo, halloo, halloo, Grigalach!

Glenorchy's proud mountains, Calchuirn and her towers,
Glenstrae, and Glenlyon, no longer are ours—
　We're landless, landless, landless, Grigalach!

But, doom'd and devoted by vassal and lord,
Macgregor has still both his heart and his sword—
 Then courage, courage, courage, Grigalach!

If they rob us of name, and pursue us with beagles,
Give their roofs to the flames, and their flesh to the eagles—
 Then vengeance, vengeance, vengeance, Grigalach!

While there's leaves in the forest, or foam on the river,
Macgregor, despite them, shall flourish for ever!
 Then gather, gather, gather, Grigalach!

Through the depths of Loch Katrine the steed shall career,
O'er the peak of Ben Lomond the galley shall steer,
And the rocks of Craig-Royston like icicles melt,
Ere our wrongs be forgot or our vengeance unfelt.
 Then gather, gather, gather, Grigalach!

ALL JOY WAS BEREFT ME.
SIR WALTER SCOTT, BART.

All joy was bereft me the day that you left me,
 And climb'd the tall vessel to sail yon wide sea;
O weary betide it! I wander'd beside it,
 And bann'd it for parting my Willie and me.

Far o'er the wave hast thou follow'd my fortune,
 Oft fought the squadrons of France and of Spain;
Ae kiss of welcome's worth twenty at parting,
 Now I ha'e gotten my Willie again.

When the sky it was mirk, and the winds they were wailing,
 I sat on the beach wi' the tear in my e'e,
And thought o' the bark where my Willie was sailing,
 And wish'd that the tempest could a' blaw on me.

Now that thy gallant ship rides at her mooring,
 Now that my wanderer's in safety at hame,
Music to me were the wildest winds' roaring,
 That e'er o'er Inch-Keith drove the dark ocean faem.

When the lights they did blaze, and the guns they did rattle,
 And blithe was each heart for the great victory,
In secret I wept for the dangers of battle,
 And thy glory itself was scarce comfort to me.

But now shalt thou tell, while I eagerly listen,
 Of each bold adventure, and every brave scar;
And, trust me, I'll smile, though my een they may glisten,
 For sweet after danger's the tale of the war.

And oh, how we doubt when there's distance 'tween lovers,
   When there's naething to speak to the heart through the e'e,
How often the kindest and warmest prove rovers,
   And the love of the faithfulest ebbs like the sea.
Till at times—could I help it?—I pined and ponder'd,
   If love could change notes like the bird on the tree—
Now I'll never ask if thine eyes may ha'e wander'd,
   Enough, thy leal heart has been constant to me.

Welcome, from sweeping o'er sea and through channel,
   Hardships and danger despising for fame,
Furnishing story for glory's bright annal,
   Welcome, my wanderer, to Jeanie and hame!

Enough, now thy story in annals of glory
   Has humbled the pride of France, Holland, and Spain;
No more shalt thou grieve me, no more shalt thou leave me,
   I never will part with my Willie again.

WHERE SHALL THE LOVER REST?

SIR WALTER SCOTT, BART.

Where shall the lover rest,
   Whom the fates sever,
From his true maiden's breast,
   Parted for ever?
Where, through groves deep and high,
   Sounds the far billow,
Where early violets die,
   Under the willow.
      Eleu loro.
   Soft shall be his pillow.

There, through the summer day,
   Cool streams are laving,
There, while the tempests sway,
   Scarce are boughs waving;
There thy rest shalt thou take,
   Parted for ever,
Never again to wake,
   Never, O never,
      Eleu loro.
   Never, O never.

Where shall the traitor rest,
   He the deceiver,
Who could win maiden's breast,
   Ruin, and leave her?

In the lost battle,
　Borne down by the flying,
Where mingles war's rattle,
　With groans of the dying,
　　Eleu loro.
There shall he be lying.

Her wing shall the eagle flap
　O'er the false-hearted;
His warm blood the wolf shall lap,
　E'er life be parted;
Shame and dishonour sit
　By his grave ever;
Blessing shall hallow it—
　Never, O never,
　　Eleu loro.
　Never, O never.

THE HUNTER'S SONG.

SIR WALTER SCOTT, BART.

My hawk is tired of perch and hood,
My idle greyhound loathes his food,
My horse is weary of his stall,
And I am sick of captive thrall.
I wish I were as I have been,
Hunting the hart in forest green,
With bended bow and bloodhound free,
For that's the life is meet for me.

I hate to learn the ebb of time,
From yon dull steeple's drowsy chime,
Or mark it as the sunbeams crawl,
Inch after inch along the wall.
The lark was wont my matins ring,
The sable rook my vespers sing;
These towers, although a king's they be,
Have not a hall of joy for me.

No more at dawning morn I rise,
And sun myself in Ellen's eyes,
Drive the fleet deer the forest through,
And homeward wend with evening dew;
A blithesome welcome blithely meet,
And lay my trophies at her feet,
While fled the eve on wing of glee—
That life is lost to love and me.

THE HEATH THIS NIGHT.

SIR WALTER SCOTT, BART.

THE heath this night must be my bed,
The bracken curtain for my head,
My lullaby the warder's tread,
   Far, far, from love and thee, Mary;
To-morrow eve, more stilly laid,
My couch may be my bloody plaid,
My vesper song, thy wail, sweet maid!
   It will not waken me, Mary!

I may not, dare not, fancy now
The grief that clouds thy lovely brow,
I dare not think upon thy vow,
   And all it promised me, Mary.
No fond regret must Norman know;
When bursts Clan-Alpine on the foe,
His heart must be like bended bow,
   His foot like arrow free, Mary.

A time will come with feeling fraught,
For, if I fall in battle fought,
Thy hapless lover's dying thought
   Shall be a thought on thee, Mary.
And if return'd from conquer'd foes,
How blithely will the evening close,
How sweet the linnet sing repose,
   To my young bride and me, Mary!

DONALD CAIRD.

SIR WALTER SCOTT, BART.

DONALD CAIRD'S come again,
Donald Caird's come again!
Tell the news in brugh and glen,
Donald Caird's come again!

Donald Caird can lilt and sing,
Blithely dance the Highland fling;
Drink till the gudeman be blind,
Fleech till the gudewife be kind;
Hoop a leglan, clout a pan,
Or crack a pow wi' ony man;
Tell the news in brugh and glen,
Donald Caird's come again.

Donald Caird can wire a maukin,
Kens the wiles o' dun-deer staukin;
Leisters kipper, makes a shift
To shoot a muir-fowl i' the drift:
Water-bailiffs, rangers, keepers,
He can wauk when they are sleepers;
Not for bountith, or reward,
Daur they mell wi' Donald Caird.

Donald Caird can drink a gill,
Fast as hostler-wife can fill;
Ilka ane that sells gude liquor
Kens how Donald bends a bicker:
When he's fou he's stout and saucy,
Keeps the kantle o' the causey;
Highland chief and Lawland laird
Maun gi'e way to Donald Caird.

Steek the aumrie, lock the kist,
Else some gear will sune be mist;
Donald Caird finds orra things
Where Allan Gregor fand the tings:
Dunts o' kebbuck, taits o' woo,
Whiles a hen and whiles a soo;
Webs or duds frae hedge or yard—
Ware the wuddie, Donald Caird!

On Donald Caird the doom was stern,
Craig to tether, legs to airn:
But Donald Caird, wi' mickle study,
Caught the gift to cheat the wuddie.
Rings o' airn, and bolts o' steel,
Fell like ice frae hand and heel!
Watch the sheep in fauld and glen,
Donald Caird's come again.

O, HUSH THEE, MY BABIE.
SIR WALTER SCOTT, BART.

O, HUSH thee, my babie, thy sire was a knight,
Thy mother a lady, both lovely and bright;
The woods and the glens, from the towers which we see,
They all are belonging, dear babie, to thee.
    O ho ro, i ri ri, cadul gu lo,
    O ho ro, i ri ri, &c.

O, fear not the bugle, though loudly it blows,
It calls but the warders that guard thy repose;
Their bows would be bended, their blades would be red,
Ere the step of a foeman draws near to thy bed,
    O ho ro, i ri ri, &c.

O, hush thee, my babie, the time soon will come,
When thy sleep shall be broken by trumpet and drum;
Then hush thee, my darling, take rest while you may,
For strife comes with manhood, and waking with day.
    O ho ro, i ri ri, &c.

O SAY NOT, MY LOVE.
SIR WALTER SCOTT, BART.

OH, say not, my love, with that mortified air,
 That your spring-time of pleasure is flown,
Nor bid me to maids that are younger repair,
 For those raptures that still are thine own.

Though April his temples may wreathe with the vine,
 Its tendrils in infancy curl'd,
'Tis the ardour of August matures us the wine,
 Whose life-blood enlivens the world.

Though thy form, that was fashion'd as light as a fay's,
 Has assumed a proportion more round,
And thy glance, that was bright as a falcon's at gaze,
 Looks soberly now on the ground—

Enough, after absence to meet me again,
 Thy steps still with ecstasy move;
Enough, that those dear sober glances retain
 For me the kind language of love.

THE MAID OF NEIDPATH.
SIR WALTER SCOTT, BART.

O LOVERS' eyes are sharp to see,
 And lovers' ears in hearing;
And love, in life's extremity,
 Can lend an hour of cheering.
Disease had been in Mary's bower,
 And slow decay from mourning,
Though now she sits on Neidpath's tower,
 To watch her love's returning.

All sunk and dim her eyes so bright,
 Her form decay'd by pining
Till through her wasted hand, at night, -
 You saw the taper shining;
By fits, a sultry hectic hue
 Across her cheek was flying;
By fits, so ashy pale she grew,
 Her maidens thought her dying.

Yet keenest powers to see and hear,
  Seem'd in her frame residing;
Before the watch-dog prick'd his ear,
  She heard her lover's riding;
Ere scarce a distant form was kenn'd,
  She knew, and waved to greet him;
And o'er the battlement did bend,
  As on the wing to meet him.

He came—he pass'd—a heedless gaze,
  As o'er some stranger glancing;
Her welcome, spoke in faltering phrase,
  Lost in his courser's prancing—
The castle arch, whose hollow tone
  Returns each whisper spoken,
Could scarcely catch the feeble moan,
  Which told her heart was broken.

LUCY'S FLITTIN.

WILLIAM LAIDLAW,

The Steward, amanuensis, and trusted friend of Sir Walter Scott. He was born at Blackhouse, in Yarrow, in 1780. He early formed the acquaintance of Sir Walter Scott and assisted him in procuring materials for the "Minstrelsy of the Scottish Border." He became steward to Sir Walter in 1817, and, except for an interval of some three years, he remained in his service till 1832. After the death of Sir Walter, he left Abbotsford to act as factor on the Ross-shire estates of Mrs. Mackenzie, of Seaforth. He died at Contin, near Dingwall, in 1845.

'Twas when the wan leaf frae the birk tree was fa'in,
  And Martinmas dowie had wound up the year,
That Lucy row'd up her wee kist wi' her a' in't,
  And left her auld maister and neabours sae dear;
For Lucy had served in the glen a' the simmer;
  She cam' there afore the flower bloomed on the pea;
An orphan was she, and they had been kind till her,
  Sure that was the thing brocht the tear to her e'e.

She gaed by the stable where Jamie was stannin';
  Richt sair was his kind heart the flittin' to see;
Fare ye weel, Lucy! quo' Jamie, and ran in;
  The gatherin' tears trickled fast frae his e'e.
As down the burn-side she gaed slow wi' the flittin',
  Fare ye weel Lucy! was ilka bird's sang;
She heard the craw sayin't, high on the tree sittin',
  And robin was chirpin't the brown leaves amang.

Oh, what is't that pits my puir heart in a flutter?
  And what gars the tears come sae fast to my e'e?
If I wasna ettled to be ony better,
  Then what gars me wish ony better to be?
I'm just like a lammie that loses its mither;
  Nae mither or friend the puir lammie can see;
I fear I ha'e tint my puir heart a'thegither,
  Nae wonder the tears fa' sae fast frae my e'e.

Wi' the rest o' my claes I ha'e row'd up the ribbon,
  The bonnie blue ribbon that Jamie ga'e me;
Yestreen, when he ga'e me't, and saw I was sabbin',
  I'll never forget the wae blink o' his e'e.
Though now he said naething but Fare ye weel, Lucy!
  It made me I neither could speak, hear, nor see:
He could na say mair but just, Fare ye weel, Lucy!
  Yet that I will mind till the day that I dee.

The lamb likes the gowan wi' dew when it's droukit;
  The hare likes the brake and the braird on the lea;
But Lucy likes Jamie,—she turn'd and she lookit,
  She thocht the dear place she wad never mair see.
Ah, weel may young Jamie gang dowie and cheerless!
  And weel may he greet on the bank o' the burn!
For bonnie sweet Lucy, sae gentle and peerless,
  Lies cauld in her grave, and will never return!

ON THE BANKS O' THE BURN.
WILLIAM LAIDLAW.

On the banks o' the burn while I pensively wander,
  The mavis sings sweetly, unheeded by me;
I think on my lassie, her gentle mild nature,
  I think on the smile o' her bonnie black e'e.

When heavy the rain fa's, and loud loud the win' blaws,
  An' simmer's gay cleadin' drives fast frae the tree;
I heedna the win' nor the rain when I think on
  The kind lovely smile o' my lassie's black e'e.

When swift as the hawk, in the stormy November,
  The cauld norlan' win' ca's the drift owre the lea;
Though bidin' its blast on the side o' the mountain,
  I think on the smile o' her bonnie black e'e.

When braw at a weddin' I see the fine lasses,
  Tho' a' neat an' bonnie, they're naething to me!
I sigh an' sit dowie, regardless what passes,
  When I miss the smile o' her bonnie black e'e.

When thin twinklin' starnies announce the gray gloamin',
When a' round the inglo's sae cheerie to see;
Then music delightfu', saft on the heart stealin',
Minds me o' the smile o' her bonnie black e'e.

When jokin', an' laughin', the lave they are merry,
Tho' absent my heart like the lave I maun be;
Sometimes I laugh wi' them, but I oft turn dowie,
An' think on the smile o' my lassie's black e'e.

Her lovely fair form frae my mind's awa' never,
She's dearer than a' this hale warld to me;
An' this is my wish, May I leave it, If ever
She row on another her love-beaming e'e.

ALAKE FOR THE LASSIE.
WILLIAM LAIDLAW.

Alake for the lassie! she's no right at a',
That lo'es a dear laddie, an' he far awa';
But the lassie has muckle mair cause to complain,
That lo'es a dear lad, when she's no lo'ed again.

The fair was just comin', my heart it grew fain
To see my dear laddie, to see him again;
My heart it grew fain, an' lap light at the thought
Of milkin' tho ewes my dear Jamie wad bught.

The bonnie gray morn scarce had open'd her e'e,
When we set to the gate a' wi' nae little glee;
I was blythe, but my mind oft misga'e me right sair,
For I hadna seen Jamie for five months an' mair.

I' the hirin' right soon my dear Jamie I saw,
I saw nae ane like him, sae bonnie and braw;
I watch'd an' baid near him, his motion to see,
In hopes aye to catch a kind glance o' his e'e.

He never wad see me in ony ae place:
At length I gaed up an' just smiled in his face,
I wonder aye yet my heart brackna in twa—
He just said, "How are ye?" and steppit awa'.

My neeber lads strive to entice me awa';
They roos'd me, an' hecht me ilk thing that was braw;
But I hatit them a', an' I hatit the fair,
For Jamie's behaviour had wounded me sair.

His heart was sae leal, and his manners sae kind!
He's someway gane wrang, he may alter his mind;
An' sud he do sae, he's be welcome to me;
I'm sure I can never like ony but he.

ALLISTER M'ALLISTER.
UNKNOWN.

O ALLISTER M'ALLISTER,
Your chanter sets us a' astir,
Then to your bags and blaw wi' birr,
  We'll dance the Highland fling.
Now Allister has tuned his pipes,
And thrang as bumbees frae their bykes,
The lads and lasses loup the dykes,
  And gather on the green.
    O Allister M'Allister, &c.

The Miller, Hab, was fidgin' fain
To dance the Highland fling his lane,
He lap as high as Elspa's wame,
  The like was never seen;
As round about the ring he whuds,
And cracks his thumbs and shakes his duds,
The meal flew frae his tail in cluds,
  And blinded a' their een.
    O Allister M'Allister, &c.

Neist rauchle-handed smiddy Jock,
A' blacken'd o'er wi' coom and smoke,
Wi' shauchlin' blear-e'ed Bess did yoke,
  That slaverin'-gabbit quean.
He shook his doublet in the wund,
His feet like hammers strack the grund,
The very moudiwarts were stunn'd,
  Nor kenn'd what it could mean.
    O Allister M'Allister, &c.

Now wanton Willie was nae blate,
For he got hand o' winsome Kate,
"Come here," quo' he, "I'll show the gate
  To dance the Highland fling."
The Highland fling he danced wi' glee,
And lap as he were gaun to flee;
Kate beck'd and bobb'd sae bonnilie,
  And tript it light and clean.
    O Allister M'Allister, &c.

Now Allister has done his best,
And weary houghs are wantin' rest,
Besides they sair wi' drouth were strest,
  Wi' dancin' sae I ween.
I trou the gauntrees gat a lift,
And round the bicker flew like drift,
And Allister that very night,
  Could scarcely stand his lane.
    O Allister M'Allister, &c.

BAILIE NICOL JARVIE.

Sung by the late Mr. Mackay, in his great character of "The Bailie" in Rob Roy, as an after song, it being often his habit to come to the footlights after the curtain had fallen on the last scene and sing it. We have heard the authorship ascribed to the late William Murray, of the Theatre Royal, Edinburgh.

You may sing o' your Wallace and brag o' your Bruce,
 And talk o' your fechtin' Red Reiver,
But whare will ye find me a man o' sic use,
 As a thorough-bred Saut Market Weaver?
Let ance Nicol Jarvie come under your view,
 At hame whare the people adore me,
Whare they made me a bailie and councillor too,
 Like my faither, the Deacon, before me.

These claverin' chiels in the clachan hard bye,
 They'll no gi'e a body but hard words,
My faith! they shall find if again they will try,
 A het poker's as guid as their braid swords;
It's as weel though to let that flee stick to the wa',
 For mayhap they may chance to claymore me,
To let sleepin' dogs lie is the best thing ava,
 Said my faither, the Deacon, before me.

My puir cousin Rob, O! his terrible wife
 Was sae proud, that she chose to disown me,
Fient a bodle cared she for a magistrate's life,
 My conscience! she was just gaun to drown me.
But if ever again in her clutches I pop,
 Puir Matty may live to deplore me,
But were I in Glasgow, I'd stick to my shop,
 Like my faither, the Deacon, before me.

Now to think o' them bangin' a bailie so high,
 To be picked at by corbies and burdies!
But if I were at Glasgow, my conscience! I'll try
 To let their craigs feel the weight o' their burdies.
But stop, Nicol! stop man! na that canna be,
 For if ane wad to hame safe restore ye,
In the Saut Market safe, I'd forget and forgie—
 Like my faither, the Deacon, before me.

ROB ROY MACGREGOR.

From the Opera of "Rob Roy."

Pardon now the bold outlaw,
 Rob Roy Macgregor, O!
Grant him mercy, gentles a',
 Rob Roy Macgregor, O!
Let your hands and hearts agree,
Set the Highland laddie free,
Make us sing wi' muckle glee,
 Rob Roy Macgregor, O!

Long the state has doom'd his fa',
 Rob Roy Macgregor, O!
Still he spurn'd the hatefu' law,
 Rob Roy Macgregor, O!
Scots can for their country die;
Ne'er frae Britain's foes they flee,
A' that's past forget—forgie,
 Rob Roy Macgregor, O!

Scotland's fear and Scotland's pride,
 Rob Roy Macgregor, O!
Your award must now abide,
 Rob Roy Macgregor, O!
Lang your favours ha'e been mine,
Favours I will no'er resign,
Welcome then for auld langsyne,
 Rob Roy Macgregor, O!

THE LASS OF GOWRIE.

A modern version of this favourite song: other versions by Lady Nairne and William Reid are inserted in their proper places.

Upon a simmer afternoon,
A wee before the sun gade down,
My lassie, in a braw new gown,
 Cam' o'er the hills to Gowrie.
The rose-bud, ting'd with morning show'r,
Blooms fresh within the sunny bow'r,
But Katie was the fairest flower
 That ever bloom'd in Gowrie.

Nae thought had I to do her wrang,
But round her waist my arms I flang,
And said, My dearie, will ye gang,
 To see the Carse o' Gowrie?

I'll tak' ye to my father's ha',
In yon green fields beside the shaw;
I'll mak' you lady o' them a',
    The brawest wife in Gowrie.

A silken gown o' siller gray,
My mither coft last new-year's day,
And buskit me frae tap to tae,
    To keep me out o' Gowrie.
Daft Will, short syne, cam' courting Nell,
And won the lass, but what befel,
Or whare she's gane, she kens hersel',
    She staid na lang in Gowrie.

Sic thoughts, dear Katie, ill combine
Wi' beauty rare, and wit like thine;
Except yoursel', my bonnie quean,
    I care for nought in Gowrie.
Since first I saw you in the sheal,
To you my heart's been true and leal;
The darkest night I fear nae de'il,
    Warlock, or witch, in Gowrie.

Saft kisses on her lips I laid,
The blush upon her cheeks soon spread
She whisper'd modestly, and said,
    O Pate, I'll stay in Gowrie!
The auld folks soon ga'e their consent,
Syne for Mess John they quickly sent,
Wha ty'd them to their heart's content,
    And now she's Lady Gowrie.

COMIN THROUGH THE RYE.

THE modern version of one of our early songs: a set, based upon the old words, but so altered by Burns as to be included in nearly every edition of his songs as his own, appears in Johnson's Museum. There are numerous other versions, verses, &c., floating about, but they are all of little value.

    Gin a body meet a body
      Comin' through the rye,
    Gin a body kiss a body,
      Need a body cry?
    Every lassie has her laddie,
      Nane, they say, ha'e I!
    Yet a' the lads they smile at me,
      When comin' through the rye.
    Amang the train there is a swain
      I dearly lo'e mysel;
    But whaar his hame, or what his name,
      I dinna care to tell.

Gin a body meet a body,
  Comin' frae the town,
Gin a body greet a body,
  Need a body frown?
Every lassie has her laddie,
  Nane, they say, ha'e I!
Yet a' the lads they smile at me,
  When comin' through the rye.
Amang the train there is a swain,
  I dearly lo'e mysel;
But whaur his hame, or what his name,
  I dinna care to tell.

BLYTHE, BLYTHE, AROUND THE NAPPIE.

DANIEL MACPHAIL,

A WORKING Cabinet Maker; he died at Glasgow about the year 1833.

BLYTHE, blythe, around the nappie,
  Let us join in social glee;
While we're here we'll ha'e a drappie—
  Scotia's sons ha'e aye been free.

Our auld forbears, when ower their yill,
  And cantie bickers round did ca',
Forsooth, they cried, anither gill!
  For sweirt we are to gang awa'.

Some hearty cock wad then ha'e sung
  An auld Scotch sonnet aff wi' glee,
Syne pledged his cogue: the chorus rung,
  Auld Scotia and her sons are free.

Thus cracks, and jokes, and sangs gaed roun',
  Till morn the screens o' light did draw:
Yet, dreich to rise, the carles roun'
  Cried, Deoch an doras, then awa'!

The landlord then the nappie brings,
  And toasts, Fu' happy a' may be,
Syne tooms the cogue: the chorus rings,
  Auld Scotia's sons shall aye be free.

Then like our dads o' auld lang syne,
  Let social glee unite us a',
Aye blythe to meet, our mou's to weet,
  But aye as sweirt to gang awa'.

LAND OF MY FATHERS.

JOHN LEYDEN,

WAS born in 1775 at Denholm in Roxburghshire. His father was a shepherd and in poor circumstances, but as John displayed remarkable talents, he managed to get him educated at the University of Edinburgh, with the view of entering the Church. When his studies were finished, though he became a licentiate, he failed to obtain a church. He edited for some time the "Scot's Magazine." He afterwards turned his attention to the study of medicine; and, having received his degree of M.D. from the University of St. Andrew's, he sailed for Madras, where he had received an appointment as Surgeon in the East India Company's service. He died at Java in 1811.

There is no more remarkable instance of perseverance and genius in the whole history of our literature than John Leyden. In antiquities, poetry, philology, in fact in every department of literature to which he seriously turned himself, he has left his mark. His Dissertation on the languages and literature of the Indo-Chinese Nations is well-known to philologists. No one can read any of his published volumes of poetry without finding the stamp of genius firmly impressed, while even in his edition of the "Complaynt of Scotland," the curious theories there brought forward at least serve to show the diligent and faithful manner in which he tried to explain the antiquities of his native land.

LAND of my fathers! though no mangrove here
O'er thy blue streams her flexile branches rear,
Nor scaly palm her finger'd scions shoot,
Nor luscious guava wave her yellow fruit,
Nor golden apples glimmer from the tree;
Land of dark heaths and mountains, thou art free.
Free as his lord the peasant treads the plain,
And heaps his harvest on the groaning wain.

Proud of his laws, tenacious of his right,
And vain of Scotia's old unconquer'd might:
Dear native valleys! may ye long retain
The charter'd freedom of the mountain swain:
Long, 'mid your sounding glades, in union sweet,
May rural innocence and beauty meet;
And still be duly heard, at twilight calm,
From every cot the peasant's chanted psalm!

Then, Jedworth, though thy ancient choirs shall fa'o,
And time lay bare each lofty colonnade,
From the damp roof the massy sculptures die,
And in their vaults thy rifted arches lie;
Still in these vales shall angel harps prolong,
By Jed's pure stream, a sweeter evening song
Than long processions, once, with mystic zeal,
Pour'd to the harp and solemn organ's peal.

THE EVENING STAR.

DR. JOHN LEYDEN.

How sweet thy modest light to view,
　Fair star! to love and lovers dear;
While trembling on the falling dew,
　Like beauty shining through the tear.

Or hanging o'er that mirror stream
　To mark each image trembling there,
Thou seem'st to smile with softer gleam
　To see thy lovely face so fair.

Though blazing o'er the arch of night,
　The moon thy timid beams outshine
As far as thine each starry light—
　Her rays can never vie with thine.

Thine are the soft enchanting hours
　When twilight lingers on the plain,
And whispers to the closing flow'rs,
　That soon the sun will rise again.

Thine is the breeze that, murmuring bland
　As music, wafts the lover's sigh;
And bids the yielding heart expand
　In love's delicious ecstasy.

Fair star! though I be doom'd to prove
　That rapture's tears are mix'd with pain;
Ah! still I feel 'tis sweet to love,—
　But sweeter to be lov'd again.

LOVE'S ADIEU.

JOSEPH GRANT.

A NATIVE of Kincardineshire. He died in 1835, aged 30. Two or three volumes of his poetry and prose essays were published during his life time.

The e'e o' the dawn, Eliza,
　Blinks over the dark green sea,
An' the moon's creepin' down to the hill tap
　Richt dim an' drowsilie;
An' the music o' the mornin'
　Is murmurin' alang the air;
Yet still my dowie heart lingers
　To catch one sweet throb mair.

We've been as blest, Eliza,
　As children o' earth can be,
Though my fondest wish has been nipt by
　The bonds o' povertie;

An' through life's misty sojourn,
 That still may be our fa',
But hearts that are linked for over
 Ha'e strength to bear it a'.

The cot by the mutterin' burnie,
 Its wee bit garden an' field,
May ha'e mair o' the blessin's o' heaven
 Than lichts on the lordliest bield.
There's mony a young brow braided
 Wi' jewels o' far aff isles,
But woe may be drinkin' the heart-springs
 While we see nought but smiles.

But adieu, my ain Eliza!
 Where'er my wanderin's be,
Undyin' remembrance will mak' thee
 The star o' my destinie;
An' weel I ken, thou loved one,
 That aye till I return
Thou'lt treasure pure faith in thy bosom
 Like a gem in a gowden urn.

EXILE OF ULDOONAN.

JOHN GRIEVE,

A TRADESMAN in Edinburgh, one of the earliest friends of The Ettrick Shepherd, who held him in great esteem. He died in 1836.

ADIEU to rock and to water-fall,
 Whose echoes start among Albyn's hills,
A long adieu, Uldoonan! and all
 Thy wildwood steeps, and thy sparkling rills.
From the dreams of my childhood and youth I awaken,
 And all the sweet visions that fancy wove;
Adieu! ye lone glens, and ye braes of green bracken,
 Endeared by friendship, and hope, and love.

The stranger came, and adversity's wind
 Blew cold and chill on my father's hearth;
I strove, but vainly, some shelter to find
 Among the fields of my father's birth:
But my desolate spirit shall never be severed
 From the home where a sister and mother once smiled,
Though within its bare walls lies the roof-tree all shivered,
 And mouldering rubbish is spread and piled.

I hear before me the waters roar;
I see the galley in yonder bay,
All ready and trim, she beckons the shore,
And seems to elude my longer stay.
Uldoonan! when lingering afar from thy valley,
At my pilgrimage close o'er the billowy brine,
Harps long will be strung, and new voices will hail thee,
Without devotion and love like mine.

POLWARTH ON THE GREEN.
JOHN GRIEVE.

'Twas summer tide; the cushat sang
 His am'rous roundelay;
And dews, like cluster'd diamonds, hang
 On flowers and leafy spray.
The coverlet of gloaming gray
 On every thing was seen,
When lads and lasses took their way
 To Polwarth on the Green.

The spirit-moving dance went on,
 And harmless revelry
Of young hearts all in unison,
 Wi' love's soft witcherie;
Their hall the open-daisied lea,
 While frae the welkin sheen,
The moon shone brightly on the glee
 At Polwarth on the Green.

Dark een and raven curls were there,
 And cheeks of rosy hue,
And finer forms, without compare,
 Than pencil ever drew;
But ane, wi' een of bonnie blue,
 A' hearts confess'd the queen,
And pride of grace and beauty too,
 At Polwarth on the Green.

The miser hoards his golden store,
 And kings dominion gain;
While others in the battle's roar
 For honour's trifles strain.
Away such pleasures! false and vain;
 Far dearer mine have been,
Among the lowly rural train,
 At Polwarth on the Green.

WHEN THE KYE COME HAME.

JAMES HOGG.

THE Ettrick Shepherd, was born in December, 1770, at a small cottage near the Parish Kirk of Ettrick, in Selkirkshire.

At the time of his birth, his father rented a small farm, but this proving unsuccessful, he returned to his original occupation of a shepherd. The son's education was therefore of a very meagre description, and when only seven years of age, he was in service as a cow herd; poor and ragged, and often hungry, but always fond of music, reading, and thinking.

In 1796, while in the service of Mr. Laidlaw of Blackhouse (father of the author of "Lucy's Flittin'"), he first committed the sin of rhyme. His rhymes, says the shepherd himself, were "songs and ballads made up for the lasses to sing in chorus, and a proud man I was when I first heard the rosy nymphs chanting my uncouth strains, and jeering me by the still dear appellation of 'Jamie the Poeter.'"

In 1801 his ambition prompted him, while in Edinburgh attending a market, to write a number of his poems from memory and print them. The tiny volume was no sooner ready than he deeply regretted his haste, it being full of typographical errors, omissions, &c.; however, he found this out too late. The volume fell still-born from the press, and the author had to pay a smart printer's bill for the gratification of seeing himself in print. He shortly afterwards became acquainted with Sir (then Mr.) Walter Scott, and through that gentleman's introduction, he arranged with Constable for the publication of a volume of poems, which accordingly appeared under the title of "The Mountain Bard."

The success of this volume, and of a small work on sheep issued about the same time, yielded him about three hundred pounds. With this he began farming; but, after struggling for three years, was so unsuccessful that he had no resource but to go to Edinburgh and support himself by his pen. He issued a sort of Poetical Miscellany, of pieces by William Laidlaw and others, besides his own. This was a failure. He then began a weekly periodical called "The Spy," which made a deal of noise but brought "little woo'" to its editor. In 1813, however, he at once established his fame and his purse by the publication of "The Queen's Wake," the best of his works.

In 1814, he received a lease of the farm of Altrive, belonging to the Duke of Buccleuch, at a merely nominal rent, and henceforth his life was divided between attending to his crops in the country and to his books in the town. He contributed to Blackwood's Magazine and other periodicals; wrote "The Pilgrims of the Sun," "Mador of the Moor," "The Poetic Mirror," and other poems, and edited the "Jacobite Relics."

In 1820, fortune so smiled on him that he married and applied for a larger farm. He was offered and accepted the farm of Mount Benger, adjoining Altrive. Here his customary ill-luck attended him; and, on the expiry of his lease, he was glad to return to his old holding.

His works from 1820 cannot be said to add much to his fame. One or two three-volume novels, several short tales and stories, and a long narrative poem called "Queen Hynde," were failures; and from 1826 he confined himself principally to revising and re-publishing the works already issued, writing for periodicals, &c., by which means he eked out the little income derived from his farm so as to support his family in comfort. He died in 1835.

The character of the Ettrick Shepherd is a strange mixture of simplicity and shrewdness. His many weaknesses were hurtful to himself only, while his genius, hospitality, and kindly spirit, endeared him to all. As a poet, though his fame rests almost wholly on his "Queen's Wake," and a number of his songs, his great ambition to be recognised as the successor of Burns has been gratified, and the name of Ettrick Shepherd has become a household one throughout all Scotland.

    Come all ye jolly shepherds
      That whistle through the glen,
    I'll tell ye of a secret
      That courtiers dinna ken.
    What is the greatest bliss
      That the tongue o' man can name?
    'Tis to woo a bonnie lassie
      When the kye come hame.

        When the kye come hame,
          When the kye come hame,
        'Tween the gloamin' and the mirk,
          When the kye come hame.

    'Tis not beneath the burgonet,
      Nor yet beneath the crown,
    'Tis not on couch of velvet,
      Nor yet on bed of down:
    'Tis beneath the spreading birch,
      In the dell without a name,
    Wi' a bonnie, bonnie lassie,
      When the kye come hame.

    There the blackbird bigs his nest
      For the mate he loves to see,
    And up upon the tapmost bough,
      Oh, a happy bird is he!
    Then he pours his melting ditty,
      And love 'tis a' the theme,
    And he'll woo his bonnie lassie,
      When the kye come hame.

    When the bluart bears a pearl,
      And the daisy turns a pea,
    And the bonnie lucken gowan
      Has fauldit up his e'e,
    Then the laverock frae the blue lift
      Draps down, and thinks nae shame
    To woo his bonnie lassie
      When the kye come hame.

Then the eye shines sae bright,
　The haill soul to beguile,
There's love in every whisper,
　And joy in every smile;
O, who would choose a crown,
　Wi' its perils and its fame,
And miss a bonnie lassie
　When the kye come hame?

See yonder pawky shepherd
　That lingers on the hill—
His yowes are in the fauld,
　And his lambs are lying still;
Yet he downa gang to rest,
　For his heart is in a flame
To meet his bonnie lassie
　When the kye come hame.

Awa' wi' fame and fortune—
　What comfort can they gi'e?—
And a' the arts that prey
　On man's life and libertie!
Gi'e me the highest joy
　That the heart o' man can frame,
My bonnie, bonnie lassie,
　When the kye come hame.

JEANIE.

JAMES HOGG.

O! my lassie, our joy to complete again,
　Meet me again in the gloamin', my dearie;
Low down i' the dell let us meet again,
　O! Jeanie, there's naething to fear ye.
Come when the wee bat flits silent and eerie;
Come when the pale face o' nature looks weary.
　　Love be thy sure defence,
　　Beauty and innocence—
O! Jeanie, there's naething to fear ye.

Sweetly blows the haw and the rowan-tree,
　Wild roses speck our thicket sae breerie;
Still, still will our bed in the greenwood be—
　O! Jeanie, there's naething to fear ye:
Note when the blackbird o' singing grows weary,
List when the beetle bee's bugle comes near ye:
　　Then come with fairy haste,
　　Light foot and beating breast—
O! Jeanie, there's naething to fear ye.

Far, far will the bogle an' brownie be;
Beauty an' truth, they daurna come near it.
Kind love is the tie of our unity;
A' maun love it, and a' maun revere it.
Love mak's the sang o' the woodland sae cheerie;
Love gars a' nature look bonnie that's near ye;
    Love mak's the rose sae sweet,
    Cowslip an' violet—
O! Jeanie, there's naething to fear ye.

LOVE IS LIKE A DIZZINESS.

JAMES HOGG.

I LATELY liv'd in quiet ease,
  An' never wish'd to marry, O;
But when I saw my Peggy's face,
  I felt a sad quandary, O:
Though wild as ony Athol deer,
  She has trepann'd me fairly, O;
Her cherry cheeks, and een sae clear,
  Harass me late an' early, O.
    O! love! love! laddie,
      Love's like a dizziness!
    It winna let a puir body
      Gang about his business!

To tell my feats this single week
  Wad mak' a curious diary, O;
I drave my cart against a dyke,
  My horses in a miry, O:
I wear my stockings white an' blue,
  My love's sae fierce and fiery, O;
I drill the land that I should plow,
  An' plow the drills entirely, O.
    O! love! love! &c.

Soon as the dawn had brought the day,
  I went to theek the stable, O;
I coost my coat, an' ply'd away
  As fast as I was able, O.
I wrought a' morning out an' out
  As I'd been redding fire, O;
When I had done, and look'd about,
  Behold it was the byre, O!
    O! love! love! &c.

Her wily glance I'll ne'er forget;
  The dear, the lovely blinkin' o't,
Has pierc'd me through and through the heart,
  And plagues me wi' the prinklin' o't;
I try'd to sing, I try'd to pray,
  I try'd to drown't wi' drinkin' o't;
I try'd wi' toil to drive't away,
  But ne'er can sleep for thinkin' o't.
    O! love! love! &c.

Were Peggy's love to hire the job,
  An' save my heart frae breakin', O,
I'd put a girdle round the globe,
  Or dive in Corryvrekin, O;
Or howk a grave at midnight dark
  In yonder vault sae eerie, O;
Or gang and spier for Mungo Park
  Through Africa sae drearie, O.
    O! love! love! &c.

Ye little ken what pains I prove!
  Or, how severe my plisky, O!
I swear I'm sairer drunk wi' love
  Than e'er I was wi' whisky, O!
For love has rak'd me fore an' aft,
  I scarce can lift a leggy, O;
I first grew dizzy, then gaed daft,
  An' now I'll dee for Peggy, O.
    O! love! love! &c.

SING ON, SING ON, MY BONNIE BIRD.

JAMES HOGG.

Sing on, sing on, my bonnie bird,
  The sang ye sang yestreen, O,
When here, aneath the hawthorn wild,
  I met my bonnie Jean, O.
My blude ran prinklin' through my veins,
  My hair began to steer, O;
My heart play'd deep against my breast,
  As I beheld my dear, O.

O weels me on my happy lot!
  O weels me o' my dearie!
O weels me on the charmin' spot,
  Where a' combin'd to cheer me.

The mavis liltit on the bush,
  The lavrock on the green, O;
The lily bloom'd, the daisy blush'd,
  But a' war nought to Jean, O.

Sing on, sing on, my bonnie thrush,
  Be neither flee'd nor eerie;
I'll wad your love sits in the bush,
  That gars ye sing sae cheerie:
She may be kind, she may be sweet,
  She may be neat and clean, O;
But O, she's but a drysome mate,
  Compar'd wi' bonnie Jean, O.

If love wad open a' her stores,
  An' a' her bloomin' treasures,
And bid me rise, an' turn an' choose,
  And taste her chiefest pleasures;
My choice wad be the rosy cheek,
  The modest beamin' eye, O;
The yellow hair, the bosom fair,
  The lips o' coral dye, O.

A bramble shade around her head,
  A burnie poplin' by, O;
Our bed the swaird, our sheet the plaid,
  Our canopy the sky, O,
And here's the burn, an' there's the bush,
  Around the flow'rie green, O;
An' this the plaid, an' sure the lass
  Wad be my bonnie Jean, O.

Hear me, thou bonnie modest moon!
  Ye starnies twinklin' high, O!
An' a' ye gentle powers aboon,
  That roam athwart the sky, O.
To see me gratefu' for the past,
  Ye saw me blest yestreen, O;
An' ever till I breathe my last
  Ye'll see me true to Jean, O.

BIRNIEBOUZLE.

JAMES HOGG.

WILL ye gang wi' me, lassie,
  To the braes o' Birniebouzle?
Baith the yird an' sea, lassie,
  Will I rob to fend ye.

I'll hunt the otter an' the brock,
The hart, the hare, an' heather cock,
An' pu' the limpet aff the rock,
   To batten an' to mend ye.

If ye'll gang wi' me lassie,
   To the braes o' Birniebouzle,
Till the day you dee, lassie,
   Want shall ne'er come near ye.
The peats I'll carry in a scull,
The cod an' ling wi' hooks I'll pull,
An' reave the eggs o' mony a gull,
   To please my dainty dearie.

Sae canty will we be, lassie,
   At the braes o' Birniebouzle,
Donald Gun and me, lassie,
   Ever sall attend ye.
Though we ha'e nowther milk nor meal,
Nor lamb nor mutton, beef nor veal,
We'll fank the porpy and the seal,
   And that's the way to fend ye.

An' ye sall gang sae braw, lassie,
   At the kirk o' Birniebouzle,
Wi' littit brogues an' a', lassie,
   Wow but you'll be vaunty!
An' you sall wear, when you are wed,
The kirtle an' the Hieland plaid,
An' sleep upon a heather bed,
   Sae cozy an' sae canty.

If ye'll but marry me, lassie,
   At the kirk o' Birniebouzle,
A' my joy shall be, lassie,
   Ever to content ye.
I'll bait the line and bear the pail,
An' row the boat and spread the sail,
An' drag the larry at my tail,
   When mussel hives are plenty.

Then come awa' wi' me, lassie,
   To the braes o' Birniebouzle;
Bonny lassie, dear lassie,
   You shall ne'er repent ye.
For you shall own a bught o' ewes,
A brace o' gaits, and byre o' cows,
An' be the lady o' my house,
   An' lads an' lasses plenty.

GOOD NIGHT AN' JOY BE WI' YOU A'!
JAMES HOGG.

The year is wearin' to the wane,
  An' day is fadin' west awa',
Loud raves the torrent an' the rain,
  An' dark the cloud comes down the shaw.
But let the tempest tout and blaw,
  Upon his loudest winter horn,
Good night an' joy be wi' you a',
  We'll maybe meet again the morn.

O we ha'e wander'd far an' wide,
  O'er Scotia's land o' firth an' fell,
An' mony a simple flower we've call'd,
  An' twined them wi' the heather-bell:
We've ranged the dingle an' the dell,
  The hamlet an' the baron's ha',
Now let us tak' a kind farewell,—
  Good night an' joy be wi' you a'!

Ye ha'e been kind as I was keen,
  An' follow'd where I led the way,
'Till ilk a poet's lore we've seen
  Of this an' mony a former day.
If e'er I led your steps astray,
  Forgi'e your minstrel ance for a';
A tear fa's wi' his parting lay—
  Good night an' joy be wi' you a'!

DONALD MACDONALD.
JAMES HOGG.

My name it is Donald Macdonald—
  I leeve in the Highlands sae grand;
I've follow'd our banner, and will do,
  Wherever my Maker has land.
When rankit amang the blue bonnets,
  Nae danger can fear me ava;
I ken that my brethren around me
  Are either to conquer or fa'.
    Brogues, and brochan, and a',
      Brochan, and brogues, and a',
    And is na her very weel aff
      Wha has brogues, and brochan, and a'?

What though we befreendit young Charlie?
  To tell it I dinna think shame;
Puir lad! he cam' to us but barely,
  And reckon'd our mountains his hame.

It's true that our reason forbade us,
But tenderness carried the day;
Had Geordie come friendless amang us,
Wi' him we had a' gane away.
    Sword, and buckler, and a',
      Buckler, and sword, and a';
    For George we'll encounter the devil,
      Wi' sword, and buckler, and a'.

And O I wad eagerly press him
The keys o' the East to retain;
For should he gi'e up the possession,
We'll soon ha'e to force them again;
Than yield up an inch wi' dishonour,
Though it were my finishin' blow,
He aye may depend on Macdonald,
Wi' his Highlandmen all in a row.
    Knees, and elbows, and a',
      Elbows, and knees, and a,'
    Depend upon Donald Macdonald,
      His knees, and elbows, and a'.

If Bonaparte land at Fort-William,
Auld Europe nae langer shall grane;
I laugh when I think how we'll gall him
Wi' bullet, wi' steel, and wi' stane:
Wi' rocks o' the Nevis and Garny
We'll rattle him aff frae our shore,
Or lull him asleep in a cairnie,
And sing him Lochaber no more!
    Stanes, and bullets, an' a',
      Bullets, and stanes, and a';
    We'll finish the Corsican callan
      Wi' stanes, and bullets, and a'.

The Gordon is gude in a hurry;
And Campbell is steel to the bane,
And Grant, and Mackenzie, and Murray,
And Cameron, will burkle to nane;
The Stuart is sturdy and wannel;
And sae is Macleod and Mackay;
And I, their gude-brither, Macdonald,
Sall never be last in the fray.
    Brogues, and brochan, and a',
      Brochan, and brogues, and a';
    And up wi' the bonnie blue bonnet,
      The kilt, and feather, and a'.

DOCTOR MUNROE.
JAMES HOGG.

"Dear Doctor, be clever, an' fling aff your beaver,
  Come, bleed me an' blister me, dinna be slow;
I'm sick, I'm exhausted, my prospects are blasted,
  An' a' driven heels o'er head, Doctor Munroe!"
"Be patient, dear fellow, you foster your fever;
  Pray, what's the misfortune that troubles you so?"
"O, Doctor! I'm ruin'd, I'm ruin'd for ever—
  My lass has forsaken me, Doctor Munroe!

"I meant to have married, an' tasted the pleasures,
  The sweets, the enjoyments from wedlock that flow;
But she's ta'en another, an' broken my measures,
  An' fairly dumfounder'd me, Doctor Munroe!
I'm fool'd, I am dover'd as dead as a herring—
  Good sir, you're a man of compassion, I know;
Come, bleed me to death, then, unflinching, unerring,
  Or grant me some poison, dear Doctor Munroe!"

The Doctor he flang aff his big-coat an' beaver,
  He took out his lance, an' he sharpen'd it so;
No judge ever look'd more decided or graver—
  "I've oft done the same, sir," says Doctor Munroe,
"For gamblers, rogues, jockeys, and desperate lovers,
  But I always make charge of a hundred, or so."
The patient look'd pale, and cried out in shrill quavers,
  "The devil! do you say so, sir, Doctor Munroe?"

"O yes, sir, I'm sorry there's nothing more common;
  I like it—it pays—but, ere that length I go,
A man that goes mad for the love of a woman
  I sometimes can cure with a lecture, or so."
"Why, thank you, sir; there spoke the man and the friend too,
  Death is the last reckoner with friend or with foe,
The lecture then, first, if you please, I'll attend to;
  The other, of course, you know, Doctor Munroe."

The lecture is said—How severe, keen, an' cutting,
  Of love an' of wedlock, each loss an' each woe,
The patient got up— o'er the floor he went strutting,
  Smil'd, caper'd, an' shook hands with Doctor Munroe.
He dresses, an' flaunts it with Bell, Sue, an' Chirsty,
  But freedom an' fun chooses not to forego;
He still lives a bachelor, drinks when he's thirsty,
  An' sings like a lark, an' loves Doctor Munroe!

CALLUM-A-GLEN.
JAMES HOGG.

Was ever old warrior of suffering so weary?
  Was ever the wild beast so bayed in his den?
The Southron blood-hounds lie in kennels so near me,
  That death would be freedom to Callum-a-Glen.
My chief they have slain, and of stay have bereft me,
My sons are all slain and my daughters have left me;
  No child to protect me, where once there was ten,
  And woe to the grey hairs of Callum-a-Glen.

The homes of my kindred are blazing to heaven,
  The bright sun of morning has blushed at the view;
The moon has stood still on the verge of the even,
  To wipe from her pale cheek the tint of the dew:
For the dew it lies red on the vales of Lochaber,
It sprinkles the cot and it flows from the pen;
  The pride of my country is fallen for ever!
  Death, hast thou no shaft for old Callum-a-Glen?

The sun in his glory has look'd on our sorrow,
  The stars have wept blood over hamlet and lea:
Oh, is there no day-spring for Scotland? no morrow
  Of bright renovation for souls of the free?
Yes: one above all has beheld our devotion;
Our valour and faith are not hid from his ken;
  The day is abiding of stern retribution
  On all the proud foes of old Callum-a-Glen.

MY LOVE SHE'S BUT A LASSIE YET.
JAMES HOGG.

My love she's but a lassie yet,
A lightsome lovely lassie yet;
  It scarce wad do
  To sit an' woo
Down by the stream sae glassy yet.
But there's a braw time coming yet,
When we may gang a-roaming yet;
  An' hint wi' glee
  O' joys to be,
When fa's the modest gloaming yet.

She's neither proud nor saucy yet,
She's neither plump nor gaucy yet;
  But just a jinking,
  Bonnie blinking,
Hilty-skilty lassie yet.

But O, her artless smile's mair sweet
Than hinny or than marmalets;
   An' right or wrang,
   Ere it be lang,
I'll bring her to a parley yet.

I'm jealous o' what blesses her,
The very breeze that kisses her,
   The flowery beds
   On which she treads,
Though wae for ane that misses her.
Then O to meet my lassie yet,
Up in yon glen sae grassy yet;
   For all I see
   Are nought to me,
Save her that's but a lassie yet!

THERE'S NAE LADDIE COMING FOR THEE.

JAMES HOGG.

There's nae laddie coming for thee, my dear Jean,
There's nae laddie coming for thee, my dear Jean,
I ha'e watch'd thee at mid-day, at morn, an' at e'en,
An' there's nae laddie coming for thee, my dear Jean.
But be nae down-hearted though lovers gang by,
Thou'rt my only sister, thy brother am I;
An' aye in my wee house thou welcome shalt be,
An' while I ha'e saxpence, I'll share it wi' thee.

O Jeanie, dear Jeanie, when we twa were young,
I sat on your knee, to your bosom I clung;
You kiss'd me, an' clasp'd me, an' croon'd your bit sang,
An' bore me about when you hardly dought gang.
An' when I fell sick, wi' a red watery e'e
You watch'd your wee brother, an' fear'd he wad dee;
I felt the cool hand, and the kindly embrace,
An' the warm trickling tears drappin' aft on my face.

Sae wae was my kind heart to see my Jean weep,
I closed my sick e'e, though I wanna asleep;
An' I'll never forget till the day that I dee,
The gratitude due, my dear Jeanie, to thee!
Then be nae down-hearted, for nae lad can feel
Sic true love as I do, or ken ye sae weel;
My heart it yearns o'er thee, and grieved wad I be
If aught were to part my dear Jeanie an' me.

I'LL NO WAKE.

JAMES HOGG.

O, MOTHER, tell the laird o't,
  Or sairly it will grieve me, O,
That I'm to wake the ewes the night,
  And Annie's to gang wi' me, O.
I'll wake the ewes my nicht about,
  But ne'or wi' ane sae saucy, O,
Nor sit my lane the lee-lang night
  Wi' sic a scornfu' lassie, O:
    I'll no wake, I'll no wake,
      I'll no wake wi' Annie, O;
    Nor sit my lane o'er night wi' ane
      Sae thraward an' uncanny, O!

Dear son, be wise an' warie,
  But never be unmanly, O;
I've heard ye tell another tale
  Of young an' charming Annie, O.
The ewes ye wake are fair enough,
  Upon the brae sae bonny, O;
But the laird himsel' wad gi'e them a'
  To wake the night wi' Annie, O.
    He'll no wake, he'll no wake,
      He'll no wake wi' Annie, O;
    Nor sit his lane o'er night wi' ane
      Sae thraward an' uncanny, O!

I tauld ye ear', I tauld ye late,
  That lassie wad trapan ye, O;
An' ilka word ye boud to say
  When left alane wi' Annie, O!
Take my advice this night for ance,
  Or beauty's tongue will ban ye, O,
An' sey your leal auld mother's skill
  Ayont the muir wi' Annie, O.
    He'll no wake, he'll no wake,
      He'll no wake wi' Annie, O,
    Nor sit his lane o'er night wi' ane
      Sae thraward an' uncanny, O!

The night it was a simmer night,
  An' oh! the glen was lanely, O,
For just as sternie's gowden e'e
  Peep'd o'er the hill serenely, O.

The twa are in the flow'ry heath,
  Ayont the muir sae flowy, O,
An' but ae plaid between them baith,
  An' wasna that right dowie, O?
    He maun wake, he maun wake,
      He maun wake wi' Annie, O;
    An' sit his lane o'er night wi' ane
      Sae thraward an' uncanny, O!

Neist morning at his mother's knee
  He blest her love unfeign'dly, O;
An' aye the tear fell frae his e'e,
  An' aye he clasp'd her kindly, O.
"Of a' my griefs I've got amends,
  In yon wild glen sae grassy, O;
A woman only woman kens,—
  Your skill has won my lassie, O.
    I'll aye wake, I'll aye wake,
      I'll aye wake wi' Annie, O,
    An' sit my lane ilk night wi' ane
      Sae sweet, sae kind, an' canny, O!"

MEG O' MARLEY.
JAMES HOGG.

O ken ye Meg o' Marley glen,
  The bonny blue-e'ed dearie?
She's play'd the deil amang the men,
  An' a' the land's grown eery.
She's stown the "Bangor" frae the clerk,
  An' snool'd him wi' the shame o't;
The minister's fa'n through the text,
  An' Meg gets a' the blame o't.

The ploughman ploughs without the sock;
  The gadman whistles sparely;
The shepherd pines amang his flock,
  An' turns his e'en to Marley;
The tailor lad's fa'n ower the bed;
  The cobler ca's a parly;
The weaver's neb's out through the web,
  An' a' for Meg o' Marley.

What's to be done, for our gudeman
  Is flyting late an' early?
He rises but to curse an' ban,
  An' sits down but to ferly.
But ne'er had love a brighter lowe
  Than light his torches sparely
At the bright e'en an' blythesome brow
  O' bonny Meg o' Marley.

THE SKYLARK.
JAMES HOGG.

Bird of the wilderness,
Blythesome and cumberless,
Sweet be thy matin o'er moorland and lea!
Emblem of happiness,
Blessed is thy dwelling-place,
Oh! to abide in the desert with thee!

Wild is thy lay and loud,
Far in the downy cloud;
Love gives it energy, love gave it birth;
Where on the dewy wing,
Where art thou journeying?
Thy lay is in heaven, thy love is on earth.

O'er fell and fountain sheen,
O'er moor and mountain green,
O'er the red streamer that heralds the day;
Over the cloudlet dim,
Over the rainbow's rim,
Musical cherub, hie, hie thee away!

Then when the gloaming comes,
Low in the heather blooms,
Sweet will thy welcome and bed of love be!
Bird of the wilderness,
Bless'd is thy dwelling-place,
Oh! to abide in the desert with thee.

I'LL SING O' YON GLEN.
JAMES HOGG.

I'll sing of yon glen o' red heather,
An' a dear thing that ca's it her hame,
Wha's a' made o' love-life together,
Frae the tie o' the shoe to the kaime.
Love beckons in ev'ry sweet motion,
Commanding due homage to gi'e;
But the shrine of my dearest devotion
Is the bend o' her bonnie e'e brae.

I fleech'd and I pray'd the dear lassie
To gang to the brakens wi' me,
But though neither lordly nor saucy,
Her answer was, "Laith wad I be.
Ah! is it nae cruel to press me
To that which wad breed my heart wae,
An' try to entice a poor lassie
The gate she's o'er ready to gae?

"I neither ha'e father nor mither,
  Good counsel or caution to gi'e,
And prudence has whisper'd me never
  To gang to the brackens wi' thee.
I neither ha'e tocher nor mailing,
  I ha'e but ae boast—I am free;
But a' wad be tint, without failing,
  Amang the green brackens wi' thee."

"Dear lassie, how can ye upbraid me,
  And by your ain love to beguile,
For ye are the richest young lady
  That ever gaed o'er the kirk-style?
Your smile that is blither than ony,
  The bend o' your sunny e'e-bree,
And the love-blinks aneath it sae bonnie
  Are five hunder thousand to me."

There's joy in the blythe blooming feature,
  When love lurks in every young line;
There's joy in the beauties of nature,
  There's joy in the dance and the wine;
But there's a delight will ne'er perish
  'Mang pleasures so fleeting and vain,
And that is to love and to cherish
  The fond little heart that's our ain.

LOOSE THE YETT.

JAMES HOGG.

Loose the yett, an' let me in,
  Lady wi' the glistening e'e,
Dinna let your menial train
  Drive an auld man out to dee.
Cauldrife is the winter even,
  See, the rime hangs at my chin;
Lady, for the sake of Heaven,
  Loose the yett, an' let me in!

Ye shall gain a virgin hue,
  Lady, for your courtesye,
Ever beaming, ever new,
  Aye to bloom an' ne'er to dee.
Lady, there's a lovely plain
  Lies beyond yon setting sun,
There we soon may meet again—
  Short the race we ha'e to run.

'Tis a land of love an' light;
  Rank or title is not there,
High an' low maun there unite,
  Poor man, prince, an' lady fair;
There, what thou on earth hast given,
  Doubly shall be paid again!
Lady, for the sake of Heaven,
  Loose the yett, an' let me in!

Blessings rest upon thy head,
  Lady of this lordly ha'!
That bright tear that thou did'st shed
  Fell nae down amang the snaw!
It is gane to heaven aboon,
  To the fount of charitye;
When thy days on earth are done;
  That blest drop shall plead for thee.

WHEN MAGGIE GANGS AWA.

JAMES HOGG.

O, what will a' the lads do
  When Maggie gangs away?
O, what will a' the lads do,
  When Maggie gangs away?
There's no a heart in a' the glen
  That disna dread the day—
O, what will a' the lads do
  When Maggie gangs away?

Young Jock has ta'en the hill for't—
  A waefu' wight is he;
Poor Harry's ta'en the bed for't,
  An' laid him doun to dee;
An' Sandy's gane unto the kirk,
  An' learning fast to pray—
And, O, what will the lads do
  When Maggie gangs away?

The young laird o' the Lang-shaw
  Has drunk her health in wine;
The priest has said—in confidence—
  The lassie was divine:
And that is mair in maiden's praise
  Than ony priest should say:
But, O, what will the lads do
  When Maggie gangs away?

The wailing in our green glen
That day will quaver high;
'Twill draw the red-breast frae the wood,
The laverock from the sky;
The fairies frae their beds o' dew
Will rise and join the lay:
An' hey! what a day 'twill be
When Maggie gangs away!

CALEDONIA.
JAMES HOGG.

Caledonia! thou land of the mountain and rock,
Of the ocean, the mist, and the wind—
Thou land of the torrent, the pine, and the oak,
Of the roebuck, the hart, and the hind:
Though bare are thy cliffs, and though barren thy glens,
Though bleak thy dun islands appear,
Yet kind are the hearts, and undaunted the clans,
That roam on these mountains so drear!

A foe from abroad, or a tyrant at home,
Could never thy ardour restrain;
The marshall'd array of imperial Rome
Essay'd thy proud spirit in vain!
Firm seat of religion, of valour, of truth,
Of genius unshackled and free,
The muses have left all the vales of the south,
My loved Caledonia, for thee!

Sweet land of the bay and the wild-winding deeps
Where loveliness slumbers at even,
While far in the depth of the blue waters sleeps
A calm little motionless heaven!
Thou land of the valley, the moor, and the hill,
Of the storm and the proud rolling wave—
Yes, thou art the land of fair liberty still,
And the land of my forefathers' grave!

OH! WEEL BEFA' THE BUSY LOOM.
FROM Blackwood's Magazine.

Oh! weel befa' the busy loom
That plies the hale day lang;
And, clicking briskly, fills the room
Wi' sic a cheery sang.
Oh! weel befa' the eident han'
That cleeds us, great and sma',
And blessings on the kind gudeman
That dearly lo'es us a'.

Our purse is low, our lot is mean,
  But waur it weel might be;
Our house is canty aye and clean,
  Our hearts frae canker free.
We fash wi' nae ambitious scheme,
  Nor heed affairs o' state;
We dinna strive against the stream,
  Or murmur at our fate.

Oh! mickle is the wealth that springs
  Frae industry and peace,
Where nae reproach o' conscience stings,
  And a' repinin's cease.
The heart will loathe the richest meat,
  If nae kind blessin's sent:
The coarsest morsel will be sweet
  When kitchen'd wi' content.

Oh! wad the Power that rules o'er life
  Impart some gracious charm,
To keep me still a happy wife,
  And shield the house frae harm.
Instead of wealth and growing care,
  I ask but health and love;
Instead of warldly wit and leir,
  Some wisdom from above.

Our bairns! the comfort o' our heart,
  Oh! may they long be spared!
We'll try by them to do our part,
  And hope a sure reward.
What better tocher can we gi'e
  Than just a taste for hame;
What better heirship, when we dee,
  Than just an honest name?

MY AIN FIRESIDE.

ELIZABETH HAMILTON,

AUTHORESS of the celebrated Scotch Story, "The Cottagers of Glenburnie." She died at Harrowgate in 1816, in her 68th year. She was authoress of several valuable and popular works in their time; but all, with the exception of her inimitable Cottagers and the song here given, are now forgotten.

I HA'E seen great anes, and sat in great ha's,
'Mang lords and fine ladies a' cover'd wi' braws;
At feasts made for princes, wi' princes I've been,
Whare the grand sheen o' splendour has dazzled my een:
But a sight sae delightfu', I trow, I ne'er spied,
As the bonnie blythe blink o' mine ain fireside;

My ain fireside, my ain fireside,
O cheery's the blink o' mine ain fireside.
    My ain fireside, my ain fireside,
    O there's nought to compare wi' ane's ain fireside.

Ance mair, gude be thanket, round my ain heartsome ingle,
Wi' the friends o' my youth I cordially mingle;
Nae forms to compel me to seem wae or glad,
I may laugh when I'm merry, and sigh when I'm sad.
Nae falsehood to dread, and nae malice to fear,
But truth to delight me, and friendship to cheer;
Of a' roads to happiness ever were tried,
There's nane half so sure as ane's ain fireside.
    My ain fireside, my ain fireside,
    O there's nought to compare wi' ane's ain fireside.

When I draw in my stool on my cosey hearthstane,
My heart loups see light I scarce ken't for my ain;
Care's down on the wind, it is clean out o' sight,
Past troubles they seem but as dreams of the night.
I hear but kenn'd voices, kenn'd faces I see,
And mark saft affection glent fond frae ilk e'e;
Nae fleetchings o' flattery, nae boastings o' pride,
'Tis heart speaks to heart at ane's ain fireside.
    My ain fireside, my ain fireside,
    O there's nought to compare wi' ane's ain fireside.

SEE THE MOON.

DANIEL WEIR,

Was born at Greenock in 1796. He began business as a bookseller there in 1815, and conducted a highly respectable business till his death in 1831.

Weir contributed to Smith's Scottish Minstrel several pleasing songs, and himself edited for a Glasgow firm three volumes of songs, &c., under the titles of "The National Minstrel," "The Sacred Lyre," and "Lyrical Gems." In these volumes the majority of his own printed pieces first appeared. A "History of Greenock" was written and published by him in 1829.

    See the moon o'er cloudless Jura
      Shining in the lake below;
    See the distant mountain towering
      Like a pyramid of snow.
    Scenes of grandeur—scenes of childhood—
      Scenes so dear to love and me!
    Let us roam by bower and wildwood,
      All is lovelier when with thee.

On Leman's breast the winds are sighing,
  All is silent in the grove,
And the flowers with dew-drops glistening
  Sparkle like the eye of love.
Night so calm, so clear, so cloudless;
  Blessed night to love and me!
Let us roam by bower and fountain,
  All is lovelier when with thee.

MARY.

DANIEL WEIR.

How dear to think on former days,
  And former scenes I've wander'd o'er;
They well deserve a poet's praise,
  In lofty rhyme they ought to soar.
How oft I've wander'd by the Clyde,
  When night obscured the landscape near,
To hear its murm'ring waters glide,
  And think upon my Mary dear.

And when the moon shot forth her light,
  Sweet glimm'ring through the distant trees,
How sweet to pass the peaceful night,
  And breathe, serene, the passing breeze.
Though grand these scenes of peace and joy,
  'Tis not for them I'd drop the tear;
Remembrance will my heart annoy,
  When thinking on my Mary dear.

Far from my friends, far from my home,
  I wander on a distant shore;
Far from those scenes I used to roam,
  And scenes perhaps I'll tread no more.
My fancy still beholds the Clyde,
  Her scenes of grandeur now appear;
What power can o'er my thoughts divide,
  From Clyde's fair banks and Mary dear.

No power on earth can change my heart,
  Or tear these scenes from out my mind;
And when this world and I shall part,
  For them I'll cast a look behind.
Swift fly the time until we meet,
  Swift fly away each day and year;
Until my early friends I greet,
  And kiss again my Mary dear!

MY LOVE, COME LET US WANDER.

DANIEL WEIR.

My love, come let us wander,
Where Raven's streams meander,
And where in simple grandeur,
   The daisy decks the plain.
Peace and joy our hours shall measure;
Come, oh come, my soul's best treasure!
Then how sweet, and then how cheerie,
Raven's braes will be, my dearie.

The silver moon is beaming,
On Clyde her light is streaming,
And, while the world is dreaming,
   We'll talk of love, my dear.
None, my Jean, will share this bosom,
Where thine image loves to blossom,
And no storm will ever sever
   That dear flower, or part us ever.

NEATH THE WAVE.

DANIEL WEIR.

'Neath the wave thy lover sleeps,
   And cold, cold is his pillow;
O'er his bed no maiden weeps,
   Where rolls the white billow.
And though the winds have sunk to rest
Upon the ocean's troubled breast,
Yet still, oh still there's left behind
A restless storm in Ellen's mind.

Her heart is on yon dark'ning wave,
   Where all she lov'd is lying,
And where around her William's grave,
   The sea-bird is crying.
And oft on Jura's lonely shore,
Where surges beat and billows roar,
She sat—but grief has nipt her bloom,
An there they made young Ellen's tomb.

DINNA ASK ME GIN I LO'E YOU.
JOHN DUNLOP.

He was born at Carmyle, in Lanarkshire, in 1755. He was for some time a merchant in Glasgow, and in 1796 held the position of Lord Provost of that city. He died at Port Glasgow, where he held the office of Collector of Customs, in 1820.

Oh! dinna ask me gin I lo'e thee;
  Troth, I daurna tell;
Dinna ask me gin I lo'e ye;
  Ask it o' yoursel'.

Oh! dinna look sae sair at me,
  For weel ye ken me true;
O, gin ye look sae sair at me,
  I daurna look at you.

When ye gang to yon braw braw town,
  And bonnier lasses see,
O, dinna, Jamie, look at them,
  Lest you should mind na me.

For I could never bide the lass,
  That ye'd lo'e mair than me;
And O, I'm sure, my heart would break,
  Gin ye'd prove false to me.

THE YEAR THAT'S AWA'.
JOHN DUNLOP.

Here's to the year that's awa'!
  We will drink it in strong and in sma';
And here's to ilk bonnie young lassie we lo'ed
  While swift flew the year that's awa'.
    And here's to ilk, &c.

Here's to the sodger who bled,
  And the sailor who bravely did fa';
Their fame is alive, though their spirits are fled
  On the wings of the year that's awa'.
    Their fame is alive, &c.

Here's to the friends we can trust,
  When the storms of adversity blaw;
May they live in our song, and be nearest our hearts,
  Nor depart like the year that's awa'.
    May they live, &c.

OH, WHY LEFT I MY HAME.

ROBERT GILFILLAN.

Was born at Dunfermline in 1798. His parents were very poor, and Robert began the "battle for bread" when his teens were a long way off. In 1811, he went to Leith, where he was engaged as an apprentice to a Cooper; when his apprenticeship was past he returned to Dunfermline, and was employed as shopman to a Grocer. In 1837, he received the appointment of Collector of Police Rates in Leith, a post which he occupied till his death, which took place in 1850.

His first volume, entitled "Original Songs," was issued in 1831, and was reprinted with about fifty additional pieces in 1835. He also contributed largely to the periodicals of the day.

Oh, why left I my hame? Why did I cross the deep?
Oh, why left I the land where my forefathers sleep?
I sigh for Scotia's shore, and I gaze across the sea,
But I canna get a blink o' my ain countrie.

The palm-tree waveth high, and fair the myrtle springs,
And to the Indian maid the bulbul sweetly sings;
But I dinna see the broom wi' its tassels on the lea,
Nor hear the lintie's sang o' my ain countrie.

Oh! here no Sabbath bell awakes the Sabbath morn,
Nor song of reapers heard among the yellow corn:
For the tyrant's voice is here, and the wail of slaverie;
But the sun of freedom shines in my ain countrie.

There's a hope for every woe, and a balm for ev'ry pain,
But the first joys of our heart come never back again,
There's a track upon the deep, and a path across the sea,
But the weary ne'er return to their ain countrie.

JANET AND ME.

ROBERT GILFILLAN.

O, wha are sae happy as me and my Janet?
O, wha are sae happy as Janet and me?
We're baith turning auld, and our walth is soon tauld,
But contentment ye'll find in our cottage sae wee.
She spins the lang day when I'm out wi' the owsen,
She croons i' the house while I sing at the plough;
And aye her blythe smile welcomes me frae my toil,
As up the lang glen I come wearied, I trow!

When I'm at a beuk she is mending the cleading,
She's darning the stockings when I sole the shoon;
Our cracks keep us cheery—we work till we're weary;
And syne we sup sowans when ance we are done.

She's baking a scone while I'm smoking my cutty,
  While I'm i' the stable she's milking the kye;
I envy not kings when the gloaming time brings
  The canty fireside to my Janet and I!
Aboon our auld heads we've a decent clay biggin,
  That keeps out the cauld when the simmer's awa';
We've twa wabs o' linen, o' Janet's ain spinning,
  As thick as dog-lugs, and as white as the snaw!
We've a kebbuck or twa, and some meal i' the girnel;
  Yon sow is our ain that plays grunt at the door;
An' *something*, I've guess'd, 's in yon auld painted kist,
  That Janet, fell bodie, 's laid up to the fore!

Nae doubt, we have haen our ain sorrows and troubles,
  Aften times pouches toom, and hearts fu' o' care;
But still, wi' our crosses, our sorrows and losses,
  Contentment, be thankit, has aye been our share;
I've an auld rusty sword, that was left by my father,
  Whilk ne'er shall be drawn till our king has a fae;
We ha'e friends ane or twa, that aft gi'e us a ca',
  To laugh when we're happy, or grieve when we're wae.

The laird may ha'e gowd mair than schoolmen can reckon,
  An' flunkies to watch ilka glance o' his e'e;
His lady, aye braw, may sit in her ha',
  But are they mair happy than Janet and me?
A' ye wha ne'er kent the straight road to be happy,
  Wha are na content wi' the lot that ye dree,
Come down to the dwellin' of whilk I've been telling,
  Ye'se learn it by looking at Janet an' me!

A CANTY SANG.

ROBERT GILFILLAN.

A canty sang, O, a canty sang,
Will naebody gi'e us a canty sang?
There's naething keeps nights frae turning owre lang
Like a canty sang, like a canty sang.

If folk wad but sing when they're gaun to flyte,
Less envy ye'd see, less anger and spite;
What saftens doun strife, and mak's love mair strang,
Like a canty sang, like a canty sang?
    Like a canty sang, &c.

If lads wad but sing when they gang to woo,
They'd come na aye hame wi' thoum i' their mou';
The chiel that wi' lasses wad be fu' thrang,
Suld learn to lilt to them a canty sang.
    A canty sang, &c.

When fools become quarrelsome ower their ale,
I'se gi'e ye a cure whilk never will fail,—
When their tongues get short an' their arms get lang,
Aye drown the din wi' a canty sang!
  A canty sang, &c.

I downa bide strife, though fond o' a spree,
Your sair wordy bodies are no for me:
A wee dribble punch, gif it just be strang,
Is a' my delight, an' a canty sang!

A canty sang, O, a canty sang,
Will naebody gi'e us a canty sang?
There's naething keeps nights frae turning ower lang
Like a canty sang, like a canty sang.

OH, TAKE ME TO YON SUNNY ISLE.
ROBERT GILFILLAN.

Oh! take me to yon sunny isle that stands in Fortha's sea,
For there, all lonely, I may weep, since tears my lot must be;
The cavern'd rocks alone shall hear my anguish and my woe,
But can their echoes Mary bring? ah! no, no, no!

I'll wander by the silent shore, or climb the rocky steep,
And list to ocean murmuring the music of the deep;
But when the soft moon lights the waves in evening's silver
 glow,
Shall Mary meet me 'neath its light? ah! no, no, no!

I'll speak of her to every flower, and lovely flowers are there,
They'll may be bow their heads and weep, for she, like them,
 was fair—
And every bird I'll teach a song, a plaintive song of woe,
But Mary cannot hear their strains?—ah! no, no, no!

Slow steals the sun a-down the sky, as loth to part with day,
But airy morn with carolling voice shall wake him forth as gay;
Yet Mary's sun rose bright and fair, and now that sun is low,
Shall its fair beam e'er grace the morn? ah! no, no, no!

But I must shed the hidden tear, lest Mary mark my care:
The stifling groan may break my heart, but it shall linger there!
I'll even feign the outward smile, to hide my inward woe,
I would not have her weep in heaven—ah! no, no, no!

MARY SHEARER.

THOMAS ATKINSON,

A BOOKSELLER in Glasgow. He died while on a voyage to Barbadoes in 1833.

She's aff and awa' like the lang summer day,
  And our hearts and our hills are now lancsome and dreary;
The sun-blinks o' June will come back ower the brae,
  But lang for blythe Mary fu' mony may weary!
      For mair hearts than mine
        Kenn'd o' nane that were dearer;
      But nane mair will pine
        For the sweet Mary Shearer!

She cam' wi' the spring just like ane o' its flowers,
  And the blue bell and Mary baith blossom'd thegither;
The bloom o' the mountain again will be ours,
  But the rose o' the valley nae mair will come hither!
      Their sweet breath is fled—
        Her kind looks still endear her;
      For the heart maun be dead
        That forgets Mary Shearer!

Than her brow ne'er a fairer wi' jewels was hung;
An e'e that was brighter ne'er glanced on a lover;
Sounds safter ne'er dropt frae an aye-saying tongue,
Nor mair pure is the white o' her bridal-bed cover.
      O! he maun be bless'd
        Wha's allowed to be near her;
      For the fairest and best
        O' her kind's Mary Shearer!

But farewell, Glenlin, and Dunoon, and Loch Striven,
  My country and kin!—since I've sae lov'd the stranger;
Where she's been maun be either a pine or a heaven,
  —Sae across the braid warld for a while I'm a ranger!
      Though I try to forget—
        In my heart still I'll wear her:—
      For mine may be yet,
        —Name and a'—Mary Shearer!

LOVE.

ASCRIBED to Robert Burns, junior, eldest son of the poet.

Ha'e ye seen, in the calm dewy morning,
  The red-breast wild warbling sae clear;
Or the low-dwelling, snow-breasted gowan,
  Surcharg'd wi' mild e'ening's soft tear?

O, then ye ha's seen my dear lassie,
 The lassie I lo'e best of a';
But far frae the hame o' my lassie,
 I'm mony a lang mile awa'.

Her hair is the wing o' the blackbird,
 Her eye is the eye o' the dove,
Her lips are the ripe blushing rose-bud,
 Her bosom's the palace of love.
Though green be thy banks, O sweet Clutha!
 Thy beauties ne'er charm me ava;
Forgive me, ye maids o' sweet Clutha,
 My heart is wi' her that's awa'.

O love, thou'rt a dear fleeting pleasure!
 The sweetest we mortals here know;
But soon is thy heav'n, bright beaming,
 O'ercast with the darkness of woe.
As the moon, on the oft-changing ocean,
 Delights the lone mariner's eye,
Till red rush the storms of the desert,
 And dark billows tumble on high.

PITY AN AULD HIGHLAN' PIPER

Ascribed to Robert Burns, junior.

OH pity an auld Highlan' piper,
 An' dinna for want let him dee:
Oh! look at my faithfu' wee doggie,
 The icicle hangs frae his e'e.

I ance had a weel theekit cot-house
 On Morvala's sea-beaten shore;
But our laird turn'd me out frae my cot-house;
 Alas! I was feckless an' puir.

My twa sons were baith press'd for sailors,
 An' brave for their kintra did fa';
My auld wife she died soon o' sorrow,
 An' left me bereft o' them a'.

I downa do ony sair wark,
 For maist bauld is my lyart auld pow,
So I beg wi' my pipes, an' my doggie,
 An' mony a place we've been through.

I set mysel' down i' the gloamin',
 An' tak' my wee dog on my knee,
An' I play on my pipes wi' sad sorrow,
 An' the tear trickles doun frae my e'e.

The tear trickles doun frae my e'e,
  An' my heart's like to break e'en in twa,
When I think on my auld wife an' bairns,
  That now are sae far far awa'.

Come in thou puir lyart auld carle,
  And here nae mair ill shalt thou dree;
As lang as I'm laird o' this manor,
  There's nane shall gae helpless frae me.

And ye shall get a wee cot-house,
  An' ye shall get baith milk an' meal;
For he that has sent it to me,
  Has sent it to use it weel.

DUNOON.

THOMAS LYLE,

A NATIVE of Paisley, where he was born in 1792. He practised as a surgeon in Glasgow till 1826, when he went to Airth in Stirlingshire. In 1853 he returned to Glasgow, where he died in 1859.

Mr. Lyle edited in 1827 a small volume of "Ancient Ballads and Songs," the result of long investigation into the popular poetry of Scotland, many pieces having been recovered from tradition by the editor and printed there for the first time. The volume is also interesting to the antiquary as containing a collection of poems by Mure of Rowallan.

SEE the glow-worm lits her fairy lamp,
  From a beam of the rising moon;
On the heathy shore at evening fall,
  'Twixt Holy-Loch, and dark Dunoon:
Her fairy lamp's pale silvery glare,
  From the dew-clad, moorland flower,
Invite my wandering footsteps there,
  At the louely twilight hour.

When the distant beacon's revolving light
  Bids my lone steps seek the shore,
There the rush of the flow-tide's rippling wave
  Meets the dash of the fisher's oar;
And the dim-seen steam-boat's hollow sound,
  As she seaward tracks her way;
All else are asleep in the still calm night,
  And robed in the misty gray.

When the glow-worm lits her elfin lamp,
  And the night breeze sweeps the hill;
It's sweet, on thy rock-bound shores, Dunoon,
  To wander at fancy's will.
Eliza! with thee, in this solitude,
  Life's cares would pass away,
Like the fleecy clouds over gray Kilmun,
  At the wake of early day.

KELVIN GROVE.

THOMAS LYLE.

LET us haste to Kelvin grove, bonnie lassie, O,
Through its mazes let us rove, bonnie lassie, O,
   Where the rose in all her pride,
   Paints the hollow dingle side,
Where the midnight fairies glide, bonnie lassie, O.

Let us wander by the mill, bonnie lassie, O,
To the cove beside the rill, bonnie lassie, O,
   Where the glens rebound the call,
   Of the roaring waters' fall,
Thro' the mountain's rocky hall, bonnie lassie, O.

O Kelvin banks are fair, bonnie lassie, O,
When in summer we are there, bonnie lassie, O,
   There, the May-pink's crimson plume,
   Throws a soft, but sweet perfume,
Round the yellow banks of broom, bonnie lassie, O.

Though I dare not call thee mine, bonnie lassie, O,
As the smile of fortune's thine, bonnie lassie, O,
   Yet with fortune on my side,
   I could stay thy father's pride,
And win thee for my bride, bonnie lassie, O.

But the frowns of fortune lower, bonnie lassie, O,
On thy lover at this hour, bonnie lassie, O,
   Ere yon golden orb of day
   Wake the warblers on the spray,
From this land I must away, bonnie lassie, O.

Then farewell to Kelvin grove, bonnie lassie, O,
And adieu to all I love, bonnie lassie, O,
   To the river winding clear,
   To the fragrant scented brier,
Even to thee of all most dear, bonnie lassie, O.

When upon a foreign shore, bonnie lassie, O,
Should I fall midst battle's roar, bonnie lassie, O,
   Then, Helen! shouldst thou hear
   Of thy lover on his bier.
To his memory shed a tear, bonnie lassie, O.

THERE LIVES A YOUNG LASSIE.

JOHN IMLAH,

AUTHOR of several volumes of poems, he was born at Aberdeen in 1799. He was employed by the celebrated firm of Broadwood of London, as a piano tuner. He died at Jamaica, whither he had gone on a visit to a relative, in 1841. None of his songs have achieved any degree of popularity except the one here given.

THERE lives a young lassie
  Far down yon lang glen;
How I lo'e that lassie
  There's nae ane can ken!
O! a saint's faith may vary,
  But faithful I'll be;
For weel I lo'e Mary,
  An' Mary lo'es me.

Red, red as the rowan
  Her smiling wee mon';
An' white as the gowan
  Her breast and her brow!
Wi' a foot o' a fairy
  She links o'er the lea;
O! weel I lo'e Mary,
  An' Mary lo'es me!

She sings sweet as onie
  Wee bird of the air,
And she's blithe as she's bonnie,
  She's guid as she's fair;
Like a lammie sae airy
  And artless is she,
O! weel I lo'e Mary,
  An' Mary lo'es me!

Where yon tall forest timmer,
  An' lowly broom bower,
To the sunshine o' simmer
  Spread verdure an' flower;
There, when night clouds the cary,
  Beside her I'll be;
For weel I lo'e Mary,
  An' Mary lo'es me.

WE'RE A' NODDIN'.

ALLAN CUNNINGHAM,

Was born at Blackwood in Nithsdale, Dumfries-shire, in 1784. When only eleven years of age he was apprenticed to an elder brother as a stone-mason, thus sharing the lot of many of the best of our Scottish song writers who had to encounter the battle of this life at a very early age.

The greatest event in Cunningham's life is his introduction to Cromek, a London engraver, and one who felt enthusiastic about Scotch poetry and poets. Cromek in 1809 visited Dumfries to procure materials for his "Reliques of Burns" then in course of preparation. The result of their acquaintance was the production of the "Remains of Nithsdale and Galloway Song," a volume professedly of songs and fragments collected among the peasantry of Nithsdale and Galloway, but being in reality, in greater part, the composition of Allan Cunningham, who succeeded in palming them upon the credulous antiquary as traditionary pieces. The ruse, however, was soon discovered on the publication of the volume.

About the time of the publication of the "Remains," Cunningham, at the desire of Cromek, removed to London, where he worked for some time as a journeyman mason. He afterwards obtained employment as foreman to Chantrey the celebrated sculptor, in whose employment he remained till his death, which took place in 1842.

As author or editor, Allan Cunningham was one of the hardest worked men of his time. In 1813 he published a volume of poems; in 1822 a dramatic poem; in 1826 a novel entitled "Paul Jones," and in 1828 another entitled "Sir Michael Scott," besides numerous other original works. He edited an edition of the works of Robert Burns with life and notes, "the Lives of the most eminent British painters, &c.," and an edition of the Songs of Scotland in 4 volumes. He also contributed largely to Blackwood's Magazine, The Athenæum, and other journals.

The family of Cunningham seems to have been one of rare talents: we have in this work presented specimens of one of his brothers' poetical powers. Two other brothers, James and Peter, were known as contributors to the literature of the day. Of his own children, the eldest was well known as author of the Handbook to London and other works; while another son, Lieut.-Colonel Cunningham, is engaged in editing a series of the British Dramatists; a task he fulfils with great judgment and discretion.

> Our gudewife 's awa',
> Now's the time to woo,
> For the lads like lasses,
> And the lasses lads too.
> The moon's beaming bright,
> And the gowan 's in dew,
> And my love 's by my side,
> And we're a' happy now.
>   And we're a' noddin',
>   Nid, nid noddin',
>   And we're a' noddin',
>   At our house at hame.

I have wale of loves,—
 Nannie rich and fair,
Bessie brown and bonnie,
 And Kate wi' curling hair;
And Bell young and proud,
 Wi' gold aboon her brow,
But my Jean has twa e'en
 That glow'r me through and through.
   And we're a' noddin', &c.

Sair she slights the lads,
 Three lie like to dee,
Four in sorrow listed,
 And five flew to the sea.
Nigh her chamber door
 A' night they watch in dool,
Ae kind word frae my love
 Would charm frae yule to yule.
   And we're a' noddin', &c.

Our gudewife 's come hame,
 Now mute maun I woo;
My true love's bright glances
 Shine a' the chamber through;
O, sweet is her voice,
 When she sings at her work,
Sweet the touch of her hand,
 And her vows in the dark.
   And we're a' noddin', &c.

JOHN GRUMLIE.

ALLAN CUNNINGHAM.

ADAPTED from the old Poem, "The Wife of Auchtermuchty."

JOHN GRUMLIE swore by the light o' the moon,
 And the green leaves on the tree,
That he could do more work in a day
 Than his wife could do in three.
His wife rose up in the morning
 Wi' cares and troubles enow—
John Grumlie bide at hame, John,
 And I'll go haud the plow.

First ye maun dress your children fair,
 And put them a' in their gear;
And ye maun turn the malt, John,
 Or else ye'll spoil the beer;

And ye maun reel the tweel, John,
  That I span yesterday;
And ye maun ca' in the hens, John,
  Else they'll all lay away.

O he did dress his children fair,
  And put them a' in their gear;
But he forgot to turn the malt,
  And so he spoil'd the beer:
And he sang loud as he reeled the tweel
  That his wife span yesterday;
But he forgot to put up the hens,
  And the hens all layed away.

The hawket crummie loot down nae milk;
  He kirned, nor butter gat;
And a' gade wrang, and nought gade right;
  He danced with rage, and grat;
Then up he ran to the head o' the knowe
  Wi' mony a wave and shout—
She heard him as she heard him not,
  And steered the stots about.

John Grumlie's wife cam hame at e'en,
  A weary wife and sad,
And burst into a laughter loud,
  And laughed as she'd been mad:
While John Grumlie swore by the light o' the moon
  And the green leaves on the tree,
If my wife should na win a penny a day,
  She's aye have her will for me.

LADY ANNE.

ALLAN CUNNINGHAM.

There's kames o' hinnie 'tween my luve's lips,
  And gowd amang her hair,
Her breists are lapt in a holy veil;
  Nae mortal e'en keek there.
What lips daur kiss, or what hand daur touch,
  Or what arm o' luve daur span,
The hinnie lips, the creamy lufe,
  Or the waist o' Lady Anne?

She kisses the lips o' her bonnie red rose,
  Wat wi' the blobs o' dew;
But nae gentle lip, nor semple lip,
  Maun touch her ladie mou'.

But a broider'd belt, wi' a buckle o' gowd,
  Her jimpy waist maun span:
Oh, she's an armfu' fit for heaven—
  My bonnie Lady Anne!

Her bower casement is latticed wi' flowers,
  Tied up wi' siller thread;
And comely sits she in the midst,
  Men's longing e'en to feed.
She waves the ringlets frae her cheek,
  Wi' her milky milky han';
And her cheeks seem touch'd wi' the finger o' God,
  My bonnie Lady Anne.

The mornin' cloud is tassel'd wi' gowd,
  Like my luve's broider'd cap;
And on the mantle that my luve wears,
  Is mony a gowden drap.
Her bonnie ee-bree's a holy arch,
  Cast by nae earthly han',
And the breath o' heaven is atween the lips
  O' my bonnie Lady Anne.

I wonderin' gaze on her stately steps,
  And I beet a hopeless flame!
To my luve, alas! she maunna stoop;
  It wad stain her honour'd name.
My e'en are bauld, they dwall on a place
  Where I daurna mint my han';
But I water, and tend, and kiss the flowers
  O' my bonnie Lady Anne.

I am but her father's gardener lad,
  And puir puir is my fa';
My auld mither gets my wee woe fee,
  Wi' fatherless bairnies twa.
But my lady comes, my lady gaes,
  Wi' a fou and kindly han';
O, the blessin' o' God maun mix wi' my luve,
  And fa' on Lady Anne.

BONNIE MARY HALLIDAY.

ALLAN CUNNINGHAM.

Bonnie Mary Halliday,
  Turn again, I call you;
If you go to the dewy wood,
  Sorrow will befall you.

The ring-dove from the dewy wood
　Is wailing sore and calling;
An' Annan water, 'tween its banks,
　Is foaming far and falling.
Gentle Mary Halliday,
　Come, my bonnie lady—
Upon the river's woody bank
　My steed is saddled ready.

And for thy haughty kinsman's threats
　My faith shall never falter—
The bridal banquet's ready made,
　The priest is at the altar.
Gentle Mary Halliday,
　The towers of merry Preston
Have bridal candles gleaming bright—
　So busk thee, love, and hasten.

Come busk thee, love, and bowne thee
　Through Tindal and green Mouswal;
Come, be the grace and be the charm
　To the proud Towers of Mochusel.
Bonnie Mary Halliday,
　Turn again, I tell you;
For wit, and grace, and loveliness,
　What maidens may excel you?

Though Annan has its beauteous dames,
　And Corrie many a fair one,
We canna want thee from our sight,
　Thou lovely and thou rare one.
Bonnie Mary Halliday,
　When the cittern's sounding,
We'll miss thy lightsome lily foot
　Amang the blythe lads bounding.

The summer sun shall freeze our veins,
　The winter moon shall warm us.
Ere the like of thee shall come again
　To cheer us and to charm us.

THE WANTON WIFE.
ALLAN CUNNINGHAM.

Nith, trembling to the reaper's sang,
　Warm glitter'd in the harvest sun,
And murmured down the lanesome glen,
　Where a wife of wanton wit did won.

Her tongue wagged wi' unhaly wit,
  Unstent by kirk or gospel bann,
An' aye she wished the kirkyard mools
  Green growing o'er her auld gudeman.

Her auld gudeman drapped in at e'en,
  Wi' harvest heuk—sair toil'd was he;
Sma' was his cog and cauld his kail,
  Yet anger never raised his e'e;
He bless'd the little, and was blithe,
  While spak' the dame, wi' clamorous tongue,
O sorrow clap your auld beld pow,
  And dance wi' ye to the mools, gudeman!

He hang his bonnet on the pin,
  And down he lay, his dool to drie;
While she sat singing in the neuk,
  And tasting at the barley bree.
The lark, 'mid morning's siller gray,
  That wont to cheer him warkward gaun,
Next morning missed amang the dew
  The blithe and dainty auld gudeman.

The third morn's dew on flower and tree
  'Gan glorious in the sun to glow,
When sung the wanton wife to mark
  His feat gaun foremost o'er the knowe.
The first flight o' the winter's rime
  That on the kirkyard sward had faun,
The wanton wife skiffed aff his grave,
  A-kirking wi' her new gudeman.

A dainty dame I wat was she,
  High brent and burnished was her brow,
'Mang lint-locks curling; and her lips
  Twin daisies dawned through honey dew:
And light and locsome in the dance,
  When ha' was het, or kirn was won;
Her breasts twa drifts o' purest snaw,
  In cauld December's bosom faun.

But lang ere winter's winds blew by,
  She skirled in her lonesome bow;
Her new gudeman, wi' hazle rung,
  Began to kame her wanton pow.
Her hearth was alokent out wi' care,
  Toom grew her kist and cauld her pan,
And dreigh and dowie waxed the night,
  Ere Beltane, wi' her new gudeman.

She dreary sits 'tween naked wa's,
  Her cheek ne'er dimpled into mirth;
Half-happit, haurling out o' doors,
  And hunger-haunted at her hearth.
And see the tears fa' frae her e'en,
  Warm happin' down her haffits wan;
But guess her bitterness of saul
  In sorrow for her auld gudeman!

A WET SHEET.
ALLAN CUNNINGHAM.

A WET sheet and a flowing sea,
  A wind that follows fast,
And fills the white and rustling sail,
  And bends the gallant mast.
And bends the gallant mast, my boys,
  While like the eagle free,
Away the good ship flies, and leaves
  Old England on the lee.

O for a soft and gentle wind!
  I heard a fair one cry;
But give to me the swelling breeze,
  And white waves heaving high:
The white waves heaving high, my lads,
  The good ship tight and free—
The world of waters is our home,
  And merry men are we.

There's tempest in yon horned moon,
  And lightning in yon cloud;
And hark the music, mariners!
  The wind is piping loud.
The wind is piping, loud, my boys,
  The lightning flashes free—
While the hollow oak our palace is,
  Our heritage the sea.

LOW GERMANIE.
ALLAN CUNNINGHAM.

As I sail'd past green Jura's isle,
  Among the waters lone,
I heard a voice—a sweet low voice,
  Atween a sigh and moan:

With ae babe at her bosom, and
  Another at her knee,
A mother wail'd the bloody wars
  In Low Germanie.

Oh woe unto these cruel wars
  That ever they began,
For they have swept my native isle
  Of many a pretty man:
For first they took my brethren twain,
  Then wiled my love frae me.
Woe, woe unto the cruel wars
  In Low Germanie.

I saw him when he sail'd away,
  And furrow'd far the brine;
And down his foes came to the shore,
  In many a glittering line:
The war-steeds rush'd amang the waves,
  The guns came flashing free,
But could nae keep my gallant love
  From Low Germanie.

Oh say, ye maidens, have ye seen,
  When swells the battle cry,
A stately youth with bonnet blue
  And feather floating high—
An eye that flashes fierce for all,
  But ever mild to me?
Oh that's the lad who loves me best
  In Low Germanie.

Where'er the cymbal's sound is heard,
  And cittern sweeter far—
Where'er the trumpet blast is blown,
  And horses rush to war;
The blithest at the banquet board,
  And first in war is he,
The bonnie lad, whom I love best,
  In Low Germanie.

I sit upon the high green land,
  When mute the waters lie,
And think I see my true love's sail
  Atween the sea and sky.
With ae bairn at my bosom, and
  Another at my knee,
I sorrow for my soldier lad
  In Low Germanie.

THERE DWALT A MAN.
ALLAN CUNNINGHAM.
The first verse is a fragment of a very old song.

THERE dwalt a man into the west,
   And O gin he was cruel,
For on his bridal night at e'en
   He gat up and grat for gruel.
They brought to him a gude sheep head,
   A napkin and a towel:
Gar tak' thae whim-whams far frae me,
   And bring to me my gruel.

But there's nae meal in a' the house,
   What will we do, my jewel?
Get up tho powk and shake it out,
   I winna want my gruel.
But there's nae milk in a' the house,
   Nor yet a spunk o' fuel:
Gae warm it in the light o' the moon,
   I winna want my gruel.

O lake-a-day for my first wife,
   Wha was baith white and rosie,
She cheer'd me aye at e'ening fa'
   Wi' something warm and cozie:
Farewell to pleasant draps o' drink,
   To butter brose and gruel;
And farewell to my first sweet wife,
   My cannie Nancy Newell.

DONALD GUNN.
DAVID WEBSTER,
Author of a volume of poems published at Paisley in 1835.

HEARD ye e'er o' Donald Gunn,
   Ance sae duddy, dowf, and needy,
Now a laird in yonder toun,
   Callous-hearted, proud, and greedy.

Up the glen aboon the linn,
   Donald met wi' Maggie Millar,
Wooed the lass amang the whins,
   Because she had the word o' siller;
Meg was neither trig nor braw,
   Had mae fauts than ane laid till her;
Donald looket ower them a',
   A' his thought was on the siller.
      Heard ye e'er, &c.

Donald grew baith braid and braw,
  Ceased to bore the whinstone quarry,
Maggie's siller pays for a',
  Breeks instead o' duddy barrie:
Though he's ignorant as a stirk,
  Though he's doure as ony donkey;
Yet, by accidental jirk,
  Donald rides before a flunkey.
     Heard ye e'er, &c.

Clachan bairnies roar wi' fright,
  Clachan dogs tak' to their trotters;
Clachan wives the pathway dicht
  To tranquillise his thraward features:
Gangrel bodies in the street
  Beck and bow to make him civil,
Tenant bodies in his debt,
  Shun him as they'd shun the devil.
     Heard ye e'er, &c.

Few gangs trigger to the fair,
  Few gangs to the kirk sae gaucie,—
Few wi' Donald can compare
  To keep the cantel o' the causie:
In his breast a bladd o' stane,
  Neith his hat a box o' brochan,
In his nieve a wally cane,
  Thus the tyrant rules the clachan.
     Heard ye e'er, &c.

TAK' IT MAN, TAK' IT.

DAVID WEBSTER.

When I was a miller in Fife,
  Losh! I thought that the sound o' the happer
Said, Tak' hame a wee flow to your wife,
  To help to be brose to your supper.
Then my conscience was narrow and pure,
  But someway by random it rackit;
For I liftet twa nievefu' or mair,
  While the happer said, Tak' it, mau, tak' it.

  Then hey for the mill and the kill,
    The garland and gear for my cogie,
  And hey for the whisky and yill,
    That washes the dust frae my craigic.

Although it's been lang in repute
  For rogues to make rich by deceiving:
Yet I see that it disna weel suit
  Honest men to begin to the thieving.
For my heart it gaed dunt upon dunt,
  Od, I thought ilka dunt it wad crackit;
Sae I flang frae my nieve what was in't,
  Still the happer said, Tak' it, man, tak' it.
    Then hey for the mill, &c.

A man that's been bred to the plough,
  Might be deav'd wi' its clamorous clapper;
Yet there's few but would suffer the sough,
  After kenning what's said by the happer.
I whiles thought it scoff'd me to scorn,
  Saying, Shame, is your conscience no chackit;
But when I grew dry for a horn,
  It changed aye to Tak' it, man, tak' it.
    Then hey for the mill, &c.

The smugglers whiles cam' wi' their packs,
  'Cause they kent that I liked a bicker,
Sae I bartered whyles wi' the gowks,
  Gi'ed them grain for a soup o' their liquor.
I had lang been accustomed to drink,
  And aye when I purposed to quat it,
That thing wi' its clapertie clink,
  Said aye to me, Tak' it, man, tak' it.
    Then hey for the mill, &c.

But the warst thing I did in my life,
  Nae doubt but ye'll think I was wrang o't,
Od, I tauld a bit bodie in Fife
  A' my tale, and he made a bit sang o't.
I have aye had a voice a' my days,
  But for singin' I ne'er gat the knack o't;
Yet I try whyles, just thinking to please
  My frien's here, wi' Tak' it, man, tak' it.
    Then hey for the mill, &c.

Now, miller and a' as I am,
  This far I can see through the matter;
There's men mair notorious to fame,
  Mair greedy than me o' the muter.
For 'twad seem that the hale race o' men,
  Or wi' safety, the ha'f we may mak' it,
Ha'e some speaking happer within,
  That says aye to them, Tak' it, man, tak' it.
    Then hey for the mill, &c.

THE FLOWER OF CALEDONIA.
JAMES BROWN.

According to Mr. Whitelaw, Brown was "well-known" in the West of Scotland in his professional capacities of musician and dancing-master. In his latter days he was afflicted with blindness, and kept a small public-house in Jamaica street, Glasgow, where he died in 1836.

Since uncle's death I've lads enow,
That never came before to woo;
But to the laddie I'll be true,
That lo'ed me first of onie, O;
I've lads enow since I gat gear,
Before, my price they'd hardly speer;
But nane to me is half so dear
As my true lover Johnnie, O.

Weel do I mind o' auld langsyne,
How they would laugh at mo and mine;
Now I'll pay them back in their ain coin,
And show them I lo'e Johnnie, O.
Weel mind I, in my youthfu' days,
How happy I've been gath'rin' slaes,
And rowin' on yon breckan braes,
Wi' the flower o' Caledonia.

The Laird comes o'er and tells my dad,
That surely I am turning mad,
And tells my mam I lo'e a lad
That's neither rich nor bonnie, O.
The Laird is but a silly gowk,
For tho' my Johnnie has nae stock,
Yet he's the flow'r o' a' the flock,
And the pride of Caledonia.

When to the Laird I wrought for fee,
He wadna look nor speak to me,
But now at breakfast, dine, and tea,
He'd fain mak' me his cronie, O;
But sure as gowd cures the heart-ache,
It's only for my siller's sake;
The mair o' me that they a' make,
The mair I lo'e my Johnnie, O.

But now my wedding day is set,
When I'll be married to my pet,
With pleasure I will pay the debt,
I've awn sae lang to Johnnie, O.
Come, fiddler, now cast aff your coat,
We's dance a reel upon the spot,
Play "Jockie's made a wedding o't,"
Or "Snod your cockernonie," O.

Now laddies keep your lasses till't,
And lasses a' your coaties kilt,
And let us ha'e a cantie lilt,
Since I ha'e got my Johnnie, O.
I've got my heart's desire at last,
Though many frowns between us past,
And since we're tied baith hard and fast,
May peace crown Caledonia!

TO A LINNET.
ROBERT ALLAN,

Was born at Kilbarchan, in Renfrewshire, in 1774. He was a muslin-weaver to trade, and while occupied at the loom composed the majority of his best pieces. He published a volume of poems in 1836, most of his pieces having already been printed in "Smith's Scottish Minstrel," and in the "Harp of Renfrewshire." He emigrated to America in 1841, and died at New York six days after his arrival.

Chaunt no more thy roundelay,
  Lovely minstrel of the grove;
Charm no more the hours away
  With thy artless tale of love.
Chaunt no more thy roundelay,
  Sad it steals upon mine ear;
Leave, O leave thy leafy spray,
  Till the smiling morn appear.

Light of heart, thou quit'st thy song,
  As the welkin's shadows lour,
Whilst the beetle wheels along,
  Humming to the twilight hour.
Not like thee, I quit the scene
  To enjoy night's balmy dream;
Not like thee, I wake again,
  Smiling with the morning beam.

A LASSIE CAM' TO OUR GATE.
ROBERT ALLAN.

A lassie cam' to our gate, yestreen,
  An' low she curtsied down;
She was lovelier far an' fairer to see
  Than a' our ladies roun'.

O whare do ye wend, my sweet winsome doo?
  An' whare may your dwelling be?
But her heart, I trow, was liken to break,
  An' the tear-drap dimm'd her e'e.

I ha'ena a hame, quo' the bonnie lassie—
I ha'ena a hame nor ha',
Fain here wad I rest my weary feet,
For the night begins to fa'.

I took her into our tapestry ha',
An' we drank the ruddy wine;
An' aye I strave, but fand my heart
Fast bound wi' love's silken twine.

I ween'd she might be the fairies' queen,
She was sae jimp and sma';
And the tear that dimm'd her bonnie blue e'e
Fell owre twa heaps o' snaw.

O whare do ye wend, my sweet winsome doo?
An' whare may your dwelling be?
Can the winter's rain an' the winter's wind
Blaw cauld on sic as ye?

I ha'ena a hame, quo' the bonnie lassie—
I ha'ena a ha' nor hame;
My father was ane o' "Charlie's" men,
An' him I daurna name.

Whate'er be your kith, whate'er be your kin,
Frae this ye mauna gae;
An' gin ye'll consent to be my ain,
Nae marrow ye shall ha'e.

Sweet maiden, tak' the siller cup,
Sae fu' o' the damask wine,
An' press it to your cherrie lip,
For ye shall aye be mine.

An' drink, sweet doo, young Charlie's health,
An' a' your kin sae dear,
Culloden has dimm'd mony an e'e
Wi' mony a saut, saut tear.

THE COVENANTER'S LAMENT.

ROBERT ALLAN.

There's nae covenant now, lassie!
There's nae covenant now!
The solemn league and covenant
Are a' broken through!
There's nae Renwick now, lassie,
There's nae gude Cargill,
Nor holy Sabbath preaching,
Upon the Martyrs' Hill!

It's naething but a sword, lassie!
  A bluidy, bluidy ane!
Waving o'er poor Scotland
  For her rebellious sin.
Scotland's a' wrang, lassie,
  Scotland's a' wrang—
It's neither to the hill nor glen,
  Lassie, we daur gang.

The Martyrs' Hill forsaken,
  In simmer's dusk, sae calm;
There nae gathering now, lassie,
  To sing the e'enin' psalm!
But the martyr's grave will rise, lassie,
  Aboon the warrior's cairn;
An' the martyr soun' will sleep, lassie,
  Aneath the waving fern!

LIFE'S A FAUGHT.
ROBERT ALLAN.

That life's a faught there is nae doubt,
  A steep and slippery brae;
And wisdom's sel', wi' a' its rules,
  Will aften find it sae.
The truest heart that e'er was made,
  May find a deadly fae,
And broken aiths and faithless vows
  Gae lovers mickle wae.

When poortith looks wi' sour disdain,
  It frights a body sair,
And gars them think they ne'er will mee
  Delight or pleasure mair.
But though the heart be e'er sae sad,
  And prest wi' joyless care,
Hope lightly steps in at the last,
  To fley awa' despair.

For love o' wealth let misers toil,
  And fret baith late and ear',
A cheerfu' heart has aye enough,
  And whiles a mite to spare.
A loal true heart's a gift frae heaven,
  A gift that is maist rare;
It is a treasure o' itsel',
  And lightens ilka care.

Let wealth and pride exalt themsel's,
 And boast o' what they ha'e,
Compar'd wi' truth and honesty,
 They are nae worth a strae.
The honest heart keeps aye aboon,
 Whate'er the world may say,
And laughs and turns its shafts to scorn,
 That ithers would dismay.

Sae let us mak' life's burden light,
 And drive ilk care awa';
Contentment is a dainty feast,
 Although in hamely ha':
It gi'es a charm to ilka thing,
 And mak's it look fu' braw,
The spendthrift and the miser herd,
 It soars aboon them a'.

But there's ae thing amang the lave
 To keep the heart in tune,
And but for that the weary spleen
 Wad plague us late and soon.
A bonnie lass, a canty wife,
 For sic is nature's law;
Without that charmer o' our lives,
 There's scarce a charm ava.

A FAREWELL SONG.

THOMAS PRINGLE,

Was born at Blacklaw, Tevioldale, in 1789. Pringle was editor of the "Edinburgh Monthly Magazine," the predecessor of "Blackwood," and afterwards was editor of a new series of the "Scots Magazine," published by Constable, of Edinburgh. The famous "Chaldee Manuscript," which appeared in the first number of "Blackwood" was written as a satire upon Pringle and one or two others.

In 1820 he emigrated to South Africa, and besides receiving a grant of land was appointed in 1823 Keeper of the Government Library in Cape Town. He also established a newspaper, but this brought him into numerous squabbles with the Local Government, and in 1826 led him to return to London. After his return he acted as Secretary to the Anti-slavery Society. He died at London in 1834.

Our native land—our native vale—
 A long and last adieu!
Farewell to bonny Teviotdale,
 And Cheviot mountains blue.

Farewell, ye hills of glorious deeds,
 And streams renown'd in song—
Farewell ye braes and blossom'd meads,
 Our hearts have lov'd so long.

Farewell the blythesome broomy knowes,
 Where thyme and harebells grow—
Farewell, the hoary, haunted howes,
 O'erhung with birk and sloe.

The mossy cave and mouldering tower
 That skirt our native dell—
The martyr's grave, and lover's bower,
 We bid a sad farewell!

Home of our love! our father's home!
 Land of the brave and free!
The sail is flapping on the foam
 That bears us far from thee!

We seek a wild and distant shore,
 Beyond the western main—
We leave thee to return no more,
 Nor view thy cliffs again!

Our native land—our native vale—
 A long and last adieu!
Farewell to bonny Teviotdale,
 And Scotland's mountains blue!

THE EWE-BUCHTING'S BONNIE.

THOMAS PRINGLE.

WITH the exception of the first stanza, which was written by Lady Grisell Baillie, (see page 56.)

O THE ewe-bughting's bonnie, baith e'ening and morn,
When our blythe shepherds play on the bog-reed and horn;
While we're milking they're lilting baith pleasant and clear;
But my heart's like to break when I think on my dear;
O the shepherds take pleasure to blow on the horn,
To raise up their flocks o' sheep soon i' the morn:
On the bonnie green banks they feed pleasant and free—
But alas! my dear heart, all my sighing's for thee!

O the sheep-herding's lightsome amang the green braes
Where Cayle wimples clear 'neath the white-blossomed slaes,
Where the wild-thyme and meadow-queen scent the saft gale,
And the cushat croods lnesomely down in the dale.
There the lintwhite and mavis sing sweet frae the thorn,
And blythe lilts the laverock aboon the green corn,
And a' things rejoice in the simmer's glad prime—
But my heart's wi' my love in the far foreign clime!

O the hay-making's pleasant, in bright sunny June—
The hay-time is cheery when hearts are in tune;
But while others are joking and laughing sae free,
There's a pang at my heart and a tear i' my e'e.
At e'en i' the gloaming, adown by the burn,
Fu' dowie, and wae, aft I daunder and mourn;
Amang the lang broom I sit greeting alane,
And sigh for my dear and the days that are gane.

O the days o' our youtheid were heartsome and gay,
When we herded thegither by sweet Gaitshaw brae,
When we plaited the rushes and pu'd the witch-bells
By the Cayle's ferny howms and on Hounam's green fells.
But young Sandy hood gang to the wars wi' the laird,
To win honour and gowd—(gif his life it be spared!)
Ah! little care I for wealth, favour, or fame,
Gin I had my dear shepherd but safely at hame!

Then round our wee cot though gruff winter sould roar,
And poortith glowr in like a wolf at the door:
Though our toom purse had barely twa boddles to clink,
And a barley-meal scone were the best on our bink;
Yet, he wi' his hirsel, and I wi' my wheel,
Through the howe o' the year we wad fen unco weel;
Till the lintwhite, and laverock, and lambs bleating fain,
Brought back the blythe time o' ewe-bughting again.

THE OLD SCOTTISH BROADSWORDS.
J. G. LOCKHART.

THE son-in-law and biographer of Sir Walter Scott.

Now there's peace on the shore, now there's calm on the sea,
Fill a glass to the heroes whose swords kept us free,
Right descendants of Wallace, Montrose, and Dundee.
    Oh, the broadswords of Old Scotland!
    And oh, the old Scottish broadswords!

Old Sir Ralph Abercromby, the good and the brave—
Let him flee from our board, let him sleep with the slave,
Whose libation comes slow while we honour his grave.
    Oh, the broadswords, &c.

Though he died not like him amid victory's roar,
Though disaster and gloom wove his shroud on the shore,
Not the less we remember the spirit of Moore.
    Oh, the broadswords, &c.

Yes, a place with the fallen the living shall claim,
We'll entwine in one wreath every glorious name,
The Gordon, the Ramsay, the Hope, and the Graham,
    All the broadswords, &c.

Count the rocks of the Spey, count the groves of the Forth,
Count the stars in the clear cloudless heaven of the north,
Then go blazon their numbers, their names and their worth,
   All the broadswords, &c.

The highest in splendour, the humblest in place,
Stand united in glory, as kindred in race,
For the private is brother in blood to his grace.
   Oh, the broadswords, &c.

Then sacred to each and to all let it be,
Fill a glass to the heroes whose swords kept us free,
Right descendants of Wallace, Montrose, and Dundee,
   Oh, the broadswords of Old Scotland!
   And oh, the old Scottish broadswords!

CAPTAIN PATON.
J. G. LOCKHART.

Touch once more a sober measure,
   And let punch and tears be shed,
For a prince of good old fellows,
   That, alack-a-day! is dead.
For a prince of worthy fellows,
   And a pretty man also,
That has left the Saltmarket
   In sorrow, grief, and woe—
Oh! we ne'er shall see the like of Captain Paton no mo'e!

His waistcoat, coat, and breeches,
   Were all cut off the same web,
Of a beautiful snuff-colour,
   Or a modest genty drab;
The blue stripe in his stocking
   Round his neat slim leg did go,
And his ruffles of the cambric fine
   They were whiter than the snow—
Oh! we ne'er shall see the like of Captain Paton no mo'e!

His hair was curled in order,
   At the rising of the sun,
In comely rows and buckles smart
   That about his ears did run;
And before there was a toupee,
   That some inches up did grow,
And behind there was a long queue
   That did o'er his shoulders flow—
Oh! we ne'er shall see the like of Captain Paton no mo'e!

And whenever we foregathered
He took off his wee three-cockit,
And he proffered you his snuff-box,
Which he drew from his side pocket,
And on Burdett or Bonaparte
He would make a remark or so,
And then along the plainstones
Like a provost he would go—
Oh! we ne'er shall see the like of Captain Paton no mo'e!

In dirty days he picked well
His footsteps with his rattan,
Oh! you ne'er could see the least speck
On the shoes of Captain Paton:
And on entering the coffee-room
About two, all men did know,
They would see him with his Courier
In the middle of the row—
Oh! we ne'er shall see the like of Captain Paton no mo'e!

Now then upon a Sunday
He invited me to dine,
On a herring and a mutton-chop
Which his maid dressed very fine;
There was also a little Malmsey
And a bottle of Bordeaux,
Which between me and the Captain
Passed nimbly to and fro—
Oh! I shall ne'er take pot-luck with Captain Paton no mo'e

Or if a bowl was mentioned,
The Captain he would ring,
And bid Nelly rin to the West-port,
And a stoup of water bring;
Then would he mix the genuine stuff
As they made it long ago,
With limes that on his property
In Trinidad did grow—
Oh! we ne'er taste the like of Captain Paton's punch no mo'e!

And then all the time he would discourse
So sensible and courteous,
Perhaps talking of last sermon
He had heard from Dr. Porteous;
Of some little bit of scandal
About Mrs. So and So,
Which he scarce could credit, having heard
The con but not the pro—
Oh! we ne'er shall see the like of Captain Paton no mo'e!

Or when the candles were brought forth,
  And the night was fairly setting in,
He would tell some fine old stories
  About Minden-field or Dettingen—
How he fought with a French Major,
  And despatched him at a blow,
While his blood ran out like water
  On the soft grass below—
Oh! we ne'er shall hear the like of Captain Paton no mo'e!

But at last the Captain sickened
  And grew worse from day to day,
And all missed him in the coffee-room,
  From which now he staid away;
On Sabbaths, too, the Wynd Kirk
  Made a melancholy show,
All for wanting of the presence
  Of our venerable beau—
Oh! we ne'er shall see the like of Captain Paton no mo'e!

And in spite of all that Cleghorn
  And Corkindale could do,
It was plain, from twenty symptoms,
  That death was in his view;
So the Captain made his test'ment
  And submitted to his foe,
And we laid him by the Ram's-horn-kirk,
  'Tis the way we all must go—
Oh! we ne'er shall see the like of Captain Paton no mo'e!

Join all in chorus, jolly boys,
  And let punch and tears be shed
For this prince of good old fellows
  That, alack-a-day! is dead;
For this prince of worthy fellows,
  And a pretty man also,
That has left the Saltmarket
  In sorrow, grief, and woe!
For it ne'er shall see the like of Captain Paton no mo'e!

MAGGY MACLANE.

JAMES MAYNE,

A nephew of Joseph Mayne, the author of Logan Braes. James was at one time a printer in Glasgow, but latterly edited a newspaper in the Island of Trinidad, where he died in 1842.

Doon i' the glen by the lown o' the trees,
Lies a wee theeket bield, like a bike for the bees;
But the binnie there skepp'd—gin ye're no dour to please—
  It's virgin Miss Maggy Maclane!
There's few seek Meg's shed noo, the simmer sun jookin';
It's aye the dry floor, Meg's— the day e'er sae drookin'!
But the heather-blabs hing whare the red blude's been shooken
  I' bruilzies for Maggy Maclane!

Doon by Meg's howf-tree the gowk comes to woo;
But the corncraik's aye fley'd at her hallan-door joo!
An' the red-breast ne'er cheeps but the weird's at his mou',
  For the last o' the roses that's gane!
Nae tryntin' at Meg's noo—nae Hallowe'en rockins!
Nae howtowdie guttlens— nae mart-puddin' yockins!
Nae bane i' the blast's teeth blaws snell up Glendockens!
  Clean bickers wi' Maggy Maclane!

Meg's auld lyart gutcher swarf'd dead i' the shawe:
Her bein, fouthy minnie,—she's aff an' awa'!
The gray on her pow but a simmerly snaw!—
  The couthy, cosh Widow Maclane!
O titties be tentie! though air i' the day wi' ye,—
Think that the green grass may ae day be hay wi' ye!—
Think o' the leal minnie—mayna be aye wi' ye!
  When sabbin' for Maggy Maclane.

Lallan' joes—Hielan' joes—Meg ance had wale;
Fo'k wi' the siller, and chiefs wi' the tail!
The yaud left the burn to drink out o' Meg's pail—
  The sheltie braw kent "the Maclane."
Awa' owre the muir they cam' stottin' an' stoicherin'!
Tramper an' traveller, a' beakin' an' broicherin'!
Cadgers an' cuddy-creels, oigherin'!—hoigherin'!
  "The lanlowpers!"—quo' Maggy Maclane.

Cowtes were to fother:—Meg owre the burn flang!
Nowte were to tether:—Meg through the wood rang!
The widow she kenn'd-na to bless or to bann!
  Sic waste o' gude wooers to hain!
Yet, aye at the souter, Meg grumph'd her! an' grumph'd her!
The loot-shouther'd wabster, she humph'd her! and humph'd her!
The lamiter tailor, she stump'd her! an' stump'd her!
  Her minnie might groo or grane!

The tailor he likit cockleekie broo ;
An' doon he cam' wi' a beck an' a boo :—
Quo' Meg,—" We'se sune tak' the clecken aff you ;"—
    An' plump ! i' the burn he's gane !
The widow's cheek redden'd ; her heart it play'd thud ! aye ;
Her garters she cuist roon' his neck like a wuddie !
She linkit him oot ; but wi' wringin' his duddies,
    Her weed-ring it's burst in twain !

Wowf was the widow—to haud nor to bing !
The tailor he's aff, an' he's coft a new ring !
Th' deil squeeze his craig's no wordy the string !—
    He's waddet auld Widow Maclane !
Auld ?—an' a bride ! Na, ye'd pitied the tea-pat !
O saut were the skadyens ! but balm's in Glenlivat !
The haggis was bockin' oot bluters o' bree-fat,
    An' hotch'd to the piper its lane !—

Doon the burnside, i' the lown o' the glen,
Meg reists her bird-lane, i' a but-an-a-ben :
Steal doon when ye dow,—i' the dearth, gentlemen,—
    Ye'se be awmous to Maggy Maclane !
Lane banks the virgin—nae white pows now keekin
Through key-hole an' cranny ; nae cash blade stan's sleekin'
His nicherin' naigie, his gaudamous seekin' !
    Alack for the days that are gane !

Lame's fa'n the souter !—some steek i' his thie !
The cooper's clean gyte, wi' a hoopin' coughee !
The smith's got sae blin'—wi' a spunk i' his e'e !—
    He's tyned glint o' Maggy Maclane !
Meg brake the kirk pew-door—Auld Beukie leuk'd near-na her !
She dunkled her pattie—Young Sneckie ne'er speir'd for her !
But the warst's when the wee mouse leuks oot, wi' a tear to her,
    Frae the meal-kist o' Maggy Maclane !

EARL MARCH.

THOMAS CAMPBELL,

THE celebrated author of "The Pleasures of Hope." He was born at Glasgow in 1777. His principal works are "The Pleasures of Hope," and "Gertrude of Wyoming ;" but some of his minor pieces, such as "The Battle of the Baltic," "Erin-go-Bragh," "The Last Man," &c., are alone sufficient to immortalise him. He died at Boulogne in 1844.

EARL March look'd on his dying child,
    And smit with grief to view her—
The youth, he cried, whom I exiled
    Shall be restored to woo her.

She's at the window many an hour,
　His coming to discover;
And her love look'd up to Ellen's bower,
　And she look'd on her lover.

But ah! so pale, he knew her not,
　Though her smile on him was dwelling;
And am I then forgot—forgot?—
　It broke the heart of Ellen.

In vain he weeps, in vain he sighs,
　Her cheek as cold as ashes;
Nor love's own kiss shall wake those eyes
　To lift their silken lashes.

NEVER WEDDING, EVER WOOING.
THOMAS CAMPBELL.

Never wedding, ever wooing,
Still a love-torn heart pursuing;
Read you not the wrongs you're doing,
　In my cheek's pale hue?
All my life with sorrow strewing,
　Wed—or cease to woo.

Rivals banish'd, bosoms plighted,
Still our days are disunited;
Now the lamp of hope is lighted,
　Now half quench'd appears,
Damp'd, and wavering, and benighted,
　'Midst my sighs and tears.

Charms you call your dearest blessing,
Lips that thrill at your caressing,
Eyes a mutual soul confessing,
　Soon you'll make them grow
Dim, and worthless your possessing,
　Not with age but woe.

WALLACE.
THOMAS CAMPBELL.

They lighted a taper at the dead of night,
　And chaunted their holiest hymn;
But her brow and her bosom were damp with affright,
　Her eye was all sleepless and dim,—
And the lady of Elderslie wept for her lord,
　When a death-watch beat in her lonely room,
When her curtain had shook of its own accord,
And the raven had flapp'd at her window board,
　To tell her of her warrior's doom.

Now sing ye the Song, and loudly pray
   For the soul of my knight so dear;
And call me a widow this wretched day,
   Since the warning of God is here.
For a night-mare rides on my strangled sleep;
   The lord of my bosom is doom'd to die;
His valorous heart they have wounded deep,
And the blood-red tears shall his country weep
   For Wallace of Elderslie.

Yet knew not his country that ominous hour,
   Ere the loud matin bell was rung,
That a trumpet of death on an English tower
   Had the dirge of her champion sung.
When his dungeon light look'd dim and red
   On the high born blood of a martyr slain,
No anthem was sung at his holy deathbed,
No weeping there was when his bosom bled,
   And his heart was rent in twain.

Oh! it was not thus when his oaken spear
   Was true to the knight forlorn,
And hosts of a thousand were scatter'd, like deer
   At the sound of the huntsman's horn.
When he strode o'er the wreck of each well-fought field,
   With the yellow-hair'd chiefs of his native land;
For his lance was not shiver'd, or helmet, or shield,
And the sword that seem'd fit for Archangel to wield,
   Was light in his terrible hand.

But, bleeding and bound, though the Wallace wight
   For his much lov'd country die,
The bugle ne'er sung to a braver Knight
   Than Wallace of Elderslie.
But the day of his glory shall never depart,
   His head unintomb'd shall with glory be palm'd,
From his blood-streaming altar his spirit shall start,
Tho' the raven has fed on his mouldering heart,
   A nobler was never embalm'd.

JULIA.

DUGALD MOORE,

A NATIVE of Glasgow, where he was born in 1805. He was apprenticed to Mr. Lumsden, stationer, and while in that gentleman's service he published his first volume, "The African and other poems" (1829). The success of this venture induced him to print again, and several other volumes were issued by him during the next ten years. He was for some time in business for himself, as bookseller and stationer in Glasgow, but died suddenly in 1841. He was interred in the Necropolis, where a handsome monument was soon erected to his memory by his admirers.

  She was a sunbeam in the storm,—
   A star that gently lifted
  Above the dark its beauteous form,
   When the dull tempest shifted.
  She loved—that passion like a spell
   With her young dreams was blended:
  The flowerets from youth's chaplet fell
   Before her spring-time ended.

  In yon church-yard, the flowers are fair
   Beneath heaven's blue expansion:—
  But a sweeter gem is lying there,
   In dark oblivion's mansion;
  The bud of promise to all eyes—
   O'er whom the wild wind dashes,—
  But she shall flourish in the skies,
   When stars and worlds are ashes.

THE CLYDE.

DUGALD MOORE.

WHEN cities of old days
But meet the savage gaze,
Stream of my early ways,
   Thou wilt roll,
Though fleets forsake thy breast,
And millions sink to rest—
Of the bright and beauteous west
   Still the soul.

When the porch and stately arch,
Which now so proudly perch
O'er thy billows, on their march
   To the sea,
Are but ashes in the shower;
Still the jocund summer hour
From his cloud will weave a bower
   Over thee.

When the voice of human power
Has ceased in mart and bower;
Still the broom and mountain flower
   Will thee bless;

And the mists that love to stray
O'er the Highlands, far away,
Will come down their deserts gray
    To thy kiss.

And the stranger brown with toil,
From the far Atlantic soil,
Like the pilgrim of the Nile,
    Yet may come,
To search the solemn heaps,
That moulder by thy deeps,
Where desolation sleeps,
    Ever dumb.

Though fetters yet should clank
O'er the gay and princely rank
Of cities on thy bank,
    All sublime;
Still thou wilt wander on,
Till eternity has gone,
And broke the dial stone
    Of old Time.

THE MITHERLESS BAIRN.
WILLIAM THOM,

BORN at Aberdeen in 1789. He was to trade a weaver, and worked at the loom in Aberdeen, Dundee, Newtyle, and finally Inverury. Some of his poetical pieces then began to attract the attention of "the great," and his fame spread. He went to London, franked by a Mr. Gordon of Knockespock, his earliest patron, and there met with a reception second only to that received by Burns in Edinburgh. He was not firm enough to stand all the flatteries and favours he received, and he returned to Scotland a broken man; unable to return again to his trade, and dependent upon the efforts of his great friends for support. His personal character has been described as generous, honest, and just. He died at Dundee in 1848.

WHEN a' ither bairnies are hush'd to their hame,
By aunty, or cousin, or frecky grand-dame,
Wha stands last an' lanely, an' sairly forfairn?
'Tis the puir dowie laddie—the mitherless bairn!

The mitherless bairnie creeps to his lane bed,
Nane covers his cauld back, or haps his bare head;
His wee hackit heelies are hard as the airn,
An' lithless the lair o' the mitherless bairn!

Aneath his cauld brow, siccan dreams hover there,
O' hands that wont kindly to kaim his dark hair!
But mornin' brings clutches, a' reckless an' stern,
That lu'e na the locks o' the mitherless bairn!

The sister wha sang o'er his saftly rock'd bed,
Now rests in the moole whare their mammie is laid;
While the father toils sair his wee bannock to earn,
An' kens na the wrangs o' his mitherless bairn.

Her spirit that pass'd in yon hour of his birth,
Still watches his lone lorn wand'rings on earth,
Recording in heaven the blessings they earn,
Wha couthilie deal wi' the mitherless bairn!

Oh! speak him na harshly—he trembles the while,
He bends to your bidding, and blesses your smile: –
In the dark hour o' anguish, the heartless shall learn,
That God deals the blow for the mitherless bairn!

LOVE.

WILLIAM THOM.

O say not—"Love will never
  Breathe in that breast again;"
That "where he bled, must ever
  All pleasureless remain."
Shall tempest-riven blossom,
  When fair leaves fall away,
In coldness close its bosom,
  'Gainst beams of milder day,
    O never!—nay
  It blooms—whene'er it may.

Though ruthless tempest tear—
  Though biting frosts subdue—
And leave no tendril where
  Love's pretty flow'rets grew;
The soil, all ravag'd so,
  Will nurture more and more,
And stately roses blow
  Where gowans droop'd before,
    Then why—O! why
Should sweet love ever die?

I WADNA GI'E MY AIN WIFE.

ALEXANDER LAING,

A NATIVE of Brechin, where he was born in 1787. He contributed largely to "Smith's Scottish Minstrel," "Harp of Renfrewshire," "Whistle Binkie," &c. He carried on the business of Flaxdressing, in his native

town, and by his industry was enabled to retire from business some time
before his death, which took place in 1857.

I wadna gi'e my ain wife
  For ony wife I see;
I wadna gi'e my ain wife
  For ony wife I see;
A bonnier yet I've never seen,
  A better canna be—
I wadna gi'e my ain wife
  For ony wife I see!

O couthie is my ingle-cheek,
  An' cheerie is my Jean;
I never see her angry look,
  Nor hear her word on ane.
She's gude wi' a' the neebours roun',
  An' aye gude wi' me—
I wadna gi'e my ain wife
  For ony wife I see!

An' O her looks sae kindlie,
  They melt my heart outright,
When o'er the baby at her breast
  She hangs wi' fond delight;
She looks intill its bonnie face,
  An' syne looks to me—
I wadna gi'e my ain wife
  For ony wife I see.

THOUGH DOWIES THE WINTER.
ALEXANDER LAING.

Though dowie's the winter sae gloomie an' drear,
O happy we've been through the dead o' the year;
An' blythe to sic bield as the burnie brae gave;
O mony a nicht ha'e we stoun frae the lave.
Now the spring-time has tane the lang e'enings awa',
We maunna be seen an' less aften I'll ca',
But May-day is coming—our wedding an a',
Sae weary na, lassie, though I gang awa'.

Our gigglet young lasses are fairly mista'en,
They ken at the place wi' his honour I've been,
An' ta'en the plough-handin' o' bonnie Broomlee,
But they kenna wha's coming to haud it wi' me.
They ken i' the e'enings I'm aften frae hame;
They say wi' a lass, 'cause I look na to them;
They jamph an' they jeer, an' they banter at me,
An' twenty they've guess'd o', but never guess'd thee.

I'll sing the haill day, when your dwellin' I'm near;
I'll whistle when ploughin' as far's you can hear,
An' aye when I see you, gin nae bodie see,
I'll blink to my lassie—my lassie to me.
An' aye till that time baith at kirk an' at fair,
In taiken o' true love, dear lassie, ye'll wear
The green-tartan rockley, my keepsake to thee—
An' I tho white owerlay ye gifted to me.

THE VALE OF CLYDE.

JOHN STRUTHERS,

Was born at East Kilbride, in 1776. He was by trade a shoemaker, but obtained a situation as "corrector of the press" in the office of Khull, Blackie, and Co. He afterwards was appointed keeper of the Stirling Library in Glasgow.

Struthers was author of several popular works. His "Poor Man's Sabbath" met with a warm reception on its appearance in 1804, and rapidly passed through several editions. His "Harp of Caledonia," in three vols., is a standard work of its class.

Admiring nature's simple charms,
  I left my humble home,
Awhile my country's peaceful plains
  With pilgrim step to roam:
I mark'd the leafy summer wave
  On flowing Irvine's side,
But richer far's the robe she wears
  Within the vale of Clyde.

I roam'd the braes of bonnie Doon,
  The winding banks of Ayr,
Where flutters many a small bird gay,
  Blooms many a flow'ret fair;
But dearer far to me the stem
  That once was Calder's pride,
And blossoms now, the fairest flower,
  Within the vale of Clyde.

Avaunt! thou life-repressing north!
  Ye withering east winds too!
But come, thou all-reviving west,
  Breathe soft thy genial dew;
Until at length, in peaceful age,
  This lovely floweret shed
Its last green leaf upon my tomb,
  Within the vale of Clyde.

ON THE WILD BRAES OF CALDER.

JOHN STRUTHERS.

On the wild braes of Calder, I found a fair lily,
  All drooping with dew in the breath of the morn,
A lily more fair never bloom'd in the valley,
  Nor rose, the gay garden of art to adorn.
Sweet, sweet was the fragrance this lily diffused,
  As blushing, all lonely, it rose on the view,
But scanty its shelter, to reptiles exposed,
  And every chill blast from the cold north that blew.

Beneath yon green hill, a small field I had planted,
  Where the light leafy hazel hangs over the burn;
And a flower such as this, to complete it, was wanted,
  A flower that might mark the gay season's return.
Straight home to adorn it, I bore this fair lily,
  Where, at morn, and at even, I have watch'd it with care;
And blossoming still, it is queen of the valley,
  The glory of spring, and the pride of the year.

ROBIN TAMSON'S SMIDDY.

ALEXANDER RODGER,

A NATIVE of East Calder, where he was born in 1784. He went to Glasgow in 1797, where he joined his maternal relatives, and at their desire apprenticed himself to a weaver. In 1819 he suffered a short imprisonment on being convicted of ill feeling to the government in consequence of literary aid he gave to one of the revolutionary newspapers which then abounded. He held a situation in the Barrowfield Works near Glasgow, for about eleven years. In 1836 he became sub-editor of the *Reformers' Gazette*, and remained in that position till his death, which took place in 1846.

My mither men't my auld breeks,
  An' wow! but they were duddy,
And sent me to get Mally shod
  At Robin Tamson's smiddy;
The smiddy stands beside the burn
  That wimples through the clachan,
I never yet gae by the door,
  But aye I fa' a-laughin'.

For Robin was a walthy carle,
  An' had ae bonnie dochter,
Yet ne'er wad let her tak' a man,
  Though mony lads had sought her;
And what think ye o' my exploit?—
  The time our mare was shoeing,
I slippit up beside the lass,
  An' briskly fell a-wooing.

An' aye she e'ed my auld breeks,
 The time that we sat crackin',
Quo' I, my lass, ne'er mind the *clouts*,
 I've new anes for the makin';
But gin ye'll just come hame wi' me,
 An' lea' the carle, your father,
Ye'se get my breeks to keep in trim,
 Mysel', an' a' thegither.

'Deed, lad, quo' she, your offer's fair,
 I really think I'll tak' it,
Sae, gang awa', get out the more,
 We'll baith slip on the back o't;
For gin I wait my father's time,
 I'll wait till I be fifty;
But na;—I'll marry in my prime,
 An' mak' a wife most thrifty.

Wow! Robin was an angry man,
 At tyning o' his dochter;
Through a' the kintra-side he ran,
 An' far an' near he sought her;
But when he cam' to our fire-end,
 An' fand us baith thegither,
Quo' I, gudeman, I've ta'en your bairn,
 An' ye may tak' my mither.

Auld Robin girn'd an' sheuk his pow,
 Gaid sooth! quo' he, you're morry,
But I'll just tak' ye at your word,
 An' end this hurry-burry;
So Robin an' our auld wife
 Agreed to creep thegither;
Now, I ha'e Robin Tamson's pet,
 An' Robin has my mither.

MY GUDEMAN SAYS AYE TO ME.

ALEXANDER RODGER.

My gudeman says aye to me,
Says aye to me, says aye to me;
My gudeman says aye to me,
 Come cuddle in my bosie!
Though wearin' auld, he's blyther still
Than mony a swankie youthfu' chiel,
And a' his aim's to see me weel,
 And keep me snug and cozie.

For though my cheeks, where roses grew,
Ha'e tint their lively glowing hue,
My Johnnie's just as kind and true
  As if I still were rosy.
Our weel-won gear he never drank,
He never lived aboon his rank,
Yet wi' a neebour blythe and frank,
  He could be as jocose aye.

We ha'e a hame, gude halesome cheer,
Contentment, peace, a conscience clear,
And rosy bairns to us mair dear.
  Than treasures o' Potosi:
Their minds are form'd in virtue's school,
Their fau'ts are check'd wi' temper cool,
For my gudeman mak's this his rule,
  To keep frae hasty blows aye.

It ne'er was siller gart us wed,
Youth, health, and love, were a' we had,
Possess'd o' these we toil'd fu' glad,
  To shun want's bitter throes aye;
We've had our cares, we've had our toils,
We've had our bits o' troubles whiles,
Yet, what o' that? my Johnnie's smiles
  Shed joy o'er a' our woes aye.

Wi' mutual aid we've trudged through life,
A kind gudeman, a cheerfu' wife;
And on we'll jog, unvexed by strife,
  Towards our journey's close, aye!
And when we're stretch'd upon our bier,
Oh may our souls, sae faithfu' here,
Together spring to yonder sphere,
  Where love's pure river flows aye.

IT'S NO THAT THOU'RT BONNIE.

ALEXANDER RODGER.

It's no that thou'rt bonnie, it's no that thou'rt braw,
It's no that thy skin has the whiteness o' snaw,
It's no that thy form is perfection itsel',
That mak's my heart feel what my tongue canna tell:
But oh! its the soul beaming out frae thine e'e,
That mak's thee sae dear and sae lovely to me.

It's pleasant to look on that mild blushing face,
Sae sweetly adorn'd wi' ilk feminine grace,
It's joyous to gaze on these tresses sae bright,
O'ershading a forehead sae smooth and sae white;
But to dwell on the glances that dart frae thine e'e,
O Jeanie! its evendown rapture to me.

That form may be wasted by lingering decay,
The bloom of that cheek may be wither'd away,
Those gay gowden ringlets that yield such delight,
By tho cauld breath o' time may be changed into white;
But the soul's fervid flashes that brighten thine e'e,
Are the offspring o' heaven, and never can die.

Let me plough the rough ocean, nor e'er touch the shore,
Let me freeze on the coast of the bleak Labradore,
Let me pant 'neath the glare of a vertical sun,
Where no trees spread their branches, nor streams ever run;
Even there, my dear Jeanie, still happy I'd be,
If bless'd wi' the light o' thy heavenly e'e.

BET OF ABERDEEN.
ALEXANDER RODGER.

How brightly beams the bonnie moon
  Frae out the azure sky,
While ilka little star aboon
  Seems sparkling bright wi' joy.
How calm the eve! how blest the hour!
  How soft the sylvan scene!
How fit to meet thee, lovely flower!
  Sweet Bet of Aberdeen.

Now let us wander through the broom,
  And o'er the flowery lea;
While simmer wafts her rich perfume
  From yonder hawthorn tree,
There on yon mossy bank we'll rest,
  Where we've sae aften been,
Clasp'd to each other's throbbing breast,
  Sweet Bet of Aberdeen.

How sweet to view that face so meek,
  That dark expressive eye;
To kiss that lovely blushing cheek,
  Those lips of coral dye;
But oh! to hear thy seraph strains,
  Thy maiden sighs between,
Makes rapture thrill through all my veins,
  Sweet Bet of Aberdeen.

Oh! what to us is wealth or rank?
Or what is pomp or power?
More dear this velvet mossy bank,
This blest ecstatic hour;
I'd covet not the monarch's throne,
Nor diamond-studded queen,
While blest wi' thee, and thee alone,
Sweet Bet of Aberdeen.

BEHAVE YOURSEL' BEFORE FOLK.

ALEXANDER RODGER.

Behave yoursel' before folk,
Behave yoursel' before folk,
And dinna be sae rude to me,
As kiss me sae before folk.
It wadna gi'e me meikle pain,
Gin we were seen and heard by nane,
To tak' a kiss, or grant you ane;
But guidsake! no before folk.
  Behave yoursel' before folk,
  Behave yoursel' before folk;
Whate'or ye do, when out o' view,
Be cautious aye before folk.

Consider, lad, how folk will crack,
And what a great affair they'll mak'
O' naething but a simple smack,
That's gi'en or ta'en before folk.
  Behave yoursel' before folk,
  Behave yoursel' before folk;
Nor gi'e the tongue o' auld or young
Occasion to come o'er folk.

It's no through hatred o' a kiss,
That I sae plainly tell you this;
But, losh! I tak' it sair amiss
To be sae teazed before folk.
  Behave yoursel' before folk,
  Behave yoursel' before folk;
When we're our lane ye may tak' ane,
But fient a ane before folk.

I'm sure wi' you I've been as free
As ony modest lass should be;
But yet it doesna do to see
Sic freedom used before folk.
  Behave yoursel' before folk,
  Behave yoursel' before folk;
I'll ne'er submit again to it—
So mind you that—before folk,

Ye tell me that my face is fair;
It may be sae—I dinna care—
But ne'er again gar't blush sae sair
  As ye ha'e done before folk.
    Behave yoursel' before folk,
    Behave yoursel' before folk;
  Nor heat my cheeks wi' your mad freaks,
  But aye be douce before folk.

Ye tell me that my lips are sweet,
Sic tales, I doubt, are a' deceit;
At ony rate, it's hardly meet
  To pree their sweets before folk.
    Behave yoursel' before folk,
    Behave yoursel' before folk;
  Gin that's the case, there's time, and place,
  But surely no before folk.

But, gin you really do insist
That I should suffer to be kiss'd,
Gae, get a license frae the priest,
  And mak' me yours before folk.
    Behave yoursel' before folk,
    Behave yoursel' before folk;
  And when we're ane, baith flesh and bane,
  Ye may tak' ten—before folk.

THE ANSWER.

Can I behave, can I behave,
  Can I behave before folk,
When, wily elf, your sleeky self
  Gars me gang gyte before folk?

In a' you do, in a' ye say,
Yo've sic a pawkie coaxing way,
That my poor wits ye lead astray,
  An' ding me doilt before folk!
    Can I behave, can I behave,
    Can I behave before folk,
  While ye ensnare, can I forbear
  To kiss you, though before folk?

Can I behold that dimpling cheek,
Whar love 'mang sunny smiles might beck,
Yet, howlet-like, my e'elids steek,
  An' shun sic light, before folk?
    Can I behave, can I behave,
    Can I behave before folk,
  When ilka smile becomes a wile,
  Enticing me—before folk?

That lip, like Eve's forbidden fruit,
Sweet, plump, an' ripe, sae tempts me to't,
That I maun pree't, though I should rue't,
　　Ay, twenty times—before folk!
　　　Can I behave, can I behave,
　　　Can I behave before folk,
　　When temptingly it offers me
　　　So rich a treat—before folk?

That gowden hair sae sunny bright;
That shapely neck o' snawy white;
That tongue, even when it tries to flyte,
　　Provokes me till't before folk!
　　　Can I behave, can I behave,
　　　Can I behave before folk,
　　When ilka charm, young, fresh, an' warm,
　　　Cries, "kiss me now"—before folk!

An' O! that pawkie, rowin' e'e,
Sae roguishly it blinks on me,
I canna, for my saul, let be,
　　Frae kissing you before folk!
　　　Can I behave, can I behave,
　　　Can I behave before folk,
　　When ilka glint conveys a hint
　　　To tak' a smack—before folk?

Ye own, that were we baith our lane,
Ye wadna grudge to grant me ane;
Weel, gin there be nae harm in't then,
　　What harm is in't before folk?
　　　Can I behave, can I behave,
　　　Can I behave before folk,
　　Sly hypocrite! an anchorite
　　　Could scarce desist—before folk!

But after a' that has been said,
Since ye are willing to be wed,
We'll ha'e a "blythesome bridal" made,
　　When ye'll be mine before folk!
　　　Then I'll behave, then I'll behave,
　　　Then I'll behave before folk;
　　For whereas then, ye'll aft get "ten,"
　　　It winna be before folk!

THE WILD GLEN SAE GREEN.

REV. HENRY S. RIDDELL,

WAS born at Sorbie, Dumfriesshire, in 1798. His father was a Shepherd, and he followed the same occupation till he managed to scrape together sufficient money to enable him to enter the University of Edinburgh. He became a licentiate of the Church of Scotland, but never took any active part in the ministry; he resided at Teviothead, where the Duke of Buccleuch generously allowed him the use of a cottage, a small annuity, and a grant of land. Mr. Riddell died in 1870.

Mr. Riddell published several volumes of poetry during his life-time, and had the rare pleasure of seeing several of his songs achieve an instant and enthusiastic popularity. "The Wild Glen sae Green," "The Crook and the Plain," and above all, the inspiriting "Scotland yet," have taken a secure position amongst our popular minstrelsy. His works are presently being edited by Dr. Brydon, of Hawick, with a view to the issue of a complete collected edition.

WHEN my flocks upon the heathy hill are lying a' at rest,
And the gloamin' spreads its mantle grey o'er the world's dewy breast,
I'll tak' my plaid and hasten through yon woody dell unseen,
And meet my bonnie lassie on the wild glen sae green.

I'll meet her by the trystin' tree that's stannin' a' alane,
Where I have carved her name upon the little moss-grey slane,
There I will clasp her to my breast, and be mair blest, I ween,
Than a' that are aneath the sky, in the wild glen sae green.

My faldin' plaid shall shield her frae the gloamin's chilly gale
The star o' eve shall mark our joy but shall not tell her tale,
Our simple tale o' tender love that tauld sae aft has been,
To my bonnie bonnie lassie in the wild glen sae green.

Oh! I could wander earth a' owre nor care for aught o' bliss,
If I might share at my return a joy sae pure as this;
And I could spurn a' earthly wealth, a palace and a queen,
For my bonnie bonnie lassie in the wild glen sae green.

SCOTLAND YET.

REV. HENRY S. RIDDELL.

GAE, bring my guid auld harp ance mair,
  Gae, bring it free and fast,
For I maun sing anither sang
  Ere a' my glee be past,
And trow ye as I sing, my lads,
  The burden o't shall be
Auld Scotland's howes, and Scotland's knowes,
  And Scotland's hills for me,—
I'll drink a cup to Scotland yet,
  Wi' a' the honours three.

The heath waves wild upon her hills,
  And, foaming frae the fells,
Her fountains sing o' freedom still,
  As they dash down the dells;
And weel I lo'e the land, my lads,
  That's girded by the sea;
Then Scotland's dales, and Scotland's vales,
  And Scotland's hills for me,—
I'll drink a cup to Scotland yet,
  Wi' a' the honours three.

The thistle wags upon the fields,
  Where Wallace bore his blade,
That gave her foeman's dearest bluid,
  To dye her auld gray plaid;
And looking to the lift, my lads,
  He sang this doughty glee,
Auld Scotland's right, and Scotland's might,
  And Scotland's hills for me,—
I'll drink a cup to Scotland yet,
  Wi' a' the honours three.

They tell o' lands wi' brighter skies,
  Where freedom's voice ne'er rang,
Gi'e me the hills where Ossian lies,
  And Coila's minstrel sang.
For I've nae skill o' lands, my lads,
  That ken nae to be free,
Then Scotland's right, and Scotland's might,
  And Scotland's hills for me,—
I'll drink a cup to Scotland yet,
  Wi' a' the honours three.

OURS IS THE LAND.
REV. HENRY S. RIDDELL.

Ours is the land of gallant hearts,
  The land of lovely forms,
The island of the mountain harp,
  The torrents, and the storms:
The land that blooms with freemen's tread,
  And withers with the slave's;
Where far and deep the green-woods spread,
  And wild the thistle waves.

Ere ever Ossian's lofty voice
  Had told of Fingal's fame;
Ere ever from their native clime
  The Roman eagles came,

Our land had given heroes birth
That durst the boldest brave,
And taught above tyrannic dust
The thistle tufts to wave.

What need we say how Wallace fought,
And how his foemen fell,
Or how on glorious Bannockburn
The work went wild and well?
Ours is the land of gallant hearts,
The land of honour'd graves,
Whose wreath of fame shall ne'er depart,
While yet the thistle waves.

THE DOWIE DENS O' YARROW.
REV. HENRY S. RIDDELL.

Oh, sisters, there are midnight dreams
That pass not with the morning,
Then ask not why my reason swims
In a brain so wildly burning.
And ask not why I fancy how
Yon wee bird sings wi' sorrow,
That blaid lies mingled with the dew,
In the dowie dens o' Yarrow.

My dream's wild light was not of night,
Nor of the dulefu' morning;
Thrice on the stream was seen the gleam
That seem'd his sprite returning:
For sword-girt men came down the glen
An hour before the morrow,
And pierced the heart aye true to mine,
In the dowie dens o' Yarrow.

Oh, there are red red drops o' dew
Upon the wild flower's blossom,
But they could na cool my burning brow,
And shall not stain my bosom.
But from the clouds o' yon dark sky
A cold cold shroud I'll borrow,
And long and deep shall be my sleep
In the dowie dens o' Yarrow.

Let my form the bluid-dyed floweret press
By the heart o' him that lo'ed me,
And I'll steal frae his lips a long long kiss
In the bower where aft he wooed me.
For my arms shall fold and my tresses shie! l
The form of my death-cold marrow,
When the breeze shall bring the raven's wing
O'er the dowie dens o' Yarrow.

THE CROOK AND PLAID.

REV. HENRY S. RIDDELL.

I winna lo'e the laddie that ca's the cart and pleugh,
Though he should own that tender love that's only felt by few;
For he that has this bosom a' to fondest love betray'd,
Is the kind and faithfu' laddie that wears the crook and plaid.

At morn he climbs the mountains wild, his fleecy flock to view,
When the larks sing in the heaven aboon, and the flowers wake
  'mang the dew,
When the thin mist melts afore the beam, ower gair and glen
  convey'd,
Where the laddie loves to wander still, that wears the crook
  and plaid.

At noon he leans him down, high on the heathy fell,
When his flocks feed a' sae bonnilie below him in the dell;
And there he sings o' faithfu' love, till the wilds around are glad;
Oh, how happy is the laddie that wears the crook and plaid!

He pu's the blooms o' heather pure, and the lily-flouir sae meek,
For he weens the lily like my brow, and the heath-bell like my
  cheek.
His words are soft and tender as the dew frae heaven shed;
And nane can charm me like the lad that wears the crook and
  plaid.

Beneath the flowery hawthorn-tree, wild growing in the glen,
He meets me in the gloamin' gray, when nane on earth can ken;
And leal and tender is his heart beneath the spreading shade,
For weel he kens the way, I trow, to row me in his plaid.

The youth o' mony riches may to his fair one ride,
And woo across a table his many-titled bride;
But we will woo beneath the tree, where cheek to cheek is laid—
Oh, nae wooer's like the laddie that rows me in his plaid!

To own the tales o' faithfu' love, oh, wha wad no comply?
Sin' pure love gi'es mair o' happiness than aught aneath the sky;
Where love is in the bosom thus, the heart can ne'er be sad;
Sae, through life, I'll lo'e the laddie that wears the crook and
  plaid.

THE WEE AULD MAN.

REV. HENRY S. RIDDELL.

About the closin' o' the day,
　The wild green woods amang, O,
A wee auld man cam' doon this way,
　As fast as he could gang, O.
He entered into this wee house,
　Where unco weel kent he, O,
That there, there lived a virtuous lass,
　And fair as fair could be, O.
　　For he had vow'd to ha'e, O,
　　　To ha'e, O, to ha'e, O,
　　For he had vow'd to ha'e, O,
　　　A wifie o' his ain, O.

He tell't the auld gudewife he'd come
　Her dochter Jean to woo, O,
And gin she would but come wi' him,
　She never would it rue, O;
For he had oxen, horse, and kye,
　And sheep upon the hill, O,
And monie a cannie thing forbye,
　That should be at her will, O.
　　For he had vow'd, &c.

The auld gudewife replied in turn,
　Up rising frae her stool, O,
The lass that would your proffer spurn,
　Would surely be a fool, O,
She to the door made anxious haste,
　And ca'd young Jeanie in, O,
And when aroun' the fire they're placed,
　The courtin' did begin, O,
　　For he had vow'd, &c.

The wee auld man tauld ower his tale
　Wi' croose and cantie glee, O;
But Jeanie's heart was hard and cauld,
　Nae love for him had she, O.
Said she, Auld gouk! you've act a part
　That I can ne'er be thine, O;
You come to woo my mither's heart,
　You come nae here for mine, O.
　　For this is no the way, O,
　　　The way, O, the way, O,
　　For this is no the way, O,
　　　A lassie's heart to win, O.

And soon a rap came to the door,
And out young Jeanie ran, O,
Said she, You may count ower your store
Wi' them that you began, O.
The wee auld man rose up in wrath,
And loud and lang he swore, O,
Syne hirsled up his shouthers baith,
And hasten'd to the door, O.
    Still vowin' he would ha'e, &c.

SCOTIA'S THISTLE.
REV. HENRY S. RIDDELL.

Scotia's thistle guards the grave,
Where repose her dauntless brave;
Never yet the foot of slave
    Has trod the wilds of Scotia!
Free from tyrants' dark control—
Free as waves of ocean roll—
Free as thoughts of minstrel's soul,
    Still roam the sons of Scotia.

Scotia's hills of hoary hue,
Heaven wraps in wreaths of blue,
Watering with it's dearest dew
    The heathy locks of Scotia.
Down each green-wood skirted vale,
Guardian spirits, lingering, hail
Many a minstrel's melting tale,
    As told of ancient Scotia.

When the shades of eve invest
Nature's dew-bespangled breast,
How supremely man is blest,
    In the glens of Scotia.
There no dark alarms convey
Aught to chase life's charms away,
There they live, and live for aye,
    Round the homes of Scotia.

Wake, my hill harp! wildly wake!
Sound by lee and lonely lake,
Never shall this heart forsake
    The bonnie wilds of Scotia.
Others o'er the ocean's foam,
Far to other lands may roam,
But for ever be my home
    Beneath the sky of Scotia.

A STEED, A STEED.

WILLIAM MOTHERWELL,

A NATIVE of Glasgow, born in the Barony Parish there in 1797. Being intended for the legal profession he was apprenticed, at the age of fifteen years, in the office of the Sheriff Clerk of Paisley. In 1819 he was appointed Sheriff Clerk Depute of Renfrew, and held that position till 1829. He then removed to Glasgow, where he was appointed editor of the *Courier*. He died suddenly in 1835.

Except the volume of his poems published in 1832 (and afterwards in 1847), the fame of William Motherwell depends almost wholly on one or two works edited by him; but while his poems have given him no mean place among the poets of Scotland, his "Harp of Renfrewshire (1819) and Minstrelsy Ancient and Modern" (1827) have established his reputation as one of the best expositors of our early popular literature.

    A STEED! a steed of matchless speede!
      A sword of metal keene!
    Al else to noble heartes is drosse—
      Al else on earth is meane.
    The neighyinge of the war-horse prowde,
      The rowlinge of the drum,
    The clangor of the trumpet lowde—
      Be soundes from heaven that come.
    And, oh! the thundering presse of knightes,
      Whenas their war-cryes swelle,
    May tole from heaven an angel bright,
      And rouse a fiend from hell.

    Then mounte! then mounte, brave gallants all,
      And don your helmes amaine;
    Deathe's couriers, fame and honour, call
      Us to the fielde againe.
    No shrewish tears shall fill our eye
      When the sword-hilt's in our hand;
    Heart-whole we'll parte, and no whit sighe
      For the fayrest of the land.
    Let piping swaine, and craven wight,
      Thus weepe and puling crye;
    Our buisnesse is like men to fighte,
      And hero-like to die!

WEARIE'S WELL.

WILLIAM MOTHERWELL.

    IN a saft simmer gloamin',
      In yon dowie dell,
    It was there we twa first met
      By Wearie's cauld well.

We sat on the brume bank
 And look'd in the burn,
But sidelang we look'd on
 Ilk ither in turn.

The corn-craik was chirming
 His sad eerie cry,
And the wee stars were dreaming
 Their path through the sky.
The burn babbled freely
 Its luve to each flower,
But we heard and we saw nought
 In that blessed hour.

We heard and we saw nought
 Above or around:
We felt that our love lived,
 And loathed idle sound.
I gazed on your sweet face
 Till tears fill'd mine e'e,
And they drapt on your wee loof—
 A warld's wealth to me!

Now the winter snaw's fa'ing
 On bare holm and lee;
And the cauld wind is strippin'
 Ilk leaf aff the tree.
But the snaw fa's not faster,
 Nor leaf disna part
Sae sune frae the bough, as
 Faith fades in your heart.

Ye've waled out anither
 Your bridegroom to be;
But can his heart luve sae
 As mine luvit thee?
Ye'll get biggings and mailins,
 And monie braw claes,
But they a' winna buy back
 The peace o' past days.

Fareweel, and for ever!
 My first luve and last ·
May thy joys be to come,
 Mine live in the past.
In sorrow and sadness,
 This hour fa's on me,
But light, as thy love, may
 It fleet over thee.

THE MERMAIDEN.

WILLIAM MOTHERWELL.

The nicht is mirk, and the wind blaws schill,
  And the white faem weets my bree,
And my mind misgi'es me, gay maiden,
  That the land we sall never see!
Then up and spak' the mermaiden,
  And she spak' blythe and free,
"I never said to my bonnie bridegroom,
  That on land we sud weddit be.

"Oh! I never said that ane erthlie priest
  Our bridal blessing should gi'e,
And I never said that a landwart bouir
  Should hald my luve and me."
And where is that priest, my bonnie maiden,
  If ane erthlie wicht is na he?
"Oh! the wind will sough, and the sea will rair,
  When weddit we twa sall be."

And where is that bouir, my bonnie maiden,
  If on land it auld na be?
"Oh! my blythe bouir is low," said the mermaiden,
  "In the bonnie green howes o' the sea:
My gay bouir is biggit o' the gude ships' keels,
  And the banes o' the drowned at sea;
The fisch are the deer that fill my parks,
  And the water waste my dourie.

"And my bouir is sklaitit wi' the big blue waves,
  And paved wi' the yellow sand,
And in my chaumers grow bonnie white flowers
  That never grew on land.
And have ye e'er seen, my bonnie bridegroom,
  A leman on earth that wuld gi'e
Aiker for aiker o' the red plough'd land,
  As I'll gi'e to thee o' the sea?

The mune will rise in half ane hour,
  And the wee bricht starns will shine;
Then we'll sink to my bouir 'neath the wan water
  Full fifty fathom and nine."
A wild, wild skreich, gi'ed the foy bridegroom,
  And a loud, loud laugh, the bride;
For the mune raise up, and the twa sank down
  Under the silver'd tide.

JEANNIE MORRISON.
WILLIAM MOTHERWELL.

I've wander'd east, I've wander'd west
  Through mony a weary way;
But never, never, can forget
  The luve o' life's young day!
The fire that's blawn on Beltane e'en,
  May weel be black gin Yule;
But blacker fa' awaits the heart
  Where first fond luve grows cule.

O dear, dear Jeanie Morrison,
  The thochts o' bygane years
Still fling their shadows ower my path,
  And blind my e'en wi' tears:
They blind my e'en wi' saut, saut tears,
  And sair and sick I pine,
As memory idly summons up
  The blithe blinks o' langsyne.

'Twas then we luvit ilk ither weel,
  'Twas then we twa did part;
Sweet time—and time! twa bairns at schule,
  Twa bairns, and but ae heart!
'Twas then we sat on ae laigh bink,
  To loir ilk ither lear;
And tones, and looks, and smiles were shed,
  Remember'd ever mair.

I wonder, Jeanie, aften yet,
  When sitting on that bink,
Cheek touchin' cheek, loof lock'd in loof,
  What our wee heads could think!
When baith bent doun ower ae braid page
  Wi' ae buik on our knee,
Thy lips were on thy lesson, but
  My lesson was in thee.

Oh mind ye how we hung our heads,
  How cheeks brent red wi' shame,
Whene'er the schule-weans, laughin', said,
  We cleek'd thegither hame?
And mind ye o' the Saturdays,
  (The schule then skail't at noon),
When we ran aff to speel the braes—
  The broomy braes o' June?

My head rins round and round about,
  My heart flows like a sea,
As ane by ane the thochts rush back
  O' schule-time and o' thee.

Oh, mornin' life! Oh, mornin' luve!
  Oh, lichtsome days and lang,
When binnied hopes around our hearts,
  Like simmer blossoms sprang!

O mind ye, luve, how aft we left
  The deavin' dinsome toun,
To wander by the green burnside,
  And hear its waters croon;
The simmer leaves hung ower our heads,
  The flowers burst round our feet,
And in the gloamin' o' the wood,
  The throssil whusslit sweet.

The throssil whusslit in the wood,
  The burn sang to the trees,
And we, with Nature's heart in tune,
  Concerted harmonies;
And on the knowe abune the burn,
  For hours thegither sat
In the silentness o' joy, till baith
  Wi' very gladness grat!

Aye, aye, dear Jeanie Morrison,
  Tears trinkled down your cheek,
Like dew-beads on a rose, yet nane
  Had ony power to speak!
That was a time, a blessed time,
  When hearts were fresh and young,
When freely gush'd all feelings forth,
  Unsyllabled—unsung!

I marvel, Jeanie Morrison,
  Gin I ha'e been to thee
As closely twined wi' earliest thochts
  As ye ha'e been to me!
Oh! tell me gin their music fills
  Thine ear as it does mine;
Oh! say gin e'er your heart grows grit
  Wi' dreamings o' langsyne?

I've wander'd east, I've wander'd west,
  I've borne a weary lot;
But in my wanderings, far or near,
  Ye never were forgot.
The fount that first burst frae this heart,
  Stills travels on its way;
And channels deeper as it rins
  The luve o' life's young day.

O dear, dear Jeanie Morrison,
  Since we were sindor'd young,
I've never seen your face, nor heard
  The music o' your tongue;
But I could hug all wretchedness,
  And happy could I dee,
Did I but ken your heart still dream'd
  O' bygane days and me!

THE BLOOM HATH FLED.
WILLIAM MOTHERWELL.

The bloom hath fled thy cheek, Mary,
  As spring's rath blossoms die,
And sadness hath o'ershadow'd now
  Thy once bright eye;
But, look on me, the prints of grief
  Still deeper lie.
    Farewell!

Thy lips are pale and mute, Mary,
  Thy step is sad and slow,
The morn of gladness hath gone by
  Thou erst did know;
I, too, am changed like thee, and weep
  For very woe.
    Farewell!

It seems as 'twere but yesterday
  We were the happiest twain,
When murmur'd sighs and joyous tears,
  Dropping like rain,
Discoursed my love, and told how loved
  I was again.
    Farewell!

'Twas not in cold and measur'd phrase
  We gave our passion name:
Scorning such tedious eloquence,
  Our heart's fond flame
And long imprisoned feelings fast
  In deep sobs came.
    Farewell!

Would that our love had been the love
  That merest worldlings know,
When passion's draught to our doom'd lips
  Turns utter woe,
And our poor dream of happiness
  Vanishes so!
    Farewell!

But in the wreck of all our hopes,
  There's yet some touch of bliss,
Since fate robs not our wretchedness
  Of this last kiss:
Despair, and love, and madness, meet
  In this, in this.
    Farewell!

THE LADY OF MY HEART.
WILLIAM MOTHERWELL.

THE murmur of the merry brook,
  As, gushingly and free,
It wimples, with its sun-bright look,
  Far down yon shelter'd lea,
Humming to every drowsy flower
  A low quaint lullaby,
Speaks to my spirit, at this hour,
  Of love and thee.

The music of the gay green wood,
  When every leaf and tree
Is coax'd by winds, of gentlest mood
  To utter harmony;
And the small birds, that answer make
  To the winds' fitful glee,
In me most blissful visions wake,
  Of love and thee.

The rose perks up its blushing cheek,
  So soon as it can see,
Along the eastern hills, one streak
  Of the sun's majesty:
Laden with dewy gems, it gleams
  A precious freight to me,
For each pure drop thereon meseems
  A type of thee.

And when abroad in summer morn,
  I hear the blythe bold bee
Winding aloft his tiny horn,
  (An errant knight perdy,)
That winged hunter of rare sweets,
  O'er many a far country,
To me a lay of love repeats,
  Its subject—thee.

And when, in midnight hour, I note
  The stars so pensively,
In their mild beauty, onward float
  Through heaven's own silent sea:

My heart is in their voyaging
To realms where spirits be,
But its mate, in such wandering,
Is ever thee.

But, oh, the murmur of the brook,
The music of the tree;
The rose with its sweet shamefaced look,
The booming of the bee;
The course of each bright voyager,
In heaven's unmeasured sea,
Would not one heart-pulse of me stir,
Loved I not thee?

HIE GERMANIE.
WILLIAM MOTHERWELL.

Oh wae be to the orders that march'd my luve awa',
And wae be to the cruel cause that gars my tears doun fa'!
Oh wae be to the bluidy wars in Hie Germanie,
For they ha'e ta'en my luve, and left a broken heart to me.

The drums beat in the mornin' afore the scriech o' day,
And the wee wee fifes piped loud and shrill, while yet the morn
  was grey;
The bonnie flags were a' unfurl'd, a gallant sight to see,
But waes me for my sodger lad that march'd to Germanie.

Oh, lang, lang is the travel to the bonnie Pier o' Leith,
Oh dreich it is to gang on foot wi' the snaw drift in the teeth!
And oh, the cauld wind froze the tear that gather'd in my e'e,
When I gaed there to see my luve embark for Germanie.

I looked ower the braid blue sea, sae lang as could be seen
As wee bit sail upon the ship, that my sodger lad was in;
But the wind was blawin' sair and snell, and the ship sail'd
  speedilie,
And the waves and cruel wars ha'e twinn'd my winsome luve
  frae me.

I never think o' dancin', and I downa try to sing,
But a' the day I spier what news kind neibour bodies bring;
I sometimes knit a stocking, if knittin' it may be,
Syne for every loop that I cast on, I'm sure to let doun three.

My father says I'm in a pet, my mither jeers at me,
And bans me for a dautit wean, in dorts for aye to be;
But little weet they o' the cause that drumles sae my e'e;
Oh thay ha'e nae winsome luve like mine in the wars o' Germanie!

PART IV.
JACOBITE SONGS.

INTRODUCTORY NOTE.

On the abdication of James II. in 1688, the Prince of Orange was called to occupy the British throne. That monarch, instead of trying to conciliate all classes of his subjects, gave mortal offence to the people of Scotland by two distinct acts affecting respectively the two great divisions of the country. The massacre of Glencoe was, rightly or wrongly, laid by the Highlanders to his account, while the commercial people of the Lowlands could never forgive his conduct in the Darien affair.

These two acts kept alive and increased the dissatisfaction felt in Scotland at the Stuart family being debarred from the throne in favour of the "Oranger." The death of King William was occasioned, as is well known, through his horse stumbling against a mole-hill, and, "The Gentleman in Black" became a standing toast with the Jacobites.

During the reign of Queen Anne, the Jacobite feeling naturally weakened, to be revived with greater intensity, when in 1714 the Elector of Hanover (descending from King James I.) succeeded to the throne. The Earl of Mar unfurled the standard of the Stuarts, but after fighting Sherrifmuir, he found he had over estimated his strength, and the rebellion was suppressed. In 1727 George II. ascended the throne, and it was during his reign that the rebellion of 1745, which so nearly cost him his crown, arose. Prince Charles Edward Stuart was the eldest son of the Chevalier de St. George (son of James II.) His mother was the granddaughter of John Sobieski, the celebrated King and hero of Poland.

The Jacobite Songs have never been properly edited; Hogg's "Relics," full of blunders and forgeries, having served as the basis for all subsequent collections. We do not yet despair of seeing these songs thrown together so as to form a history of the two rebellions in song and ballad. An attempt has been made here to arrange them in this form, but the limited space at our command, and the popular nature of the work, would not allow anything but the better and more popular songs to be given, leaving aside, of course, rhymes and pasquils innumerable, which often serve to give a better idea of events than even the smooth pages of our ordinary histories.

YOU'RE WELCOME WHIGS.

Composed probably about the time of the Revolution of 1688, when, as Mr. Robert Chambers remarks, the Jacobites "lost power, but acquired wit."

You're welcome, Whigs, from Bothwell Brigs,
  Youre malice is but zeal, boys;
Most holy sprites, the hypocrites,
  'Tis sack ye drink, not ale, boys
I must aver, ye cannot err,
  In breaking God's commands, boys
If ye infringe bishops' or kings',
  You've heaven in your hands, boys.

Suppose ye cheat, disturb the state,
  And steep the laud wi' blood, boys;
If secretly your treachery
  Be acted, it is good, boys.
The fiend himsel', in midst o' hell,
  The pope, with his intrigues, boys,
You'll equalize in forgeries;
  Fair fa' you, pious Whigs, boys.

You'll God beseech, in homely speech,
  To his coat-tail you'll claim, boys;
Seek lippies of grace frae his gawcie face,
  And bless and not blaspheme, boys.
Your teachers they can kiss and pray,
  In zealous ladies' closets;
Your wits convert by Venus' art;
  Your kirk has holy roset.

Which death will tie promiscuously,
  Her members on the vale, boys,
For hornèd beasts the truth attest,
  That live in Annandale, boys.
But if one drink, or shrewdly think
  A bishop ere was saved,
No charity from presbytrye,
  For that need once be cravèd.

You lie, you lust, you break your trust,
  And act all kinds of evil,
Your covenant makes you a saint,
  Although you live a devil.
From murders, too, as soldiers true,
  You are advancèd well, boys;
You fought like devils, your only rivals,
  When you were at Dunkeld, boys.

Your wondrous things great slaughter brings,
　　You kill'd more than you saw, boys;
At Pentland hills ye got your fills,
　　And now you seem to craw, boys.
Let wabsters preach, and ladies teach
　　The art of cuckoldry, boys,
When cruel zeal comes in their tail,
　　Then welcome presbytrye, boys.

King William's hands, with lovely bands,
　　You're decking with good speed, boys;
If you got leave, you'll reach his sleeve,
　　And then have at his head, boys.
You're welcome, Jack, we'll join a plack,
　　To drink your last confusion,
That grace and truth we may possess
　　Once more without delusion.

BONNIE DUNDEE.
SIR WALTER SCOTT.

To the Lords of Convention 'twas Claverhouse spoke,
"Ere the king's crown go down there are crowns to be broke
So each cavalier who loves honour and me,
Let him follow the bonnet of Bonnie Dundee.
　　Come, fill up my cup, come, fill up my can,
　　Come, saddle my horses, and call out my men,
　　Come, open the West Port, and let me gae free,
　　And it's room for the bonnets of Bonnie Dundee."

Dundee he is mounted, he rides up the street,
The bells are rung backward, the drums they are beat,
But the Provost, douce man, said, just e'en let him be,
The toun is well quit of that deil of Dundee.
　　Come, fill up, etc.

As he rode down the sanctified bends of the Bow,
Each carlin was flyting and shaking her pow;
But some young plants of grace, they look'd couthie and slee,
Thinking—Luck to thy bonnet, thou bonnie Dundee!
　　Come, fill up, etc.

With sour-featured saints the Grassmarket was panged,
As if half of the west had set tryste to be hanged;
There was spite in each face, there was fear in each e'e,
As they watch'd for the bonnet of bonnie Dundee.
　　Come, fill up, etc.

The cowls of Kilmarnock had spits and had spears,
And lang-hafted gullies to kill cavaliers;
But they shrunk to close-heads, and the causeway left free,
At a toss of the bonnet of Bonnie Dundee.
    Come, fill up, etc.

He spurred to the foot of the high castle rock,
And to the gay Gordon he gallantly spoke;
"Let Mons Meg and her marrows three volleys let floe,
For love of the bonnets of bonnie Dundee."
    Come, fill up, etc.

The Gordon has askèd him whither he goes;—
"Wheresoever shall guide me the soul of Montrose,
Your grace in short space shall have tidings of me,
Or that low lies the bonnet of bonnie Dundee.
    Come, fill up, etc.

"There are hills beyond Pentland, and streams beyond Forth;
If there's lords in the Southland, there's chiefs in the North,
There are wild dunniewassals three thousand times three,
Will cry *Hoigh!* for the bonnets of bonnie Dundee.
    Come, fill up, etc.

"Away to the hills, to the woods, to the rocks,
Ere I own a usurper, I'll crouch to the fox,
And tremble, false Whigs, though triumphant ye be,
You have not seen the last of my bonnet and me.
    Come, fill up," etc.

He waved his proud arm, and the trumpets were blown,
The kettle-drums clash'd, and the horsemen rode on,
Till on Ravelston crags, and on Clermiston lee,
Died away the wild war notes of bonnie Dundee.
    Come, fill up my cup, come, fill up my can,
    Come, saddle my horses, and call up my men,
    Fling all your gates open, and let me gae free,
    Sae 't is up with the bonnets of Bonnie Dundee.

BATTLE OF KILLICRANKIE.

WHILE England quietly submitted to the change of government, a desperate struggle was going on in Scotland. Graham of Claverhouse, Viscount Dundee, raised the standard of the King, and, backed by the clans, commenced a brief campaign on behalf of his Royal master. The only meeting between the rival forces at all worthy of notice, was that celebrated in the following song, The Battle of Killicrankie, fought July 17, 1689, between 8000 Highlanders under Dundee, and the English army of some 5000 men under General Hugh Mackay. The Battle was short and decisive in favour of the Highlanders, Mackay's troops being beaten back on all points with heavy loss. The fruits of the victory were lost to King James through the death of Claverhouse, who was mortally wounded early in the fight.

CLAVERS and his Highlandmen,
  Came down upon the raw, man,
Who, being stout, gave many a clout,
  The lads began to claw then.
With sword and targe into their hand,
  Wi' which they were na slaw, man,
Wi' mony a fearful heavy sigh,
  The lads began to claw, then.

O'er bush, o'er bank, o'er ditch, o'er stank,
  She flang amang them a', man;
The Butter-box got mony knocks,
  Their riggings paid for a' thon.
They got their paiks, wi' sudden straiks,
  Which to their grief they saw, man;
Wi' clinkum clankum o'er their crowns,
  The lads began to fa' then.

Her skipt about, her leapt about,
  And flung amang them a', man;
The English blades got broken heads,
  Their crowns were cleav'd in twa then.
The durk and door made their last hour,
  And prov'd their final fa', man;
They thought the devil had been there,
  That play'd them sic a paw then.

The solemn league and covenant,
  Cam whigging up the hills, man,
Thought Highland trews durst not refuse
  For to subscribe their bills then:
In Willie's name they thought nae ane
  Durst stop their course at a', man,
But her nain-sell, wi' mony a knock,
  Cried, "Furich, whigs awa', man."

Sir Evan-Dhu, and his men true,
  Came linking up the brink, man;
The Hogan Dutch they feared such,
  They bred a horrid stink then.
The true Maclean, and his fierce men,
  Came in amang them a', man;
Nane durst withstand his heavy hand,
  All fled and ran awa' then.

Och on a ri, och on a ri,
  Why should she lose King Shames, man?
Och rig in di, och rig in di,
  She shall break a' her banes then;
With *furichinish*, and stay a-while,
  And speak a word or twa, man,
She's gi' a straik out o'er the neck,
  Before ye win awa' then.

O fy for shame, ye're three for ane,
  Her nane-sell's won the day, man;
King Shames' red coats should be hung up,
  Because they ran awa' then:
Had bent their brows, like Highland trues,
  And made as lang a stay, man,
They'd sav'd their king, that sacred thing,
  And Willie'd run away then.

KILLICRANKIE.

(ANOTHER VERSION.)

FROM JOHNSON'S MUSEUM, probably touched up by BURNS.

  WHARE ha'e ye been sae braw, lad?
    Whare ha'e ye been sae brankie, O?
  Whare ha'e ye been sae braw, lad?
    Came ye by Killicrankie, O?
      An ye had been whare I ha'e been
        Ye wadna been sae cantie, O;
      An ye had seen what I ha'e seen,
        I' the braes o' Killicrankie. O.

  I faught at land, I faught at sea,
    At hame I faught my auntie, O;
  But I met the devil and Dundee,
    On the braes o' Killicrankie, O;
      An ye had been, etc.
  The bauld Pitcur fell in a furr,
    And Clavers gat a clankie, O,
  Or I had fed an Athol gled
    On the braes o' Killicrankie, O.
      An ye had been, etc.

  O fie, Mackay, what gart ye lie
    I' the bush ayont the brankie, O?
  Ye'd better kiss'd King Willie's loof,
    Than come to Killicrankie, O.
      It's nae shame, it's nae shame,
        It's nae shame to shank ye, O;
      There's sour slaes on Athol braes,
        And deils at Killicrankie, O.

IT WAS A' FOR OUR RIGHTFU' KING.

ASCRIBED to Captain Ogilvie, a cadet of the house of Inverquharity. He took part in the Battle of the Boyne, in the service of King James, and accompanied his Royal master into France, being one of a hundred gentlemen who voluntarily agreed to attend their king in exile. He was killed in some engagement on the Rhine.

"It was a' for our rightfu' king
  We left fair Scotland's strand!
It was a' for our rightfu' king
  We e'er saw Irish land, my dear,
  We e'er saw Irish land.

Now a' is done that men can do,
  An' a' is done in vain:
My love an' native land fareweel,
  For I maun cross the main, my dear,
  For I maun cross the main."

He turn'd him right an' round about,
  Upon the Irish shore,
An' ga'e his bridle-reins a shake
  With, "Adieu for evermore, my dear,
  With, Adieu for evermore."

The sodger frae the wars returns,
  The sailor frae the main;
But I hae parted frae my love,
  Never to meet again, my dear,
  Never to meet again.

When day is gane, an' night is come,
  An' a' folk bound to sleep,
I think on him that's far awa,
  The lee-lang night, an' weep, my dear,
  The lee-lang night, an' weep.

TO DAUNTON ME.

To daunton me, to daunton me,
Ken ye the things that would daunton me?
O eighty-eight and eighty-nine,
And a' the dreary years sin' syne,
With cess, and press, and Presbytrie,
Guid faith these had like to hae dauntoned me!

But to wanton me, to wanton me,
Do you ken the things that would wanton me?
To see guid corn upon the rigs,
And a gallows hie to hang the Whigs,
And the right restored where the right should be,
O these are the things that would wanton me!

To wanton me, to wanton me,
Ken you what maist would wanton me?
To see King James at Edinburgh cross,
Wi' fifty thousand foot and horse,
And the usurper forced to flee,
O this is what maist would wanton me.

HERE'S TO THE KING.

The feelings of the Jacobites, under whatever disadvantage, always turned towards the Exiled family. The following song may be taken as illustrating the sly manner in which their loyalty was sung, without, of course, laying themselves open to a charge of treason.

Here's to the king, sir,
Ye ken wha I mean, sir,
And to every honest man,
 That will do 't again!

Fill, fill your bumpers high,
Drain, drain your glasses dry,
Out upon him, fye! oh, fye!
 That winna do 't again!

Here's to the chieftains
Of the Scots Highland clans!
They hae done it mair than anes,
 And will do 't again.

When you hear the trumpet sound
Tuttie taitie to the drum,
Up your swords, and down your guns,
 And to the rogues again!

Here's to the king of Swede,
Fresh laurels crown his head!
Fye on every sneaking blade,
 That winna do 't again!

But to mak things right now,
He that drinks maun fight too,
To shew his heart's upright too,
 And that he 'll do 't again!

Sometimes the following verse was added:

Weel may we a' be,
Ill may we never see,
Here's to the king
 And the guid companie!

CARLE, AN' THE KING COME.

A MORE outspoken burst than the last. The air is very popular, and numerous songs, Jacobitical and otherwise, have been written for it.

CARLE, an' the king come,
Carle, an' the king come,
Thou shalt dance, and I will sing,
    Carle, an' the king come.
An' somebody were come again,
Then somebody maun cross the main,
And ev'ry man shall ha'e his ain,
    Carle, an' the king come.

I trow we swapped for the worse,
We ga'e the boot and better horse,
And that we'll tell them at the cross,
    Carle, an' the king come.
When yellow corn grows on the rigs,
And a gibbet's built to hang the Whigs,
O then we will dance Scottish jigs,
    Carle, an' the king come.

Nae mair wi' pinch and drouth we'll dine,
As we ha'e done—a dog's propine,
But quaff our waughts o' bouzy wine,
    Carle, an' the king come.
Cogie, an' the king come,
Cogie, an' the king come,
I'se be fou, and thou'se be toom,
    Cogie, an' the king come.

WILLIE THE WAG.

A SATIRE on King William.

O, I HAD a wee bit mailin,
    And I had a good gray mare,
And I had a braw bit dwalling,
    Till Willie the wag came here.
He waggit me out o' my mailin,
    He waggit me out o' my gear,
And out o' my bonny black gowny,
    That ne'er was the waur o' the wear.

He fawn'd and he waggit his tale,
    Till he poison'd the true well-e'e;
And wi' the wagging o' his fause tongue,
    He gart the brave Monmouth die.

He waggit us out o' our rights,
    And he waggit us out o' our law,
And he waggit us out o' our king;
    O that grieves me the warst of a'.

The tod rules o'er the lion,
    The midden's aboon the moon,
And Scotland maun cower and cringe
    To a fause and a foreign loon.
O walyfu' fa' the piper
    That sells his wind sae dear!
And O walyfu' fa' the time
    When Willie the wag came here!

WHAT'S THE RHYME TO PORRINGER.

O WHAT'S the rhyme to porringer?
Ken ye the rhyme to porringer?
King James the Seventh had ae dochter,
And he ga'e her to an Oranger.
Ken ye how he requited him?
Ken ye how he requited him?
The lad has into England come,
And ta'en the crown in spite o' him.

The dog, he sanna keep it lang,
    To flinch we 'll mak' him fain again;
We 'll hing him hie upon a tree,
    And James shall hae his ain again.
Ken ye the rhyme to grasshopper?
Ken ye the rhyme to grasshopper?
A hempen rein, and a horse o' tree,
A psalm-book and a presbyter.

THIS IS NO MY HOUSE.

O THIS is no my ain house,
    I ken by the biggin o't;
For bow-kail thrave at my door-check,
    And thristles on the riggin o't.
A carle came wi' lack o' grace,
Wi' unco gear and unco face;
And sin' he claim'd my daddy's place,
    I downa bide the triggin o't.

Wi' routh o' kin, and routh o' reek,
My daddy's door it wadna steek;
But bread and cheese were his door-check,
    And girdle cakes the riggin o't.
    O this is no my ain house, etc.

My daddy bag his housie weel,
By dint o' head and dint o' heel,
By dint o' arm and dint o' steel,
  And muckle weary priggin o't.
    O this is no my ain house, etc.

Then was it dink, or was it douce,
For ony cringing foreign goose
To claucht my daddie's wee bit house,
  And spoil the hamely triggin o't?
    O this is no my ain house, etc.

Say, was it foul, or was it fair,
To come a hunder mile and mair,
For to ding out my daddy's heir,
  And dash him wi' the whiggin o't?
    O this is no my ain house, etc.

OVER THE SEAS AND FAR AWA.

When we think on the days of auld,
When our Scots lads were true as bauld,
O weel may we weep for our foul fa',
And grieve for the lad that's far awa!
    Over the seas and far awa,
    Over the seas and far awa,
O weel may we maen for the day that's gane,
    And the lad that's banish'd far awa.

Some traitor lords, for love o' gain,
They drove our true king owre the main,
In spite o' right, and rule, and law,
And the friends o' him that's far awa.
    Over the seas and far awa, etc.

A bloody rook frae Brunswick flew,
And gather'd devil's birds eneuch;
Wi' kingmen's blude they gorge their maw'!
O dule to the louns sent Jamie awa!
    Over the seas and far awa, etc.

And cruel England, leal men's dread
Doth hunt and cry for Scottish bludo
To hack, and head, and hang, and draw,
And a' for the lad that's far awa.
    Over the seas and far awa, etc.

There's a reade in heaven, I read it true,
There's vengeance for us on a' that crew,
There's blude for blude to ane and a'
That sent our bonnie lad far awa.

Over the seas and far awa,
Over the seas and far awa,
He'll soon be here that I loe dear,
And he's welcome hame frae far awa!

I HA'E NAE KITH, I HA'E NAE KIN.

"THIS is a very sweet and curious little old song, but not very easily understood. The air is exceedingly simple, and the verses highly characteristic of the lyrical songs of Scotland."—Hogg's Jacobite Relics, vol. I., p. 218.

I HA'E nae kith, I ha'e nae kin,
 Nor ane that's dear to me,
For the bonny lad that I lo'e best,
 He's far ayont the sea.
He's gane wi' ane that was our ain,
 And we may rue the day,
When our king's ae daughter came here,
 To play sic foul play.

O gin I were a bonny bird,
 Wi' wings that I might floe,
Then I wad travel o'er the main,
 My ae true love to see;
Then I wad tell a joyfu' tale
 To ane that's dear to me,
And sit upon a king's window,
 And sing my melody.

The adder lies i' the corbie's nest,
 Aneath the corbie's wame,
And the blast that reaves the corbie's brood
 Shall blaw our good king hame.
Then blaw ye east, or blaw ye west,
 Or blaw ye o'er the faem,
O bring the lad that I lo'e best,
 And ane I darena name!

SUCH A PARCEL OF ROGUES IN A NATION.
ROBERT BURNS.

A FEELING among the people that the Scottish Members of Parliament were peculiarly susceptible of corruption, and that through underhand means they had been induced to assent to the union between the two kingdoms in 1702, seems to have found vent in the following song. The charge of corruption has we think been disproved, but there is no doubt that the Act was received in Scotland with great bitterness, and passed amid deep grumblings and even threats.

    FAREWEEL to a' our Scottish fame,
      Fareweel our ancient glory;
    Fareweel e'en to the Scottish name,
      Sae fam'd in martial story.
    Now Sark rins ower the Solway sands,
      And Tweed rins to the ocean,
    To mark where England's province stands:
      Such a parcel of rogues in a nation!

    What force or guile could not subdue,
      Through many warlike ages,
    Is wrought now by a coward few,
      For hireling traitor's wages.
    The English steel we could disdain,
      Secure in valour's station,
    But English gold has been our bane:
      Such a parcel of rogues in a nation!

    O would or I had seen the day
      That treason thus could sell us,
    My auld gray head had lain in clay,
      Wi' Bruce and loyal Wallace!
    By pith and power, to my last hour
      I'll make this declaration,
    We're bought and sold for English gold:
      Such a parcel of rogues in a nation!

FY LET US A' TO THE TREATY.

A SATIRICAL song on the principal personages in connection with the Act of Union.—Air, "Fy let us a' to the bridal."

    Now fy let us a' to the treaty,
      For there will be wonders there,
    For Scotland is to be a bride, sir,
      And wed to the Earl of Stair.
    There's Queensberry, Seafield, and Mar, sir,
      And Morton comes in by the bye;
    There's Loudon, and Leven, and Weems, sir,
      And Sutherland, frequently dry.

    There's Roseberry, Glasgow, and Duplin,
      And Lord Archibald Campbell, and Ross;
    The president, Francis Montgomery,
      Wha ambles like ony paced horse.

There's Johnstoun, Dan Campbell, and Ross, lad,
  Whom the court hath had still on their bench;
There's solid Pitmedden and Forgland,
  Wha design'd jumping on to the bench.

There's Ormistoun and Tillicoultrie,
  And Smollett for the town of Dumbarton;
There's Arniatoun, too, and Carnwathie,
  Put in by his uncle L. Warton;
There's Grant, and young Pennicook, sir,
  Hugh Montgomery, and Davy Dalrymple;
There's one who will surely bear bouk, sir,
  Prestongrange, who indeed is not simple.

Now the Lord bless the jimp one-and-thirty,
  If they prove not traitors in fact,
But see that their bride be well drest, sir,
  Or the devil take all the pack.
May the devil take all the hale pack, sir,
  Away on his back with a bang;
Then well may our new-buskit bridie
  For her ain first wooer think lang.

THERE'LL NEVER BE PEACE SIN' JAMIE'S AWA'.

By Carnousie's auld wa's, at the close of the day,
An auld man was singing, wi' locks thin and grey,
And the burden o' his sang, while the tears fast did fa',
Was, there'll never be peace sin' Jamie's awa'.

Our kirk's gaen either to ruin again,
Our state's in confusion, and bravely we ken,
Tho' we darena weel tell wha's to blame for it a',
And we'll never see peace sin' Jamie's awa'.

Our auld honest master, the laird o' the lan',
He bauldly set off at the head o' the clan,
But the knowes o' Carnousie again he ne'er saw,
An a's gaen to wrock sin' Jamie's awa'.

THERE'LL NEVER BE PEACE UNTIL JAMIE COMES HAME.

ROBERT BURNS.

FOUNDED on the old words.

By yon castle wa', at the close o' the day,
I heard a man sing, though his head it was grey;
And as he was singing, the tears down came,
There'll never be peace until Jamie comes hame.

The church is in ruins, the state is in jars,
Delusions, oppressions, and murderous wars;
We darena weel say't, but we ken wha's to blame;
There'll never be peace until Jamie comes hame.

My seven braw sons for Jamie drew sword,
And now I greet round their green beds in the yird;
It brak the sweet heart o' my faithfu' auld dame;
There'll never be peace until Jamie comes hame.
Now life is a burden that bows me down,
Sin' I tint my bairns, and he tint his crown;
But till my last moments my words are the same,
There'll never be peace until Jamie comes hame.

THE BLACKBIRD.

FROM RAMSAY'S TEA TABLE MISCELLANY. The Blackbird was the Old Pretender, who was known among his adherents by that title, derived from the darkness of his complexion. It has been claimed by Mr. Samuel Lover and others as of Irish origin, but on no other grounds than "conjecture."

ONCE on a morning of sweet recreation,
   I heard a fair lady a-making her moan,
With sighing and sobbing, and sad lamentation,
   Aye singing, "My Blackbird for ever is flown!
He's all my heart's treasure, my joy, and my pleasure,
   So justly, my love, my heart follows thee;
And I am resolved, in foul or fair weather,
   To seek out my Blackbird, wherever he be.

"I will go, a stranger to peril and danger,
   My heart is so loyal in every degree;
For he's constant and kind, and courageous in mind:
   Good luck to my Blackbird, wherever he be!
In Scotland he's loved and dearly approved,
   In England a stranger he seemeth to be;
But his name I'll advance in Britain or France;
   Good luck to my Blackbird, wherever he be!

"The birds of the forest are all met together,
   The turtle is chosen to dwell with the dove,.
And I am resolved, in foul or fair weather,
   Once in the spring-time to seek out my love.
But since fickle Fortune, which still proves uncertain,
   Hath caused this parting between him and me,
His right I'll proclaim, and who dares me blame?
   Good luck to my Blackbird, wherever he be!"

LADY KEITH'S LAMENT.

Lady Mary Drummond, wife of Lord Keith, is supposed to be the heroine and authoress of this song. "She was so strongly attached to the exiled family," says Hogg, "that, on the return of her two sons to Scotland, she would never suffer them to enjoy any rest till they engaged actively in the cause of the Stuarts."—Air, Boyne Water.

I may sit in my woe croo house,
    At the rock and the reel to toil fu' dreary;
I may think on the day that's gane,
    And sigh and sab till I grow weary.
I ne'er could brook, I ne'er could brook,
    A foreign loon to own or flatter;
But I will sing a ranting sang,
    That day our king comes ower the water.

O gin I live to see the day,
    That I ha'e begg'd, and begg'd frae Heaven,
I'll fling my rock and reel away,
    And dance and sing frae morn till even:
For there is ane I winna name,
    That comes the reigning bike to scatter;
And I'll put on my bridal gown,
    That day our king comes ower the water.

I ha'e seen the gude auld day,
    The day o' pride and chieftain glory,
When royal Stuarts bore the sway,
    And ne'er heard tell o' Whig nor Tory.
Though lyart be my locks and grey,
    And eild has crook'd me down—what matter?
I'll dance and sing ae ither day,
    That day our king comes ower the water.

A curse on dull and drawling Whig,
    The whining, ranting, low deceiver,
Wi' heart sae black, and look sae big,
    And canting tongue o' clishmaclaver.
My father was a good lord's son,
    My mother was an earl's daughter,
And I'll be Lady Keith again,
    That day our king comes ower the water.

AWA, WHIGS, AWA.

The air of this song is very old and very popular. Part of the verses are also as old as the time of Charles I. but it is one of those elastic songs which may be added to or abridged to suit passing events. "There is a tradition that at the battle of Bothwell Bridge, the Piper to Clavers' own troop of horse, stood on the brink of the Clyde playing it with great glee;

but, being struck with a bullet, either by chance or in consequence of an aim taken, as is generally reported, he rolled down the bank in the agonies of death; and always, as he rolled over the bag, so intent was he on this old party tune, that, with determined firmness of fingering, he made the pipes to yell out two or three notes of it, till at last he plunged into the river and was carried peaceably down the stream among a great number of floating whigs." Hogg's Jacobite Relics, vol. i., p. 259. The fourth and fifth verses are by Burns.

> Awa, Whigs, awa,
> Awa, Whigs, awa,
> Ye're but a pack o' traitor loons,
> Ye'll ne'er do good at a.'
> Our thristles flourish'd fresh and fair,
> And bonny bloom'd our roses;
> But Whigs came like a frost in June,
> And wither'd a' our posies.
>   Awa, Whigs, etc.
>
> Our sad decay in kirk and state
> Surpasses my describing;
> The Whigs cam' o'er us for a curse,
> And we ha'e done wi' thriving.
>   Awa, Whigs, etc.
>
> A foreign Whiggish loon brought seeds
> In Scottish yird to cover,
> But we'll pu' a' his dibbled leeks,
> And pack him to Hanover.
>   Awa, Whigs, etc.
>
> Our ancient crown's fa'n i' the dust,
> Deil blind them wi' the stoure o't;
> And write their names i' his black beuk,
> Wha ga'e the Whigs the power o't.
>   Awa, Whigs, etc.
>
> Grim vengeance lang has ta'en a nap,
> But we may see him wauken;
> Gude help the day when royal heads
> Are hunted like a maukin!
>   Awa, Whigs, etc.
>
> The deil he heard the stoure o' tongues,
> And ramping cam' amang us;
> But he pitied us sae curs'd wi' Whigs,
> He turn'd and wadna wrang us.
>   Awa, Whigs, etc.

The deil sat grim amang the reek,
  Thrang buddling brunstane matches;
And croon'd 'mang the benk-taking Whigs,
  Scraps of auld Calvin's catches.

Awa, Whigs, awa,
  Awa, Whigs, awa,
Ye'll run me out o' wun spunks,
  Awa, Whigs, awa.

THE WEE, WEE GERMAN LAIRDIE.

Hogg's Version of this best of all the Jacobite Satirical Songs. It is based upon that by Allan Cunningham in Cromek's Remains, which in its turn was based upon an older song or probably songs. In Cunningham's Poems and Songs, published in 1847 under the editorship of his Son, it is inserted as one of his productions.

Wha the deil hae we gotten for a king,
  But a wee, wee German lairdie!
An' when we gaed to bring him hame,
  He was delving in his kail-yairdie:
Sheughing kail, and laying leeks,
But the hose and but the breeks
Up his beggar duds he cleeks,
  The wee, wee German lairdie!

And he's clapt down in our gudeman's chair,
  The wee, wee German lairdie!
And he's brought fouth o' foreign trash,
  And dibbled them in his yairdie:
He's pu'd the rose o' English loons,
And brake the harp o' Irish clowns,
But our Scots thristle will jag his thumbs
  The wee, wee German lairdie.

Come up amang the Highland hills,
  Thou wee, wee German lairdie,
And see how Charlie's lang-kail thrives,
  That he dibbled in his yairdie:
And if a stock ye daur to pu',
Or haud the yoking of a pleugh,
We'll break your sceptre o'er your mou',
  Thou wee bit German lairdie!

Our hills are steep, our glens are deep,
  No fitting for a yairdie;
And our norlan' thristles winna pu',
  For a wee, wee German lairdie!

And we've the trenching blades o' weir,
 Wad lib ye o' your German gear,
And pass ye 'neath the claymore's sheer,
 Thou feckless German lairdie!
Auld Scotland! thou'rt owre cauld a hole
 For nursing siccan vermin;
But the very dogs o' England's court
 Can bark and howl in *German!*
Then keep thy dibble in thy ain hand,
 Thy spade, but and thy yairdie;
For wha the deil now claims our land
 But a wee, wee German lairdie.

YE WHIGS ARE A REBELLIOUS CREW.

A SATIRE, general and personal, against the Hanoverian Government and King. The two last verses relate to domestic squabbles among the members of the royal family. *Feckie* is Frederick, Prince of Wales.

Ye Whigs are a rebellious crew,
 The plague of this poor nation;
Ye give not God nor Cæsar due;
 Ye smell of reprobation.
Ye are a stubborn perverse pack,
 Conceiv'd and nurs'd by treason;
Your practices are foul and black,
 Your principles 'gainst reason.

Your Hogan Mogan foreign things,
 God gave them in displeasure;
Ye brought them o'er, and call'd them kings;
 They've drain'd our blood and treasure.
Can ye compare your king to mine,
 Your Geordie and your Willie?
Comparisons are odious,
 A toadstool to a lily.

Our Darien can witness bear,
 And so can our Glenco, sir;
Our South Sea it can make appear,
 What to your kings we owe, sir.
We have been murder'd, starv'd, and robb'd,
 By those your kings and knav'ry,
And all our treasure is stock-jobb'd,
 While we groan under slav'ry.

Did e'er the rightful Stuart's race
 (Declare it, if you can, sir,)
Reduce you to so bad a case?
 Hold up your face, and answer.

Did he whom ye expell'd the throne,
　Your islands e'er harass so,
As these whom ye have plac'd thereon,
　Your Brunswick and your Nassau?
By strangers we are robb'd and shamm'd,
　This you must plainly grant, sir,
Whose coffers with our wealth are cramm'd,
　While we must starve for want, sir.
Can ye compare your kings to mine,
　Your Geordie and your Willie?
Comparisons are odious,
　A bramble to a lily.

Your prince's mother did amiss,
　This ye have ne'er denied, sir,
Or why liv'd she without a kiss,
　Confin'd until she died, sir?
Can ye compare your queen to mine?
　I know ye're not so silly :
Comparisons are odious,
　A dockan to a lily.

Her son is a poor matchless sot,
　His own papa ne'er lov'd him;
And Feckie is an idiot,
　As they can swear who prov'd him.
Can ye compare your prince to mine,
　A thing so dull and silly?
Comparisons are odious,
　A mushroom to a lily.

THE SOW'S TAIL TO GEORDIE!

This song has always been very popular. The Sow was a name given on account of her enormous figure, to Madam Kilmansegge, Countess of Darlington, one of the favourite mistresses of George I. Full advantage was taken by the Jacobites of the unclean habits of the court, and songs, libels, and every possible manner of abuse, was shouted about the public streets, and often even in hearing of the royal household. The following song will serve as a specimen of those emanating from Scotland.

It's Geordie's now come hereabout,
　O was light on his sulky snout!
A pawky sow has found him out,
　And turn'd her tail to Geordie.
　　The sow's tail is till him yet,
　　A sow's birse will kill him yet,
　　The sow's tail is till him yet,
　　　The sow's tail to Geordie

It's Geordie he came up the town,
Wi' a bunch o' turnips on his crown;
"Aha!" quo' she, "I'll pull them down,
And turn my tail to Geordie."
    The sow's tail is till him yet, etc.

It's Geordie he gat up to dance,
And wi' the sow to take a prance,
And aye she gart her hurdies flaunce,
And turn'd her tail to Geordie.
    The sow's tail is till him yet, etc.

It's Geordie he gaed out to hang,
The sow came round him wi' a bang:
"Aha!" quo' she, "there's something wrang;
I'll turn my tail to Geordie."
    The sow's tail is till him yet, etc.

The sow and Geordie ran a race,
But Geordie fell and brake his face:
"Aha!" quo' she, "I've won the race,
And turn'd my tail to Geordie."
    The sow's tail is till him yet, etc.

It's Geordie he sat down to dine,
And wha came in but Madam Swine?
"Grumph! Grumph!" quo' she, "I'm come in time,
I'll sit and dine wi' Geordie."
    The sow's tail is till him yet, etc.

It's Geordie he lay down to die;
The sow was there as weel as he:
"Umph! Umph!" quo' she, "he's no for me,"
And turn'd her tail to Geordie.
    The sow's tail is till him yet, etc.

It's Geordie he gat up to pray,
She mumpit round and ran away:
"Umph! Umph!" quo' she, "he's done for aye,"
And turn'd her tail to Geordie.
    The sow's tail is till him yet, etc.

MY DADDY HAD A RIDING MARE:

THE riding mare represents Great Britain, and the riders are the various sovereigns who occupied the throne after the abdication of James II. The "Unco loon" is King William III. Queen Anne, and her Hanoverian Successors are taken up in order. "The Sow" has been explained in the previous song.

My daddy had a riding mare,
 And she was ill to sit,
And by there came an unco loon,
 And slippit in his fit.
He set his fit into the st'rup,
 And gripped sickerly;
And aye sinsyne, my dainty mare,
 She flings and glooms at me.

This thief he fell and brain'd himsel',
 And up gat couthy Anne;
She gripp'd the mare, the riding gear
 And halter in her hand:
And on she rade, and fast she rade,
 O'er necks o' nations three;
Feint that she ride the aiver stiff,
 Sin' she has geck'd at me!

The Whigs they ga'e my *Auntie* draps
 That hasten'd her away,
And then they took a cursed oath,
 And drank it up like whey:
Then they sent for a bastard race,
 Whilk I may sairly rue,
And for a horse they've got an ass,
 And on it set a sow.

Then hey the ass, the dainty ass,
 That cocks aboon them a'!
And hey the sow, the dainty sow,
 That soon will get a fa'!
The graith was ne'er in order yet,
 The bridle wasna worth a doit;
And mony ane will get a bite,
 Or cuddy gangs awa.

PETTICOAT'S LOOSE.

It's Hanover, Hanover, fast as you can over,
   Hey gudeman, away gudeman;
It's Hanover, Hanover, fast as you can over,
   Bide na here till day gudeman.
For there is a harper down i' the north,
Has play'd a spring on the banks o' Forth,
And aye the owre-word o' the tune
   Is, awa', gudeman, awa', gudeman,
   It's Hanover, Hanover, etc.

It's Feddy maun strap, and Robin maun string,
And Killy may wince, and fidge, and fling,
For Kenny has loos'd her petticoat string,
   Gae tie't again, gae tie't again.
   It's Hanover, Hanover, etc.

O Kenny my kitten, come draw your mitten,
   And dinna be lang, and dinna be lang;
For petticoat's loose, and barrie is slitten,
   And a's gane wrang, and a's gane wrang.
   It's Hanover, Hanover, etc.

THE CUCKOO.

A FINE allegorical Song. The Cuckoo refers to the Chevalier de St. George, though why so designated we have been unable to trace.

The cuckoo's a bonny bird, when he comes home,
The cuckoo's a bonny bird when he comes home,
He'll fley away the wild birds that hank about the throne,
My bonny cuckoo, when he comes home.
The cuckoo's the bonny bird, and he'll hae the day;
The cuckoo's the royal bird, whatever they may say;
Wi' the whistle o' his mou', and the blink o' his e'e,
He'll scare a' the unco birds awa frae me.

The cuckoo's a bonny bird, when he comes home,
The cuckoo's a bonny bird, when he comes home,
He'll fley away the wild birds that hank about the throne,
My bonny cuckoo, when he comes home.
The cuckoo's a bonny bird, but far frae his hame;
I ken him by the feathers that grow upon his kaine;
And round that double kame yet a crown I hope to see,
For my bonny cuckoo he is dear to me.

2 L

DONALD MACGILLAVRY.

JAMES HOGG.

Donald's gane up the hill hard and hungry;
Donald comes down the hill wild and angry;
Donald will clear the gouk's nest cleverly:
Here's to the king and Donald Macgillavry.
Come like a weigh-bauk, Donald Macgillavry,
Come like a weigh-bauk, Donald Macgillavry;
Balance them fair, and balance them cleverly:
Off wi' the counterfeit, Donald Macgillavry.

Donald's run o'er the hill but his tether, man,
As he were wud, or stung wi' an ether, man;
When he comes back, there are some will look merrily:
Here's to King James, and Donald Macgillavry.
Come like a weaver, Donald Macgillavry,
Come like a weaver, Donald Macgillavry,
Pack on your back, and elwand see cleverly:
Gie him full measure, my Donald Macgillavry.

Donald has foughten wi' reif and roguery;
Donald has dinner'd wi' banes and beggary:
Better it were for Whigs and Whiggery
Meeting the devil than Donald Macgillavry.
Come like a tailor, Donald Macgillavry,
Come like a tailor, Donald Macgillavry:
Push about, in and out, thimble them cleverly,
Here's to King James, and Donald Macgillavry!

Donald's the callan that brooks nae tangleness;
Whigging, and prigging, and a' newfangleness,
They maun be gane: he winna be baukit, man;
He maun hae justice, or faith he'll tak' it, man.
Come like a cobbler, Donald Macgillavry,
Come like a cobbler, Donald Macgillavry,
Beat them, and bore them, and lingel them cleverly:
Up wi' King James and Donald Macgillavry!

Donald was mumpit wi' mirds and mockery;
Donald was blinded wi' blads o' property;
Arles ran high, but makings were naething, man:
Lord, how Donald is flyting and fretting, man!
Come like the devil, Donald Macgillavry,
Come like the devil, Donald Macgillavry,
Skelp them and scaud them that prov'd sae unbritherly:
Up wi' King James, and Donald Macgillavry!

JAMIE THE ROVER.

THE tenth of June was the birthday of the Chevalier de St. George, here celebrated under the name of Jamie the Rover. "Auchindown," says Hogg, "is neither more nor less than an old ruinous Castle in Glen-Fiddich, in Banffshire, and it would appear that these festivals in honour of the exiled sovereign had been among the last entertainments given there; for about that very time the Castle ceased to be inhabited, and we hear of the Knights of Auchindown no more. The building is extremely ancient, no one knows when it was built, or by whom."

OF all the days that's in the year,
The tenth of June I love most dear,
When our white roses will appear,
 For sake of Jamie the Rover.
In tartans braw our lads are drest,
With roses glancing on their breast;
For among them a' we love him best,
 Young Jamie they call the Rover.

As I came in by Auchindown,
The drums did beat, and trumpets sound,
And aye the burden o' the tune
 Was, Up wi' Jamie the Rover!
There's some wha say he's no the thing,
And some wha say he's no our king;
But to their teeth we'll rant and sing,
 Success to Jamie the Rover!

In London there's a huge black bull,
That would devour us at his will;
We'll twist his horns out of his skull,
 And drive the old rogue to Hanover.
And hey as he'll rout, and hey as he'll roar,
And hey as he'll gloom, as heretofore!
But we'll repay our auld black score,
 When we get Jamie the Rover.

O wae's my heart for Nature's change,
And ane abroad that's forced to range!
God bless the lad, where'er he remains,
 And send him safely over!
It's J. and S., I must confess,
Stands for his name that I do bless:
O may he soon his own possess,
 Young Jamie they call the Rover!

LOCHMABEN GATE.

ON the 29th May, 1714, there was a horse race held at Lochmaben, and which drew together a great number of spectators. "After the race the Popish and Jacobite gentry, such as Francis Maxwell of Tinwald, John

Maxwell, his brother; Robert Johnston of Wamphray, Robert Carruthers of Ramerscales, the Master of Burleigh (who was under sentence of death for murder, and had made his escape out of the Tolbooth of Edinburgh a little before he was to have been executed), with several others whom I could name, went to the cross, where in a very solemn manner, before hundreds of witnesses, with drums beating and colours displayed, they did, upon their knees, drink their king's health!"—*Rae's History of the Rebellion.*

As I came by Lochmaben gate,
  It's there I saw the Johnstons riding;
Away they go, and they fear'd no foe,
  With their drums a-beating, colours flying.
All the lads of Annandale
  Came there, their gallant chief to follow;
Brave Burleigh, Ford, and Ramerscale,
  With Winton and the gallant Rollo.

I asked a man what meant the fray?
  "Good sir," said he, "you seem a stranger:
This is the twenty-ninth of May;
  Far better had you shun the danger.
These are rebels to the throne,
  Reason have we all to know it;
Popish knaves and dogs each one,
  Pray pass on, or you shall rue it."

I look'd the traitor in the face,
  Drew out my brand and ettled at him:
"Deil send a' the whiggish race
  Downward to the dad that gat 'em!"
Right sair he gloom'd, but naething said,
  While my heart was like to scunner,
Cowards are they born and bred,
  Ilka whinging, praying sinner.

My bonnet on my sword I bare,
  And fast I spurr'd by knight and lady,
And thrice I waved it in the air,
  Where a' our lads stood rank'd and ready.
"Long live King James!" aloud I cried,
  "Our nation's king, our nation's glory!"
"Long live King James!" they all replied,
  "Welcome, welcome, gallant Tory!"

There I shook hands wi' lord and knight,
  And mony a braw and buskin'd lady:
But lang I'll mind Lochmaben gate,
  And a' our lads for battle ready.
And when I gang by Locher Brigs,
  And o'er the moor, at een or morrow,
I'll lend a curse unto the Whigs,
  That wrought us a' this dool and sorrow.

THE AULD STUARTS BACK AGAIN.

PROBABLY written about the time of the outbreak of 1715. Glasgow, Ayr, Irvine, Kilmarnock, and the rest of the Western towns were particularly zealous on behalf of the reigning family, and so fall under the whip of the satirist in the first part of the song. The latter part refers to a meeting of the principal Jacobite Chiefs convened by the Earl of Mar, and held at his Castle of Braemar, August 26, 1715. Among those present at this council were, the Marquis of Huntly (eldest son of the Duke of Gordon), the Marquis of Tullibardine (eldest son of the Duke of Athol), Earls of Nithsdale, Marischal Traquair, Errol, Southesk, Carnwath, Seaforth, Linlithgow; Viscounts Kilsyth, Kenmure, Kingston, and Stormount; Lords Rollo, Duffus, Drummond, Strathallan, Ogilvie, and Nairn; besides a large attendance of Chiefs and Chieftains representing the Clans.

THE auld Stuarts back again,
The auld Stuarts back again;
Let howlet Whigs do what they can,
  The Stuarts will be back again.
Wha cares for a' their creeshy duds,
And a' Kilmarnock's sowen suds?
We'll whack their hydes and fyle their fuds,
  And bring the Stuarts back again.

There's Ayr and Irvine, wi' the rest,
And a' the cronies i' the west,
Lord! sic a scaw'd and scabbit nest,
  How they'll set up their crack again
But wad they come, or dare they come,
Afore the bagpipe and the drum,
We'll either gar them a' sing dumb,
  Or "Auld Stuarts back again."

Give ear unto my loyal sang,
A' ye that ken the right frae rang,
And a' that look and think it lang
  For auld Stuarts back again.
Were ye wi' me to chace the rae,
Out owre the hills and far away,
And saw the Lords were there that day,
  To bring the Stuarts back again.

There ye might see the noble Mar,
Wi' Athol, Huntly, and Traquair,
Seaforth, Kilsyth, and Auldubair,
  And mony mae, whatreck, again.
Then what are a' their westland crews?
We'll gar the tailors tack again;
Can they forestand the tartan trews,
  And auld Stuarts back again?

THE CHEVALIER'S MUSTER ROLL.

"THERE can be little doubt but this song, denominated *The Chevalier's Muster Roll*, has been made and sung about the time when the Earl of Mar raised the standard for King James in the North; but it is so far from being a complete list, that many of the principal chiefs are left out, as Athol, Broadalbine, Ogilvie, Keith, Stuart, &c., &c. It therefore appears evident to me, that it has been adapted for some festive meeting where all the names of those present were introduced, without regard to the others; and I have not the least doubt that every name mentioned in the song applied to some particular person, though it is impossible, at this distance of time, to trace each one with certainty."—*Hogg*.

LITTLE wat ye wha's coming,
Little wat ye wha's coming,
Little wat ye wha's coming,
Jock an' Tam[1] an' a's coming.

Duncan's coming, Donald's coming,
Colin's coming, Ronald's coming,
Dougal's coming, Lauchlan's coming,
Alaster and a's coming.
  Little wat ye wha's coming,
  Jock an' Tam an' a's coming.

Borland[2] and his men's coming,
Cameron[3] and M'Lean's[4] coming,
Gordon[5] and M'Gregor's coming,
Ilka dunywastle's coming,
  Little wat ye wha's coming,
  M'Gillivray[6] and a's coming.

Wigton's coming, Nithsdale's coming,
Carnwarth's coming, Kenmure's coming,
Derwentwater and Forster's coming,
Widdrington and Nairn's coming,
  Little wat ye wha's coming,
  Blithe Cowhill[7] and a's coming.

The Laird of M'Intosh[8] is coming,
M'Crabie an' M'Donald's coming,
M'Kenzie and M'Pherson's coming,
And the wild M'Craw's coming.
  Little wat ye wha's coming,
  Donald Gun and a's coming.

---

[1] Supposed to mean the Lowlands generally. [2] A Chieftain of the Clan Macintosh. [3] Of Lochiel. [4] Sir John McLean. [5] Marquis of Huntly. [6] Supposed to be McGillivray, head of one of the Clan Chaltan. [7] The names in this stanza are those of the Lowland Chiefs. [8] The Chief of the Clan.

They gloom, they glour, they look sae big,
At ilka stroke they'll fell a Whig:
They'll fright the fuds o' the Pockpuds,
For mony a buttock bare's coming.
  Little wat ye wha's coming,
  Jock and Tam an' a's coming.

THE STANDARD ON THE BRAES O' MAR.

ALEXANDER LAING, of Brechin.

THE standard on the braes o' Mar,
  Is up and streaming rarely;
The gathering pipe on Loch-na-gar,
  Is sounding lang and sairly.
    The Highlandmen
    Frae hill and glen,
    In martial hue,
    With bonnets blue,
    With belted plaids
    And burnish'd blades,
Are coming late and early.

Wha wadna join our noble chief,
  The Drummond and Glengarry,
Macgregor, Murray, Rollo, Keith,
  Panmure, and gallant Harry?
    Macdonald's men,
    Clan-Ranald's men,
    Mackenzie's men,
    Macgillavry's men,
    Strathallan's men,
    The Lowlan' men,
Of Callander and Airly.

Fy! Donald, up and let's awa',
  We canna langer parley,
When Jamie's back is at the wa',
  The lad we lo'e sae dearly.
    We'll go—we'll go
    And meet the foe
    And fling the plaid,
    And swing the blade,
    And forward dash,
    And hack and slash—
And fleg the German Carlie.

THE BATTLE OF SHERRIFMUIR,

Was fought near Dunblane, Perthshire, on the 13th November, 1715, between the Hanoverian forces under the Duke of Argyll, and the Jacobite under the Earl of Mar. The battle at its close was undecided and both sides claimed victory. All the solid advantages, however, remained with the royal troops.

> There's some say that we wan,
> Some say that they wan,
> And some say that nane wan at a', man;
> But one thing I'm sure,
> That at Sherramuir,
> A battle there was, that I saw, man:
> And we ran, and they ran,
> And they ran, and we ran,
> And we ran, and they ran awa', man.
>
> Argyll[1] and Belhaven,[2]
> Not frighted like Leven,[3]
> Which Rothes[4] and Haddington[5] saw, man;
> For they all, with Wightman,[6]
> Advanced on the right, man,
> While others took flight, being raw, man:
> And we ran, and they ran, etc.
>
> Lord Roxburgh[7] was there,
> In order to share
> With Douglas,[8] who stood not in awe, man;
> Voluntoerly to ramble
> With Lord Loudoun Campbell,[9]
> Brave Ilay[10] did suffer for a', man:
> And we ran, and they ran, etc.
>
> Sir John Shaw,[11] that great knight,
> With broadsword most bright,
> On horseback he briskly did charge, man;
> A hero that's bold,
> None could him withhold,
> He stoutly encountered the targemen:
> And we ran, and they ran, etc.
>
> For the cowardly Whittam,[12]
> For fear they should cut him,
> Seeing glittering broadswords with a pa', man,

---

[1] John, Second Duke of Argyll. [2] Lord Belhaven. [3] David Leslie, Earl of Leven.
[4,5] Earls of Rothes and Haddington. [6] Major General in the Royal Army.
[7] Fifth Duke of Roxburgh. [8] Duke of Douglas. [9] Third Earl of Loudon.
[10] Earl of Ilay, brother to the Duke of Argyll. [11] Sir John Shaw of Greenock.
[12] Major-General in the Royal Army.

And that in such thrang,
Made Baird aide-de-camp,
And from the brave clans ran awa, man:
    And we ran, and they ran, etc.

The great Colonel Dow
Gade foremost, I trow,
When Whittam's dragoons ran awa, man:
Except Sandy Baird,
And Naughtan the laird,
Their horse shaw'd their heels to them a', man:
    And we ran, and they ran, etc.

Brave Mar[1] and Panmure[2]
Were firm, I am sure,
The latter was kidnapt awa, man,
With brisk men about,
Brave Harry retook
His brother, and laughed at them a', man:
    And we ran, and they ran, etc.

Brave Marshall[3] and Lithgow,[4]
And Glengarry's pith too,[5]
Assisted by brave Loggia,[6] man,
And Gordons the bright,
So boldly did fight,
That the red-coats took flight and awa', man:
    And we ran, and they ran, etc.

Strathmore[7] and Clanronald,[8]
Cry'd still, "Advance, Donald,"
Till both of these heroes did fa', man;
For there was such hashing,
And broadswords a-clashing,
Brave Forfar[9] himself got a claw, man:
    And we ran, and they ran, etc.

Lord Perth[10] stood the storm,
Seaforth[11] but lukewarm,
Kilsyth[12] and Strathallan[13] not slow, man;
And Hamilton[14] pled,
The men were not bred,
For he had no fancy to fa', man:
    And we ran, and they ran, etc.

---

[1] The Earl of Mar. [2] The Hon. Henry Maule of Kellie.
[3] George Keith, tenth Earl Marischal. [4] Earl of Calendar and Linlithgow.
[5] Archibald Macdonald, chief of Glengarry. [6] Drummond of Logie-Almond.
[7] John Lyon, fifth Earl of Strathmore and Kinghorn.
[8] Ronald Macdonald of Clanronald. [9] Archibald Douglas, second Earl of Forfar.
[10] James, Lord Drummond. [11] William Mackenzie, fifth Earl of Seaforth.
[12] William, Lord Kilsyth. [13] William, Lord Strathallan.
[14] George Hamilton, Lieut.-General under the Earl of Mar.

Brave gen'rous Southesk,[1]
Tullibardine[2] was brisk,
Whose father, indeed, would not draw, man,
Into the same yoke,
Which served for a cloak,
To keep the estate 'twixt them twa, man:
And we ran, and they ran, etc.

Lord Rollo[3] not fear'd,
Kintore[4] and his beard,
Pitsligo[5] and Ogilvie,[6] a', man,
And brothers Balfours,
They stood the first showers,
Clackmannan and Burleigh[7] did claw, man:
And we ran, and they ran, etc.

But Cleppan[8] fought pretty,
And Strowan[9] the witty,
A poet that pleases us a', man;
For mine is but rhyme,
In respect of what's fine,
Or what he is able to draw, man:
And we ran, and they ran, &c.

For Huntly[10] and Sinclair,[11]
They both play'd the tinkler,
With consciences black as a craw, man;
Some Angus and Fifemen,
They ran for their life, man,
And ne'er a Lot's wife there at a', man:
And we ran, and they ran, etc.

Then Laurie the traitor,
Who betray'd his master,
His king and his country, and a', man,
Pretending Mar might,
Give orders to fight,
To the right of the army awa', man:
And we ran, and they ran, etc.

Then Laurie for fear,
Of what he might hear,
Took Drummond's best horse and awa', man,
'Stead of going to Perth,
He crossed the Firth,
Alongst Stirling bridge, and awa', man;
And we ran, and they ran, etc.

---

[1] James, fifth Earl of Southesk. [2] William Murray, Marquis of Tullibardine. [3] Robert, Lord Rollo. [4] William, Earl of Kintore. [5] Lord Forbes of Pitsligo. [6] James, Lord Ogilvie, eldest son of the Earl of Airlie. [7] Lord Burleigh. [8] Major Clephane of the Jacobite Army. [9] Robertson of Strowan, Chief of the clan. [10] Marquis of Huntly. [11] James, Master of Sinclair.

To London he press'd,
And there he profess'd,
That he behav'd best of them a', man;
And so, without strife,
Got settled for life,
Ten hundred a-year to his fa', man:
  And we ran, and they ran, etc.

In Borrowstounness
He resides with disgrace,
Till his neck stand in need of a thraw, man,
And then, in a tether,
He'll swing from a ladder,
And go off the stage with a pa', man:
  And we ran, and they ran, etc.

Rob Roy there stood watch [1]
On a hill, for to catch
The booty, for aught that I saw, man,
For he ne'er advanc'd,
From the place he was stano'd,
Till no more was to do there at a', man:
  And we ran, and they ran, etc.

So we all took the flight,
And Moubray the wright,
And Lethem the smith was a bra' man,
For he took a fit
Of the gout, which was wit,
By judging it time to withdraw, man:
  And we ran, and they ran, etc.

And trumpet M'Lean,
Whose breeks were not clean,
Thro' misfortune he happen'd to fa', man,
By saving his neck,
His trumpet did break,
And came off without musick at a', man:
  And we ran, and they ran, etc.

So there such a race was,
As ne'er in that place was,
And as little chase was at a', man;
From each other they run
Without touk of drum,
They did not make use of a paw, man:
  And we ran, and they ran, etc.

[1] The celebrated outlaw.

Whether we ran, or they ran,
  Or we wan, or they wan,
Or if there was winning at a', man,
  There no man can tell,
  Save our brave Genarall,
Who first began running of a', man,
  And we ran, and they ran, etc.

Wi' the Earl o' Seaforth,
  And the Cock o' the North[1];
But Florence ran fastest of a', man,
  Save the laird o' Phinaven,
  Who aware to be even
Wi' any general or peer o' them a', man,
  And we ran, and they ran, etc.

BATTLE OF SHERRAMUIR.

SECOND VERSION,

APPEARED originally as a street song, under the title of "A Dialogue between Will Lickladle and Tom Cleancogue, twa shepherds who were feeding their flocks on the Ochil Hills on the day the battle of Sherramuir was fought." Its author was the Rev. John Barclay of Muthill, who died in 1798.

W. O CAM ye here the fight to shun,
  Or herd the sheep wi' me, man?
Or were ye at the Sherramuir,
  Or did the battle see man?
T. I saw the battle sair and teugh,
  And reeking red ran mony a sheugh:
My heart for fear ga'e sough for sough,
To hear the thuds, and see the cluds
O' clans frae woods, in tartan duds,
  Wha glaum'd at kingdoms three, man.

The redcoat lads, wi' black cockades,
  To meet them warna slaw, man;
They rush'd, and push'd, and blood out gush'd,
  And mony a bouk did fa', man.
The great Argyll led on his files,
I wat they glanc'd for twenty miles;
They hough'd the clans like ninepin kyles,
They hack'd and hash'd, while braid swords clash'd,
And through they dash'd, and hew'd, and smash'd,
  Till fey men died awa, man.

---

[1] A popular name for the Duke of Gordon.

But had ye seen the philabegs,
  And skyrin tartan trews, man,
When in the teeth they dar'd our Whigs,
  And covenant true blues, man;
In lines extended lang and large,
When baigonets o'erpower'd the targe,
And thousands hasten'd to the charge;
Wi' Highland wrath, they frae the sheath
Drew blades o' death, till, out o' breath,
  They fled like frighted dows, man.

W. O how deil, Tam, can that be true?
  The chace gaed frae the north, man?
I saw mysel, they did pursue
  The horsemen back to Forth, man,
And at Dumblane, in my ain sight,
They took the brig wi' a' their might,
And straight to Stirling wing'd their flight;
But, cursed lot! the gates were shut,
And mony a huntit, poor redcoat,
  For fear amaist did swarf, man.

T. My sister Kate cam' up the gate
  Wi' crowdie unto me, man;
She swore she saw some rebels run
  To Perth and to Dundee, man.
Their left hand gen'ral had nae skill,
The Angus lads had nae gude will,
That day their neighbours' blude to spill;
For fear by foes that they should lose
Their cogues o' brose, they scar'd at blows,
  And hameward fast did flee, man.

They've lost some gallant gentlemen
  Amang the Highland clans, man:
I fear my Lord Panmure is slain,
  Or in his en'mies' hands, man.
Now wad ye sing this double flight,
Some fell for wrang, and some for right,
And mony bade the warld gude-night,
Say pell and mell, wi' muskets knell,
How Tories fell, and Whigs to hell
  Flew aff in frighted bands, man.

UP AN' WARN A', WILLIE.

When we gaed to the braes o' Mar,
  And to the weapon-shaw, Willie,
Wi' true design to serve our king,
  And banish Whigs awa', Willie
    Up and warn a', Willie,
      Warn, warn a';
For lords and lairds came there bedeen,
  And vow but they were braw, Willie.
    Up and warn a', Willie,
      Warn, warn a';
    Then second sighted Sandy said,
      We'd do nae gude at a', Willie.

But when the army join'd at Perth,
  The bravest e'er ye saw, Willie,
We didna doubt the rogues to rout,
  Restore our king an' a', Willie.
    Up and warn a', Willie,
      Warn, warn a';
The pipers play'd frae right to left,
  O whirry Whigs awa', Willie.

But when the standard was set up,
  Right fierce the wind did blaw, Willie;
The royal nit upon the tap
  Down to the ground did fa, Willie.
    Up and warn a', Willie,
      Warn, warn a';
To hear my canty Highland sang
  Relate the thing I saw, Willie.

But when we march'd to Sherramuir,
  And there the rebels saw, Willie,
Brave Argyll attacked our right,
  Our flank and front, and a', Willie.
    Up and warn a', Willie,
      Warn, warn a';
Traitor Huntly soon gave way,
  Seaforth, St. Clair, and a', Willie.

But brave Glengarry on our right,
  The rebels' left did claw, Willie,
He there the greatest slaughter made
  That ever Donald saw, Willie.
    Up and warn a', Willie,
      Warn, warn a';
And Whittam fyl'd his breeks for fear,
  And fast did rin awa, Willie.

For he ca'd us a Highland mob,
  And swore he'd slay us a', Willie;
But we chas'd him back to Stirling brig,
  Dragoons and foot and a', Willie.
    Up and warn a,' Willie,
      Warn, warn a';
    At length we rallied on a hill,
      And briskly up did draw, Willie.

But when Argyll did view our line,
  And them in order saw, Willie,
He straight gaed to Dumblane again,
  And back his left did draw, Willie.
    Up and warn a', Willie,
      Warn, warn a';
    Then we to Auchterarder march'd
      To wait a better fa', Willie.

Now if ye speir wha wan the day,
  I've tell'd you what I saw, Willie,
We baith did fight, and baith were beat,
  And baith did rin awa', Willie.
    Up and warn a', Willie,
      Warn, warn a';
    For second sighted Sandy said
      We'd do nae good at a', Willie.

LAMENT.

AFTER the Battle of Sherriffmuir, Mar retreated to Perth, and the army soon afterwards dispersed, leaving the Duke of Argyll to traverse the country without opposition. A number of the insurgents escaped to France, while those who were captured, were either executed, or sent into exile.

  Hard fate that I should banish'd be,
    And rebel call'd with scorn,
  For serving of the kindest prince
    That ever yet was born.
  O my king, God save my king,
    Whatever me befall!
  I would not be in Huntly's case,
    For honours, lands, and all.

  My target and my good claymore
    Must now lie useless by;
  My plaid and trews I heretofore
    Did wear most cheerfully.
    O my king, etc.

So cheerfully our king cam o'er,
  Sent Ecklin to the North;
But treach'rously he was betray'd
  By Huntly and Seaforth.
    O my king, etc.

O the broom, the bonny bonny broom,
  The broom of the Cowdenknowes!
I wish these lords had staid at hame,
  And milked their minnies' ewes,
    O my king, etc.

O wretched Huntly, hide thy head!
  Thy king and country's gone,
And many a valiant Scot hast thou
  By villany undone,
    O my king, etc.

Farewell, Old Albion. I must take
  A long and last adieu;
Or bring me back my king again,
  Or farewell hope and you.
    O my king, etc.

Set our true king upon the throne
  Of his ancestors dear,
And send the German cuckold home
  To starve with his small gear.
    O my king, etc.

Then happy days in peace we'll see,
  And joy in every face;
Confounded all the Whigs shall be,
  And honest men in place:
O my king, God save my king,
  Whatever me befall!
I would not be in Huntly's case,
  For honours, lands, and all.

KENMURE'S ON AND AWA.

WILLIAM, Viscount Kenmure, was leader of the Jacobite forces in the south of Scotland in 1715. He was defeated at Preston, and conveyed to London as a prisoner, where he was beheaded on the 24th February, 1716. This song is partly by Burns.

O KENMURE'S on and awa, Willie,
  O Kenmure's on and awa;
And Kenmure's lord's the bravest lord
  That ever Galloway saw.

Success to Kenmure's band, Willie!
Success to Kenmure's band!
There's no a heart that fears a Whig,
That rides by Kenmure's hand.

There's a rose in Kenmure's cap, Willie,
There's a rose in Kenmure's cap,
He'll steep it red in ruddie heart's blude,
Afore the battle drap.
Here's him that's far awa, Willie,
Here's him that's far awa,
And here's the flower that I lo'e best,
The rose that's like the snaw.

O Kenmure's lads are men, Willie,
O Kenmure's lads are men,
Their hearts and swords are metal true,
And that their faes shall ken.
They'll live, or die wi' fame, Willie,
They'll live, or die wi' fame;
And soon wi' sound o' victorie
May Kenmure's lord come hame.

His lady's cheek was red, Willie,
His lady's cheek was red,
When she saw his steely jupes put on,
Which smell'd o' deadly feud.
Here's Kenmure's health in wine, Willie,
Here's Kenmure's health in wine;
There ne'er was a coward o' Kenmure's blude,
Nor yet o' Gordon's line.

LORD DERWENTWATER'S FAREWELL.

JAMES RADCLIFF, Earl of Derwentwater, was another of the victims of the affair at Preston. He was beheaded at London. "Derwentwater," says Smollet, "was an amiable youth, brave, open, generous, hospitable, and humane. His fate drew tears from the spectators, and was a great misfortune to the country in which he lived. He gave bread to multitudes of people whom he employed on his estate: the poor, the widow, and the orphan, rejoiced in his bounty." "This" adds Hogg, "is an amiable character, and though smirched with the foulness of rebellion, smells sweetly of heaven."

FAREWELL to pleasant Ditson Hall,
My father's ancient seat;
A stranger now must call thee his,
Which gars my heart to greet.

Farewell each kindly well-known face,
  My heart has held so dear:
My tenants now must leave their lands,
  Or hold their lives in fear.

No more along the banks of Tyne,
  I'll rove in autumn gray;
No more I'll hear, at early dawn,
  The lav'rocks wake the day:
Then fare-thee-well, brave Witherington,
  And Forster ever true.
Dear Shaftsbury, and Errington,
  Receive my last adieu.

And fare-thee-well, George Collingwood,
  Since fate has put us down,
If thou and I have lost our lives,
  Our king has lost his crown.
Farewell, farewell, my lady dear,
  Ill, ill thou counsell'dst me:
I never more may see the babe
  That smiles upon thy knee.

And fare-thee-well, my bonny gray steed,
  That carried me aye so free;
I wish I had been asleep in my bed,
  The last time I mounted thee.
The warning bell now bids me cease;
  My trouble's nearly o'er;
Yon sun that rises from the sea,
  Shall rise on me no more.

Albeit that here in London town
  It is my fate to die,
O carry me to Northumberland,
  In my father's grave to lie:
There chant my solemn requiem
  In Hexham's holy towers,
And let six maids of fair Tynedale
  Scatter my grave with flowers.

And when the head that wears the crown,
  Shall be laid low like mine,
Some honest hearts may then lament
  For Radcliff's fallen line.
Farewell to pleasant Ditson Hall,
  My father's ancient seat;
A stranger now must call thee his,
  Which gars my heart to greet.

OWER THE HILLS AN' FAR AWAY.

Ower the hills and far away,
It's ower the hills and far away;
Ower the hills and ower the sea
The wind has blawn my plaid frae me.
My tartan plaid, my ae good sheet,
That keepit me frae wind and weet,
And held me bien baith night and day,
Is ower the hills and far away.

There was a wind it cam to me,
Ower the south and ower the sea,
And it has blawn my corn and hay,
Ower the hills and far away.
It blew my corn, it blew my gear,
It neither left me kid nor steer,
And blew my plaid, my only stay,
Ower the hills and far away.

But though 't has left me bare indeed,
And blawn my bonnet off my head,
There's something hid in Highland brae;
It hasna blawn my sword away.
Then ower the hills and ower the dales,
Ower all England and through Wales,
The broadsword yet shall bear the sway,
Ower the hills and far away.

HOW LANG SHALL OUR LAND.

WILLIAM MESTON,
Tutor to the young Earl Mareschall, and a victim to the failure of the '15.

How lang shall our land thus suffer distresses,
Whilst traitors, and strangers, and tyrants oppress us!
How lang shall our old, and once brave warlike nation,
Thus tamely submit to a base usurpation?
Thus must we be sad, whilst the traitors are vaudie,
Till we get a sight of our ain bonnie laddie.
 Thus must we be sad, whilst the traitors are vaudie,
 Till we get a sight of our ain bonny laddie.

How lang shall we lurk, how lang shall we languish,
With faces dejected, and hearts full of anguish?
How lang shall the Whigs, perverting all reason,
Call honest men knaves, and loyalty treason?
Thus must we be sad, whilst the traitors are vaudie,
Till we get a sight of our ain bonnie laddie.
 Thus must we be sad, etc.

O Heavens, have pity! with favour present us;
Rescue us from strangers that sadly torment us,
From Atheists, and Deists, and Whiggish opinions;
Our king return back to his rightful dominions:
Then rogues shall be sad, and honest men vaudie,
When the throne is possess'd by our ain bonny laddie.
    Then rogues shall be sad, etc.

Our vales shall rejoice, our mountains shall flourish;
Our church, that's oppressed, our monarch will nourish;
Our land shall be glad, but the Whigs shall be sorry,
When the king gets his own, and Heaven the glory.
Then rogues shall be sad, but the honest men vaudie,
When the throne is possess'd by our ain bonny laddie.
    The rogues shall be sad, etc.

SOMEBODY.

This first appeared in Hogg's Jacobite Relics; and, though he does not own it, in all probability was written by him. From the failure of the rising in 1715, to the landing of Prince Charles Edward, the thoughts of the Jacobite party were always bent on the return of the exiled family.

    My heart is sair, I daurna tell,
    My heart is sair for somebody;
    I would walk a winter's night,
      For a sight o' somebody.
      Och hon for somebody!
      Och hey for somebody!
    I wad do—what wad I not,
      For the sake o' somebody!

    If somebody were come again,
    Then somebody maun cross the main,
    And ilka ane will get his ain,
    And I will see my somebody.
      Och hon, etc.

    What need I kame my tresses bright
    Or why should coal or candle-light
    E'er shine in my bower day or night,
      Since gane is my dear somebody?
      Och hon, etc.

    Oh! I hae grutten mony a day
    For ane that's banish'd far away:
    I canna sing, and maunna say,
      How sair I grieve for somebody.
      Och hon, etc.

WELCOME ROYAL CHARLIE.

On the 25th July, 1745, Charles Edward Stuart, the "Bonnie Prince Charlie" of the Jacobites, and the "Young Pretender" of the Hanoverians, landed at Borodale and began what must now be regarded as one of the most desperate and romantic campaigns in modern history. The more ardent Highland Chiefs at once welcomed him with all the ardour of their nature, but several still advised delay. Charles, however, had virtually thrown away his scabbard, and declined this; and overcoming their scruples, after a few preliminary movements the clans were declared ready, and the standard was raised in the Valley of Glenfinnan. "The spot," says Mr. Chambers, "selected for the rearing of the standard, was a little eminence in the centre of the vale. The Marquis of Tullibardine, whose rank entitled him to the honour, pitched himself on the top of this knoll, supported by two men, on account of his weak state of health. He then flung upon the mountain breeze that flag which, shooting like a streamer from the north, was soon to spread such omens of woe and terror over the peaceful vales of Britain."—*History of the Rebellion of 1745-6*, p. 48, 1869.

> When France had her assistance lent,
> Our darling prince to us she sent,
> Towards the north his course he bent,
> His name was Royal Charlie.
>   But, O, he was lang o' coming,
>   O, he was lang o' coming,
>   O, he was lang o' coming;—
>   Welcome Royal Charlie!
>
> When he upon the shore did stand,
> The friends he had within the land
> Came down and shook him by the hand,
> And welcom'd Royal Charlie.
>   Wi' "O, ye've been lang o' coming," etc.
>
> The dress that our Prince Charlie had
> Was bonnet blue and tartan plaid;
> And O he was a handsome lad!
> Few could compare wi' Charlie.
>   But O, he was lang o' coming, etc.

THE GATHERING OF THE CLANS.

> Come along, my brave clans,
>   There's nae friends sae staunch and true;
> Come along, my brave clans,
>   There's nae lads sae leal as you.
> Come along, Clan-Donuil,
>   Frae 'mang your birks and heather braes;
> Come with bold Macalister,
>   Wilder than his mountain raes.

Gather, gather, gather,
  From Loch Morar to Argyle;
Come from Castle Tuirim,
  Come from Moidart and the isles.
Macallan is the hero
  That will lead you to the field;
Gather, bold Siolallain,
  Sons of them that never yield.

Gather, gather, gather,
  Gather from Lochaber glen:
Mac-Mic-Rannail calls you;
  Come from Taroph, Roy, and Spean.
Gather, brave Clan-Donuil,
  Many sons of might you know;
Lenochan's your brother,
  Auchterechtan and Glencoe.

Gather, gather, gather,
  'Tis your prince that needs your arm:
Though Macconnel leaves you,
  Dread no danger or alarm.
Come from field and foray,
  Come from sickle and from plough;
Come from cairn and correi,
  From deer-wake and driving to.

Gather, bold Clan-Donuil;
  Come with haversack and cord;
Come not late with meal or cake,
  But come with dirk, and gun, and sword.
Down into the Lowlands,
  Plenty bides by dale and burn,
Gather, brave Clan-Donuil,
  Riches wait on your return.

GATHERING OF ATHOL.

Wha will ride wi' gallant Murray?
  Wha will ride wi' Geordie's sel?
He's the flow'r o' a' Glenisla,
  And the darlin' o' Dunkel'.
See the white rose in his bonnet!
  See his banner o'er the Tay!
His gude sword he now has drawn it,
  And has flung the sheath away.

Every faithful Murray follows;
  First of heroes! best of men!
Every true and trusty Stewart
  Blythely leaves his native glen.

Athol lads are lads of honour,
　Westland rogues are rebels a';
When we come within their border,
　We may gar the Campbells claw.

Menzies he's our friend and brother;
　Gask and Strowan are nae slack!
Noble Perth has ta'en the field,
　And a' the Drummonds at his back.

Let us ride wi' gallant Murray,
　Let us fight for Charlie's crown;
From the right we'll never sinder,
　Till we bring the tyrants down.

Mackintosh, the gallant soldier,
　Wi' the Grahams and Gordons gay,
They have ta'en the field of honour,
　Spite of all their chiefs could say.

Bend the musket, point the rapier,
　Shift the brog for Lowland shoe,
Scour the durk, and face the danger;
　Mackintosh has all to do.

COME YE BY ATHOL.
JAMES HOGG.

Come ye by Athol, lad wi' the philabeg
Down by the Tummel or banks o' the Garry,
Saw ye the lads wi' their bonnets and white cockades,
Leaving their mountains to follow Prince Charlie.
　Follow thee! Follow thee! wha wadna follow thee?
　Lang hast thou loved and trusted us fairly!
　Charlie, Charlie, wha wadna follow thee,
　King o' the Highland hearts, bonnie Prince Charlie.

I ha'e but ae son, my gallant young Donald,
But if I had ten they should follow Glengarry!
Health to McDonnell and gallant Clan Ronald,
For these are the men that will die for their Charlie.
　Follow thee! Follow thee! &c.

I'll to Lochiel and Appin, and kneel to them,
Down by Lord Murray and Roy of Kildarlie;
Brave McIntosh, he shall fly to the field wi' them;
These are the lads I can trust wi' my Charlie.
　Follow thee! Follow thee! &c.

Down through the Lowlands, down wi' the Whigamore,
Loyal true Highlanders, down wi' them rarely!
Ronald and Donald, drive on wi' the broad claymore,
Over the necks of the foes o' Prince Charlie.
　Follow thee! Follow thee! &c.

WHA'S FOR SCOTLAND AND CHARLIE?

O WHA'S for Scotland and Charlie?
O wha's for Scotland and Charlie?
   He's come o'er the sea
   To his ain countrie;
Now wha's for Scotland and Charlie?
   Awa', awa', auld carlie,
   Awa', awa', auld carlie,
   Gi'e Charlie his crown,
   And let him sit down,
Whare ye've been sae lang, auld carlie.

It's up in the morning early,
It's up in the morning early,
   The bonnie white rose;
   The plaid and the hose,
Are on for Scotland and Charlie.
The swords are drawn now fairly,
The swords are drawn now fairly,
   The swords they are drawn,
   And the pipes they ha'e blawn
A pibroch for Scotland and Charlie.

The flags are fleein' fu' rarely,
The flags are fleein' fu' rarely,
   And Charlie's awa'
   To see his ain ha',
And to bang his faes right sairly.
Then wha's for Scotland and Charlie?
O wha's for Scotland and Charlie?
   He's come o'er the sea
   To his ain countrie;
Then wha's for Scotland and Charlie?

WHA WADNA FIGHT FOR CHARLIE?

  WHA wadna fight for Charlie?
    Wha wadna draw the sword?
  Wha wadna up and rally,
    At their royal prince's word?

Think on Scotia's ancient heroes,
  Think on foreign foes repell'd
Think on glorious Bruce and Wallace,
  Wha the proud usurpers quell'd.
    Wha wadna, etc.

Rouse, rouse, ye kilted warriors!
Rouse, ye heroes of the north!
Rouse, and join your chieftain's banners,
'Tis your prince that leads you forth!
    Wha wadna, etc.

Shall we basely crouch to tyrants?
Shall we own a foreign sway?
Shall a royal Stuart be banish'd
While a stranger rules the day?
    Wha wadna, etc.

See the northern clans advancing!
See Glengarry and Lochiel!
See the brandish'd broad-swords glancing?
Highland hearts are true as steel.
    Wha wadna, etc.

Now our prince has rear'd his banner;
Now triumphant is our cause;
Now the Scottish lion rallies;
Let us strike for prince and laws.
    Wha wadna, etc.

WHA'LL BE KING BUT CHARLIE?

LADY NAIRNE.

THE news frae Moidart cam' yestreen
Will soon gar mony ferlie;
That ships o' war hae just come in,
And landed royal Charlie.
Come through the heather, around him gather,
  Ye're a' the welcomer early;
Around him cling, wi' a' your kin,
  For wha'll be king but Charlie?
    Come through the heather, around him gather,
    Come Ronald, come Donald, come a' thegither,
    And crown your rightfu' lawful king,
    For wha'll be king but Charlie?

The Highland clans, wi' sword in hand,
Frae John o' Groats to Airly,
Hae to a man declar'd to stand
Or fa' wi' royal Charlie.
    Come through the heather, etc.

The Lowlands a', baith great and sma',
Wi' mony a lord and laird, hae
Declar'd for Scotia's king an' law,
And spier ye wha but Charlie?
    Come through the heather, etc.

There's ne'er a lass in a' the land
  But vows baith late and early,
To man she'll ne'er gie heart or hand,
  Wha wadna fecht for Charlie.
    Come through the heather, etc.

Then here's a health to Charlie's cause,
  And be't complete and early;
His very name my heart's blood warms
  To arms for royal Charlie!
    Come through the heather, etc.

ROYAL CHARLIE.

The wind comes frae the land I love,
  It moves the flood fu' rarely;
Look for the lily on the lea,
  And look for royal Charlie.

Ten thousand swords shall leave their sheaths,
  And smite fu' sharp and sairly;
And Gordon's might, and Erskine's pride,
  Shall live and die wi' Charlie.

The sun shines out—wide smiles the sea,
  The lily blossoms rarely;
O yonder comes his gallant ship,
  Thrice welcome, royal Charlie!

"Yes, yon's a good and gallant ship,
  Wi' banners flaunting fairly;
But should it meet your darling Prince,
  'Twill feast the fish wi' Charlie."

Wide rustled she with silks in state,
  And waved her white hand proudlie,
And drew a bright sword from the sheath,
  And answered high and loudlie:—

"I had three sons and a good lord,
  Wha sold their lives fu' dearlie;
And wi' their dust I'd mingle mine,
  For love of gallant Charlie.

"It wad hae made a hail heart sair,
  To see our horsemen flying;
And my three bairns, and my good lord,
  Among the dead and dying:

"I snatched a banner—led them back—
  The white rose flourish'd rarely:
The deed I did for royal James
  I'd do again for Charlie."

COME BOAT ME O'ER.

Come boat me o'er, come row me o'er,
Come boat me o'er to Charlie;
I'll gie John Ross anither bawbee
To ferry me o'er to Charlie.
    We'll o'er the water, we'll o'er the sea,
    We'll o'er the water to Charlie;
    Come weel, come wo, we'll gather and go,
    And live or die wi' Charlie.

It's weel I lo'e my Charlie's name,
Though some there be abhor him;
But O to see Auld Nick gaun hame,
And Charlie's face before him!
    We'll o'er the water, etc.

I swear by moon and stars sae bright,
And sun that glances early,
If I had twenty thousand lives,
I'd gie them a' for Charlie.
    We'll o'er the water, etc.

I ance had sons, but now hae nane;
I bore them toiling sairly;
And I wad bear them a' again,
And lose them a' for Charlie;
    We'll o'er the water, we'll o'er the sea,
    We'll o'er the water to Charlie;
    Come weel, come wo, we'll gather and go,
    And live or die wi' Charlie.

MACLEAN'S WELCOME.

From the Gaelic, by James Hogg.

Come o'er the stream, Charlie, dear Charlie, brave Charlie,
Come o'er the stream, Charlie, and dine with Maclean;
And though you be weary, we'll make your heart cheery,
And welcome our Charlie and his loyal train.
We'll bring down the track deer, we'll bring down the black steer,
The lamb from the breckan, and doe from the glen:
The salt sea we'll harry, and bring to our Charlie,
The cream from the bothy, and curd from the pen.
    Come o'er the stream, Charlie, etc.

And you shall drink freely the dews of Glen Sheerly,
That stream in the star-light when kings do not ken,
And deep be your meed of the wine that is red,
To drink to your sire, and his friend the Maclean.
    Come o'er the stream, Charlie, etc.

O'er heath-bells shall trace you, the maids to embrace you,
 And deck your blue bonnet with flowers of the brae ;
And the loveliest Mary in all Glen M'Quarry
 Shall lie in your bosom till break of the day.
  Come o'er the stream, Charlie, etc.

If aught will invite you, or more will delight you,
 'Tis ready, a troop of our bold Highlandmen
Shall range on the heather with bonnet and feather,
 Strong arms and broad claymores three hundred and ten.
  Come o'er the stream, Charlie, etc.

THE RESTORATION.

To curb usurpation, by th' assistance of France,
With love to his country, see Charlie advance!
He's welcome to grace and distinguished this day,
The sun brighter shines, and all nature looks gay.
 Your glasses charge high, 't is in great Charlies' praise!
 To his success your voices and instruments raise.

Approach, glorious Charles, to this desolate land,
And drive out thy foes with thy mighty hand;
The nations shall rise, and join as one man,
To crown the brave Charles, the Chief of the Clan.
 Your glasses, etc.

In his train see sweet Peace, fairest queen of the sky,
Ev'ry bliss in her look, ev'ry charm in her eye,
Whilst oppression, corruption, vile slav'ry and fear,
At his wish'd-for return never more shall appear.
 Your glasses, etc.

Whilst in Pleasure's soft arms millions now court repose,
Our hero flies forth, though surrounded with foes ;
To free us from tyrants ev'ry danger defies,
And in Liberty's cause he conquers or dies!
 Your glasses, etc.

How hateful's the tyrant who lives by false fame,
To satiate his pride sets our country in flame,
How glorious the prince, whose great generous mind,
Makes true valour consist in relieving mankind!
 Your glasses, etc.

Ye brave clans, on whom we just honour bestow,
O think on the source whence our dire evils flow!
Commanded by Charles, advance to Whitehall,
And fix them in chains who would Britons enthral.
 Your glasses, etc.

TO DAUNTON ME.

To daunton me an' me sae young,
An' gude King James's eldest son !
O that's the thing that ne'er can be,
For the man's unborn that'll daunton me !
O set me ance on Scottish land
An' gie me my braidsword in my hand,
Wi' my bonnet blue aboon my bree,
An' shaw me the man that'll daunton me.

It's nae the battle's deadlie stoure,
Nor friends proived fause that'll gar me cower;
But the reckless hand o' povertie,
O! that alane can daunton me.
High was I born to kingly gear,
But a cuif came in, my cap to wear,
But wi' my braidsword I'll let him see
He's nae the man to daunton me.

O I hae scarce to lay me on,
Of kingly fields were ance my ain;
Wi' the moorcock on the mountain-bree,
But hardship ne'er can daunton me.
Up came the gallant chief Lochiel,
An' drew his glaive o' nut-brown steel,
Says, "Charlie, set your fit to me,
An' shaw me wha will daunton thee!"

YOUNG CHARLIE IS A GALLANT LAD.

Young Charlie is a gallant lad,
As e'er wore sword and belted plaid;
And lane and friendless though he be,
He is the lad that shall wanton me.
At Moidart our young prince did land,
With seven men at his right hand,
And a' to conquer nations three:
That is the lad that shall wanton me.

O wae be to the faithless crew
That frae our true king took his due,
And banish'd him across the sea;
Nae wonder that should daunton me.
But, Charlie lad, ere it be lang,
We'll shaw them a' the right frae wrang;
Argyle and a' our faes shall see
That nane on earth can daunton thee.

Then raise the banner, raise it high;
For Charles we'll conquer or we'll die:
The clans a' leal and true men be,
And shaw me wha will daunton thee!
Our gude King James shall soon come hame,
And traitors a' be put to shame;
Auld Scotland shall again be free;
O that's the thing wad wanton me!

THE PIPER O' DUNDEE.

The piper came to our town,
To our town, to our town,
The piper came to our town,
  And he played bonnilie.
He played a spring the laird to please,
A spring brent new frae yont the seas;
And then he ga'e his bags a wheeze,
  And played anither key.
    And wasna he a roguey,
      A roguey, a roguey,
    And wasna he a roguey,
      The piper o' Dundee?

He played "The welcome ower the main,"
And "Ye'se be fou and I'se be fain,"
And "Auld Stuarts back again,"
  Wi' muckle mirth and glee.
He played "The Kirk," he played "The Quier,"
"The Mullin Dhu" and "Chevalier,"
And "Lang awa', but welcome here,"
  Sae sweet, sae bonnilie.

It's some gat swords, and some gat nane,
And some were dancing mad their lane,
And mony a vow o' weir was taen
  That night at Amulrie!
There was Tullibardine and Burleigh,
And Struan, Keith, and Ogilvie,
And brave Carnegie, wha but he,
  The piper o' Dundee?

HE'S OWRE THE HILLS.

He's ow're the hills that I lo'e weel;
He's owre the hills we darena name,
He's owre the hills ayont Dumblane,
Wha soon will get his welcome hame.

My father's gane to fight for him,
My brithers winna bide at hame,
My mither greets and prays for them,
And 'daed she thinks they're no to blame.
    He's owre the hills, &c.

The Whigs may scoff, the Whigs may jeer,
But, ah! that luve maun be sincere,
Which still keeps true whate'er betide,
An' for his sake leaves a' beside.
    He's owre the hills, &c.

His right these hills, his right these plains;
O'er Highland hearts secure he reigns;
What lads e'er did, our lads will do:
Were I a lad, I'd follow him too.
    He's owre the hills, &c.

Sae noble a look, sae princely an air,
Sae gallant and bold, sae young and sae fair;
Oh! did you but see him, ye'd do as we've done;
Hear him but ance, to his standard you'll run.
    He's owre the hills, &c.

JOHNNIE COPE.

On the intelligence of the rising of the clans reaching the government, Sir John Cope, Commander-in-Chief of the forces in Scotland, was instructed to take measures for the public safety, and at once organise the troops under his command and march to meet the rebels. He left Stirling on the 24th August, intending to march to Fort Augustus, and making that his headquarters. He found his march through the Highlands as bad and dangerous as though he were in the middle of an enemy's country. His horses and baggage were stolen at night, and false intelligence was readily given him by the natives. The roads too, were not of the best, and Sir John's army travelled, as became a royal army, with plenty of luxuries. Almost rendered desperate at his increasing troubles, Sir John abandoned his intention of making Fort Augustus his headquarters, and turning aside marched on Inverness, which he reached on the 29th August. The enemy gladly seized the opportunity, and left Sir John to proceed in safety, while they marched quickly and safely upon the lowlands. The Highlanders entered Perth on the 3rd September, where Prince Charles was proclaimed Regent, and on the 18th of the same month, after a slight resistance on the part of the magistrates, the city of Edinburgh was in his hands. The king was proclaimed at the Cross, and the Palace of Holyrood was once more inhabited by a Stuart.

Sir John Cope soon saw the effect of his move on Inverness, and lost no time in trying to repair it. His troops were sent by sea and landed at Dunbar, where, meeting with reinforcements he marched on Edinburgh. The Highland army advanced to meet him, and the two armies met at Preston-pans about seven or eight miles from Edinburgh. It is needless to narrate the easy victory gained by the Highlanders, Sir John seems to have headed the retreat of the Royal troops in person, and Scotland was for the moment fairly in the possession of the Stuarts.

> Sir John Cope trode the north right far,
> Yet ne'er a rebel he cam naur,
> Until he landed at Dunbar,
> Right early in the morning.
>   Hey, Johnnie Cope, are ye wauking yet?
>   Or are ye sleeping, I would wit?
>   O haste ye, get up for the drums do beat:
>   O fye, Cope, rise in the morning!
>
> He wrote a challenge from Dunbar,
> "Come fight me, Charlie, an ye daur;
> If it be not by the chance of war,
> I'll give you a merry morning."
>   Hey Johnnie Cope, etc.
>
> When Charlie look'd the letter upon,
> He drew his sword the scabbard from,
> "So heaven restore to me my own,
> I'll meet you, Cope, in the morning."
>   Hey, Johnnie Cope, etc.
>
> Cope swore with many a bloody word,
> That he would fight them gun and sword;
> But he fled frae his nest like a weel-scar'd bird,
> And Johnnie he took wing in the morning.
>   Hey Johnnie Cope, etc.
>
> It was upon an afternoon,
> Sir John march'd into Preston town,
> He says, "My lads, come lean you down,
> And we'll fight the boys in the morning."
>   Hey, Johnnie Cope, etc.
>
> But when he saw the Highland lads
> Wi' tartan trews and white cockades,
> Wi' swords and guns, and rungs and gauds,
> O Johnnie took wing in the morning!
>   Hey, Johnnie Cope, etc.
>
> On the morrow when he did rise,
> He look'd between him and the skies;
> He saw them wi' their naked thighs,
> Which fear'd him in the morning.
>   Hey, Johnnie Cope, etc.

O then he fled into Dunbar,
Crying for a man-of-war;
He thought to have pass'd for a rustic tar,
And gotten awa in the morning.
   Hey, Johnnie Cope, etc.

Sir John then into Berwick rade,
Just as the deil had been his guide;
Gi'en him the world, he wadna staid
T' have foughten the boys in the morning!
   Hey, Johnnie Cope, etc.

Said the Berwickers unto Sir John,
"O what's become of all your men?"
"I' faith," says he, "I dinna ken;
I left them a' this morning."
   Hey, Johnnie Cope, etc.

Says Lord Mark Kerr, "Ye are na blate,
To bring us the news o' your ain defeat,
I think you deserve the back o' the gate:
Get out o' my sight this morning."
   Hey, Johnnie Cope, etc.

JOHNNIE COPE.

This version was written by Adam Skirving, a farmer at Garleton, in Haddingtonshire. He was born in 1719, and died in 1803. There are numerous versions of this song, the air being a favourite one, and often sung. Each singer abridges and adapts the words to his own taste.

Cope sent a challenge frae Dunbar,
"Come, Charlie, meet me an ye dare,
And I'll teach you the art of war,
If you'll meet wi' me i' the morning."
   Hey, Johnnie Cope, are ye wauking yet?
   Or are your drums a-beating yet?
   If ye were waking I would wait
   To gang to the coals i' the morning.

When Charlie look'd the letter upon,
He drew his sword the scabbard from,
"Come follow me, my merry merry men,
And we'll meet Johnnie Cope i' the morning."
   Hey, Johnnie Cope, etc.

Now, Johnnie, be as gude's your word,
Come let us try baith fire and sword,
And dinna rin awa like a frighted bird,
That's chased frae it's nest i' the morning.
   Hey, Johnnie Cope, etc.

When Johnnie Cope he heard of this,
He thought it wadna be amiss
To hae a horse in readiness,
To flee awa i' the morning.
    Hey, Johnnie Cope, etc.

Fy, now, Johnnie, get up and rin:
The Highland bagpipes make a din,
It's best to sleep in a hale skin,
For 'twill be a bluidie morning.
    Hey, Johnnie Cope, etc.

When Johnnie Cope to Dunbar came,
They speer'd at him, "Where's a' your men?"
"The deil confound me gin I ken,
For I left them a' i' the morning."
    Hey, Johnnie Cope, etc.

Now, Johnnie, troth ye were na blate,
To come wi' the news o' your ain defeat,
And leave your men in sic a strait,
So early in the morning.
    Hey, Johnnie Cope, etc.

"I' faith," quo' Johnnie, "I got a fleg,
Wi' their claymores and philabegs;
If I face them again, deil break my legs!
So I wish you a very gude morning."
    Hey, Johnnie Cope, etc.

COPE'S TRAVELS.

General Cope is now come down,
    And all his men in order;
For to fight our noble Prince,
    Upon the Highland border.
But when he to the Highlands came,
    He wearied with the ground, man;
And when he heard the Prince was there,
    He took his heels and ran, man.

From Inverness to Lochabers,
    And there he staid a while, man,
From Lochabers to Turriff went,
    For he was 'fraid to fight, man.
From Turriff to Old Meldrum,
    And since to Aberdeen, man,
And staid a while in Aberdeen,
    Encamp'd on Windmill Brae, man.

Syne took shipping, sailed to sea,
　Upon a Sabbath-day, man,
And at Dunbar was forced to land,
　For there he ran away, man.
With all his force baith men and horse,
　Went up to Prestonpans, man;
There they thought that they were men,
　But they prov'd to be nane, man.

OUR GALLANT PRINCE IS NOW COME HAME.

Our gallant prince is now come hame
　To Scotland, to proclaim his daddie:
May Heav'n protect the royal name
　Of Stuart, and the tartan plaidie!
O my bonnie Highland laddie,
　My handsome, charming Highland laddie!
May Heaven still guard, and him reward,
　Wi's bonnet blue and tartan plaidie!

When first he landed on our strand,
　The gracefu' looks o' that brave laddie
Made every Highland heart to warm,
　And lang to wear the tartan plaidie.
　　O my bonnie, etc.

When Geordie heard the news belyve,
' That he was come before his daddie,
He thirty thousand pounds would give,
　To catch him in his tartan plaidie.
　　O my bonnie, etc.

But Geordie kend the better way,
　To stay at hame wi' his braw lady,
Wha canna fight, he needs must pay,
　To ward the glent o' Highland plaidie.
　　O my bonnie, etc.

He sent John Cope unto the north,
　Wi' a' his men for battle ready;
But Charlie bauldly sallied forth,
　Wi' bonnet blue and belted plaidie.
　　O my bonnie, etc.

Cope rade a race to Inverness,
　And fand the prince gane south already,
Like lion bold, all uncontroll'd
　Wi' belt and brand, and tartan plaidie.
　　O my bonnie, etc.

Cope turn'd the chase, and left the place;
  The Lothians was the next land ready;
And then he swore that at Gladsmuir
  He wad disgrace the Highland plaidie.
    O my bonnie, etc.

Says he, "My lads, I tell you true,
  I'm sorry that they're sae unready;
Small is the task we have to do,
  To catch this rebel in his plaidie."
    O my bonnie, etc.

The prince he rose by break of day,
  And blythely was he buskit ready:
"Let's march," said he; "Cope langs to see
  The bonnet blue and belted plaidie."
    O my bonnie, etc.

They were na slack, nae flinching back;
  In rank and file they marched steady;
For they were bent, with one consent,
  To fight for him that wore the plaidie.
    O my bonnie, etc.

But soon John Cope cried to his men,
  "For gudesake turn, ye dogs, and speed ye,
And let each man 'scape as he can,
  The deil confound the tartan plaidie!"
    O my bonnie, etc.

Some rade on horse, some ran on foot;
  Their heels were light, their heads were giddy:
But late or air, they'll lang nae mair
  To meet the lad wi' the Highland plaidie.
    O my bonnie, etc.

Now where is Cope, wi' a' his brag?
  Say, is the craven gane already?
O leeze me on my bonnie lad,
  His bonnet blue and belted plaidie!
    O my bonnie, etc.

NOW CHARLES ASSERTS HIS FATHER'S RIGHT.

Now Charles asserts his father's right,
  And thus establishes his own,
Braving the dangers of the fight,
  To cleave a passage to the throne.
The Scots regain their ancient fame,
  And well their faith and valour show,
Supporting their young hero's claim
  Against a powerful rebel foe.

The God of battle shakes his arm,
  And makes the doubtful victory shine;
A panic dread their foes disarm;
  Who can oppose the will divine?
The rebels shall at length confess
  Th' undoubted justice of the claim,
When lisping babes shall learn to bless
  The long-forgotten Stuart's name.

CHARLIE HE'S MY DARLING.

The Highlanders re-entered Edinburgh after the battle amid great rejoicing. Jacobitism, which before was afraid to show its head, was now paraded in every corner. The ladies, especially, took up the cause of the young Chevalier with the utmost enthusiasm, and were loud in their expressions of admiration of his appearance and bravery.

'Twas on a Monday morning,
  Right early in the year,
That Charlie came to our town,
  The young Chevalier.
    And Charlie he's my darling,
    My darling, my darling,
    And Charlie he's my darling,
    The young Chevalier.

As he was walking up the street,
  The city for to view,
O there he spied a bonnie lass,
  The window looking through.
    And Charlie he's my darling, etc.

Sae light's he jumped up the stair,
  And tirl'd at the pin;
And wha sae ready as hersel
  To let the laddie in!
    And Charlie he's my darling, etc.

He set his Jenny on his knee,
  All in his Highland dress;
For brawly weel he kenn'd the way
  To please a bonnie lass.
    And Charlie he's my darling, etc.

It's up yon heathery mountain,
  And down yon scraggy glen,
We daurna gang a milking
  For Charlie and his men.
    And Charlie he's my darling, etc.

AS I CAM' DOWN THE CANONGATE.

From Cromek's remains of Nithsdale and Galloway Song.

As I cam' down the Canongate,
The Canongate, the Canongate,
As I cam' down the Canongate,
I heard a lassie sing,
   Merry may the keel row,
   The keel row, the keel row,
   Merry may the keel row,
   The ship that my love's in.

My love has breath o' roses,
O' roses, o' roses,
Wi' arms o' lily posies,
To fauld a lassie in.
   O merry etc.

My love he wears a bonnet,
A bonnet, a bonnet,
A snawy rose upon it,
A dimple on his chin,
   O merry, etc.

THE WHITE COCKADE.

My love was born in Aberdeen,
The bonniest lad that e'er was seen:
But now he's made our hearts fu' sad,
He's taen the field wi' his white cockade.
   O he's a ranting roving blade!
   O he's a brisk and bonnie lad!
   Betide what may my heart is glad
   To see my lad wi' his white cockade.

O leeze me on the philabeg,
The hairy hough and garton'd leg!
But aye the thing that blinds my e'e
Is the white cockade aboon the bree.
   O he's a ranting roving blade, etc.

I'll sell my rock, I'll sell my reel,
My rippling-kame, and spinning-wheel,
To buy mysel' a tartan plaid,
A braid sword, durk, and white cockade.
   O he's a ranting roving blade, etc.

I'll sell my rokely and my tow,
My good gray mare and hawkit cow,
That every loyal Scottish lad
May take the field wi' his white cockade.
O he's a ranting roving blade!
O he's a brisk and bonnie lad;
Betide what may, my heart is glad,
To see my lad wi' his white cockade.

TO YOUR ARMS.

To your arms, to your arms, my bonnie Highland lads!
  To your arms, to your arms, at the touk of the drum!
The battle trumpet sounds, put on your white cockades,
  For Charlie, the great prince regent, is come.
There is not the man in a' our clan,
  That would nuckle to the lad that is five feet ten;
And the tune that we strike on the tabor and pipe
  Is "The king shall enjoy his own again."

To your arms, to your arms! Charlie yet shall be our king!
  To your arms' all ye lads that are loyal and true!
To your arms, to your arms! His valour nane can ding,
  And he's on to the south wi' a jovial crew:
Good luck to the lads that wear the tartan plaids!
  Success to Charlie and a' his train!
The right and the wrang they a' shall ken ere lang,
  And the king shall enjoy his own again.

The battle of Gladsmuir it was a noble stour,
  And weel do we ken that our young prince wan;
The gallant Lowland lads, when they saw the tartan plaids,
  Wheel'd round to the right, and away they ran;
For Master Johnnie Cope, being destitute of hope,
  Took horse for his life, and left his men;
In their arms he put no trust, for he knew it was just
  That the king should enjoy his own again.

To your arms, to your arms, my bonnie Highland lads!
  We winna brook the rule o' a German thing:
To your arms, to your arms, wi' your bonnets and your plaids,
  And hey for Charlie and our ain true king!
Good luck shall be the fa' o' the lad that's awa,
  The lad whose honour never yet knew stain:
The wrang shall gae down, the king get the crown,
  And ilka honest man his own again.

WI' A HUNDRED PIPERS.
LADY NAIRNE.

Wi' a hundred pipers an' a' an' a',
Wi' a hundred pipers an' a' an' a',
We'll up an' gie them a blaw, a blaw,
Wi' a hundred pipers an' a' an' a'.
Oh it's owre the Border awa' awa',
Its ower the Border awa' awa',
We'll on and march to Carlisle ha';
Wi' its yetts, its castle an' a' an' a'.

Oh ! our sodger lads looked braw, looked braw,
Wi' their tartans, kilts, an' a' an' a',
Wi' their bonnets, an' feathers, an' glitterin' gear,
An' Pibrochs soundin' sweet and clear;
Will they a' return to their ain dear glen,
Will they a' return, our Hielan' men,
Second-sichted Sandy looked fu' wae
An' mithers grat as they march'd away.
    Wi a hundred pipers, etc.

Oh wha is for'most o' a' o' a';
Oh wha does follow the blaw, the blaw;
Bonnie Charlie the king o' us a', hurra !
Wi' his hundred pipers an' a' an' a'.
His bonnet an' feather he's wavin' high,
His prancin' steed seems maist to fly,
The nor' win' plays wi' his curly hair,
While the pipers blaw in an' unco flare.
    Wi' a hundred pipers, etc.

The Esk was swollen sae red an' sae deep,
But shouther to shouther the brave lads keep,
Twa thousand swam owre to fell English ground,
An' danced themsel's dry to the pibroch's sound.
Dumfounder'd, the English saw, they saw,
Dumfounder'd, they heard the blaw, the blaw,
Dumfounder'd they a' ran awa', awa',
From the hundred pipers an' a' an' a'.
    Wi' a hundred pipers, etc.

THERE GROWS A BONNIE BRIER BUSH.
LADY NAIRNE.

There grows a bonnie brier bush in our kail yard,
And white are the blossoms o't in our kail yard,
Like wee bit cockauds, to deck our hieland lads,
And the lassies lo'e the bonnie bush in our kail yard.

An' it's hame, an' it's hame, to the north countrie,
An' it's hame, an' it's hame, to the north countrie,
Where my bonnie Jean is waiting for me,
Wi' a heart kind an' true, in my ain countrie.

But were they a' true that were far awa'?
O' were they a' true that were far awa'?
They drew up wi' glaikit Englishers at Corlisle ha',
And forgot auld frien's that were far awa.

Ye'll come nae mair, Jamie, where aft ye have been,
Ye'll come nae mair, Jamie, to Atholl's green,
O'er weel ye lo'ed the dancin' at Carlislo ha',
And forgot the hieland hills, that were far awa.

I ne'or lo'ed a dance but on Atholl's green,
I ne'er lo'ed a lassie, but my dorty Jean,
Sair, sair against my will, did I bide sno lang awa,
And my heart was aye in Atholl's green, at Carlisle hn'.

The brier bush was bonnie ance in our kail yard,
The brier bush was bonnie ance in our kail yard,
A blast blew ower the hill, that ga'e Atholl's flowers a chill,
And the bloom's blawn aff the bonnie bush in our kail yard.

FALKIRK MUIR.

On the 31st October, after being largely reinforced, Charles continued his march southwards. The army which left Edinburgh amounted to about 6000 men, 3000 of whom were Highlanders, and 500 cavalry. They passed through Carlisle, Kendal, Lancaster, Preston, Wigan, Manchester, and Macclesfield, and on the 4th December the advanced portion of the army took possession of Derby, followed immediately after by the whole force. The position had now become critical. Three armies were opposed to them; one under the command of the Duke of Cumberland, another under Marshal Wade, while a third was stationed to defend London. The Highland Leaders became alarmed at fighting in an unknown country, and counselled a retreat to the North, there to await the royal forces. This was stoutly opposed by Charles, who almost implored them to continue the advance. A council of war was held on the 5th, at which Lord George Murray expressed the opinion, that they were about to be attacked by three Royal armies, amounting to about 30,000 men, while their own numbers did not now exceed 5000—for the English Jacobites had not joined the Prince's standard with the same enthusiasm as their Northern compatriots; and the retreat, in spite of all Charles' protestations, seems to have been unanimously agreed upon. The retreat was conducted with much secrecy and dispatch; and it was not till they reached Falkirk that they were met by a Royal army under General Hawley, and after a short struggle the Royalists suffered a complete defeat. Hawley, who had been loud in his denunciations of Cope's incapability, and who had openly

wished to show how easily the Highland rabble could be dispersed, received
deservedly a good share of the satire of the Rebel rhymsters. Cope's misfortunes may be pitied, but Hawley smacks too much of the bully to
merit the smallest show of sympathy.

    Up and rin awa, Hawley,
    Up and rin awa, Hawley;
    The philabegs are coming down
     To gie your lugs a claw, Hawley;
    Young Charlie's face at Dunipace,
     Has gien your mou' a thraw, Hawley;
    A blasting sight for bastard wight,
     The warst that e'er he saw, Hawley.
     Up and rin awa, etc.

  Gae dight your face, and turn the chase,
   For fierce the wind does blaw, Hawley;
  And Highland Geordie's at your tail,
   Wi' Drummond, Perth, and a', Hawley.
  Had ye but staid wi' lady's maid
   An hour, or maybe twa, Hawley,
  Your bacon bouk and bastard snout,
   Ye might hae sav'd them a', Hawley.
    Up and rin awa, etc.

  Whene'er you saw the bonnets blue
   Down frae the Torwood draw, Hawley,
  A wisp in need did you bestead,
   Perhaps you needed twa, Hawley.
  And General Husk, that battle-busk,
   The prince o' warriors a', Hawley,
  With whip and spur he cross'd the furr,
   As fast as he could ca', Hawley.
    Up and rin awa, etc.

  I hae but just ae word to say,
   And ye maun hear it a', Hawley;
  We came to charge wi' sword and targe,
   And nae to hunt ava, Hawley.
  When we came down aboon the town,
   And saw nae faes at a', Hawley,
  We couldna, sooth! believe the truth,
   That ye had left us a', Hawley.
    Up and rin awa, etc.

  Nae man bedeen believ'd his een,
   Till your brave back he saw, Hawley,
  That bastard brat o' foreign cat
   Had neither pluck nor paw, Hawley.

We didna ken but ye were men
  Wha fight for foreign law, Hawley:
Gae fill your wame wi' brose at hame,
  It fits you best of a', Hawley.
    Up and rin awa, etc.

The very frown o' Highland loon,
  It gart you drap the jaw, Hawley,
It happ'd the face of a' disgrace,
  And sicken'd Southron maw, Hawley.
The very gleam o' Highland flame,
  It pat ye in a thaw, Hawley,
Gae back and kiss your daddie's miss;
  Ye're nought but cowards a', Hawley.
    Up and scour awa, Hawley,
    Up and scour awa, Hawley:
    The Highland dirk is at your doup,
    And that's the Highland law, Hawley.

THE HIGHLANDMEN CAME DOWN THE HILL.

The Highlandmen came down the hill,
  And owre the knowe wi' right gude will:
Now Geordie's men may brag their fill,
  For wow but they were braw, man!
They had three gen'rals o' the best,
Wi' lairds, and lords, and a' the rest,
Chiels that were bred to stand the test,
  And couldna rin awa, man.

The Highlandmen are savage loons,
Wi' barkit houghs and burly crowns;
They canna stand the thunder-stoun's
  Of heroes bred wi' care, man—
Of men that are their country's stay,
These Whiggish braggarts of a day.
The Highlandmen came down the brae
  The heroes were not there, man!

Says brave Lochiel, "Pray, have we won?
I see no troop, I hear no gun."
Says Drummond, "Faith, the battle's done,
  I know not how nor why, man.
But, my good lords, this thing I crave,
Have we defeat these heroes brave?"
Says Murray, "I believe we have:
  If not, we're here to try, man."

But tried they up, or tried they down,
There was no foe in Falkirk town,
Nor yet in a' the country roun',
  To break a sword at a', man.
They were sae bauld at break o' day,
When tow'rd the west they took their way;
But the Highlandmen came down the brae,
  And made the dogs to blaw, man.

A tyke is but a tyke at best,
A coward ne'er will stand the test,
And Whigs at morn wha cock'd the crest,
  Or e'en had got a fa', man.
O wae befa' these northern lads,
Wi' their braidswords and white cockades!
They lend sic hard and heavy blads,
  Our Whigs nae mair can craw, man.

CULLODEN.

AFTER the battle of Falkirk, the Highlanders continued their retreat, and on the 18th February, 1746, entered Inverness. On the 25th of February, the Duke of Cumberland's army entered Aberdeen, and both sides engaged in petty skirmishes in their district, till on the 8th April, the Duke marched upon the northern capital. The Highland army advanced to Drummossie Moor, about five miles to meet him, and on the 16th April, 1746, engaged in the celebrated battle of Culloden, which resulted as is well known in the complete defeat of the Highland army. "The battle of Culloden lasted little more than forty minutes, most of which brief space of time was spent in distant firing, and very little in the active struggle. It was as complete a victory as possible on the part of the Royal army, and any other result would have been very discreditable to the English army. Its numbers and condition for fighting were so superior, their artillery did so much for them, and the plan of the battle was so much in their favour, that to have lost the day would have argued a degree of misbehaviour for which even Preston-pans and Falkirk had not prepared us."—*Chambers's History of the Rebellion*, 1869, p. 801.

FAIR lady, mourn the memory
  Of all our Scottish fame!
Fair lady, mourn the memory
  Ev'n of the Scottish name!
How proud were we of our young prince,
  And of his native sway!
But all our hopes are past and gone,
  Upon Culluden day.

There was no lack of bravery there,
  No spare of blood or breath,
For, one to two, our foes we dar'd,
  For freedom or for death.

The bitterness of grief is past,
　Of terror and dismay :
The die was risk'd, and foully cast,
　Upon Culloden day.

And must thou seek a foreign clime,
　In poverty to pine,
No friend or clansman by thy side,
　No vassal that is thine?
Leading thy young son by the hand,
　And trembling for his life,
As at the name of Cumberland
　He grasps his father's knife.

I cannot see thee, lady fair,
　Turn'd out on the world wide ;
I cannot see thee, lady fair,
　Weep on the bleak hill side.
Before such noble stem should bend
　To tyrant's treachery,
I'll lay thee with thy gallant sire,
　Beneath the beechen tree.

I'll hide thee in Clan-Ronald's isles,
　Where honour still bears away;
I'll watch the traitor's hovering sails,
　By islet and by bay :
And ere thy honour shall be stain'd,
　This sword avenge shall thee,
And lay thee with thy gallant kin,
　Below the beechen tree.

What is there now in thee, Scotland,
　To us can pleasure give ?
What is there now in thee, Scotland,
　For which we ought to live?
Since we have stood, and stood in vain,
　For all that we held dear,
Still have we left a sacrifice
　To offer on our bier.

A foreign and fanatic sway
　Our Southron foes may gall;
The cup is fill'd, they yet shall drink,
　And they deserve it all.
But there is nought for us or ours,
　In which to hope or trust,
But hide us in our fathers' graves,
　Amid our fathers' dust.

CURSES.

Scotland and England must be now
  United in a nation,
And we must all perjure and vow,
  And take the abjuration.
The Stuarts' ancient freeborn race,
  Now we must all give over;
And we must take into their place
  The bastards of Hanover.

Curs'd be the Papists who withdrew
  The king to their persuasion:
Curs'd be that covenanting crew,
  Who gave the first occasion.
Curs'd be the wretch who seiz'd the throne,
  And marr'd our constitution;
And curs'd be they who helped on
  That wicked revolution.

Curs'd be those traitorous traitors who,
  By their perfidious knavery,
Have brought our nation now into
  An everlasting slavery.
Curs'd be the Parliament, that day,
  Who gave their confirmation;
And curs'd be every whining Whig,
  For they have damn'd the nation.

BONNIE LADDIE.

The barbarities inflicted upon the Highlanders after Culloden by the Royal army, were not lost sight of by the Jacobite wits in their distress. Certainly the Duke of Cumberland allowed his army to conduct themselves more like a body of savages than "Christian soldiers," and the poets of the party have revenged themselves by sending him down to posterity with a reputation for cruelty as fixed as the evil character given to Macbeth or Richard III. by Shakspeare.

Geordie sits in Charlie's chair,
  Bonnie laddie, Highland laddie;
Deil tak' him gin he hide there,
  My bonnie laddie, Highland laddie;
Charlie yet shall mount the throne,
  Bonnie laddie, Highland laddie;
Weel ye ken it is his own,
  My bonnie laddie, Highland laddie.

Weary fa' the Lawland loon,
  Bonnie laddie, Highland laddie,
Wha took frae him the British crown,
  My bonnie laddie, Highland laddie.

But leeze me on the kilted claus,
　Bonnie laddie, Highland laddie,
That fought for him at Preston-pans,
　My bonnie laddie, Highland laddie.

Ken ye the news I hae to tell,
　Bonnie laddie, Highland laddie?
Cumberland's awa to hell,
　My bonnie laddie, Highland laddie.
When he came to the Stygian shore,
　Bonnie laddie, Highland laddie;
The deil himsel' wi' fright did roar,
　My bonnie laddie, Highland laddie.

When Charon grim came out to him,
　Bonnie laddie, Highland laddie;
"Ye're welcome here, ye devil's limb!"
　My bonnie laddie, Highland laddie.
They pat on him a philabeg,
　Bonnie laddie, Highland laddie,
And unto him they ca'd a peg,
　My bonnie laddie, Highland laddie.

How he did skip and he did roar,
　Bonnie laddie, Highland laddie:
The deils ne'er saw sic sport before,
　My bonnie laddie, Highland laddie.
They took him neist to Satan's ha',
　Bonnie laddie, Highland laddie,
To lilt it wi' his grandpapa,
　My bonnie laddie, Highland laddie.

The deil sat girnin in the neuk,
　Bonnie laddie, Highland laddie,
Riving sticks to roast the duke,
　My bonnie laddie, Highland laddie.
They pat him neist upon a spit,
　Bonnie laddie, Highland laddie,
And roasted him baith head and feet,
　My bonnie laddie, Highland laddie.

Wi' scalding brunstane and wi' fat,
　Bonnie laddie, Highland laddie,
They flamm'd his carcase weel wi' that,
　Bonnie laddie, Highland laddie.
They ate him up baith stoop and roop,
　Bonnie laddie, Highland laddie;
And that's the gate they serv'd the duke,
　My bonnie laddie, Highland laddie.

THE WAES O' SCOTLAND.
ALLAN CUNNINGHAM.

When I left thee, bonny Scotland,
  O thou wert fair to see!
Fresh as a bonny bride in the morn,
  When she maun wedded be.
When I came back to thee, Scotland,
  Upon a May morn fair,
A bonny lass sat at our town end,
  Kaming her yellow hair.

"Oh hey! oh hey!" sung the bonny lass,
  "Oh hey! and wae is me!
There's siccan sorrow in Scotland,
  As een did never see.
Oh hey! oh hey! for my father auld!
  Oh hey! for my mither dear!
And my heart will burst for the bonny lad
  Wha left me lanesome here."

I had gane in my ain Scotland
  Mae miles than twa or three,
When I saw the head o' my ain father
  Coming up the gate to me.
"A traitor's head!" and "a traitor's head!"
  Loud bawl'd a bloody loon;
But I drew frae the sheath my glaive o' weir,
  And strack the reaver down.

I hied me hume to my father's ha',
  My dear auld mither to see;
But she lay 'mang the black eizels,
  Wi' the death-tear in her e'e.
"O wha has wrought this bloody wark?
  Had I the reaver here,
I'd wash his sark in his ain heart's blood,
  And gie't to his dame to wear."

I hadna gane frae my ain dear hame
  But twa short miles and three,
Till up came a captain o' the Whigs
  Says, "Traitor, bide ye me!"
I grippit him by the belt sae braid,
  It birsted i' my hand,
But I threw him frae his weir-saddle,
  And drew my burlie brand.

"Shaw mercy on me!" quo' the loon,
  And low he knelt on knee:
But by his thigh was my father's glaive
  Whilk gude King Bruce did gie;

And buckled round him was the broider'd belt
Whilk my mither's hands did weave,
My tears they mingled wi' his heart's blood,
And reek'd upon my glaive.

I wander a' night 'mang the lands I own'd,
When a' folk are asleep,
And I lie o'er my father and mither's grave
An hour or twa to weep.

O, fatherless and mitherless,
Without a ho' or hame,
I maun wander througn dear Scotland,
And bide a traitor's blame.

ON GALLIA'S SHORE.
HAMILTON OF BANGOUR.

On Gallia's shore we sat and wept,
When Scotland we thought on,
Robbed of her bravest sons, and all
Her ancient spirit gone.

Revenge! the sons of Gallia said,
Revenge your native land;
Already your insulting foes
Crowd the Batavian strand.

How shall the sons of freedom e'er
For foreign conquest fight;
For power, how wield the sword unsheath'd,
For liberty and right?

If thee, oh Scotland, I forget,
Even with my latest breath,
May foul dishonour stain my name,
And bring a coward's death.

May sad remorse of fancied guilt
My future days employ,
If all thy sacred rights are not
Above my chiefest joy.

Remember England's children, Lord,
Who on Drummossie day,
Deaf to the voice of kindred love,
Raze, raze it quite, did say.

And thou, proud Gallia, faithless friend,
Whose ruin is not far,
Just Heaven, on thy devoted head,
Pour all the woes of war.

2 o

When thou thy slaughter'd little ones,
And ravish'd dames shall see,
Such help, such pity, may'st thou have,
As Scotland had from thee.

FAREWELL TO GLEN-SHALLOCH.

JAMES HOGG.

Translated from the Gaelic.

Farewell to Glen-Shalloch,
  A farewell for ever!
Farewell to my wee cot,
  That stands by the river!
The fall is loud-sounding,
  In voices that vary,
And the echoes surrounding
  Lament with my Mary.

I saw her last night,
  'Mid the rocks that enclose them,
With a babe at her knee
  And a babe at her bosom:
I heard her sweet voice
  In the depth of my slumber,
And the song that she sung
  Was of sorrow and cumber.

"Sleep sound, my sweet babe,
  There is nought to alarm thee;
The sons of the valley
  No power have to harm thee.
I'll sing thee to rest
  In the balloch untrodden,
With a coronach sad
  For the slain of Culloden.

"The brave were betray'd,
  And the tyrant is daring
To trample and waste us,
  Unpitying, unsparing.
Thy mother no voice has,
  No feeling that changes,
No word, sign, or song,
  But the lesson of vengeance.

"I'll tell thee, my son,
  How our laurels are withering:
I'll gird on thy sword
  When the clansmen are gathering;

I'll bid thee go forth
  In the cause of true honour,
And never return
  Till thy country hath won her.

"Our tower of devotion
  Is the home of the reaver;
The pride of the ocean
  Is fallen for ever;
The pines of the forest,
  That time could not weaken,
Is trod in the dust,
  And its honours are shaken.

"Rise, spirits of yore,
  Ever dauntless in danger!
For the land that was yours
  Is the land of the stranger.
O come from your caverns,
  All bloodless and hoary,
And these fiends of the valley
  Shall tremble before ye!"

THE FRASERS IN THE CORREL

"Where is your daddy gane, my little May?
Where has our lady been a' the lang day?
Saw you the red-coats rank on the hall green?
Or heard ye the horn on the mountain yestreen?"
"Ye auld carle graybeard, spier na at me;
Gae spier at the maiden that sits by the sea.
The red-coats were here, and it wasna for good,
And the ravon's turn'd hoarse wi' the waughting o' blood.

"O listen, auld carle, how roopit his note!
The blood of the Fraser's too hot for his throat,
I trow the black traitor's of Sassenach breed;
They prey on the living, and he on the dead.
When I was a baby, we ca'd him in joke,
The harper of Errick, the priest of the rock;
But now he's our mountain companion no more,
The slave of the Saxon, the quaffer of gore."

"Sweet little maiden, why talk you of death?
The raven's our friend, and he's croaking in wrath:
He will not pick up from a bonnetted head,
Nor mar the brave form by the tartan that's clad.
But point me the cliff where the Fraser abides,
Where Foyers, Culduthill, and Gorthaly hides.
There's danger at hand, I must speak with them soon,
And seek them alone by the light of the moon."

"Auld carle graybeard, a friend you should be,
For the truth's on your lip, and the tear i' your e'e;
Then seek in the correi that sounds on the brae,
And sings to the rock when the breeze is away.
I sought them last night with the haunch of the deer,
And far in yon cave they were hiding in fear:
There, at the last crow of the brown heather-cock,
They pray'd for their prince, kneel'd, and slept on the rock.

"O tell me, auld carle, what will be the fate
Of those who are killing the gallant and great?
Who force our brave chiefs to the correi to go,
And hunt their own prince like the deer or the roe?"
"My sweet little maiden, beyond yon red sun
Dwells one who beholds all the deeds that are done:
Their crimes on the tyrants one day he'll repay,
And the names of the brave shall not perish for aye."

THE LOVELY LASS O' INVERNESS.
ROBERT BURNS.

The lovely lass o' Inverness,
  Nae joy nor pleasure she can see;
For e'en and morn she cries, alas!
  And aye the saut tear blinds her e'e.
Drummossie moor! Drummossie day,
  A waefu' day it was to me;
For there I lost my father dear,
  My father dear and brethren three.

Their winding sheet's the bluidy lea,
  Their graves are growing green to see,
And by them lies the dearest lad
  That ever blest a woman's e'e.
Now wae to thee thou cruel lord,
  A bluidy man I trow thou be;
For monie a heart thou hast made sair,
  That ne'er did wrang to thine or thee.

THERE LIVED A LASS IN INVERNESS.
ALLAN CUNNINGHAM.

There liv'd a lass in Inverness,
  She was the pride of a' the town;
Blithe as the lark on gowan tass,
  When frae the nest it's newly flown.

At kirk she wan the auld folks' love,
　At dance she wan the laddies' een;
She was the blithest o' the blithe
　At wooster trystes or Hallowe'en.

As I came in by Inverness,
　The simmer sun was sinking down,
O there I saw the weel-faur'd lass,
　And she was greeting through the town.
The grayhair'd men were a' i' the streets,
　And auld dames crying (sad to see):
The flower o' the lads o' Inverness
　Lie bluidy on Culloden lea.

She tore her haffet links o' gowd,
　And dighted aye her comely e'e.
My father lies at bluidy Carlisle,
　At Preston sleep my brethren three;
I thought my heart could haud nae mair,
　Mae tears could never blind my e'e;
But the fa' o' ane has burst my heart—
　A dearer ane there ne'er could be.

He trysted me o' love yestreen,
　O' love tokens he gave me three;
But he's faulded i' the arms of weir,
　O, ne'er again to think o' me.
The forest flowers shall be my bed,
　My food shall be the wild berrie,
The fa'ing leaves shall hap me ower,
　And wauken'd again I winna be.

O weep, O weep, ye Scottish dames,
　Weep till ye blind a mither's e'e;
Nae reeking ha' in fifty miles,
　But naked corses, sad to see.
O spring is blithesome to the year,
　Trees sprout, flowers bud, and birds sing hie;
But O, what spring can raise them up
　Whose bluidy weir has seal'd the e'e.

The hand of God hung heavy here,
　And lightly touch'd foul tyrannie;
It strack the righteous to the ground,
　And lifted the destroyer hie.
But there's a day, quo' my God in prayer,
　When righteousness shall bear the gree;
I'll rake the wicked low i' the dust,
　And wauken, in bliss, the gude man's e'e.

THE HIGHLAND WIDOW'S LAMENT.

Oh! I am come to the low countrie!
 Ochon, ochon, ochrie!
Without ae penny in my purse,
 To buy a meal to me.

It wasna sae in the Highland hills,
 Ochon, ochon, ochrie!
Nae woman in the country wide
 Sae happy was as me:

For then I had a score of kye,
 Ochon, ochon, ochrie!
Feeding on yon hill sae high,
 And giving milk to me!

And there I had three score o' yowos,
 Ochon, ochon, ochrie!
Skipping on yon bonnie knowes,
 And casting woo to me.

I was the happiest o' the clan:
 Sair, sair may I repine;
For Donald was the bravest man,
 And Donald he was mine.

Till Charlie he came ower at last,
 Sae far, to set us free:
My Donald's arm it wanted was
 For Scotland and for me.

Their waefu' fate what need I tell?
 Right to the wrang did yield;
My Donald and his country fell
 Upon Culloden field.

I hae nocht left me now ava,
 Ochon, ochon, ochrie!
But bonnie orphan lad-weans twa,
 To seek their bread wi' me.

But I hae yet a tocher-band,
 Ochon, ochon, ochrie!
My winsome Donald's dirk and brand,
 Into their hands to gie.

And still ae blink o' hope is left,
 To lighten my auld e'e;
To see my bairns gie bluidy crowns
 To them gart Donald die.

Ochon, ochon, oh, Donald, oh!
Ochon, ochon, ochrie!
Nae woman in the world wide
Sae wretched now as me!

THE EXILE'S LAMENT.

FRAE the friends and land I love,
  Driven by fortune's felly spite;
Frae my best belov'd I rove,
  Never mair to taste delight:
Never mair maun hope to find
  Ease frae toil, relief frae care.
When remembrance racks the mind,
  Pleasure but unveils despair.

Brightest climes shall mirk appear,
  Desert ilka blooming shore,
Till the fates, nae mair severe,
  Friendship, love, and peace restore;
Till revenge, wi' laurell'd head,
  Bring our banish'd hame again,
And ilka loyal bonny lad
  Cross the seas and win his ain.

A LAMENT.

A SOLDIER, for gallant achievements renown'd,
  Revolv'd in despair the campaigns of his youth;
Then beating his bosom, and sighing profound,
  That malice itself might have melted to ruth—
"Are these," he exclaim'd, "the results of my toil,
  In want and obscurity thus to retire?
For this did compassion restrain me from spoil,
  When earth was all carnage, and heav'n was on fire?

"My country is ravag'd, my kinsmen are slain,
  My prince is in exile, and treated with scorn,
My chief is no more—he hath suffer'd in vain—
  And why should I live on the mountain forlorn?
O woe to Macconnal, the selfish, the proud,
  Disgrace of a name for its loyalty famed!
The curses of heaven shall fall on the head
  Of Callum and Torquil, no more to be named.

"For had they but join'd with the just and the brave,
  The Campbell had fallen, and Scotland been free;
That traitor, of vile usurpation the slave,
  The foe of the Highlands, of mine, and of me.

The great they are gone, the destroyer is come,
  The smoke of Lochaber has redden'd the sky:
The war-note of freedom for ever is dumb;
  For that have I stood, and with that I will die.

"The sun's bright effulgence, the fragrance of air,
  The varied horizon henceforth I abhor.
Give me death, the sole boon of a wretch in despair,
  Which fortune can offer, or nature implore."
To madness impelled by his griefs as he spoke,
  And darting around him a look of disdain,
Down headlong he leapt from a heaven-towering rock,
  And sleeps where the wretched forbear to complain.

LENACHAN'S FAREWELL.

Fare-thee-well, my native cot,
  Bothy o' the birken tree!
Sair the heart and hard the lot
  O' the lad that parts wi' thee.
Thee, my grandsires fondly rear'd,
  Then thy wicker-work was full:
Mony a Campbell's glen he clear'd,
  Hit the buck and hough'd the bull.

In thy green and grassy crook
  Mair lies hid than crusted stanes;
In thy bien and weirdly nook
  Lie some stout Clan-Gillian banes.
Thou wert aye the kinsman's hame,
  Routh and welcome was his fare;
But if serf or Saxon came,
  He cross'd Murich's hirst nae mair.

Never hand in thee yet bred
  Kendna how the sword to wield;
Never heart of thine had dread
  Of the foray or the field:
Ne'er on straw, mat, bulk, or bed,
  Son of thine lay down to die;
Every lad within thee bred,
  Died 'neath heaven's open eye.

Charlie Stuart he came here,
  For our king, as right became:
Wha could shun the Bruce's heir?
  Wha could tine our royal name?

Firm to stand, and free to fa',
  Forth he marched right valiantlie.
Gane is Scotland's king and law!
  Woe to the Highlands and to me!

Freeman yet, I'll scorn to fret,
  Here nae langer I maun stay;
But when I my hame forget,
  May my heart forget to play!
Fare-thee-well, my father's cot,
  Bothy o' the birken tree!
Sair the heart and hard the lot
  O' the lad that parts wi' thee.

WAES ME FOR PRINCE CHARLIE.
WILLIAM GLEN.

WHEN all hope of winning the battle of Culloden had passed, Prince Charles was led from the field, and began that series of wanderings, the details of which have been often given to the public, and by none more vividly than by Mr. Robert Chambers, who concludes his sketch by saying: "For upwards of five months he had skulked as a proscribed fugitive through the mountains and seas of the West Highlands, often in the most imminent danger of being taken, and generally exposed to severe personal hardships. The narrowness of his own escapes is shown strikingly in the circumstance of so many persons being taken immediately after having contributed to his safety. The reader must have already accorded all due praise to the people who, by their kindness and fidelity, had been the chief means of working out his deliverance. Scarcely any gentleman to whom he applied for protection, or to aid in effecting his movements, refused to peril their own safety on his account; hundreds, many of whom were in the humblest walk of life, had been entrusted with the secret, yet, if we overlook the beggar boy in South Uist, and the dubious case of Barrisdale, none had attempted to give him up to his enemies. Thirty thousand pounds had been offered in vain for the life of one human being, in a country where the sum would have purchased a princely estate."— History of the Rebellion of 1745-6, p. 440.

A WEE bird came to our ha' door,
  He warbled sweet and clearly,
And aye the o'ercome o' his sang
  Was "Wae's me for Prince Charlie!"
Oh! when I heard the bonnie bonnie bird,
  The tears came drapping rarely,
I took my bannet aff my head,
  For weel I lo'ed Prince Charlie.

Quo' I, "My bird, my bonnie bonnie bird,
  Is that a tale ye borrow?
Or is't some words ye've learnt by rote,
  Or a lilt o' dool and sorrow?"

"Oh! no, no, no!" the wee bird sang,
  "I've flown sin morning early;
But sic a day o' wind and rain!—
  Oh! wae's me for Prince Charlie!

"On hills that are by right his ain,
  He roams a lonely stranger;
On ilka hand he's press'd by want,
  On ilka side by danger.
Yestreen I met him in a glen,
  My heart near bursted fairly,
For sadly chang'd indeed was he—
  Oh! wae's me for Prince Charlie!

"Dark night came on, the tempest howl'd
  Out owre the hills and valleys;
And whare was't that your prince lay down,
  Whase hame should been a palace?
He row'd him in a Highland plaid,
  Which cover'd him but sparely,
And slept beneath a bush o' broom—
  Oh! wae's me for Prince Charlie!"

But now the bird saw some redcoats,
  And he shook his wings wi' anger:
"O this is no a land for me,
  I'll tarry here nae langer."
A while he hover'd on the wing,
  Ere he departed fairly:
But weel I mind the fareweel strain;
  'Twas "Wae's me for Prince Charlie!"

PRINCE CHARLIE'S LAMENT.

Ascribed to Daniel Weir of Greenock.

The storm is raging o'er the Kyle,
  And o'er thy glen, dark Auchnacary,
Your Prince has travell'd many a mile,
  And knows not where to go or tarry.
He sees, far in the vale below,
  The wounded soldier home returning;
And those who wrought this day of woe,
  Are round yon watchfire dimly burning.

O Scotland lang shall rue the day
  She saw Culloden drench'd and gory;
The sword the bravest hearts may stay,
  But some will tell the mournful story.
Amidst those hills that are mine ain,
  I wander here a houseless stranger;
With nought to shield me from the rain,
  And every hour beset with danger.

Howl on, ye winds, the hills are dark,
  There shrouded in a gloomy covering;
Then haste thee o'er the sea, my bark,
  For bloodhounds are around me hov'ring.
O Scotland, Scotland, fare thee well,
  Farewell ye hills, I dare not tarry;
Let hist'ry's page my suff'rings tell,
  Farewell! Clanronald and Glengary.

WELCOME TO SKYE.

Prince Charles left the mainland, and wandered about the island of Skye. It was in Uist that Flora Macdonald began her romantic adventures with Prince Charles, and it was in Skye she left him. The "Twa Bonnie Maidens" alluded to Flora Macdonald and to Prince Charles, who for sometime disguised himself as her maid-servant.

There are twa bonny maidens,
And three bonny maidens,
Come over the Minch,
And come over the main,
Wi' the wind for their way,
And the corroi for their hame:
Let us welcome them bravely
Unto Skye again.
Come along, come along,
Wi' your boatie and your song,
You twa bonny maidens,
And three bonny maidens;
For the night it is dark,
And the red-coat is gone,
And you're bravely welcome
To Skye again.

There is Flora, my honey,
So dear and so bonny,
And one that is tall,
And comely withal;
Put the one as my king,
And the other as my queen,
They're welcome unto
The Isle of Skye again.
Come along, come along,
Wi' your boatie and your song,
You twa bonny maidens,
And three bonny maidens;
For the lady of Macoulain
She lieth her lane,
And you're bravely welcome
To Skye again.

Her arm it is strong,
And her petticoat is long,
My one bonny maiden,
And twa bonny maidens;
But their bed shall be clean,
On the heather mast crain;
And they're welcome unto
The Isle of Skye again.
Come along, come along,
Wi' your boatie and your song,
You one bonny maiden,
And twa bonny maidens
By the sea-moullit's nest
I will watch o'er the main;
And you're dearly welcome
To Skye again.

There's a wind on the tree,
And a ship on the sea,
My twa bonny maidens,
My three bonny maidens:
On the lea of the rock
Your cradle I shall rock;
And you're welcome unto
The Isle of Skye again.
Come along, come along,
Wi' your boatie and your song,
My twa bonny maidens,
And three bonny maidens:
More sound shall you sleep,
When you rock on the deep;
And you'll aye be welcome
To Skye again.

THE CHEVALIER'S LAMENT.

ROBERT BURNS.

The small birds rejoice in the green leaves returning,
   The murmuring streamlet runs clear through the vale,
The hawthorn trees blow in the dews of the morning,
   And wild scattered cowslips bedeck the green dale.
But what can give pleasure, or what can seem fair,
   When the lingering moments are numbered by care,
     No flowers gaily springing,
     Or birds sweetly singing,
   Can soothe the sad bosom of joyless despair.

The deed that I dared could it merit their malice,
A king and a father to place on his throne;
His right are those hills, and his right are these valleys,
Where the wild beasts find shelter, but I can find none.
But 'tis not my sufferings, thus wretched, forlorn,
My brave gallant friends, 'tis your ruin I mourn.
 Your deeds proved so loyal,
 In hot bloody trial,
Alas! can I make it no better return.

BONNIE CHARLIE'S NOW AWA'.

On the 10th September, 1746, Prince Charles Edward, after nearly six months' wanderings throughout the Highlands and Islands, embarked on board "L'Hereux," and bade farewell for ever to Scottish ground. About one hundred and thirty followers are said to have accompanied him to France. And so ended the celebrated rebellion of 1745, a rebellion which shook the throne of the reigning family to its centre, and gave rise to feelings of bitterness on the part of the defeated party, which required several generations to efface. Long after the Prince had left the country the Highlandmen entertained hopes of his return with a sufficient force to enable them to repay the wanton cruelties which had been inflicted on them by the royal army, under the Duke of Cumberland. The conduct of Prince Charles in his after life, it is needless to mention, was such as to remove all trace of that nobleness of soul which so enchanted all who came in contact with him in his early career. He died at Florence in 1788.

Royal Charlie's now awa',
 Safely owre the friendly main;
Mony a heart will break in twa,
 Should he ne'er come back again.
  Will you no come back again?
  Will you no come back again?
  Better lo'ed you'll never be,
  And will you no come back again?

Mony a traitor 'mang the isles
 Brak' the band o' nature's law;
Mony a traitor, wi' his wiles,
 Sought to wear his life awa'.
  Will he no come back again?
  Will he no come back again?
  Better lo'ed he'll never be,
  And will he no come back again?

The hills he trode were a' his ain,
 And bed beneath the birken tree;
The bush that hid him on the plain,
 There's none on earth can claim but he.
  Will he no come back again? etc.

Whene'er I hear the blackbird sing,
　Unto the e'ening sinking down,
Or merle that makes the woods to ring,
　To me they hae nae ither soun'
　　Than, will he ne'er come back again, etc.

Mony a gallant sodger fought,
　Mony a gallant chief did fa';
Death itself were dearly bought,
　A' for Scotland's king and law.
　　Will he no come back again? etc.

Sweet the lav'rock's note and lang,
　Lilting wildly up the glen;
And aye the o'ercome o' the sang
　Is, "Will he no come back again?"
　　Will he no come back again? etc.

BONNIE CHARLIE'S NOW AWA'.
LADY NAIRNE.

BONNY Charlie's now awa',
Safely owre the friendly main;
Mony a heart will break in twa,
Should he ne'er come back again.
　　Will ye no come back again?
　　Will ye no come back again?
　　Better lo'ed ye canna be,
　　Will ye no come back again?

Ye trusted in your Hielan' men,
They trusted you, dear Charlie,
They kent you hidin' in the glen,
Your cleadin' was but barely.
　　Will ye no, &c.

English bribes were a' in vain,
An' e'en tho' puirer we may be,
Siller canna buy the heart
That beats aye for thine an' thee.
　　Will ye no, &c.

We watch'd thee in the gloamin' hour,
We watch'd thee in the mornin' grey;
Tho' thirty-thousand pounds they'd gie;
Oh! there is nane that wad betray.
　　Will ye no, &c.

Sweet the laverock's note an lang,
Lilting wildly up the glen,
But aye to me, he sings ae sang,
Will ye no come back again?
　　Will ye no, &c.

FLORA MACDONALD'S LAMENT.

JAMES HOGG.

FAR over yon hills of the heather so green,
  And down by the correi that sings to the sea,
The bonnie young Flora sat sighing her lane,
  The dew on her plaid and the tear in her e'e.
She look'd at a boat which the breezes had swung
  Away on the wave, like a bird of the main;
And aye as it lessen'd, she sighed and she sung,
  "Farewell to the lad I shall ne'er see again!
Farewell to my hero, the gallant and young!
  Farewell to the lad I shall ne'er see again!

"The moorcock that crows on the top of Ben-Connal,
  He kens o' his bed in a sweet mossy hame;
The eagle that soars o'er the cliffs of Clan Ronald,
  Unaw'd and unhunted, his eiry can claim;
The solan can sleep on his shelve of the shore;
  The cormorant roost on his rock of the sea:
But, oh! there is ane whose hard fate I deplore;
  Nor house, ha', nor hame, in his country has he.
The conflict is past, and our name is no more;
  There's nought left but sorrow for Scotland and me.

"The target is torn from the arm of the just,
  The helmet is cleft on the brow of the brave,
The claymore for ever in darkness must rust,
  But red is the sword of the stranger and slave:
The hoof of the horse, and the foot of the proud,
  Have trod o'er the plumes in the bonnet of blue.
Why slept the red bolt in the breast of the cloud,
  When tyranny revell'd in blood of the true?
Farewell, my young hero, the gallant and good!
  The crown of thy fathers is torn from thy brow."

LAMENT OF FLORA MACDONALD.

WHY, my Charlie, dost thou leave me,
  Dost thou flee thy Flora's arms?
Were thy vows but to deceive me,
  Valiant o'er my yielding charms?
All I bore for thee, sweet Charlie,
  Want of sleep, fatigue, and care;
Brav'd the ocean late and early,
  Left my friends, for thou wast fair.

Sleep, ye winds that waft him from me;
  Blow, ye western breezes, blow—
Swell the sail; for I love Charlie—
  Ah! they whisper, Flora, no.
Cold she sinks beneath the billow,
  Dash'd from yonder rocky shore;
Flora, pride and flower of Isla,
  Ne'er to meet her Charlie more.

Dark the night, the tempest howling,
  Bleak along the western sky;
Hear the dreadful thunders rolling,
  See the forked lightning fly.
No more we'll hear the maid of Isla,
  Pensive o'er the rocky steep;
Her last sigh was breathed for Charlie!
  As she sunk into the deep.

BANNOCKS O' BARLEY.

Bannocks o' bear meal, bannocks o' barley,
Here's to the Highlandman's bannocks o' barley!
Wha in a brulzie will first cry "a parley?"
Never the lads wi' the bannocks o' barley!
  Bannocks o' bear meal, bannocks o' barley,
  Here's to the Highlandman's bannocks o' barley.

Wha drew the gude claymore for Charlie?
Wha cow'd the lowns o' England rarely?
And claw'd their backs at Falkirk fairly?—
Wha but the lads wi' the bannocks o' barley!
  Bannocks o' bear meal, etc.

Wha when hope was blasted fairly,
Stood in ruin wi' bonnie Prince Charlie?
And 'neath the Duke's bluidy paws dreed fu' sairly.?
Wha but the lads wi' the bannocks o' barley!
  Bannocks o' bear meal, etc.

LEWIE GORDON.

DR. ALEXANDER GEDDES.

Lewis, third son of the Duke of Gordon, declared for Prince Charles, in 1745. He was attainted, and died in France in 1754.

Oh! send Lewie Gordon hame,
And the lad I daurna name;
Though his back be at the wa',
Here's to him that's far awa!
  Och hon! my Highland man,
  Och, my bonny Highland man;
  Weel would I my true-love ken,
  Amang ten thousand Highland men.

Oh! to see his tartan-trews,
Bonnet blue, and laigh-heel'd shoes;
Philabeg aboon his knee;
That's the lad that I'll gang wi'!
  Och hon! etc.

The princely youth of whom I sing,
Is fitted for to be a king;
On his breast he wears a star;
You'd tak' him for the god of war.
  Och hon! etc.

Oh to see this princely one
Seated on a royal throne!
Disasters a' would disappear,
Then begins the jub'lee year!
  Och hon! etc.

HERE'S A HEALTH.

Here's a health to them that's away,
Here's a health to them that's away,
Here's a health to him that was here yestreen,
But duretna bide till day.
O wha winna drink it dry?
O wha winna drink it dry?
Wha winna drink to the lad that's gane,
Is nane o' our company.

Let him be swung on a tree,
Let him be swung on a tree;
Wha winna drink to the lad that's gane,
Can ne'er be the man for me.
It's good to be merry and wise,
It's good to be honest and true,
It's good to be aff wi' the auld king,
Afore we be on wi' the new.

2 P

HERE'S HIS HEALTH IN WATER.

Although his back be at the wa',
  Another was the fau'tor;
Although his back be at the wa',
  Yet here's his health in water.
He gat the skaith, he gat the scorn,
  I lo'e him yet the better;
Though in the muir I hide forlorn,
  I'll drink his health in water.
Although his back be at the wa',
  Yet here's his health in water.

I'll maybe live to see the day
  That hands shall get the halter,
And drink his health in usquebae,
  As I do now in water.
I yet may stand as I hae stood,
  Wi' him through ront and slaughter,
And bathe my hands in scoundrel blood,
  As I do now in water.
Although his back be at the wa',
  Yet here's his health in water.

THOUGH GEORDIE REIGNS IN JAMIE'S STEAD.

Though Geordie reigns in Jamie's stead,
  I'm griev'd, yet scorn to shaw that;
I'll ne'er look down, nor hang my head
  To rebel Whig, for a' that.
For a' that, and a' that,
  And thrice as muckle's a' that,
He's far beyond Dumblane the night,
  That shall be king for a' that.

He wears a broadsword by his side,
  And weel he kens to draw that;
The target and the Highland plaid,
  The shoulder belt, and a' that:
A bonnet bound with ribbons blue,
  The white cockade and a' that,
The tartan hose and philabeg,
  Which makes us blythe, for a' that.

The Whigs think a' that weal is won,
  But, faith, they maunna fa' that;
They think our loyal hearts dung down,
  But we'll be blythe, for a' that,

For still we trust that Providence
  Will us relieve from a' that,
And send us hame our gallant prince:
  Then we'll be blythe, for a' that.

But O what will the Whigs say syne,
  When they're mista'en in a' that?
When Geordie maun fling by the crown,
  And hat, and wig, and a' that?
The flames will get baith hat and wig,
  As often they've done a' that;
Our Highland lad will get the crown,
  And we'll be blythe, for a' that.

Then will your braw militia lads
  Rewarded be for a' that,
When they fling by their black cockades;
  A hellish badge I ca' that.
As night is banish'd by the day,
  The white shall drive awa that;
The sun shall then his beams display,
  And we'll be blythe, for a' that.

OH! HE'S BEEN LANG O' COMING.

THE youth that should hae been our king,
Was dress'd in yellow, red, and green,
A braver lad ye wadna seen,
  Than our brave royal Charlie.
    Oh! he's been lang o' coming,
    Lang, lang, lang o' coming,
    Oh! he's been lang o' coming,
      Welcome royal Charlie.

At Falkirk and at Prestonpans,
Supported by the Highland clans,
They broke the Hanoverian bands.
  For our brave royal Charlie.
    Oh! he's been lang, etc.

The valient chief, the brave Lochiel,
He met Prince Charlie on the dale;
Then, O! what kindness did prevail,
  Between the Chief and Charlie.
    Oh! he's been lang, etc.

O come and quaff along wi' me,
And drink a bumper, three times three,
To him that's come to set us free,
  Huzy! rejoice for Charlie.
    Oh! he's been lang, etc.

We darena brew a peck o' maut,
But Geordie says it is a faut;
And to our kail cannot get saut,
    For want of royal Charlie.
      Oh! he's been lang, etc.

Now our good king abroad is gone,
A German whelp now fills the throne,
And whelps it is denied by none,
    Are brutes compared to Charlie.
      Oh! he's been lang, etc.

Now our good king is turned awa',
A German whelp now rules us a';
And tho' we're forc'd against our law,
    The right belongs to Charlie.
      Oh! he's been lang, etc.

If we had but our Charlie back,
We wadna fear the German's crack;
Wi' a' his thieving, hungry pack,
    The right belongs to Charlie.
      Oh! he's been lang, etc.

O, Charlie come and lead the way,
No German whelp shall bear the sway,
Tho' ilka dog maun hae his day;
    The right belongs to Charlie.
      Oh! he's been lang, etc.

THE EMIGRANT.

May morning had shed her first streamers on high,
O'er Canada, opening all pale on the sky!
Still dazzling and white was the robe that she wore,
Except where the mountain wave lash'd on the shore.

Far heaved the young sun, like a lamp on the wave,
And loud screamed the gull o'er his foam-beaten cave,
When an old lyart swain on a headland stood high,
With the staff in his hand, and the tear in his eye.

His old tartan plaid, and his bonnet so blue,
Declared from what country his lineage he drew;
His visage so wan, and his accents so low,
Announced the companion of sorrow and woe.

"Ah, welcome thou sun, to thy canopy grand,
And to me, for thou com'st from my dear native land!
Again dost thou leave that sweet isle of the sea,
To beam on these winter-bound valleys and me!

"How sweet in my own native valley to roam,
Each face was a friend's, and each house was a home;
To drag our live thousands from river to bay,
Or chase the dun deer o'er the mountains so gray.

"Now forced from my home and my blithe halls away,
The son of the stranger has made them a prey:
My family and friends to extremity driven,
Contending for life both with earth and with heaven.

"My country," they said—"but they told me a lie,
Her valleys were barren, inclement her sky;
Even now in the glens, 'mong her mountains so blue,
The primrose and daisy are blooming in dew.

"How could she expel from those mountains of heath,
The clans who maintained them in danger and death;
Who ever were ready the broadsword to draw,
In defence of her honour, her freedom, and law.

"We stood by our Stuart, till one fatal blow
Loosed ruin triumphant, and valour laid low;
The lords whom we trusted, and lived but to please,
Then turned us adrift to the storms and the seas.

"O gratitude! where didst thou linger the while?
What region afar is illumed with thy smile?
That orb of the sky for a home will I crave,
When yon sun rises red on the Emigrant's grave!"

HAME, HAME, HAME.

ALLAN CUNNINGHAM.

Hame, hame, hame, hame fain wad I be,
O hame, hame, hame to my ain countrie!
There's an eye that ever weeps, and a fair face will be fain,
As I pass through Annan Water with my bonnie bands again.
When the flower is i' the bud and the leaf upon the tree,
The lark shall sing me hame in my ain countrie.

Hame, hame, hame, hame fain wad I be,
O hame, hame, hame to my ain countrie!
The green leaf o' loyalty's beginning for to fa',
The bonny white rose it is withering an a';
But I'll water't wi' the blude of usurping tyrannie,
An' green it will grow in my ain countrie.

Hame, hame, hame, hame fain wad I be,
O hame, hame, hame to my ain countrie!
There's nought now frae ruin my countrie can save,
But the keys of kind heaven to open the grave,
That a' the noble martyrs wha died for loyaltie,
May rise again and fight for their ain countrie.

Hame, hame, hame, hame fain wad I be,
O hame, hame, hame to my ain countrie!
The great now are gane, a' who ventured to save,
The new grass is growing aboon their bloody grave;
But the sun through the mirk, blinks blythe in my e'e—
"I'll shine on ye yet in your ain countrie."

HILL OF LOCHIEL.

JAMES HOGG.

Long have I pined for thee;
Land of my infancy,
Now will I kneel on thee,
   Hill of Lochiel;
Hill of the sturdy steer,
Hill of the roe and deer,
Hill of the streamlet clear,
   I love thee well.

When in my youthful prime,
Correi and crag to climb,
Or towering cliff sublime
   Was my delight;
Scaling the eagle's nest,
Wounding the raven's breast,
Skimming the mountain's crest,
   Gladsome and light.

When at the break of morn,
Proud o'er thy temples borne,
Rythed the red-deer's horn,
   How my heart beat!
Then, when with stunned leap,
Roll'd he adown the steep,
Never did hero reap
   Conquest so great.

Then rose a bolder game,
Young Charlie Stuart came,
Cameron, that loyal name
   Foremost must be:

Hard then our warrior meed,
Glorious our warrior dead,
Still we were doom'd to bleed
  By treachery.

Then did the red blood stream,
Then was the broadsword's gleam,
Quench'd in fair freedom's beam,
  No more to shine.
Then was the morning's brow,
Red with the fiery glow,
Fell hall and hamlet low,
  All that were mine.

Then was our maiden young,
First aye in battle strong,
Fir'd at her prince's wrong,
  Forc'd to give way:
Broke was the golden cup,
Gone Caledonia's hope,
Faithful and true men drop,
  Fast in the clay.

Fair in a hostile land,
Stretch'd on a foreign strand,
Oft has the tear-drop bland,
  Scorch'd as it fell.
Once was I spurn'd from thee,
Long have I mourn'd for thee,
Now I'm return'd to thee,
  Hill of Lochiel.

www.ingramcontent.com/pod-product-compliance
Lightning Source LLC
Chambersburg PA
CBHW021225300426
44111CB00007B/428